AA004093

SENSORDEVICES 2018

The Ninth International Conference on Sensor Device Technologies and Applications

September 16 - 20, 2018

Venice, Italy

SENSORDEVICES 2018 Editors

Paulo E. Cruvinel, Embrapa Instrumentation, Brazil
Manuela Vieira, CTS-UNINOVA, Portugal
Manuel Augusto Vieira, Electronics inside the Electronic Telecommunication and Computer Department of ISEL, Lisbon, Portugal
Arcady Zhukov, University Basque Country, Spain
Ivan Miguel Serrano Pires, University of Beira Interior - Covilhã, Portugal
Vittorio M.N. Passaro, PhD, Associate Professor, Politecnico di Bari, Italy
Vítor Carvalho, PhD, IPCA-EST-2Ai & Algoritmi Research Centre, Portugal

Printed from e-media with permission by:

Curran Associates, Inc.
57 Morehouse Lane
Red Hook, NY 12571

Some format issues inherent in the e-media version may also appear in this print version.

Printed by Curran Associates, Inc. (2018)

International Academy, Research, and Industry Association (IARIA)
412 Derby Way
Wilmington, DE 19810

Phone: (408) 893-6407
Fax: (408) 527-6351

petre@iaria.org

Additional copies of this publication are available from:

Curran Associates, Inc.
57 Morehouse Lane
Red Hook, NY 12571 USA
Phone: 845-758-0400
Fax: 845-758-2633
Email: curran@proceedings.com
Web: www.proceedings.com

Table of Contents

SENSORDEVICES 2018

Forward

The Ninth International Conference on Sensor Device Technologies and Applications (SENSORDEVICES 2018), held between September 16, 2018 and September 20, 2018 in Venice, Italy, continued a series of events focusing on sensor devices themselves, the technology-capturing style of sensors, special technologies, signal control and interfaces, and particularly sensors-oriented applications. The evolution of the nano-and microtechnologies, nanomaterials, and the new business services make the sensor device industry and research on sensor-themselves very challenging.

Most of the sensor-oriented research and industry initiatives are focusing on sensor networks, data security, exchange protocols, energy optimization, and features related to intermittent connections. Recently, the concept of Internet-of-things gathers attention, especially when integrating IPv4 and IIPv6 networks. We welcomed technical papers presenting research and practical results, position papers addressing the pros and cons of specific proposals, such as those being discussed in the standard fora or in industry consortia, survey papers addressing the key problems and solutions on any of the above topics short papers on work in progress, and panel proposals.

We take here the opportunity to warmly thank all the members of the SENSORDEVICES 2018 technical program committee, as well as all the reviewers. The creation of such a high quality conference program would not have been possible without their involvement. We also kindly thank all the authors who dedicated their time and effort to contribute to SENSORDEVICES 2018. We truly believe that, thanks to all these efforts, the final conference program consisted of top quality contributions.

We also gratefully thank the members of the SENSORDEVICES 2018 organizing committee for their help in handling the logistics and for their work that made this professional meeting a success.

We hope that SENSORDEVICES 2018 was a successful international forum for the exchange of ideas and results between academia and industry and to promote further progress in the field of sensor device technologies and applications. We also hope that Venice, Italy provided a pleasant environment during the conference and everyone saved some time to enjoy the unique charm of the city.

SENSORDEVICES 2018 Chairs

SENSORDEVICES Steering Committee

Sergey Y. Yurish, International Frequency Sensor Association (IFSA), Spain
Hiroo Wakaumi, Tokyo Metropolitan College of Industrial Technology, Japan
Jeong-Woo Choi, Sogang University, Korea
Jerzy P. Lukaszewicz, Nicoulaus Copernicus University, Torun, Poland
Daniele Zonta, University of Strathclyde, UK

SENSORDEVICES 2018
Committee

SENSORDEVICES Steering Committee

Sergey Y. Yurish, International Frequency Sensor Association (IFSA), Spain
Hiroo Wakaumi, Tokyo Metropolitan College of Industrial Technology, Japan
Jeong-Woo Choi, Sogang University, Korea
Jerzy P. Lukaszewicz, Nicoulaus Copernicus University, Torun, Poland
Daniele Zonta, University of Strathclyde, UK
Eiji Higurashi, University of Tokyo, Japan
Jean Paul Salvestrini, GeorgiaTech Lorraine, USA
Giovanni Pau, Kore University of Enna, Italy

SENSORDEVICES 2018 Research/Industry Chairs

Winfried Vonau, Kurt-Schwabe-Institut für Mess- und Sensortechnik e.V. Meinsberg, Germany
Paulo E. Cruvinel, Embrapa Instrumentation, Brazil
Dan Wilson, Southern Research Station - Center for Bottomland Hardwoods Research, USA
Yanxia Hou, Institut Nanosciences et Cryogénie | CEA-Grenoble, France
Yoseph Bar-Cohen, Jet Propulsion Laboratory | NASA, USA
Yurong Jiang, Hewlett-Packard Labs, USA
Irinela Chilibon, National Institute of Research and Development for Optoelectronics, Romania

SENSORDEVICES 2018 Technical Program Committee

Ahmed N Abdalla, FTECK, UMP, Malaysia
Iyad Abuhadrous, Palestine Technical College, Palestine
Ahmed Alfadhel, Rochester Institute of Technology, USA / Research Products Development Company (RPDC), Saudi Arabia
Amir R. Ali, German University in Cairo, Egypt
Itziar G. Alonso González, University of Las Palmas de Gran Canaria (ULPGC), Spain
Jesús B. Alonso Hernández, Institute for Technological Development and Innovation in Communications (IDeTIC) | University of Las Palmas de Gran Canaria (ULPGC), Spain
Fabrice Andrieux, Lancaster University, UK
Darius Andriukaitis, Kaunas University of Technology (KTU), Lithuania
Djamila Aouada, University of Luxembourg, Luxembourg
Francisco J. Arcega, University of Zaragoza, Spain
Ammar Aryan, Université de Caen Basse-Normandie, France
Ripendra Awal, Prairie View A&M University, USA
Yoseph Bar-Cohen, Jet Propulsion Laboratory | NASA, USA
Ramón Barber Castaño, University Carlos III of Madrid, Spain
Juan Bautista Talens Felis, Universitat Politècnica de València, Spain
Michal Borecki, Warsaw University of Technology, Poland
Manuel José Cabral dos Santos Reis, University of Trás-os-Montes e Alto Douro, Portugal
Antonio José Calderón Godoy, University of Extremadura, Spain

Alfonso Gómez Espinosa, Tecnológico de Monterrey Campus Querétaro, Mexico
Friederike J. Gruhl, Karlsruhe Institute of Technology (KIT) | Institute of Microstructure Technology (IMT), Germany
Banshi D. Gupta, Indian Institute of Technology Delhi, New Delhi, India
Fengshou Gu, University of Huddersfield, UK
Jan Havlík, Czech Technical University in Prague, Czech Republic
Yigang He, Hefei University of Technology, China
Eiji Higurashi, University of Tokyo, Japan
Carmen Horrillo Güemes, CSIC, Madrid, Spain
Yanxia Hou, Institut Nanosciences et Cryogénie | CEA-Grenoble, France
Kun Mean Hou, Laboratoire LIMOS UMR 6158 CNRS, France
Wen-Jyi Hwang, National Taiwan Normal University, Taiwan
M. Ichchou, Ecole Centrale de Lyon, France
Raul Igual, EUPT | University of Zaragoza, Teruel, Spain
Emmanuel Iwuoha, University of Western Cape, South Africa
Alberto Izquierdo Fuente, Universidad de Valladolid, Spain
Gotan Jain, K.K.H.A. Arts, S.M.G.L. Commerce and Science College, Chandwad, India
Yurong Jiang, Hewlett-Packard Labs, USA
Yunho Jung, Korea Aerospace University, Korea
Hirokatsu Kataoka, AIST, Japan
Jin (Wei) Kocsis, University of Akron, USA
Priscila M. Kosaka, Instituto de Microelectrónica de Madrid (CSIC), Spain
Sapozhnikova Kseniia, D. I. Mendeleyev Institute for Metrology, St.Petersburg, Russia
Anil Kumar, CSIR-CEERI, Pilani, India
Raj Kumar, University of Oslo, Norway
Narito Kurata, Tsukuba University of Technology, Japan
Dong-Weon Lee, Chonnam National University, Korea
Gyu Myoung Lee, Liverpool John Moores University, UK
Kevin Lee, School of Science and Technology - Nottingham Trent University, UK
Martin Lenzhofer, CTR Carinthian Tech Research AG, Austria
Sylvie Lesoille, Andra, France
Dawei Li, Donghua University, Shanghai, China
Tianliang Li, Nanyang Technological University, Singapore
Diego Ettore Liberati, National Research Council of Italy, Italy
Qing Lin, Soongsil University, Korea
Thurmon Lockhart, Arizona State University, USA
Wen-Shiung Lour, National Taiwan Ocean University, Taiwan
Gilles Lubineau, PSE/KAUST, Saudi Arabia
Jerzy P. Lukaszewicz, Nicoulaus Copernicus University, Torun, Poland
Mai S. Mabrouk, Misr University for Science and Technology, Egypt
Luca Maiolo, Institute for Microelectronics and Microsystems - National Research Council (IMM-CNR), Roma, Italy
Oleksandr Makeyev, Diné College, USA
Piero Malcovati, University of Pavia, Italy

Copyright Information

Optimization of Giant Magnetoimpedance Effect in Co-rich Magnetic Microwires

Paula Corte-León, Lorena Gonzalez-Legarreta, Valentina Zhukova, Mihail Ipatov, Julian Gonzalez
Department Materials Physics, Univ. Basque Country, UPV/EHU, 20018 San Sebastian, Spain
e-mail: paula.corte@ehu.eus, lorena.glegarreta@gmail.com, valentina.zhukova@ehu.es, mihail.ipatov@ehu.eus, julianmaria.gonzalez@ehu.es

Juan Maria Blanco
Department Applied Physics I, Univ. Basque Country, EUPDS, UPV/EHU, 20018, San Sebastian, Spain
e-mail: juanmaria.blanco@ehu.es

Arcady Zhukov
Department Materials Physics, Univ. Basque Country, UPV/EHU, 20018 San Sebastian and Ikerbasque, Bilbao Spain
e-mail: arkadi.joukov@ehu.es

Abstract—**Processing of the Co-rich glass-coated microwire by Joule-heating allows considerable improvement of magnetic softness and Giant Magneto-Impedance (GMI) effect. At optimal Joule heating conditions, we observed GMI ratio up to 650%, low magnetic anisotropy field of about 25 A/m and coercivity of about 2 A/m. Observed experimental dependencies are discussed considering various factors affecting the magnetic properties of studied microwire upon Joule heating: induced magnetic anisotropy, internal stresses relaxation and radial distribution of magnetic anisotropy.**

Keywords- giant magnetoimpedance effect, magnetic microwires; magnetic softness.

I. INTRODUCTION

Giant Magneto-Impedance (GMI) effect presenting one of the highest sensitivities to applied magnetic field has become a topic of great attention owing to it interest for development of cost effective magnetic field sensors and devices [1]-[7].

In most of publications [1]-[8], the expression for the GMI effect through the GMI ratio, $\Delta Z/Z$, defined as:

$$\Delta Z/Z = [Z(H) - Z(H_{max})] / Z(H_{max}), \quad (1)$$

is used.

The highest GMI ratio up to 650 %, as well as magnetic field sensitivity up to 10%/A/m were reported experimentally for amorphous magnetic Co-rich microwires [9] [10]. These achievements allowed to develop a number of extremely sensitive magnetic sensors and magnetometers using magnetic wire presenting GMI effect [5][6][11]-[13].

Theoretically predicted maximum GMI ratio is about 3000% [14] that is few times superior to the experimentally reported maximum ΔZ/Z-values [9][10]. Therefore, it is expected that experimentally reported GMI effect can be considerably improved by preparation technology improvement, as well as by using of effective post-processing methods. It is clear that the use of magnetic materials with higher GMI effect can improve the performance of magnetic devices. Consequently, considerable efforts have been paid to study the post-processing on GMI ratio of various magnetic materials [4] [7][15]-[18].

Developed GMI sensors present excellent magnetic field sensitivity, quick response and low power consumption [5]. However, one of the weak points of the GMI sensors is the size [5][19]. The demagnetizing factor and hence the diameter of magnetic wires is the limiting factor [7][20]. Therefore, thin magnetically soft wires are highly demanded for development of the GMI sensors.

The thinnest magnetic wires with ferromagnetic metallic nucleus diameter from 0.05 to 80 μm covered by glass coating can be prepared using Taylor-Ulitovsky method [4] [7][21].

Presence of glass-coating results in elevated magnetoelastic anisotropy [22]-[25]. The common way for improvement of the magnetic softness is a careful selection of chemical composition of metallic alloy allowing achievement of vanishing magnetostriction coefficient [4] [10]. However, experimentally observed GMI ratio values are still considerably lower than theoretically predicted optimized GMI ratio (about 3000%) [14][26]. As showed elsewhere, the value of GMI ratio is intrinsically related to magnetic softness [27]. Therefore, further efforts for optimization of magnetic softness are expected to improve the GMI ratio in amorphous wires.

The most common post-processing of magnetic materials usually consists of annealing [4]. However, conventional annealing of Co-rich originates considerable magnetic hardening hence deterioration of GMI effect [4][7][10][28]. Observed changes of magnetic properties induced by the conventional annealing in Co-rich microwires have been explained considering change of the magnetostriction coefficient value and sign as well as modification of the domain structure and remagnetization process mechanism related to the stresses relaxation [10][28].

On the other hand, GMI ratio enhancement has been reported after stress-annealing or Joule heating of Co-rich microwires at certain annealing conditions [7]. This difference has been associated to the induced magnetic anisotropy. The origin of the anisotropy induced by stress or magnetic field annealing of amorphous materials has been previously attributed the directional ordering of atomic pairs, compositional and topological short- range ordering or back stresses [29]-[31].

Consequently, it is expected that the GMI ratio can by improved by the Joule. Up to now, only a few experimental results on effect of Joule heating on GMI effect have been reported [7]

Consequently, in this paper we systematically studied the influence of Joule heating on magnetic properties and GMI effect of Co-rich glass-coated microwires.

In the section Experimental details, we present the description of the experimental techniques used for the sample preparation and characterization, while in the Experimental results and discussion, we describe the results on the effect of Joule heating on hysteretic properties and the GMI effect of Co-rich microwires.

II. Experimental Details

We studied the influence of Joule heating on magnetic properties and GMI effect of $Co_{67}Fe_{3.9}Ni_{1.4}B_{11.5}Si_{14.5}Mo_{1.6}$ amorphous glass-coated microwires (total diameter, D= 26.6 μm, metallic nucleus diameter, d=25.6 μm) prepared by Taylor-Ulitovsky method described elsewhere [1][4][7].

The hysteresis loops were measured by the fluxmetric method as described in previous publications on magnetic microwires [7]. We represent the hysteresis loops as the dependence of normalized magnetization, M/M_{Hmax} (where M is the sample's magnetic moment at given magnetic field, H, and M_{Hmax} is the sample's magnetic moment at the maximum magnetic field amplitude, H_m) versus magnetic field, H.

We employed the DC current values, I, of 30 and 40 mA selected in order to avoid the deterioration of magnetic properties related to the crystallization. Employed current densities (58.3 and 77.7 A/mm^2 for 30 and 40 mA respectively) were clearly below the value that can produce magnetic hardening and/or crystallization of the samples [32].

All the measurements have been performed for the same sample. We have measured the hysteresis loops and GMI effect in the as-prepared sample, then the same sample has been annealed. All the measurements have been performed after each annealing and then the same sample has been annealed again. Finally, we obtained the dependencies of maximum GMI ratio, $\Delta Z/Z_{max}$ on frequency, f, at different annealing time, t_{ann}.

The impedance and its magnetic field dependence were evaluated using the micro-strip sample holder previously described elsewhere [16][26]. The microwire impedance, Z, was evaluated from the reflection coefficient S_{11} measured by the vector network analyzer (Agilent N5230A).

The GMI ratio, $\Delta Z/Z$, is defined using eq. (1). Use of aforementioned technique allows to measure GMI effect in the extended frequency range (up to 1 GHz).

III. Experimental Results and Discussion

As-prepared $Co_{67}Fe_{3.9}Ni_{1.5}B_{11.5}Si_{14.5}Mo_{1.6}$ microwire presents quite soft magnetic properties characterized by hysteresis loop with low coercivity (about 7 A/m) typical for glass-coated microwires with low and negative magnetostriction coefficient (see Figure 1).

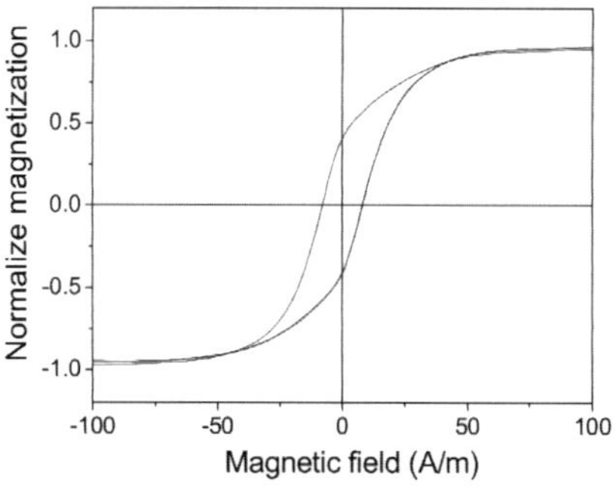

Figure 1. Hysteresis loop of as-prepared $Co_{67}Fe_{3.9}Ni_{1.5}B_{11.5}Si_{14.5}Mo_{1.6}$ amorphous glass-coated microwire.

Consequently, high GMI ratio (with $\Delta Z/Z_{max}$≈550% at f=300 MHz) is observed, even for as-prepared $Co_{67}Fe_{3.9}Ni_{1.4}B_{11.5}Si_{14.5}Mo_{1.6}$ microwire (see Figure 2).

As-prepared $Co_{67}Fe_{3.9}Ni_{1.4}B_{11.5}Si_{14.5}Mo_{1.6}$ microwire

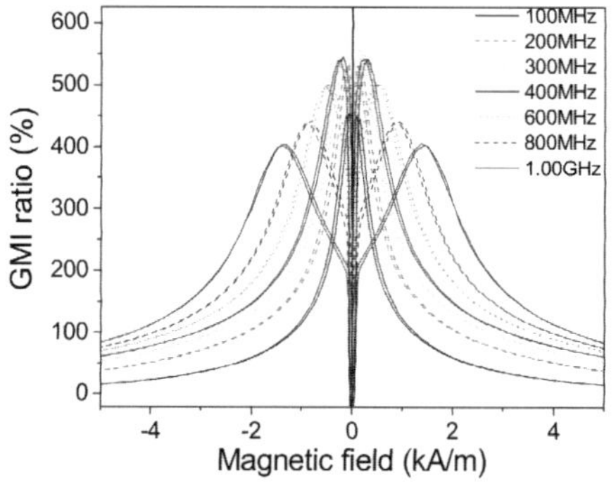

Figure 2. $\Delta Z/Z$(H) dependencies measured in as-prepared $Co_{67}Fe_{3.9}Ni_{1.4}B_{11.5}Si_{14.5}Mo_{1.6}$ microwire at different frequencies.

presents double-peak $\Delta Z/Z(H)$ dependence previously reported for Co-rich magnetic wires with low negative magnetostriction coefficient usually associated to weak circumferential magnetic anisotropy [4][7][27].

After Joule heating at certain conditions, we observed increase of maximum GMI ratio, $\Delta Z/Z_{max}$, as shown for example for the sample annealed at 40 mA for 3 and 5 min (Figures.3a and 3b). At this annealing condition $\Delta Z/Z_{max}$ ≈650% is observed. However, increasing the annealing time $\Delta Z/Z_{max}$ decreases (see Figure. 3c for 40 mA, t_{ann}=10 min).

Similarly, considered magnetic softening is observed after Joule heating at certain conditions: as-compared to as-

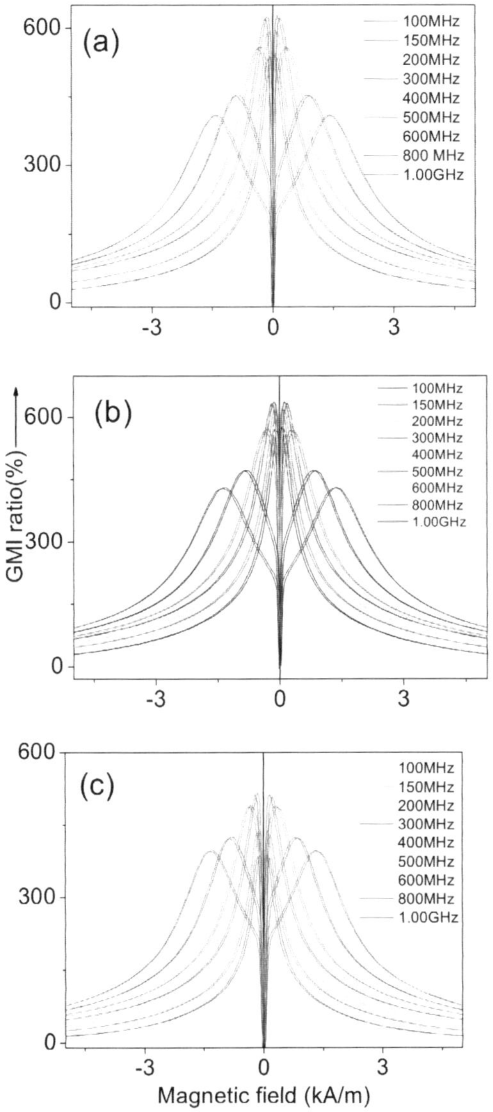

Figure 3. $\Delta Z/Z(H)$ dependencies measured in annealed at 40 mA for 3 min (a), 5 min (b) and 10 min (c) $Co_{67}Fe_{3.9}Ni_{1.4}B_{11.5}Si_{14.5}Mo_{1.6}$ microwire at different frequencies.

prepared sample Joule heated sample present lower coercivity, of about 2 A/m (see Figure 4a).

Additionally, from Figure 4a, it can be observed that current annealed sample presents lower magnetic anisotropy field, H_k, of about 25 A/m. Similar magnetic properties ($H_c \approx$ 2 A/m and $H_k \approx 32$ A/m) are also observed for current annealed microwire at 30 mA for 3 min (see Figure 4b). But further increasing of annealing time (at I= 30 mA) results in slight increasing of coercivity (up to 6 A/m at t_{ann}= 20 min) and of magnetic anisotropy field (up to 75 A/m) (see Figure. 4c).

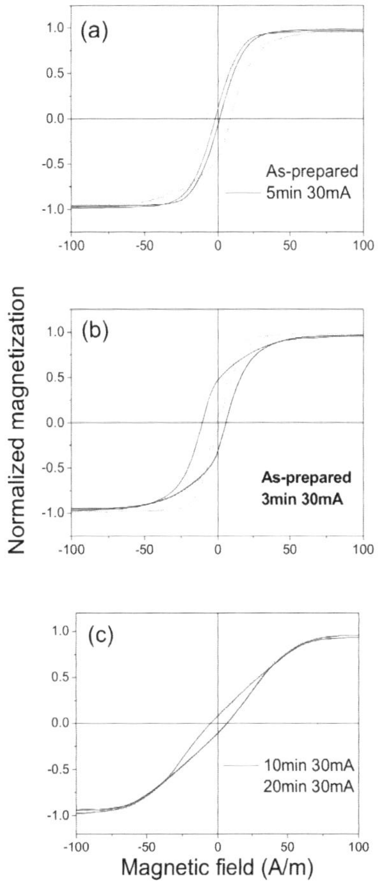

Figure 4. Hysteresis loops of as-prepared and current annealed at 30 mA and 40 mA for 5 min (a), 3 min (b) 10 and 20 min (c) $Co_{67}Fe_{3.9}Ni_{1.5}B_{11.5}Si_{14.5}Mo_{1.6}$ amorphous glass-coated microwire

The evolution of the magnetic anisotropy field, H_k, after current annealing is presented in Figure 5.

The observed results are summarized in Figure 6 where the maximum GMI ratio $\Delta Z/Z_{max}$, is plotted versus the

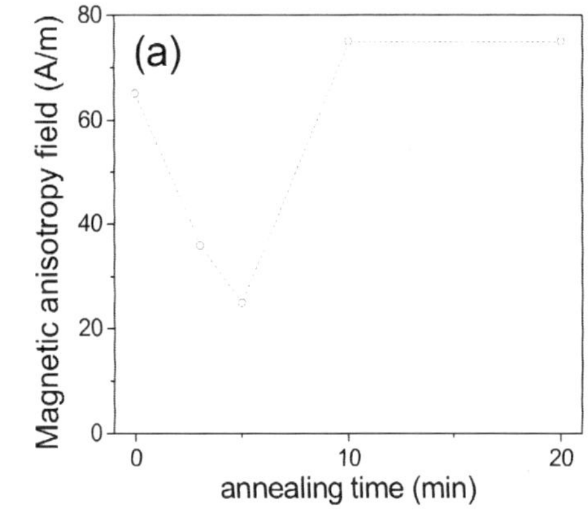

Figure 5. Dependence of the magnetic anisotropy field on Joule annealing time at I=30 mA for $Co_{67}Fe_{3.9}Ni_{1.4}B_{11.5}Si_{14.5}Mo_{1.6}$ microwire.

frequency, $\Delta Z/Z_{max}(f)$, for different annealing conditions. As it can be observed, we achieved remarkable improvement of $\Delta Z/Z_{max}$ from 550% (observed for as-prepared sample) up to 650% (achieved after current annealing at 30mA or 40 mA for short annealing time of 3 and 5 min). Superior $\Delta Z/Z_{max}$ is observed in a whole frequency range, although the optimum frequency where $\Delta Z/Z_{max} \approx 650\%$ in current annealed samples is about 200 MHz, while for as-prepared samples the highest $\Delta Z/Z_{max} \approx 550\%$ is observed at about 300 MHz (see Figure 6).

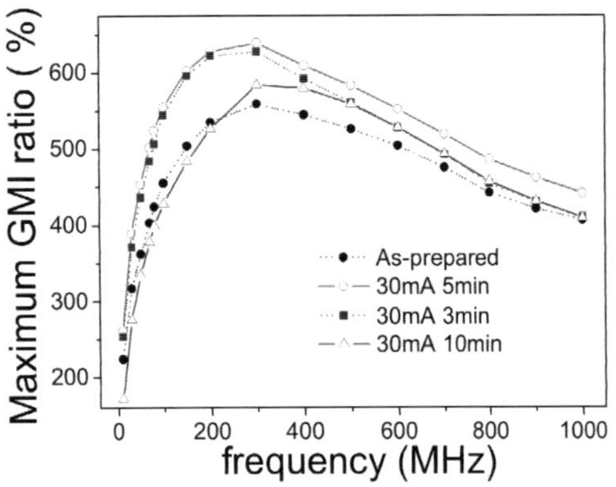

Figure 6. $\Delta Z/Z_{max}(f)$ dependences observed in $Co_{67}Fe_{3.9}Ni_{1.4}B_{11.5}Si_{14.5}Mo_{1.6}$ microwire current annealed at different annealing conditions

The observed influence of current annealing on magnetic softness of $Co_{67}Fe_{3.9}Ni_{1.5}B_{11.5}Si_{14.5}Mo_{1.6}$ glass-coated microwire must be attributed not only to the sample heating, but also to the circumferential magnetic field H_{circ} (associated to the current I flowing through the sample).

The aforementioned circumferential magnetic field, H_{circ}, produced by the current (Oersted field) in the surface of the metallic nucleus can be evaluated as following:

$$H_{circ}=I/2\pi r \qquad (2)$$

where I is the current value, r- radial distance.

Evaluated values of H_{circ} on the surface of studied microwire are $H_{circ} \approx 0.375$ kA/m and 0.5 kA/m for I=30 mA and 40 mA respectively for studied microwire. These H_{circ} –values are clearly superior to the H_k–values evaluated from the hysteresis loops (see Figure 2) and hence can affect the magnetization near the surface during the current annealing.

It is worth mentioning that the Oersted field changes from 0 in the microwire axis to its maximum value in the surface. Therefore, the thin layer in the surface of metallic nucleus is affected by the Oersted magnetic field during the Joule heating. In fact, this layer is involved in the GMI effect.

As mentioned above, it is known that the annealing in presence of magnetic field can considerably affect the magnetic anisotropy of amorphous materials [29]-[36]. The macroscopic magnetic anisotropy is originated by a preferred magnetization direction during the annealing and previously discussed considering the directional ordering of atomic pairs or compositional short- range ordering, as well as the topological short-range ordering [29]-[36].

For the present studies of microwire containing Fe, Co and Ni, the pair ordering looks rather reasonable. We must assume that the evolution of magnetic properties and GMI effect must be affected by the competition of induced magnetic anisotropy related to the presence of the Oersted field as well as stress relaxation and related change of the magnetostriction coefficient reported for conventional furnace annealing [7].

Therefore, it is expected that the current annealing can considerably affect the GMI performance and the hysteresis loops of the studied microwires. We believe that this circumferential magnetic field does not allow magnetic hardening previously reported for conventional furnace annealing of Co-rich microwires [7][18][28].

IV. CONCLUSIONS

We have investigated the influence of Joule heating on GMI ratio of $Co_{67}Fe_{3.9}Ni_{1.5}B_{11.5}Si_{14.5}Mo_{1.6}$ glass-coated microwire. From the obtained dependence, we determined the optimal current annealing conditions and obtained considerable improvement of $\Delta Z/Z_{max}$ –values from 550% to about 650% after appropriate current annealing conditions. Additionally, current annealed microwires present excellent magnetic softness with low magnetic anisotropy field of about 25 A/m and coercivity of 2 A/m.

The observed dependencies have been discussed considering magnetic anisotropy induced by circular magnetic anisotropy during current annealing, internal stresses relaxation and radial distribution of magnetic anisotropy.

ACKNOWLEDGMENT

This work was supported by Spanish MINECO under MAT2013-47231-C2-1-P, by the Government of the Basque Country under the Elkartek (RTM 4.0) project and by the University of Basque Country under the scheme of "Ayuda a Grupos Consolidados" (Ref. PPG17/35). The authors thank for technical and human support provided by SGIker of UPV/EHU (Medidas Magneticas Gipuzkoa) and European funding (ERDF and ESF).

REFERENCES

[1] M. Vazquez, H. Chiriac, A. Zhukov, L. Panina, and T. Uchiyama, "On the state-of-the-art in magnetic microwires and expected trends for scientific and technological studies", Phys. Status Solidi A, vol. 208, pp. 493-501, 2011.

[2] M. Knobel, M. Vazquez, and L. Kraus, "Giant magnetoimpedance", Handbook of magnetic materials, ed. E. Bruck, vol. 15, pp. 497-563, 2003.

[3] M. H. Phan and H. X. Peng, "Giant magnetoimpedance materials: Fundamentals and applications", Progr. Mater. Sci., vol. 53, pp. 323-420, 2008.

[4] A. Zhukov, M. Ipatov, and V. Zhukova, "Advances in Giant Magnetoimpedance of Materials", Handbook of Magnetic Materials, ed. K.H.J. Buschow, vol. 24 ch. 2, pp. 139, 2015.

[5] K. Mohri, T. Uchiyama, L. P. Shen, C. M. Cai, and L. V. Panina, "Amorphous wire and CMOS IC-based sensitive micro-magnetic sensors (MI sensor and SI sensor) for

intelligent measurements and controls", J. Magn. Magn. Mater., vol. 249, pp. 351-356, 2002.

[6] Y. Honkura, "Development of amorphous wire type MI sensors for automobile use", J. Magn. Magn. Mater., vol. 249, pp. 375-381, 2002.

[7] A. Zhukov, M. Ipatov, M. Churyukanova, A. Talaat, J.M. Blanco and V. Zhukova, "Trends in optimization of giant magnetoimpedance effect in amorphous and nanocrystalline materials", J. Alloys Compd., vol. 727, pp. 887-901, 2017.

[8] R. Beach and A. Berkowitz, "Giant magnetic field dependent impedance of amorphous FeCoSiB wire", Appl. Phys. Lett., vol. 64, pp. 3652-3654, 1994.

[9] K. R. Pirota, L. Kraus, H. Chiriac, and M. Knobel, "Magnetic properties and GMI in a CoFeSiB glass-covered microwire", J. Magn. Magn. Mater., vol. 21, pp. L243-L247, 2000.

[10] A. Zhukov, V. Zhukova, J. M. Blanco, and J. Gonzalez, "Recent research on magnetic properties of glass-coated microwires", J. Magn. Magn. Mater., vol. 294, pp.182-192, 2005.

[11] T. Uchiyama, K. Mohri, and Sh. Nakayama, "Measurement of Spontaneous Oscillatory Magnetic Field of Guinea-Pig Smooth Muscle Preparation Using Pico-Tesla Resolution Amorphous Wire Magneto-Impedance Sensor", IEEE Trans. Magn., vol. Mag-47, pp. 3070-3073, 2011.

[12] S. Gudoshnikov et al., "Highly sensitive magnetometer based on the off-diagonal GMI effect in Co-rich glass-coated microwire", Phys. Status Solidi A, vol. 211, pp. 980–985, 2014.

[13] L. Ding et al.,, "Development of a high sensitivity GiantMagneto-Impedance magnetometer: comparison with a commercial Flux-Gate", IEEE Sensors, vol. 9, pp. 159-168, 2009.

[14] L. Kraus, "Theory of giant magneto-impedance in the planar conductor with uniaxial magnetic anisotropy", J. Magn. Magn. Mater., vol. 195, pp. 764-778, 1999.

[15] L. Kraus, Z. Frait, K. R. Pirota, and H. Chiriac, "Giant magnetoimpedance in glass-covered amorphous microwires", J. Magn. Magn. Mater., vol. 254–255, pp. 399–403, 2003.

[16] A. Zhukov, A. Talaat, M. Ipatov, and V. Zhukova, "Tailoring of High Frequency Giant Magnetoimpedance Effect of amorphous Co-rich microwires", IEEE Magn. Lett., vol. 6, 2500104, 2015.

[17] A. F. Cobeño, A. Zhukov, J. M. Blanco, and J. Gónzalez, "Giant magneto-impedance effect in CoMnSiB amorphous microwires", J. Magn. Magn. Mater., vol. 234, L359-L365, 2001.

[18] A. Zhukov, K. Chichay, A. Talaat, V. Rodionova, J.M. Blanco, M. Ipatov and V. Zhukova, "Manipulation of magnetic properties of glass-coated microwires by annealing", J. Magn. Magn. Mater., vol. 383, pp. 232–236, 2015.

[19] K. Mohri, T. Uchiyama, L. V. Panina, M. Yamamoto, and K. Bushida, "Recent Advances of Amorphous Wire CMOS IC Magneto-Impedance Sensors: Innovative High-Performance Micromagnetic Sensor Chip", Journal of Sensors vol. 2015, p. 718069, 2015.

[20] A. P. Zhukov, M. Vázquez, J. Velázquez, H. Chiriac, and V. Larin, "The remagnetization process of thin and ultrathin Fe-rich amorphous wires", J. Magn. Magn. Mater., vol. 151, pp. 132-138, 1995.

[21] H. Chiriac, S. Corodeanu, M. Lostun, G. Ababei, and T-A. Óvári, "Rapidly solidified amorphous nanowires", J. Appl. Phys., vol. 107, 09A301, 2010.

[22] A. S. Antonov, V. T. Borisov, O. V. Borisov, A. F. Prokoshin, and N. A. Usov, "Residual quenching stresses in glass-coated amorphous ferromagnetic microwires", J. Phys. D: Appl. Phys., vol. 33, pp. 1161-1168, 2000.

[23] A. Zhukov et al., "Ferromagnetic resonance and Structure of Fe-based Glass-coated Microwires", J. Magn. Magn. Mater., vol. 203, pp. 238-240, 1999.

[24] S. A. Baranov, V. S. Larin, and A. V. Torcunov, "Technology, Preparation and Properties of the CastGlass-Coated Magnetic Microwires" Crystals, vol 7, p. 136 , 2017.

[25] H. Chiriac, T-A. Ovari, and A. Zhukov, "Magnetoelastic anisotropy of amorphous microwires", J. Magn. Magn. Mater., vol. 254–255, pp. 469–471, 2003.

[26] M. Ipatov, V. Zhukova, A. Zhukov, J. González, and A. Zvezdin, "Low-field hysteresis in the magnetoimpedance of amorphous microwires", Phys. Rev. B, vol 81, p. 134421, 2010.

[27] N. A. Usov, A. S. Antonov, and A. N. Lagar`kov, "Theory of giant magneto-impedance effect in amorphous wires with different types of magnetic anisotropy", J. Magn. Magn. Mater., vol. 185, pp.159-173, 1998.

[28] A. Zhukov, A. Talaat, M. Ipatov, J. M. Blanco, and V. Zhukova, "Tailoring of magnetic properties and GMI effect of Co-rich amorphous microwires by heat treatment", J. Alloys Compd., vol. 615, pp. 610–615, 2014.

[29] F. E. Luborsky and J. L. Walter, "Magnetic Anneal Anisotropy in Amorphous Alloys", IEEE Trans. Magn., vol. Mag-13, pp. 953-956, 1977.

[30] J. Haimovich, T. Jagielinski, and T. Egami, "Magnetic and structural effects of anelastic deformation of an amorphous alloy", J. Appl. Phys., vol. 57, pp. 3581-3583, 1985.

[31] V. Zhukova et al., "Tailoring of magnetoimpedance effect and magnetic softness of Fe-rich glass-coated microwires by stress- annealing", Sci. Rep., vol. 8, p.3202, 2018.

[32] V. Zhukova et al., "Tailoring of magnetic properties of glass coated microwires by current annealing", J. Non-Cryst. Solids, vol. 287, pp. 31-36, 2001.

[33] O. V. Nielsen and H. J. V. Nielsen, "Stress and field-induced magnetic anisotropy in metallic glasses with positive or negative λ_s", Solid Stat. Commun., vol. 35, pp. 281-284, 1980.

[34] T. Miyazaki and M. Takahashi, "Magnetic annealing effect of amorphous $(Fe_{1-x}Co_x)_{77}Si_{10}B_{13}$ alloys", J Appl. Phys., vol. 17, pp.1755-1763, 1978.

[35] M. J. Garcia Prieto et al., "Glass coated Co-rich Amorphous Microwires with Improved Permeability", Sensors & Actuators A, vol. 81/1-3, pp. 227-231, 2000.

[36] V. Zhukova et al., "Grading the magnetic anisotropy and engineering the domain wall dynamics in Fe-rich microwires by stress-annealing", Acta Materialia, vol. 155, pp.279-285, 2018.

Tunning the Giant Magnetoimpedance Effect in Fe-rich Magnetic Microwires by Stress-annealing

Paula Corte-León, Lorena Gonzalez-Legarreta, Valentina Zhukova, Mihail Ipatov,
Department Materials Physics, Univ. Basque Country, UPV/EHU, 20018 San Sebastian, Spain
e-mail: paula.corte@ehu.eus, lorena.glegarreta@gmail.com, valentina.zhukova@ehu.es, mihail.ipatov@ehu.eus

Juan Maria Blanco
Department Applied Physics I, Univ. Basque Country, EUPDS, UPV/EHU, 20018, San Sebastian, Spain
e-mail: juanmaria.blanco@ehu.es

Arcady Zhukov
Department Materials Physics, Univ. Basque Country, UPV/EHU, 20018 San Sebastian and Ikerbasque, Bilbao Spain
e-mail: arkadi.joukov@ehu.es

***Abstract*— The Giant Magneto-Impedance (GMI) effect is one of the most promising phenomena for creation of miniaturized magnetic sensors and magnetometers. We propose a route for development of cost-effective magnetically soft microwires for GMI applications. Stress-annealing of the Fe-rich glass-coated microwire allows considerable improvement of magnetic softness and giant Magneto-Impedance effect. Observed experimental dependencies are discussed considering various factors affecting the magnetic properties of the studied microwire upon stress-annealing: induced magnetic anisotropy and internal stresses relaxation.**

Keywords- giant magnetoimpedance effect; magnetic microwires; magnetic softness.

I. INTRODUCTION

Studies of Giant Magneto-Impedance (GMI) effect have attracted considerable attention of the scientific community and industries over the past two decades owing to a number of technological applications such as magnetic sensors, memories and devices, smart composites for remote stress and temperature monitoring, health monitoring, etc. [1]-[5].

Usually, magnetic field dependences of impedance, Z, is expressed through the GMI ratio [6][7], $\Delta Z/Z$, defined as:

$$\Delta Z/Z \quad = [Z\,(H) \; - \; Z\,(H_{max})] \,/\, Z\,(H_{max}), \qquad (1)$$

where H_{max} is the maximum applied DC magnetic field.

The GMI effect is one of the most promising phenomena for creation of sensitive and inexpensive magnetic sensors and magnetometers. The main interest in GMI effect is related to one of the largest magnetic field sensitivities (up to 10 %/A/m) among non-cryogenic effects [1]-[5][8][9].

The development of magnetic materials presenting the highest GMI effect is essentially relevant for aforementioned applications of the GMI effect in magnetic sensors and devices [1]-[5]. The highest GMI effect is reported for Co-rich magnetic wires where $\Delta Z/Z$ -values of about 600% are achieved [8][9]. But, for most industrial applications, the use of Co-based alloys might be an obstacle since Co belongs to critical materials, being therefore at risk of supply constraints, financially costly and price volatile [10].

On the other hand, for most of emerging applications, the miniaturized magnetic sensors are requested [3]-[5]. Therefore, the development of cost-effective magnetically soft microwires without Co is highly demanded for prospective applications [1][6].

Less expensive Fe-rich glass-coated microwires are good candidates. However, usually highly magnetostrictive as-prepared Fe-rich amorphous glass-coated microwires present rectangular hysteresis loop characterized by low circumferential magnetic permeability and therefore present low GMI effect [3][5][9]. Experimentally, it was confirmed that the domain structure of Fe-rich microwires consists of a large axially magnetized single domain surrounded by the outer domains with radial magnetization orientation [11]. Such domain structure is related to a magnetoelastic anisotropy, i.e., high internal stresses with preferentially axial component and high and positive magnetostriction coefficient.

One of the possibilities is the diminishing of the magnetostriction coefficient by devitrification of amorphous precursor after appropriate annealing [12]-[14]. However, Finemet-type nanocrystalline materials are rather brittle.

Recently, an alternative method has been reported, allowing magnetic softening of Fe-rich microwires through the induced magnetic [15][16]. One of the main advantages of this method is that excellent mechanical properties of amorphous microwires are maintained.

Consequently, in this paper, we present our recent experimental results on effect of stress-annealing on magnetic properties and high frequency GMI effect of Fe-rich glass-coated microwires.

In the section Experimental details, we present the description of the experimental techniques used for the sample preparation and characterization, while in the Experimental results and discussion we describe the results on the effect of conventional and stress annealing on hysteretic properties and GMI effect of Fe-based microwires.

II. EXPERIMENTAL DETAILS

We studied the influence of stress-annealing on magnetic properties and GMI effect of $Fe_{75}B_9Si_{12}C_4$ amorphous glass-coated microwires (total diameter, D = 26.6 μm, metallic nucleus diameter, d = 25.6 μm) prepared by Taylor-Ulitovsky method described elsewhere [5][9].

The samples have been annealed using a conventional furnace. In the case of stress-annealing, the mechanical load has been attached to the end of the sample during the anneling.

The values of stresses applied during the annealing have been calculated as previously described elsewhere [16]:

$$\sigma_m = \frac{K.P}{K\ S_m + S_{gl}};\ \sigma_{gl} = \frac{P}{K\ S_m + S_{gl}} \qquad (2)$$

where $k = E_2/E_1$, E_2 is the Young modulus of the metal, E_1 is the Young modulus of the glass at room temperature, P is the mechanical load applied during the annealing, and S_m and S_{gl} are the cross sections of the metallic nucleus and glass coating respectively. The estimated values of applied stress are calculated using (2) is $\sigma_m \approx 900$ MPa.

The hysteresis loops were measured by the fluxmetric method as described in previous publications on magnetic microwires [5]. We represent the hysteresis loops as the dependence of normalized magnetization, M/M_{Hmax} (where M is the sample's magnetic moment at given magnetic field, H, and M_{Hmax} is the sample's magnetic moment at the maximum magnetic field amplitude, H_m) versus magnetic field, H.

The microwire impedance, Z, was evaluated from the reflection coefficient S_{11} measured by the vector network analyzer using the micro-strip sample holder as previously described [16][17]. This technique allows to extend the frequency range for GMI characterization up to GHz range.

The GMI ratio, $\Delta Z/Z$, is defined using (1).

III. EXPERIMENTAL RESULTS AND DISCUSSION

As expected from previous knowledge on magnetic properties of Fe-rich microwires [16], as-prepared $Fe_{75}B_9Si_{12}C_4$ microwires present perfectly rectangular hysteresis loops (Figure 1).

Conventional annealing (without stress) does not affect the overall hysteresis loop shape, although some decrease of coercivity after annealing is appreciated (Figure 1).

However, after stress-annealing, we observed drastic changes of hysteresis loops and hence magnetic properties of studied $Fe_{75}B_9Si_{12}C_4$ microwires. The hysteresis loops change from perfectly rectangular to linear with quite low coercivity (see Figures 2a-2c). The coercivity, H_c, and remanent magnetization decrease with increasing of the annealing temperature, T_{ann}.

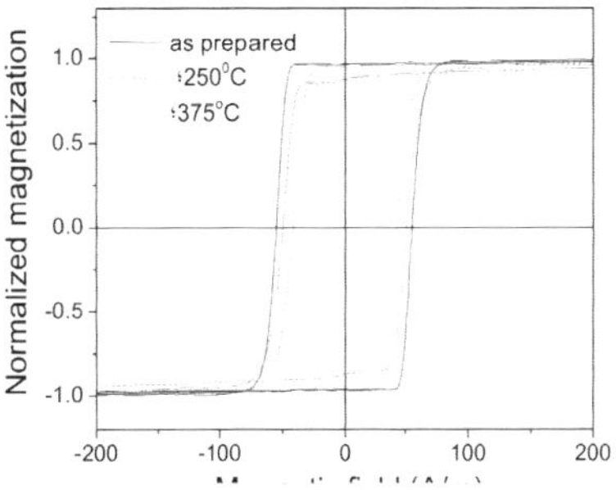

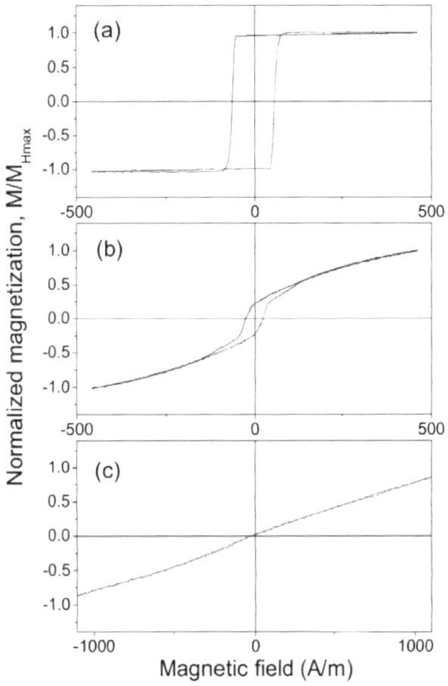

Figure 2. Hysteresis loops as-prepared (a), annealed at 250 °C (b), and 300 °C (c) for 1 h $Fe_{75}B_9Si_{12}C_4$ microwires.

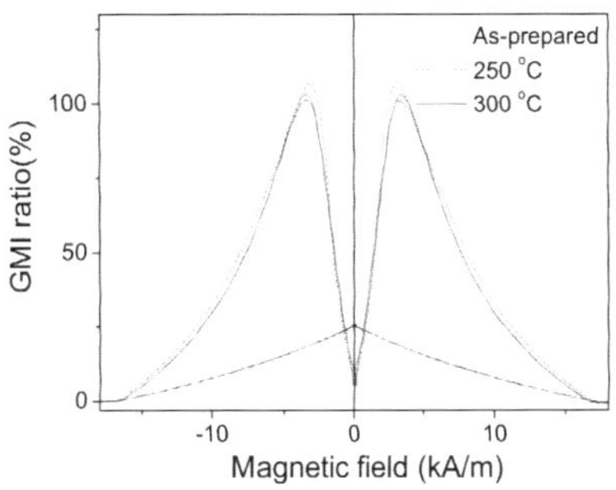

Figure 3. Dependence of GMI ratio, on annealing temperature measured for $Fe_{75}B_9Si_{12}C_4$ microwires at 700 MHz.

The observed modification of the hysteresis loops reflects change of magnetic anisotropy from axial to transverse. Consequently, the hysteresis loops of stress-annealed Fe-rich microwires are quite similar those of Co-rich microwires in which the remagnetization process in axial direction is associated to the magnetization rotation [16].

It is worth mentioning that the transversal magnetic anisotropy in stress-annealed Fe-rich microwires can be tuned by the temperature of stress-annealing (see Figure 1).

As reported elsewhere, magnetic field dependence of GMI ratio is intrinsically related to the type of magnetic anisotropy [18][19]. Therefore, as expected, the GMI ratio value and the magnetic field dependence of studied microwires are rather different. Drastic increasing of GMI ratio after stress-annealing can be appreciated from Figure 3.

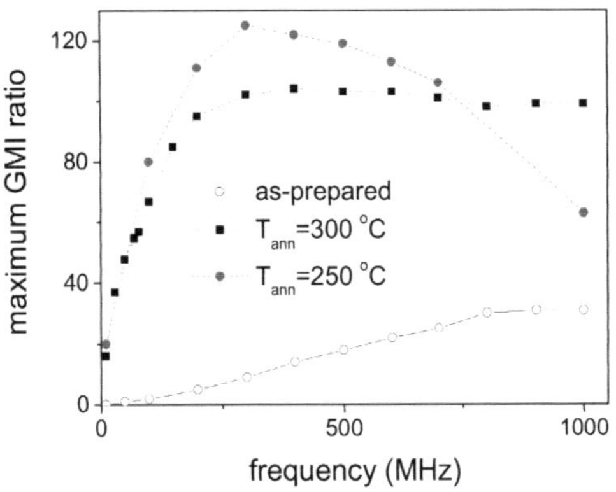

Figure 4. Frequency dependence of maximum GMI ratio for as-prepared and stress-annealed $Fe_{75}B_9Si_{12}C_4$ microwires.

Moreover, the $\Delta Z/Z(H)$ dependencies of as-prepared and stress-annealed samples are essentially different. Stress-annealed samples present double-peak $\Delta Z/Z(H)$ dependencies predicted for the samples with transverse magnetic anisotropy, while decay of $\Delta Z/Z$ versus H typical for axial magnetic anisotropy is observed in as-prepared sample.

As previously reported elsewhere, for each particular magnetic material, there is an optimal frequency range where the GMI effect presents the highest values [16][17][20]. The optimal frequency is related to the sample dimensions (diameter), as well as to the magnetic anisotropy. The observed improvement of GMI ratio is present in a wide frequency range. For comparison, frequency dependencies of maximum GMI ratio on measured frequency are presented in Figure 4.

As can be appreciated from Figure 4, GMI ratio in $Fe_{75}B_9Si_{12}C_4$ microwires stress-annealed at all studied conditions (T_{ann}) is almost one order of magnitude higher than in as-prepared $Fe_{75}B_9Si_{12}C_4$ microwires. The most noticeable is the enhancement of $\Delta Z/Z_m$ -values observed for the frequency band of about 300 MHz, where more than one order increasing of the GMI ratio (up to $\Delta Z/Z_m \approx 125\%$) by stress-annealing is achieved (Figure 4). In the sample stress-annealed at T_{ann} = 300 °C for t_{ann} = 60 min the GMI ratio values of about 100% are observed in a wide frequency band from 200 MHz up to 1 GHz (Figure 4).

Considerable enhancement of GMI ratio observed in stress-annealed Fe-rich microwires must be attributed to transverse magnetic anisotropy evidenced from comparison of hysteresis loops of as-prepared and stress –annealed microwires and $\Delta Z/Z(H)$ dependencies (Figures 2, 3).

The rectangular hysteresis loop observed in as-prepared Fe-rich microwires (Figures 1, 2a) with positive magnetostriction coefficient is commonly attributed to the axial magnetic anisotropy related to the magnetoelastic anisotropy [21]-[23]. From provided simulation [23][24], as well as from indirect experimental studies involving change of magnetic properties upon chemical etching [5][25] of glass-coating or stress relaxation by annealing [5][26], it is confirmed that the axial internal stresses in glass-coated microwires arising during the preparation process are the highest within the most part of the metallic nucleus.

From previous studies, it is known that stresses and/or magnetic field annealing considerably affects the magnetic properties of amorphous materials originated by a macroscopic induced magnetic anisotropy [27]-[29].

The origin of induced magnetic anisotropy of amorphous materials has been discussed in terms of the directional ordering of atomic pairs or compositional short- range ordering [27]-[31], as well as the compositional and topological short range ordering [30][31]. The mentioned pair ordering is commonly considered for amorphous alloys containing at least two magnetic elements [27]-[29]. However, topological short range ordering (also known as structural anisotropy) involves the angular distribution of the atomic bonds and small anisotropic structural rearrangements at temperatures near the glass transition temperature [30].

For the present case of $Fe_{75}B_9Si_{12}C_4$ amorphous microwires containing only one magnetic element (Fe) the pair ordering and the compositional short- range ordering mechanisms of stress- induced magnetic anisotropy are not very likely. Therefore, the contribution of topological short range ordering looks more likely. Additionally, in the case of glass-coated microwires, the presence of the glass-coating associated to strong internal stresses [21]-[23] is relevant for formation of the macroscopic magnetic anisotropy. Consequently, previously the origin of stress-induced anisotropy in Fe-rich ($Fe_{74}B_{13}Si_{11}C_2$) amorphous microwires has been discussed considering "back stresses" giving rise to the redistribution of the internal stresses after stress-annealing [32].

Consequently, the observed transversal magnetic anisotropy induced by stress annealing can be explained considering either increasing to back stresses or aforementioned topological short range ordering.

The advantage of above described effective approach allowing improvement of magnetic softness and high frequency GMI effect of Fe-rich microwires is that the proposed stress-annealing allows to retain superior mechanical properties of amorphous materials, i.e., plasticity and flexibility.

It is worth mentioning that the observed stress-induced anisotropy is rather stable and cannot be removed completely by the subsequent annealing: as recently described [16], only a portion of such stress-annealing induced anisotropy can be eliminated by subsequent annealing without stress.

IV. CONCLUSION

In this work, we present studies of magnetic properties and GMI effect of Fe o-rich microwires.

Considerable enhancement of magnetic softness and GMI effect of Fe-rich microwires has been observed after stress- annealing. For the interpretation of the observed effect of stress annealing, we considered internal stresses relaxation after annealing and interplay of compressive stresses and axial internal stresses after stress annealing. Consequently, appropriate annealing is the effective method for improvement of magnetic softness, domain wall dynamics and GMI effect of glass-coated microwire.

ACKNOWLEDGMENT

This work was supported by Spanish MINECO under MAT2013-47231-C2-1-P, by the Government of the Basque Country under the scheme of "Ayuda a Grupos Consolidados" (Ref.: IT954- 16) and under Elkartek RTM 4.0 project. Technical and human support provided by SGIker (UPV/EHU,) is gratefully acknowledged.

REFERENCES

[1] Novel Functional Magnetic Materials, Fundamentals and Applications (editor A. Zhukov), Springer Series in Materials Science, vol. 231, Springer International Publishing, 2016, ISSN 0933-033X, DOI: 10.1007/978-3-319-26106-5.

[2] M. H. Phan and H. X. Peng, "Giant magnetoimedance materials: Fundamentals and applications", Prog. Mater. Sci., vol. 53, pp. 323-420, 2008.

[3] A. Zhukov, M. Ipatov and V. Zhukova, "Advances in Giant Magnetoimpedance of Materials", Handbook of Magnetic Materials, ed. K.H.J. Buschow, vol. 24 ch. 2, pp. 139-236, 2015.

[4] K. Mohri, T. Uchiyama, L. P. Shen, C. M. Cai and L. V. Panina, "Amorphous wire and CMOS IC-based sensitive micro-magnetic sensors (MI sensor and SI sensor) for intelligent measurements and controls", J. Magn. Magn. Mater., vol. 249, pp. 351-356, 2002.

[5] A. Zhukov et al., "Trends in optimization of giant magnetoimpedance effect in amorphous and nanocrystalline materials", J. Alloys Compd., vol. 727, pp. 887-901, 2017.

[6] L. V. Panina and K. Mohri, "Magneto-impedance effect in amorphous wires", Appl. Phys. Lett., vol. 65, pp. 1189-119, 1994.

[7] R. Beach and A. Berkowitz, "Giant magnetic field dependent impedance of amorphous FeCoSiB wire", Appl. Phys. Lett., vol. 64, pp. 3652-3654, 1994.

[8] K. R. Pirota, L. Kraus, H. Chiriac and M. Knobel, "Magnetic properties and GMI in a CoFeSiB glass-covered microwire", J. Magn. Magn. Mater., vol. 21, pp. L243-L247, 2000.

[9] A. Zhukov, V. Zhukova, J. M. Blanco and J. Gonzalez, "Recent research on magnetic properties of glass-coated microwires", J. Magn. Magn. Mater., vol. 294, pp. 182-192, 2005.

[10] D. Peck, P. Kandachar and E. Tempelman, "Critical materials from a produce design perspective", Mater. Design, vol. 65, pp. 147-159, 2015.

[11] Yu. Kabanov, A. Zhukov, V. Zhukova and J. Gonzalez, "Magnetic domain structure of microwires studied by using the magneto-optical indicator film method", Appl. Phys. Lett., vol. 87, p. 142507, 2005.

[12] A. P. Zhukov et al., "Effect of Nanocrystallization on Magnetic Properties and GMI Effect of Microwires", IEEE Trans. Magn., vol. 50 (6), p. 2501905, 2014.

[13] A. Talaat et al., "Engineering of Magnetic Softness and Magnetoimpedance in Fe-Rich Microwires by Nanocrystallization", JOM, vol. 68(6), pp. 1563-1571, 2016.

[14] C. Dudek, A. L. Adenot-Engelvin, F. Bertin and O. Acher, "Engineering of the magnetic Finemet based nanocristalline glass-coated microwires", J. Non-Cryst Solids, vol. 353, pp. 925-927, 2007.

[15] V. Zhukova et al., "Engineering of magnetic softness and giant magnetoimpedance effect in Fe-rich microwires by stress-annealing", Scr. Mater., vol. 14, pp. 10–14, 2018.

[16] V. Zhukova et al., "Tailoring of magnetoimpedance effect and magnetic softness of Fe-rich glass-coated microwires by stress-annealing", Sci. Reports, vol. 8, p. 3202, 2018.

[17] A. Zhukov, A. Talaat, M. Ipatov and V. Zhukova, "Tailoring of High Frequency Giant Magnetoimpedance Effect of amorphous Co-rich microwires", IEEE Magn. Lett., vol. 6, 2500104, 2015.

[18] N. A. Usov, A. S. Antonov and A. N. Lagar`kov, "Theory of giant magneto-impedance effect in amorphous wires with different types of magnetic anisotropy", J. Magn. Magn. Mater., vol. 185, pp. 159-173, 1998.

[19] P. Aragoneses, A. Zhukov, J. Gonzalez, J. M. Blanco and L. Dominguez, "Effect of AC driving current on Magneto-Impedance effect", Sens. Actuators A, vol. 81/1-3, pp. 86-90, 2000.

[20] D. Ménard, M. Britel, M. P. Ciureanu A. and A. Yelon, "Giant magnetoimpedance in a cylindrical conductor", J. Appl. Phys., vol. 84, pp. 2805–2814, 1998.

[21] A. S. Antonov, V. T. Borisov, O. V. Borisov, A. F. Prokoshin and N. A. Usov, "Residual quenching stresses in glass-coated amorphous ferromagnetic microwires", J. Phys. D: Appl. Phys., vol. 33, pp. 1161-1168, 2000.

[22] A. Zhukov, M. Vázquez, J. Velázquez, A. Hernando and V. Larin, "Magnetic properties of Fe-based glass-coated microwires", J. Magn. Magn. Mater., vol. 170, 323-330, 1997.

[23] H. Chiriac, T-A. Ovari and A. Zhukov, "Magnetoelastic anisotropy of amorphous microwires", J. Magn. Magn. Mater., vol. 254–255, pp. 469–471, 2003.

[24] A. Zhukov et al., "Ferromagnetic resonance and Structure of Fe-based Glass-coated Microwires", J. Magn. Magn. Mater., vol. 203, pp. 238-240, 1999.

[25] C. F. Catalan et al., "Effect of glass coating on magnetic properties of amorphous microwires", Rapidly Quenched &

Metastable Materials, Materials Science & Engineering A, Supplement pp. 438-441, 1997.
[26] A. Zhukov et al., "Manipulation of magnetic properties of glass-coated microwires by annealing", J. Magn. Magn. Mater., vol. 383, pp. 232–236, 2015.
[27] F. E. Luborsky and J. L. Walter, "Magnetic Anneal Anisotropy in Amorphous Alloys", IEEE Trans. Magn., vol. Mag-13, No2, pp. 953-956, 1977.
[28] J. Haimovich, T. Jagielinski, and T. Egami, "Magnetic and structural effects of anelastic deformation of an amorphous alloy", J. Appl. Phys., vol. 57, pp. 3581-3583, 1985.
[29] O. V. Nielsen and H. J. V. Nielsen, "Stress and field-induced magnetic anisotropy in metallic glasses with positive or negative λ_s", Solid Stat. Commun., vol. 35, pp. 281-284, 1980.
[30] T. Jagielinski, "Flash annealing of amorphous alloys", IEEE Trans. Magn. vol. Mag-19, pp. 1925-1927, 1983.
[31] T. Miyazaki and M. Takahashi, "Magnetic annealing effect of amorphous $(Fe_{1-x}Co_x)_{77}Si_{10}B_{13}$ alloys", J Appl. Phys., vol. 17, pp. 1755-1763, 1978.
[32] A. Zhukov, V. Zhukova, V. Larin, J. M. Blanco and J. Gonzalez, "Tailoring of magnetic anisotropy of Fe-rich microwires by stress induced anisotropy", Physica B, vol. 384, pp. 1-4, 2006.

Technological Chain for Tuning of Magnetic Properties of Glass Covered Microwire for Sensor Application

Alexander Chizhik, Arkady Zhukov, Julian Gonzalez, Paula Corte-Leon
Dept. of Physical Materials
University of the Basque Country, UPV/EHU
San Sebastian, Spain
email: oleksandr.chyzhyk@ehu.es, arkadi.joukov@ehu.eus, julianmaria.gonzalez@ehu.eus, paula.corte@ehu.eus

Andrzej Stupakiewicz
University of Bialystok
Bialystok, Poland
email: and@uwb.edu.pl

Abstract—**The technological chain of precise tuning of magnetic properties of amorphous microwires has been established for the first time. The main elements of chain are the chemical composition, geometrical proportions, thermal annealing, mechanical stress and crossed magnetic fields. The relevance and importance of the establishment of the tuning chain is determined by the wide application of magnetic microwires is magnetic sensors.**

Keywords-Soft magnetic materials; Amorphous magnetic wires; Magneto-optic Kerr effect.

I. INTRODUCTION

Amorphous magnetic wires present a number of properties suitable for technical applications, such as giant magnetoimpedance (GMI) effect or magnetic bistability associated with fast domain wall propagation [1]–[4]. Amorphous magnetic wires are also important when using new highly accurate switching sensing devices. Consequently, various types of magnetic wires have been widely investigated during last years [1]–[9].

Our study was directed to select the essential properties to establish a repeatable control of the key technological parameters of magnetic microwires. We recognized that, at each steps of the chain, we change and manipulate the limited number of the properties. Therefore, by increasing the number of the elements of the technological chain, we make the magneto-electric system of the microwire more predictable.

The main idea of our work is the presentation of the technological chain providing the tuning of the basic properties of glass covered microwires. Preliminary, we selected microwire samples with different compositions and geometry to establish in the best way the each step of the process chain.

The structure of the paper is the following: Section II is devoted to the experimental details, Section III – to the composition and annealing, Section IV – influence of torsion stress, Section V – influence of crossed magnetic field, Section VI – conclusions.

II. EXPERIMENTAL DETAILS

The study of the magnetization reversal in the surface of microwires has been performed by means of the optical polarizing microscopy working in reflective mode using the longitudinal magneto-optical Kerr effect (MOKE) configuration [10] [11]. The surface hysteresis loops were obtained from the MOKE intensity for different values of the external magnetic field applied in the axial direction (H_{ax}) as a result of the MOKE images processing [10].

A pair of Helmholtz coils provided an axial magnetic field H_{ax}. The circular magnetic field was originated by the electric current flowing along the microwire. The mechanical torsion stress has been applied. While one of the wire ends was mechanically fixed the second end was rotary stressed to apply the stress with different angle.

Samples annealing has been performed in a conventional furnace below the crystallization temperature and Curie temperature. All the thermal treatments were performed in air because metallic nucleus is coated by the insulating and continuous glass coating. The microwire was heated, annealed and slowly cooled with the furnace under the tensile stress.

Bulk hysteresis loops have been measured by flux-metric method. We represent the normalized magnetization, M/M_s as a function of the axial magnetic field, H, where M is the magnetic moment at given magnetic field and M_s is the magnetic moment of the sample at the maximum magnetic field amplitude. We measured the dependence of the impedance, Z, and GMI ratio, $\Delta Z/Z$, on the magnetic field by using specially designed micro-strip sample holder placed inside a sufficiently long solenoid that creates a homogeneous magnetic field. Z_{MAX} is the value of the impedance measured when the axial magnetic field H was maximal.

III. COMPOSITION AND ANNEALING

The selection of nominal composition and the conditions of the thermal annealing are the basic steps of technological chain. At the first step of the technological route, we demonstrate the role of the microwire composition. Taking into account that the Co-based and Fe-based wires (that is, a wire in which the Co or Fe content is maximal relative to other chemical elements) are the main elements of the wire-based sensors we selected the following samples: $Co_{69.16}Fe_{4.1}B_{11.81}Si_{13.84}Cr_{1.09}$ with metallic nucleus diameter d=25,6 µm and total diameter D=30,2 µm (sample I) and $Fe_{65}B_{15}Si_{15}C_5$ with d=30 µm and D=34,4 µm (sample II). The sample II was annealed in the presence of tensile stress.

Figure 1 shows the magnetic hysteresis loops (Fig. 1a)) and GMI dependencies (Fig. 1b)) of the sample I while the Figure 2 presents the experimental dependencies obtained in the sample II.

The magnetic behaviour is different for these microwires. The magnetization reversal in the as-cast sample I reflects the magnetization rotation contribution while as-cast sample II demonstrates the magnetic bistability. The annealing process reverses the picture: the annealed sample I becomes magnetically bistable while the annealed sample II looses the bistability.

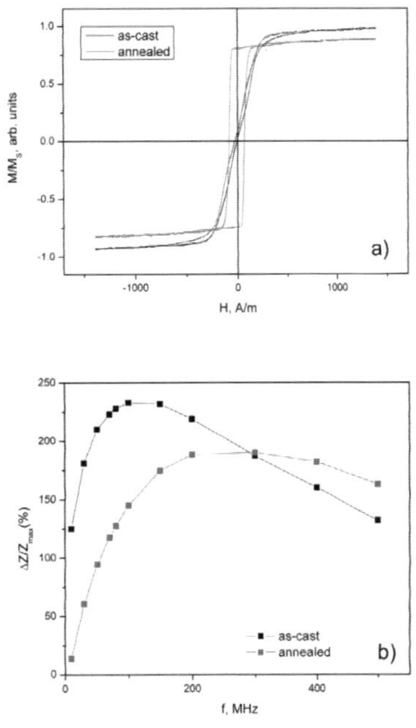

Figure 1. a) bulk hysteresis loops and b) GMI of as-cast and annealed microwire obtained in sample I.

The annealing influences in the opposite manner on the GMI effect in two studied samples (Figs. 1b and 2b). For Co-rich wire, the GMI (Fig. 1b)) of annealed microwire is basically lower than of the as-cast sample [12]. It is associated with to the axial magnetic anisotropy induced by the thermal annealing.

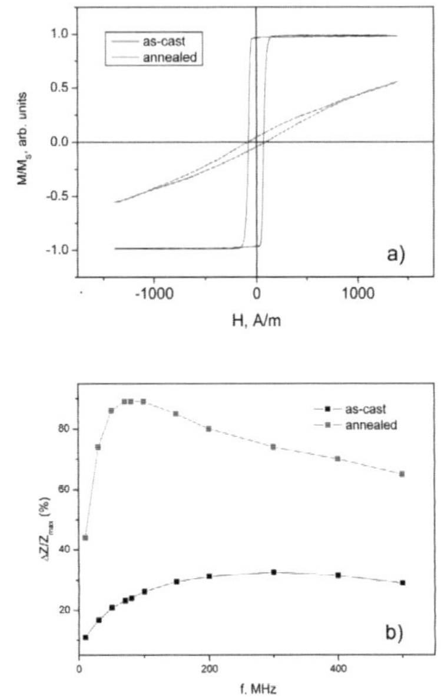

Figure 2. a) bulk hysteresis loops and b) GMI of as-cast and annealed microwire obtained in sample II.

The wire annealed in the presence of the tensile stress demonstrates the rectangular hysteresis loop (Fig. 1a) normally observed in the wires with positive magnetostriction constant. For Fe-rich wire, the increase of GMI ratio (Fig. 2b)) is related to the partial crystallization and change of sign of the magnetostriction constant [13]. The annealing in the presence of stress is related to stress relaxation and considerable effect of internal stresses on magnetostriction [14] [15]. We assume that the stress relaxation induced by annealing can change the magnetostriction sign. On the other, hand under applying stresses we can reduce the magnetostriction constant.

IV. TORSION STRESS

Here, we present the influence of the torsion stress on the magnetization reversal. First, we have demonstrated that the magnetization reversal in the surface of the wire repeats the magnetization reversal in the volume both for as-cast and annealed samples. Figure 3 presents the longitudinal MOKE hysteresis loops for the as-cast and annealed sample I. The shape of these curves coincides with the shape of magnetic hysteresis (Fig. 1a)).

Applying the torsion stress we have demonstrated the possibility of the transformation of the hysteresis of type a) to the hysteresis of type b).

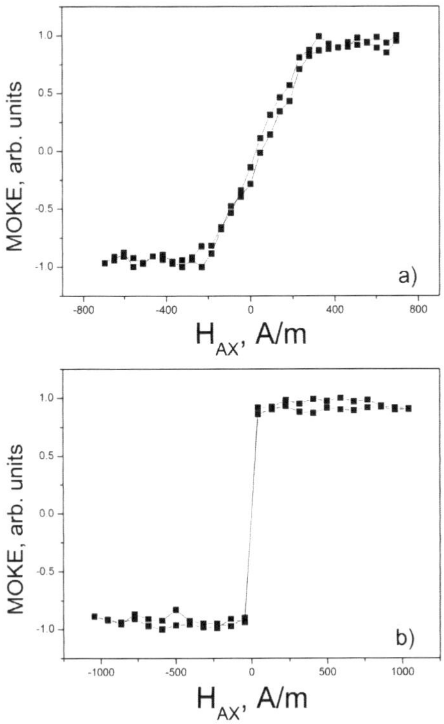

Figure 3. Surface MOKE hysteresis loops obtained in a) as-cast sample I, b) annealed sample I.

Taking into account the importance of thermal stability of the sensors operation, we could remark the following. Generally, the hysteresis loop consists of fluent rotation of the magnetization and sharp jumps. The relation between these two parts of magnetization reversal depends on the temperature. In some wires this effect is observed even when approaching only 50 ^{o}C.

Figure 4 shows the stress induced transformation of the MOKE hysteresis of the as-cast sample I. In the presence of the stress, the jump of the magnetization appears and increases. In such a way, the hysteresis loop takes the shape of the annealed wire (Fig. 3b). The evident jumps of the surface magnetization are observed in the presence of the high torsion stress (the curve with "star" points in the Fig. 4).

V. Crossed Magnetic Field

The final step of the tuning is the application of the crossed magnetic field. Figure 5 shows the MOKE dependencies on circular magnetic field with the presence of DC axial magnetic field acted as an external parameter.

Without the axial field the jump between two circularly magnetized states takes place (line with rectangular black points). The DC axial magnetic field moves the hysteresis loop along the circular field axis. The direction and the value of the shift depend definitely on the sign and the value of the axial field. This shift reflects the change of the angle of helicality of surface magnetic structure.

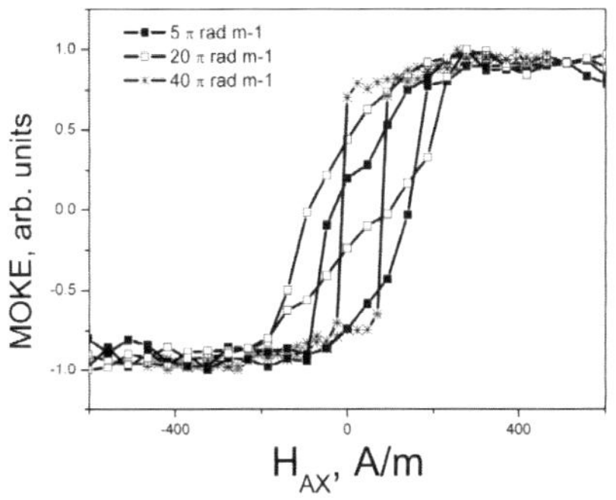

Figure 4. Surface MOKE hysteresis loops obtained in presence of torsion stress of different value in as cast sample I.

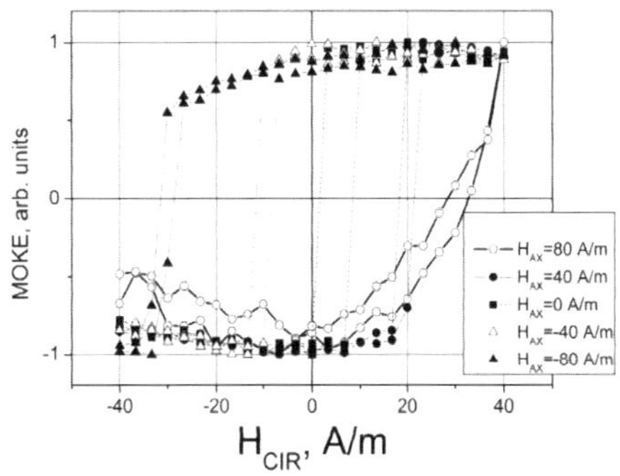

Figure 5. Surface MOKE hysteresis reflecting the magnetization reversal process obtained in a circular field in the presence of DC axial field H_{AX}. Sample I.

The angle between the circular axis of the wire and surface magnetization changes in the presence of axial filed. In such a way, the angle of surface helical structure is smoothly and reversibly adjusted by the DC axial field. This fine tuning of the helical structure is considered as a key method of the control of GMI sensor because the applied experimental configuration of "circular field + DC axial field" is totally coincide with the field configuration of the GMI sensors.

VI. Conclusions

The technical chain of the adjustment of the magnetic and electric properties of magnetic microwire for sensor application is demonstrated. The un-reversible elements of the chain are the chemical composition, geometric metal-glass proportion and the thermal treatment. The reversible units necessary for the fine tuning are the mechanical stress, in particular torsion stress, and the vector sum of crossed circular and axial magnetic fields.

Creation of such type of chains extends the possibility of the control of the main properties of microwires permitting the realization of the predicted parameters of magnetic sensors. The main parameters which could be predicted are the frequency and magnetic field ranges of the stable operation of sensors. Also the range of the sensitivity to external stresses and the level of stress saturation could be determined.

The disadvantage of the proposed scenario is the impossibility of the creation of the universal chain. Different types of the microwires need different elements of the technical chain.

ACKNOWLEDGMENT

We acknowledge support from the National Science Centre Poland under grant DEC-2016/22/M/ST3/00471. This work was supported by Spanish MINECO under MAT2013-47231-C2-1-P, and MAT2013-48054-C2-2-R, by the Government of the Basque Country under the scheme of "Ayuda a Grupos Consolidados" (Ref.: IT954-16), A.C. acknowledges the financial support of the Program of Mobility of the Investigating Personnel Basque Government MV_2017_1_0003.

REFERENCES

[1] Novel Functional Magnetic Materials, Fundamentals and Applications (editor A. Zhukov), Springer Series in Materials Science, vol. 231, Springer International Publishing, 2016, ISSN 0933–033X.

[2] L. V. Panina and K. Mohri, "Magneto-impedance effect in amorphous wires," Appl. Phys. Lett., vol. 65, pp. 1189-1191, Aug. 1994, doi:10.1063/1.112104.

[3] A. Zhukov, M. Ipatov and V. Zhukova, Advances in Giant Magnetoimpedance of Materials, Handbook of Magnetic Materials, ed. K. H. J. Buschow, 24: chapter 2, pp. 139–236, 2015.

[4] I. Ogasawara and S. Ueno, "Preparation and properties of amorphous wires," IEEE Trans. Magn., vol. 31, pp. 1219-1223, Feb. 1995, doi: 10.1109/20.364811.

[5] P. Rudkowski, G. Rudkowska and J. O. Strom-Olsen, "The fabrication of fine metallic fibers by continuous melt-extraction and their magnetic and mechanical properties," Mater. Sci. Eng., vol. A 133, pp. 158-161, Mar. 1991, dpi: 10.1016/0921-5093(91)90038-O.

[6] V. Zhukova, A. Zhukov, V. Kraposhin, A. Prokoshin and J. Gonzalez, "Magnetic properties and GMI of soft melt-extracted magnetic amorphous fibers," Sensors and Actuators (A), vol. 106, pp. 225-229, Sept. 2003, doi: 10.1016/S0924-4247(03)00172-9.

[7] K. Mohri, T. Uchiyama, L. P. Shen, C. M. Cai and L. V. Panina, "Amorphous wire an CMOS IC-based sensitive micro-magnetic sensors (MI sensor and SI sensor) for intelligent measurements and controls," J. Magn. Magn. Mater., vol. 249, pp. 351-356, Aug. 2001, doi: 10.1016/S0304-8853(02)00558-9.

[8] V. Matko V. and R. Šafarič, "Major improvements of quartz crystal pulling sensitivity and linearity using series reactance," Sensors, vol. 9, pp. 8263-8270, Oct. 2009, doi: 10.3390/s91008263.

[9] V. Matko, "Next generation AT-cut quartz crystal sensing devices," Sensors, 2011, vol. 5, pp. 4474-4482, Apr. 2011, doi: 10.3390/s110504474.

[10] A. Stupakiewicz, A. Chizhik, M. Tekielak, A. Zhukov, J. Gonzalez and A. Maziewski, "Direct imaging of the magnetization reversal in microwires using all-MOKE microscopy," Rev. Sci. Instrum., vol. 85, id. 103702, Oct. 2014, doi: 10.1063/1.4896758.

[11] A. Chizhik and J. Gonzalez, Magnetic Microwires: A Magneto-Optical Study. Pan Stanford Publishing Pte. Ltd., Singapore, 2014, ISBN 978-981-4411-26-4.

[12] A. Zhukov, K. Chichay, A. Talaat, V. Rodionova, J. M. Blanco, M. Ipatov and V. Zhukova, "Manipulation of magnetic properties of glass-coated microwires by annealing," J. Magn. Magn. Mater., vol. 383, pp. 232-236, June 2015, doi: 10.1016/j.jmmm.2014.10.003.

[13] V. Zhukova, J. M. Blanco, M. Ipatov, M. Churyukanova, S. Taskaev and A. Zhukov, "Tailoring of magnetoimpedance effect and magnetic softness of Fe-rich glass-coated microwires by stress- annealing," Sci. Reports, vol. 8, id. 3202, Feb. 2018, doi: 10.1038/s41598-018-21356-3.

[14] A. Zhukov, M. Churyukanova, S. Kaloshkin, V. Semenkova, S. Gudoshnikov, M. Ipatov, A. Talaat, J.M. Blanco and V. Zhukova, "Effect of annealing on magnetic properties and magnetostriction coefficient of Fe Ni-based amorphous microwires", J. Alloys and Compounds, vol. 651, pp. 718-723, Aug. 2015, doi: 10.1016/j.jallcom.2015.08.151.

[15] M. Churyukanova, V. Zhukova, A. Talaat, J.J. del Val, S. Kaloshkin, E. Kostitcyna, E. Shuvaeva, V. Sudarchikova and A. Zhukov, "Studies of thermal and magnetic properties of Fe-based amorphous and nanocrystalline glass coated microwires," J. Alloys and Compounds, vol. 615, pp. S256-S260, Jan. 2014, doi: 10.1016/j.jallcom.2013.12.030.

The Development of ASIC Type GSR Sensor Driven by GHz Pulse Current

Yoshinobu Honkura
Magnedesign Corporation,
Nagoya, Japan
E-mail: yoshinobu.honkura@magnedesign.co.jp

Shinpei Honkura
Nanocoil Corporation,
Nagoya, Japan
E-mail:shinpei.honkura@nanocoil.co.jp

***Abstract*—In this paper, we observed the GSR effect driven by GHz pulse current expressed by sine functionality to increase with increasing of the pulse current frequency. These features are explained by spin rotation with GHz rotation speed.**

Keywords-GSR sensor; GMI sensor; GHz pulse.

I. INTRODUCTION

Highly sensitive micro magnetic sensors based on amorphous wire, such as FG sensor [1] introduced in 1987, GMI sensor [2] introduced in 1999 and GSR sensor [3] introduced in 2015, have progressed in both of sensitivity and size for extending Internet of Things (IoT) applications. FG sensor and MI sensor have been used for electronics compass [1][2][4], for automotive use, and smart phones [7]. These three types of sensors are based on the same principle allowing to measure the voltage Vc of the coil surrounding the amorphous wire proportional to the external magnetic field on passing pulse current through the wire, resulting that they have the same element structures of these sensors and the same design of these electronics circuits.

The sensitivity is expected in principle to be dependent on $Vc \infty \sqrt{f} \cdot N \cdot \mu H$, where f means frequency, N is col turn numbers and μ is wire permeability. These pulse current frequencies of FG sensor, MI sensor and GSR sensor have increased from KHz pulse and MHz pulse [9] to GHZ pulse in turn. It resulted that GSR sensor shows the largest sensitivity per element volume.

The deference of frequency brings different electro-magnetic phenomena, even if the same amorphous wires are used. FG sensor detects the rotation of axial magnetization generated in whole cross section of the wire induced by KHz pulse current. MI sensor based on skin effect induced by MHz pulse current detects the rotation of axial magnetization of the skin layer of the wire which is arisen by the movement of 90 degree magnetic wall [9] existing close to the surface [5]. GSR sensor detects a new phenomenon to make the spin rotation of the electronic spin existing on the surface with tilt angle toward axis direction dependent on the magnetic field which is arisen by GHz pulse current so that it can give a sine functional output relationship between coil voltage and magnetic field as well as good linearity, no hysteresis and low noise. We named the above new phenomenon GSR effect.

The sensitivity of GSR sensor is increased with the increase of the coil turn numbers per length, which can be made by 3 dimensional photolithography technique [9] to produce fine pitched micro coil. The micro coil with the coil pitch of 5.5μm and the diameter of 16μm is produced by this new technique. Current GMI sensor has the coil pitch of 30 μm and the diameter of 32μm. The new coil has 6 times smaller coil pitch than that of conventional coil. At the same time, the micro coil is produced directly on the protective film of ASIC surface [9], so that this new process can develop a very small ASIC type GSR sensor without the assembling process with ASIC and the element.

This paper presents 1) the features of GSR sensor, 2) a new process to produce micro coil and 3) development of various ASIC type GSR sensors suitable for different applications.

II. RESEARCH ON GSR EFFECT

A. Principle of GSR effect

The principle of GSR effect induced in the amorphous wire with zero magneto-striction is explained using Figure 1. The wire has a special magnetic domain structure [6] which consists of surface domains with circular spin, axis magnetic domains and 90 degree domain wall existing between two domains. When external magnetic field is applied to the wire along axis direction, electronic spins in surface domains tilt toward the axial direction with the angle dependent on the magnetic field strength. The axis magnetic domains induce axial direction magnetization. GHz pulse current passes through the wire to make strong circular magnetic field and makes only spin rotation with GHz angular velocity but no movement of the domain wall because of strong skin effect induced by GHz current pulse. Figure 2 shows the typical plan structure of GSR element which has one glass coated amorphous wire, 2 wire electrodes and 2 coil electrodes with the size of length of 0.16mm and width of 0.23mm. Figure 3 shows an observed result of the wire voltage and the coil voltage induced by GHz pulse current. The peak coil

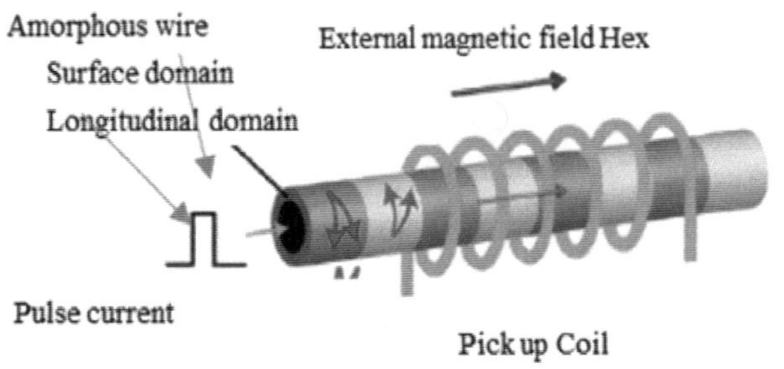

Figure 1. Principle of GSR Effect

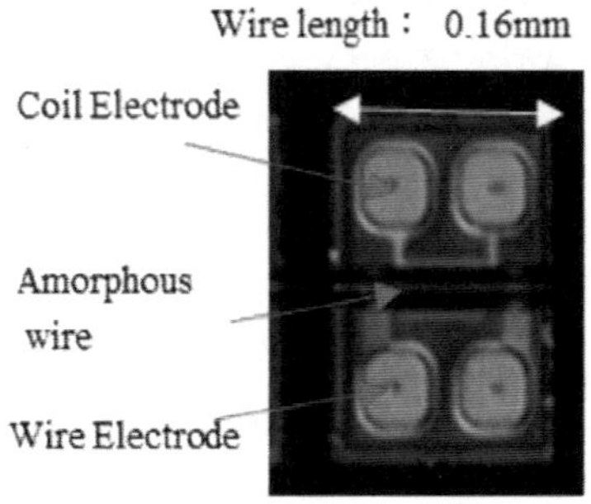

Figure 2. Structure of GSR Element

voltage is induced on the sharp edges of rising and falling of the wire pulse current. It is predicted that 1) GSR effect might increase the coil voltage with the increase of frequency of GHz pulse current and coil turn numbers. 2) The spin rotation not accompanied with domain wall movements could improve magnetic properties of magnetic noise, hysteresis and linearity as well as sensitivity.

B. Experimental Procedure

The present GSR element shown in Figure 2 is equipped with a wire with a composition of $Co_{50.7}Fe_{8.1}B_{13.3}Si_{10.3}$ [8] and the permeability of 1800 with a diameter of 10μm. The tested GSR elements have length of 0.16mm, 0.45mm and 0.96mm, wire resistance of 3Ω、 8Ω, 4.5Ω and 13Ω、 coil turn numbers of 14, 32, 66 and 148 and coil resistance of 80Ω、 210Ω, 360Ω and 810Ω respectively.

The block diagram and ASIC of electronics circuit for GSR sensor in Figure 4(a) is similar to a conventional GMI circuit [1][2][10] but ASIC used in this research has improvements as follows. The pulse generator can generate pulse currents with frequency of1GHz to 3GHz. An electronic switch can operate at a very small interval of 0.1nsec between on and off. An adjustment circuit can control a detection timing from 0 to 4 nsec by interval of 0.1 nsec. The analog circuit has band width of 500 KHz and AD converter has 16 bits. The I2C communication is used to send data to MCU. Consumption current is about 0.4mA @ ODR of 5KHz.

The experiments using GSR sensor produced by connecting with ASIC and GSR elements by wire bonding(Figure 4(b)) are carried out to examine the effects of pulse frequency, detection timing, coil turn numbers and effective permeability on magnetic properties such as sensitivity, relationship between magnetic field and col voltage, measuring rage, linearity, noise and hysteresis. The effect of frequency is examined by changing transition time of pulse current Δt from 0.2nsec to 1 nsec where pulse frequency f is defined by $f=1/2\Delta t$.

C. Results on Features of Coil Voltage of GSR Sensor

A coil voltage of GSR sensor [3] observed under a frequency of 1.5GHz takes a maximum value about the time of 1 nsec and then decreases. The maximum value increases

Figure 3. Observed Coil Voltage

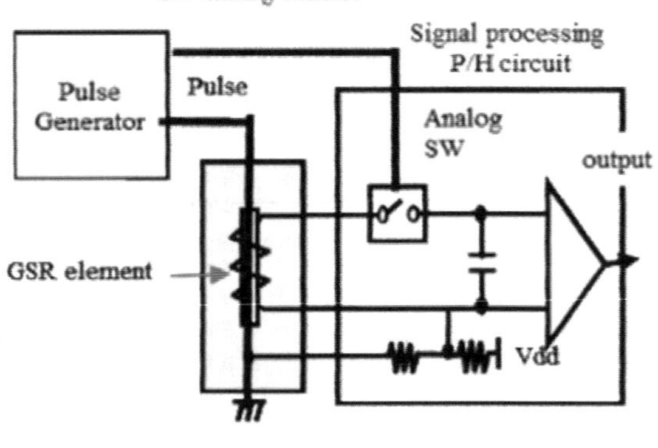

a) Block diagram

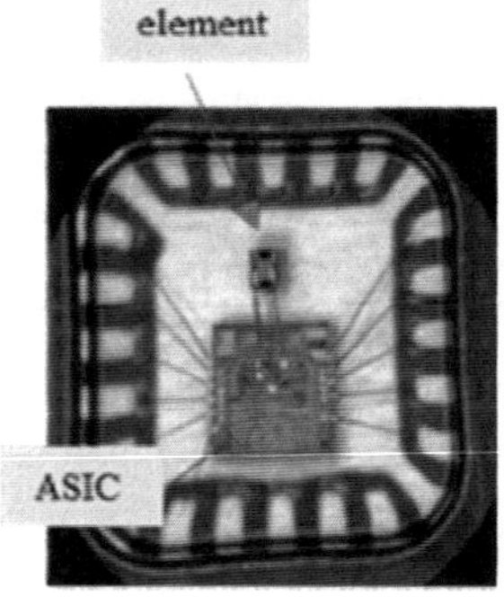

a)ASIC used in the test

Figure 4. The Circuit of GSR Sensor

with increase of magnetic field and takes opposite value by positive and negative. It is noted that coil voltages at H=0 A/m which means electric signal voltage is very small compared to that at H=720 A/m which means magnetic signal voltage. A relationship between the coil voltage and the magnetic field at the maximum detection timing of the falling process is shown in Figure 5. There is a surprising result that the relationship ship has a sin function expressed by an equation as $V=V_0 \cdot \sin(\pi H/2Hm)$ where Hm is defined as the field strength taking Vmax. The experimental data results show that Hm is nearly equal to the anisotropy Hk of the amorphous wire, that is, Hm = 0.96Hk.

measuring range of GMI sensor is one of big disadvantage.

D. Results on Sensitivity of GSR Sensor

The effect of pulse current frequency on the sensitivity of GSR sensor type of length =0.26mm is studied by changing from 1GHz to 3GHz as shown in Figure 7(a). The coil voltage increases with the increase of frequency following saturation over 3GHz. The spins existing in the surface at the angular velocity ω ($= 2\pi f$) and the high speed spin rotation excited by GHz pulse current makes the big coil voltage $V(=-\Delta\varphi/\Delta t)$. The reason to take saturation over 3GHz is because the actual frequency of the pulse current

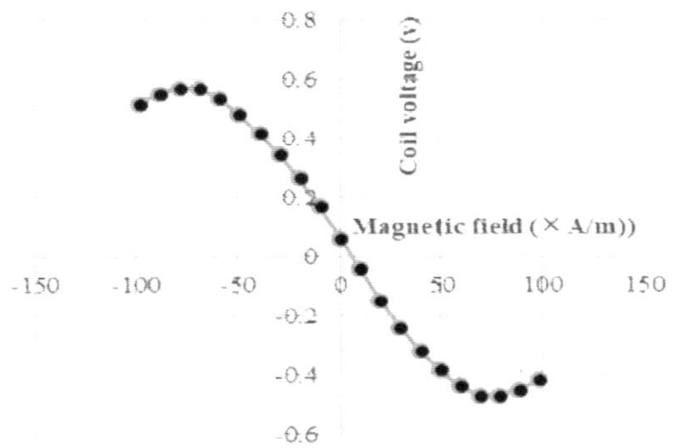

Figure 5. Coil Voltage vs Magnetic Field

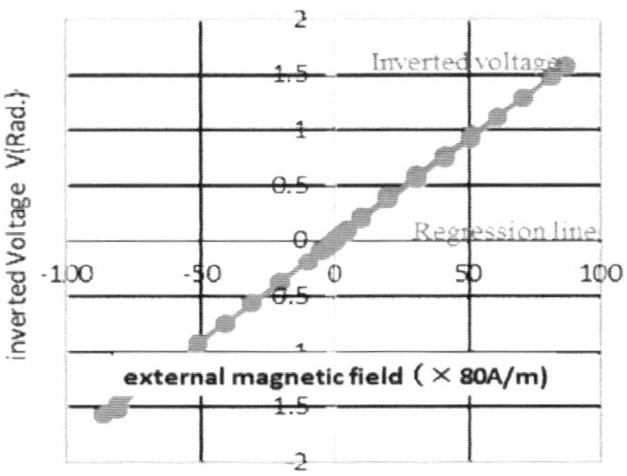

Figure 6. Inverted Coil Voltage vs Regression Line

Figure 6 shows both linear lines of an inversed voltage by $\pi H/2Hm=\arcsin(V/V_0)$ and a regression line. It is found the linear relationship between coil voltage and magnetic field gives good linearity of 0.5% FS and an extension of the measuring range of 960 A/m (linear approximation) to 7200 A/m (dependent on Hm) .On the contrary, GMI sensor output is based on BH curve of amorphous wire without mathematical equation so that a collinear approximation is used not to extend the measuring range. The narrow

passing through the wire becomes lower than input frequency due to the strong eddy current. The sensitivity increases proportional to coil turn numbers as shown in Figure 7(b), where coil turn numbers change from 16 turns to 148 turns keeping their wire lengths of 0.96mm. The influences of increase of coil resistance and parasitic capacitance accomplished with increase of coil turn numbers are not affected as long as present test conditions. The sensitivity increases proportional to effective permeability as

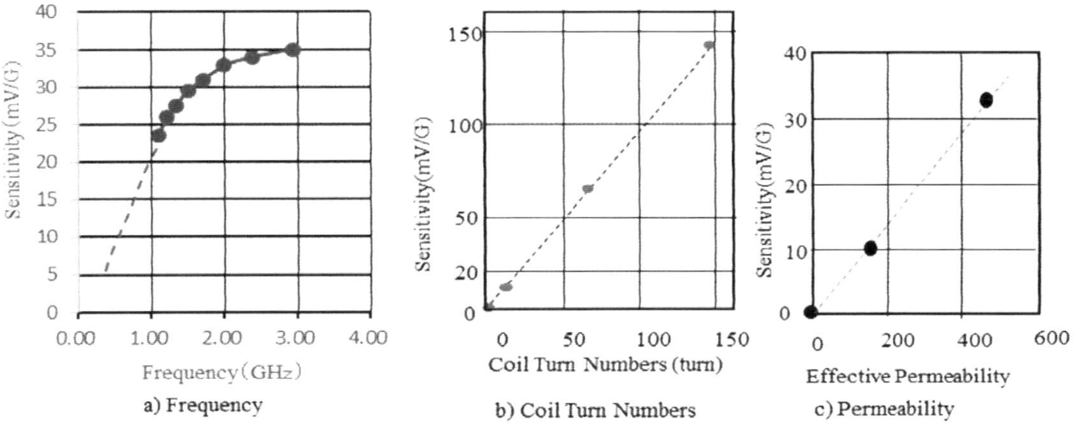

Figure 7. Effect of Frequency, Coil Turn Numbers and Effective Permeability on Sensitivity

shown in Figure 7(c), where wires tested with intrinsic permeability of 1800 and the diameter of 10 μm has effective permeability of 150 and 460 controlled by wire length of 0.16mm and 0.26mm respectively keeping coil turn numbers of 14. It is found that the sensitivity of GSR sensor is effected by pulse frequency, detection type of falling or rising, coil turn numbers and effective permeability.

E. Results on Other Magnetic Properties

It is surprised the rising detection of GSR sensor makes no hysteresis as well as falling detection. GSR effect detects only spin rotation around the wire surface so that hysteresis does not occur. On the contrary, GMI sensor shows a big hysteresis [11] in the case of rising detection because it detects axial magnetization to have the big hysteresis. Rising detection is important for developing high ODR type GSR sensor of over

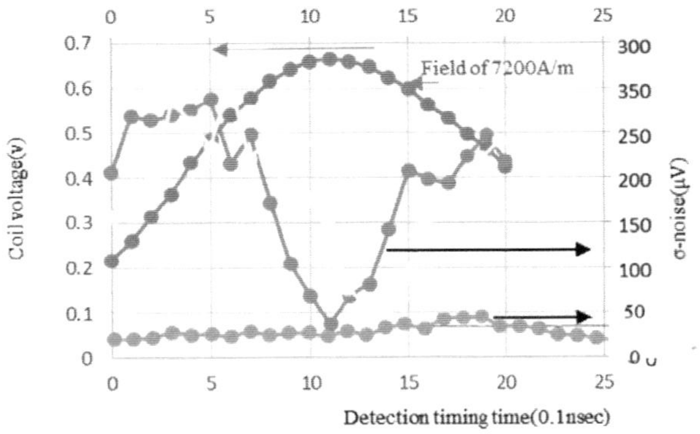

Figure 8. Detection Timing vs σ-Noise

1MHz. It means GSR sensor has bigger potential ability than GMI sensor.

Figure 8 shows the result that σ-noise becomes small to 40μV under H=7200 A/m when falling detection is carried out around peak position of the coil voltage. It means the magnetic noise of GSR sensor occurs only 10μV because the ASIC has own noise of 30 μV. The frequency of pulse current takes the designated GHz frequency around peak position but around the initial and ending time of pulse current it rises or falls slowly to take low frequency of KHz to MHz. High frequency generates spin rotation accompanied with low noise. Low frequency induces domain wall movement to make big noise proportional to magnetic field strength.

Figure 9 shows effects of tension treatment [10] at room temperature on the sin functional relationship between the coil voltage and the magnetic field. When the tension changes from 76kg/mm2 to 10 kg/mm2, the sin function shows distortion from sine function. The reason is probably that the tension might enrich the surface domain with circular spins and press the 90 degree domain wall into the inside of the wire so that the movement of magnetic walls are suppressed and GSR effect to give the correct sine function might occur dominantly.

F. Summary of the Results

We observed GSR effect based on the spin rotation of electron spins_existing in surface circular magnetic domain driven by GHz pulse current. The effect makes new features that coil voltage increases with pulse frequency to make big sensitivity and its relationship with magnetic field and coil voltage has the sin functionality to extend the range of linearity as well as it gives non hysteresis and low noise. These features are explained by spin rotation not accompanied with magnetic wall movements.

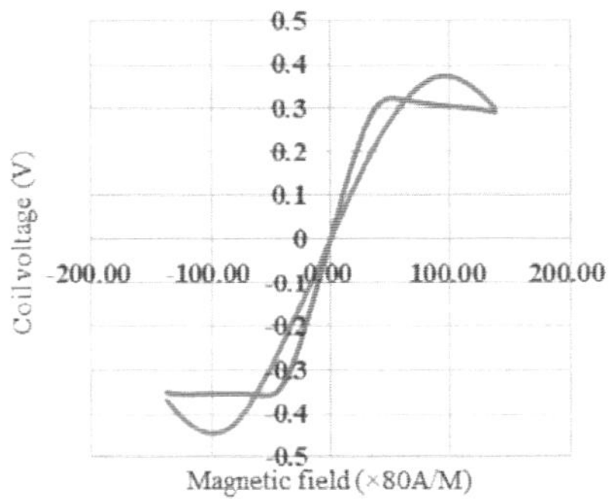

Figure 9. Effects of Tension on Coil Voltage

III. DEVELOPMENT OF 3 DIMENSIONAL PHTOGRAPHY PROCESS FOR A MICRO COIL

We developed a 3 dimensional photography process to produce a micro coil and to put it on the ASIC surface directly. The size of GSR sensor can be drastically downsized by one piece assembling with the element and ASIC as shown in Figure 10. The element is produced through a following process shown in Figure 11 where a glass coated amorphous wire with a diameter of 10μm has a composition of $Co_{50.7}Fe_{8.1}B_{13.3}Si_{10.3}$ and permeability of 1800.

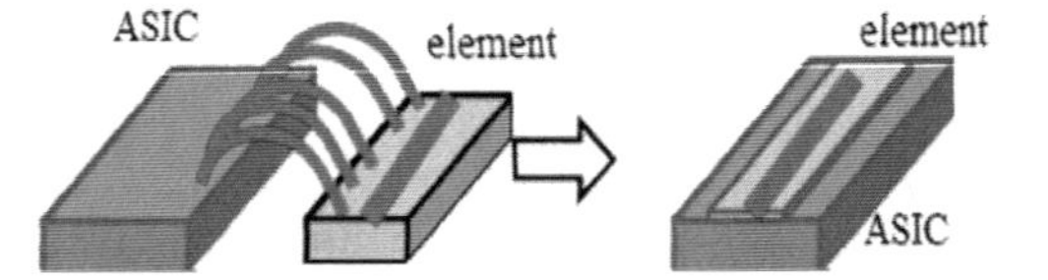

Figure 10. One Piece Assembling with ASIC and GSR Element

The first step is to form a resign film with the thickness of 10 μm and then to make a groove with a width of 18μm and a depth of 7μm on the film by RIE etching. Second step is to produce a bottom coil pattern (Figure 12) with a coil pith of 5.5μm. The 3 dimensional photolithography makes wire pattern on convex- concave plane controlled by diffraction phenomenon between mask lattice and convexo-concave plane in Figure 13. The coil pitch of 5.5μm can be formed by the combination with mask lattice pitch of 5.5μm and groove depth of 7 μm using the light wave length of 700 nm.

Third step is to set the amorphous wire along the groove using a wire aliment machine in Figure 14. This machine can apply the tension of from 50kg/mm2 to 100kg/mm2 o the wire with the diameter of 10 μm for improving linearity of GSR sensor and can align wires with the aliment interval of ± 1 μm accuracy using the wire as a base line for aliment. Fourth step is to mold the wire using an adhesive resist. Fifth step is to produce a wire coil pattern (Figure 15) with a coil pith of 5.5μm using 3 dimensional photolithography on the adhesive resist.

The above process can produce a micro coil with the coil pitch of 5.5μm、 the coil diameter of 16μm、 the wire length of 0.10mm to 2mm and coil turn numbers of 10 turn to 1000 turns on the ASIC surface. GSR sensor can achieve the micro size keeping the good sensor performance.

IV. DEVELOPMENT OF ASIC TYPE GSR SENSOR FOR VARIOUS APPLICATIONS

Various prototype GSR Elements are produced shown in Figure.16. They are divided into one axis type with the length of 0.16mm, 0.45mm and 0.99mm, two axis type and 3axis type.

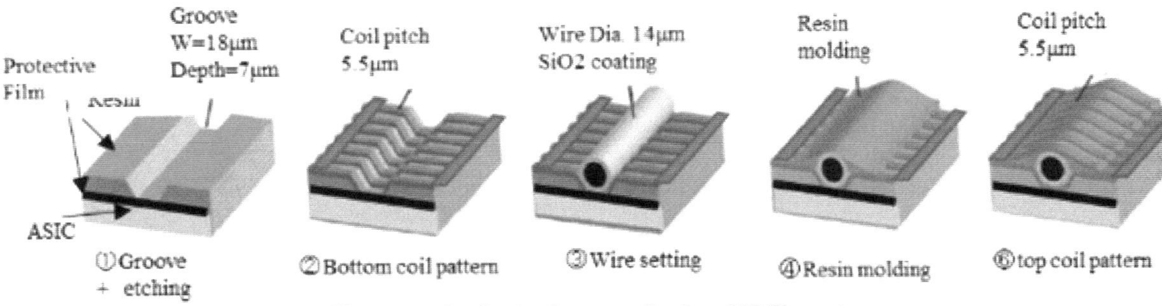

Figure 11. Production Process to Produce GSR Element

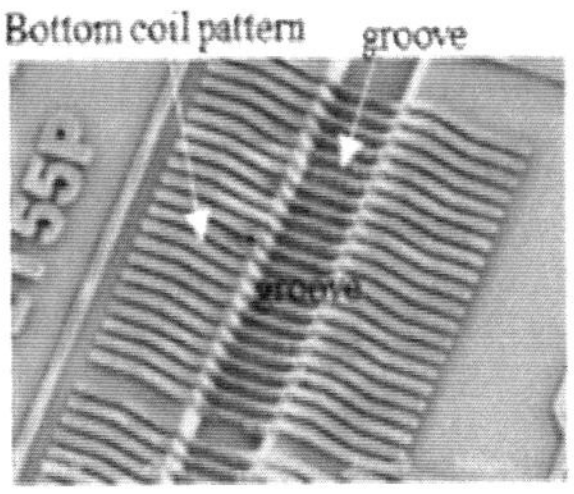

Figure 12. Bottom Coil Pattern on the Groove

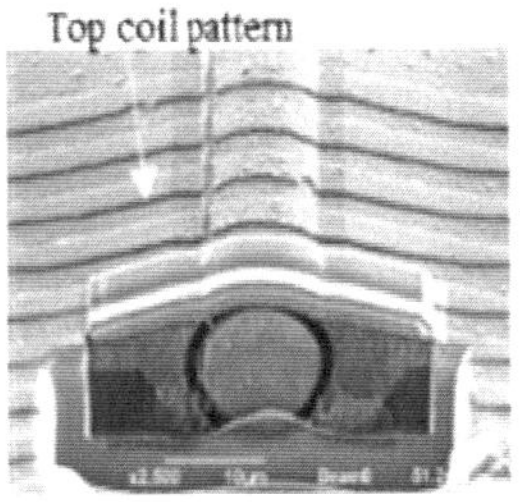

Figure 15. Top Coil Pattern on the Convex

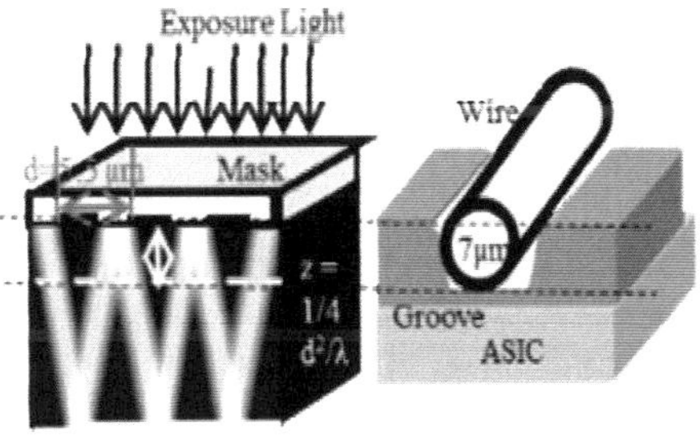

Figure 13. Diffraction Phenomena by Mask Lattice

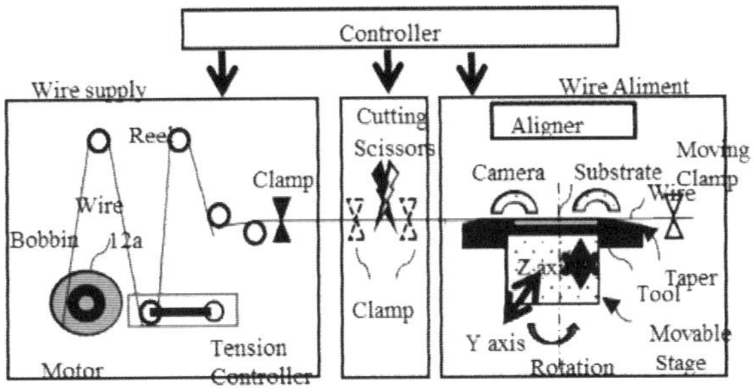

Figure 14. Wire Aliment Machine with the Tension of 76 kg/mm2

Some prototype GSR sensors suitable for specified applications [7] [9] are produced by combination with these elements and the ASIC. The properties of these prototype GSR sensors are shown in Table 1. It is notice that the examination have been carried out using one ASIC which means that their performance are not optimized for all elements. This paper suggests that GSR sensor has good potentiality for some specified applications.

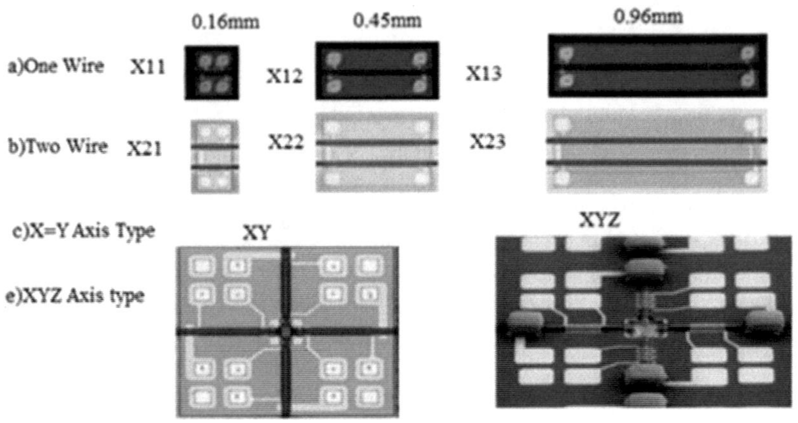

Figure 16. Various Prototype GSR Element

A. *Automotive Use Application or Robot Industries*

These applications request high accuracy and precise magnetic sensors of 16 to 18 bits which needs to equip wide measuring rang of over 80G as well as high sensitivity, good linearity, no hysteresis, low noise, low consumption and wide bandwidth of over 500KHz. Types of X11, X12 and X13 with the wire length of 0.16mm can give the wide measuring range of over 80G and the good linearity of o.1%FS, almost no hysteresis, low σ-noise of 2mG to6mG, low current consumption of 0.4mA and 2.4mG(240nT)/LSB in condition of analog circuit bandwidth of 500KHz and ODR of 5KHz. In addition it is well known that amorphous wire type sensors equip strong reliability and temperature stability against outside atmosphere such temperature, magnetic damage and mechanical stress.

GMI sensor had been expected to be most promising sensor for automotive use, but it is not used because of its narrow measuring range of 12G. The prototype of GSR sensor has wide measuring range of over 80G as well as high total performance 100 times better than that of commercial ASIC type GMI sensor. Here the total performance is calculated by performance index of S/N ratio ×measuring range ×element size.

B. *Small Size GSR Sensor for in the Body Use*

GSR sensor can make very small size possible because GSR element can be produced directly on ASIC surface. The size of GSR sensor can make the same size of the ASIC size of 1.2mm ×1.2mm ×0.1mm which is used in this paper. That means it is promising for in body navigation use.

The magnetic devices with σ-noise of over 10mG for in the body navigation such as catheters, endoscope and so on are used , but they have the poor positioning accuracy of 1-2mm.

TABLE 1. PERFORMANCE OF VARIOUS ASIC TYPE GSR SENSORS

Types	Element Size Length(mm) ×Width (mm)	Resistance Wire/Coil	Coil Turn Numbers	Sensitivity	σNoise @5KHz		S/N Ratio	Measuring Range	Typical Applications Futures
		Ω	turn	mV/G	μV	mG		A/m	
X11	0.16×0.23	3/80	14	10	60	6	167	6400	Automotive Wide range
X12	0.45×0.23	7/330	64	63	60	1	1050	2400	Positioning sensitivity
X13	0.90×0.23	14/740	148	140	140	1	1000	Over 800	nT meter High sensitivity
X21	0.22×0.34	6/140	28	13	35	2.7	370	6400	Automotive Wide range
XY	0.26×0.3 XY:0.6×0.6	6/160	32	30	70	2 (1.4)	430	4000	Encoder 2D
XYZ	0.26×0.3 XYZ:0.6×0.6	6/80	14	16	60	3.8 (2.7)	270	4000	Gyro Compass 3D compass
*MI	0.60×0.35	10/1	16	3.3	70	7	47	960	compass

* Estimated value from Published Data

If types of X12 and X13 with the length of 0.45 mm and 0.90mm respectively with σ-noise of 1mG @ ODR of 5KHz is used, it is expected that the positioning accuracy will improve to under 0.1mm . These applications request long and thin shape sensor. These requests are favorable for direct on-chip type of GSR sensor because wire is long.

C. Compass for Smart Phone and Mobile Computer

Types of XY and XYZ are operated to output 5 data such a X1,X2,Y1,Y2 and temperature @ODR of 1KHz. Type XY for 2D compass consists two X axis coil (X1 and X2) and two Y axis coil (Y1 and Y2) to obtain the magnetic field at the center position by averaging to have noise of 1.4 mG @ ODR of 1KHz and the range of 50G. Type XYZ for 3D compass consists of 2D compass and permalloy parts to detect Z axis magnetic field. The sensitivity for Z axis magnetic field is adjusted by the height of the permalloy part. It is important to form a magnetic circuit by direct connection with the wire and the permalloy parts. It has noise of 2.7mG@ ODR of 1KHz and the range of 50G.

Types of XY and XYZ are designed suitable for next generation type compass which requests noise of under 1mG @ODR of 200Hz and measuring range of 24G compared to current specification of noise of under 10 mG@ ODR of 50 Hz and the range of 12G. The specification means about 20 times higher than conventional one. Types of XY and XYZ are not satisfied to the specification but if ASIC performance or GSR element design are changed to make ODR from 1KHz to 200Hz and the measuring range 50G to 24 G, σ-noise will decrease from 1.4 ～2.7 to about 0.3 ～0.7 to be satisfied with the next generation type compass. Next generation type compass will have high speed and high accuracy so that it can calculate real time 3 dimensional attitude. That is, the next generation type compass will mean a magnetic Gyro-Compass with gyro functionality without Vibration gyro. This type of GSR sensor must be promising for smart phone mobile computer, drone, robots and goggles.

D. pT Sensor for Detecting Biomagnetism

The sensitivity of GSR sensor can increase with the coil turn numbers increased by the long wires or 4 wires of GSR element. Gsr sensor must be promising for these applications. However, the wire resistance of long coil becomes more than 2KΩ so that we need to make a high power electronic circuit with VDD of 5V.

V. CONCLUSION

We found GSR effect based on spin rotation forced by GHz pulse current which makes new features with big sensitivity and the sin functional relationship with magnetic field as well as good linearity, non-hysteresis and low noise. We developed the production technology to produce micro coils directly formed on the ASIC surface which make small size GSR sensor possible. Some prototypes of ASIC type GSR sensor have been produced in consideration for applications such as automotive use, in the body use, gyro –compass use and medical use. It is concluded that GSR sensors have big potentiality to become promising magnetic sensor for many applications.

ACKNOWLEDGMENT

This work was financially supported by the subsidized projects of METI, NEDO and Aichi prefecture of Japan. We wish to acknowledge these supports.

REFERENCES

[1] Y. Akane, "Magnetic sensors" Japan Patent No.2617498(1987)

[2] K. Mohri "A micro magnetic sensor based on MI effect" , Japan Patent No.3645116 (1999)

[3] Y.Honkura, "High Sensitive Micro sized Magnetometer", United States Patent No: US 9,857,436 B2, Jan. 2, 2018

[4] Y. Honkura; "The Development of MI sensor and its Applications to Mobile Pone"; AES2012, 2012

[5] K. Mohri, "Science and technology on magnetic sensors" , Corona Publishing Co. LTD , 1998

[6] Yu. Kabanov, A. Zhukov, V. Zhukova and J. Gonzalez, "Magnetic domain structure of microwires studied by using the magneto-optical indicator film method, Appl. Phys. Lett. 87, p142507, 2005

[7] Y. Honkura: "chaptrer 3: Electronics compass and motion sensor using MI sensor", new magnetic sensors and their applications, Triceps Co. Ltd, 2013

[8] A. Zhukov, M. Ipatov, M.Churyukanova, A. Talaat, J.M. Blanco and V.Zhukova, "Trends in optimization of giant magnetoimpedance effect in amorphous and nanocrystalline materials" , J. Alloys Compound. 727 (2017) 887-901

[9] Y. Honkura: "chapter 5 section4: Development of high sensitive micro magnetic sensor based on GSR effect" , 「new magnetic sensors and their applications」 Technical Information Institute Co. LTD (2018)

[10] Y. Honkura; "Equipment and the method to line up magnetic wires on Si wafer, Japanese Patent No. 5839530 (2015)

[11] Y. Honkura: "Magnetic sensor", Japan patent No.3801194(2006)

High Performance GMI Sensor for Biomagnetic Field Measurement

Tsuyoshi Uchiyama and Jiaju Ma
Department of Electronics
Nagoya University
Nagoya, Japan
e-mail: tutiyama@nuee.nagoya-u.ac.jp, ma.jiaju@i.mbox.nagoya-u.ac.jp

***Abstract*—In this paper, we present a high performance Giant Magneto-Impedance (GMI) sensor for biomagnetic field measurement. We used a first order gradiometer based on amorphous wire GMI sensor for measuring the cardiac magnetic field and the brain magnetic field. The measured results of a cardiac magnetic field perpendicular to the breast plane (cardio apex position) and simultaneously recorded Electrocardiography (ECG) are shown. The spontaneous brain activity (Alpha rhythm) measurements were carried out on a female subject by GMI sensor and simultaneously recorded Electroencephalography (EEG).**

Keywords-amorphou wire; GMI sensor; MCG; MEG.

I. INTRODUCTION

Superconducting interferential devices (SQUID) have been used as measuring tools for biomagnetic signals from human beings. Magnetocardiography (MCG) is a non-invasive and non-contact technique for the diagnosis of heart diseases. The existing experimental data and clinical data revealed the MCG is more sensitive (in comparison with the methods based on the measurement of electric potentials) to local currents that are generated at the interfaces of myocardium fragment with different electrophysiological properties. The technology for recording non-invasive cranial nerve activity that requires no liquid helium and high spatial resolution has been around for over 30 years. Recently, the use of different types of magnetic sensors, such as Tunnel Magneto-Resistance (TMR) sensor and atomic magnetometer are being studied for Magnetoencephalography (MEG).

In the present study, we report measurement results for MCG and MEG based on magnetoimpedance (MI) sensor that can be operating in an unshielded environment and at room temperature. This paper is organized as follows. Section II is dedicated to the description of the theoretical basis of GMI effect and the structures of complementary metal–oxide–semiconductor (CMOS) MI sensor. Section III presents the results of MCG measurements and spontaneous brain activity measurements via the new MI sensor system. Finally, a general conclusion is given in Section IV.

II. GMI SENSOR

We used the amorphous wire (manufactured by UNITIKA Ltd.) with composition of FeCoSiB. The wire was cold-drawn to around 30 um diameter from the as-quenched state of approximately 130 um diameter and then tension-annealed. The remarkable GMI effect occurs in the amorphous wire because the high frequency AC current passing through the amorphous wire leads to the skin effect. The impedance of the wire depends on the skin depth. In general, the skin depth is related to the permeability of soft magnetic materials. Therefore, the impedance has dependence on the magnetic field through change in permeability.

Using both pick-up coil and analogue switch for the signal processing, the temperature stability and linearly of the CMOS MI sensor was remarkably improved. The magnetic sensors using GMI element in combination with pick-up coil have been reported by several groups as Off-Diagonal GMI sensor [1][2]. More recently, we have successfully developed a high performance magnetic sensor having 2pT resolutions at 1Hz based on Off-Diagonal GMI sensor [3]. In order to cancel out the effect of environmental magnetic field noise, we have developed a first order gradiometer for biomagnetic field measurement. In the gradiometer, the amorphous wire has two coils: a sensing coil and a reference coil.

III. RESULTS

MCG measurements by MI gradiometer were carried out for a men subject (aged 54) in sitting position. We measured MCG at the point of the chest surface 25mm on the left hand side of subject from a pit of the stomach. Figure 1(a) illustrates the experimental set up in this study. The MI gradiometer is placed on the wooden table and we measure the perpendicular magnetic field component (Bz) to the chest surface. D is the distance from chest surface to the front edge of the MI gradiometer. Figure 1(b) represents simultaneous measurement of ECG and MCG signals, when the distance D is approximately 4 mm. In this case, we can identify sharp magnetic peak which corresponds to peak in R wave of ECG. Negative magnetic peak is observed following the T wave in ECG.

The spontaneous brain activity (Alpha rhythm) measurements were carried out on a female subject. The subject was with eyes open during the first 8 s of the recording. Then, the subject was instructed to close her eyes for the remaining 8 s of the recording. As expected, the alpha rhythm signals simultaneously measured by EEG and MI sensor were significantly attenuated when the subject opens her eyes, and intensified with eyes closed. The subject's α wave MEG signal has a main frequency component of 10-11 Hz and the maximum amplitude is about 25 pTrms. Significant susceptibility of MI sensor to spontaneous brain activity was confirmed by signal / noise of 8/1, as shown in Figure 2.

IV. CONCLUSION

The noise level of the developed GMI gradiometer, which can operate in an unshielded environment and at room temperature, was 30pT root-mean-square (rms) in a 40Hz bandwidth. In this study, measurement of MCG (by GMI sensor) and ECG was carried out simultaneously. We can identify sharp magnetic peak with strength of approximately 100pT, which was corresponded to peak in ECG R wave. We also tried to measure the brain magnetic field of female subject. The alpha rhythm signals simultaneously measured by EEG and MEG (by GMI sensor) were significantly attenuated when the subject opens eyes, and intensified with eyes close.

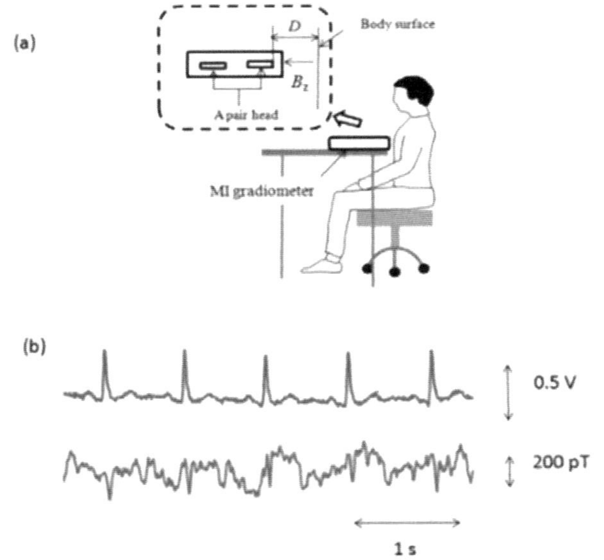

Figure 1. Set up for MCG measurement in (a). Simultaneous measurement of ECG and MCG in (b).

REFERENCES

[1] S. Gudoshnikov, N. Usov, A. Nozdrin, M. Ipatov, A. Zhukov and V. Zhukova, "Highly sensitive magnetometer based on the off-diagonal GMI effect in Co-rich glass-coated microwire", Phys. Status Solidi A 211, No. 5, pp. 980–985.

[2] B. Dufay, S. Saez, C. P. Dolabdjian, A. Yelon, and D. Menard, "Characterization of an optimized off-diagonal GMI-based magnetometer", IEEE Sensors Journal, vol. 13, No. 1, pp. 379-388, 2013.

[3] J. Ma and T. Uchiyama, "High Performance Single Element MI Magnetometer with Peak to Peak Voltage Detector by Synchronized Switching", IEEE Trans. Magn., vol. 53, no. 11, 4003404, November 2017.

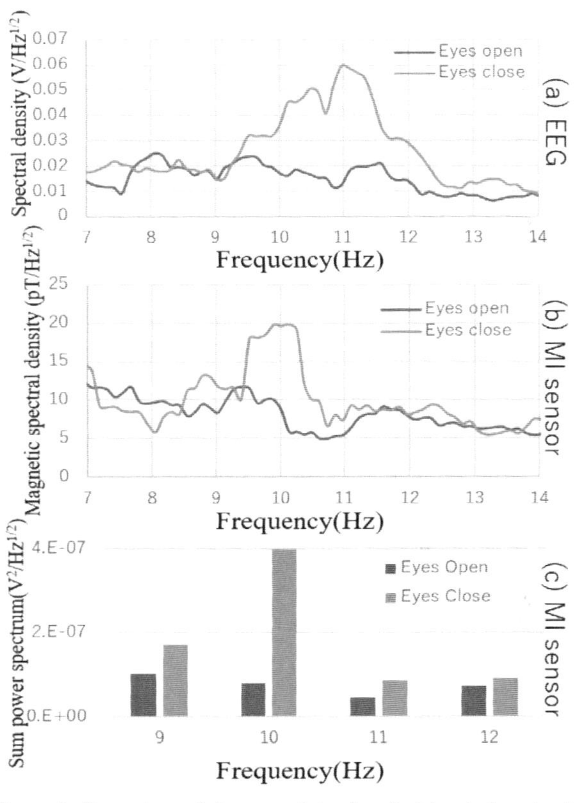

Figure 2. Comparison of the spectral density of alpha rhythm signals simultaneously measured by EEG and MI sensor between eyes opening and closing. (a) EEG. (b) measured by MI sensor. (c) the sum power spectrum level of MI sensor recording.

New Advances in Quartz Enhanced Photoacoustic Spectroscopy for Gas Sensing Applications

Giansergio Menduni, Arianna Elefante, Pietro Patimisco, Angelo Sampaolo, Marilena Giglio, Vincenzo Spagnolo
PolySense Lab – Physics Dept., Polytechnic and University of Bari
Bari, Italy
email: giansergio.menduni@poliba.it; arianna.elefante@uniba.it; pietro.patimisco@poliba.it; angelo.sampaolo@uniba.it; marilena.giglio@uniba.it vincenzoluigi.spagnolo@poliba.it

Vittorio M. N. Passaro
Photonics Research Group, Dept. Of Electrical and Information Engineering, Polytechnic di Bari,
Bari, Italy
email: vittorio.passaro@poliba.it

Abstract—**In this paper, we review the latest advancements in Quartz-Enhanced Photo-Acoustic Spectroscopy (QEPAS) for trace-gas sensing. Starting from the QEPAS basic physical principles, we analyze and discuss the influence of Quartz Tuning Forks (QTFs) geometry on their optoacoustic transducer performance. Subsequently, we provide an overview of the latest developments in QEPAS sensing technology employing custom QTFs and novel micro-resonator configurations. Finally, we report on a novel QEPAS approach allowing simultaneous dual-gas detection.**

Keywords-Quartz-enhanced photoacoustic spectroscopy; gas sensing; custom quartz tuning fork; acoustic resonators; dual-gas detection.

I. INTRODUCTION

In the last few years, gas sensing has gathered an increasing attention for both industrial applications and academia research. Examples of gas sensing applications are: industrial production (like methane/ethane detection in drilling) [1], automotive industry (like detection of polluting gases from vehicles) [2], medical applications (breath analysis) [3], indoor air quality supervision (like detection of carbon monoxide) [4], environmental monitoring (like greenhouse gas monitoring) [5].

A wide range of non-optical gas detection approaches have been proposed, like laboratory analytical equipment, semiconductor gas sensors and electrochemical devices [6]. Optical sensors can offer higher sensitivity [7], selectivity and long-term stability, and are characterized by a long lifetime and short response time, allowing real-time and in-situ detection.

Optical gas sensors are mainly based on Lambert-Beer's law of light absorption processes. Photoacoustic spectroscopy is one of the most sensitive optical sensing techniques. It is based on the detection of acoustic waves, generated as a consequence of the modulated absorption of light from a specific targeted gas. Absorbed light excites the gas target molecules into higher energy levels that relax non-radiatively and generate heat and thereby an increase of pressure in the localized region of the excitation light beam. The modulated absorption generates pressure waves, which can be detected by a microphone.

Quartz-Enhanced Photo-Acoustic Spectroscopy (QEPAS) is an alternative approach to photoacoustic detection of trace gas utilizing a Quartz Tuning Fork (QTF) as a sharply resonant acoustic transducer to detect weak photoacoustic excitation and allowing the use of extremely small volumes [8][9]. Such an approach removes restrictions imposed on the gas cell by the acoustic resonance conditions. QEPAS is a very sensitive technique, for several gases limit of detection of few parts per billion have been achieved [9]. A record sensitivity of 50 part per trillion (ppt) in 1sec integration time has been demonstrated for SF_6 detection [10], while implementing an intracavity-based QEPAS system a detection limit of 900 ppt in 1sec has been achieved for CO_2 trace detection [11][12]. Here, we review the latest advancements in QEPAS for trace-gas sensing. In Section II, we report on QEPAS sensing using custom QTFs, in Section III we discuss the results obtained using single-tube micro-resonator systems, and in Section IV we report on QEPAS results obtained using QTFs operating at the 1st overtone flexural mode. We conclude the work in Section V.

II. QEPAS WITH CUSTOM QTFS

Prior to 2013, all the QEPAS sensors reported in the literature employed commercial standard QTFs operating at the fundamental in-plane flexural resonant mode, with a frequency of ~ 32.7 kHz. However, the standard QTFs structure and its operating frequency were optimized for timing purposes and not for spectroscopic applications. With the aim of determining the dependence of the QTF parameters and performance on their relevant dimensions and identify the optimal design for optoacoustic gas sensing, we designed and tested a set of QTFs with different values of spacing between the prongs, their length and thickness, and crystal thickness. A photograph of one of the realized QTFs is shown in Figure 1.

Figure 1. Photograph of custom QTFs. The space between the prongs is 1.5 mm.

We assessed the dependence of the resonance frequency, the related Q-factor, the fork stiffness, the spring constant, and the electrical resistance from the QTF dimensions [13][14]. We also identified the optoacoustic gas sensing figures of merit and studied their dependence from the QTFs relevant dimensions. For QEPAS applications, our results show that the QTF resistivity R should be kept low and the resonance Q-factor as high as possible. Both conditions can be obtained by increasing the QTF crystal thickness w and the ratio T/L between the prong thickness T and length L. However, the resonance frequency increases as T/L^2, and it should not exceed 40 kHz. Moreover, the smallest possible prong spacing must be chosen to enhance the amplitude of the acoustic wave incident on the internal prong surface, avoiding that the focused laser beam illuminates the QTF. Therefore, the optimal prong spacing selection is mainly determined by the wavelength of the exciting laser beam and its spatial quality.

III. SINGLE-TUBE MICRO-RESONATOR SYSTEMS

Acoustic micro-resonators are important components to improve the performance of QEPAS sensors [8][13]. Among the different QEPAS spectrophone configurations, the on-beam one showed the strongest acoustic coupling efficiency between the QTF and the microresonator (mR), resulting in an optimum signal to noise (SNR) gain factor of ~ 30 [9] for a standard 32 kHz-QTF. The on-beam spectrophone configuration consists of two stainless steel tubes with the QTF inserted between them. The possibility to operate with custom QTFs with a prong spacing of up to 1.5 mm, opens the way to the implementation of a single-tube mR configuration in an on-beam QEPAS spectrophone (SO-QEPAS configuration). By implementing the SO-QEPAS configuration we demonstrated that it is possible to achieve a signal-to-noise amplification factor of ~130 in comparison with the bare QTF [15].

IV. QEPAS WITH QTF OPERATING IN THE 1ST OVERTONE FLEXURAL MODE

In QEPAS sensing, the resonance frequency of the QTF must be limited below 40 kHz to ensure that the transfer of the excess energy absorbed by the target gas follows efficiently the fast modulation of the incident laser radiation [9]. The custom QTF we have realized are characterized by a fundamental resonance frequency up to one order of magnitude lower with respect to the standard 32 kHz-QTF [13][14]. However, the 1st overtone modes frequencies are also reduced with a decrease of the fundamental resonance frequency to ~ 3kHz. This opened the way to the implementation of QTF overtone flexural modes for QEPAS trace gas sensing.

A typical calculated vibration profile of the QTF prongs at the 1st overtone flexural mode for maxima displacements conditions is shown in Figure 2 as a function of the distance from the support base for the first overtone mode.

The 1st overtone flexural mode can be modeled as 2-coupled point-masses, each one positioned at an antinode and oscillating in counter-phase. The two antinodes identify the position of the maximum vibration amplitudes along the prong. When the focusing spot is located at the antinodes points of the vibration profile, where the maximum vibration amplitude is allowed, the QEPAS signal is maximized.

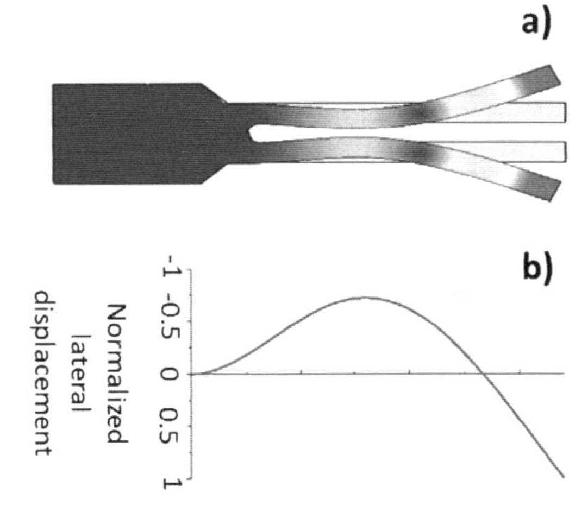

Figure 2. Deformation of the QTF prongs (a) and normalized lateral displacement for a QTF first overtone mode (b).

By optimizing the QTF design, it is possible to favor the first overtone flexural mode operation with respect to the fundamental mode one in terms of QEPAS signal [16],[17].

A. *Single-tube micro-resonator coupled with QTF 1st overtone flexural mode*

The length of the mR is correlated with the sound wavelength, given by $\lambda = v/f$, where v is the sound speed (343 m/s in air). Thereby, implementing dual-tube or single-tube mR for QTFs having resonance frequency < 10 kHz becomes challenging. As an example, for a frequency as low as 5 kHz, $\lambda = 6.86$ cm. The optimal length for a single-tube mR falls between $\lambda/2$ and λ, closer to $\lambda/2$., because of the mR acoustic coupling with the QTF [9]. These lengths make optical alignment challenging when operating with mid-IR and inhibits operations with a THz laser. However, since the 1st overtone frequency is about 6.2 times higher than the fundamental one, operating at the 1st overtone will require a significantly more than six times reduced mR length. The first demonstration of a QEPAS system implementing a QTF operating at the 1st overtone flexural mode and coupled with a single-tube mR is reported in [18]. Benefiting from the high overtone resonance frequency (17.7 kHz) and the quasi 1st harmonic acoustic standing waves generated in the SO-QEPAS configuration, the AmR length was reduced to 14.5 mm. The signal enhancement in the overtone resonance mode in this SO-QEPAS configuration leads to an overall sensitivity enhancement factor of ~380 with respect to the bare custom QTF operating in the fundamental resonance mode.

B. *Double antinode excited QEPAS*

Since the 1st overtone flexural mode can be modeled as 2-coupled point-masses, each one positioned at an antinode and oscillating in counter-phase, it can be possible to excite the two resonance antinode points of a custom QTF operated at the 1st overtone resonance mode simultaneously using one laser source and two dual-tubes mRs. This approach named double antinode excited quartz-enhanced photoacoustic spectroscopy (DAE-QEPAS) has been demonstrated for the first time in [19]. Two sets of acoustic mRs were optimized and assembled at two separated 1st overtone antinode points of the QTF to improve the spectrophone performance. With the two antinodes excited by one laser source, the DAE-QEPAS spectrophone attained a sensitivity gain factor of ~ 100 times and ~3 times with respect to the 1st overtone resonances of the bare custom QTF and a standard on-beam QEPAS spectrophone, respectively.

C. *Simultaneous dual-gas QEPAS detection*

QEPAS sensors require a proper design to perform chemical analysis of a multi-component gas mixture due to the fact that the QTF cannot recognize the molecular species responsible for the generation of the pressure waves. Very recently, this limitation has been overcome by realizing a dual-gas QEPAS sensing system based on a QTF frequency division multiplexing technique [20]. The QTF in a dual-gas QEPAS sensor is excited simultaneously at the fundamental and 1st overtone flexural modes by two independently modulated lasers. The two target gases are detected via demodulation of the custom QTF piezoelectric signal at the fundamental frequency $f0$ and the 1st overtone frequency $f1$, respectively, by means of two lock-in amplifiers. The capability of the QEPAS sensor to perform simultaneous dual-gas spectral detection was demonstrated by implementing a DFB laser source targeting an acetylene (C_2H_2) and a diode laser targeting a H_2O absorption line and reaching normalized noise equivalent absorption factors in the 10^{-7} $cm^{-1} \cdot W/Hz^{1/2}$ range. Further improvements of dual-gas QEPAS sensors performances will be achieved by adding dual- or single-tube acoustic micro-resonators to enhance the generated photo-acoustic wave intensity.

V. CONCLUSIONS

Recent developments in quart-enhanced photoacoustic spectroscopy were reviewed. Compared with a standard 32 kHz-QTF, the custom QTFs result in better sensing performance, considering also that they allowed to implement large prongs spacing (up to 1.5 mm) making the optical alignment less critical, especially with laser sources having limited spatial beam quality. The simultaneous reduction of the fundamental resonances modes down to 3 kHz in custom QTFs opened the way to the use of the 1st overtone mode for QEPAS sensing. Since the 1st overtone mode is characterized by two antinodes positions, new approaches, such as the double antinode excited QEPAS and simultaneous dual-gas detection by exciting simultaneously the QTF at the fundamental and the 1st overtone flexural modes, have been demonstrated.

ACKNOWLEDGMENT

The authors from Dipartimento Interateneo di Fisica di Bari acknowledge the financial support from THORLABS GmbH, within PolySense, a joint-research laboratory.

REFERENCES

[1] A. Sampaolo et al., "Interband cascade laser based quartz-enhanced photoacoustic sensor for multiple hydrocarbons detection," Proc. SPIE 10540, Quantum Sensing and Nano Electronics and Photonics XV, 2018, 105400C; doi: 10.1117/12.2288336

[2] C. Di Franco et al., "Optical and electronic NOx sensors for applications in mechatronics," Sensors, vol. 9, pp. 3337-3356, 2009.

[3] P. R. Fortes, J. F. S. Petruci, and I. M. Raimundo, "Optical Gas Sensors for Exhaled Breath Analysis," SPIE Press, Bellingham, Washington, 2017.

[4] X. Liu et al., "A Survey on Gas Sensing Technology," Sensors, vol. 12, pp. 9635-9665, 2012.

[5] J. Hodgkinson and R. P. Tatam, "Optical gas sensing: a review," Meas. Sci. Technol., Vol. 24, 012004, 2013.

[6] E. Bakker and M. Telting-Diaz, "Electrochemical Sensors," Anal. Chem., Vol. 74, pp. 2781–2800, 2002.

[7] I. Galli et al., "Molecular Gas Sensing Below Parts Per Trillion: Radiocarbon-Dioxide Optical Detection," Phys. Rev. Lett., Vol. 107, 270802, 2011.

[8] P. Patimisco, A. Sampaolo, L. Dong, F. K. Tittel, and V. Spagnolo, "Recent advances in quartz enhanced photoacoustic sensing," Appl. Phys. Rev., Vol. 5, 011106, 2018.

[9] P. Patimisco, G. Scamarcio, F. K. Tittel, and V. Spagnolo, "Quartz-Enhanced Photoacoustic Spectroscopy: A Review," Sensors, Vol. 14, pp. 6165-6206 (2014).

[10] V. Spagnolo, P. Patimisco, S. Borri, G. Scamarcio, B. E. Bernacki, and J. Kriesel, "Part-per-trillion level SF6 detection using a quartz enhanced photoacoustic spectroscopy based sensor with single-mode fiber-coupled quantum cascade laser excitation," Opt. Lett., Vol. 37, pp. 460-462, 2012.

[11] S. Borri et al., "Intracavity quartz-enhanced photoacoustic sensor," Appl. Phys. Lett., Vol. 104, 091114, 2014.

[12] P. Patimisco et al., "High finesse optical cavity coupled with a quartz-enhanced photoacoustic spectroscopic sensor," Analyst, Vol. 140, pp. 736-743, 2015.

[13] P. Patimisco et al., "Quartz–enhanced photoacoustic spectrophones exploiting custom tuning forks: a review", Adv. Phys. X, Vol. 2, pp. 169-187, 2016.

[14] P. Patimisco et al., "Analysis of the electro-elastic properties of custom quartz tuning forks for optoacoustic gas sensing," Sensors and Actuators B, Vol. 227, pp. 539-546, 2016.

[15] H. Zheng et al., "Single-tube on-beam quartz-enhanced photoacoustic spectroscopy," Opt. Lett., Vol. 41, pp. 978-981, 2016.

[16] A. Sampaolo et al., "Quartz-enhanced photoacoustic spectroscopy exploiting tuning fork overtone modes," Appl. Phys. Lett., Vol. 107, 231102, 2015.

[17] F. K. Tittel et al., "Analysis of overtone flexural modes operation in quartz-enhanced photoacoustic spectroscopy," Opt. Ex., Vol.24, pp. A682-A692, 2016.

[18] H. Zheng et al., "Overtone resonance enhanced single-tube on-beam quartz enhanced photoacoustic spectrophone," Appl. Phys. Lett., Vol. 109, 111103, 2016.

[19] H. Zheng et al., "Double antinode excited quartz-enhanced photoacoustic spectrophone," Appl. Phys. Lett., Vol 110, 021110, 2017.

[20] H. Wu et al., "Simultaneous dual-gas QEPAS detection based on a fundamental and overtone combined vibration of quartz tuning fork," Appl. Phys. Lett., Vol. 110, 121104, 2017.

Concept of Optical Sensor Utilising the Far Field Pattern Radiated by Periodic Grating Strips Over Silica Cladding on the Silicon Wire Waveguide

Vittorio M. N. Passaro

Photonics Research Group
Dipartimento di Ingegneria Elettrica e dell'Informazione
Politecnico di Bari,
Bari, Italy
e-mail: vittorio.passaro@poliba.it

Francesco De Leonardis

Photonics Research Group
Dipartimento di Ingegneria Elettrica e dell'Informazione
Politecnico di Bari,
Bari, Italy
e-mail: francesco.deleonardis@poliba.it

Andrei Tsarev*,**

*Laboratory of Optical Materials and Structures,
Rzhanov Institute of Semiconductor Physics, SB RAS,
Novosibirsk, Russia
e-mail: tsarev@isp.nsc.ru

**Laboratory of Semiconductor and Dielectric Materials,
Physics Department
Novosibirsk State University
Novosibirsk, Russia
e-mail: a.tsarev@nsu.ru

Eugeny Kolosovsky

Laboratory of Optical Materials and Structures,
Rzhanov Institute of Semiconductor Physics, SB RAS,
Novosibirsk 630090, Russia
e-mail: kolos@isp.nsc.ru

Abstract—**This paper describes the novel concept of the optical sensor, which utilizes the physical nature of the light propagating in a silicon wire with the periodic segmented grating placed in the waveguide vicinity over the silica buffer. In specific cases, this segmented grating works as a virtual leaky waveguide, which radiates power as an outcoming optical beam having small both wavelength band and beam divergence. The radiation angle strongly depends on the refractive index of the grating environment. Thus, this device can be used as an optical sensor with the readout to be arranged by measuring the far field pattern in the focal plate of the lens, which is placed near the sensor element. The device concept is verified by direct numerical modelling through the Finite Difference Time Domain (FDTD) method.**

Keywords-silicon wire; segmented grating; far fiald patern; optical sensor; numerical modeling; FDTD method.

I. INTRODUCTION

The most popular optical sensors are based on the high precision measuring the optical wavelength that propagates in the photonic structure and whose properties depend on the environment of the sensor element. It can be done by a tunable laser with a fine linewidth or by launching into the waveguide the optical beam, which contains a broad wavelength range, say, from the super-luminescence diode, and measuring the transmitting signal by the Optical Spectrum Analyzer (OSA). Both these variants provide the possibility to develop advanced optical sensors with the sensitivity depending on the design of optical element and the spectrum resolution of the tunable laser or the OSA. Both of these readout schemes are rather costly, which prevents the wide spread of these sensor technologies.

The current paper presents the new concept of the optical sensor design. The idea of this sensor comes from the background of optical phenomena, which takes place in the silicon wire with the periodic segmented grating evanescently coupled through the silica buffer.

When the guided optical beam, which contains a broad spectral range, arrives in the grating area (see Figure 1), different optical processes can occur, depending on the ratio between the optical wavelength λ_0 and the grating period Λ [1]. In this paper, we will not discuss the well-known effect of the Bragg reflection to the guided wave propagating in a silicon wire in the opposite direction and the broadband interaction with radiation modes that provides the outcoming optical wave with the radiation angle depending on the optical wavelength. Our investigation is focused on the resonance-type interaction of incoming guided wave with the virtual leaky wave that is supported by the periodic grating structure, coupled by the evanescent field with the underplayed silicon wire. We call this type of diffraction regime "abnormal blocking" [2]. It is interested to note that this interaction is a resonance type, like a Bragg reflection, and it is supported by the outcoming optical beam, like a coupling with the radiated modes. However, in contrast to the last process, the coupling to radiated modes has a resonance feature and thus this effect of "abnormal blocking" can be used for sensing applications [2].

The paper is structured as follows. In Section II we define the sensor design and features, while in Section III we summarize the conclusions.

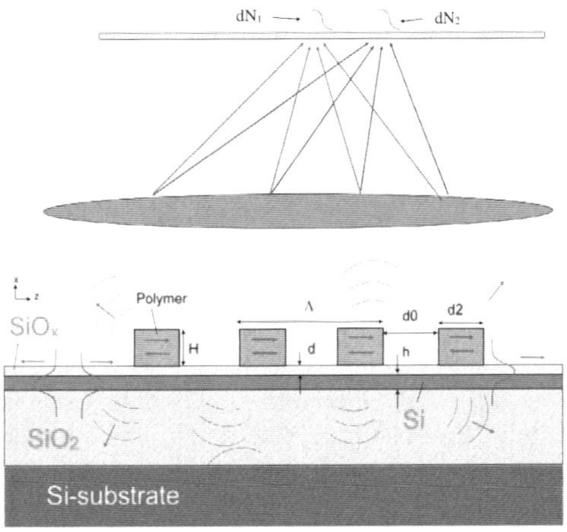

Figure 1. The principal design of optical sensor based on the interaction of the guided wave with the virtual leaky wave of the segmented grating. Here, $\Lambda = d0 + d2$ is the period of grating, H and d2 are the height and the width of the segmented grating, d0 is the spacing between the strips, d and h are the waveguide and buffer heights, respectively.

II. SENSOR DESIGN AND FEATURES

The principle of this type of sensor is based on the utilization of the radiated feature of coupling the guided to the virtual leaky wave, which takes place in the segmented grating structure placed in the vicinity of the silicon wire waveguide. This interaction has the maximum effect when the well-known Bragg condition on conservation of the momentum is satisfied:

$$N_L = \pm N_g - p \cdot \lambda / \Lambda = n_0 \cdot \sin(\varphi) \quad (1)$$

where N_L and N_g are effective indices of the leaky and guided waves of the silicon waveguide with the segmented grating structure, p is the diffraction order of the grating, φ and n_0 are the radiated angle (relative to the structure normal) and the refractive index of the grating environment, say, the water for the case of a liquid sensor, respectively.

The changing of the grating environment index by the amount dN leads to the change in the condition (1) of diffraction observation. This change is the subject of the measurement by the optical sensor. The main sensor parameters could be derived from Eq. (1) in the form of the following set of equations:

$$\partial N_L/\partial n = \pm \partial N_g/\partial n - \partial\lambda/\partial n \cdot p/\Lambda \quad (2)$$

$$S_n = \partial\lambda/\partial n = \Lambda/p \cdot (\partial N_L/\partial n \mp \partial N_g/\partial n) \quad (3)$$

$$\varphi_n = \partial\varphi/\partial n = - p/[\Lambda\, n_0 \cdot \cos(\varphi)] \quad (4)$$

Eq. (2) is characterized by the mode index sensitivity of the sensor. In order to improve the sensitivity, one can use the waveguide near the cutoff, the slot [3][4] or segment waveguide structures [5]. Eq. (3) describes the homogeneous sensitivity of the typical sensor, which works by measuring the Drop wavelength of the structure. The last Eq. (4) corresponds to the homogeneous sensitivity feature of our sensor, which measures the small index variation by the determination of the diffraction angle of the radiated power, which is generated during the interaction of guided and virtual leaky waves. This effect of "abnormal blocking" [2] has a resonance feature and thus this radiated angle φ has also the resonance behavior on the optical wavelength. By the analysis of the far field diffraction, corresponding to the condition of realization of the "abnormal blocking", one can get information about the index change in the grating vicinity. This analysis can be done by using the field distribution in the focal plate of the lens obtained by the charge-coupled device (CCD) camera.

The structure design, which is under investigation, is shown in Figure 1. The silicon wire having the height h = 250 nm and the width w = 450 nm is placed on a thick 2 μm silicon dioxide buffer. It corresponds to the optical waveguide, which supports a transverse electric (TE)-polarized single mode (electric field in the plane of the waveguide). The segmented structure is achieved by the periodic (Λ = 1.3 μm) strips from polymer SU-8 (index n_p=1.56) with length 0.50 μm, height H = 1.0 μm and width W=1.0 μm and which is separated from the silicon waveguide by a silica overlayer from a flowable oxide (FOx) having height d = 200 nm and index 1.4.

This structure is investigated by numerical modeling, which has been performed using the Finite Difference Time Domain (FDTD) method through the commercial software package RSoft-SYNOPSYS [6]. In order to examine the long structure, we utilize FDTD under the two dimensional (2D) approximation based on the effective index method (EIM) [7], as in Figure 2. Previously, we have shown that the EIM method has a fundamental limitation [8][9], which takes place when trying to analyze the pulsed excitation of waveguide structures by 2D FDTD method.

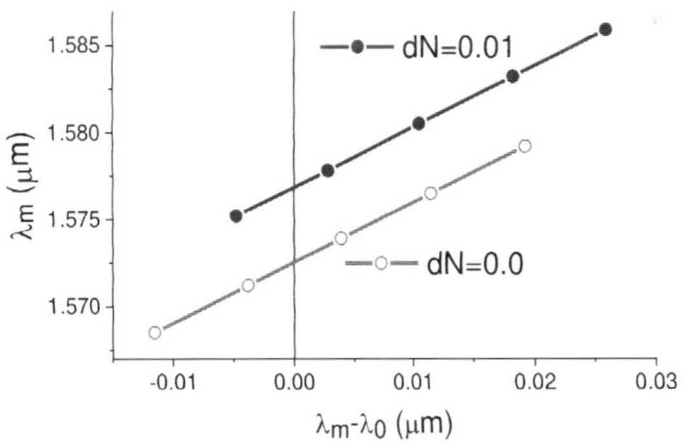

Figure 2. The algorithm for the dispersion compensation for two-dimensional simulation by FDTD method using EIM.

The reason is that the two-dimensional EIM approximation does not take into account the waveguide dispersion, which is the fundamental feature in the propagation of a short pulse containing a wide spectral composition. Therefore, the classical EIM can be used only for the monochromatic excitation of a waveguide.

We found an original solution to this problem. The presence of waveguide dispersion leads to the fact that the wavelengths of anomalous blocking λ_m found using the 2D FDTD modeling depend on the wavelength λ_0, at which the impulse excitation and spectrum analysis of the waveguide structure is carried out. However, for the case when $\lambda_m = \lambda_0$ this value is exactly equal to the desired value. Therefore, by constructing the dependence λ_0 on the difference λ_0-λ_m and having determined the values λ_0 at the zero coordinate (see Figure 2), it is possible to find the wavelengths of the anomalous blocking for different values of the perturbation of the refractive index of the environment. This optical wavelength (determined for different values of the environment indices and structure parameters) is used for all simulations. This algorithm allows to determine the correct values S_n and φ_n, by 2D FDTD plus EIM.

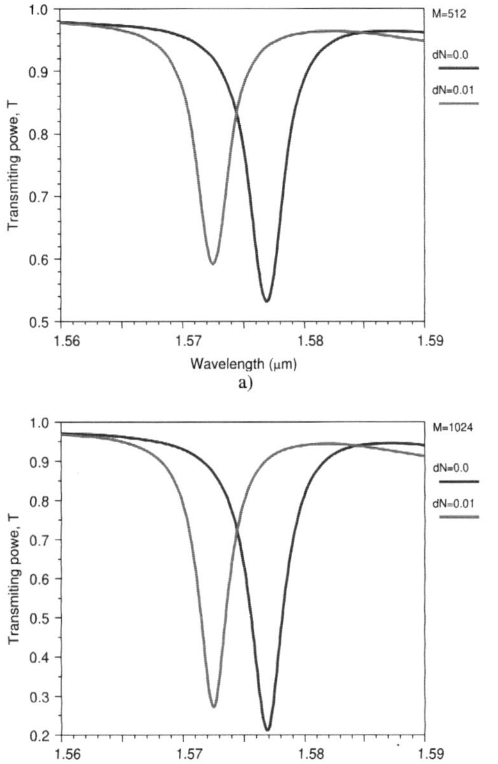

Figure 3. Transmitting power (T) relative to the input signal of the guided wave, which propagates along the silicon wire with segmented grating: a) M=512, b) M=1024.

The sensor element, based on segmented grating over the silicon waveguide, can be used through different readout schemes. The traditional variant based on measuring the transmitted spectrum is illustrated in Figure 3 for different number of segments M=512 and M=1024. One can see that the suppression of the Drop wavelength is increased with increasing the grating length (Λ×M), but this does not increase the filter resolution (half width 3.3 nm), which is restricted by the optical decay of the leaky wave supported by the grating. Nevertheless, by measuring the optical wavelength, one can determine the index variation. For the case of water environment, we have the homogeneous sensitivity $Sn=\partial\lambda/\partial n$ = 440 nm/RIU. For the case of an Optical Spectrum Analyzer (OSA) resolution of 0.01 nm, it provides the sensor resolution of 1.3 10^{-5} RIU.

Similar sensitivity can be achieved by measuring the far field distribution of the optical wave, radiated by the grating structure, in regime of "abnormal blocking" effect. In order to prove this statement, we plot in Figure 4 the angle variation of the far field pattern of radiated power, corresponding to the 20 different wavelengths around the drop wavelength of "abnormal blocking". These far field patterns produce the index-dependent variations in the power distribution in the focal plate of the lens (see Figure 5), which could be measured by the matrix photodetector.

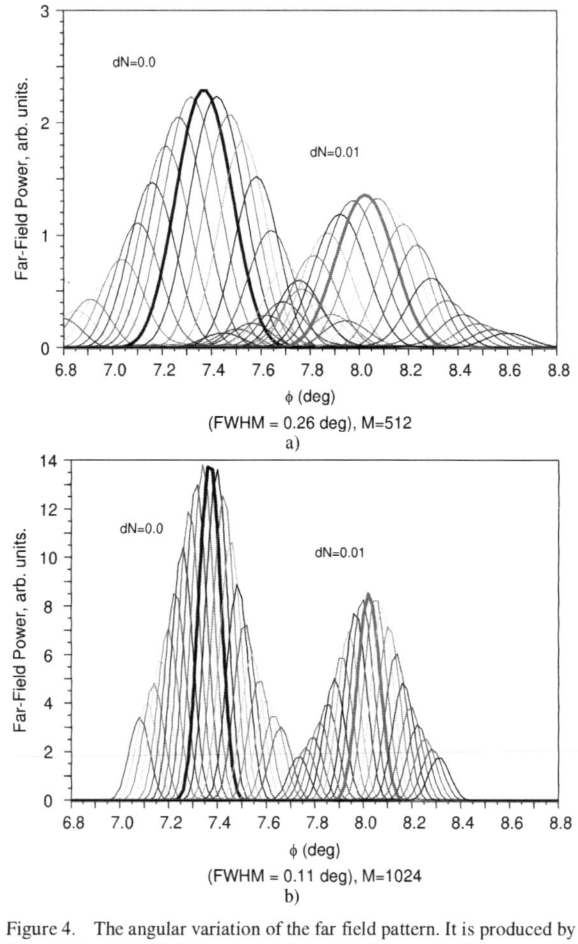

Figure 4. The angular variation of the far field pattern. It is produced by the guided wave, which propagates along the silicon wire with segmented grating: a) M=512; b) M=1024.

The thick lines in Figure 4 correspond to the far field of the monochromatic wave incidence at drop wavelengths 1.5768 μm and 1.5725 μm for dN=0.0 and dN=0.01, respectively.

The structure has a limited bandwidth (3.3 nm) of wavelength response (see Figure 3). Thus, the part of the optical wave at different wavelengths (around the drop one) will be also scattered by the grating and will propagate at different angles (see (4)). These additional far field patterns are shown as thin lines in Figure 4 and Figure 5. They also increase the beam divergence relative to monochromatic wave. Our analysis proves that this device is suitable for measuring the small variation of the refractive index of the grating environment. Besides, the sensor resolution is increased with increasing the number of segments in the grating. For 1024 segments, the angle deviation for dN=0.01 is twice the optical beam divergence.

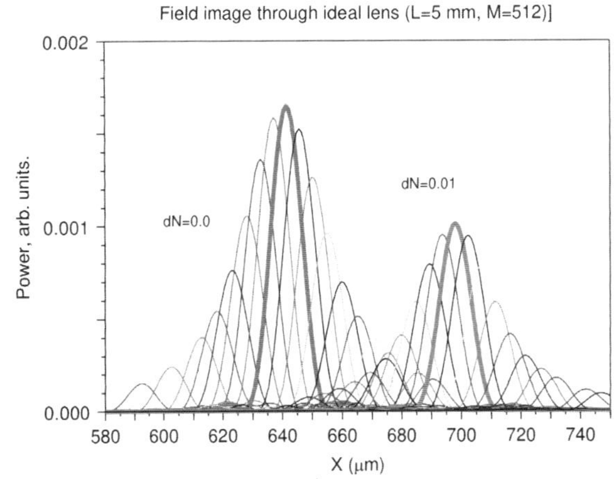

a)

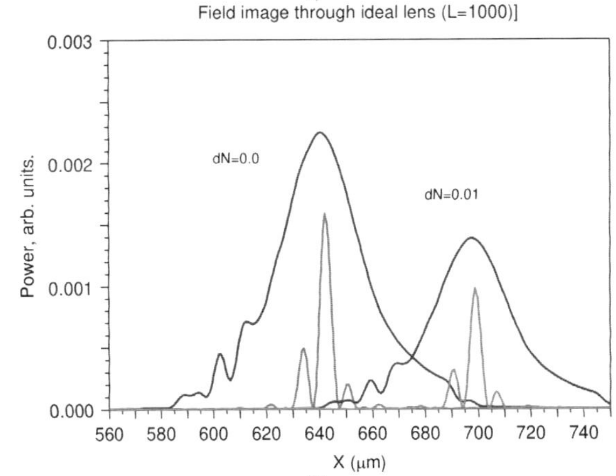

b)

Figure 5. The power distribution in the focal plate of the ideal lens having the focal length 5 mm for the case of M=512 and different index variations dN=0.0 and dN=0.01 of the environment (water): a) a set of far field patterns corresponding to different optical wavelengths around the Drop one; b) the total power distribution (as a sum of 20 different wavelengths), which has to be measured by the photodector array.

It means that under the same condition (the ratio of the Drop resolution to the pattern half width) the proposed sensor will provide 1.5 better resolution than in the OSA readout of the same device, with an arrangement for measuring the far field pattern much simpler and cheaper.

III. CONCLUSION

We have proposed and carried out numerical modelling of a novel type of optical sensor, which utilizes a segmented periodic structure over the silicon wire. The tunnel coupling of the guided wave to the segmented structure provides excitation of the virtual leaky wave in the periodic segmented structure. The last radiates the power as an outgoing optical beam. This process has a resonance nature and takes place at small wavelength range (around 3.3 nm), thus the outgoing optical beam has a small divergence (0.33 degree), which makes possible to determine small index environmental variations by measuring the change in the far field pattern distribution. This can be accomplished by commercial CCD arrays placed in the focal plate of the lens in an optical solution much simpler and cheaper than a tunable laser or an OSA.

ACKNOWLEDGMENT

The work had got a partial support by the Russian project RFMEFI58117X0026 in the part of using RSoft software by SYNOPSYS [6] for FDTD simulations.

REFERENCES

[1] D. Marcuse, "Directional couplers made of nonidentical asymmetric slabs. Part II: Grating-assisted couplers," J. Lightwave Technol., vol. LT-5, pp. 268-273, 1987.

[2] E. A. Kolosovskii and A. V. Tsarev, "Abnormal blocking of a guided mode propagating in a silicon optical waveguide with periodic tunnel coupling", Quantum Electron., vol. 47, pp. 58–64, 2017.

[3] F. Dell'Olio and V. M. N. Passaro, "Optical sensing by optimized silicon slot waveguides," Opt. Express, vol. 15, pp. 4977-4993, 2007.

[4] T. Claes et al., "Label-free biosensing with a slot-waveguide-based ring resonator in silicon on insulator," IEEE Photon. J., vol. 1, pp. 197–204, 2009.

[5] J. Flueckiger et al., "Sub-wavelength grating for enhanced ring resonator biosensor," Opt. Express, vol. 24, pp. 15672-15686, 2016.

[6] Rsoft FullWave by SYNOPSYS, single license (2018).

[7] K. S. Chiang, "Dual effective-index method for the analysis of rectangular dielectric waveguides," Appl. Opt., vol. 25, pp. 2169-2174, 1986.

[8] A. Tsarev, "Modified effective index method to fit the phase and group index of 3D photonic wire waveguide," Opt. Lett., vol. 38, pp. 293-295, 2013.

[9] L. O'Faolain and A. Tsarev, "Experimental demonstration of original optical filter based on multiply coupled waveguides," Opt. Lett., vol. 39, pp. 3627-3629. 2014.

Silicon Photonics for Mid-Infrared Sensing

D. J. Rowe, Y. Qi, V. Mittal, A. Osman, Z. Qu,
Y. Wu, M. Banakar, J. Soler Penades, J. S. Wilkinson,
M. Nedeljkovic, G. Z. Mashanovich
Optoelectronics Research Centre
University of Southampton
Southampton, UK
e-mail: g.mashanovich@soton.ac.uk

A. Sánchez-Postigo, J. G. Wangüemert-Pérez,
A. Ortega-Moñux, R. Halir, Í. Molina-Fernández
Dpto. Ingeniería de Comunicaciones
Universidad de Málaga
Malaga, Spain

Abstract—**In this paper, we review our recent work on Si and Ge material platforms suitable for mid-infrared sensing. We investigate Silicon-on-Insulator, Germanium-on-Silicon, suspended Si and suspended Ge. Design, fabrication and characterisation results for various passive devices are discussed. We also show preliminary results on integration of microfluidic channels with the Silicon-on-Insulator platform.**

Keywords-silicon; germanium; mid-infrared;waveguides.

I. INTRODUCTION

The mid-infrared (MIR) wavelength region contains strong absorption bands of many molecules and substances and is therefore of great interest for various sensing applications [1]. Silicon and germanium are suitable material platforms for the MIR as they are transparent in this wavelength range and are readily available with well established fabrication techniques mostly employed for the realisation of near-IR photonic devices [2].

As the MIR wavelength range is very broad (2-15 μm) and different applications can target different wavelengths within the MIR, development of non-standard material platforms may be needed. SOI is the most popular platform in the NIR and is low loss up to ~3.8 μm [3]. To utilise the full transparency of Si, buried oxide layer can be removed resulting in a suspended Si structure. In this paper we report our approach based on subwavelength gratings [4][5]. Several research groups have reported Ge-on-Si and SiGe waveguides with operation up to 8.5 μm [6-8]. However, such waveguides have limited evanescent field which may result in low sensitivity of transducers based on these platforms. Suspended Ge is an alternative platform for sensing [9] and here we discuss our preliminary result on this platform. Finally, we show integration of microfluidic PDMS channels and SOI waveguides and measurement of aqueous solutions of IPA.

The paper is organised as following. A review of several MIR platforms is given in Section II. Section III describes suspended Si and suspended Ge platforms. Integration of MIR photonic circuits with microfluidic channels is given in Section IV. Finally, Section V contains conclusions.

II. STANDARD PLATFORMS

The SOI platform has been extensively used for NIR devices, photonic integrated circuits and systems [10]. It is therefore a preferred platform in silicon photonics and we have conducted an extensive investigation into its suitability for the MIR. We have shown that this platform can be used up to ~4 μm due to large SiO_2 material loss beyond ~ 3.6 μm [3]. A number of MIR devices have been realised in this platform, for example waveguides with loss of ~1 dB/cm, spectrometers [2], modulators [9], detectors [11][12], integrated sources [13] etc. This platform can also be used for sensing as shown for example in [14] and in Section IV of this paper. To increase refractive index contrast and also transparency range, pedestal Si and suspended Si can be used as shown in Section II.

The main appeal of Ge as a MIR material is its superior spectral transparency compared to Si that spans from 2 to 15 μm. Ge also has other interesting characteristics such as larger carrier mobility, thermo-optic and non-linear coefficients compared to Si. The most popular approach for fabrication of Ge-based MIR platform has been CVD growth of Ge on Si wafers. Various Ge thicknesses have been used with reported losses typically around 2 dB/cm and with best results as low as 0.6 dB/cm [15].

Ge-rich SiGe waveguides have also been demonstrated and sub dB/cm losses shown [8]. The main advantage of this approach is the possibility to have a gradual change of Ge concentration in the SiGe alloy thus reducing defect concentration that can affect the GOS platform losses.

Although these platforms should have low losses up to 11 or 12 μm, larger values have been observed beyond 8.5-9 μm [6-8] and therefore further investigation is needed. These platforms have another drawback: to enable low propagation losses thicker Ge and SiGe top layers are required resulting in high optical mode confinement in the core and low evanescent field as shown in Figure 1 for a GOS waveguide. This results in low interaction of the optical mode with an analyte and thus lower sensitivity. Suspended Ge can offer solution to this problem as discussed in the next section.

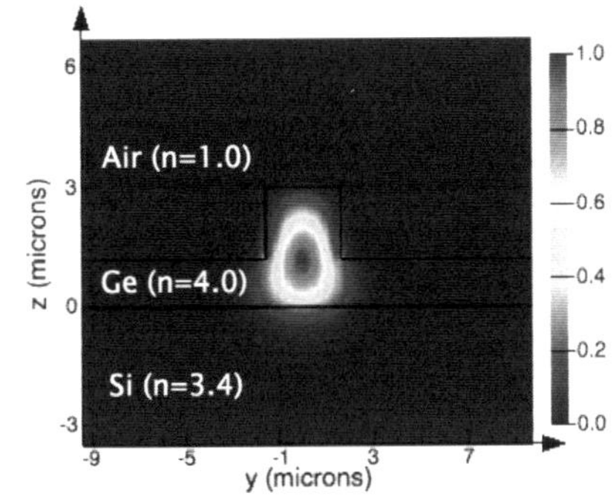

Figure 1. GOS waveguide: optical mode is well confined in the waveguide resulting in low evanescent field.

III. SUSPENDED PLATFORMS

A. Suspended Si

Si is transparent up to 8 µm and to realise Si-based photonics circuits that operate to a wavelength as long as 8 µm there are two solutions: a) Si is bonded to a substrate that has the same or larger transparency range and b) the buried oxide (BOX) in SOI is removed and suspended Si formed. Here, we discuss b).

The most obvious solution is to form a rib waveguide and holes on both sides of the rib that can be used for wet selective etching of the BOX layer. This requires two dry etch steps to form the rib and holes and also careful positioning of the holes such not to cause scattering of the optical mode. It can also result in bending of the slab region for larger structures, such as Multi-Mode Interference (MMI) splitters or Mach-Zehnder Interferometers (MZIs), depending on the thickness of the slab region.

A better solution is to place the holes in close proximity to the core, to increase the mode-analyte interaction, to improve mechanical stability and to simplify the fabrication process. We have developed such an approach based on subwavelength gratings as shown in Figure 2. The subwavelength gratings act as lateral claddings and access points for HF removal of the BOX.

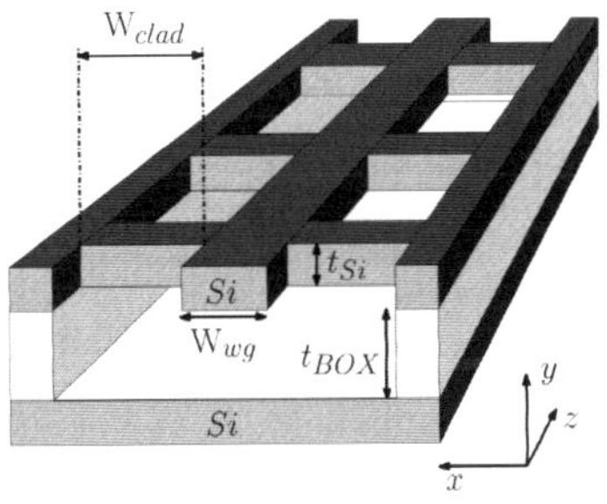

Figure 2. Suspended Si waveguide with subwavelength grating cladding.

There are several contradictory requirements when designing such structures. To reduce scattering caused by the sidewall roughness the waveguide core W_{wg} should be wide. This can result in multimode propagation and/or downward bending of the waveguide. The cladding width W_{clad} should be relatively large to reduce the leakage loss but on the other hand small to reduce downward bending. Subwavelength holes should be large enough to enable liquid HF penetration and subsequent BOX removal, however also small enough not to reduce Si side supports that are important to mechanical stability of the structure. If these Si supports are too wide they can increase mode leakage to the slab region.

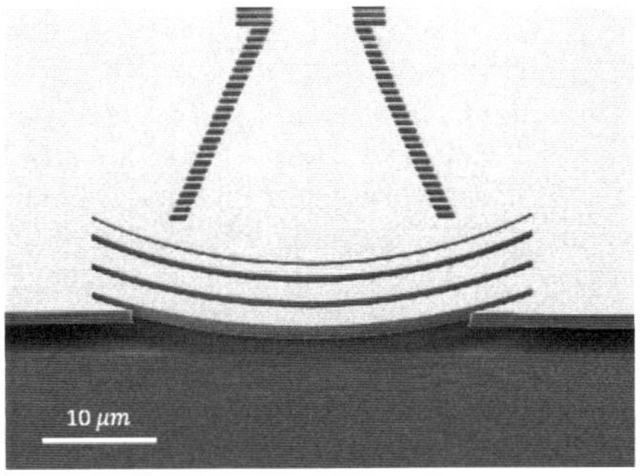

Figure 3. Part of a supsended grating coupler for suspended Si photonic circuits operating at a wavelength of 7.7 µm [16].

It is clear from the previous paragraph that extensive simulations are required to optimise dimensions of various photonic devices based on the subwavelength grating design. We have conducted such an optimisation and fabricated devices operating at 3.8 [5] and 7.7 µm [16], achieving propagation losses of 0.8 dB/cm and 3.1 dB/cm, respectively, low bending losses, low insertion losses for MMIs, MZIs, and good coupling efficiency for surface grating couplers (Figure 3). It should be pointed out that Si material loss at 7.7 µm is 2.1 dB/cm, and leakage loss for this particular waveguide is 0.1 dB/cm, meaning that the 'actual' waveguide loss is 0.9 dB/cm which is very similar to the 3.8 µm result of 0.8 dB/cm [5]. This demonstrates a robust fabrication method.

B. Suspended Ge

To suspend Ge, the same two approaches can be implemented: rib waveguide configuration (Figure 4) or subwavelength grating approach discussed in the previous section (Figure 2). We have applied the former, and we are currently working on the latter.

In terms of the substrate, Si or SOI can be used. In our approach, we have used the SOI substrate because it results in a well defined air channel under the Ge rib waveguide (Figure 4).

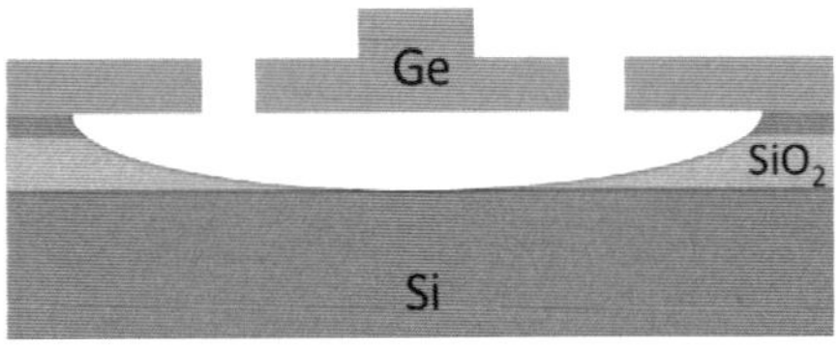

Figure 4. Suspended Ge waveguide on thin SOI platform.

The waveguides were fabricated using 6" Ge-on-SOI wafers with a 1 μm Ge layer grown by RPCVD on 50 nm SOI. The BOX thickness was 3 μm. Rib waveguides were designed for single mode propagation at λ = 7.7 μm. The dimensions were: height (H) = 1 μm, width (W) = 3.5 μm and etch depth (D) = 300 nm. The initial SOI substrate consisted of a 250 nm thick layer of Si on a 3 μm thick layer of SiO_2. It was thinned to 50nm Si using oxidation. The waveguides were patterned using e-beam lithography. They were then defined by dry etching using ICP. A second e-beam lithography step followed in order to define the holes, which were etched down to the BOX. The sample then underwent two wet etch steps. First, the sample was immersed in 1:7 HF, which removed the BOX. Then it was immersed in a 25% aqueous solution of Tetramethyl-ammonium Hydroxide (TMAH) at room temperature, which resulted in a removal of the 50 nm thick Si layer.

The waveguides were measured using the effective cut-back method. Waveguides of different lengths were fabricated for the propagation loss measurement. The measured value was 2.65 dB/cm at λ = 7.7 μm. Our future work will address waveguides for longer wavelengths and development of other passive devices in this platform and its implementation for sensing.

IV. Integration with Microfluidic Channels

Strip waveguides were fully etched in 500 nm silicon on 3 μm silica with a silica cladding. The mode profile was optimised using Lumerical for maximum sample interaction and to prevent cross-talk. Spirals were used to reduce footprint while providing a range of interaction lengths, where the sample-waveguide interaction length was determined by a window in the silica cladding. Gratings were optimised for operation at λ = 3.8 μm.

PDMS microfluidic channels were prepared using Sylgard 184 and a 3D printed resin mould. The channel had 3000 x 100 μm cross-section and 30 mm length. The channel was made excessively wide for simple manual alignment with the sensing windows, although we subsequently designed a mount to aid alignment and reduce channel width. An O_2 plasma was used for surface modification to covalently bond the PDMS and SiO_2 cladding.

DI water and IPA solutions were prepared at volume fractions of 20, 40, 60, 80 and 100% and delivered using a syringe pump. A tunable QCL source and detector were coupled to waveguide gratings using fluoride mid-infrared fibres. A lock-in amplifier and chopper were used to reduce noise. A LabVIEW program was used to synchronise the laser wavelength sweep with data collection.

The normalised power spectra of water-IPA solutions relative to water are shown in Figure 5, showing the expected IPA absorption at λ = 3.76 μm. All measurements were performed using a 100 μm interaction length. By using longer interaction lengths smaller concentrations of aqueous solutions of IPA (~1%) can be achieved.

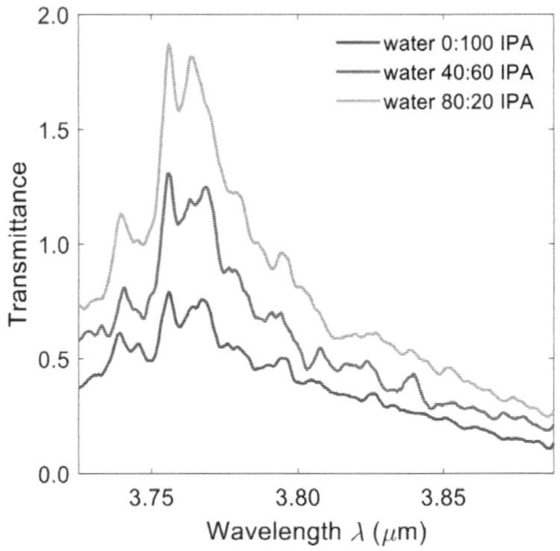

Figure 5. Transmittance of water-IPA solutions relative to water, showing the expected IPA absorption at λ = 3.76 μm.

V. Conclusions

Low loss waveguides and other photonic devices have been realised in SOI, GOS, suspended Si and suspended Ge platforms. Which platform will be used depends on the application in question and appropriate wavelength range. Work is underway to integrate these platforms with microfluidic channels for detection of various substances that have strong absorption bands in the MIR.

Acknowledgment

This work was supported by the EPSRC in the UK through the following projects: National Hub in High Value Photonic Manufacturing (EP/N00762X/1), Electronic-Photonic Convergence (EP/N013247/1), MIGRATION (EP/L01162X/1), and CORNERSTONE (EP/L021129/1), and by the Royal Academy of Engineering (RF201617/16/33).

References

[1] R. Soref, "Mid-infrared photonics in silicon and germanium," Nature Photonics, vol. 4, pp. 495-497, 2010.

[2] G. Z. Mashanovich et al., "Silicon photonic waveguides and devices for near- and mid-IR applications," IEEE Journal of Selected Topics in Quantum Electronics, vol. 21, pp. 1-12, 2015.

[3] M. Nedeljkovic et al., "Silicon photonic devices and platforms for the mid-infrared" Optical Materials Express, vol. 3, pp. 1205–1214, 2013.

[4] J. Soler Penades et al., "Suspended SOI waveguide with sub-wavelength grating cladding for mid-infrared," Optics Letters, vol. 39, pp. 5661-5664, 2014.

[5] J. Soler Penades et al., "Suspended silicon mid-infrared waveguide devices with subwavelength grating metamaterial cladding," Optics Express, vol. 24, pp. 22908-22916, 2016.

[6] M. Brun et al., "Low loss SiGe graded index waveguides for mid-IR applications," Optics Express, vol. 22, pp. 508, 2014.

[7] M. Nedeljkovic et al., "Germanium-on-silicon waveguides operating at mid-infrared wavelengths up to 8.5 μm," Optics Express, vol. 25, pp. 27431-27441, 2017.

[8] J. M. Ramirez et al., "Graded SiGe waveguides with broadband low-loss propagation in the mid infrared," Optics Express, vol. 26, pp. 870-877, 2018.

[9] G. Z. Mashanovich et al., "Group IV mid-infrared photonics," *Optical Materials Express* (in press)

[10] D. Thomson et al., "Roadmap on silicon photonics," Journal of Optics, vol. 18, 073003, 2016.

[11] J. J. Ackert, et al., "High-speed detection above the telecommunication windows with monolithic silicon photodiodes," Nature Photonics, vol. 9, pp. 393-396, 2015.

[12] M. Muneeb et al., "III-V-on-silicon integrated micro-spectrometer for the 3 μm wavelength range," Optics Express, vol. 24, pp. 9465-9472, 2016.

[13] A. Spott et al., "Quantum cascade laser on silicon," Optica, vol. 3, p. 545, 2016.

[14] P. Tai Lin at al., "Label-free glucose sensing using chip-scale mid-infrared integrated photonics," Advanced Materials, vol. 4, pp. 1755–175, 2016.

[15] M. Nedeljkovic et al., "Surface-grating-coupled low-loss Ge-on-Si rib waveguides and multimode interferometers," IEEE Photonics Technology Letters, vol. 27, pp. 1040-1043, 2015.

[16] J. Soler Penadés et al., "Suspended silicon waveguides for long-wave infrared wavelengths," Optics Letters, vol. 43, pp. 795-798, 2018.

Chemical Sensors in Plastic Optical Fibers

Luigi Zeni and Nunzio Cennamo
Department of Engineering
University of Campania Luigi Vanvitelli
Aversa, Italy
e-mail: luigi.zeni@unicampania.it;
nunzio.cennamo@unicampania.it

Maria Pesavento
Department of Chemistry
University of Pavia
Pavia, Italy
e-mail: maria.pesavento@unipv.it

Abstract—**Plastic Optical Fibers (POFs) are especially advantageous due to their excellent flexibility, simple manufacturing and handling procedures, great numerical aperture, large diameter, and the fact that plastic is able to withstand smaller bend radii than glass. Sensors based on POFs and Molecularly Imprinted Polymers (MIPs) are presented in the selective detection of different analytes. The developed POF-MIP sensors represent a simple approach to low-cost sensing. In this work we have recalled a chemical sensor for furfural (2-FAL) detection in power transformer insulating oil, with a Limit Of Detection (LOD) of about 4μM.**

Keywords-plastic optical fibers; chemical sensors; molecularly imprinted polymers; optical fiber sensors.

I. Introduction

Surface Plasmon Resonance (SPR) is a very sensitive method for determining refractive index variations at the interface between a metal layer and a dielectric medium. Thus, it is a transduction technique particularly suitable for marker free sensors, in which the dielectric is a receptor layer with refractive index depending on its interaction with a particular substrate. In the scientific literature, several review papers describe plasmonic sensor platforms and their applications [1]-[6].

Jorgenson et al. realized SPR sensors in optical fibers without prisms [7], in which the metal layer was directly deposited on the core of an optical fiber. The SPR sensors in optical fiber allow for remote sensing and for reduced dimension and price of the whole sensor system. At the beginning, the optical fibers employed were made of glass, but more recently plastic or special optical fibers have been used too [7]-[17]. The Plastic Optical Fibers (POFs) present exceptional flexibility, simple manipulation, large numerical aperture, big diameter. Also, they are able to withstand smaller bend radii than glass fibers. Therefore, POFs are particularly advantageous for the realization of low-cost SPR sensors [16]. SPR sensors based on optical fibers show a noticeably high sensitivity, due to the fact that they are able to detect even small variations of refractive index of the medium (dielectric) in contact with the metal layer [18]-[21]. When biological or artificial receptors are present at the metal-dielectric interface, they selectively capture the analyte present in the sample under test, and a local variation of the dielectric's refractive index in contact with the metal film is produced.

Different structures have been proposed for SPR sensors based on optical fibers [5]. D-shaped POF platforms have been successfully developed by our research group for different analytes and different receptors such as antibodies, aptamers and Molecularly Imprinted Polymers (MIP) too [22]-[28].

The flat part of the D-shaped platform is suitable for an easy deposition of the receptors, in particular MIPs, and makes it possible to perform the determination in a drop, instead of requiring complex flux devices. It has been shown that MIPs are easily produced over gold by in-situ polymerization, forming thin and firm receptor layers, which are suitable for SPR detection by the D-shaped POF platforms [24]-[28].

The D-shaped POF platforms are obtained by a hand polishing procedure, which could lead to a somewhat irreproducible morphology of the D-shaped region (roughness and total depth). Previous investigations showed that this could strongly influence the performance of the platform [29][30].

MIPs are synthetic receptors with many favorable aspects with respect to bio-receptors, such as an easier and faster preparation, the possibility of application outside the laboratory, for example under environmental conditions, a longer durability [31][32].

The advantage of the MIPs combined with SPR D-shaped POF platform is that they can be directly formed on a flat gold surface by depositing a drop of prepolymeric mixture directly over gold film, spinning by a spin coater machine and in situ polymerization [24]-[28], without modifying the surface (functionalization and passivation), as needed for the bio-receptors [22][23]. Besides, their refractive index can in principle be modulated in order to be suitable for the SPR transduction.

Taguchi et al. presented a different interesting approach for Bisphenol A (BPA) detection, exploiting molecularly imprinted nanoparticles combined with a slab optical waveguide [33]. This approach is similar to that used in the Kretschmann configuration but exploiting optical fibers combined with a slab waveguide.

In this work, we reported as the combination of a D-shaped POF and an MIP receptor is an effective way to obtain a highly selective and sensitive SPR optical chemical sensor. Several examples of applications of this optical chemical sensor have been demonstrated, as for example the selective detection of trinitrotoluene (TNT), for security applications [24], of furfural (furan-2-carbaldehyde) and dibenzyl disulfide (DBDS) in power transformer insulating oil, for industrial applications [25][28], of L-nicotine [27] in clinical applications, and perfluorinated alkylated substances (PFAs) in environmental monitoring applications [26].

The rest of the paper is structured as follows. In Section 2, we have presented an optical platform based on plastic optical fibers. In Section 3, we have reported a particular synthetical receptor: the Molecularly Imprinted Polymer. In Section 4, we have illustrated an example of a chemical-optical sensor based on an SPR-POF platform combined with an MIP receptor. We have concluded the work in Section 5.

II. SPR-POF PLATFORM

The D-shaped POF platform was realized as described in [16], the size of the POF is 980 μm of core (1 mm in diameter). Summarily, our SPR platform is made by removing the cladding of POF (along half circumference), spin coating a buffer layer on the exposed core and finally sputtering a thin gold film [16]. Figure 1 shows the SPR-POF sensor and the outline of the manufacturing steps. The final length of sensing region is about 10 mm. The photoresist layer is about 1,500 nm thick and the gold film is about 60 nm, presenting a good adhesion to the substrate too.

The buffer layer is made of photoresist (Microposit S1813), with a refractive index greater than that of the POF's core (PMMA). This buffer layer improves the performances of the SPR sensor and the gold film adhesion on the platform.

The selectivity is obtained by placing a specific receptor (for example MIP) for the considered analyte in tight contact with the gold surface (see Figure 1).

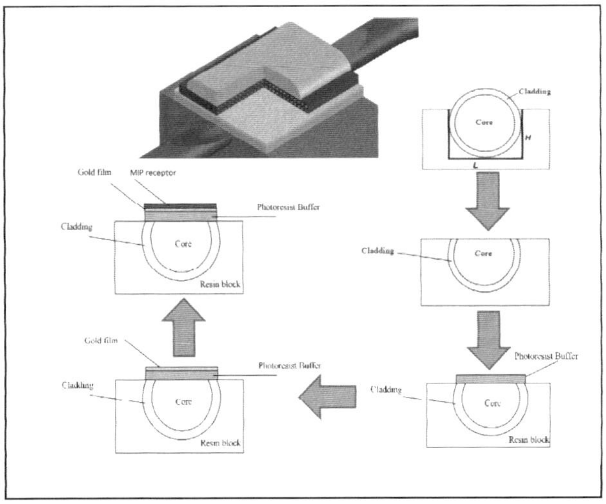

Figure 1. SPR sensor platform based on D-shaped POF.

The experimental setup consists of a halogen lamp (HL–2000–LL, Ocean Optics) illuminating the optical chemical sensor and a spectrum analyzer (USB2000+UV–VIS spectrometer, Ocean Optics) connected to a computer, as shown in Figure 2. The spectral emission of the lamp ranges from 360 nm to 1700 nm and the spectrometer is sensitive from 300 nm to 1050 nm.

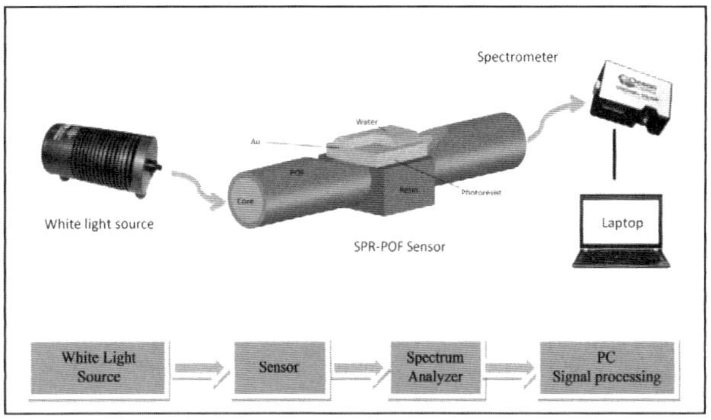

Figure 2. Experimental setup.

Usually, in the bio-chemical applications, a small amount of solution with analyte (about 50 μL) was dropped over the sensing area (MIP layer, the chemical receptor) and the spectrum recorded after about ten minutes incubation. The transmission curves along with data values were displayed online on the computer screen and saved with the help of advanced software provided by Ocean Optics. Each experimental value is the average of 5 subsequent measurements. The signal processing is obtained by Matlab and OriginPro 8.5 software.

III. MIP RECEPTORS

For the characterized optical chemical sensors [24]-[28], based on SPR-POF-MIPs, the MIP receptor layer has been obtained by three simple steps (see Figure 3).

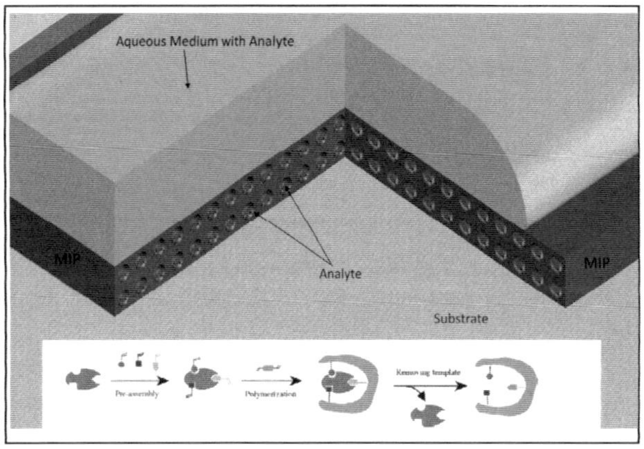

Figure 3. MIP receptor layer outline.

In particular, we have used these steps:

1) About 50 μL of the prepolymeric mixture were dropped over the flat optical sensing region (D-shaped area) and spun for 1 min at about 700 rpm, by a spin coater machine;

2) Thermal polymerization was then carried out for 16 h at 80 °C, by oven;

3) The template was extracted by repeated washings with 96% ethanol.

Figure 3 shows the outline of the MIP receptor layer with a summary of these manufacturing steps (the porous solid obtained by polymerization of the aggregate substrate-coordinating monomers after extraction of the template from the selective site).

IV. An Example of SPR-POF-MIP Sensor

As an example, we report on the results of the exploitation of an MIP receptor on a D-shaped POF for furfural detection in power transformer insulating oil. Furfural (2-FAL) has been considered among several furanic compounds possibly present in used transformer oils, since it is usually the most prominent component of paper decomposition in power transformer [28].

The gold planar surface over the D-shaped POF (SPR active surface) was washed with ethanol and then dried in a thermostatic oven at 60 °C prior to depositing the sensing layer, a specific MIP layer. The prepolymeric mixture for MIP was prepared according to the classical procedure reported in [28] with only slight modifications. Divinylbenzene (DVB), the cross-linker, was also the solvent in which the functional monomer (that is, methacrylic acid, MAA), and the template, furfural (2-FAL) are dissolved [25][28].

Figure 4 shows the spectra of the SPR-POF-MIP sensor for 2-FAL detection, where at about 860 nm a red-shift is present for increasing concentration of analyte (2-FAL) from 0 ppm to 0.193 ppm.

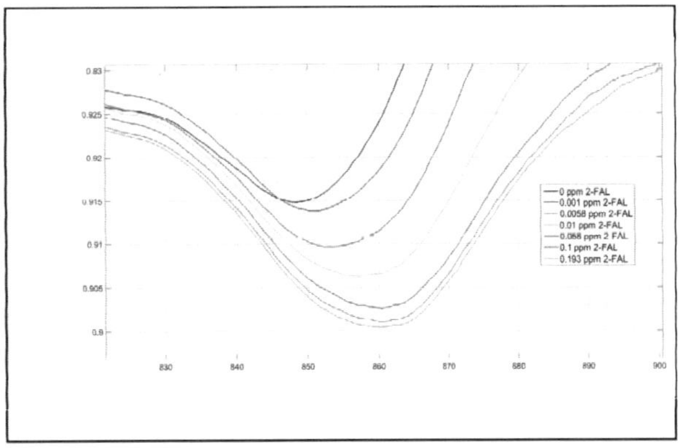

Figure 4. SPR spectra obtained for different concentrations of 2-FAL in oil.

The shift of resonance wavelength indicates that the refractive index in contact with the gold surface is increased. The dependence of the minimum wavelength on the 2-FAL concentration is evident.

Figure 5 shows the dose response curves for 2-FAL (ppm) in oil, in semi-log scale, and the Hill fitting to the experimental data, obtained by the red shift resonances shown in Figure 4.

Figure 5 shows that the experimental data are well fitted by the Hill equation, and, from the Hill parameters, we obtained a sensitivity at low concentration of about $6{\cdot}10^7$ (nm/M) and a Limit Of Detection of about 4 (μM) [25][34].

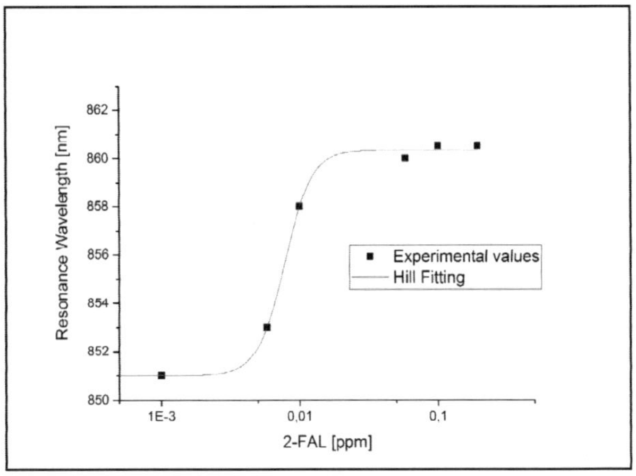

Figure 5. Resonance wavelength (nm) versus 2-FAL concentration (ppm) in oil, in semi-log scale, and Hill fitting of data.

Standardization curves like those reported in Figure 5 are generally used for chemo and biosensors, and their physical meaning can be linked to the fact that the absorption occurs by combination at specific sites, when the quantity of receptor sites available for the combination with the substrate is restricted [24]-[28][34].

V. Conclusions

We have reported on the ability of a low-cost SPR-POF sensor platform to be exploited in chemical applications based on MIP receptors.

The SPR-POF-MIP sensor systems are easy to use, small size and low-cost. As a paradigm, we have recalled the results for furfural detection in power transformer insulating oil.

References

[1] J. Homola, "Present and future of surface plasmon resonance biosensors," Anal. Bioanal. Chem., vol. 377, pp. 528–539, 2003.

[2] A. Leung, P.M. Shankar, and R. Mutharasan, "A review of fiber-optic biosensors," Sens. Act B: Chem., vol. 125, pp. 688–703, 2007.

[3] K. Anuj, R.J. Sharma, and B.D. Gupta, "Fiber-optic sensors based on surface Plasmon resonance: a comprehensive review," IEEE Sens. J., vol. 7, pp. 1118–1129, 2007.

[4] J. Homola, S.S. Yee, and G. Gauglitz, "Surface plasmon resonance sensors: review," Sens. Act B: Chem., vol. 54, pp. 3-15, 1999.

[5] C. Caucheteur, T. Guo, and J. Albert, "Review of plasmonic fiber optic biochemical sensors: improving the limit of detection," Anal and bioanal chemistry, vol. 407, pp. 3883-3897, 2015.

[6] M. C. Estevez, M. A. Otte, B. Sepulveda, and L. M. Lechuga, "Trends and challenges of refractometric nanoplasmonic biosensors: A review," Analytica Chimica Acta, vol. 806, pp. 55-73, 2014.

[7] R.C. Jorgenson and S.S. Yee, "A fiber-optic chemical sensor based on surface plasmon resonance," Sens. Act B: Chem., vol. 12, pp. 213–220, 1993.

[8] E. Klantsataya, P. Jia, H. Ebendorff-Heidepriem, T.M. Monro, and A. François, "Plasmonic Fiber Optic Refractometric Sensors: From Conventional Architectures to Recent Design Trends," Sensors, vol. 17, pp. 12, 2017.

[9] X.D. Wang and O.S. Wolfbeis, "Fiber-Optic Chemical Sensors and Biosensors (2008-2012)," Anal. Chem.," vol. 85, pp. 487-508, 2013.

[10] X.D. Wang and O.S. Wolfbeis, "Fiber-Optic Chemical Sensors and Biosensors (2013-2015)," Anal. Chem., vol. 88, pp. 203–227, 2016.

[11] D.J. Monk and D.R. Walt, "Optical fiber-based biosensors," Anal. Bioanal. Chem., vol. 379, pp. 931–945, 2004.

[12] A. Trouillet, C. Ronot-Trioli, C. Veillas, and H. Gagnaire, "Chemical sensing by surface plasmon resonance in a multimode optical fiber," Pure App. Opt., vol. 5, pp. 227-237, 1996.

[13] B.D. Gupta and R.K. Verma, "Surface plasmon resonance-based fiber optic sensors: Principle, probe designs, and some applications," Journal of Sensors, vol. 2009, pp. 1–12, 2009.

[14] M.E. Bosch, A.J.R. Sánchez, F.S. Rojas, and C.B. Ojeda, "Recent development in optical fiber biosensors," Sensors, vol. 7, pp. 797–859, 2007.

[15] A. Abdelghani et al., "Surface plasmon resonance fiber-optic sensor for gas detection," Sens. Act B: Chem., vol. 39, pp. 407–410, 1997.

[16] N. Cennamo, D. Massarotti, L. Conte, and L. Zeni, "Low cost sensors based on SPR in a plastic optical fiber for biosensor implementation," Sensors, vol. 11, pp. 11752–11760, 2011.

[17] M. Piliarik, J. Homola, Z. Manikova, and J. Čtyroký, "Surface Plasmon Resonance Sensor Based on a Single-Mode Polarization-Maintaining Optical Fiber," Sens. Actuat. B Chem., vol. 90, pp. 236–242, 2003.

[18] M. Kanso, S. Cuenot, and G. Louarn, "Sensitivity of optical fiber sensor based on surface plasmon resonance: Modeling and experiments," Plasmonics, vol. 3, pp. 49–57, 2008.

[19] Y.S. Dwivedi, A.K. Sharma, and B.D. Gupta, "Influence of design parameters on the performance of a SPR based fiber optic sensor," Plasmonics, vol. 3, pp. 79–86, 2008.

[20] M. Iga, A. Sek, and K. Watanabe, "Gold thickness dependence of SPR-based hetero-core structured optical fiber sensor," Sens. Act B: Chem., vol. 106, pp. 363–368, 2005.

[21] A.K. Sharma and B.D. Gupta, "On the sensitivity and signal to noise ratio of a step-index fiber optic surface plasmon resonance sensor with bimetallic layers," Opt. Commun., vol. 245, pp. 159–169, 2005.

[22] N. Cennamo et al., "An innovative plastic optical fiber based biosensor for new bio/applications. The case of celiac disease," Sens. Act. B: Chem., vol. 176, pp. 1008–1014, 2013.

[23] N. Cennamo et al., "An easy way to realize SPR aptasensor: A multimode plastic optical fiber platform for cancer biomarkers detection," Talanta, vol. 140, pp. 88–95, 2015.

[24] N. Cennamo et al., "Sensors based on surface plasmon resonance in a plastic optical fiber for the detection of trinitrotoluene," Sens. Act. B: Chem., vol. 118, pp. 221-226, 2013.

[25] N. Cennamo et al., "Markers detection in transformer oil by plasmonic chemical sensor system based on POF and MIPs," IEEE Sens. J., vol. 16, pp. 7663-7670, 2016.

[26] N. Cennamo et al., "A Molecularly Imprinted Polymer on a Plasmonic Plastic Optical Fiber to detect perfluorinated compounds in water," Sensors, vol. 18, pp. 1836, 2018.

[27] N. Cennamo, G. D'Agostino, M. Pesavento, and L. Zeni, "High selectivity and sensitivity sensor based on MIP and SPR in tapered plastic optical fibers for the detection of L-nicotine," Sensors and Actuators B., Vol. 191, pp. 529–536, 2014.

[28] N. Cennamo, L. De Maria, G. D'Agostino, L. Zeni, and M. Pesavento, "Monitoring of Low Levels of Furfural in Power Transformer Oil with a Sensor System Based on a POF-MIP Platform," Sensors, vol. 15, pp. 8499-8511, 2015.

[29] K. Gasior, T. Martynkien, and W. Urbanczyk, "Effect of constructional parameters on the performance of a surface plasmon resonance sensor based on a multimode polymer optical fiber," Appl. Opt., vol. 53, pp. 8167-8174, 2014.

[30] K. Gasior, T. Martynkien, G. Wojcik, P. Mergo, and W. Urbanczyk, "D-shape polymer optical fibers for surface plasmon resonance sensing," Opto-Electronics Review, vol. 25, pp. 1–5, 2017.

[31] L. Uzun and A.P.F. Turner, "Molecularly-imprinted polymers sensors: realising their potential," Biosens. Bioelectron., vol. 76, pp. 131–144, 2016.

[32] K. Haupt and K. Mosbach, "Molecularly imprinted polymers and their use in biomimetic sensors," Chem. Rev., vol. 100, pp. 2495–2504, 2000.

[33] Y. Taguchi, E. Takano, and T. Takeuchi, "SPR Sensing of Bisphenol A Using Molecularly Imprinted Nanoparticles Immobilized on Slab Optical Waveguide with Consecutive Parallel Au and Ag Deposition Bands Coexistent with Bisphenol A-Immobilized Au Nanoparticles," Langmuir, vol. 28, pp. 7083–7088, 2012.

[34] B.I. Burganov, A.V. Lobanov, I.A. Borisov, and A.N. Reshetilov, "Criterion for Hill equation validity for description of biosensor calibration curves," Anal. Chim. Acta, vol. 427, pp. 11-19, 2001.

Low Index Photonic Membrane Textile for Personal Thermoregulation

Salim Assaf, Yan Pennec, Alexander Korovin, Anthony Treizebre, Vincent Thomy, Bahram Djafari-Rouhani
IEMN Université de Lille
Villeneuve d'Ascq, France
E-mail: Salim.Assaf@univ-lille1.fr; yan.pennec@univ-lille1.fr; alexander.korovin@iemn.univ-lille1.fr; Anthony.Treizebre@univ-lille1.fr; Vincent.Thomy@iemn.univ-lille1.fr; Bahram.Djafari-Rouhani@univ-lille1.fr

Abstract— **The effect of a photonic polymer membrane in the Mid InfraRed (MIR) range for passive personal heating regulation is demonstrated. We show that, by designing the holes' diameters and periods of the membrane, we are able to reflect up to 17% of the emission of the human body in the wavelength range [7.5, 11.5] µm. The work presented here has been performed theoretically with the help of the Finite Element Method. The origin of the reflectivity comes from guided and resonant modes belonging to the excitation of the photonic membrane. Integrated to a textile, such a membrane can greatly mitigate the energy demand for indoor heating and ultimately contributes to the relief of the climate issues.**

Keywords- photonic polymer membrane; personal heating regulation; human body; MIR; textile; reflectivity; numerical calculations; Finite Element Method.

I. INTRODUCTION

A large part of the building energy consumption is attributed to temperature control using Heating, Ventilation and Air Conditioning (HVAC) systems [1]. A decrease in this consumption, even slightly, will contribute to both environmental protection and costs saving. One way is to support building insulation; another way is to control the energy consumption by personal thermoregulation [2]. Toward this end, personal thermoregulation properties have been recently developed, not only in extreme environments for military personnel, athletes or emergency medical service personnel [3], but for the majority of people who spend their time in a sedentary state. The personal thermal management has been defined through different devices, wearable like normal clothes, but capable to control the body comfort. Personal cooling textile have been developed using synthetic polymer fibers with low IR absorbance [4][5] or able to enhance the radiative dissipation by nanoporous polyethylene film [6]. The opposite effect, i.e. personal heating textiles, have also been studied. In this case, the personal thermal management has been controlled by the integration of metallic nanowires embedded in the textile that reduce the energy waste from the human body. Such textiles not only reflect the human body infrared radiation, but also allow Joule heating to complement the passive insulation [7]-[9]. Realizing heating and cooling properties within a same structure and without any energy input still remains a tremendous challenge. Very recently, Hsu et al. [10] investigated a dual-mode textile for human body radiative heating using a bilayer thermal emitter embedded inside an IR-transparent nanoPE that can perform both passive radiative heating and cooling using the same piece of textile. A reversible humidity sensitive clothing for personal thermoregulation was also proposed using shape memory polymer [11]. The smart textile has been designed to reversibly adapt the thermal insulation functionality, thus permitting the air flow and reducing the humidity level and the apparent temperature. Therefore, a tremendous effort is necessary to develop smart wearable thermoregulating textiles which can reversibly respond to the immediate temperature feeling of the wearer.

Photonic crystals, proposed in 1987 by Eli Yablonovitch [12] are periodic structures based on patterns whose dimensions are close to the working wavelength. The control and manipulation of waves in photonic crystals are achieved by the generation of band gaps in the Bragg regime for in plane waves. Photonic crystal slabs can also interact with external radiations in complex and interesting ways. Of particular importance here is the presence of resonances within the plate which present a high confined electromagnetic field [13]-[15]. Such interaction is usually presented as Fano phenomenon that occurs when a discrete localized state becomes coupled to a continuum of states [16]. The resonances of the plate can then couple to external radiation and provide an efficient way to channel light from within the slab to the external environment. In addition, the resonances can significantly affect the transmission and reflection of externally incident light, resulting in complex resonant line shapes that are useful in filter applications [17]. Very recently, such property was introduced in topics related to plasmonic [18], electromagnetic metamaterial [19][20], and for different optomechanic [21] or sensing [22][23] applications.

We investigate here the properties of a photonic crystal membrane, tailored in the MIR range, useful for personal heating regulation. The BCB (Benzocyclobutene) is the polymer which compose the photonic membrane. The objective is to increase the reflectance in the MIR range, playing with the geometrical parameters of the membrane. We first describe the photonic polymer membrane under consideration and its physical and geometrical parameters. Then, we show the calculation of the reflective spectrum and study its behavior as a function of the geometrical parameters. The rest of the paper is structured as follows. After this introduction, we describe in Section 2 the design and detail the simulation of the photonic membrane. Then, we conclude the paper in Section 3.

II. DESIGN AND SIMULATION OF A PHOTONIC POLYMER MEMBRANE

As seen schematically Figure 1a, the human body electromagnetic wave is launched from the top and interacts with the photonic membrane. The photonic membrane, embedded in air, is made of a polymer (BCB) and drilled following a triangular array of holes (Figure 1b). We took into consideration the absorption of the BCB by using its complex refractive index. The geometrical parameters involved in the study are the lattice parameter *P*, the hole's diameter *D* and the thickness of the membrane *h*. All numerical results have been performed with the help of the Finite Element Method (FEM) for which the elementary unit cell for the calculation of the transmission, reflection and absorption spectra are sketched Figure 1b. At each side of the unit cell, perfect matching layers (PML) are applied to absorb all outgoing waves while on the plane of the membrane periodic boundary conditions are used to build the infinite periodic membrane.

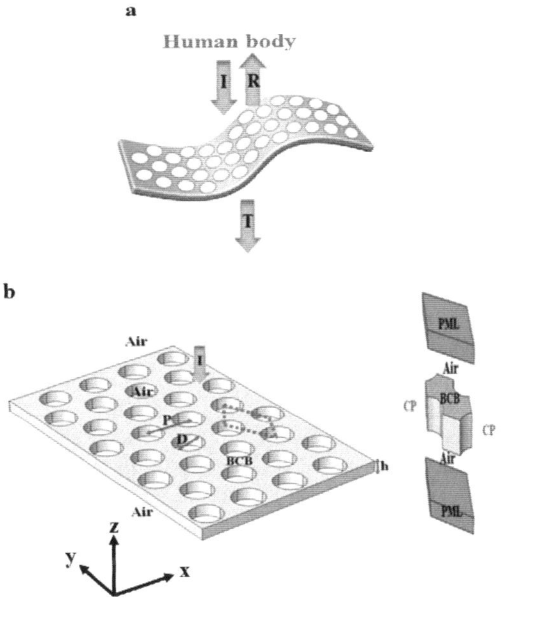

Figure 1. a) Principal scheme of the system with the direction of the incident (I), reflective (R) and transmitive (T) electromagnetic waves. b) (left) 3D view of the BCB membrane where h is the thickness, D the diameter and P the period. (Right) Elementary unit cell used for the FEM calculation with the absorbing (PML) and periodic (CP) boundary conditions.

Figure 2a presents, as a reference, the behavior of a not structured BCB membrane of thickness 4µm, and records the reflection, transmission and absorption curves, reported respectively in black, blue and red. One can see that almost 80% of the signal emitted is transmitted through the membrane. At the wavelengths close to 8 µm, 9.5 µm and 12µm, several dips appear in the transmission curve which correspond to absorption peaks inside the membrane. A small amplitude of reflection (lower than 20%) appears in the reflection spectrum with a zero reflection at 6µm. This variation is due to the Fabry Perot oscillations inside the BCB membrane of finite thickness. We now structure the membrane, considering a triangular array of holes with the geometrical parameters *P* = 7 µm, *D* = 5.5 µm, and h = 4 µm and record, as before, the reflection (black), transmission (blue) and absorption (red) coefficients (Figure 2b). We find that the spectrum is drastically affected in the wavelength range [6, 7.5] µm. To get a deeper insight, the reflection coefficient is magnified in the inset of Figure 2b. One can see that the reflection comes from the existence of two main peaks and a small one in the middle. To understand their origin, we perform the calculation of the distribution of the electric field in the unit cell at the wavelengths 6.08 µm, 6.41 µm and 6.88 µm corresponding respectively to the three features (Figure 2c). The two high reflection peaks come from the excitation of the guided modes, which spread over the BCB membrane. One is antisymmetric while the other is symmetric with respect to the middle plane of the membrane. The small peak in the middle corresponds to an antisymmetric mode strongly confined inside the air hole. One can note that this localized mode, in interaction with the emitted continuum, gives rise to a peak of asymmetric shape in the reflection spectrum. Such physical properties are known as a Fano resonance [15].

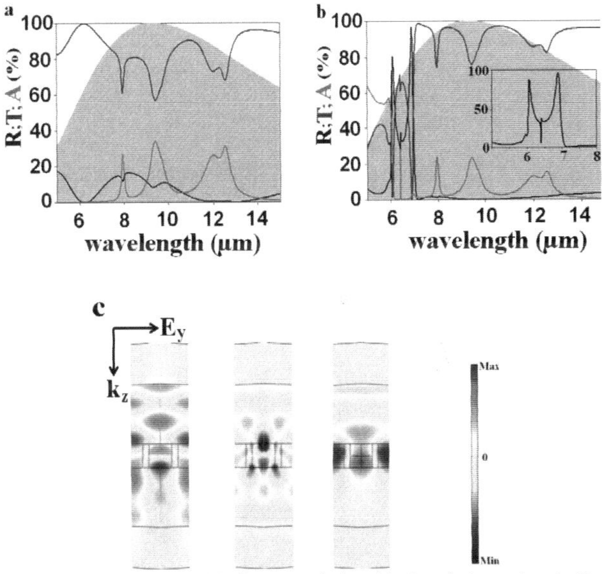

Figure 2. a) Reflection (black), transmission (blue) and absorption (red) coefficients through a) the non-structured membrane with h = 4 µm and b) the structured membrane with P = 7 µm, D = 5.5 µm, and h = 4 µm. The grey hatched area represents the emissivity of the human body at 37°C. c) Representation of the electric field Ey at the wavelengths λ =6.08 µm ; λ = 6.41 µm, and λ = 6.88 µm, corresponding respectively to the three features in the inset of b).

Figures 2a and 2b show the emissivity of the human body at 37°C calculated from the Planck law and represented with the grey hatched area. One can see that, with the chosen set of geometrical parameters, the reflection curve has been affected in the lower part of the emissive spectrum. In Figure 3a, the geometrical parameters of the photonic structure have been changed with P = 9 µm and D = 6.5 µm. One can see that the peaks of reflection shift to the higher wavelength and now reach the area where the maximum of the emissive spectrum is expected. It remains that the shape of the signal is the same, composed of two main peaks and the Fano shape resonance in between. Nevertheless, the amplitude has decreased, due to the presence of the polymer absorption which was not present in the previous case.

We then demonstrated that the resonant modes of the low index polymer membrane can be used to produce a reflection in the MIR range. To get a quantitative representation of the global reflection as a function of the geometrical parameters, we define an efficiency coefficient, η, which corresponds to a numerical integration of the reflection over a wavelength range under consideration, normalized with respect to the emissivity of the human body. So, all the efficiency factors should be comprised between 0 and 1, with a maximum of reflection when $\eta = 1$. This factor is explained through the following formula:

$$\eta = \frac{\int_{\lambda_{min}}^{\lambda_{max}} E_\lambda . R_\lambda . d\lambda}{\int_{\lambda_{min}}^{\lambda_{max}} E_\lambda} \quad (1)$$

where E_λ is the human body emissivity at the wavelength λ and R_λ is the structure's reflectance over the wavelength range [λ_{min} = 7.5 µm, λ_{max} = 11.5 µm].

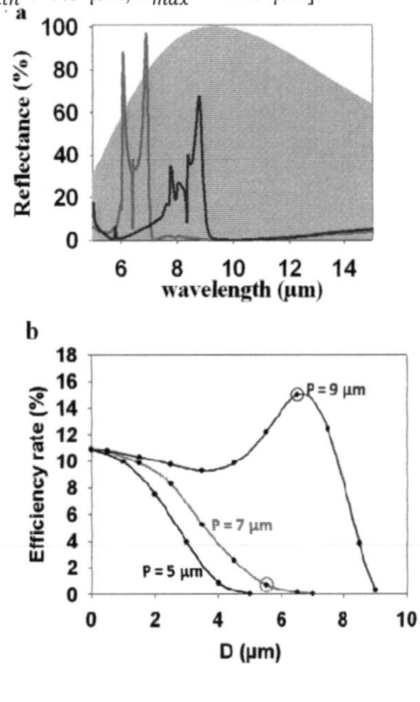

Figure 3. a) Reflection spectra for: P = 7 µm and D = 5.5 µm (red curve) and P = 9 µm and D = 6.5 µm (blue curve) with h = 4 µm b) Evolution of the efficient rate η as a function of D, for three periods P (h = 4 µm). The circled dots correspond to the position of the two reflection spectra in a).

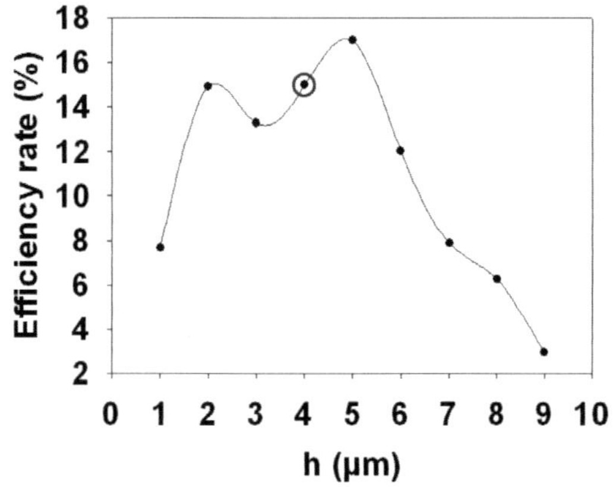

Figure 4. Evolution of the efficiency reflection coefficient η as a function of h, with P = 9 µm and D = 6.5 µm. The circled dot corresponds to the position of the blue reflection spectrum in a).

Figure 3 shows the evolution of the efficiency coefficient (in %) as a function of the diameter of the holes, for different periods and for a constant thickness of the membrane, h = 4 µm. One can see that η clearly depends of the geometrical parameters and a maximum of reflectance (~15 %) is reached for a period P = 9 µm and a diameter D = 7 µm. The origin of the variation of η comes from the shift of the two peaks described in the previous section through the wavelength range [7.5, 11.5] µm, which presents the higher level of emissivity of the human body. Figure 4 represents the behavior of the efficiency coefficient as a function of the thickness of the membrane. The circled blue dot in the curve corresponds to the maximum of the efficiency obtained from Figure 3 corresponding to the geometrical parameters P = 9 µm, D= 6.5 µm and h = 4 µm. One can see that the response of the efficiency coefficient is robust with respect to the thickness variation of the membrane and even more the efficiency can still be increased, reaching 17% of reflectivity.

III. CONCLUSION

The effect of reflectance of a photonic membrane of low refractive index on the human body emission at 37°C has been theoretically investigated in the MIR range. We showed that the reflectivity depends on the geometrical parameters of the membrane and found the occurrence of three peaks of reflection whose origin is due to the structuring of the membrane. One origin is due to the photonic guided modes inside the membrane, the second one comes from the local excitation of the electromagnetic field inside the air holes. The dependence of the geometrical parameters has been quantitatively highlighted through the definition of an efficiency coefficient. We found that the BCB membrane can reflect up to 17% of the emission in the wavelength range [7.5, 11.5] µm which correspond to the maximum of the human body emissivity.

We are currently studying the effect of the physical parameters considering the behavior of the refractive index of both the membrane and the environment on the reflectivity rate. Also, the work is ongoing toward an experimental demonstration. This work paves the way for the design of a smart responsive photonic membrane which dynamically modifies its reflectance in response to external stimuli like temperature or humidity.

ACKNOWLEDGMENT

We thank Semi Lab for performing the refractive index measurement. S.A. thanks the society DAMART France for partial financial support of his PhD. This work was supported by the European Commission project Phototex under the INTERREG program France - Wallonie - Vlaanderen.

REFERENCES

[1] K. J. Chua, S. K. Chou, W. M. Yang, and J. Yan, "Achieving better energy-efficient air conditioning – A review of technologies and strategies," *Appl. Energy*, vol. 104, pp. 87–104, Apr. 2013.

[2] R. F. Rupp, N. G. Vásquez, and R. Lamberts, "A review of human thermal comfort in the built environment," *Energy Build.*, vol. 105, pp. 178–205, Oct. 2015.

[3] M. M. Yazdi and M. Sheikhzadeh, "Personal cooling garments: a review," *J. Text. Inst.*, vol. 105, no. 12, pp. 1231–1250, 2014.

[4] J. K. Tong, X. Huang, S. V. Boriskina, J. Loomis, Y. Xu, and G. Chen, "Infrared-Transparent Visible-Opaque Fabrics for Wearable Personal Thermal Management," *ACS Photonics*, vol. 2, no. 6, pp. 769–778, Jun. 2015.

[5] P. B. Catrysse, A. Y. Song, and S. Fan, "Photonic Structure Textile Design for Localized Thermal Cooling Based on a Fiber Blending Scheme," *ACS Photonics*, vol. 3, no. 12, pp. 2420–2426, Dec. 2016.

[6] P.-C. Hsu *et al.*, "Radiative human body cooling by nanoporous polyethylene textile," *Science*, vol. 353, no. 6303, pp. 1019–1023, Sep. 2016.

[7] P.-C. Hsu *et al.*, "Personal Thermal Management by Metallic Nanowire-Coated Textile," *Nano Lett.*, vol. 15, no. 1, pp. 365–371, Jan. 2015.

[8] Z. Yu, Y. Gao, X. Di, and H. Luo, "Cotton modified with silver-nanowires/polydopamine for a wearable thermal management device," *RSC Adv.*, vol. 6, no. 72, pp. 67771–67777, 2016.

[9] L. Cai *et al.*, "Warming up human body by nanoporous metallized polyethylene textile," *Nat. Commun.*, vol. 8, no. 1, Dec. 2017.

[10] P.-C. Hsu *et al.*, "A dual-mode textile for human body radiative heating and cooling," *Sci. Adv.*, vol. 3, no. 11, p. e1700895, Nov. 2017.

[11] Y. Zhong *et al.*, "Reversible Humidity Sensitive Clothing for Personal Thermoregulation," *Sci. Rep.*, vol. 7, p. 44208, Mar. 2017.

[12] E. Yablonovitch, "Inhibited Spontaneous Emission in Solid-State Physics and Electronics," *Phys. Rev. Lett.*, vol. 58, no. 20, p. 4, 1987.

[13] V. N. Astratov *et al.*, "Resonant coupling of near-infrared radiation to photonic band structure waveguides," *J. Light. Technol.*, vol. 17, no. 11, pp. 2050–2057, Nov. 1999.

[14] V. Pacradouni, W. J. Mandeville, A. R. Cowan, P. Paddon, J. F. Young, and S. R. Johnson, "Photonic band structure of dielectric membranes periodically textured in two dimensions," *Phys. Rev. B*, vol. 62, no. 7, pp. 4204–4207, Aug. 2000.

[15] A. R. Cowan, P. Paddon, V. Pacradouni, and J. F. Young, "Resonant scattering and mode coupling in two-dimensional textured planar waveguides," *J. Opt. Soc. Am. A*, vol. 18, no. 5, p. 1160, May 2001.

[16] M. F. Limonov, M. V. Rybin, A. N. Poddubny, and Y. S. Kivshar, "Fano resonances in photonics," *Nat. Photonics*, vol. 11, no. 9, pp. 543–554, Sep. 2017.

[17] P. Markoš, "Fano resonances and band structure of two-dimensional photonic structures," *Phys. Rev. A*, vol. 92, no. 4, Oct. 2015.

[18] B. Luk'yanchuk *et al.*, "The Fano resonance in plasmonic nanostructures and metamaterials," *Nat. Mater.*, vol. 9, no. 9, pp. 707–715, Sep. 2010.

[19] A. B. Khanikaev, C. Wu, and G. Shvets, "Fano-resonant metamaterials and their applications," *Nanophotonics*, vol. 2, no. 4, Jan. 2013.

[20] Y. Yang, I. I. Kravchenko, D. P. Briggs, and J. Valentine, "All-dielectric metasurface analogue of electromagnetically induced transparency," *Nat. Commun.*, vol. 5, p. 5753, Dec. 2014.

[21] K. A. Yasir and W.-M. Liu, "Controlled Electromagnetically Induced Transparency and Fano Resonances in Hybrid BEC-Optomechanics," *Sci. Rep.*, vol. 6, no. 1, Sep. 2016.

[22] S. Amoudache *et al.*, "Optical and acoustic sensing using Fano-like resonances in dual phononic and photonic crystal plate," *J. Appl. Phys.*, vol. 119, no. 11, p. 114502, Mar. 2016.

[23] N. S. King *et al.*, "Fano Resonant Aluminum Nanoclusters for Plasmonic Colorimetric Sensing," *ACS Nano*, vol. 9, no. 11, pp. 10628–10636, Nov. 2015.

Evanescent Field Sensors Based on Si Photonics

Concept and Characterization

Andreas Tortschanoff, Christian Ranacher, Cristina Consani
Carinthian Tech Research AG
Villach, Austria
e-mail: andreas.tortschanoff@ctr.at

Thomas Grille
Infineon Technologies Austria AG
Villach, Austria
e-mail: thomas.grille@infineon.com

Abstract— **We present a detailed study of Si-based optical waveguides, which can be used as evanescent field sensors for the quantitative analysis of various gases and liquids. Waveguides were fabricated and experimentally characterized. Direct quantitative comparison of simulation with experimental results of directional coupling structures allows fine-tuning of the optical material parameters and provides important input for future sensor design. The concept was validated with quantitative CO_2 measurements.**

Keywords - silicon photonics; evanescent field sensor; directional coupler; integrated sensor.

I. Introduction

Interest for integrated gas sensors, which could be used in mobile devices has grown over the last years and provides the motivation for investigating Si-based photonics in the mid-infrared spectral range [1]. One approach uses waveguide structures and evanescent field infrared absorption as the sensor principle [2]. The measurement principle is shown in Figure 1. Mid-Infrared radiation from a quantum cascade laser is guided to the structure via an optical fiber. Diffraction gratings and taper structures on both ends of the waveguide are used for coupling the light into and out of the waveguide. Part of the waveguide is in contact with the sample-gas and there absorption occurs in the evanescent field of the transmitted mode.

The devised active structures are silicon strip waveguides, which are in contact with the gas, so that the evanescent field gets absorbed. For a good understanding and further optimization of the sensor performance, a thorough characterization of these photonic structures is crucial. Here, we present results from simulation and experiments, where we characterized damping, mode profiles, and coupling. Comparison of simulation and experimental results also allows a fine-tuning of the simulation parameters, which is important for further optimization. Finally, our first measurements with CO_2 demonstrate the feasibility of gas measurements with this type of evanescent field sensors.

The rest of this paper is organized as follows. Section II describes experimental procedures and the fabrication of the structures. Section III presents and discusses the first results we obtained and Section IV summarizes our work and presents first conclusions from this work in progress.

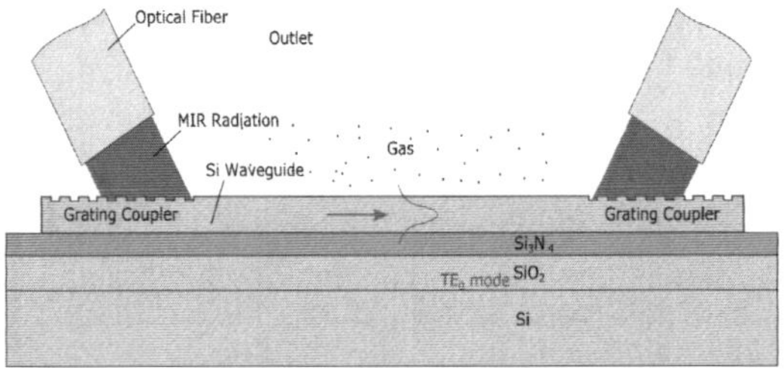

Figure 1. Schematic representation of the measurement idea. (see text for details)

II. Experimental

The devised sensor test structures are silicon strip waveguides on a silicon nitride-layer, deposited on SiO_2, which can be fabricated with standard semiconductor processes to provide a fully integrated CMOS (Complementary metal-oxide-semiconductor) compatible sensor.

Simulations where carried out using COMSOL-Multiphysics in order to determine favorable dimensions of the waveguide and the grating coupler. The waveguides were

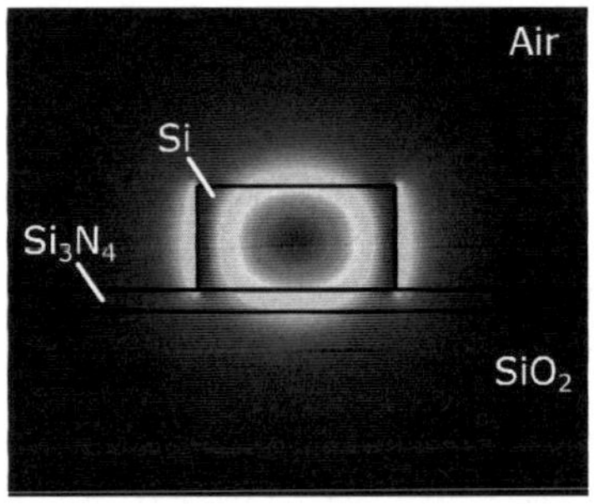

Figure 2. Field distribution of the electromagnetic field in the strip waveguide for the fundamental quasi-TE mode (a) and quasi-TM mode (b). The plot shows results for the configuration with 140 nm Si_3N_4.

designed for the absorption band of CO_2 at 4.26 µm. The dimensions of the waveguide were chosen for single-mode wave propagation. The calculated mode profiles for a strip waveguide on a silicon nitride membrane are shown in Figure 2. The influence of different Si_3N_4 layer thicknesses on damping and mode profiles was investigated. The width and height of the waveguides are 1.4 µm and 660 nm, respectively.

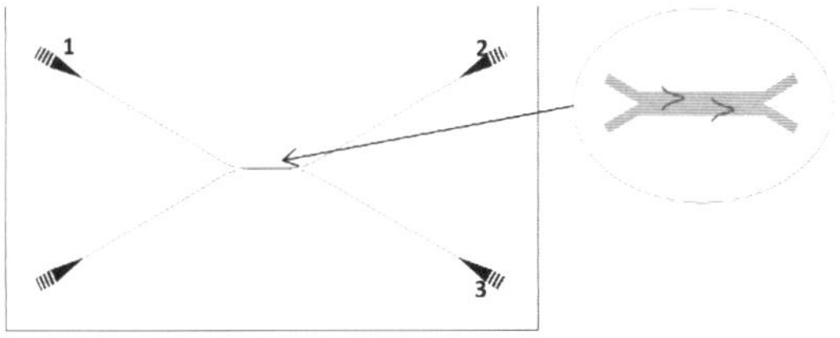

Figure 3. Scheme of the directional coupler structure. The inset on the right shows the details of the coupling region..

There are large uncertainties, with regard to the optical parameters, because the optical properties of the thin layers of poly-Si and Si_3N_4 strongly depend on the details of the deposition method. For experimental characterization of the mode properties, directional couplers were designed and fabricated, which are very sensitive to the exact shape of the mode. A direct comparison between experiments and simulation allows fine-tuning the optical parameters for the simulation. The basic outline of these structures is shown in Figure 3. A grating launch-pad with a subsequent taper structure is used to couple light in and out. Light is coupled in at port 1 and detectors are placed at port 2 ("through-port") and 3 ("drop-port"). For the structures measured in this paper, the gap between the waveguides was 400nm.

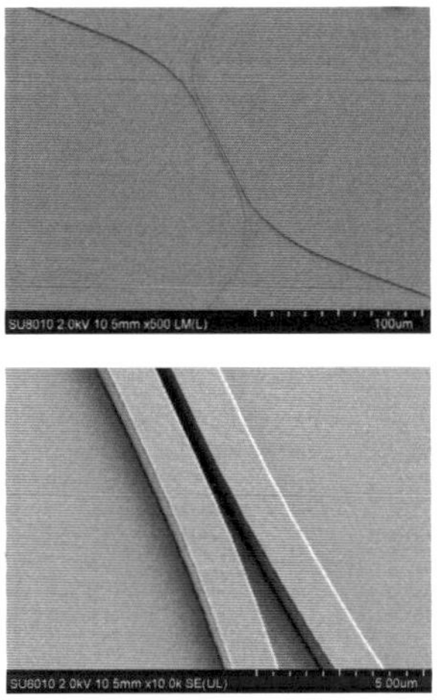

Figure 4. SEM analysis of the strip waveguide directional coupler.

Measurements on structures with different interaction lengths allow quantitative comparison of the experimental results with the simulation.

Details of the fabrication process can be found in [3]. In short, the structures were manufactured using low pressure chemical vapor deposition, lithography and etching. A 2 µm thick SiO_x layer and subsequently a Si_3N_4 layer of some nanometers were deposited onto a silicon substrate. On top of the Si_3N_4 an amorphous silicon layer was deposited which was annealed at 700 C° to achieve a polycrystalline silicon layer. Finally, the waveguide structures, as well as the gratings, where etched into the polycrystalline silicon layer.

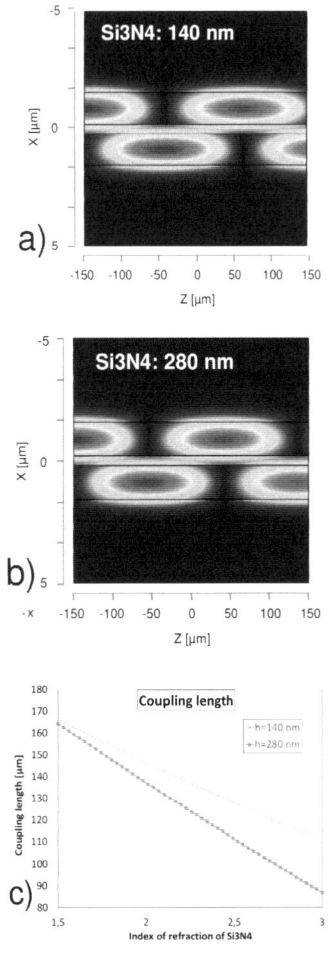

Figure 5. (a), (b) Representative simulation results for directional coupler structures with a Si_3N_4 layer thickness as indicated. The amplitude of the electric field is plotted. Optical parameters were taken from the COMSOL database. (c) Dependence of the coupling length on the index of refraction of Si_3N_4, used in the simulations.

The waveguide characterization, as well as the gas measurements, was carried out using a custom test-bench, described in detail in [4]. In short, it comprises a Quantum Cascade Laser (QCL) as radiation source, optical fibers, a stage for placing the test chips, and mercury cadmium telluride (MCT) detectors. The beam was guided from the laser to the device and from the device to the detector via optical fibers with core diameters of 100 µm and 450µm, respectively.

While the characterization of the intrinsic losses was carried out on wafer-level, the gas measurements were carried out on single chips. The single test chips were placed in a 3D printed gas cell, which comprised a gas inlet and a holder for the test chip. The top of the cell provided openings for the optical fibers, which also served as outlet for the gas. During the gas measurements the cell was flushed with CO_2/N_2 mixtures at a total flow rate of 100 ml/min using two mass flow controllers.

All characterization measurements were performed at 2400 cm^{-1}, which is just outside the CO_2 absorption band in order to avoid an influence of the ambient CO_2 concentration. For the absorption measurements, the laser was tuned to a position within the CO_2 band at about 2363 cm^{-1}, where maximal absorption was observed.

III. RESULTS

Figure 4 shows pictures from scanning electron microscopy validating the fabrication quality. The surface roughness of the Si structures and the Si3N4 layer, as well as the topography of the strip waveguides were also investigated using atomic force microscopy, which revealed that the surface roughness is about 1 nm at measurement positions (on the top of the Si layer as well as on the SiO2 and the Si3N4 layer).

To measure the intrinsic losses, the transmitted IR radiation was measured on four waveguides with different lengths (5.0 mm, 7.5 mm, 10.0 mm and 12.5 mm), for each configuration of Si3N4 layer thickness (0nm, 140nm and 280nm). For every thickness, the transmitted intensity through the four waveguides was recorded, which allows to calculate the intrinsic damping, without contributions from losses at the coupling structures and the taper [5]. The damping increases with increasing Si_3N_4 thickness and is on the order of 4-5 dB/cm.

Most importantly, we performed measurements on directional couplers. These results are very sensitive to the exact shape of the mode and allow a direct comparison between experiments and simulation. Besides academic interest, this is important because it allows fine-tuning of the optical parameters for the simulation, and, in addition, such coupling structures will be important building blocks for more complex sensor designs. Figures 5(a) and 5(b) show the simulation results for two different thicknesses of the Si_3N_4 layer. From this, we estimated the coupling length for maximal energy transfer between the waveguides to be 110µm and 95µm for thicknesses of the Si_3N_4-layer of 140 nm and 280 nm, respectively. Figure 5(c) shows the calculated dependence of the coupling length as a function of layer thickness. Based on these simulations, test-structures with interaction lengths of 70, 110, and 150 µm were designed and fabricated. In the experiments, we found a mismatch of about 20% with regard to the initial estimates. However, fine-tuning of the optical parameters by some percent provides excellent overlap between experiment and simulation. This is shown in Figure 6. Here, the curves show the simulated relative intensities at the through-port and the drop-port as a function of propagation length for three different layer-thicknesses of Si_3N_4. The markers show the experimental results measured on structures with interaction lengths of 70, 110, and 150 µm and different thickness of the Si_3N_4 layer. The values for the refractive indices of Si and Si_3N_4 used in the simulations were n_{Si}=3.525 and n_{Si3N4}=1.92 respectively.

(a)

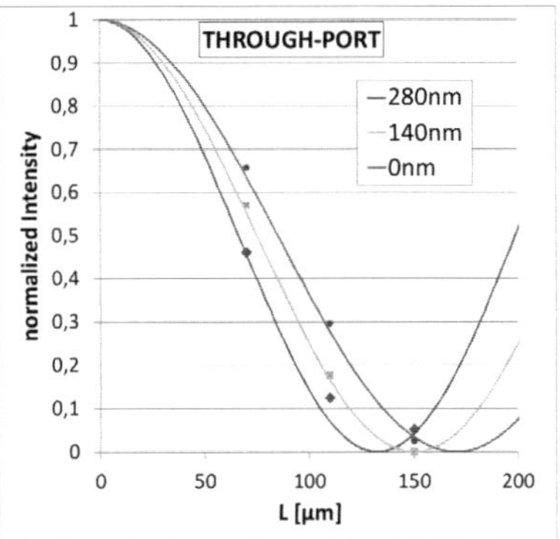

(b)

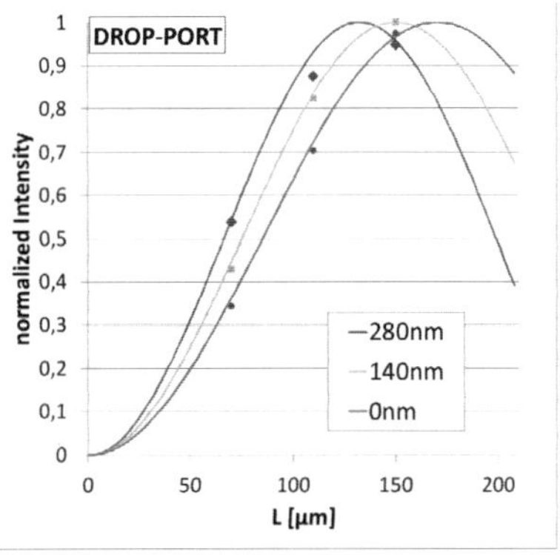

Figure 6. Comparison of simulation with experimental results. The curves show the simulated relative intensities at (a) the through-port and (b) the drop-port for three different layer-thicknesses.

Finally, in order to test the sensing capability of the strip waveguide, quantitative CO_2 measurements were conducted using a strip waveguide in the form of a meander with a length of 2 cm. The QCL was tuned to a wavelength where we observed maximal CO_2 absorption. The position of the fibers for in- and out-coupling was adjusted in order to optimize the coupling and achieve a high signal at the detector. The sensor chip was placed in a gas cell, which was flushed using mixtures of N_2/CO_2 of different concentrations. Free-beam absorption, which occurs between the fibers and the waveguide was characterized with a reference measurement and compensated for. In these measurements [5], it was possible to sense CO_2 concentrations down to 500 ppm, which is already in the range of the typical workplace CO_2 concentrations and well below the exposure limits.

IV. CONCLUSIONS

We presented a detailed design and characterization of silicon strip waveguides. Among others, our results indicate that the index of refraction of the deposited poly-silicon is about 3% higher in our structures, compared to literature values of bulk silicon. The waveguides feature damping characteristics of 4-5 dB/cm, depending on the details of the layer structure and can be used for CO2 monitoring, which was demonstrated with actual measurements. Based on these results, we will proceed in designing and optimizing the next generation of waveguide structures for evanescent field sensing.

ACKNOWLEDGMENT

This project has been supported by the COMET K1 centre ASSIC Austrian Smart Systems Integration Research Center. The COMET Competence Centers for Excellent Technologies- Program is supported by BMVIT, BMDW and the federal provinces of Carinthia and Styria.

REFERENCES

[1] V. Lavchiev and B. Jakoby, "Photonics in the Mid-Infrared: Challenges in Single-Chip Integration and Absorption" Sensing, IEEE J. of Selected Topics in Quantum Electronics, vol 23, pp. 452-463, 2017 .

[2] C. Ranacher et al., "A photonic silicon waveguide gas sensor using evanescent-wave absorption," in SENSORS, 2016 IEEE. IEEE, pp. 1–3, 2016.

[3] U. Hedenig et al., "Characterization of Si Mid-Infrared Photonic Components for Chemical and Gas Sensing", AMA Sensors 2015 Proceedings, pp. 356-360, 2015.

[4] C. Ranacher et al., "Spectroscopic gas sensing using a silicon slab waveguide," Procedia Engineering, vol. 168, pp. 1265–1269, 2016.

[5] C. Ranacher et al., "Characterization of Evanescent Field Gas Sensor Structures Based on Silicon Photonics", IEEE Photonics Journal (submitted)

1D MEMS Micro-Scanning LiDAR

Norbert Druml, Ievgeniia Maksymova, Thomas Thurner, Diederik van Lierop,
Marcus Hennecke and Andreas Foroutan
Infineon Technologies Austria AG, Graz, Austria
email:{norbert.druml, ievgeniia.maksymova, thomas.thurner, diederik.vanlierop, marcus.hennecke, andreas.foroutan}@infineon.com

***Abstract*—Light Detection and Ranging (LiDAR) sensor technology will be the major enabler for automated transportation. As all major OEMs in transportation outline, only by fusing the sensor data of LiDAR, Radar, and cameras, a holistic and robust environment perception can be achieved. However, most of today's available long-range LiDAR solutions are complex and costly, which impedes a broad integration into affordable vehicles and robots. This work details the recently emerged and currently most promising technology towards a low-cost, long-range, robust, and automotive certified LiDAR system: the micro-scanning 1D MEMS-mirror LiDAR. In this work, we depict not only a proposed future 1D LiDAR system design and involved ASIC concepts, we also showcase a very first realized LiDAR prototype which will pave the way towards the future >200m and <200$ LiDAR perception system.**

***Keywords*—LiDAR; direct Time-of-Flight; 1D MEMS mirror; micro-scanning**

I. INTRODUCTION

Highly automated transportation will usher in a major paradigm shift in transportation. It will not only enable radically new use-cases and applications, but will also significantly increase safety for passengers and road users in general. In order to achieve the future goal of highly automated vehicles, various redundant and diverse sensor types are required in order to enable robust environment perception during all possible weather conditions. According to industry and academia, the Light Detection and Ranging (LiDAR) technology will be the key enabler, in conjunction with Radar and cameras, for robust and holistic environment perception (see also [1] and [2]). Figure 1 depicts the basic building blocks of a LiDAR system realizing the direct Time-of-Flight sensing principle: a central system controller triggers the emission of a laser pulse. This laser pulse is reflected by the scenery and is eventually received by a photo diode. The laser pulse's Time-of-Flight, which is measured with the help of fast running counters, directly correlates with the distance between scenery and sensor, thus enabling three-dimensional environment perception.

Today, there are several automotive qualified LiDAR technologies available targeting, e.g., the short-range use-case of emergency breaking. However, when it comes to the long-range (>200m) and low-cost (<200$) automotive use-case, there is still a major gap in technology. So far, there has not been any suitable technology identified that will cover these two essential requirements at the same time. Thanks to the latest technological and manufacturing advances in the field of

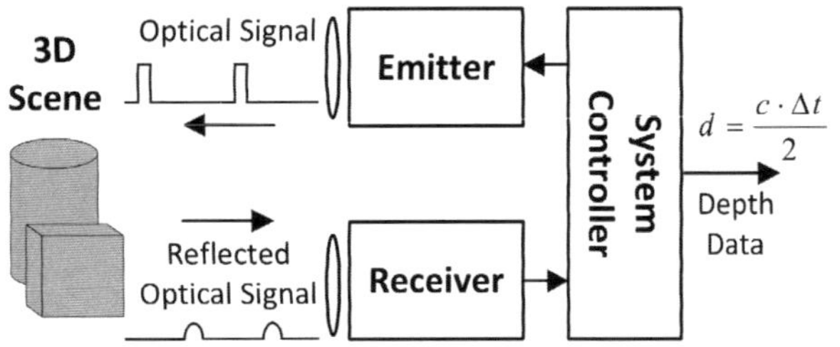

Figure 1. Basic principle of the LiDAR environment perception technology.

Micro-Electro-Mechanical Systems (MEMS), promising new LiDAR concepts based on MEMS mirrors are emerging. These very small mirrors of, e.g., 2x2mm size are employed to deflect the LiDAR system's laser beam into the scenery. Thus, a robust near-solid-state approach is given that enables not only highly accurate and optical-/power-efficient laser deflection, but also enables cost-efficient LiDAR system solutions.

This work presents in detail the 1D micro-scanning MEMS-based LiDAR solution and therefore makes the following fundamental contributions:

- It presents from semiconductor point of view the latest conceptual and technological advances in automotive 1D MEMS micro-scanning LiDAR.
- It showcases a first highly-integrated LiDAR prototype based on the 1D MEMS micro-scanning approach.
- It provides a clear vision towards the future long-range (>200m) and low-cost (<200$) LiDAR system for automotive and robotic applications.

This paper is structured as follows. Section II gives a short introduction into the related work covering the topic of the latest LiDAR technologies. In Section III, our vision of a 1D micro-scanning LiDAR is presented. Section IV depicts a very first working 1D micro-scanning LiDAR prototype. Finally, our results are concluded and some details about our future work are given in Section V.

II. RELATED WORK

LiDAR technologies, which are currently explored by industry and academia, can be fundamentally categorized as depicted in Figure 2. The most important conceptual difference concerns the scanning or staring way of perceiving the environment [3]. Staring-based solutions are available in the market and proved to be robust and mature. Although staring-based solutions can be manufactured in a cost-efficient way, they are constrained in terms of field-of-view and maximum measurement range (up to approximately 60m) due to eye- and skin-safety regulations. Flash LiDAR sensors are commercially available through companies like Continental or LeddarTech [4]. Flash LiDARs illuminate the whole scenery at once and employ a detector array or matrix for receiving the reflected light [5]. They are commonly used for short-range use-cases, such as blind spot detection or emergency breaking. Similar to the flash LiDARs, the multi-beam approaches [6] are used for short-range applications.

In contrast to the staring principle, the scan-based approaches divert a collimated laser beam to the target and thus illuminate a small fraction of the scenery at once. By moving the beam position, a 3D surround image of the entire scenery can be generated. Because the whole laser energy is focused in a point or a line instead of the whole field-of-view, better signal-to-noise ratio (SNR) and thus longer measurement distances are achievable. Velodyne, a pioneer in the field of rotating LiDAR scanners, came up with a very first solution for the DARPA Robotic Car Races [7] in 2007. This system achieved a measurement range of up to 120m, 20 frames per second, and a horizontal field-of-view of 360°. Since then, spinning

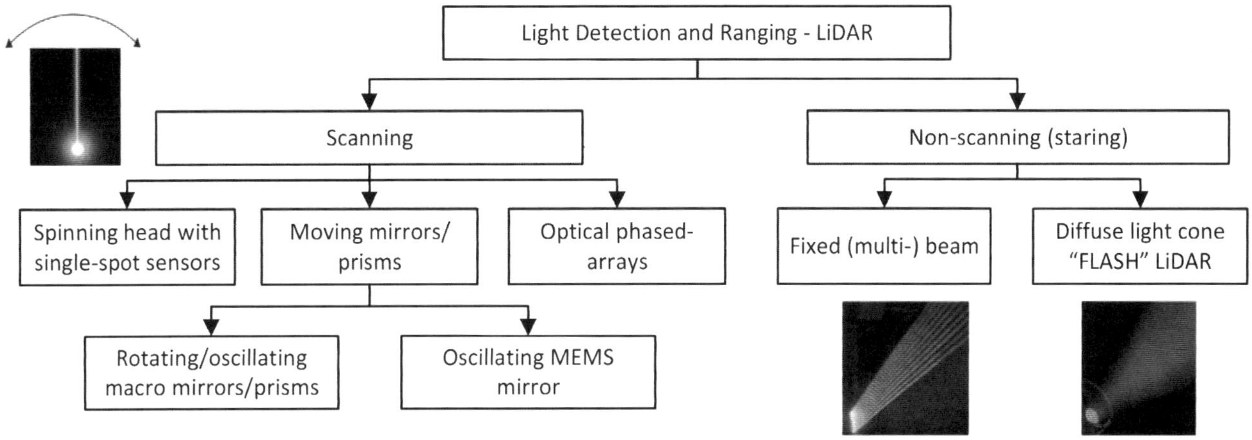

Figure 2. Fundamental classification of various LiDAR concepts.

heads and rotating/oscillating macro mirrors/prisms solutions have further improved in terms of performance, resolution, and robustness. For example, LiDAR systems from Velodyne achieve measurement ranges of 200m with a horizontal field-of-view of 360°. However, their main drawbacks are high costs and moving macro components that degrade the form factor and that hinder a lean car integration.

A novel concept which is currently explored by academia and industry is optical phased arrays [8]. The major advantage of this novel approach is the possibility for electronic laser beam forming (similar to phased array antennas in Radar), thus omitting the integration of any moving or rotating mechanical parts required for deflecting of beams in a traditional way. However, preliminary research results show that there is still a critical technological gap concerning the efficiency of the photonic integrated circuits. This efficiency degradation, which is in the range of a high double digit percentage, represents a major limitation for long-range LiDAR applications.

The currently most promising concept towards a realizable low-cost (<200$), long-range (>200m), robust, automotive qualified LiDAR environment perception is the micro-scanning MEMS mirror concept. As summarized by Holmstrom et al. [9], there are various types of MEMS-scanner concepts. A crucial differentiating factor is whether one moving axis (as depicted by Krastev et al. [10]) or two moving axes (such as [11] or [12]) are implemented. While the 1D approach typically deflects a vertical laser beam line into the scenery and performs a horizontal scanning (see also Figure 3), the 2D concept deflects a laser point or narrow line and performs vertically as well as horizontally scanning. Furthermore, there are mirrors which are driven in resonance (robust against shocks and vibration, instantaneous measurement of the position for all angles is not required) or without resonance (prone to shocks and vibrations, difficult to control due to the inevitable ringing which needs to be suppressed by a control loop). This work focuses on the resonant 1D MEMS mirror, because this specific setup enables higher scanning frequencies compared to 2D approach and provides high robustness against external perturbations (such as shocks and vibrations which are given in transportation).

Summarizing, even though the LiDAR research community is highly active, there is still a huge gap concerning a realizable long-range and low-cost solution. Therefore, this paper provides a highly relevant and important contribution to the ongoing discussion in this important field of research.

III. 1D MEMS-based Automotive LiDAR

Currently, the most promising approach towards a long-range, low-cost, robust, and automotive qualified LiDAR system is enabled through the micro-scanning 1D MEMS mirror concept. In the following, this solution (as depicted in Figure 3) is detailed.

A. *Requirements*

Requirements for a long-range LiDAR sensor are, from OEM and Tier 1 perspective, still in a dynamic development process and differ a lot. Thus, some partly representative requirements can be summarized as follows:

- 120° horizontal field-of-view and 16° vertical field-of-view
- 20cm distance resolution, 0.1° horizontal and 0.5° vertical resolution
- 200m measurement range
- 20 frames per second of field-of-view's point cloud
- 200$ system costs
- ASIL-C and laser class 1 guaranteeing functional-, eye-, and skin-safety
- High robustness against shocks and vibrations

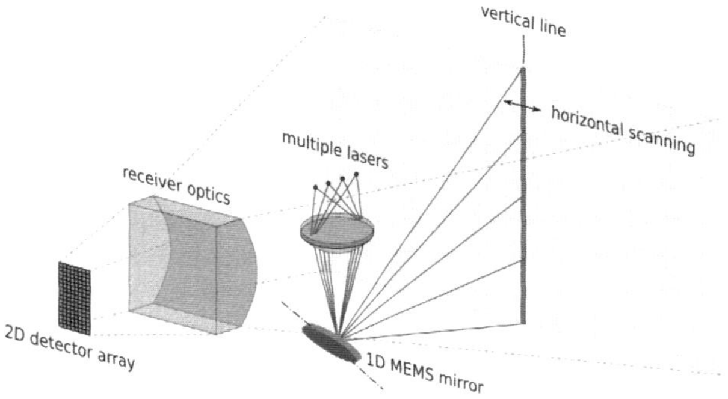

Figure 3. 1D micro-scanning LiDAR illuminating the scenery with a vertical laser beam line and scanning horizontally.

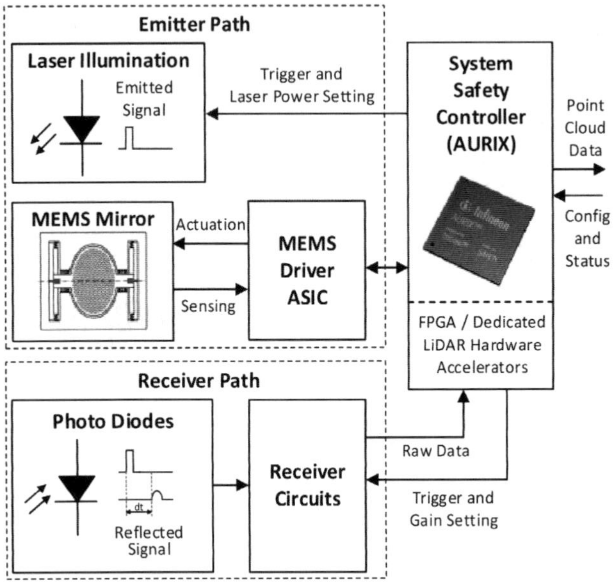

Figure 4. System concept of a potential future 1D MEMS-based automotive LiDAR system.

B. Design Space Considerations

Given these requirements, the design space of MEMS mirrors considerable favors the 1D scanning approach over a 2D scanning approach. By deflecting a vertical laser beam line horizontally, a sweet spot in terms of signal-to-noise ratio and sampling rates is achieved compared to 2D mirrors (slower line-by-line sampling) and Flash LiDARs (degraded signal-to-noise values at long ranges due to eye-safety limitations). This is of special importance when considering the maximum possible laser pulse repetition rates of affordable laser sources, which is in the range of 100kHz. Given a modest field-of-view of, e.g., 400 x 80 pixel, a 2D scanning solution requires a laser pulse-repetition-frequency of 640kHz in order to achieve 20fps (without taking signal averaging for improved SNR into account). When taking into account also the flight time of light (e.g., $2\mu s$ for 300m), 2D scanning is regarded as an unfavorable approach in order to meet the automotive frame-rate and SNR requirements. In contrast, the 1D approach, which scans with each laser beam trigger one complete vertical line, enables the integration of affordable 100kHz pulse-repetition-frequency lasers, and thus making the <200$ vision feasible. The achieved high frame-rates can then be exploited for scene oversampling in order to further improve the signal quality. In addition to pulse repetition frequency and SNR considerations, an automotive LiDAR system has to be robust against shocks and vibrations. Here, oscillating scanning solutions provide more robustness compared to non-oscillating approach. In particular, the 1D oscillating scanning solution provides highest robustness by design. Summarizing, based on currently available technologies, 2D micro-scanning and Flash LiDARs hardly fulfill the requirements for robust, long-range, and low-cost LiDAR systems.

C. Overall System Concept and Chipset

Figure 4 depicts the system concept of a potential future 1D MEMS-based automotive LiDAR system. This chipset is composed of the oscillating 1D MEMS mirror and its MEMS Driver ASIC, a System Safety Controller, a laser illumination unit, an (1D or 2D) array of photo diodes (such as avalanche photo diodes (APDs) or single-photon avalanche diodes (SPADs)), and Receiver Circuits. The main purpose of MEMS Driver ASIC is to sense, actuate, and control the oscillating MEMS mirror. Furthermore, it implements crucial functional safety features and provides an essential MEMS phase clock that is used to synchronize the whole system to the movement of the mirror. The MEMS Driver ASIC's phase clock and safety signals are provided to the central System Safety Controller. This System Safety Controller synchronizes with the MEMS phase clock and triggers the laser illumination unit according to a laser-shoot-pattern. At the same time, the System Safety Controller triggers the Receiver Circuits in order to capture the laser beam reflections. The Receiver Circuits samples and digitizes the reflected laser light. The Receiver Circuits' output data is then forwarded to the System Safety Controller. Finally, the System Safety Controller performs the final signal processing (e.g., calculation of the point cloud), which may be carried out hardware accelerated either with an FPGA or dedicated hardware units, and sends the data to a central ADAS ECU or sensor fusion box.

Figure 5. Fabricated and packaged 1D MEMS Mirror.

D. MEMS Mirror

The central element of the whole LiDAR system design is given by the 1D oscillating MEMS mirror and its MEMS Driver ASIC. The MEMS mirror, as it is depicted in Figure 5, implements an electrostatic comb drive approach [13] with a very high Q factor of approximately 150. By applying a voltage of, e.g., 100V to the comb fingers, an electric force is applied by the capacitance structure that pulls the rotor towards its zero position. Switching off this high-voltage after the rotor crossed the zero position, let's the mirror swing towards its maximum deviation. When reaching the maximum deviation, high-voltage is again switched on. Figure 6 depicts the very concise response curve if the frequency of the high voltage actuation is changed. Starting with an actuation frequency f_{start} and reducing it, let's the operation point move on the lower resonance curve. While being on the lower resonance curve the phase relation between actuation voltage and mirror is positive, which means that the mirror and its zero crossing follow the actuation voltage. If the actuation frequency is further reduced until it reaches f_{jump}, a jump in the phase relation and in the mirror's deviation angle is observable. At the top resonance curve, the phase relation between actuation voltage and mirror is now negative, which implies that the actuation voltage follows the mirror and its zero crossing. If the actuation frequency is now increased, also the mirror's deviation angle increases. Finally, when surpassing a maximum stable frequency, the working point drops back to the lower resonance curve. Therefore, the response

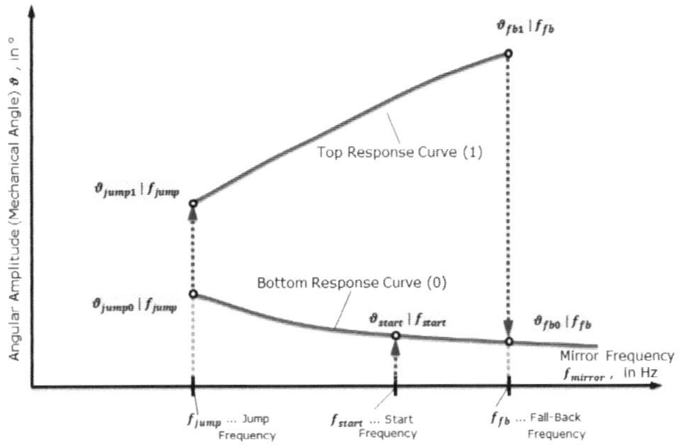

Figure 6. MEMS mirror response curve. Changing the actuation frequency results in a non-linear change in mirror' oscillation angle.

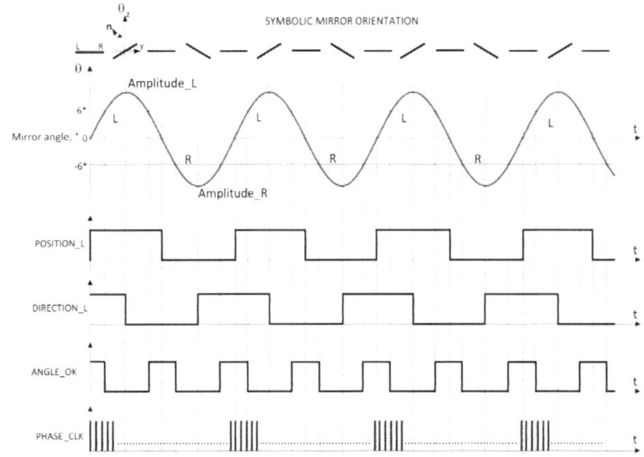

Figure 7. MEMS position and safety signaling of the MEMS Driver ASIC.

curve describes the mechanical behavior of the MEMS mirror as a non-linear harmonic oscillator.

Depending on the mirror design (mechanical design, leaf springs, comb drive structure, etc.), deviation angles of more than +/-15°are achievable. Thanks to the mirror's high Q factor, its oscillator design, and the one-dimensional rotation axis, a laser beam deflection solution is given that provides high robustness against external perturbations (such as shocks or car vibrations). Furthermore, thanks to its conventional mirror design, the laser beam can be deflected almost losslessly and with high pulse-repetition frequencies (which is an essential enabler for oversampling of the environment).

E. MEMS Driver ASIC

The crucial task of the MEMS Driver ASIC is to sense, actuate, and control the movement of the MEMS mirror. Actuation of the mirror is carried out by simply switching on / off the mirror's high-voltage at the right point in time. However, in order to perform this high-voltage switching on / off properly, precisely sensing of the mirror position is essential. Since the mirror's comb fingers form a capacitance that varies with the mirror's position, position sensing is carried out by measuring this position dependent capacitance. Such kind of capacitance sensing can be performed with various measurement principles. One feasible measurement principle is the usage of trans-impedance converters in order to convert the capacitor's current flows into voltages levels. These voltage levels can then be analog-to-digital converted and can be processed by digital analysis and control circuits.

In general, the MEMS mirror can be operated either in open control-loop or closed control-loop, cf. [14]. While the open control-loop mode actuates the mirror with a defined frequency without taking advantage of any control strategies, the closed control-loop mode implements two important control strategies:

- A phased-locked loop precisely follows the movement (phase) of the oscillating MEMS mirror.
- An amplitude control loop ensures that the maximum deflection angle of the MEMS mirror stays constant.

With the help of these two control loops, a robust scan shape can be guaranteed. In order to signal the central System Safety Controller (which triggers the laser beam firing) the momentary position of the MEMS mirror, the following important signals are provided: *POSITION_L* (mirror is either on the left or right side) and *DIRECTION_L* signals (mirror moves either towards the left or right side) provide precise information of the mirror's momentary position, as illustrated in Figure 7. When the mirror crosses its zero position, the position signal changes. When the mirror is at its maximum deflection angle, the direction signal changes. A *PHASE_CLK* signal, which counts in equi-temporal steps from 0 to n_{max} during one mirror swing, provides a precise and high-frequent phase information of the momentary mirror position. These three signals are not only crucial for the system controller in order to decide at which mirror position to trigger the laser beam firing, but also to enable an efficient way to track the MEMS mirror. As a consequence, the precision of these signals directly influences the whole LiDAR system's measurement accuracy. In addition to these tracking signals, an *ANGLE_OK* signal is provided by the MEMS Driver ASIC in order to notify the system controller whether the angle setpoint is reached or not. This notification is crucial for ensuring functional-, eye-, and skin-safety: if and only if both the MEMS mirror and the MEMS Driver ASIC operate properly within their specified set of parameters, then laser shooting is permitted.

F. Photo Diodes and Receiver Circuits

The LiDAR system's receiving part (which is primarily defined through an 1D or 2D array of photo diodes, Receiver Circuits, and hardware-accelerated signal processing) is absolutely crucial in order to achieve the required SNR and maximum distance requirements. The number of implemented photo diodes defines vertical resolution, which is not constrained by our system architecture. In the shown receiver signal chain, the Receiver Circuits' main purpose is to amplify the received electrical current from the array of photo diodes with the help of high-performance amplifiers. This amplification circuit has to implement not only a high dynamic range (in order to detect targets in near vicinity and far away), but shall also support adjustable gain settings, short recovery times (in order to detect a weak pulse directly after a strong pulse), and low electrical/optical cross-talk between channels. After amplification of the sensed analog signals, a high-speed conversion to the digital domain is required. At this point, the LiDAR system's design space critically expands by selecting the ADCs' resolution and sampling rate: more than 1-Bit ADC resolution is required for signal amplitude analyses (in order to detect for example lane markings), high sampling rates are required for more accurate range resolutions (e.g., 1.5 GHz for 10cm range resolution). Given a modest laser pulse-repetition rate of, e.g., 100kHz

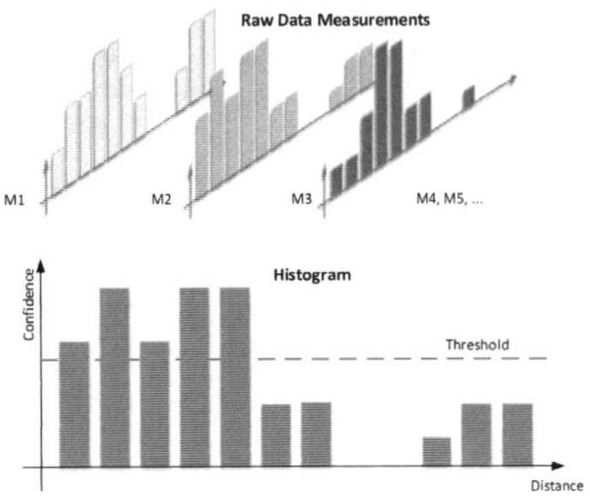

Figure 8. Increasing confidence by oversampling and histogram evaluation.

and 32 vertical pixels, results according to (1) in several GBit/s of raw data.

$$RawData = PRF \cdot VPixels \cdot ADC_{Res} \cdot ADC_{Rate} \quad (1)$$

After acquisition of the raw sensor data, a lot of effort (in terms of computational resources and power dissipation) has to be spent in order to compute a robust 3D point cloud. Such a signal processing chain can include various types of computations, e.g., averaging of several measurements, evaluation of histograms, usage of matched filtering, etc. The aim of these signal processing steps is not only on improving the LiDAR system's SNR and on mitigating interferences from sunlight and other LiDARs, but also on reducing the final data rate towards the System Safety Controller or a central sensor fusion box. Figure 8 highlights the benefits of signal averaging and histogram evaluations: SNR and confidence increase, while data rates decrease at the same time by factors. These fundamental LiDAR signal processing steps define a very active research arena impacted by both academia and industry. Moreover, further important research questions arise when aiming for an optimized system partitioning: what kind of signal processing shall be integrated into Receiver Circuits, a potential FPGA, the System ASIC, and a central sensor fusion box in order to minimize data rates while maintaining as much data- and algorithm-flexibility as possible.

G. System Safety Controller

Infineon Technologies' AURIX can be employed as the central System Safety Controller. AURIX is a 32-Bit System-on-Chip, compliant to various standards, such as IEC 61508, ISO 26262, and ISO 25119, and is used in particular in automotive and industrial domains as a *Safety Element out of Context* (SEooC) for applications such as electric power steering, airbag control, etc. In the given 1D MEMS micro-scanning LiDAR system, AURIX is not only employed to monitor the integrity of the MEMS mirror, MEMS Driver, and Receiver Circuits, but also to monitor power supply, control signals, and the LiDAR data stream. Apart from functional safety features, the AURIX also implements hardware and software for controlling and signal processing. In particular the laser scan pattern is controlled by the AURIX by triggering lasers and the Receiver Circuits at well defined points in time. With regards to signal processing, the task of AURIX is to compute and provide 3D point cloud data for dedicated ADAS and sensor fusion ECUs. Depending on the OEMs' / Tier1s' requirements, not only the pre-processed LiDAR point cloud data is provided, but for example also each pixel's most relevant multi-hit targets. As highlighted in Figure 4, the next generation AURIX safety controllers will also support dedicated LiDAR hardware accelerators that will further enhance and speed-up LiDAR signal processing.

IV. Prototype

Based on the presented 1D MEMS micro-scanning LiDAR concept and the proposed system partitioning (see Figure 4), we realized a very first working prototype. Please note that due to disclosure policies, currently only some overview results can be provided. Figure 9 and Figure 10 showcase the assembled and opened prototype. Only thanks to the miniaturizing of emitter path (MEMS mirror, MEMS Driver ASIC) and receiver path (photo diodes, Receiver Circuits, signal processing FPGA, AURIX Safety Controller), such a small form factor is achievable. Moreover, the LiDAR prototype implements advanced hardware-accelerated signal processing techniques, which makes its sensing capabilities unaffected by interferences from other LiDAR systems, which is a crucial requirement for a broad adoption in transportation. The output of this LiDAR prototype is a 3D point cloud with more than 20 frame per seconds. Due to the

Figure 9. 1D MEMS mirror based LiDAR prototype.

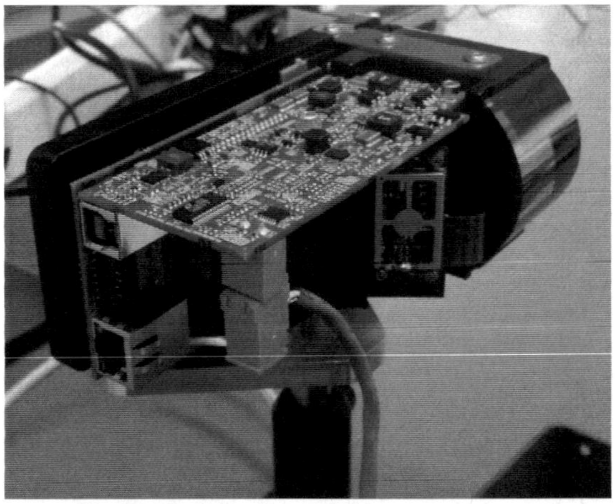

Figure 10. LiDAR prototype implementing optics, lasers, controllers, MEMS mirror, Receiver Circuits, MEMS Driver ASIC, and signal processing.

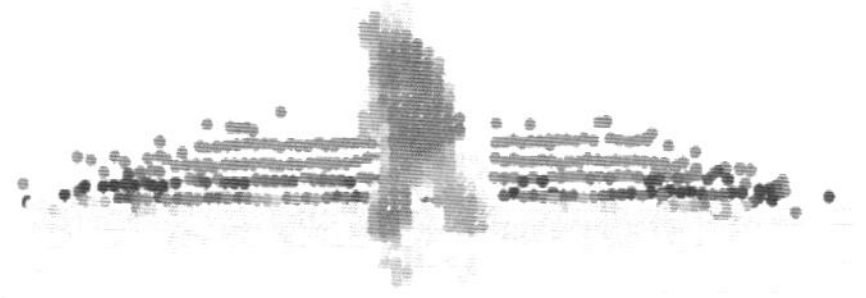

Figure 11. A clearly classifiable pedestrian detected in a few meters distance of the LiDAR system. Visualization is performed with ROS Robot Operating System.

usage of standardized data formats, the 3D point cloud data can be easily visualized with freely available software tools such as ROS Robot Operating System (cf. [15]). Finally, Figure 11 shows the ROS visualization of a pedestrian crossing the LiDAR's field-of-view, and Figure 12 depicts a standard indoor lab scenery and its 3D point cloud representation.

V. CONCLUSIONS

Light Detection and Ranging (LiDAR) sensor technology will be the major enabler for automated transportation. Only by fusing the sensor data of LiDAR, Radar, and cameras, a holistic and robust environment perception can be achieved. As outlined, currently there is major gap concerning a realizable long-range and low-cost LiDAR solution.

This work detailed the recently emerged and currently most promising approach towards a low-cost, long-range, robust, and automotive LiDAR system: the micro-scanning 1D MEMS mirror LiDAR. We depicted not only the vision of a potential future system design and its required ASIC concepts, we also showcased a very first realized 1D LiDAR prototype. Given the presented results, a quantum leap towards the future >200m and <200$ LiDAR perception system and the future revolution in transportation was made.

Our future work fully focuses on advancing the semiconductor components of the the micro-scanning 1D MEMS mirror LiDAR in order to make our vision happen.

ACKNOWLEDGMENT

The authors would like to thank the ECSEL Joint Undertaking and the Austrian Federal Ministry for Transport, Innovation and Technology which funded the PRYSTINE project under the grant agreement n° 783190.

Furthermore, the authors would like to thank all LiDAR colleagues from Infineon Technologies in the Netherlands, Germany, and Austria for their valuable contributions.

REFERENCES

[1] Frost & Sullivan, "LIDAR-based Strategies for Active Safety and Automated Driving from Major OEMs in Europe and North America," August 2015.

[2] R. Rasshofer and K. Gresser, "Automotive Radar and Lidar Systems for Next Generation Driver Assistance Functions," *Advances in Radio Science*, vol. 3, no. B. 4, pp. 205–209, 2005.

[3] H. Winner, S. Hakuli, and G. Wolf, *Handbuch Fahrerassistenzsysteme: Grundlagen, Komponenten und Systeme für aktive Sicherheit und Komfort*. Springer-Verlag, 2011.

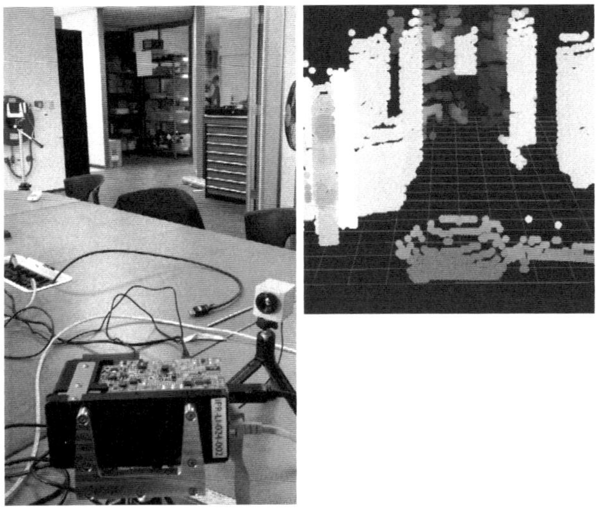

Figure 12. Standard lab scenery and its 3D point cloud visualized with ROS Robot Operating System.

[4] *Spec sheet: Leddar Vu Compact fixed-beam lidar sensor module*, LeddarTech Inc., 2016.

[5] T. E. Laux and C.-I. Chen, "3D flash LIDAR vision systems for imaging in degraded visual environments," in *SPIE Defense+ Security*, vol. 9087. International Society for Optics and Photonics, 2014.

[6] R. Liebske, *SRL 1 Short Description*, Continental, August 2012.

[7] J. R. McBride, J. C. Ivan, D. S. Rhode, J. D. Rupp, M. Y. Rupp, J. D. Higgins, D. D. Turner, and R. M. Eustice, "A Perspective on Emerging Automotive Safety Applications, Derived from Lessons Learned through Participation in the DARPA Grand Challenges," *Journal of Field Robotics*, vol. 25, no. 10, pp. 808–840, 2008.

[8] C. DeRose, R. Kekatpure, D. Trotter, A. Starbuck, J. Wendt, A. Yaacobi, M. Watts, U. Chettiar, N. Engheta, and P. Davids, "Electronically controlled optical beam-steering by an active phased array of metallic nanoantennas," *Optics express*, vol. 21, no. 4, pp. 5198–5208, 2013.

[9] S. T. Holmstrom, U. Baran, and H. Urey, "MEMS laser scanners: a review," *Journal of Microelectromechanical Systems*, vol. 23, no. 2, pp. 259–275, 2014.

[10] K. Krastev, H. van Lierop, H. Soemers, R. Sanders, and A. Nellissen, "MEMS scanning micromirror," September 2013, US Patent 8,526,089.

[11] T. Sandner, T. Grasshoff, M. Schwarzenberg, and H. Schenk, "Quasi-static microscanner with linearized scanning for an adaptive 3D-laser camera," in *International Conference on Optical MEMS and Nanophotonics (OMN)*. IEEE, 2013, pp. 103–104.

[12] R. Moss, P. Yuan, X. Bai, E. Quesada, R. Sudharsanan, B. L. Stann, J. F. Dammann, M. M. Giza, and W. B. Lawler, "Low-cost compact MEMS scanning ladar system for robotic applications," in *Laser Radar Technology and Applications XVII*, vol. 8379, 2012.

[13] P. Deng and W. Ma, "Nonlinearity investigation of the MEMS scanning mirror with electrostatic comb drive," in *IEEE International Conference on Nano/Micro Engineered and Molecular Systems (NEMS)*, September 2014, pp. 212–215.

[14] B. Borovic, A. Liu, D. Popa, H. Cai, and F. Lewis, "Open-loop versus closed-loop control of MEMS devices: choices and issues," *Journal of Micromechanics and Microengineering*, vol. 15, no. 10, August 2005.

[15] M. Quigley, K. Conley, B. Gerkey, J. Faust, T. Foote, J. Leibs, R. Wheeler, and A. Y. Ng, "ROS: an open-source Robot Operating System," in *ICRA workshop on open source software*, vol. 3, no. 3.2, 2009, p. 5.

Light-Fidelity (Li-Fi)

Optical Sensing and Detection in Large Indoor Environements

Manuela Vieira, Manuel Augusto Vieira, Paula Louro, Alessandro Fantoni
ADETC/ISEL/IPL,
R. Conselheiro Emídio Navarro, 1959-007
Lisboa, Portugal
CTS-UNINOVA
Quinta da Torre, Monte da Caparica, 2829-516,
Caparica, Portugal

e-mail: mv@isel.ipl.pt, mv@isel.pt, plouro@deetc.isel.pt, afantoni@deetc.isel.ipl.pt

Pedro Vieira
ADETC/ISEL/IPL,
R. Conselheiro Emídio Navarro, 1959-007
Lisboa, Portugal
Instituto das Telecomunicações
Instituto Superior Técnico, 1049-001,
Lisboa, Portugal
e-mail: pvieira@isel.pt

***Abstract*— In this work, a Light Emitting Diode (LED) assisted navigation system for large environments is presented. The LEDs are used both for room illumination purposes and as transmitters if modulated at high frequencies. The payload data together with the identifiers, IDs, assigned to the physical location of the transmitters are broadcast using an On-Off Keying (OOK) modulated scheme. The mobile receiver is a double p-i-n/pin SiC photodetector with light controlled filtering properties. Coded multiplexing techniques for supporting communications and navigation together on the same channel are analysed. A demonstration of fine-grained indoor localization is simulated. Different indoor layouts for the LEDs are considered. Square and hexagon mesh are tested, and a 2D localization design, demonstrated by a prototype implementation, is presented. The results showed that the LED-aided Visible Light Communication (VLC) navigation system makes possible not only to determine the position of a mobile target inside the unit cell but also in the network and concomitantly to infer the travel direction in time.**

Keywords- Visible Light Communication; Indoor positioning; Square and hexagonal topologies; SiC technology; optical sensor; transmitter; receiver; Multiplex/demultiplex techniques.

I. INTRODUCTION

With the rapid advancement of smart equipment, location based services that employ different kinds of communication and positioning technologies have started to develop. Although Global Positioning System (GPS) works extremely well in an open-air localization, it does not perform effectively in indoor environments, due to the inability of GPS signals to penetrate building materials. Nowadays, indoor positioning methods are mainly based on Wi-Fi, Bluetooth, Radio-frequency identification (RFID), Visible Light Communications (VLC) and inertia navigation [1]-[5]. Although many methods are available, they require dense coverage of WiFi access points or expensive sensors, like high-performance cameras, to guarantee the localization accuracy.

VLC is a data transmission technology [6]-[8]. VLC can easily be employed in indoor environments, such as offices, homes, hospitals, airplanes/airports and conference rooms. Compared with other positioning methods, indoor VLC based positioning has advantages, since it can use the existing LED lighting infrastructure with simple modifications.

In the following, we propose to use modulated visible light, carried out by white low cost LEDs, to provide globally consistent signal-patterns and engage indoor localization. The LEDs are capable of switching to different light intensity levels at a very fast rate. The switching rate is fast enough to be imperceptible by the human eye. This functionality can be used for communication where the data is encoded in the emitting light in different ways [9]. A photodetector can receive the modulated signals and decode the data. This means that the LEDs serve twofold for providing illumination as well as for communications.

Research is necessary to design LED arrangements that can optimize communication performance while meeting the illumination constraints for a variety of indoor layouts, using four-code assignment for the LEDs in an extended square or diamond mesh. The main idea is to divide the space into spatial beams originating from the different light sources, and identify each beam with a unique timed sequence of light signals. The receiver, equipped with an a-SiC:H pinpin photodiode, determines its physical position by detecting and decoding the light signals. The overlap of different light beams at the receiver is used as an advantage to increase the positioning accuracy. Fine-grained indoor localization can enable several applications; in supermarkets and shopping malls, exact location of products can greatly improve the customer's shopping experience and enable customer analytics and marketing [10][11].

The use of Red-Green-Blue (RGB) LEDs is a promising solution as they offer the possibility of Wavelength Division Multiplexing (WDM), which can enhance the transmission data rate. A WDM receiver has been developed [12][13]. The device is based on tandem a-SiC:H/a-Si:H pin/pin light controlled filter. When different visible signals are encoded in the same optical transmission path, the device multiplexes the different optical channels, performs different filtering processes (amplification, switching, and wavelength conversion) and finally decodes the encoded signals recovering the transmitted information.

In this paper, a LED-assisted indoor positioning and navigation VLC system, for large indoor environment is proposed. The paper is organized as follow. After the introduction (Section I), in Section II, the system configuration is presented. The principle of the positioning scheme and the algorithm to decode the information are described and experimental results are presented, in Section III. A 2D localization design, demonstrated by a prototype implementation is tested. Fine-grained indoor localization is demonstrated using square and hexagonal topologies. Finally, in Section IV, conclusions are addressed. The proposed, composed data transmission and indoor positioning, involves wireless communication, smart sensoring and optical sources network, building up a transdisciplinary approach framed in cyber-physical systems.

II. SYSTEM CONFIGURATION

LED bulbs work as transmitters, broadcasting the information. An optical receiver extracts its location to perform positioning and, concomitantly, the transmitted data from each transmitter. Multiple LEDs can transmit simultaneously to the same receiver using joint transmission. To synchronize the signals from multiple LEDs, the transmitters use different ID´s, such that the signal is constructively at the receiver.

A. Shapes and topologies

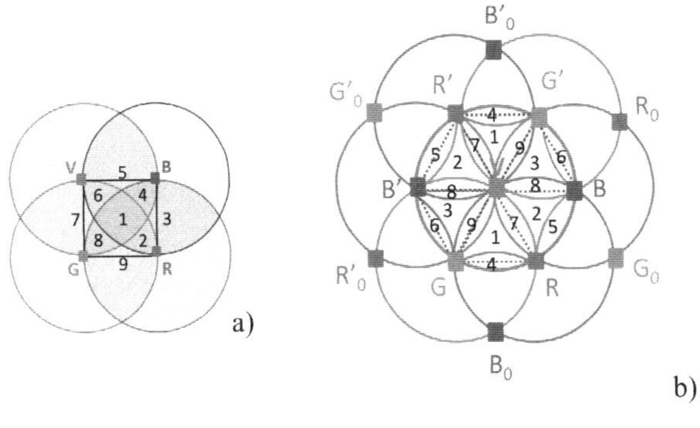

Figure 1. Top-down view of unit cells (LED array = RGBV color spots) having each one four modulated RGBV-LEDs located at the corners of the grid. a) Square cell. b) First hexagon ring.

The unit cells, for the analyzed topologies, are displayed in Figure 1. In Figure 1a, the proposed LED arrangement employs four modulated LEDs placed at the corners of a square grid. In Figure 1b, a cluster of three diamond cells sharing the violet node, fill the space with a hexagon, leading to the hexagonal topology.

The estimated distance from the ceiling lamp to the receiver is used to generate a circle around each transmitter on which the device must be located in order to receive the transmitted information (generated location and coded data).

TABLE 1. FINE-GRAINED CELL TOPOLOGY.

Footprints regions	Square topology	Hexgonal topology
P#1	RGBV	RGV R'G'V
P#2	RGB	RBV R'B'V
P#3	RG	G'BV GB'V
P#4	RBV	RGB_0V $R'G'B'_0V$
P#5	BV	RG_0BV $R'G'_0B'V$
P#6	GBV	$R_0G'BV$ $R'_0GB'V$
P#7	GV	RGBV R'G'B'V
P#8	RGV	RG'BV R'GB'V
P#9	RG	RGB'V R'GB'V

In all topologies, the grid sizes were chosen to avoid overlap in the receiver from adjacent grid points. To improve its practicality, the tested geometric scenario for the calculations, in both topologies, uses a grid in smaller size (2 cm between adjacent nodes). To receive the information from several transmitters, the receiver must be positioned where the circles from each transmitter overlap, producing at the receiver, a MUX signal that, after demultiplexing, acts twofold as a positioning system and a data transmitter. The generated regions, defined onwards as footprints, are pointed out in Figure 1 and reported in Table 1. In the hexagonal topology, each node has six neighbors, so, eighteen footprints are possible. Twelve at the edges of the six equilateral triangles where four circles overlap (#P4 to #P9) and six at their centroids (#P1 to #P3), where only three channels are received. Taking into account the XY symmetry (Figure 1b), the R, G and B nodes and their symmetric (R'G'B') must be considered. When the received channels come from outside the hexagon edges (first ring), the nodes are label with *0* (see Figure 1b). When the signal comes only from one LED, the coordinates of the LED are assigned to the device's reference point. If the device receives multiple signals, *i.e.*, if it is in an overlapping region of two or more LEDs, it finds the centroid of the received coordinates and stores it as the reference point. This is the so called fine-graining of the unit cell.

For data transmission commercially available white RGB-LEDs and a violet (V: 400 nm) LED were used. The output spectrum of the white LED contains three peaks assigned to the colours red (R: 626 nm), green (G: 530 nm) and blue (B: 470 nm), that mixed together provide the white perception to the human eye. Each chip, in the trichromatic LED, can be switched *on* and *off* individually for a desired bit sequence. The luminous intensity is regulated by the driving current for white perception. They exhibit a wide divergence angle (2x60°), since they are also designed for general lighting and allow a wide delivery of the VLC signal around the surrounding area. The driving current of each emitter is controlled independently, suppling the respective coding sequence and frequency [14]. In both topologies, the driving current of the emitters having the same wavelength was always the same.

B. *Cellular topologies for large environments*

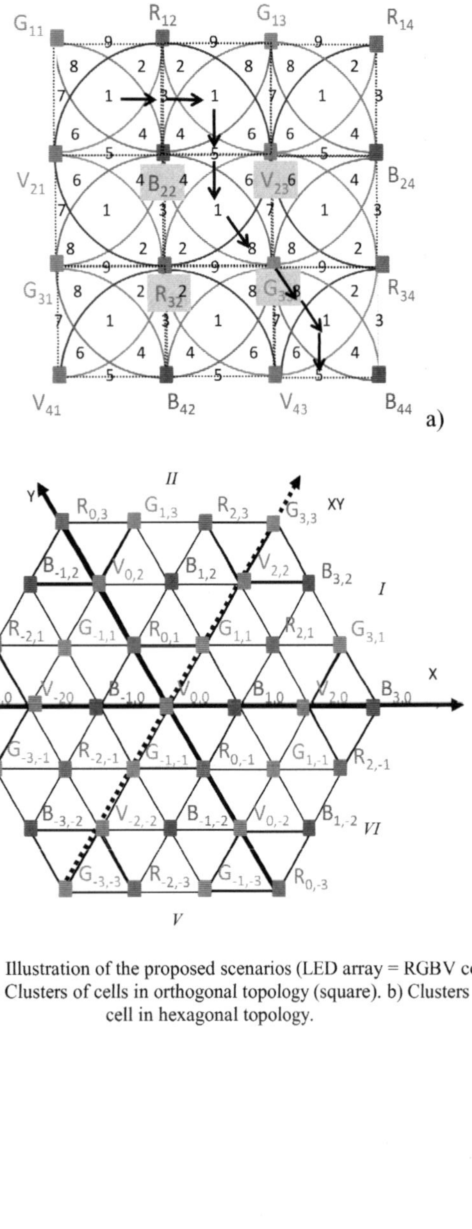

Figure. 2. Illustration of the proposed scenarios (LED array = RGBV color spots): a) Clusters of cells in orthogonal topology (square). b) Clusters of cell in hexagonal topology.

When the rooms are very large, such as in supermarkets or large shopping malls, the positioning technique (four-code assignment for the LEDs), is applied in the whole room [15]. Two topologies were set for the unit cell: the square, (Figure 2a) and the hexagon (Figure 2b). In the first, the proposed LED arrangement employs four modulated LEDs placed at the corners of a square grid. The unit cell $C_{i,j}$ is repeated in the horizontal and vertical directions in order to fill all the space. In the second topology (Figure 2b), the hexagon, the same LED array was used, but in a no-orthogonal system. We select a pair inclined at 120 degrees to be the axes, labelled as X and Y. We have readdressed the nodes, in the oblique Cartesian system. Consequently, in both topologies, each node, $X_{i,j}$, carries its own color, X, (RGBV) as well as its ID position in the network (i,j).

C. *The OOK modulation scheme*

The modulation of the emitted light was done through the modulation of the driving electrical current of the semiconductor chips of each LED. An on-off keying modulation scheme was used. The frame structures are illustrated in Figure 3, for both topologies.

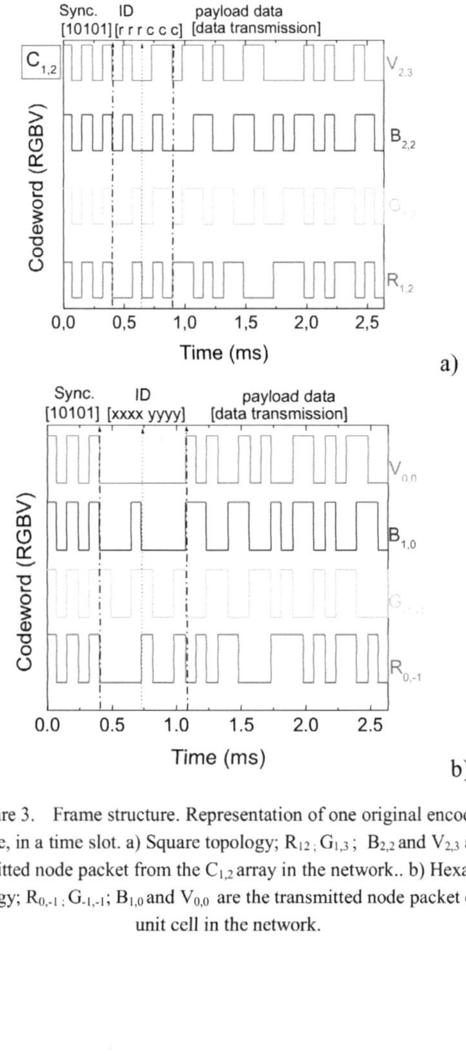

Figure 3. Frame structure. Representation of one original encoded message, in a time slot. a) Square topology; R_{12} ; $G_{1,3}$; $B_{2,2}$ and $V_{2,3}$ are the transmitted node packet from the $C_{1,2}$ array in the network.. b) Hexagonal topology; $R_{0,-1}$; $G_{-1,-1}$; $B_{1,0}$ and $V_{0,0}$ are the transmitted node packet of the unit cell in the network.

For both, the frame is built based on three separate blocks; the synchronism (Sync), the ID address of the transmitter (ID) and the message to transmit (payload data). The first five bits are used for time synchronization. The same synchronization header [10101], in an ON-OFF pattern, is imposed simultaneously to all the emitters. Each color signal (RGBV) carries, its own ID-BIT, so, the next bits give the coordinates of the emitter inside the array ($X_{i,j}$). Cell's IDs are encoded using a binary representation for the decimal number. In the square topology (Figure 3a), six bits are used: the first three for the binary code of the line and the other three for the column. In the hexagonal topology (Figure 1b to code the positive and the negative coordinates "sign and magnitude" representation was used, setting bit to *0* is for a positive number, and setting it to *1* is for a negative number. The remaining bits in the number indicate the absolute value. So, the next eight bits (ID) are assigned, respectively, to the *x* and *y* coordinate (*i,j*) of the emitter in the array (Figure 3b). For instance, R_{12} emitter sends a six ID_BIT [001 010] in the square topology while in the hexagonal one the eight ID bits are [0001 0010]. For both, the last bits, in the frame, are reserved for the message send by the X_{ij} node (payload data).

D. *The VLC receiver*

The VLC receiver is a two terminal, p-i'(a-SiC:H)-n/p-i(a-Si:H)-n photodiode packed in two transparent conductive contacts (TCO). The deposition conditions, optoelectronic characterization and device optimization are described in [13]. The configuration and operation is illustrated in Figure 4.

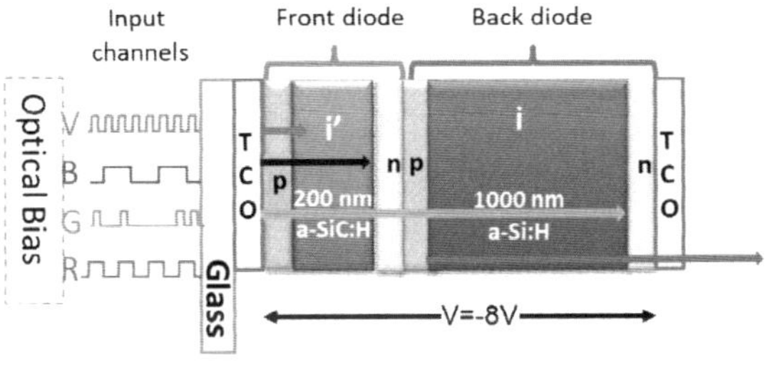

Figure 4. Double pi'n/pin configuration and device operation.

The device operates within the visible range using for data transmission the modulated low power light supplied simultaneously by the RGBV LEDs located at the nodes of the array. A mix of R, G, B, and V pulsed communication channels (input channels; transmitted data), each one with a specific bit sequence, impinges on the device and are absorbed accordingly to their wavelengths (see arrows in the figure). The combined optical signal (MUX signal; received data) is analyzed by reading out the generated photocurrent under negative applied voltage and violet background lighting, applied from the front side of the receiver [12] [16].

III. Experimental Results and Discussion

A. *Coding/Decoding techniques*

In Figure 5, the normalized received data due to the mixture of the four R, G, B, and V input channels, i.e., the MUX code signal in a stamp time, are displayed, for the square topology. In Figure 5a, the bit sequence was chosen to allow all the on/off sixteen (2^4) possible combinations of the four input channels. For three times slots (t_1, t_2, t_3), in Figure 5b, the MUX signal acquired by a receiving positions P#3, P#1, and P#5 (see Table 1), is displayed. The decoded packet of transmitted information is presented in the top of both figures.

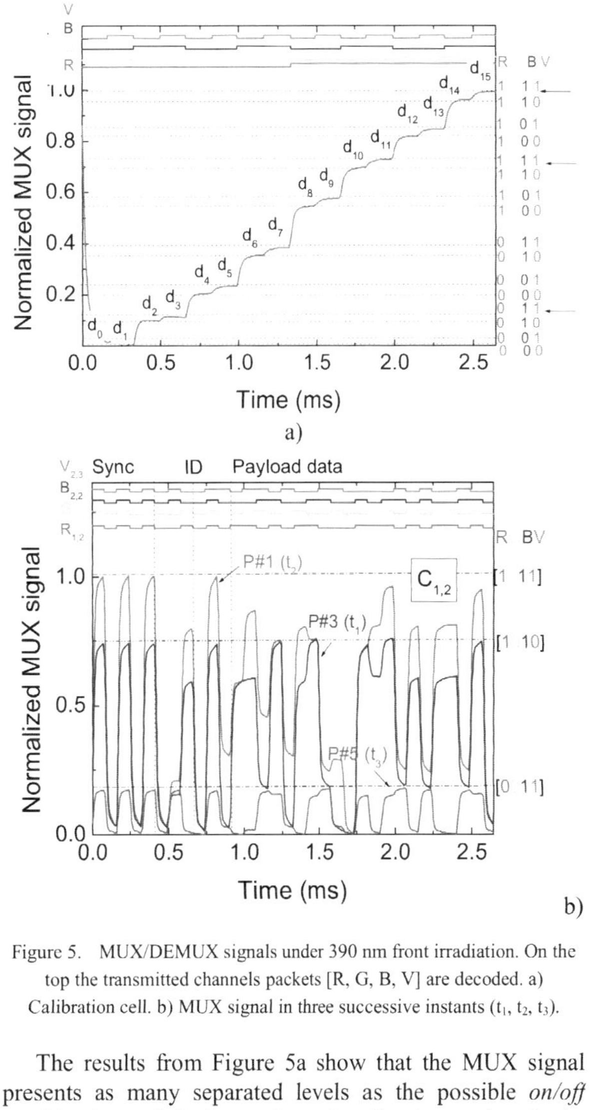

Figure 5. MUX/DEMUX signals under 390 nm front irradiation. On the top the transmitted channels packets [R, G, B, V] are decoded. a) Calibration cell. b) MUX signal in three successive instants (t_1, t_2, t_3).

The results from Figure 5a show that the MUX signal presents as many separated levels as the possible *on/off* combinations of the input channels, allowing to decode the transmitted information [17]. All the ordered levels (d_0-d_{15}) are pointed out at the correspondent levels, and are displayed as horizontal dotted lines. On the right hand side of Figure 5a, the match between MUX levels and the 4 bits binary code assigned to each level is shown. Hence, by assigning each output level to a 4-digit binary code, [X_R, X_G, X_B, X_V], with X=1 if the channel is *on* and X=0 if it is *off*, the signal can be decoded. The MUX signal presented in Figure 5a is used for calibration purposes. Comparing the calibrated levels with the different generated levels (Figure 5b), in the same frame of time, a simple algorithm [18] is used to decode the multiplex signals. After decoding the MUX signals, the localization of the receiver is straightforward. Taking into account, the frame structure (Figure 3), the position of the receiver inside the navigation cell and its ID in the network is revealed [19]. The ID position, in the unit cell, comes directly from the synchronism block, where all the received channels are, simultaneously, *on* or *off*. The 4-bit binary code ascribed to the higher level identifies the receiver position in the unit cell (Table 1). Those binary codes are displayed in the right hand of the Figure 5b. For instance, the level [1010] corresponds to the level d_{10} where the red and the blue channels are simultaneously *on* (see arrow in Figure 5a). The same happens to the other footprints (P#1 and P#5). Each decoded message carries, also, the node address of the transmitter. So, the next block of six bits, in the square topology or eight in the hexagonal one, gives de ID of the received node. In P#5 the location of the transmitters, in the network, are $B_{2,2}$ and $V_{2,3}$ while in P#1 the assigned transmitters are $R_{1,2}$, $G_{1,3}$, $B_{2,2}$ and $V_{2,3}$. The last block is reserved for the transmission of the message (payload data). A stop bit (0) is used always at the end of each frame.

B. LED-aided navigation system

The input of the aided navigation system is the MUX signal, and the output is the system state estimated at each time step (Δt). As a proof of concept, the suitability of the proposed navigation data bit transition was tested, in the lab [20]. The solution was to move the receiver along a known pattern path as described in Figure 2a, the arrows illustrate the simulated path in successive instants. The signal acquisition on the different generated locations was performed and the transition actions were correlated by calculating the ID position codes in the successive instants.

Taking into account Figure 5b, results show that, as the receiver moves between generated point regions, the received information pattern changes. Note that, between two consecutive data sets, there is one navigation data bit transition (a channel is missing or added). We observe that when the receiver initially moves from P#3 to P#1, the green, $G_{1,3}$ and the violet, $V_{2,3}$, channels are added and the 4-bynary bit code changes from [1010] to [1111].

In Figure 6a, the arrows illustrate the simulated path, in the hexagon topology, at six successive instants (t_1 to t_6). Figure 6b, displays the MUX signals acquired at t_1, t_2 and t_3. At the right hand of the figure, the 4-bit binary codes are pointed out at the correspondent levels.

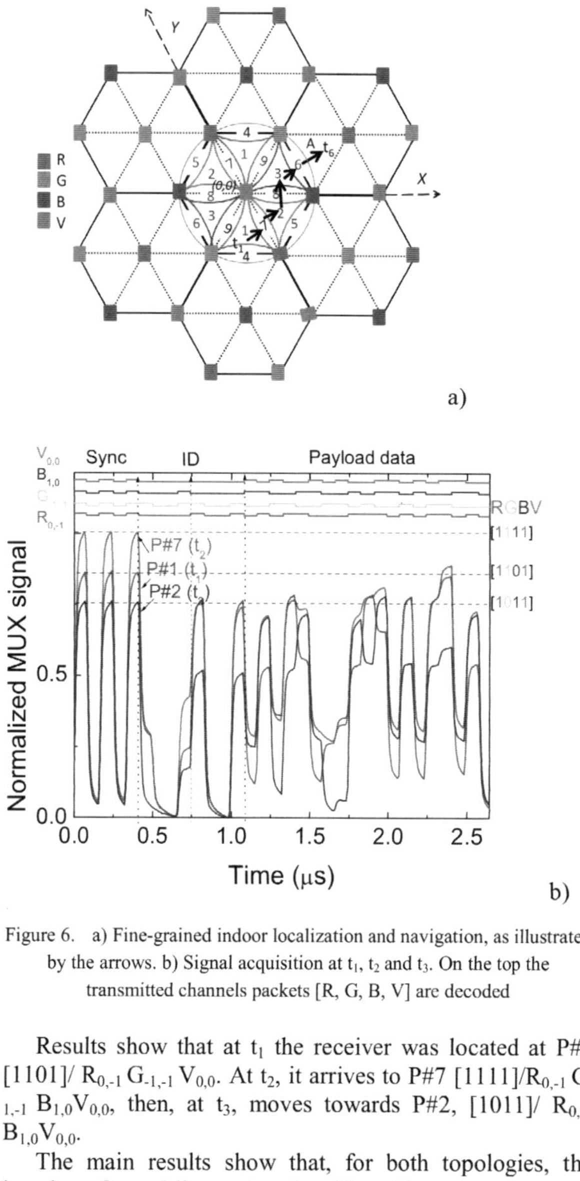

Figure 6. a) Fine-grained indoor localization and navigation, as illustrated by the arrows. b) Signal acquisition at t_1, t_2 and t_3. On the top the transmitted channels packets [R, G, B, V] are decoded

Results show that at t_1 the receiver was located at P#1 [1101]/ $R_{0,-1}$ $G_{-1,-1}$ $V_{0,0}$. At t_2, it arrives to P#7 [1111]/$R_{0,-1}$ $G_{-1,-1}$ $B_{1,0}V_{0,0}$, then, at t_3, moves towards P#2, [1011]/ $R_{0,-1}$ $B_{1,0}V_{0,0}$.

The main results show that, for both topologies, the location of a mobile receiver is achieved based on the LED-based navigation system. At the client's end, positioning bits are decided by the received MUX signal (wavelengths and ID address of the received channels). Fine grained localization was achieved by detecting the wavelengths of the received channels in each cell (Table 1). Nine sub-regions fill each square cell while in the hexagonal, due to the existing XY symmetry, eighteen possible sub-regions can be designed. The use of the square, hexagonal or both topologies depends on the layout of the environment.

IV. CONCLUSIONS AND FUTURE TRENDS

We have proposed a VLC LED-assisted navigation system for large indoor environments. For illumination purposes, data transmission and positioning, white LEDs were used. An a-SiC:H/a-Si:H pin/pin SiC optical MUX/DEMUX mobile receiver decodes the data and based on the synchronism and ID of the joint transmitters it infers its path location. A four-code assignment for the LEDs was proposed. Two cellular networks were tested and compared: the square and the hexagon. The results show that, in large indoor environments, the use of VLC technology allows different cellular topologies, where both location and data transmission are achieved. The choice of one or both topologies depends mainly on the layout of the environment.

ACKNOWLEDGEMENTS

This work was sponsored by FCT – Fundação para a Ciência e a Tecnologia, within the Research Unit CTS – Center of Technology and systems, reference UID/EEA/00066/2013 and by projects: IPL/2017/PPGDiode/ISEL, IPL/2017/SMART_VeDa/ISEL and IPL/2017/EmGraph/ISEL.

REFEEENCES

[1] C. Yang, and H. R. Shao, "WiFi-based indoor positioning," IEEE Commun. Mag., vol. 53, No. 3, pp.150–157, Mar. 2015.

[2] X. Y. Lin, T. W. Ho, C. C. Fang, Z. S. Yen, B. J. Yang, and F. Lai, "A mobile indoor positioning system based on iBeacon technology," in Proc. Int. Conf. IEEE Eng. Med. Biol. Soc., pp. 4970–4973, 2015.

[3] C. H. Huang, L. H. Lee, C. C. Ho, L. L. Wu, and Z. H. Lai, "Real-time rfid indoor positioning system based on kalman filter drift removal and heron-bilateration location estimation," IEEE Trans. Instrum. Meas., vol. 64, no. 3, pp. 728–739, Mar. 2015.

[4] N. U. Hassan, A. Naeem, M. A. Pasha, T. Jadoon, and C. Yuen, "Indoor positioning using visible led lights: A survey,"ACM Comput. Surv., vol. 48, pp. 1–32, 2015.

[5] R. Haarle, "A survey of indoor inertial positioning systems for pedestrians," Commun. Surv. IEEE Commun. Surveys Tuts., vol. 15, no. 3, pp.1281–1293, 2013.

[6] E. Ozgur, E. Dinc., and O. B. Akan, "Communicate to illuminate: State-of-the-art and research challenges for visible light communications," Physical Communication pp.17 72–85, 2015.

[7] K. Panta and J. Armstrong, "Indoor localisation using white LEDs,"Electron. Lett. 48(4), pp. 228–230, 2012.

[8] T. Komiyama, K. Kobayashi, K. Watanabe, T. Ohkubo, and Y. Kurihara, "Study of visible light communication system using RGB LED lights," in Proceedings of SICE Annual Conference, IEEE, 2011, pp. 1926–1928.

[9] S. Schmid, G. Corbellini, S. Mangold, and T. R. Gross, "An LED-to-LED Visible Light Communication system with software-based synchronization," in 2012 IEEE Globecom Workshops, pp. 1264–1268, 2012.

[10] A. Jovicic, J. Li, and T. Richardson, "Visible light communication: opportunities, challenges and the path to market," Communications Magazine, IEEE, vol. 51, no. 12, pp. 26–32, 2013.

[11] S T. Komine and M. Nakagawa, "Fundamental analysis for visible-light communication system using led lights," Consumer Electronics, IEEE Transactions on, vol. 50, no. 1, pp. 100–107, 2004.

[12] M. Vieira, P. Louro, M. Fernandes, M. A. Vieira, A. Fantoni and J. Costa, "Three Transducers Embedded into One Single SiC Photodetector: LSP Direct Image Sensor, Optical Amplifier and Demux Device" Advances in Photodiodes InTech, Chap.19, pp. 403-425, 2011.

[13] M. A. Vieira, P. Louro, M. Vieira, A. Fantoni, and A. Steiger-Garção, "Light-activated amplification in Si-C tandem devices: A capacitive active filter model" IEEE sensor journal, 12, No. 6, pp.1755-1762, 2012.

[13] M. A. Vieira, M. Vieira, P. Louro, L. Mateus, and P. Vieira, "Indoor positioning system using a WDM device based on a-SiC: H technology," Journal of Luminescence 191, pp. 135-138, 2017.

[15] M. Vieira, M. A. Vieira, P. Vieira, and P. Louro "Coupled data transmission and indoor positioning by using transmitting trichromatic white LEDs and a SiC optical MUX/DEMUX mobile receiver," Proc. SPIE. 10231, Optical Sensors 2017, 102310G. doi: 10.1117/12.2265189 (2017).

[16] M. A. Vieira, M. Vieira, V. Silva, P. Louro, J. Costa, "Optical signal processing for data error detection and correction using a-SiCH technology" Phys. Status Solidi C 12, No. 12, pp. 1393–1400, 2015.

[17] M. A. Vieira, M. Vieira, V. Silva, P. Louro, and M. Barata, "Optoelectronic logic functions using optical bias controlled SiC multilayer devices". MRS Proceedings, 1536, pp. 91-96, 2013.

[18] M. A. Vieira, M. Vieira, M., J. Costa, P. Louro, M. Fernandes, and A. Fantoni, "Double pin Photodiodes with two Optical Gate Connections for Light Triggering: A capacitive two-phototransistor model," in Sensors & Transducers Journal Vol. 10, Special Issue, February 2011, pp. 96-120, 2011.

[19] M. A. Vieira, M. Vieira, P. Louro, V. Silva, P. Vieira, "Optical signal processing for indoor positioning using a-SiCH technology," Opt. Eng. 55 (10), 107105 (2016), doi: 10.1117/1.OE.55.10.107105, 2016.

[20] M. Vieira, M. A. Vieira, P. Louro, A. Fantoni, P. Vieira, "Visible light communication technology for fine-grained indoor localization," Proc. SPIE 10538, Optical Interconnects XVIII, 105380A, February 2nd, 2018.

A Low-Voltage Folded-Cascode OP Amplifier with a Dynamic Switching Bias Circuit

Hiroo Wakaumi

Tokyo Metropolitan College of Industrial Technology
Tokyo, Japan
email: waka781420j@ab.auone-net.jp

***Abstract*—Wideband filters employing Operational Amplifiers (OP Amps) are required in sensing devices such as video cameras for environment sensing. A high-speed low-voltage Folded-Cascode (FC) OP Amp with a Dynamic Switching Bias (DSB) circuit capable of processing video signals, which enables low power consumption, high gain with wide bandwidths, and a wide dynamic range, was proposed. Through simulations, it was shown that the OP Amp with the reduced 3-V power supply is able to operate at a 14.3 MHz dynamic switching rate, allowing processing video signals, and a dissipated power of 57 % compared to that in the conventional 5-V power DSBFC OP Amp while keeping a 0.6 V wide output dynamic range. The response of the 2nd-order switched capacitor Low-Pass Filter (LPF) tested as its application was near the theoretical frequency response within frequencies below 5 MHz. The power dissipation of this LPF was also reduced to 56.8 % of that in the switched capacitor LPF with the conventional 5-V power DSBFC OP Amp.**

Keywords-CMOS; operational amplifier; dynamic switching; switched capacitor circuit; filter.

I. INTRODUCTION

Wideband filters are essential for signal processing in video electronic appliances. Specifically, a wideband Low-Pass Filter (LPF) is needed in sensing devices such as a CCD (Charge-Coupled Device) camera with a monitor handling a wide bandwidth video signal of over 2 MHz. The CMOS (Complementary MOS) Switched Capacitor (SC) techniques suitable for realizing analog signal processing ICs (Integrated Circuits), have promising use in video signal bandwidth circuits. It has been demonstrated that SC techniques using CMOS Operational Amplifiers (OP Amps) are useful for implementing analog functions such as filters [1]-[4]. Although CMOS OP Amps are suitable for such filter ICs, the use of several OP Amps results in large power consumption. Especially, the power consumption of OP Amps in high speed operation becomes large because they have wideband properties. There is a possibility that this causes unstable operation.

Until now, several approaches have been considered to decrease the power consumption of OP Amps, including the development of ICs that work at low power supply voltages [5][6]. In the two-stage Folded-Cascode (FC) OP Amp operating at the low power of 1 V [6], resistive biasing and capacitive level shifter are required to increase the output voltage swing. The requirement of four resistors for the resistive biasing makes it difficult to realize as an IC. A clocked current bias scheme for FC OP Amps suitable for achieving a wide dynamic range has typically been proposed to decrease the power consumption of the OP Amp [7][8]. Since the circuit requires complicated four-phase bias-current control pulses and biasing circuits, it is not suitable for the high speed operation and results in a large layout area.

Recently, the author proposed an FC CMOS OP Amp with a Dynamic Switching Bias circuit (DSBFC OP Amp), of simple configuration, to provide low power consumption while maintaining high speed switching operation suitable for processing video signals [9]. This OP Amp operating at the 5-V power supply voltage is not necessarily enough for use in low-voltage signal processing applications under the progress of miniaturization of equipment. That is, the development of OP Amps with a still lower power supply voltage is expected to decrease their power dissipation.

In this paper, a Low-Voltage (LV) DSBFC OP Amp with the 3-V power supply voltage is proposed, which enables low power consumption and is suitable for achieving wide bandwidths and realizing as an IC. The point of view in design for architecture and operation of the LV DSBFC OP Amp is discussed in Section II. Simulation results for performance of the LV DSBFC OP Amp are shown in Section III. As an application example of this OP Amp, its practicability for a 2nd-order SC Butterworth LPF is also evaluated in Section IV. Finally, conclusions of this work are summarized in Section V.

II. LOW-VOLTAGE DSB OP AMP CONFIGURATION

Figure 1 shows a configuration of an LV DSBFC OP Amp, in which the power supply voltages ($\pm$1.5 V) were reduced to 60 % of the previous ones ($\pm$2.5 V). The DSB method is also used for implementing low power consumption. When the power supply voltage is simply reduced, their gains are restrained and bandwidth becomes low. So, in the newly developed circuit, each FET (Field Effect Transistor) size of the LV DSBFC OP Amp was optimized to achieve high-speed switching operation of 14.3 MHz. This OP Amp has a DSB circuit suitable for low power dissipation and an FC OP Amp to achieve a wide dynamic range even in low power supply voltages. The DSB

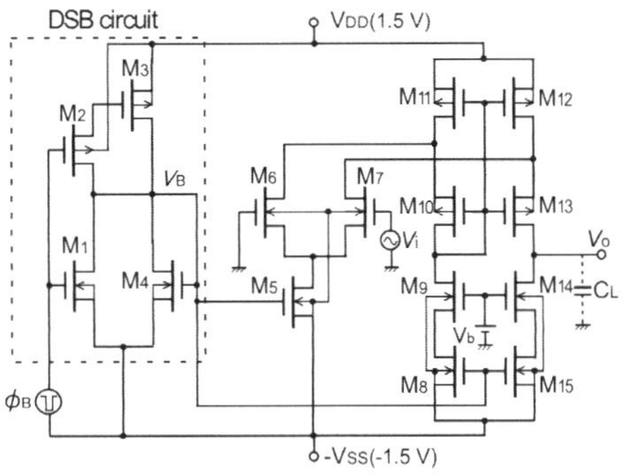

Figure 1. Configuration of the low-voltage DSBFC OP Amp.

TABLE I. LOW-VOLTAGE DSBFC OP AMP DESIGNED VALUES.

FET	W/L (μm/μm)	FET	W/L (μm/μm)
M_1	15/2.5	M_6, M_7	2000/2.5
M_2	30/2.5	M_8, M_{15}	92/2.5
M_3	50/4	M_9, M_{14}	1055/2.5
M_4	44/6	M_{10}, M_{13}	2000/2.5
M_5	187/2.5	M_{11}, M_{12}	390/2.5

circuit consists of a bias circuit of M_1-M_4. The FC OP Amp consists of a current mirror of M_{10}-M_{13} and current sources of M_8, M_9, M_{14}, and M_{15}. The current sources M_5, M_8, and M_{15} of the FC OP Amp are controlled by switching a bias voltage V_B of the DSB circuit dynamically from V_B* to -1.5 V to reduce the power consumption still more. Table I shows its designed values. A minimum channel length of p-MOS FETs and n-MOS FETs is 2.5 μm. In order to achieve almost the same transconductance g_m as that in the conventional 5-V power DSBFC OP Amp, a channel width W of M_{11} and M_{12} and that of M_{10} and M_{13}, in p-MOS current mirror circuits, were increased by nearly fourfold and twofold, respectively. Each W of n-MOS current sources M_9, M_{14}, M_8, and M_{15} was increased by nearly one and a half. The bias voltage of V_B* at the on state of the FC OP Amp was adjusted to nearly 0 V (larger than the conventional one) to decrease W of the current source M_5 maintaining a high switching speed of the DSB circuit. W of M_1-M_3 was increased by over twofold. W of M_4 was adjusted to an optimum value. The bias voltage Vb of the current source consisting of M_9 and M_{14} was set at 0.15 V.

In the DSB circuit, when an external control pulse ϕ_B driving an inverting switching circuit of M_1-M_4 is -1.5 V, the OP Amp turns on by setting V_B at an appropriate level of nearly 0 V by enabling M_3 and M_4 to operate in the saturation region, and operates normally as an operational amplifier. Conversely, when ϕ_B becomes 1.5 V, the OP Amp turns off by setting V_B at nearly -1.5 V, enabling M_1 to operate in a low impedance and M_3 in a high impedance. This high impedance status of M_3 occurs because the gate of M_3 is set at a potential determined by the capacitive coupling between gate and source of M_2 and between gate and drain of M_3 at the transition of ϕ_B to 1.5 V. Therefore, the OP Amp does not dissipate power at all during this off

TABLE II. TYPICAL PERFORMANCES FOR THE LOW-VOLTAGE 3-V POWER AND CONVENTIONAL 5-V POWER DSBFC OP AMPS. C_L=1 PF.

Performance parameters	3V power DSBFC OP Amp - this work	5V power DSBFC OP Amp
Power supply voltages	±1.5 V	±2.5 V
Switching frequency *fs*	14.3 MHz	14.3 MHz
Open loop gain Ao	47.1 dB	51 dB
Phase margin θ	32.8 degrees	34.2 degrees
Unity gain frequency *fu*	603.7 MHz	709 MHz
Slew rate SR (C_L=10 pF)	131 V/μs	140 V/μs
Settling time ts	10 ns	12 ns
Distortion THD (*fin* =10 kHz, *Vo* =0.6 Vp-p)	0.73%	0.40%
Power dissipation (C_L=5 pF) in 50 % switching duty ratio	9.3 mW	16.3 mW

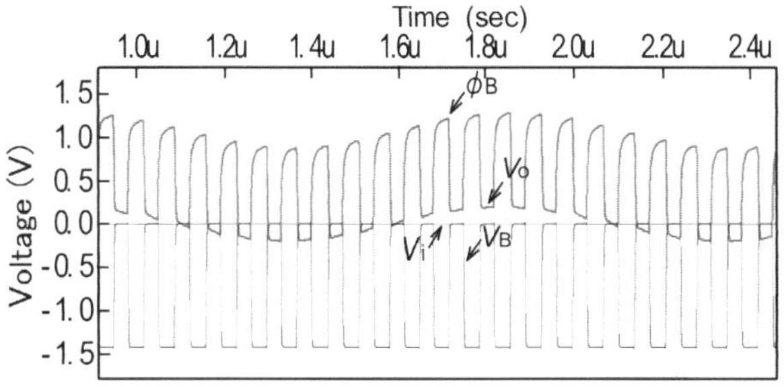

Figure 2. Simulation waveforms of the low-voltage DSBFC OP Amp. Input signal frequency f_{in}=1 MHz, V_{in}=1 mV, fs=14.3 MHz, C_L=2 pF.

period, which brings about low power consumption.

III. Simulation Results

The LV DSBFC OP Amp performance was tested through SPICE simulations. The power supply voltages V_{DD} and Vss are 1.5 V. Typical performances compared with those of the conventional DSBFC OP Amp with a power supply of 5 V are shown in Table II. The values of parameters of open loop gain, phase margin, unity gain frequency, slew rate, and settling time are almost the same as those in the conventional 5-V power DSBFC OP Amp. As the inherent static nonlinearity of the LV DSBFC OP Amp, the total harmonic distortion THD for the 10 kHz input signal, enabling 0.6 Vp-p to output, was 0.73 %, which is a little large compared to the conventional one. However, this is less than 1 %.

The LV DSBFC OP Amp operated in a dynamic switching mode with a Duty Ratio (DR) of 50 % and a switching frequency, *fs*, of 14.3 MHz as shown in Figure 2. The output sine wave voltage for the input signal of 1 mV was nearly equal to that in the static operation mode of this OP Amp. Like this, the distortion by the dynamic operation seems to be hardly seen. In the dynamic switching operation mode of 50 % duty ratio, the power dissipation was 9.3 mW, which is 66 % of that observed in the static operation mode as shown in Figure 3. This is also 57 % of that of the conventional 5-V power DSBFC OP Amp. This shows this OP Amp's extremely low power consumption characteristics due to the reduced effect of power supply voltages (60 % of that in the

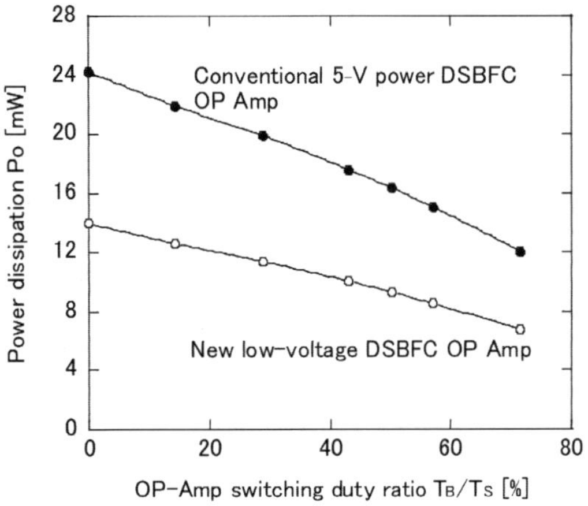

Figure 3. Power dissipation vs. OP-Amp switching duty ratio in the DSB mode. fs=14.3 MHz, C_L=5 pF.

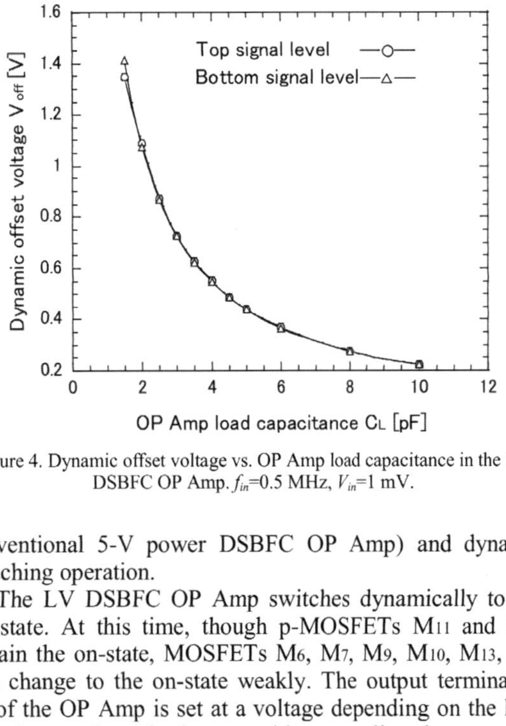

Figure 4. Dynamic offset voltage vs. OP Amp load capacitance in the LV DSBFC OP Amp. f_{in}=0.5 MHz, V_{in}=1 mV.

conventional 5-V power DSBFC OP Amp) and dynamic switching operation.

The LV DSBFC OP Amp switches dynamically to the off state. At this time, though p-MOSFETs M_{11} and M_{12} remain the on-state, MOSFETs M_6, M_7, M_9, M_{10}, M_{13}, and M_{14} change to the on-state weakly. The output terminal of Vo of the OP Amp is set at a voltage depending on the load capacitance through the capacitive coupling between the drain and the gate of the MOSFET M_{13}. So, a large output swing in Vo occurs at the off-state transition. A dynamic offset voltage V_{off} (defined as the difference of the on-state and the off-state output voltages) at the off-state transition of the OP Amp vs. load capacitance C_L was tested (Figure 4). In small load capacitances less than 1.5 pF, top and bottom signal levels of the dynamic off swing do not match. This causes distortion at an output signal of the OP Amp. Therefore, we can see that the load capacitance C_L over 2 pF is desirable for its operation.

IV. Application to SC LPF

To demonstrate the practicability of the above low-voltage DSBFC OP Amp, the feasibility of its application in a 2nd-order SC IIR (Infinite Impulse Response) LPF with the Butterworth frequency characteristic was tested. When a sampling frequency fs=14.3 MHz (equal to four times of NTSC (National Television System Committee) color sub-carrier frequency 3.58 MHz) and a cutoff frequency fc=2 MHz, respectively, were chosen for this LPF, the discrete-time transfer function is given by [10]

$$H(z) = -\frac{0.1174(1+z^{-1})^2}{1-0.8252z^{-1}+0.2946z^{-2}}. \quad (1)$$

The circuit configuration and operation waveforms realizing this transfer function are shown in Figures 5 and 6, respectively [10]. This filter consists of a sample-hold circuit with a holding capacitor C_1 and a CMOS sampling switch controlled by ϕ_{SH}, CMOS switches ϕ_1, ϕ_2 for charge transfer, capacitors A-E, G, and I, and two LV DSBFC OP Amps (OP Amps 1 and 2). The sampling switch was designed to a channel width / channel length W/L=105/2.5 (μm/μm) for each of p-MOSFET and n-MOSFET. Other CMOS switches were designed to 75/2.5 (μm/μm). CMOS switches are turned on and off by non-overlapping two-phase clock pulses ϕ_1, ϕ_2, swinging from -1.5 V to 1.5 V. These sampling and CMOS switches were designed to have a balanced structure with each equal L and W of p-MOS and n-MOS FETs to delete a feed-through phenomenon. This phenomenon is easy to be caused by a capacitive coupling between gate and output terminals.

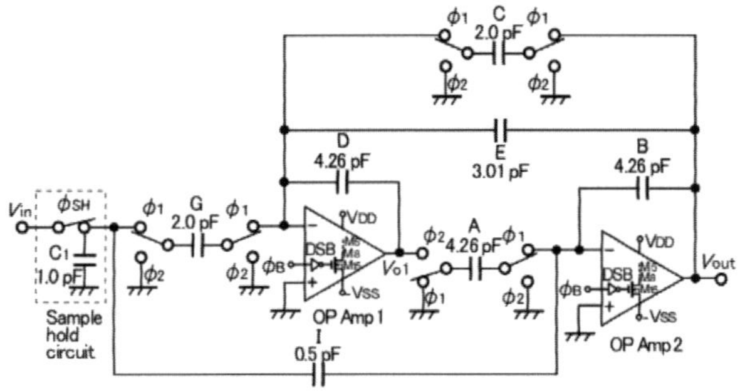

Figure 5. Configuration of the 2nd-order SC LPF.

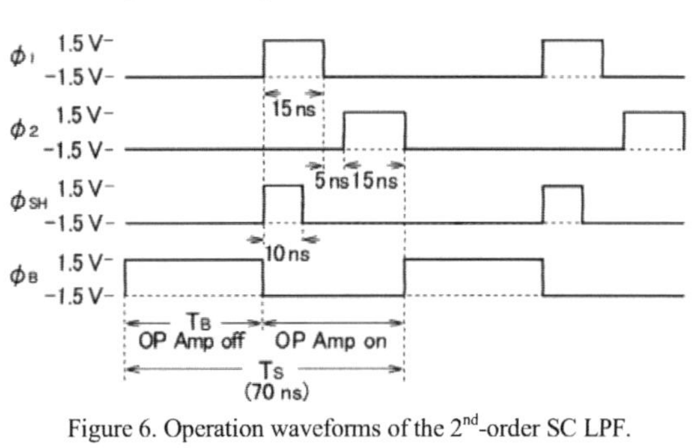

Figure 6. Operation waveforms of the 2nd-order SC LPF.

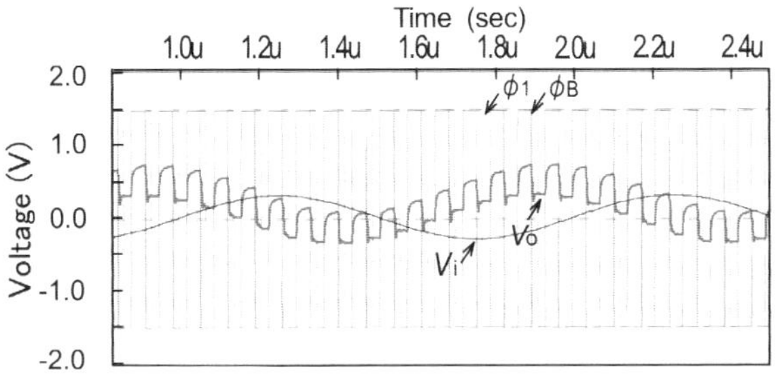

Figure 7. Simulation waveforms for the 2nd-order SC LPF. V_{in}=0.3 V_0-p, f_{in}=1 MHz, C_L=4 pF.

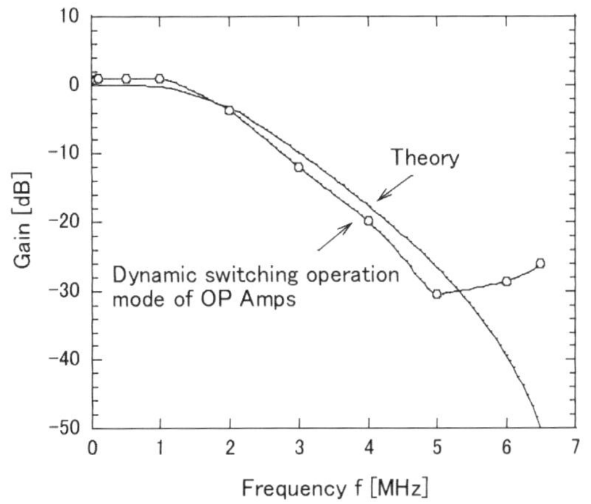

Figure 8. Frequency response of the SC LPF in the DSB mode of the OP Amp. T_B=35 ns.

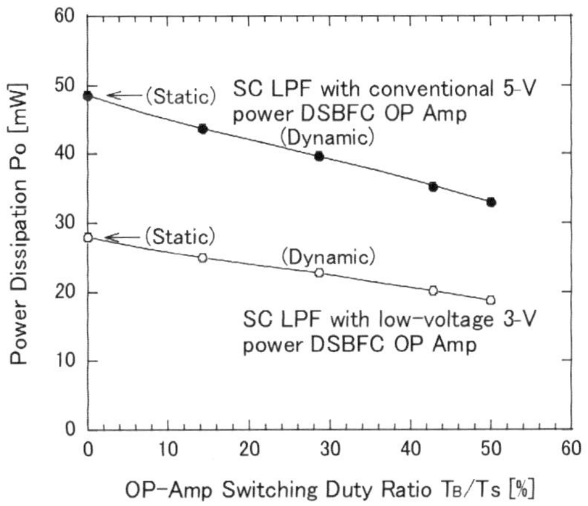

Figure 9. Power dissipation vs. OP Amp switching duty ratio in the 2nd-order SC LPF. f_{in}=1 MHz.

Major CMOS process parameters are given as a gate insulating film thickness t_{ox}=50 nm, a p-MOSFET threshold voltage V_{TP}=-0.6 V, and an n-MOSFET threshold voltage V_{Tn}=0.6 V.

Operation waveforms for an input signal of 1 MHz with an amplitude of 0.3 V and an output load of 4 pF are shown in Figure 7. In the dynamic switching operation, an output load of the LV DSBFC OP Amp increases to nearly 5 pF including internal capacitances of the SC LPF. For the pass-band frequency signal (≦2MHz), almost the same signal as the input one was obtained. The frequency response of the SC LPF in the dynamic switching operation of the LV DSBFC OP Amp is shown in Figure 8. The frequency response was near the theoretical one from 100 kHz to near 5 MHz. In the high frequency range over 6 MHz, it deteriorated due to a sampling phase effect. The gain below -26 dB was obtained at over 6 MHz within a stop-band. Though this stop-band gain is not enough, it is expected to be improved by making the roll-off steeper through the increase of filter order.

Power dissipation vs. OP Amp switching duty ratio in the 2nd-order SC LPF is shown in Figure 9. The power dissipation of the SC LPF itself decreased in proportion to the off period T_B of the OP Amp. In the dynamic switching operation mode of T_B=35 ns (DR=50 %), the power dissipation of the SC LPF (18.7 mW) was reduced to 66.8 % as compared to that in the static operation of the OP Amps (28.0 mW). Thus, the dynamic switching operation of the LV DSBFC OP Amp is useful for reducing the power dissipation of the SC LPF. This power dissipation was 56.8 % compared to that in the SC LPF using the conventional 5-V power DSBFC OP Amp (32.9 mW). This low power characteristic was realized by the low power supply voltages and dynamic switching operation.

V. Conclusions and Future Work

A high-speed low-voltage Folded-Cascode (FC) OP Amp with a Dynamic Switching Bias (DSB) circuit capable of processing video signals, which enables low power consumption, high gain with wide bandwidths, and a wide dynamic range, was proposed. Through simulations, it was shown that the OP Amp with the reduced 3-V power supply is able to operate at a 14.3 MHz dynamic switching rate, allowing processing video signals, and a dissipated power of 57 % compared to that in the conventional 5-V power DSBFC OP Amp while keeping a 0.6 V wide output dynamic range. The response of the 2nd-order Switched Capacitor Low-Pass Filter (SC LPF) tested as its application was near the theoretical frequency response within frequencies below 5 MHz. The power dissipation of this LPF was also reduced to 56.8 % of that in the SC LPF with the conventional 5-V power DSBFC OP Amp.

Thus, it was confirmed that the 3-V power DSBFC OP Amp is useful for high speed operation, low power consumption, and greatly reducing the power dissipation of the SC LPF. This circuit should be useful for the realization of low-power wide-band signal processing ICs. It is also noteworthy that the performance is expected to be improved still more by employing MOSFETs with a minimum shorter channel length than 2.5 μm used in this work.

As the future work, the study on the increase of the filter order remains, because the frequency response will be improved to a practical level by increasing this one. However, there might be a limitation in the filter order, because two OP Amps per one order LPF must be used and so power dissipation will increase in proportion to the filter order.

REFERENCES

[1] R. Gregorian and W. E. Nicholson, "CMOS Switched-Capacitor Filters for a PCM Voice CODEC," IEEE Journal of Solid-State Circuits, vol. SC-14, no. 6, pp. 970-980, Dec. 1979.

[2] R. Dessoulavy, A Knob, F. Krummenacher, and E. A. Vittoz, "A Synchronous Switched Capacitor Filter," IEEE Journal of Solid-State Circuits, vol. SC-15, no. 3, pp. 301-305, June 1980.

[3] A. Iwata, H. Kikuchi, K. Uchimura, A. Morino, and M. Nakajima, "A Single-Chip Codec with Switched-Capacitor Filters," IEEE Journal of Solid-State Circuits, vol. SC-16, no. 4, pp. 315-321, Aug. 1981.

[4] J.-T. Wu, Y.-H. Chang, and K.-L. Chang, "1.2 V CMOS Switched-Capacitor Circuits," in 1996 IEEE International Solid-State Circuits Conf. Digest of Technical Papers-42nd ISSCC, pp. 388-389, 479.

[5] Z. Kun, W. Di, and L. Zhangfa, "A High-Performance Folded Cascode Amplifier," in 2011 International Conference on Computer and Automation Engineering-ICCAE 2011, IPCSIT, vol. 44, pp. 41-44, 2012.

[6] S. H. Mirhosseini and A. Ayatollahi, "A Low-Voltage, Low-Power, Two-Stage Amplifier for Switched-Capacitor Applications in 90 nm CMOS Process," Iranian Journal of Electrical & Electronic Engineering, vol. 6, no. 4, pp. 199-204, Dec. 2010.

[7] D. B. Kasha, W. L. Lee, and A. Thomson, "A 16-mW, 120-dB Linear Switched-Capacitor Delta-Sigma Modulator with Dynamic Biasing," IEEE J. Solid-State Circuits, vol. 34, no. 7, pp. 921-926, July 1999.

[8] H.-L. Chen, Y.-S. Lee, and J.-S. Chiang, "Low Power Sigma Delta Modulator with Dynamic Biasing for Audio Applications," in 50th Midwest Symposium on Circuits nad Systems 2007-MWSCAS 2007, pp. 159-162.

[9] H. Wakaumi, "A Folded-Cascode OP Amplifier with a Dynamic Switching Bias Circuit," Engineering Letters, vol. 23, no. 2, pp. 92-97, June 2015.

[10] H. Wakaumi, "A Switched-Capacitor Low-Pass Filter with Dynamic Switching Bias OP Amplifiers," ASTES Journal, vol. 2, no. 6, pp. 100-106, Nov. 2017.

Low Profile Circularly Polarized Antenna with Large Coverage for Multi-Sensor Device Links Optimisation

Mohamad Majed, Youssef Sbeity
University of Limoges
ENSIL-ENSCI
Limoges, France
E-mail : mohamad.majed@etu.unilim.fr
youssef.sbeity@etu.unilim.fr

Michele Lalande, Bernard Jecko
University of Limoges
XLIM Lab
Limoges, France
E-mail : michele.lalande@xlim.fr
bernard.jecko@xlim.fr

***Abstract*-Multi-sensor devices are well connected to each other and to the microcontrollers via wireless links. This technology introduces the interfacing problems not only in terms of signal processing, but also in the Electromagnetic (EM) links to perform Multi-sensor, Sensor arrays, Identification, Localization, Tracking, and Multiple Input Multiple Output (MIMO) Radar applications. Because of the unpredictable sensor positioning, the link antennas must work in circular polarization, have large coverage and a small thickness to be located on walls, ceilings, platforms, etc. To satisfy these conditions, this paper presents a new kind of low profile antenna with circular polarization able to cover a large area. The use of Electronic Band Gap Low Profile Metamaterial (LP-EBG) satisfies all these specifications together.**

Keywords-Sensor; Radar; Circular Polarization; Antenna; Miniature; Larger Aperture Angle.

I. Introduction

Today, multi-sensors are extensively used for many applications including: temperature control in a building, identification, localization, tracking, remote sensing, and MIMO radars.

All these wireless technologies need reliable links with microcontrollers, base station and other links for ad-hoc sensors techniques. Such applications involve link antennas with circular polarization because the sensor positions cannot be mastered. In addition, they need antennas with large coverage to minimize the number of sensors and the cost. Large coverage means a large aperture angle but of a small gain. There is no problem by the gain decrease because of the radiated power, which is always limited by the Equivalent Isotropic Radiated Power (EIRP) specifications. Hence, the decrease of the working band must be controlled.

These antennas will be located on Printed Circuit Board (PCB), walls, ceilings, Internet of Things (IoT) boxes, etc. Consequently, they must have a low profile. To achieve these characteristics together, an original antenna based on the Electronic Band Gap (EBG) antenna concept [1] was designed in this paper. This is a low profile antenna with a thickness around $\lambda/10$ and transversal dimensions usually included between 1.5λ and 0.1λ. This antenna can work in a linear or circular polarization and it is possible to multiply the space coverage by 2 or 3 times in its miniaturized form.

The rest of the paper is structured as follows. Section 2 describes a small low profile antenna design, followed by the circular Pixel characteristics in Section 3. Antenna miniaturization to increase the aperture angle is explained in Section 4 and Section 5 sheds light on the Radio Frequency Identification (RFID) application and ground coverage. The work is concluded in Section 6, followed by references.

II. Small Low Profile Antenna Design

A Low Profile EBG antenna [2] is a resonant high gain air cavity (Figure 1.a) inserted between a ground plane and a semi-reflective surface usually a Frequency Selective Surface (FSS). A small antenna is built with the same characteristics (see Figure 1.b) by introducing vertical walls in such structure. This small antenna is called "Pixel" because it has already been used in its square shape as Pixel in the Agile Radiating Matrix Antenna (ARMA) concept [3].

The new air cavity antenna (Pixel) is fed by a patch that is printed on a dielectric slab or by any other probe being located on the cavity (Figure 1.c). The dimensions of the final structure with a square shape [3] can be chosen to be between 1.5λ and 0.1λ, and other shapes can be used besides a circular one, as shown further in the paper.

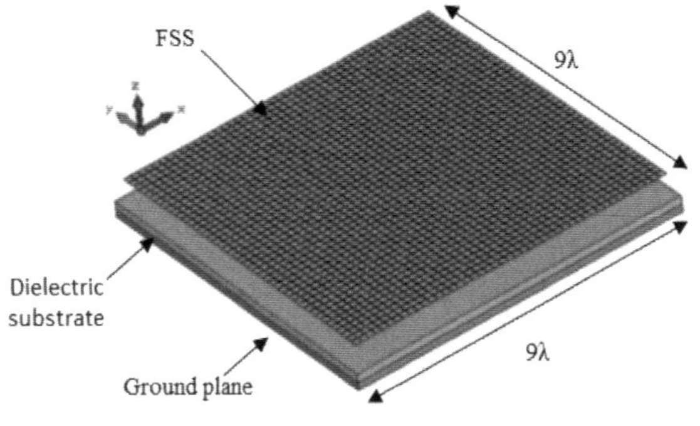

Figure 1.a EBG Antenna

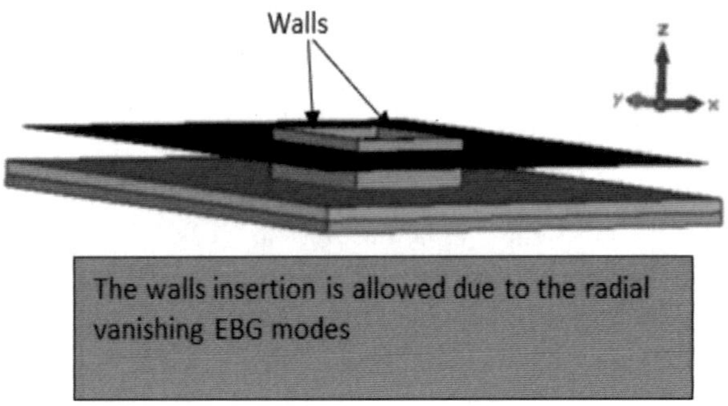

Figure 1.b Walls limited cavity antenna

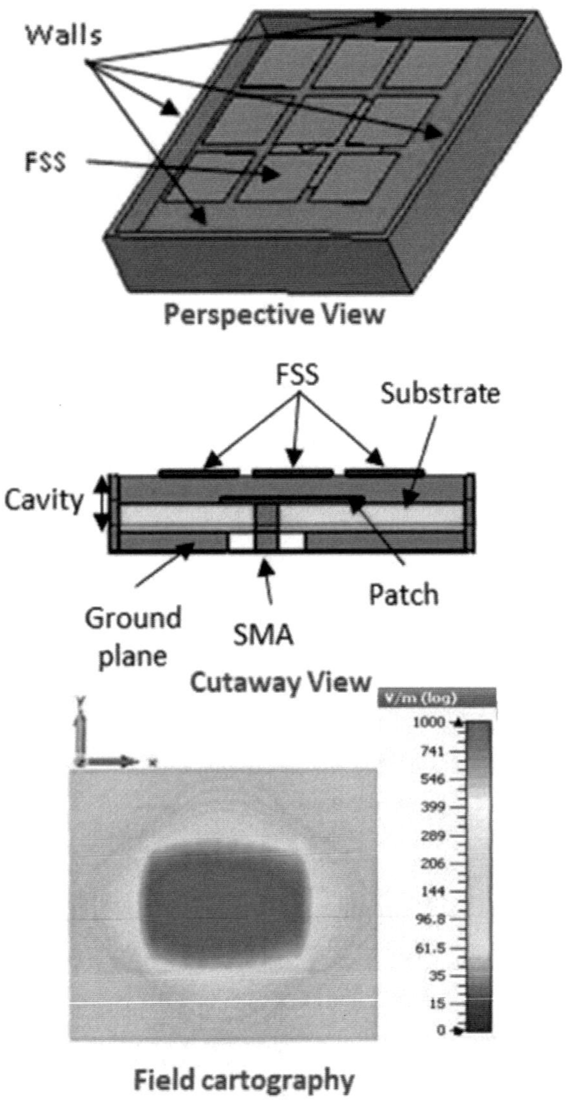

Figure 1.c Final antenna with its corresponding radiating surface ES field cartography

III. Circular Pixel characteristics

To show the main characteristics, a circularly shaped Pixel antenna with a $\lambda/2$ diameter fed by a circular patch is designed (Figure 2). The antenna is fed by four ports [4] polarization circuit in order to obtain a good circular polarized radiation pattern.

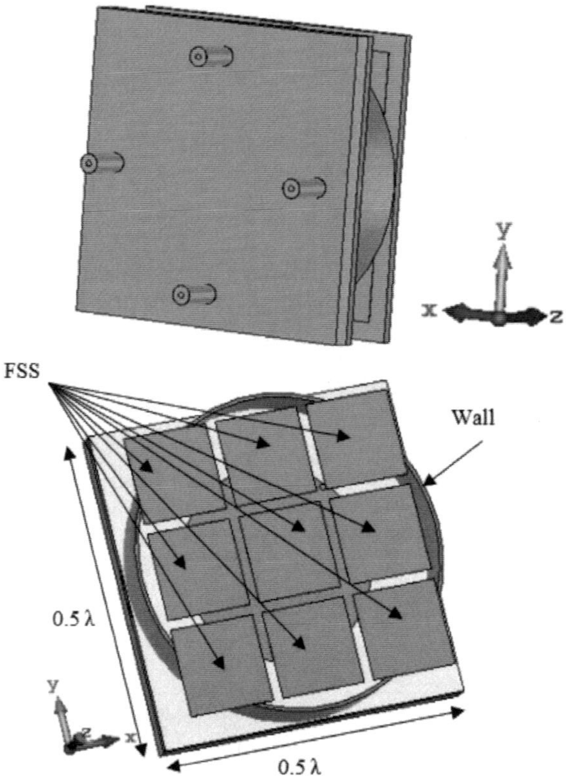

Figure 2.a Circularly shaped Pixel antenna above a square ground plane

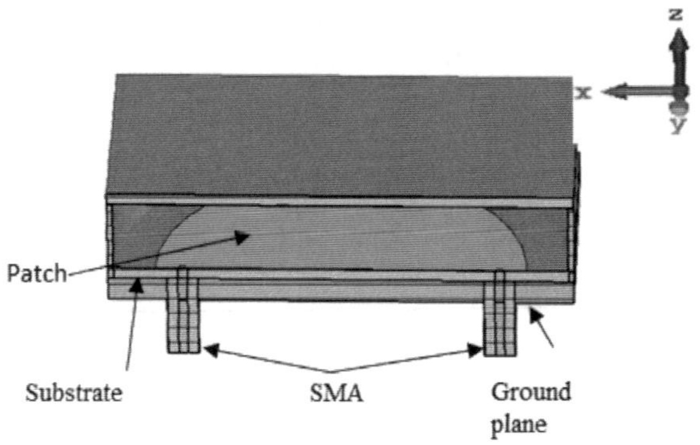

Figure 2.b Cut view: plane containing two feeding coaxial cables.

The Return Loss S_{11} parameter evolution as a function of the frequency (Figure 3.a) shows a large bandwidth: 18% but the aperture angle is only about 103° (Figure 3.b) with a λ/2 diameter of the "Pixel". The axial ratio is presented in Figure 3.c.

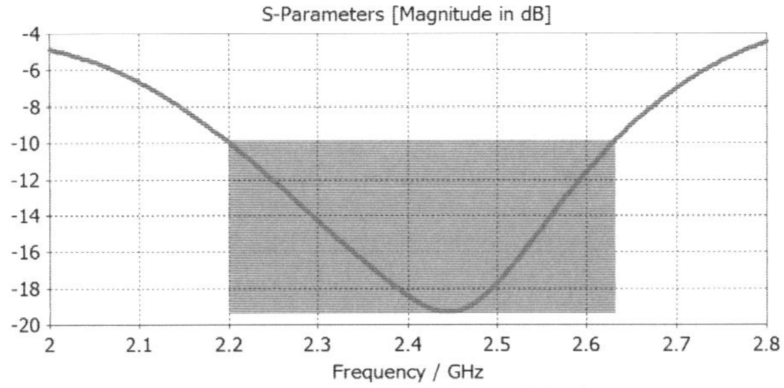

Figure 3.a S11 parameter as a function of the frequency

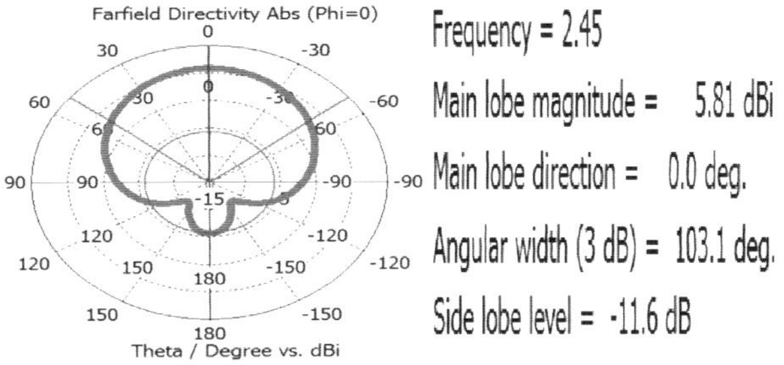

Figure 3.b Antenna gain evolution

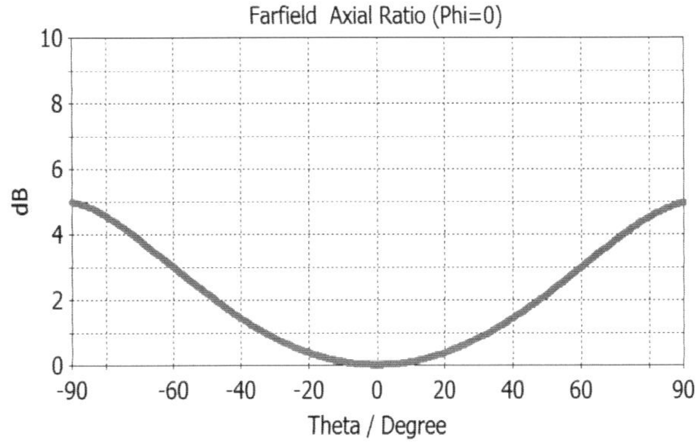

Figure 3.c Axial ratio

Axial Ratio: <3 dB for +-60 degrees. This indicates that the deviation from circular polarization is less than 3 dB over the specified angular range.

IV. ANTENNA MINIATURIZATION TO INCREASE THE APERTURE ANGLE

To increase the aperture angle of the antenna, the diameter of the Pixel antenna is reduced to 0.2λ (Figure 4). Consequently, the feeding patch dimensions must be highly reduced by introducing a new substrate with a high permittivity Ɛ = 10 (Arlon). This new antenna is called Mini Antenna "MINA" and the characteristics are demonstrated in a linear polarization design as seen in Figure 4.

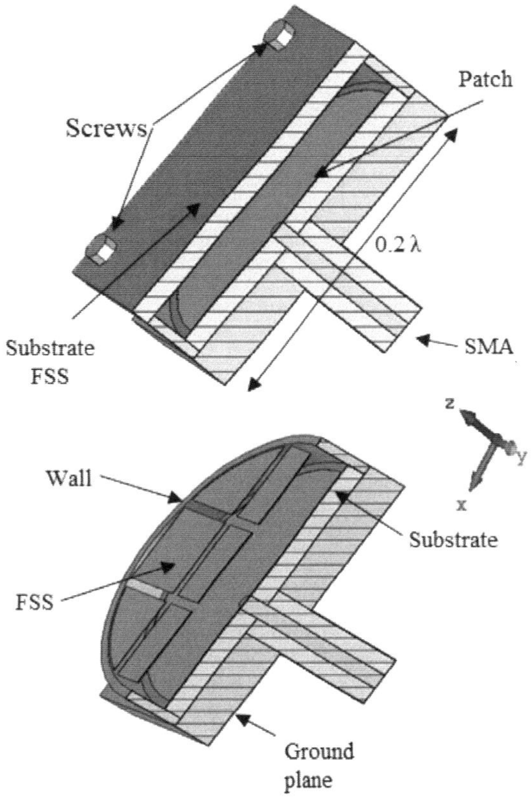

Figure 4. Half cut-view of the MINA (with and without the FSS substrate).

Concerning these conditions, the bandwidth is strongly reduced as shown in Figure 5.a: 0.5% (should be improved to match with the application bandwidth) but the aperture angle is large, as expected (Figure 5.b).

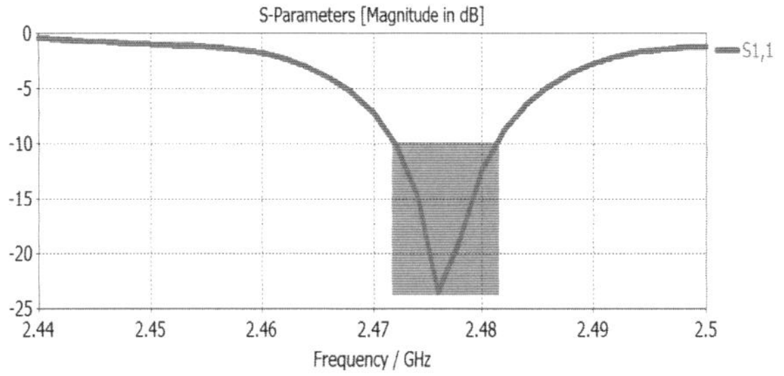

Figure 5. a S11 parameter as a function of the frequency

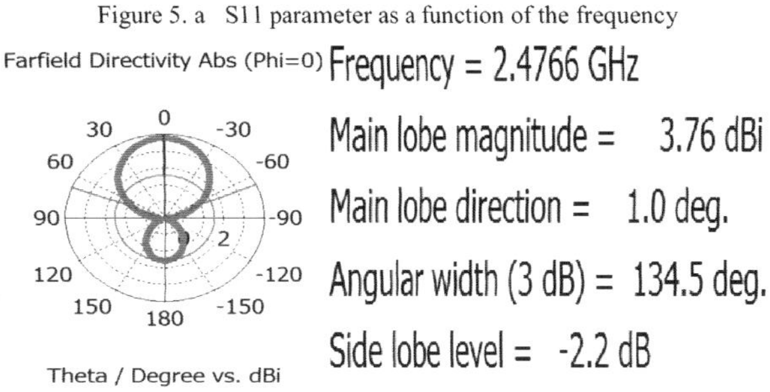

Figure 5.b Gain evolution as a function of the Θ angle for all the ϕ planes.

V. GROUND COVERAGE

To illustrate the operation, let us consider MINA as a reader antenna for a simple Radio Frequency Identification (RFID) application. It is located on the roof of a large shopping center area. The miniaturized MINA solution offers a coverage multiplied by four, as shown in Figure 6, when the 0.5λ and the 0.2λ structures are compared. Instead of using 4 readers, the number of the prepared tags is multiplied by 4 and only one reader is used.

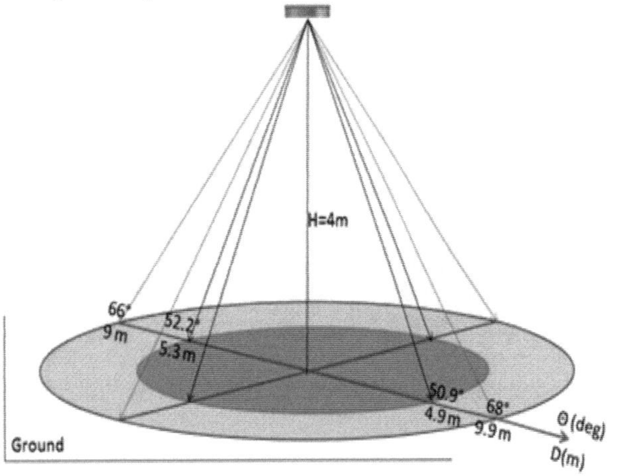

Figure 6. Ground coverage obtained with the 2 antennas: 0.5λ Pixel and the 0.2λ MINA.

VI. CONCLUSION

A new kind of low profile antenna was presented in this paper. The behavior is deduced from the usage of an EBG metamaterial, which allows to build planar antennas with large or small surfaces (1.5λ to 0.2λ).

For low frequency sensor-to-microcontroller links, the use of this solution is only limited by the antenna size and for high frequency solutions (sub millimeter ones) it is limited by the manufacturing technology. Such link antennas are particularly suitable for coverage of multi-sensor applications.

REFERENCES

[1] C. Menudier, M. Thevenot, T. Monediere, and B. Jecko "EBG Resonator Antennas: State of Art and Prospect" Antenna Theory and Techniques, 6th International Conference IEEE, pp.37-43. Sevastopol, Ukraine, September,2007.

[2] M. S. Toubet et al. "Wide Bandwidth, High-Gain, and Low-Profile EBG Prototype for High Power Applications," Antennas and Wireless Propagation Letters, IEEE , vol.10, no. 1362-1365, 2011.

[3] B. Jecko, E. Arnaud, H. Abou Taam, and A. Siblini "The ARMA concept: Comparison of AESA and ARMA technologies for agile antenna design.": Fermat Journal vol 20, pp.1-7, 2017.

[4] A. Siblini, B. Jecko, H. AbouTaam, M. Rammal, and A. Bellion "New Circularly Polarized Matrix Antenna for Space Applications" Wireless Telecommunications Symposium (WTS) IEEE, pp.1-4, London, 2016.

[5] A. Siblini, B. Jecko, and E. Arnaud "Multimode Reconfigurable Nano-Satellite Antenna for PDTM Application," Antennas and Propagation, 11th European Conference EUCAP, pp.542-545, Paris 2017.

Sensors-Based Stereo Image System for Precision Control of Weed in the Agricultural Industry

Bruno M. Moreno[1,2], Paulo E. Cruvinel[1,2,3]

[1] Embrapa Instrumentation (CNPDIA), P.O. Box 741, 13560-970, São Carlos, SP, Brazil
[2] Electrical and Computer Engineering Program, University of São Paulo, São Carlos, SP, Brazil
[3] Computer Science Program, Federal University of São Carlos, São Carlos, SP, Brazil
Emails: bruno.moraes.moreno@usp.br; paulo.cruvinel@embrapa.br

Abstract—**This contribution proposes a solution for agricultural weed control based on stereo digital image sensors domain-oriented devices, technologies, and applications. In the world, agriculture has been developed by combining the production, value aggregation, environmental and social responsibility. The sector is primarily responsible to supply food for people, as well as fibers and energy. To keep such results, farmers have faced the need to seek, increasing the rational use of inputs, as is the use of pesticides, plant regulators, and liquid fertilizers. This paper presents a discussion related to the design and development of stereo image sensors for precision spraying to control weed species in agricultural crops, i.e., based on advances in sensor's instrumentation and image processing. The yield of a crop can vary depending on the species of invasive plants involved, its percentage of occupation by area, competition period, stage of development of the crop and soil, as well as weather conditions. In this context, the selection of an adequate image sensor can result in better recognition process, i.e., improvement in sprayer quality at variable rates based on management zones.**

Keywords–Camera sensors; Embedded platform; Stereo vision; Image sensor; Decision making; Weed control; Agricultural industry.

I. Introduction

The current agriculture must face the challenge of increasing production in response to the demand of the growing population. Based on this directive and under the precision-based management, an increasing use of remote sensing technologies have been used to attend the rural areas. Additionally, embedded instruments and analog and digital cameras are found frequently, as well as series of computer modelling to aid decision-making based on the site-specific management, which has brought improvements related to the management systems that can promote the rationalization in terms of the application of inputs, decreased production costs, and impacts on the environment [1] [2]. Among the steps aimed at rationalizing the use of agricultural inputs, one may find the application of pesticides, which has required major efforts since its processes are related not only to the treatment of the pests into a cultivated area, but also related to the care about its possible impacts in both the cultivated area, as well as in adjacent areas [3]. The idea related to the technification of the agricultural processes to improve production methods has been gaining ground in recent decades. Real-time process monitoring and control, along with advances in positioning systems, can provide more details of the fields of production and therefore can improve the decision-making based on variability of the processes in agricultural production. The agricultural production chain starts from the adaptation to the land to the sale of the product in the supermarket. Within this chain, there are several involved processes that have important relevance in order to obtain the minimization of environmental impact, better efficiency in the amount of production and quality of the final product.

The clearest example of these processes is the application of agricultural pesticides in pulverized form, in which is necessary to improve safety and efficiency of application, for agricultural pest control. The spraying of agricultural pesticides is used in most large-scale production crops and requires precision and effectiveness to avoid the impact it may have on the soil, the crop and the environment, if not applied in a responsible way and with the highest quality standards. To obtain an efficient agricultural spraying the factors, such as efficiency of the applied chemical, factors which come from the weather conditions, biological factors and the quality of the application must be considered. Thus, several studies are based on the search for quality and efficiency of the chemical products [4]. Also, there is a large number of scientists working on biological and climatic factors which can affect the quality and efficiency of the production. On the other hand, several works show the importance of the application, from the point of view of the used methods, the machinery and the automation of the application processes. In addition, technological advances and the evolution of embedded systems to aid decision-making processes have provided to agriculture a new way of seeing the rural property, where the consideration of spatial and temporal variability of soil and plants have improved the concepts related to the risk management in agriculture, i.e., the way to find efficiency and cost minimization in the use of agricultural inputs. Furthermore, in this context, and taking into account advanced trends, sensors-based technologies can provide appropriate tools to achieve solutions and to implement the strategies above mentioned. In precision agriculture area, sensor-based technologies play an important role.

In this context, the precision agriculture area has been seeking sensor-based technologies to improve agricultural processes, and such field of knowledge is playing today an important role. One technology with the use of camera sensors that adds more information to decision making in the agricultural field is the one based on stereo vision methods. These methods can be used for various applications, and there are studies that analyze the vision at night for the development of an advanced driver assistance system, monitor the conditions of long pipelines with autonomous robots, and assist in the reconstruction of virtual plant leaf model [5]–[7]. This paper presents a method based on the use of a customized stereo image sensor for the precision application of herbicides to control weed in an agricultural field. The rest of the paper is structured as follows. Section II presents the mathematical theory behind the selection of the image sensors, based on the transfer functions. Section III discusses the stereo vision methods and the materials used. Section IV presents the results and discussions. Finally, we conclude our work in Section V.

II. Theory Behind the Selection of Image Sensors for Agricultural Weed Control

The camera function has been widespread applied for various circumstances [8] [9]. Lens and cameras designers encounter challenges for developing systems with high image quality. The major concern is how to optimize the lens parameters such as curvatures and thicknesses to get high image quality, for example, a high image resolution. Several optimizations have been proposed to improve the aberrations of lens systems [10]–[12]. The Modulation Transfer Function (MTF) is the amplitude term of Optical Transfer Function (OTF) that is similar to the transfer function of linear system. The transfer function is regarded as a major characteristic in the linear system. There are some proposals that present their methods to approach the transfer function [13]–[15]. A simple one is to receive the impulse response at output as input being an impulse signal. This impulse response is related to the transfer function. Using the same procedure, a point source is respected as the impulse signal to help estimate the image response in a lens system. The image of point source shown in the image plane is called the point spread function (PSF), which is the inverse Fourier transform of the OTF. Therefore, the MTF applied to determine the image resolution could be derived from the amplitude term of the Fourier transform of the PSF. MTF is in principle classified into three categories: scanning method, autocorrelation, and crossrelation methods. Of these, the scanning method seems to be most commonly used in many fields, and the Line Spread Functions (LSF) measurement is equally preferable because it can be obtained with a simple slit, and it is measure of fundamental definition.

The MTF can be evaluated from either the geometrical optics or diffraction calculation. Ray tracing methods are widely applied to simulate the image response of object point source in the image system. Using the irradiance model, Lin and Liu [16] presented a MTF computation method without counting the number of rays traveling to each grid. Tseng et al. [17] proposed skew ray tracing method to simulate the geometrical PSF, i.e., using a homogeneous coordinate transformation matrix.

In this paper, the use of a camera in agricultural environment can be defined taking into account the calculation of the LSF of the camera lens and MTF, which represents the magnitude response of the optical system to sinusoids of different spatial frequencies, i.e., retrieved by Fourier transform of the LSF. Several key aspects of optical instrumentation are related with the implementation of a linear source for a given optical system, the impact of the finite size of the source on the measurement, and the choice of the optical elements to image the response of specific patterns of plants and its relation with the lens used in the camera. By taking a linear source the solution to measure the MTF is in 1D, orthogonally to the direction of the line. This can be proven considering a given source $S(x,y) = \delta(x).C$, and a lens of diameter equal to (a), that means:

$$R(k_x,k_y) = \int\int_{-a/2}^{a/2} \delta(x) C e^{j(k_x x + k_y y)} dx dy \quad (1)$$

The response of the objective can be expressed as the square of the Fourier transform of the product of the source with the aperture of the lens $R^2(k_x,k_y)$, with (k_x,k_y) the spatial frequencies associated with the spatial coordinator (x,y). Besides, looking for a solution of (1) and solving the integral by parts is possible to reach:

$$R^2(k_x,k_y) \alpha \frac{sin^2(ak_y)}{(ak_y)^2} \quad (2)$$

Equation (2) corresponds to the LSF. The Fourier Transform of the LSF then gives the 1D MTF in the yy-direction.

III. Materials and Methods

A. Stereo Vision

The stereo vision system used in this work is based on the use of two cameras with the aim of simulating the human vision system and obtain depth of objects, with the camera plane as a reference. The depth is resulted through the comparison of the objects position between each captured image.

The simplest way of comparing the images is guaranteed when the cameras are coplanar and aligned, as shown in Figure 1. The variables defined by the camera are the baseline b and the focal distance f. The $P(X,Y,Z)$ represents a point that would be recorded by the two cameras and $u_L = (X_L, Y_L)$ and $u_R = (X_R, Y_R)$ are the projections of this point in each image. From the concepts of geometry and similarity of triangles, it is possible to obtain:

$$\frac{X_L}{f} = \frac{X}{Z} \Rightarrow X_L = \frac{Xf}{Z} \quad (3)$$

$$\frac{-X_R}{f} = \frac{b-X}{Z} \Rightarrow X_R = \frac{(X-b)f}{Z} \quad (4)$$

$$Y_L = Y_R = \frac{fY}{Z} \quad (5)$$

Considering that the difference between the x coordinates in each image is equal to $d = X_L - X_R$, where d is the disparity, (3) and (4) can be rewritten as:

$$X = \frac{bX_L}{d} \quad (6)$$

$$Y = \frac{bY_L}{d} \quad (7)$$

$$Z = \frac{bf}{d} \quad (8)$$

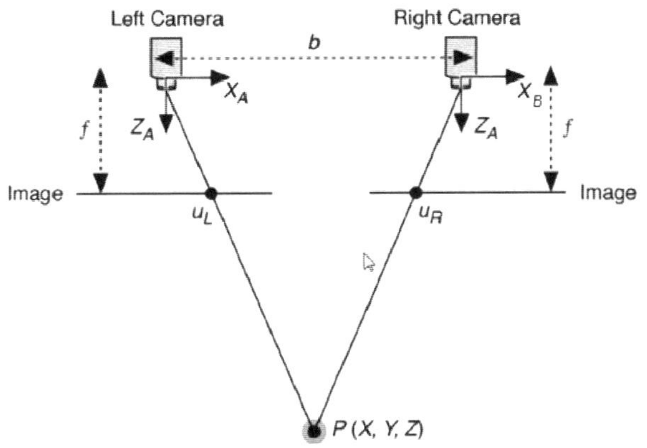

Figure 1. Stereo vision model (taken from [18]).

It is then realized that the depth of the point in relation to the plane of the cameras can be found from three parameters. The focal distance f and the baseline b could be defined previously and are held constant. Thus, to find the depth of objects in the image, it is enough to find the disparity of all the pixels, what we call disparity map.

It is also important to note the distortion that variations in the disparity map can cause in the depth estimation, i.e., verify the measurement obtained accuracy. So, for a variation in depth, it is possible to find [18]:

$$\Delta Z = Z - \frac{bf}{d + \Delta d} = \frac{Z^2 \Delta d}{bf + Z\Delta d} \approx \frac{Z^2 \Delta d}{bf} \tag{9}$$

According to (9), to decrease the distortions, the variable Z cannot be very large while b and f cannot be very small. Since f is an intrinsic feature of the camera, the system is then planned so that b is a distance that allow the desired Z, in order to have less distortion.

So, the problem becomes to find the desired map of disparity. Therefore, to find the map, one must take into account the corresponding pixels of one of the images in the other, of course, if it exists. As the system configuration ensures that the Y coordinate between the images is the same (guaranteed by the synchronization between the cameras to ensure the validity of (5)), given a pixel (x_i, y_i) in image 1, one must look for the pair (x_j, y_i) in image 2 to obtain the local disparity, which is given by $|x_j - x_i|$.

The difficulties in solving the correspondence problem could be presented in the form of ambiguities (more than one matching pair) generated from regions with similar characteristics as texture and color intensity. Furthermore, the method considers that the luminous intensity received by both cameras of a given object will be the same, despite the variation in angle observed (i.e., the surfaces analyzed follow Lambert's law for emission), and the cameras have the same properties on the receiver, such as the gain and the bias. Another problem is the presence of hidden points between the cameras, which means that one point in one image does not correspond to another because it is visible only by one the camera. Such effect is called as occlusion.

Today, the stereo methods are well used and researched, especially where the region of interest has enough information to avoid ambiguities, with wider disparity maps. The basic procedures to implement such methods are as follows [19]:

1) Preprocess the images (optional).
2) For each disparity under consideration, compute all pixels for matching.
3) Consider to aggregate support spatially (only in non-global methods).
4) Across all disparities, compute and find the best correspondent match.
5) Compute a sub-pixel disparity estimate (optional).

The first step consist of preparing both images for analysis and can be done via hardware or software. The captured image can have high noise or even low noise, the last one possibly caused by the camera bias. One way to remove these image noises is to decrease the resolution (hardware filtering) or apply bandpass filters in the algorithm (filtering by software). In this work, it was used an averaging filtering as procedure to eliminate errors caused during the images acquisition and recording, sometimes treated for the captured images having differentiated illumination. This operation is useful to deal with random noise [20].

For the second step, it is possible to use global methods, where the image as a whole is analyzed (increases the accuracy and also the processing time); local methods, where the area used for calculation a pixel disparity is restricted; and hybrid methods, derived from local methods. Regardless of which is chosen, the first step of any dense stereo matching algorithm is a similarity measure that compares pixel values to determinate its correspondence. The most common pixel-based matching costs include sums of squared intensity differences (SSD) and absolute intensity differences (SAD), but there are also methods which are invariant in relation to gain and camera bias, to scale and to illumination, such as the Census Transform [21] [22].

In global stereo matching methods, the goal is to find a solution d that minimizes the global energy $E(d)$ in (11), where $E_d(d)$ measure how the disparity function d agrees with the input image pair, with L being the initial matching cost, and $E_s(d)$ encodes the smoothness assumptions made by the algorithm.

$$E(d) = E_d(d) + \lambda * E_s(d) \tag{10}$$

$$E_d(d) = \sum_{(x,y)} L(x, y, d(x, y)) \tag{11}$$

Meanwhile, the local methods utilize a support region in the disparity space image $L(x, y, d)$, described in (12), to aggregate the matching cost. It is important that the selected support region is large enough to contain texture variability and small enough to not contain many depth discontinuities.

$$L(x, y, d) = w(x, y, d) * L_0(x, y, d) \tag{12}$$

To ensure that the best matching pair of pixels are selected in the local methods, the easiest way is to choose the lowest cost associated with each pair of pixels in a given disparity, a strategy known as "winner-take-all" (WTA). Although it may happen that only one image has single correspondence (reference image) while the other has points paired to multiple pixels, this can be done correctly via dynamic programming, as cooperative algorithms with symmetric constraints. The partial occlusion can also be treated by explicit pairing a pixel in the reference image to a group of pixels in the other one.

Finally, the estimation of sub-pixel disparity works to estimate the disparity at the points where it cannot be found, as occlusion points. With methods such as iterative gradient and interpolation using discrete disparity values, these points also earn a specific disparity and then increase the resolution of the stereo vision system, especially when the disparity variation is smooth. Another post-process tool applied to the disparity map is the association of confidence levels at each pixel depth estimation.

The stereo vision algorithm used to validate the captured images is a Fast SAD local method, which performs pixelwise matching based on a maximum disparity and a windows size entered by the user [23].

B. Raspberry Pi Architecture

The embedded platform Raspberry Pi has been considered fit for use due to its compact format, good processing and low cost, even if the use in computer vision area is new. The Raspberry Pi used was the Raspberry Pi 1 model B, which features 26 GPIO pins, Ethernet connect, two USB connectors, HDMI output and power supply via micro USB. Others features are shown in Table I. To ensure sufficient storage space for digital images to be recorded, it is necessary to use a SD card of at least 8 GB. The kernel used was Raspbian, offered by the manufacturer. The power system provides a voltage of 5 V and a maximum current of 2 A, which is sufficient because in tests it has been analyzed that the basic current for use of the Raspberry is between 300 mA and 550 mA, while each camera Pi requires approximately 250 mA when activated.

The kernel Raspbian is a version of the Debian Hard Float, which supports different program languages, such as Python. The command for capturing the images inserted via terminal enables the software code to record in each Raspberry the image captured by the cameras, via serial communication.

C. Acquisition of the Digital Images

According to official information, the properties of the camera Pi template 1.3 follow the information presented in Table II.

The implemented stereo system consists in the two Camera Pi in the same plane and with equal height, connect via CSI on the Raspberry Pi and correctly powered. It is chosen to use a fixed resolution to capture the images and convert them to grayscale before the stereo vision algorithm, although it will be select only the region of interest. Anyway, the RGB images will also be held in memory because the color is being used as an attribute for the weed's segmentation. The first necessary step to allow the use of the stereo vision system is to calibrate the cameras, which consist of images taken from a frame obtained from a chessboard to extract their intrinsic characteristic. The stereo matching is part of a high-level system, as shown in Figure 2.

To acquire the digital images in the agricultural field, we used the developed stereo digital camera, for validation, which allowed images having 640 x 480 pixels. Also, there was used a wooden frame measuring 0.5 x 0.5 m, which served as a scale factor for characterizing the size of the plants. Figure 3 shows the details of the arrangement for the experimental plots in the agricultural area.

TABLE I. RASPBERRY PI 1 MODEL B FEATURES

Processor	BCM2835 ARM1176JZFS		
Clock	700 MHz	GPIO	26 pins
Memory	512 MB RAM	Ethernet	1 conector
USB Ports	2 USB 2.0 ports	HDMI	1 conector
Camera serial interface (CSI)		Display serial interface (DSI)	
3.5mm jack for audio out		SD card slot	

TABLE II. CAMERA HARDWARE SPECIFICATIONS

Size	25 x 24 x 9 mm
Still resolution	5 MP
Video modes	1080p30, 720p60, 640x480p60/90
Sensor	OmniVision OV5647
Sensor resolution	2592 x 1944 pixels
Sensor image area (W_s x H_s)	3.76 x 2.74 mm
Pixel size	1.4 μm x 1.4 μm
Optical size	1/4"
Full-frame SLR lens equivalent	35 mm
S/N ratio	36 dB
Dynamic range	67 dB @ (times of gain equal to 8)
Fixed focus	1 m - ∞
Focal length	3.60 0.01 mm
Horizontal field of view (HFOV)	53,50 $\pm$ 0,13
Vertical field of view (VFOV)	41.41 $\pm$ 0.11
Focal ratio (F-stop)	2.9

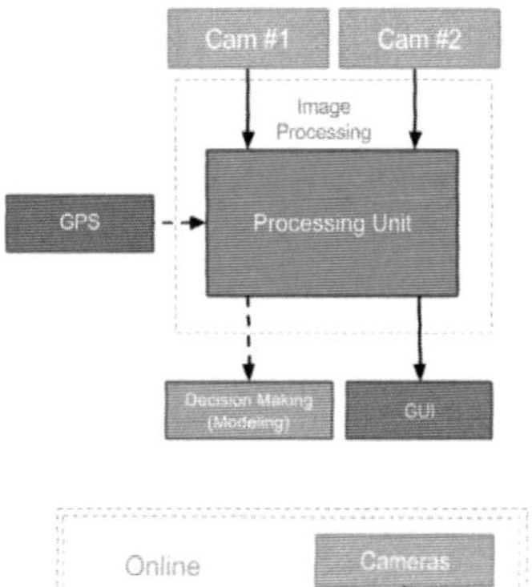

Figure 2. High-level system architecture diagram (taken from [18]).

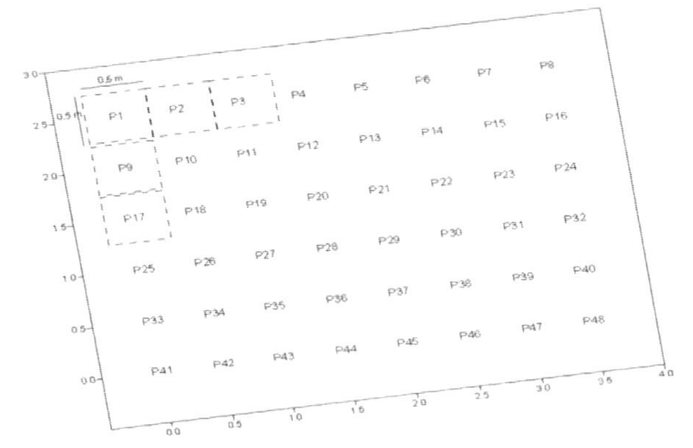

Figure 3. Details of the arrangement for validation based on the use of plots (from P1 to P48) in an agricultural area.

For weed recognition, the moment invariants method has been used, i.e., based on its application for each stereo image obtained from the plots. In fact, any geometrical pattern can be represented by a density distribution function, with respect to a pair of axes fixed in the visual field [24]. Based on such concept, the patterns can also be represented by their two-dimensional moments, with respect to the pair of fixed axes. Such moments of any order can be obtained by a number of methods [25]–[27]. Using the relations between central moments and ordinary moments, the central moments can also be obtained. In addition, by normalizing the central moments in size by using the similitude moment invariants a set of moment invariants can still be used to characterize patterns. Obviously, these are independent of the pattern position in the visual field and also independent of the pattern size. The algorithm for weed recognition based on both the stereo digital images and moment invariants is presented elsewhere [28].

Additionally, after the weed recognition process in each plot, the percentages of occupancy in such areas were considered to estimate a map of weed distribution based on the use of geostatistics. In such way it was possible to calculate the semivariogram, as well as constructing the map related to the management zones for the precision application at variable rate of the herbicide. The semivariogram depicts the spatial autocorrelation of the measured sample points. Once each pair of location is plotted, a model is fit through them. There are certain characteristics that are commonly used to describe these models [29]–[31].

IV. RESULTS AND DISCUSSIONS

With the assembled stereo vision system, as shown in Figure 4, the image quality analysis of the system modulation was evaluated by the Modulation Transfer Function (MTF) of one Camera Pi. To obtain the MTF, it was taken a image containing a linear white-to-black edge, converted the RGB image to grayscale and analyzed the normalized intensity values in a perpendicular line to the edge. The resulting profile is shown as the raw Edge Spread Function (ESF) in Figure 5a, compared with a gaussian smoothed ESF. After this, the LSF was calculated by the derivate of the ESF as shown in Figure 5b and the Fast Fourier Transform (FFT) was used to obtain the MTF, as shown in Figure 5c. Thus, the quantitative evaluation of the system is demonstrably good because of the MTF.

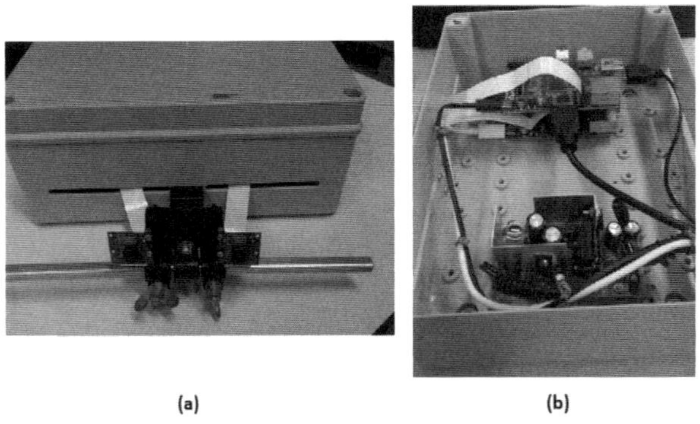

Figure 4. Implementation of the stereo system, where (a) is the stereo rig with the cameras and (b) the two Raspberry Pi on the top and a rectifier on the bottom.

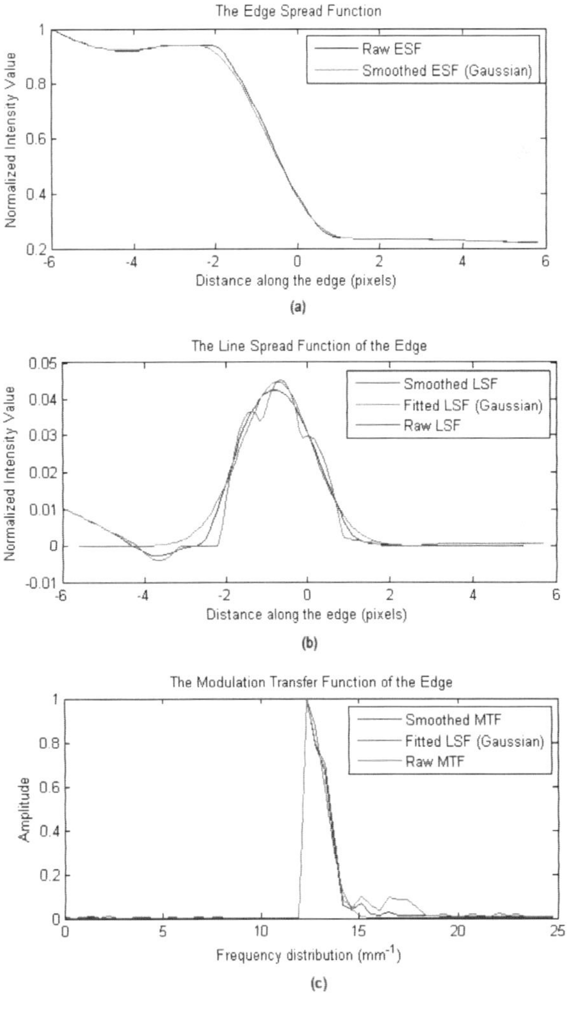

Figure 5. (a) The density profile of an edge; (b) The line spread function (LSF) of this edge; (c) The resultant modulation transfer function (MTF).

It was also desirable to verify whether the values of the field of view provided by the manufacturer are in agreement, as shown in Table II. For this, it was considered the pixel size of 1.4 μm x 1.4 μm, the focal length 3.6 mm, and the sensor resolution of 2592 x 1944 pixels were correct to evaluate the validity of the system, such as:

$$W_s = (s_x)(W) = (1.4\mu)(2592) = 3.63\ m$$
$$H_s = (s_y)(H) = (1.4\mu)(1944) = 2.72\ m$$
$$D_s = \sqrt{W_s^2 + H_s^2} = 4.54\ mm$$
$$HFOV = 2\arctan(W_s 2f) = 53.5^\circ$$
$$VFOV = 2\arctan(H_s 2f) = 41.4^\circ$$
$$DFOV = 2\arctan(D_s 2f) = 64.4^\circ$$

From Table II, it is also possible to obtain $D_s = 4.65$ mm, $DFOV = 65.7^\circ$, and so far such calculated values are in agreement with those provided by the cameras manufacturer.

The next step was to set the stereo system parameters. Considering that the distance between the camera plane and the captured image is equal to 50 cm, a good baseline to avoid distortions and to ensure a good stereo representation can be considered as equal to 6 cm, as inferred in Figure 6, obtained by the variation of b and Z in (8) and (9), respectively. Such result also has shown that the maximum disparity was around 300 pixels.

Besides, the fast SAD stereo method was chosen because offered a reasonable accurate stereo matching associated with a low processing time. The sub-pixels accuracy could be used to refine the results, although they significantly increased the processing time. Additionally, the pseudo-code of the algorithm can be observed in Figure 7.

With the parameters configured, the left and right images were obtained by each Raspberry Pi and its camera, as shown in Figure 8, with Figure 9 as the composite of the images with a red-cyan effect, which allows one to be able to view the image as a 3D shape with the aid of special glasses that has different filters in each lens.

Next, the images were entered as inputs of the chosen stereo vision method. The settings used were the maximum disparity equal to 300 and a window size equal to 5, adequate to catch the small details of the image.

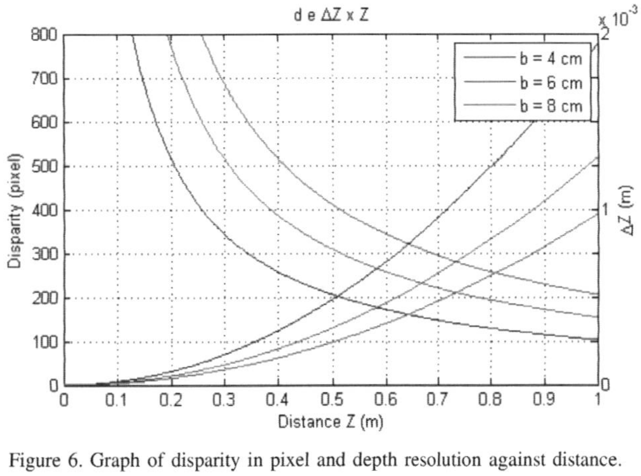

Figure 6. Graph of disparity in pixel and depth resolution against distance.

In addition, we obtained the map of disparity as a result (Figure 10), with association of the values of the baseline and the focal length. Therefore, the depth could be calculated through Equation (8). The entire process can be summarized according to the flowchart in Figure 11. Such flowchart presents aspects related to: the preparation of the hardware for images acquisition; the data transfer to the memory, which can be not only in the Raspberry architectures but also in other external computer; as well as the image processing algorithm for stereo vision and weed recognition.

Begin

Set parameters (window size w and number of disparities n);

Read image sizes; they must have the same height and width;

Initiate the disparity map, matching cost, pixel cost and window cost with zero values;

Calculate pixel cost for the n disparities using the absolute difference of two images;

Calculate integral cost of the pixel cost with cumulative sums;

Calculate window cost using the integral cost convoluted with a matrix h (h is a square matrix of size w with $h(1,1) = h(w,w) = 1$, $h(1,w) = h(w,1) = -1$ and otherwise equal to zero);

Search disparity value by finding the minimum window cost;

If specified, do the subpixel interpolation using polynomial fit;

end.

Figure 7. Stereo matching pseudo-code algorithm.

Figure 8. The images captured by the cameras from the agricultural area.

Figure 9. Red-cyan composite view of the stereo image, in which the 3D shape can be observed with the aid of special glasses.

Figure 12 and 13 show, respectively, the resulting semivariogram based on a Gaussian fitting, and the resulting map for the occupancy of the weed species *Bidens pilosa* in the whole agricultural area used as a pilot for validation.

In general, the herbicide isopropylamine salt of glyphosate is used to control invasive plants and the dose used is of the order of 3 L/hectare. This in practice occurs when the occupation rate of these invasive plants is in the order of 100% in relation to the crop area. Therefore, for the validation pilot that contains 48 plots with a total area of 12 m^2, only 3.6 mL of this agrochemical would be necessary. However, from the acquisition of the images and the digital recognition of the invasive plant patterns, as well as based on the prescription map obtained by the interpolation procedure, it is possible to observe the real occupancy rate in each plot, and the necessary volumes of this agrochemical for an effective localized control, as presented in Table III.

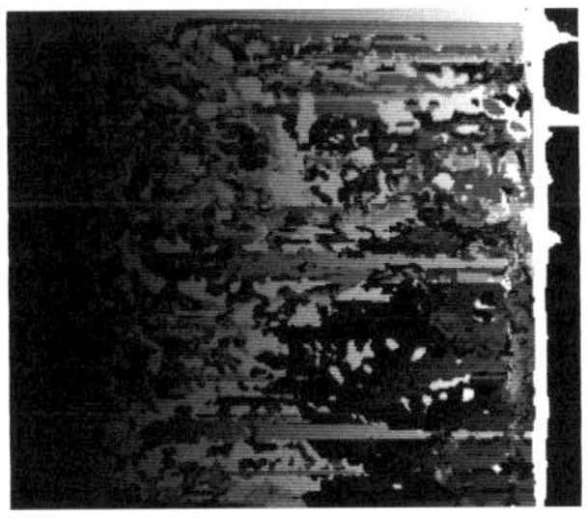

Figure 10. Disparity map.

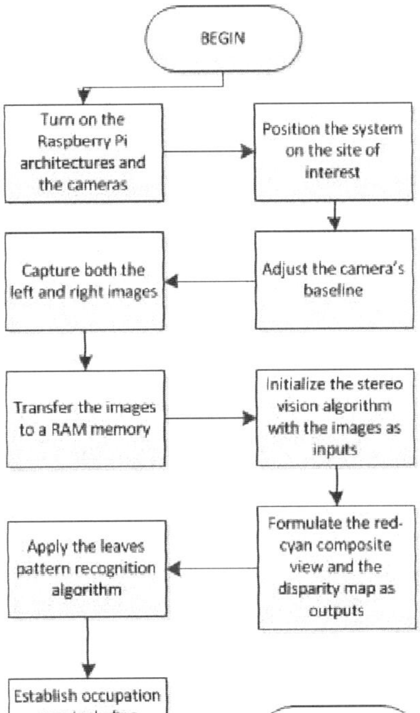

Figure 11. Image capture and processing flow.

In the traditional agricultural management systems, it is still necessary for someone to actually walk through the crops for analyzing the presence or absence of the weeds to support decision making in the crop area.

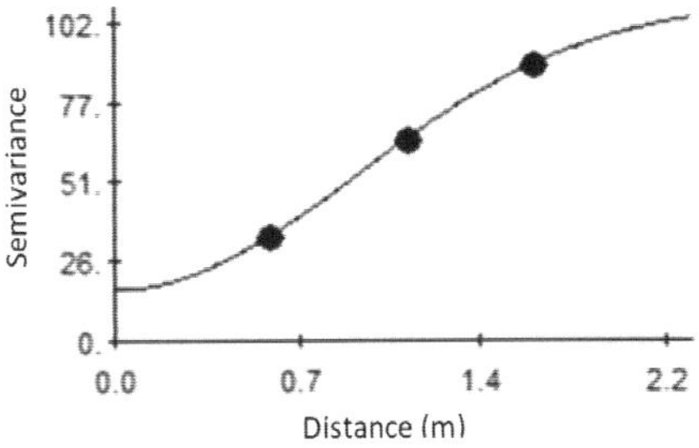

Figure 12. Semivariogram for the occupancy rate of the weed species *Bidens pilosa* (Model: Gaussian, $C_0 = 16.5$; $C_1 = 92.3$; $A = 1.3$). The model parameters are respectively represented by C_0 = nugget effect, C_1 = structural variance, and A = the range in meters.

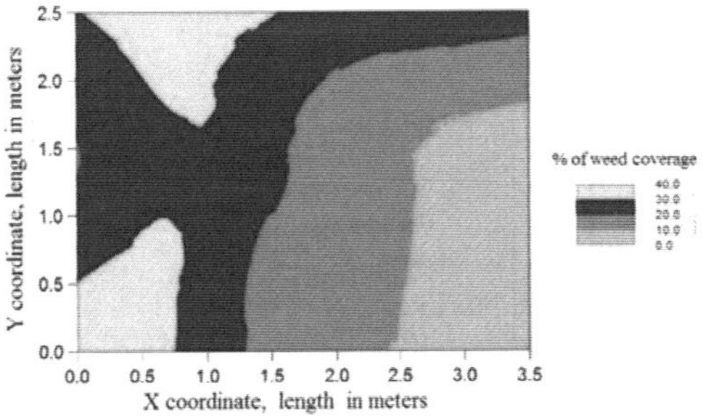

Figure 13. Map for the occupancy of the species *Bidens pilosa* in the whole plot area, i.e., based on the weed pattern recognition and the interpolation process.

TABLE III. THE CALCULATED VOLUME OF THE PRODUCT (HERBICIDE) TO BE APPLIED TO VARIABLE RATE DEPENDING ON THE TOTAL COVERAGE PROVIDED BY THE OCCURRENCE OF THE WEED IN THE PLOTS.

Experimental Plot From P1 to P24	Volume (ml) at precision application	Experimental Plot From P25 to P48	Volume (ml) at precision application
P1	0.040	P25	0.033
P2	0.045	P26	0.035
P3	0.045	P27	0.037
P4	0100	P28	0.027
P5	0.040	P29	0.035
P6	0.043	P30	0.025
P7	0.041	P31	0.031
P8	0.040	P32	0.017
P9	0.037	P33	0.047
P10	0.032	P34	0.057
P11	0.036	P35	0.046
P12	0.033	P36	0.026
P13	0.021	P37	0.039
P14	0.021	P38	0.100
P15	0.023	P39	0.029
P16	0.024	P40	0.100
P17	0.025	P41	0.047
P18	0.035	P42	0.049
P19	0.044	P43	0.048
P20	0.032	P44	0.034
P21	0.029	P45	0.100
P22	0.027	P46	0.035
P23	0.020	P47	0.029
P24	0.019	P48	0.030

However, based on the stereo vision system, one is able to collect images to be analyzed autonomously, in order to obtain information for the prescription of maps for weed control based on herbicides application at variable rate.

V. CONCLUSIONS

The results have shown the usefulness of the developed stereo vision system customized for agricultural application, which is able to provide quality images, as a well to allow a depth model of plants, allied with a low cost portable embedded platform. Therefore, the identification of the weed species, integrated with the occupancy rate, its spatial distribution and depth defined a new approach to weed control, based on the precision application of herbicides into management zones. Besides, the case studied presented the opportunities to minimize costs and environmental impacts, as well as the promotion of the gains in competitiveness.

Future works can be found based on the developed stereo vision system customized for agricultural application taken into account its integration with a machine learning platform in order to aggregate intelligence in the decision making for automatic weed control in agriculture.

ACKNOWLEDGMENT

The authors would like to thank the Embrapa Instrumentation for providing the resources for conducting this research (grants project 01.14.09.001.05.05).

REFERENCES

[1] J. Behmann, A. Mahlein, T. Rumpf, C. Rmer, and L. Plmer, "A review of advanced machine learning methods for the detection of biotic stress in precision crop protection," Precision Agriculture, vol. 16, 06 2015, pp. 239–260.

[2] B. S. Blackmore and C. P. Blackmore, "People, robots and systemic decision making," J. V. Stafford, Ed. Netherlands: Wageningen Academic Publishers, 2007, pp. 433–439, http://oro.open.ac.uk/10032/ [accessed in: July 17th, 2018].

[3] J. C. Christofoletti, "Considerations on the technology for pesticides application." Technical bulletin, vol. 5, 1999, p. 14.

[4] S. Vieira, J. Hatfield, D. R. Nielsen, and J. W. Biggar, "Geostatistical theory and application to variability of some agronomical properties," Hilgardia, vol. 51, 06 1983, pp. 1–75.

[5] Y. Xu, Q. Long, S. Mita, H. Tehrani, K. Ishimaru, and N. Shirai, "Real-time stereo vision system at nighttime with noise reduction using simplified non-local matching cost," IEEE Intelligent Vehicles Symposium (IV), June 2016, pp. 998–1003.

[6] K. Rumyantsev, S. Kravtsov, I. Korovin, and G. Schaefer, "A statistical method for estimating the accuracy of scene reconstruction using a collinear digital stereo vision system," 6th International Conference on Informatics, Electronics and Vision and 7th International Symposium in Computational Medical and Health Technology (ICIEV-ISCMHT), Sept 2017, pp. 1–4.

[7] Z. C. Liu, L. H. Xu, and C. F. Lin, "An improved stereo matching algorithm applied to 3d visualization of plant leaf," 8th International Symposium on Computational Intelligence and Design (ISCID), vol. 2, Dec 2015, pp. 354–358.

[8] M. Liang, X. Huang, C. Chung-Hao, G. Zheng, and A. Tokuta, "Robust calibration of cameras with telephoto lens using regularized least squares," Mathematical Problems in Engineering, 2014.

[9] L. Wang, F. Duan, K. Lv, and S. Chen, "Fisheye-lens-based visual sun compass for perception of spatial orientation," Mathematical Problems in Engineering, 2014.

[10] Y. C. Fang, C. M. Tsai, J. MacDonald, and Y. C. Pai, "Eliminating chromatic aberration in gauss-type lens design using a novel genetic algorithm," Applied Optics, vol. 46, no. 13, May 2007, pp. 2401–2410, http://ao.osa.org/abstract.cfm?URI=ao-46-13-2401 [accessed in: July 17th, 2018].

[11] Y. C. Fang and C. M. Tsai, "Miniature lens design and optimization with liquid lens element via genetic algorithm," Journal of Optics A: Pure and Applied Optics, vol. 10, no. 7, 2008, http://stacks.iop.org/1464-4258/10/i=7/a=075304 [accessed in: July 17th, 2018].

[12] C. C. Chen, C. M. Tsai, and Y. C. Fang, "Optical design of lcos optical engine and optimization with genetic algorithm," Journal of Display Technology, vol. 5, no. 8, Aug 2009, pp. 293–305.

[13] N. Baddour, "Multidimensional wave field signal theory: Mathematical foundations," AIP Advances, vol. 1, no. 2, 2011, https://aip.scitation.org/doi/abs/10.1063/1.3596359 [accessed in: July 17th, 2018].

[14] K. F. Chen and F. L. Yan, "On the integration schemes of retrieving impulse response functions from transfer functions," Mathematical Problems in Engineering, 2010.

[15] M. Li, S. C. Lim, and S. Chen, "Exact solution of impulse response to a class of fractional oscillators and its stability," Mathematical Problems in Engineering, 2011.

[16] P. Lin and C. Liu, "Geometrical mtf computation method based on the irradiance model," Applied Physics B, vol. 102, no. 1, Jan 2011, pp. 243–249, https://doi.org/10.1007/s00340-010-4349-3 [accessed in: July 17th, 2018].

[17] K. Tseng, C. Kung, T. Liao, and H. Chang, "Calculation of modulation transfer function of an optical system by using skew ray tracing," Transactions of the Canadian Society for Mechanical Engineering, vol. 33, 09 2009, pp. 429–442.

[18] N. S. Rosa, P. E. Cruvinel, and J. M. Naime, "Stereo vision embedded system proposal for plant phenotyping," International Journal of Semantic Computing, vol. 11, no. 03, 2017, pp. 293–309, https://www.worldscientific.com/doi/abs/10.1142/S1793351X17400116 [accessed in: July 17th, 2018].

[19] D. Scharstein, View Synthesis Using Stereo Vision. Berlin, Heidelberg: Springer-Verlag, 1999.

[20] A. Konieczka, J. Balcerek, and A. Dbrowski, "Iterative average filtering for image denoising," Signal Processing: Algorithms, Architectures, Arrangements, and Applications (SPA), Sept 2013, pp. 302–305.

[21] R. Szeliski, Computer Vision: Algorithms and Applications, 1st ed. Berlin, Heidelberg: Springer-Verlag, 2010.

[22] J. Lee, D. Jun, C. Eem, and H. Hong, "Improved census transform for noise robust stereo matching," Optical Engineering, vol. 55, 2016, https://doi.org/10.1117/1.OE.55.6.063107 [accessed in: July 17th, 2018].

[23] W. Abbeloos, "Real-time stereo vision," Master's thesis, Karel de Grote-Hogeschool University College, Belgium, May 2010, unpublished.

[24] Y. S. Abu-Mostafa and D. Psaltis, "Recognitive aspects of moment invariants," Pattern Analysis and Machine Intelligence IEEE Transactions, vol. PAMI-6, 1984, pp. 698–706.

[25] H. Ming-Kuei, "Visual pattern recognition by moment invariants," Information Theory, IRE Transactions, vol. 8, 1962, pp. 179–187.

[26] M. R. Teaque, "Image analysis via the general theory of moments," Journal of the Optical Society of America, vol. 70, 1980, pp. 920–930.

[27] J. F. Boyce and W. J. Hossack, "Moment invariants for pattern recognition," Pattern Recognition Letters, vol. 1, 1983, pp. 451–456.

[28] P. E. Cruvinel and D. Karam, "Development of variable rate herbicide application maps for maize crops (zea mays l.) based on computational vision and occupation of broad leaf weed," In: Brazilian Congress of Precision Agriculture (ConBAP), 2010, p. 4.

[29] P. Diamond and M. Armstrong, "Robustness of variograms and conditioning of kriging matrices," Journal of the International Association of Mathematical Geology, vol. 16, 1984, pp. 809–822.

[30] A. McBratney, R. Webster, and T. Burgess, "The design of optimal sampling schemes for local estimation and mapping of regionalized variables," I. Theory and method. Computers and Geosciences, vol. 7, 1981, pp. 331–334.

[31] J. Warnes and B. Ripley, "Problems with likelihood estimation of covariance functions of spatial gaussian processes," Biometrika, vol. 74, 1987, pp. 640–642.

Reliability Assessment of New and Updated Consumer-Grade Activity and Heart Rate Monitors

Salome Oniani
Faculty of Informatics and Control Systems
Georgian Technical University
Tbilisi, Georgia
E-mail: s.oniani@gtu.ge

Sandra I. Woolley
School of Computing and Mathematics
Keele University
Staffordshire, UK
E-mail: s.i.woolley@keele.ac.uk

Ivan Miguel Pires[*,**] and Nuno M. Garcia[*]
[*] Instituto de Telecomunicações,
Universidade da Beira Interior
Covilhã, Portugal
[**] Altranportugal
Lisbon, Portugal
E-mails: impires@it.ubi.pt, ngarcia@di.ubi.pt

Tim Collins
School of Engineering
Manchester Metropolitan University
Manchester, UK
E-mail: t.collins@mmu.ac.uk

Sean Ledger and Anand Pandyan
School of Health and Rehabilitation
Keele University
Staffordshire, UK
E-mails: s.j.ledger@keele.ac.uk, a.d.pandyan@keele.ac.uk

Abstract— **The aim of this paper is to address the need for reliability assessments of new and updated consumer-grade activity and heart rate monitoring devices. This issue is central to the use of these sensor devices and it is particularly important in their medical and assisted living application. Using an example lightweight empirical approach, experimental results for heart rate acquisitions from Garmin VivoSmart 3 (v4.10) smartwatch monitors are presented and analyzed. The reliability issues of optically-acquired heart rates, especially during periods of activity, are demonstrated and discussed. In conclusion, the paper recommends the empirical assessment of new and updated activity monitors, the sharing of this data and the use of version information across the literature.**

Keywords- wearable sensing; activity monitoring; ambulatory heart rate, inter-instrument reliability.

I. INTRODUCTION

Consumer-grade wearable monitoring devices are used across a spectrum of health, well-being and behavioral studies, as well as clinical trials. For example, the U.S. Library of Medicine ClinicalTrials.gov database reports nearly 200 "Completed" to "Not yet recruiting" trials involving Fitbit devices (search accessed 01/05/2018). However, the manufacturers of these devices are generally very clear regarding the intended applications and suitability of their devices, and do not make misleading clinical claims. For example, Garmin Vivosmart "Important Safety and Product Information" [1] advises that the device is for *"recreational purposes and not for medical purposes"* and that *"inherent limitations"* may *"cause some heart rate readings to be inaccurate"*, similarly, Fitbit device "Important Safety and Product Information" declares that the device is *"not a medical device"* and *"accuracy of Fitbit devices is not intended to match medical devices or scientific measurement devices"* [2]. Given that these devices *are* being used in clinical applications, and with future clinical applications anticipated [3], it is important that device reliability is assessed.

In terms of meeting user expectations, it is noteworthy that, at the time of writing, Fitbit's motion to dismiss a class action has been denied. The complaint alleged *"gross inaccuracies and recording failures"* [4] because *"products frequently fail to record any heart rate at all or provide highly inaccurate readings, with discrepancies of up to 75 bpm"* [5]. Indeed, ambulatory heart rate acquisition from optical sensors is known to be very challenging [6]. One of the main challenges is the range of severe interference effects caused by movement [7][8]. Optical heart rate signals can also be affected by skin color [9] and aging [10]. Yet, optical heart rate acquisition remains a desirable alternative to chest strap electrocardiogram (ECG) monitoring in consumer-level activity monitors, where comfortability, ease-of-use and low cost are prioritized.

After selection of an activity monitor model based on recorded parameters, study requirements and deployment needs [11], the calibration and validation of wearable monitors [12][13] can be onerous. Best practice requires a substantial time and resource investment for researchers to calibrate and validate sufficiently large numbers of their devices with a large and diverse cohort of representative users performing a range of anticipated activities. At the same time, commercial monitors can frequently and automatically update both software and firmware that can alter device function, data collection and data reporting, potentially compromising previous validation. But, of course, manufacturers are under no obligation to report the detail of their proprietary algorithms or the specifics of version changes.

Devices that have the same model name, but operate with different software and firmware versions, are distinct devices; they should not be treated as identical devices. Ideally, devices would be clearly differentiated in the literature with data for manufacturer, model *and* version data. While there may be limited (if any) opportunity for researchers to reversion commercial device software to repeat published experiments, the provision of version information would, at least, limit the potential for incorrect aggregations of data for devices that operate with different software and firmware versions.

A number of studies have reported on the validity of different monitoring device models. For example, Fokkema et al. [14] reported on the step count validity and reliability of ten different activity trackers. Thirty-one healthy participants performed 30-minute treadmill walking activities while wearing ten activity trackers. The research concluded that, in general, consumer activity trackers perform better at an average (4.8 km/h) and vigorous (6.4 km/h) walking speed than at slower walking speeds.

In another study, Wahl et al. [15] evaluated the validity of eleven wearable monitoring devices for step count, distance and Energy Expenditure (EE) with participants walking and running at different speeds. The study reported results with the commonly used metrics: Mean Absolute Percentage Error (MAPE) and IntraClass Correlation (ICC) showing that most devices, except Bodymedia Sensewear, Polar Loop, and Beurer AS80 models, had good validity (low MAPE, high ICC) for step count. However, for distance, all devices had low ICC (<0.1) and high MAPE (up to 50%), indicating poor validity. The measurement of EE was acceptable for Garmin, Fitbit and Withings devices (comprising Garmin Vivofit; Garmin Vivosmart; Garmin Vivoactive; Garmin Forerunner 920XT; Fitbit Charge; Fitbit Charge HR; Withings Pulse Ox Hip; Withings Pulse Ox Wrist) which had low-to-moderate MAPEs. The Bodymedia Sensewear, Polar Loop, and Beurer AS80 devices had high MAPEs (up to 56%) for all test conditions.

There is a growing number of similar studies that compare different recordings from different models of consumer activity monitors. However, across this literature, and in reviews of this literature [16], it is common practice to provide version data for the software used for statistical analyses of device performance, but it is not common practice to report version information for the devices themselves. As an example of device ambiguity, a reference to "Garmin Vivosmart" could refer to either Garmin Vivosmart 3 or Garmin Vivosmart HR. The date of a given publication might help disambiguate the model variant but will not help identify the version. The Vivosmart HR had 14 versions from 2.10 to 4.30 over approximately 30 months (each update comprising between 1 and 11 items, such as, *"improved calculation of Intensity Minutes"* and *"Various other improvements"*) [17]. At the time of writing, the Garmin Vivosmart 3 (v4.10) is the latest of 9 versions.

In Section II of this paper, a lightweight approach for device assessment is presented using the Garmin Vivosmart 3 smartwatch as an example device; the results of an experimental assessment are presented in Section III. Recommendations for device assessment are discussed in Section IV and, conclusions and recommendations for further work are summarized in Section V.

II. METHOD AND MATERIALS

Four Garmin Vivosmart 3 smartwatches (all versioned SW v4.10 throughout the data acquisitions during May 2018) were worn, as shown in Figure 1, by four healthy researcher participants, P1-P4 outlined in Table I, during the treadmill walking activities summarized in Table II. The walking speeds: slow, moderate, fast and vigorous, were selected based on reports in the literature [18][19] and were performed on an h/p/cosmos Pulsar treadmill. To support reproducibility [20], we report further details about materials in the appendix.

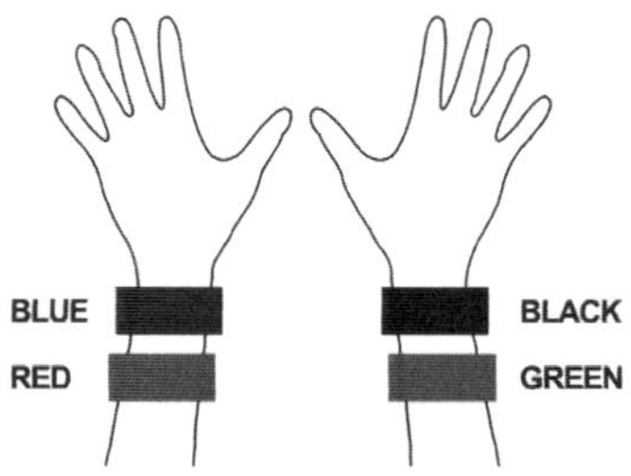

Figure 1. Activity monitor positions (color-coded for reference).

TABLE I. PARTICIPANT SUMMARY

Participant	Age (yrs)	Gender	Height (m)	Weight (kg)	BMI
P1	25	Female	1.69	58	20.03
P2	54	Female	1.62	65	24.7
P3	47	Male	1.75	70	22.8
P4	28	Male	1.70	76	26.2

TABLE II. THE WALKING ACTIVITY SCHEDULE

Time (minutes)	20	20	20	20
Activity	Slow walking (2.4 km/h)	Moderate walking (3.2 km/h)	Fast Walking (4.8 km/h)	Vigorous walking (6.4 km/h)

All participants reported regularly partaking brisk-intensive exercise outside largely sedentary academic/working roles. Participant 1 was ambidextrous. All other participants were right-handed. (Ethical approval for "Health Technology Assessment and Data Analytics", ERP2329" was obtained from Keele University.)

The slow walking activity was prefaced by two minutes of standing with arms down. Pulse readings were taken from a Polar H10 chest strap ECG monitor at 1-minute intervals throughout the activity.

Data (from the logged Garmin .FIT files) was downloaded from the watches after each activity and converted into .CSV formats and imported into Excel. Dates and times were converted from the Garmin 16- and 32-bit timestamps used in the .FIT file [21] into standard Excel date-time serial numbers.

Mean Absolute Percentage Error (MAPE) and the IntraClass Correlation (ICC) [22] were used to compare the heart rate recordings from the watches with the baseline ECG device. Step counts were also acquired and analyzed but, due to limitations of space, are not reported here.

III. Results

Figure 2 shows the heart rate recordings for P1-P4 from the treadmill walking activities. Variability in recorded values can be seen at both slower and faster walking speeds and, notably, differs between participants. For analysis of the acquired data we calculated the MAPE (compared with the ECG chest strap reference) and ICC values listed in Table III. As shown, treadmill acquisitions for participants P2 and P3 produced higher MAPEs (including MAPEs over 10%: the level often taken as the upper bound of "acceptable" errors) and lower ICCs. This could, in part, be attributed to the increased age of participants P2 and P3 compared to P1 and P4. As shown in Figure 2, for P2 there were some abnormally low but sparse heart rate recordings from the "blue" device and, to a lesser extent, the "red" device. For P3, the "blue" device recorded decreasing heart rates when the actual heart rate increased during the vigorous walking activity. This produced a near zero ICC.

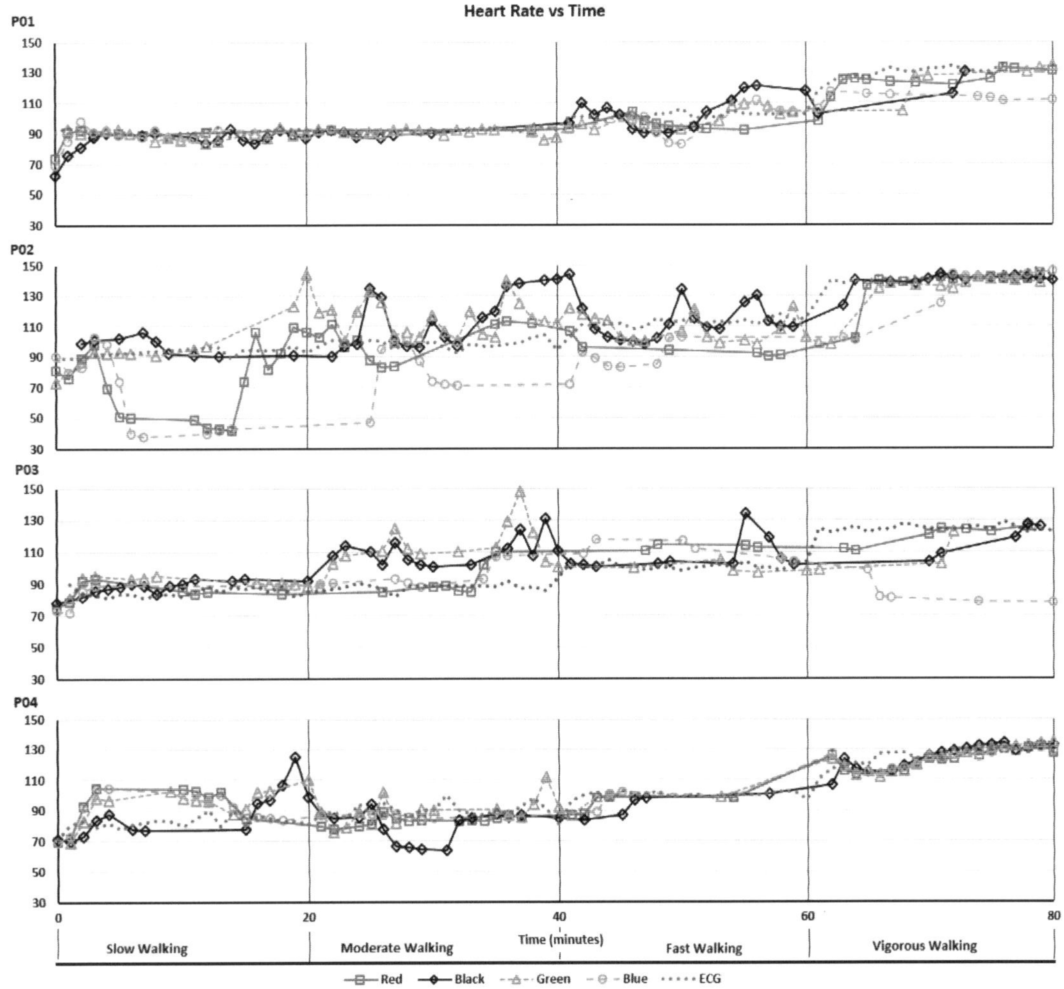

Figure 2. Heart rate recordings acquired during treadmill walking activities.

TABLE III. VALUES OF MAPE AND ICC FROM TREADMILL WALKING ACTIVITIES

Participant	*Black*		*Blue*		*Green*		*Red*	
ID	*MAPE*	*ICC*	*MAPE*	*ICC*	*MAPE*	*ICC*	*MAPE*	*ICC*
P1	7.08%	0.68	7.13%	0.71	4.34%	0.81	5.62%	0.90
P2	9.60%	0.69	15.55%	0.67	11.94%	0.58	13.42%	0.71
P3	13.00%	0.47	14.00%	0.02	16.00%	0.19	9.00%	0.84
P4	8.69%	0.84	6.14%	0.91	8.04%	0.86	7.57%	0.89

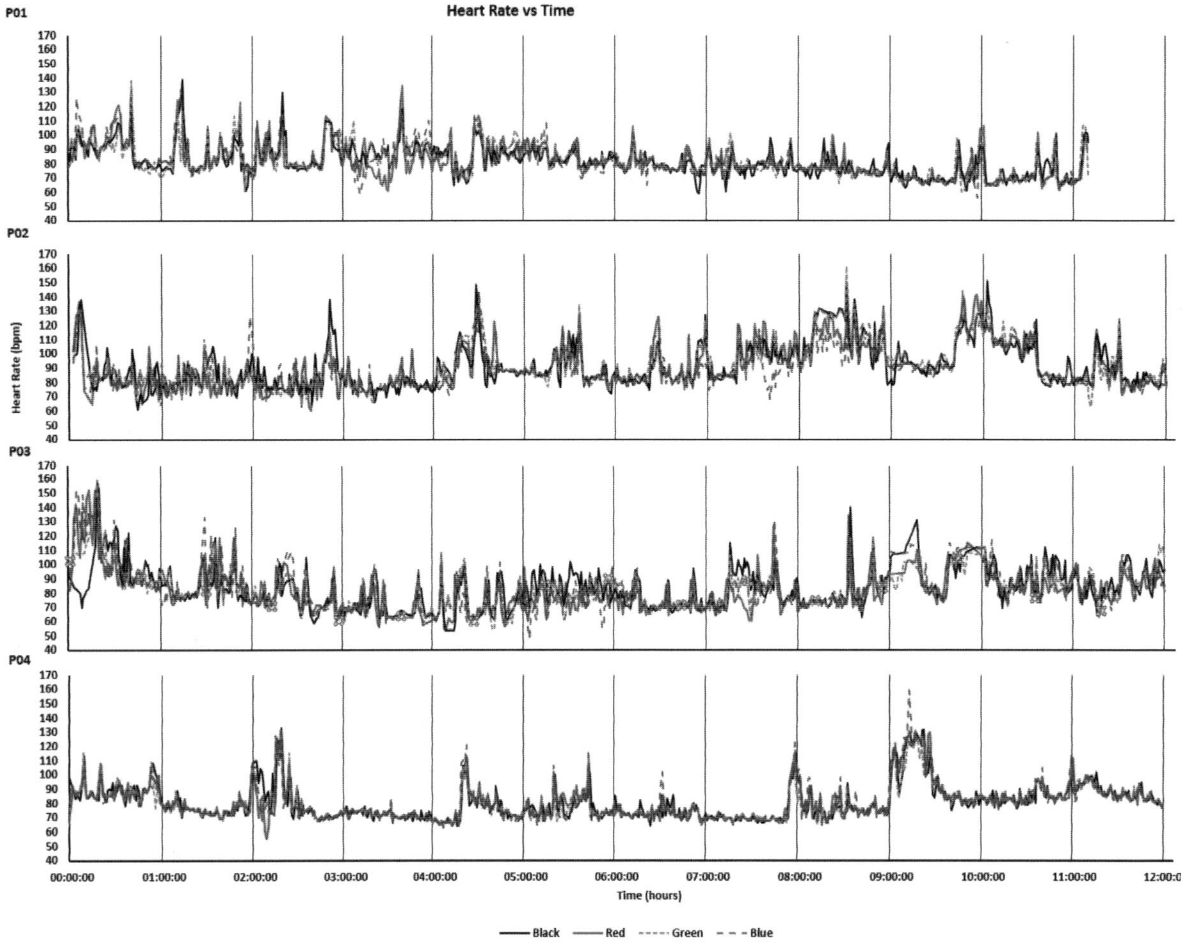

Figure 3. Heart rate recordings acquired during 12-hr everyday living.

The devices were also worn by participants for 12-hour periods during uncontrolled everyday activities. The recorded heart rates are shown in Figure 3. Intraclass correlations and confidence intervals for treadmill walking and 12-hr use are plotted, respectively, in Figures 4 and 5. As anticipated, these indicated poor performance during the treadmill activity. However, as shown in Figure 5, the devices performed more consistently during the prolonged acquisitions of activities of everyday living, when activity levels were generally lower on average.

IV. DISCUSSION

The lightweight assessment approach exemplified here is not, and could not be, prescriptive. A useful approach must incorporate participants and activities that have relevance to the intended study; otherwise, it would have little value. It is also important to ensure that the duration of activities is sufficient for devices to record enough data. We established 20-minute durations empirically for each treadmill walking speed by monitoring the frequency of logged readings and expanding the window to ensure several readings would be logged for each speed. For other devices where, for example, per-minute records are available, the activity duration could be reduced.

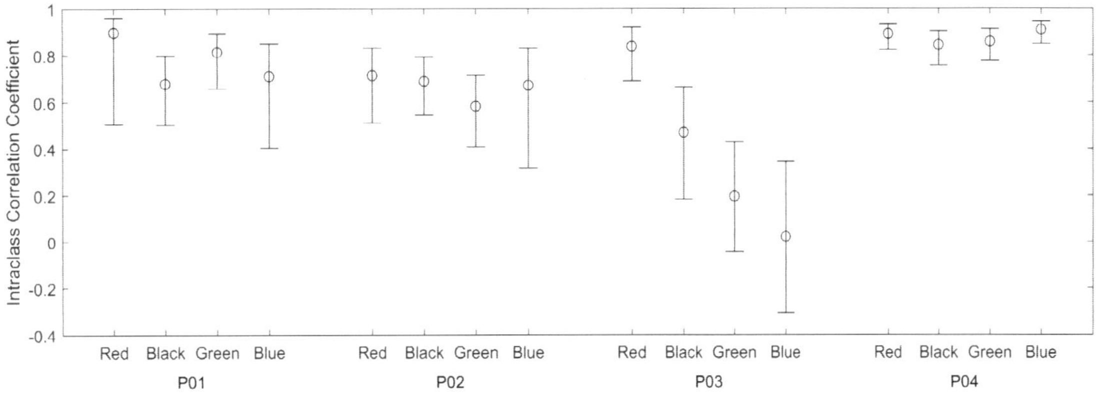

Figure 4. ICC for each device compared with ECG chest strap baseline recordings with 90% confidence intervals for treadmill activities.

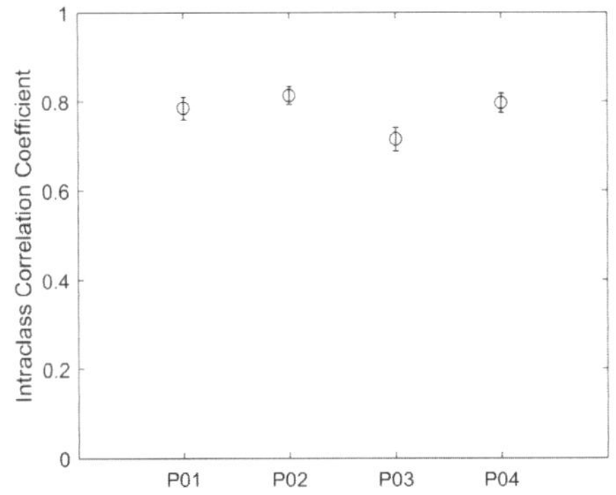

Figure 5. Inter-instrument ICC values for 12-hrs everyday living.

Of course, a comprehensive reliability assessment would be preferable to the approach outlined here. Similarly, this lightweight empirical approach is preferable to no assessment at all or reliance on outdated, irrelevant or unreproducible reports in the literature. Of the several limitations of the presented approach, there was, intentionally, a small number of participants, a limited sample of unrepeated activities and there were no reference recordings for the 12-hr everyday activity. (Reference readings from finger-worn pulse oximeters were attempted, but the devices repeatedly failed to maintain accurate readings). However, with just four participants and two activity acquisitions, we were able to quickly and simply obtain an insight into the reliability of the devices *at their current version*, have an appreciation of their limitations and, also, a degree of confidence regarding their potential for study acquisitions.

V. CONCLUSION AND FUTURE WORK

There is much scope for further work to improve reproducibility across the activity monitoring domain and to assist researchers evaluate and re-evaluate new and updated devices. We have demonstrated an empirical approach to device assessment that provides an example lightweight assessment that is not onerous and could easily be repeated as and when devices are updated.

Despite issues associated with reliable optical heart rate acquired from the wrist during activity, we might hope that future and updated consumer devices would i) be better at identifying erroneous values and avoid reporting them and ii) be better at correctly estimating values. It would be unwise to assume all device upgrades will necessarily result in improved device performance in all aspects, however, future research into sensor positioning, sensor array configurations, multi-sensor fusions and advanced signal processing techniques could significantly contribute to improved sensing reliability.

The U.S. Food and Drug Administration has established a new "Digital Health Software Precertification (Pre-Cert) Program" [23] that aspires toward a more agile approach to digital health technology regulation. It recognizes the *"iterative characteristics"* of new consumer devices [24]. In addition, the Consumer Technology Association recently defined CTA-2065; a new protocol to test and validate the accuracy of heart rate monitoring devices under the conditions of everyday living – from dynamic indoor cycling to sedentary lifestyles. We recommend that there is also some means to enable and encourage the sharing of version-by-version device reliability assessment data between manufacturer/s, users and researchers.

In a systematic review of consumer-wearable activity trackers, Everson et al. [16], recommend that *"future studies on the measurement properties of the trackers should be sure to initialize the tracker properly and indicate in the publication how this was done so others can replicate the process. Providing the specific tracker type, date purchased, and date tested would also be important."* We additionally recommend that full device details, including software and firmware versions, are reported in the literature.

ACKNOWLEDGEMENT

The authors wish to thank Professor Fiona Polack, Software and Systems Engineering Research, Keele

University for her valuable input and support in resourcing this work. The authors also thank Professor Barbara Kitchenham for her advice on protocol design and statistics.

The authors also wish to acknowledge contributions from FCT project UID/EEA/50008/2013 and COST Actions IC1303 (AAPELE – Architectures, Algorithms and Protocols for Enhanced Living Environments) and IC1401 (Memristors - Devices, Models, Circuits, Systems and Applications (MemoCiS)).

APPENDIX

The further material details were as follows:

Garmin Vivosmart 3 software/firmware versions: SW: v4.10; TSC: v1.10; SNS: v5.90. Devices were initialized according to the arm worn and all data was taken directly from logged .FIT files. Devices were purchased on 9th March 2018 and acquisitions made during May 2018. Their serial numbers were as follows: Black – 560185378, Red – 560185383, Blue – 560640435, Green – 560639717.

The treadmill was an h/p/cosmos Pulsar treadmill, h/p/cosmos Sports & Medical Gmbh, Nussdorf-Traunstein, Germany. (cos100420b; ID: X239W80479043; OP19: 0319 1139)

Polar H10 chest heart rate monitor (FCC ID: INW1W; Model: 1W; IC: 6248A-1W; SN: C7301W0726005; ID: 14C00425; Firmware: 2.1.9 and data acquired via Polar Beat 2.5.3.

REFERENCES

[1] Garmin Vivosmart 2016, "Important safety and product information," Instruction Leaflet supplied with Vivosmart 3 (v4.10), 190-02068-01_0D

[2] Fitbit, "Important safety and product information," Last Updated March 20, 2017, [Online]. Available from: https://www.fitbit.com/uk/legal/safety-instructions 2018.06.02

[3] M. M. Baig, H. GholamHosseini, A. A. Moqeem, F. Mirza, and M. Lindén, "A systematic review of wearable patient monitoring systems–current challenges and opportunities for clinical adoption," Journal of Medical Systems, vol. 41(7): 115, pp. 1-9, 2017.

[4] Business Wire, "Federal court denies Fitbit's motion to dismiss class action lawsuit alleging gross inaccuracies and recording failures in PurePulse™ heart rate monitors, June 05, 2018: [Online]. Available from: https://www.businesswire.com/news/home/20180605006652/en/Federal-Court-Denies-Fitbits-Motion-Dismiss-Class 2018.06.02

[5] Lieff Cabraser Civil Justice Blog, June 5, 2018, [Online]. Available from: https://www.lieffcabraser.com/2018/06/federal-court-denies-fitbit-motion-to-dismiss-class-action-lawsuit-inaccuracies-purepulse-heart-rate-monitors/ 2018.06.07

[6] M. Lang, "Beyond Fitbit: A critical appraisal of optical heart rate monitoring wearables and apps, their current limitations and legal implications," Albany Law Journal of Science & Technology 28(1), pp. 39-72, 2017.

[7] Z. Zhang, "Heart rate monitoring from wrist-type photoplethysmographic (PPG) signals during intensive physical exercise," In Signal and Information Processing (GlobalSIP), IEEE Global Conference on, pp. 698-702, December 2014.

[8] Z. Zhang, Z. Pi, and B. Liu, "TROIKA: A general framework for heart rate monitoring using wrist-type photoplethysmographic signals during intensive physical exercise," IEEE Transactions on Biomedical Engineering, vol. 62(2), pp. 522-531, 2015.

[9] W. T. Cecil, K. J. Thorpe, E. E. Fibuch, and G. F.Tuohy, "A clinical evaluation of the accuracy of the Nellcor N-100 and Ohmeda 3700 pulse oximeters," Journal of Clinical Monitoring, vol. 4(1), pp. 31-36, 1988.

[10] K. S. Hong, K. T. Park, and J. M. Ahn, "Aging index using photoplethysmography for a healthcare device: comparison with brachial-ankle pulse wave velocity," Healthcare Informatics Research, vol. 21(1), pp. 30-34, 2015.

[11] T. Collins, S. Aldred, S. I. Woolley, and S. Rai, "Addressing the deployment challenges of health monitoring devices for a dementia study," In Proceedings of the 5th EAI International Conference on Wireless Mobile Communication and Healthcare, pp. 202-205, 2015.

[12] D. R. Bassett Jr, A. V. Rowlands, and S. G. Trost, "Calibration and validation of wearable monitors", Medicine and Science in Sports and Exercise, 44(1 Suppl 1), p.S32, 2012.

[13] P. Freedson, H. R. Bowles, R. Troiano, and W. Haskell,. "Assessment of physical activity using wearable monitors: recommendations for monitor calibration and use in the field," Medicine and Science in Sports and Exercise, vol. 44(1 Suppl 1):S1-S4, pp. 1-6, 2012.

[14] T. Fokkema, T. J. Kooiman, W. P. Krijnen, C. P. Van Der Schans, and M. De Groot, "Reliability and validity of ten consumer activity trackers depend on walking speed," Medicine and Science in Sports and Exercise, 49(4), pp. 793-800, 2017.

[15] Y. Wahl, P. Düking, A. Droszez, P. Wahl, and J. Mester, "Criterion-validity of commercially available physical activity tracker to estimate step count, covered distance and energy expenditure during sports conditions," Frontiers in Physiology, vol. 8:725, pp. 1-12, 2017.

[16] K. R. Evenson, M. M. Goto, and R. D. Furberg, "Systematic review of the validity and reliability of consumer-wearable activity trackers," International Journal of Behavioral Nutrition and Physical Activity, vol. 12(1):159, pp. 1-22, 2015.

[17] Garmin 2018, "Updates & Downloads: vivosmart HR software - version 4.30 as of March 7, 2018," [Online]. Available from: https://www8.garmin.com/support/download_details.jsp?id=9527 2018.05.30

[18] P. M. Grant, P.M. Dall., S. I. Mitchell, and M. H.Granat, "Activity-monitor accuracy in measuring step number and cadence in community-dwelling older adults," Journal of Aging and Physical Activity, 16(2), pp. 201-214, 2008.

[19] J. Takacs, et al. "Validation of the Fitbit One activity monitor device during treadmill walking," Journal of Science and Medicine in Sport, vol. 17(5), pp. 496-500, 2014.

[20] S. Krishnamurthi and J. Vitek, "The real software crisis: Repeatability as a core value," Communications of the ACM, vol. 58(3), pp. 34-36, 2015.

[21] Garmin, 2018. FIT Software Development Kit (version 20.56.00), [Online]. Available from: https://www.thisisant.com/resources/fit 2018.06.02

[22] K. O. McGraw and S. P. Wong, "Forming inferences about some intraclass correlation coefficients," Psychological methods, vol. 1(1), p. 30-46, 1996.

[23] U.S. Food and Drug Administration "Digital health software precertification (pre-cert) program," [Online]. Available from: https://www.fda.gov/MedicalDevices/DigitalHealth/DigitalHealthPreCertProgram/ucm567265.htm 2018.06.13

[24] "CTA announces standard to improve heart rate monitoring in wearables," May 2, 2018, [Online]. Available from: https://www.cta.tech/News/Press-Releases/2018/May/CTA-Announces-Standard-to-Improve-Heart-Rate-Monit.aspx 2018.06.1

Hydriney: A Mobile Application to Help in the Control of Kidney Stones Disease

Tânia Valente*, Ivan Miguel Pires*,**, Nuno M. Garcia** and Nuno Pombo**
* Altranportugal
Lisbon, Portugal
** Instituto de Telecomunicações,
Universidade da Beira Interior
Covilhã, Portugal
e-mails: tania.ss.valente@gmail.com, impires@it.ubi.pt, ngarcia@di.ubi.pt and ngpombo@di.ubi.pt

João Orvalho
Instituto Politécnico de Coimbra
Coimbra, Portugal
e-mail: orvalho@esec.pt

Abstract— **Nephrolithiasis disease requires the management and registration of the different values on a daily basis. These values include the monitoring of daily water consumption and the urinary pH, which should be registered in a mobile application. One of the authors of this paper had the disease and decided to design and develop the Hydriney application. This application meets the needs of people who want to manage all aspects of nephrolitiasis condition and keep it under control. The application tracks almost all aspects of the kidney stones treatment and provides detailed reports, charts, and statistics to share with the urologist. The user should set the daily goals and transcribe the medicine prescription to the mobile application. Then, the application will help him to automate the records for better decision-making in treatment of kidney stones disease. This paper shows that nephrolithiasis management is a health area where Hydriney can enhance the quality of life for people living with this condition.**

Keywords- mHealth; Hydriney; Nephrolithiasis; Water Consumption; Urinary pH; kidney Stones; Uralyt-U; Calcium oxalate; Calcium phosphate; Uric acid.

I. Introduction

One of the most common problems in the urology clinical area is the nephrolithiasis disease, popularly known as kidney stones (see Figure 1). Mobile devices (*e.g.*, smartphones, tablets, and other specific devices) may help in the control of the treatment of this disease [1].

Kidney stones are solid crystals formed from the salts in urine and affect up to 5% of the world population and the lifetime risk of passing a kidney stone is about 8-10% [2]. A kidney stone is caused by a disruption in the balance between solubility and precipitation of salts in the kidneys and the urinary tract.

Some metabolic disorders, genetic conditions, and dietary choices might contribute to their development. A stone forms when urine is in a "supersaturated" state with insoluble crystal-forming substances composed of calcium (Ca), calcium oxalate (CaOx), calcium phosphate (CaP) and uric acid, due to the dehydration or genetic predisposition to over-excrete these ions in the urine [4].

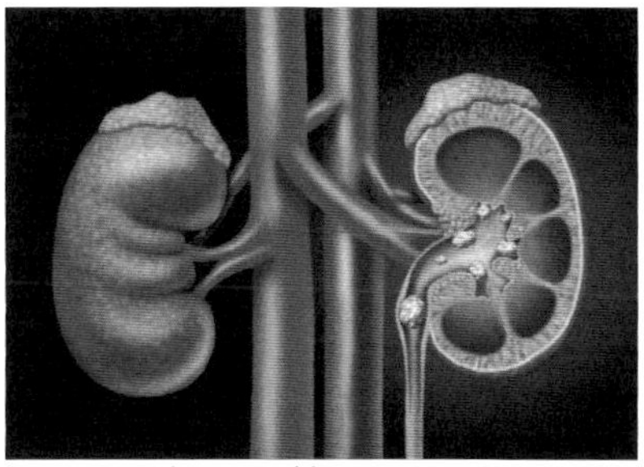

Figure 1. Kidney stones [3]

One of the most common reasons why people get kidney stones is the lack of sufficient water in the body. The body must produce at least 2 liters of urine to reduce risks of kidney stones to half [5]. People who live in warm climates and those who sweat a lot may be at higher risk than others.

Going to the doctor and taking medications are important, but not sufficient for optimal care. Individuals with kidney stones can reduce the short and long term impact of the disease by practicing self-management skills. Using mobile health technology makes it easier to control kidney stones disease. Regarding mobile applications for kidney stones, it has been found that most existing solutions are to a specific feature "food/diet". There is the mobile application named "StoneMD" [6] that was created by urologists and developers and that presents a list of foods (calcium, oxalate and citrates) classified and categorized according to the oxalate content/nutritional guidelines. If the patient has been diagnosed with an oxalate stone condition, there is the application named "oxaBrow" that can help him to manage his Oxalate Diet [7].

There are also several applications for medication like "Medisafe" [8] and water consumption control like "Waterlogged" [9]. "Medisafe" is one of the most popular medication management apps today working as a virtual pillbox on patient's smartphone. "Waterlogged" allows the user to set reminders for himself at scheduled intervals to drink some water. In order to have a complete and suitable app, the Hydriney application was developed.

The rest of this paper is organized as follows. Section II describes the methods of diagnosis and the types of kidney stones. Section III presents the existent treatment methods. Section IV presents the mobile application developed. Finally, Section V presents the conclusions of this project.

II. DIAGNOSIS AND TYPES OF KIDNEY STONES

The kidney stones diagnosis is suspected by the typical symptom of abdominal pain. Often, kidney stones are found on an X-Ray or ultrasound taken of someone who complains of blood in the urine. Imaging tests, including the X-Rays, are usually done to confirm the diagnosis (See Figure 2) [10].

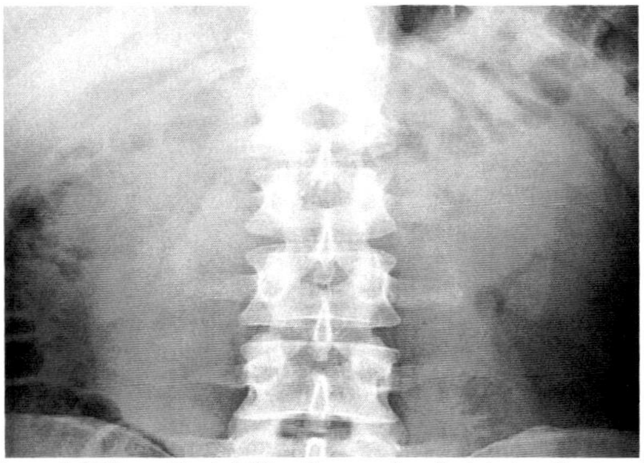

Figure 2. X-Ray with visibility of an opacity of calcic tonality, in red, suggesting the presence of a kidney stone at 1cm outside the left kidney [10]

Radiologists should measure the size of a kidney stone to help estimate the chance it will pass on its own. Stones measuring less than 4mm will pass on their own. Kidney stones develop when the urine cannot dilute all of the substances in it, like Calcium and Uric acid. As example, in Figure 3, a Calcium Oxalate stone dehydrate is presented.

Figure 3. Surface of a kidney stone with tetragonal crystals of Weddellite [11]

There are three major types of kidney stones, including: Calcium (Ca), Struvite and Acid Uric stones. These are:

- Calcium (Ca)
  - The most common type of kidney stones, that usually are in the form of Calcium Oxalate (CaOx);
  - Oxalate is a naturally occurring substance found in food and is also made daily by the liver [12];
  - Calcium stones may also occur in the form of Calcium Phosphate (CaP);
  - Calcium Phosphate (CaP) stones are much less common and typically develop in patients with metabolic or hormonal disorders [12];
  - Calcium stones form in an alkaline urine with a pH higher than 7.
- Struvite
  - Struvite stones form in response to an infection, such as a bacterial urinary tract infection;
  - These stones can grow quickly and become quite large and occur most commonly in women [12].
- Uric acid stones
  - These stones tend to form in patients with hyperuricosuria and gout diseases.
  - About 15-20% of patients with uric acid stones have a history of gout [13];
  - With an urinary pH of less than 5.5, uric acid is poorly soluble, but solubility increases with a pH greater than 6.5 [14];
  - These stones are not as visible on a plain X-ray.

III. TREATMENT OF KIDNEY STONES

The treatment of kidney stones depends on the type. There are medications that the urologist doctor can prescribe to allow the stone to pass naturally. For stones with a size less than 2.5cm, there is the procedure lithotripsy that uses shock waves to break the stone into smaller pieces. Then, the pieces can be more easily expelled from the body. For most people with recurrent kidney stones, a combination of drinking enough fluids, avoiding urinary infections, and specific treatment with medications will significantly reduce or stop new stone formation.

Certain medicines, such as Acalka, reduce calcium excretion and decrease the chance of having another calcium stone. For people who have a high level of uric acid in their urine, or who make uric acid stones, the medicine Uralyt-U will usually stop the formation of new stones. This medicine re-dissolves any crystals that are already present in the urine. The administration method of Uralyt-U includes granules (1 g/dose), that should be taken, 3 times per day and dissolved in a glass of water and then drunk. Uralyt-U has a special indicator paper, which consists on yellow paper strips and a color scale within the range of 5.6 to 8 (See Figure 4). Lower numbers are more acidic and higher numbers are less acidic. The patient should bring the table every time he visits the doctor.

Figure 4. Test stripes of Uralyt-U medicine

At the main meals (every morning, midday and in the evening), before taking each dose, the patient should dip one paper strip into the fresh urine for a few seconds. The color of the strip will change and then it should be compared with the color scale. After matching the paper strip with the color scale, the user should register the urinary pH value measure in a traditional table.

IV. APPLICATION

The Hydriney application allows the patient to use it as a "personal schedule" of the kidney stones disease. Hydriney has innovative features to help improve life with kidney stones disease. There is a left side menu following the Google design pattern with the following features: Profile; Medication; Consumption of H2O; pH of Urine (See Figure 5).

A. Profile

When the application starts, the user is re-directed to the "Profile" module. This module, presented in Figure 6, focuses on individual parameters like height, weight, age and daily water goal, in liters (l). The user must register his weight and height for the automatic calculation of the Body Mass Index (BMI).

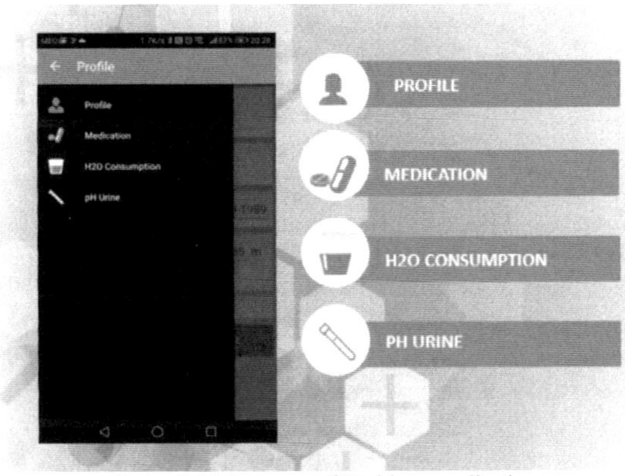

Figure 5. Main screen of Hydriney application

B. Water

Goals and reminders really help throughout the day. Hydriney reminds the user to drink according to the progress which is filled with the volumes consumed.

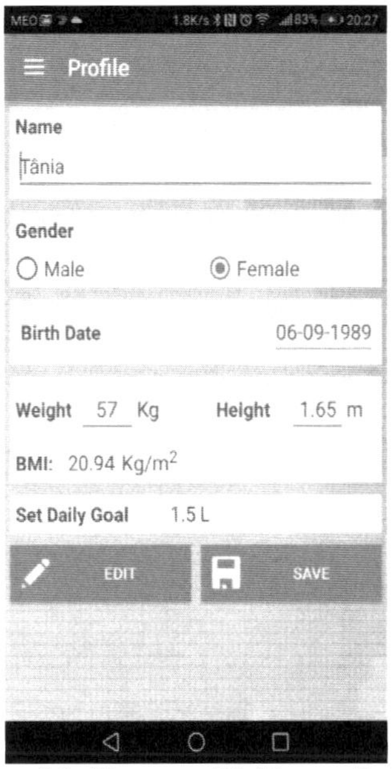

Figure 6. Profile screen of Hydriney application

Increasing water intake is important to ensure an urinary volume of approximately 2.5 liters per day that is associated with the reduced urinary supersaturation with CaOx and a significant reduction in stone recurrence [15]. H2O Consumption's feature (See Figure 7) allows the registration of water intake with notifications about the need to drink water. The screen is divided into two tabs: "Today" and "History". The "Today" tab allows the user to record, throughout the day, the water consumption. The user must press the bottle (s) corresponding to the water volume that he has just to drink. There are 5 bottle standard sizes: 1.5L, 1L, 0.5L, 0.33L, and 0.10L.

As the user registers what he drinks, the progress chart updates, in real time, the percentage of drinking water in relation to the daily goal (see Figure 6). There are also automatic notifications to remember the user to drink water, helping him to drink more water. After entering the values, the application shows in the "History" tab the detailed history chart of water consumption related to today, latest month and last year.

C. Medication

It is not always easy to keep the right time in memory taking a medicine or administering of dosage required during the treatment. The Hydriney application allows the user to detail the schedule of medicines, the dosage options (pills, boxes, and others) and medication intervals. This module development was inspired by the format of pill boxes with dividers (See Figure 8).

The screen has four divisions/boxes grouped by shift - morning, afternoon, evening and dawn. Adding the medications to the med cabinet, the user can see any interactions between them.

Each box displays the name of the medicine to take, the time to take and the flag whether it has already been taken or not.

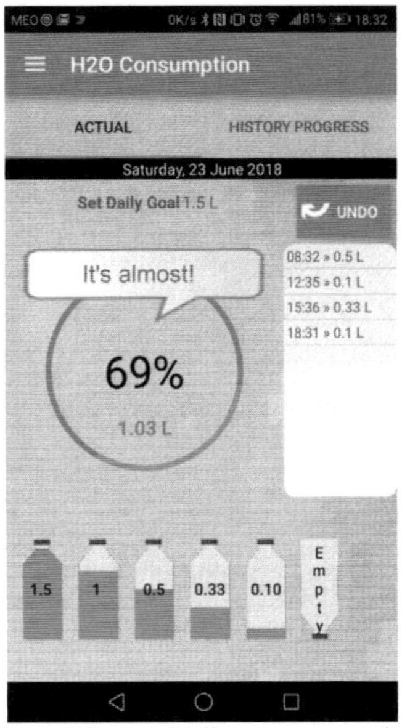

Figure 7. Screen of daily water consumption

D. *pH Measurement*

A metabolic evaluation starts with a 24-h urinary pH profile, because pH is used to measure urine acidity [16]. A lower urinary pH level increases the risk of the presence of different types of kidney stones, promoting the formation of calcium oxalate (CaOx) and uric acid stones (UA) [16]. The alkalization of the urine is important for the treatment of uric acid stones [16].

After matching the paper strip with the color scale, the patient should insert the value measured in the "pH Urine" module (See Figure 9).

As it was previously mentioned, patients taking Uralyt-U need to measure and record the urinary pH 3 times per day: before breakfast, before lunch and before dinner.

This feature makes it easier to record the urinary pH, replacing the traditional paper table. Thus, it is easier not only to register in itself but also the grouping and organization by phases of the day. When entering pH measurements, there is also a "History" tab that shows a chart with the evolution of the urinary pH. Figure 10 shows a scatter chart with the evolution of urinary pH for one month.

The charts improve the understanding of data oscillations registered and promote the better disease's self-monitoring, improving the apprehension of the patient's condition by the doctor.

Figure 8. Screen of daily medication reminders

Figure 9. Screen of daily pH measurements

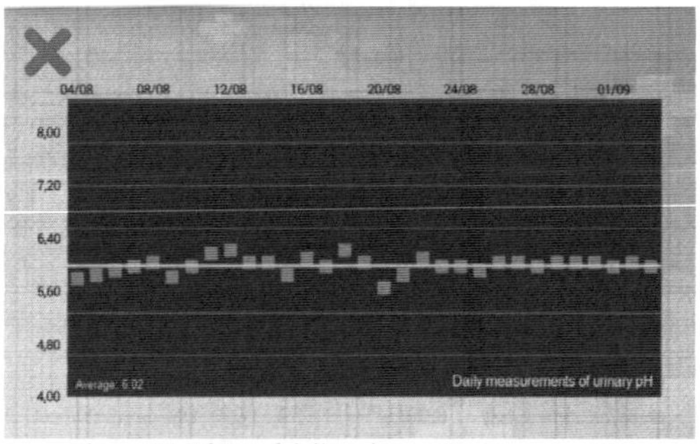

Figure 10. Chart of daily urinary pH measurements

V. Discussion and Conclusions

In this paper we have presented Hydriney, an application tailored for patients with nephrolithiasis. It can effectively help patients with their daily tasks. The Hydriney application will not replace the patient's doctor, but will greatly facilitate the care of the patient and will help reduce the risk of a possible stone recurrence.

If patients track different parameters relevant to kidney stones self-management, they might start noticing different correlations, for example, between their pH Urine and water intake.

This mobile application promises to bring benefits and opportunities to the treatment and prevention of kidney stones disease for a better quality of life. Using this app the user can then take readings, store results, set up timed interval logging, or schedule reminders for particular logs he need to complete. The mobile application tracks almost all aspects of the disease treatment and provides detailed reports, charts and statistics.

By looking for patterns or trends in patients results, the doctor could make changes on the disease treatment plan of patients.

Hardware and software tools are now making it easier for patients to take greater control. As future work, we intend to develop a pH probe using the Arduino platform to interface the Hydriney application. The sensor will be immersed in the urine sample to read the pH variation. After reading it, the data will be transmitted to the microcontroller present in the Arduino platform. Then, the Bluetooth integration will connect the data to the Hydriney application that will allow the user to keep track accurately his urinary pH. The pH sensor will transmit live readings and captures data in real-time.

Acknowledgments

This work was supported by FCT project UID/EEA/50008/2013. The authors would also like to acknowledge the contribution of the COST Actions IC1303 – AAPELE – Architectures, Algorithms and Protocols for Enhanced Living Environments, and CA16226 – Indoor living space improvement: Smart Habitat for the Elderly.

References

[1] P. S. Sousa et al., "mHealth Sensors and Applications for Personal Aid", in: Sasan Adibi (ed.), Mobile Health: A Technology Road Map (New York: Springer International Publishing 2015), pp. 266-267.

[2] F. Doe and B. Brenner, "Nephrolithiasis. Harrison's Principles of Internal Medicine". 10th ed. New York, NY, McGraw-Hill International Book Co, v. 2: pp. 1672-1678, 1983.

[3] H. Concept, "Human Kidney Stones Medical Concept Stock Illustration - Illustration of sick, section: 99255328", Dreamstime.com, 2018. [Online]. Available: https://www.dreamstime.com/stock-illustration-human-kidney-stones-medical-concept-as-organ-painful-crystaline-mineral-formations-as-medicine-symbol-cross-image99255328. [Accessed: 28- Jun- 2018].

[4] H. Han et al., "Nutritional management of kidney stones (nephrolithiasis)", Clinical nutrition research, v. 4(3): pp. 137-152, 2015.

[5] J. Lemann et al., "Urinary oxalate excretion increases with body size and decreases with increasing dietary calcium intake among healthy adults", Kidney international, v. 49(1): pp. 200-208, 1996.

[6] B. Becker, "[A mobile app for patients suffering from kidney stones]. - PubMed - NCBI", Ncbi.nlm.nih.gov, 2018. [Online]. Available: https://www.ncbi.nlm.nih.gov/pubmed/29713752. [Accessed: 28-Jun-2018].

[7] "oxaBrow", Oxabrow.com, 2018. [Online]. Available: http://www.oxabrow.com/. [Accessed: 28-Jun-2018].

[8] "Medisafe", Medisafe.com, 2018. [Online]. Available: https://medisafe.com/. [Accessed: 28-Jun-2018].

[9] "Waterlogged: Tracking My Water Consumption - Walt In PA", Walt in PA, 2018. [Online]. Available: http://www.waltinpa.com/2015/09/17/waterlogged-tracking-my-water-consumption/. [Accessed: 28- Jun- 2018].

[10] "Kidney Stone X Ray", Getty Images, 2018. [Online]. Available: https://www.gettyimages.pt/detail/fotografia-de-not%C3%ADcias/intravenous-urography-of-a-35-year-old-man-fotografia-de-not%C3%ADcias/169370479#intravenous-urography-of-a-35yearold-man-abdomen-without-preparation-picture-id169370479. [Accessed: 28- Jun- 2018].

[11] "File:Surface of a kidney stone with tetragonal crystals of Weddellite (calcium oxalate dihydrate). REM 21.jpg - Wikimedia Commons", Commons.wikimedia.org, 2018. [Online]. Available: https://commons.wikimedia.org/wiki/File:Surface_of_a_kidney_stone_with_tetragonal_crystals_of_Weddellite_(calcium_oxalate_dihydrate)._REM_21.jpg. [Accessed: 28-Jun-2018].

[12] "Kidney stones - Symptoms and causes", Mayo Clinic, 2018. [Online]. Available: https://www.mayoclinic.org/diseases-conditions/kidney-stones/symptoms-causes/syc-20355755. [Accessed: 28-Jun-2018].

[13] L. Beara-Lasic, M. H. Pillinger, and D. S. Goldfarb, "Advances in the management of gout: critical appraisal of febuxostat in the control of hyperuricemia", International journal of nephrology and renovascular disease, v. 3: pp. 1, 2010.

[14] E. N. Taylor, M. J. Stampfer, and G. C. Curhan, "Dietary factors and the risk of incident kidney stones in men: new insights after 14 years of follow-up", Journal of the American Society of Nephrology, v. 15(12): pp. 3225-3232, 2004.

[15] L. Borghi et al., "Urinary volume, water and recurrences in idiopathic calcium nephrolithiasis: a 5-year randomized prospective study", The Journal of urology, 1996. 155(3): pp. 839-843.

[16] R. A. Anderson, "A complementary approach to urolithiasis prevention", World journal of urology, v. 20(5): pp. 294-301, 2002.

An Efficient Machine Learning-based Elderly Fall Detection Algorithm

Faisal Hussain, Muhammad Basit Umair and Muhammad Ehatisham-ul-Haq
Department of Computer Engineering
University of Engineering and Technology (UET)
Taxila, Pakistan
e-mails: faisal.hussain.engr@gmail.com, basitumair@gmail.com and ehatishamuet@gmail.com

Ivan Miguel Pires*,**, Tânia Valente*, Nuno M. Garcia** and Nuno Pombo**
* Altranportugal
Lisbon, Portugal
** Instituto de Telecomunicações,
Universidade da Beira Interior
Covilhã, Portugal
e-mails: impires@it.ubi.pt, tania.ss.valente@gmail.com, ngarcia@di.ubi.pt and ngpombo@di.ubi.pt

Abstract— **Falling is a commonly occurring mishap with elderly people, which may cause serious injuries. Thus, rapid fall detection is very important in order to mitigate the severe effects of fall among the elderly people. Many fall monitoring systems based on the accelerometer have been proposed for the fall detection. However, many of them mistakenly identify the daily life activities as fall or fall as daily life activity. To this aim, an efficient machine learning-based fall detection algorithm has been proposed in this paper. The proposed algorithm detects fall with efficient sensitivity, specificity, and accuracy as compared to the state-of-the-art techniques. A publicly available dataset with a very simple and computationally efficient set of features is used to accurately detect the fall incident. The proposed algorithm reports and accuracy of 99.98% with the Support Vector Machine (SVM) classifier.**

Keywords- Elderly Fall Detection; Human Fall Detection; Wearable Fall Detection System; Fall Monitoring System; SisFall Dataset; Machine Learning Algorithms; KNN; SVM.

I. INTRODUCTION

The number of people who are elder and living alone in the world has been increasing continuously in western countries [1]. Different problems occur with the elderly people and one of them is falling. Fall is the most common issue among the elderly people of age ≥ 65. Falls are commonly defined as "inadvertently coming to rest on the ground, floor or other lower level, excluding intentional change in position to rest in furniture, wall or other objects" [2]. One-third of the people who are over 65 years old have an average one fall per year, two-third of them have a risk of falling again [3], and this number increases with age.

According to the World Health Organization (WHO) report [2], falls are the second leading cause of unintentional or accidental death [2] [4]. One bad fall can mean a long hospital stay, permanent disability, painful rehabilitation, a loss of independent life, or worse.

For over two decades, the experts from both technological and medical fields are working on reducing the consequences of fall by reducing the response time and providing better treatment upon occurrence of a fall. Falls are considered among one of the most hazardous incidents that can happen to an elderly person.

This topic is included in the research for the creation of different systems related to the Ambient Assisted Living Systems (AAL), where the development of a framework for the identification of Activities of Daily Living (ADL) and their environment was previously studied [5]–[9].

Falls can affect the quality of life among the elderly people by resulting in many hazardous health issues such as fractures and spinal cord injury and decline in mobility and activity. One serious consequence of falling is the "long-lie", defined as remaining on the ground or floor for more than an hour after a fall, which can cause death.

Elderly having age more than 65, suffer the greatest number of fatal falls. It is said that every year approximately 646000 individuals die from falls globally of which over 80% are in low and middle-income countries [4]. The death rates due to the unintentional falls are increasing over the globe. In the U.S., approximately 30,000 elderly people aged ≥ 65 died due to unintentional fall during the year 2016 [10]. Figure 1 shows the death rates per 100,000 population for elderly aged 65 and more from the year 2000 to 2015. It can be observed that this rate is continuously increasing with an average of 4.9% per annum. Moreover, the death ratio in elderly men is higher as compared to the elderly women [11].

The consequences of fall are not only confined to severe physical injuries, but psychological grievances as well. These psychological consequences include anxiety, activity disorder, depression, factitious activity restriction and fear of falling.

Fear of falling is one of the major psychological issues in elderly people, which restricts their daily life activities. About 60% of the elderly people restrict their daily living activities due to the fear of fall [12]. This activity restriction may lead to meager gait balance and muscle weakness, which ultimately affects the mobility and independence of the elderly people, and, as a result, the falling incident happens again. Figure 2 illustrates the fall cycle that may happen again and again due to fear of fall.

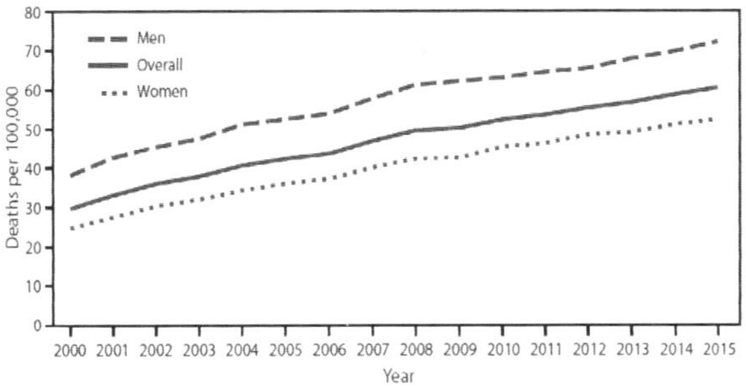

Figure 1. Death Rate in U.S. Due to Fall Incidents from 2000 to 2015 [11]

As the age increases and the human body becomes weaker, the chances fall occurrence also increase. Approximately 30 to 50% of people living in long-term care institutions fall each year, and 40% of them experience the fall again [13]. Falls exponentially increase with age-related biological changes. The incidence of some fall injuries, such as fractures and spinal cord injury, have markedly increased by 131% during the last three decades [13].. It is estimated that by the year 2050 one or more in each group of five people will be aged 65 years or above [14]. So, if the preventive measures are not taken in immediate future then the number of injuries caused by falls will increase significantly.

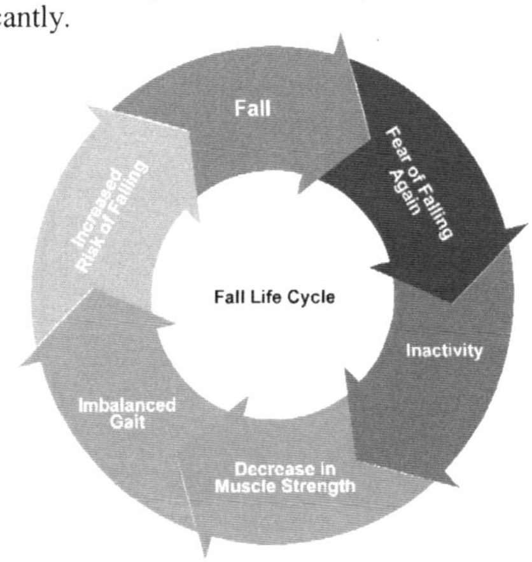

Figure 2. Fall Life Cycle

The severe and long-lasting effects of falling can be diminished by detecting the fall earlier and providing the medical assistance timely. Thus, a fall monitoring system can help in mitigating these problems by generating an emergency alert upon the occurrence of the fall incident. For this purpose, many solutions have been proposed for fall detection. Many fall monitoring systems based on accelerometer and gyroscope have also been proposed for fall detection. However, many of them mistakenly identify the daily life activities as fall or fall as daily life activity. To this aim, an efficient machine learning-based fall detection algorithm has been proposed in this paper.

The rest of this paper is organized as follows. Section II describes the related work. Section III describes the methodology used. Section IV addresses the results obtained. Finally, Section V concludes the article along with the acknowledgement.

II. Related Work

A fall incident occurs whenever a person loses his/her balance and is unable to stay erect. When a young person losses balance, then he/she has the strength to recover his/her balance, but when an elderly person losses his/her balance then it is very difficult for him/her to recover as he/she is physically frail at that age. There are many factors that can cause the fall. All the factors that can be the cause of falls are called risk factors for fall. In fact, fall occurrence is the result of a complex interaction of many factors.

The risk of falling and the number of factors are interrelated i.e. the risk of falling increases as the number of factors increases. The risk factors are categorized into three main types: behavioural, environmental and biological risk factors, as shown in Figure 3.

Behavioural risk factors are related to human actions, emotions and activities of daily life. These factors are controllable through the strategic intervention. For example, if a person falls due to excess intake of drugs, alcohol then this habit or behaviour can be modified by strategic treatment.

Environmental risk factors originate from the surrounding environment of a person. Slippery floors, insufficient lighting and cracked pathways are some of the major environmental risk factors.

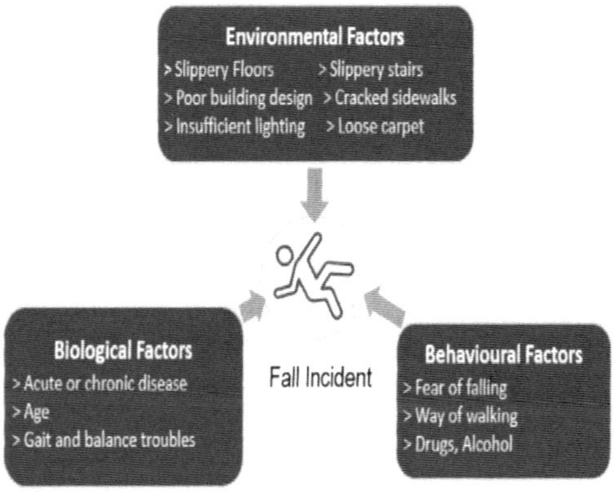

Figure 3. Fall Risk Factors

Biological risk factors are related to age, gender and physical health of a person. Some biological risk factors include: chronic and acute diseases, diabetes, heart problems, eyesight disorders, high or low blood pressure, gait and balance disorders. The biological factors like age and gender are uncontrollable, however, the diseases can be alleviated or controlled through their proper treatment and the physical health can also be improved.

There are two research tracks in the human fall-related domain: falling detection (FD) and falling prevention (FP) [15]. In the falling detection domain, the main focus is to reduce the rescue time after the fall incident occurred. In the falling prevention domain, the main focus is to predict fall through gait and balance analysis.

Fall detection systems are very helpful in reducing the response time after the falling incident. Fall prevention systems are very helpful in stopping and avoiding future falls. Human fall-related systems are classified into three types on the basis of sensor deployment, i.e. camera-based systems, ambient-based systems and wearable systems. Due to expensive hardware cost, camera-based and ambient-based devices are rarely used. Wearable devices are commonly used which use inertial measurement units like accelerometers and gyroscope. With the invention of micro-electro-mechanical system, wearable devices can be implemented to be small and lightweight.

K. Chaccour *et al.* [15] proposed a global classification scheme for both FDS and FPS. They categorized both FDS and FPS on the basis of sensor deployment, into three types: wearable based systems (WS), non-wearable based systems (NWS) and fusion or hybrid-based systems (FS). In the wearable based systems, sensors are deployed on the body of an elderly person for falling detection or falling prevention purpose. Mostly, these are deployed on waist or wrist. However, in the non-wearable based systems, sensors (*i.e.,* ambient, vision or RF sensors) are deployed in the surrounding environment rather than on the human body. On the other hand, the fusion or hybrid-based systems consist of both wearable and non-wearable sensors. J. T. Perry *et al.* [16] classified FDS on the basis of the accelerometer technique. They classified FDS methods into three types: methods that measure acceleration, methods that combine acceleration with other sensor data and methods that do not measure acceleration at all. R. Igual *et al.* [17] divided fall detection systems into wearable devices and context-aware systems.

Different data processing techniques are used in fall detection systems. These techniques depend upon the parameters extracted from the sensors. Mainly two types of data processing techniques are used in are used in FDS: analytical methods and machine learning methods.

A. Analytical Methods

Analytical methods use statistical techniques for fall prediction or fall prevention. These methods are based upon traditional techniques for the classification of data. Some famous analytical techniques for data processing are: Thresh-Holding [18][19], Fuzzy Logic [20], Hidden Markov model [21], and Bayesian Filtering [22]. All these techniques are used to classify the falls from non-falls. Among these methods, Thresh-Holding technique is mostly used. In this technique, fall is reported or predicted when peaks or specific shape features are detected in the data signals. This method is mostly used in wearable based systems. Ambient-based systems use event sensing techniques to monitor and track the vibrational data, while camera-based systems use image processing techniques to identify falls.

B. Machine Learning Methods

Machine learning methods predict or detect the falls through complex algorithms. These complex algorithms are used to get close insight on data for predicting the falls. In machine learning methods, firstly, the algorithm is trained on a feature set extracted from the dataset then it is used for testing real-time data. Some famous machine learning algorithms used for detection or prediction of falls are: Support Vector Machine [23] Multilayer Perceptron [24], K-Nearest Neighbors [25], Naive Bayes [26], and others. These methods are used to gain insights of data for detection and even prediction of future falls.

III. METHODOLOGY

The proposed methodology uses a machine learning approach for the fall detection. SisFall [19], a publicly available dataset, is used for the training and testing of the proposed algorithm on the falling or non-falling activities. There are four major steps of the proposed methodology i.e. Data collection, Preprocessing, Feature Extraction, and Fall Detection, as shown in Figure 4.

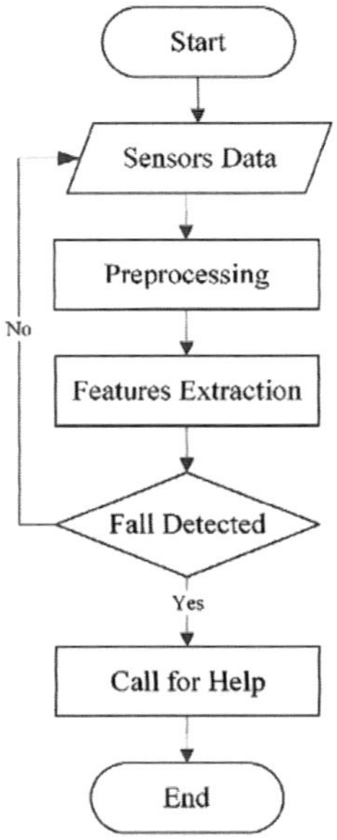

Figure 4. Flow Chart of the Proposed Methodology

1) Data Collection. The first step of the proposed methodology is to collect data that is to be used in further stages after the preprocessing. It is a very challenging task to collect data in real time by the people especially performing activities by the elderly people. Many researchers have collected data for fall activities and activities of daily life. Different datasets are available, but most of them have activities performed by only young participants. For an efficient elderly fall detection system, the dataset should contain the falls and daily life activities performed by the elderly people also. So, we found SisFall [27] dataset which contains both young and elderly participants.

SisFall is a fall and movement dataset that is used in this study. SisFall dataset contains 4505 files out of which 1798 files include 15 types of falls and 2707 files include 19 types of ADL performed by 23 young adults of age 19 to 30 years and 15 elderly people of age 60 to 75 years. All the activities are recorded at sampling rate Fs = 200 Hz using a wearable device mounted at the waist of the participant, having three motion sensors i.e. two accelerometers and one gyroscope.

2) Data Preprocessing. Once the data is acquired, the next step is to preprocess the data in order to remove the unwanted noise from the signal so that better classification can be performed by the machine learning algorithms. There are different filters used [14] but, in this methodology, we used a fourth order low pass infinite impulse response (IIR) Butterworth filter with the cut-off frequency Fc = 5Hz because it is simple and has low computational cost.

3) Feature Extraction. Once the raw signal is preprocessed, the next step is to extract the features for the purpose of classification. We extracted six features from the preprocessed data. These features include maximum amplitude, minimum amplitude, mean amplitude, Variance, kurtosis and skewness of the signal. These features along with mathematical expressions are mentioned in Table I. Each feature is extracted on three sensors data which includes two accelerometers and one gyroscope along three axis x-axis, y-axis and z-axis. The size of one feature for a single sensor along the three axis is [1(# of samples) x 1(# of features) x 3(# of axis)]. In this way, the size of all six features along with all three axis for each single sensor becomes [1(# of samples) x 6 (# of features) x 3(# of axis)] = [1 x 18] for one sample. Consequently, we come up with a final feature vector of size [1 x 54] for all three sensors along all three axis across one sample.

TABLE I. SET OF FEATURES EXTRACTED FOR FALL DETECTION

Features	Equation
Maximum Amplitude	$\max\,(\,a[k]\,)$
Minimum Amplitude	$\min\,(\,a[k]\,)$
Mean Amplitude	$\mu = \frac{1}{N}\sum a[k]$
Variance	$\sigma^2 = \frac{1}{N}\sum (a[k]-\mu)^2$
Kurtosis	$K = {m_4}/{(m_3)^2}$
Skewness	$S = {m_3}/{(m_3)^{\frac{2}{3}}}$

4) Fall Detection. After the feature extraction, the next step is to classify the activity whether it is a fall or not. The fall detection problem is a binary classification problem i.e. we have to classify the activity as fall or non-fall (i.e. ADL) activity. Hence, we divided the whole dataset into two classes i.e. Class-1 for fall activity and Class-2 for non-fall (i.e. ADL) activities. All the feature vectors that were extracted from the samples collected in the dataset by performing falls were labelled as Class-1 while all the feature vectors that were extracted from the samples collected by performing ADL were labelled as Class- 2. In this way, the total number of samples in Class-1 is 1798 for falls and the total number of samples in Class-2 is 2707 for ADL.

After labelling the feature vector of samples, we then applied the 10-fold cross-validation scheme in order to make the machine learning classifier a better predictive model and to diminish the bias. Finally, we used four machine learning classifiers in order to evaluate the performance of the proposed scheme. These algorithms include Decision Tree (DT), Logistic Regression (LR), K-Nearest Neighbor (KNN) with K=1 based on Euclidean distance and Support Vector Machine (SVM) classifier with Quadratic kernel function. The results are given in Section IV.

IV. RESULTS AND DISCUSSIONS

A. Method of Analysis

The performance of the proposed algorithm is analyzed on the basis of three commonly used performance metrics, i.e., sensitivity, specificity and accuracy. These are defined as:

1) Sensitivity (SE). It will measure the capacity of the system to detecting falls. It is the ratio of true positives to the total number of falls. Mathematically, it can be written as in (1).

$$SE = \frac{TP}{TP+FN} \times 100 \quad (1)$$

2) Specificity (SP). It is the capacity of the system to detect falls only when they occur. Mathematically, it can be written as in (2).

$$SP = \frac{TN}{TN+FP} \times 100 \quad (2)$$

3) Accuracy. It is the ability of the system to differentiate between falls and no-falls. Mathematically, it can be written as in (3).

$$Accuracy = \frac{TP+TN}{TP+FN+TN+FP} \times 100 \quad (3)$$

where *TP* refers to True Positive, *i.e.,* fall occurs and the algorithm detects it, *TN* refers to True Negative, *i.e.,* fall doesn't occur & algorithm does not detect a fall, *FP* refers to False Positive, *i.e.,* fall does not occur but the algorithm reports a fall, and *FN* refers to False Negative, *i.e.,* fall occurs but the algorithm does not detect it.

B. Results and Discussion

The experiments are performed using MATLAB R2016a. In order to analyze the extracted features, we used four machine learning classifiers (i.e., DT, LR, KNN and SVM), for fall detection, which has been evaluated on the bases of above-discussed parameters. The confusion matrices of these classifiers are shown in Figure 5.

Confusion Matrix - 1			Confusion Matrix - 2		
DT	**Predicted**		**LR**	**Predicted**	
Actual	***Fall***	***ADL***	**Actual**	***Fall***	***ADL***
Fall	1776	22	***Fall***	1778	20
ADL	22	2685	***ADL***	8	2699
Confusion Matrix - 3			**Confusion Matrix - 4**		
KNN	**Predicted**		**SVM**	**Predicted**	
Actual	***Fall***	***ADL***	**Actual**	***Fall***	***ADL***
Fall	1794	4	***Fall***	1797	1
ADL	0	2707	***ADL***	0	2707

Figure 5. Confusion Matrices of DT, LR, KNN and SVM Classifiers

The 10-fold cross-validation scheme is used for the training and testing, i.e., the dataset is divided into 10-folds randomly in such a way that every time 9-fold for training and 1-fold for testing. Hence, the entire dataset is used for both training and testing. Table II shows the results of the four machine learning classifiers. These parameters are calculated using confusion matrices shown in Figure 5.

TABLE II. FALL DETECTION RESULTS OF THE PROPOSED ALGORITHM

Classifier	SE	SP	Accuracy
DT	98.78%	99.19%	99.02%
LR	98.88%	99.70%	99.38%
KNN	99.78%	100%	99.91%
SVM	99.94%	100%	99.98%

From the Table II, it can be noted that based upon the extracted set of features, among the four machine learning classifiers, SVM performs better as compared to three classifiers in sensitivity, specificity, and accuracy. The performance of the proposed SVM-based scheme is also compared to the state-of-the-art techniques as shown in Table III.

TABLE III. RESULT COMPARISON OF THE PROPOSED ALGORITHM WITH THE STATE-OF-THE-ART TECHNIQUES

Research Study	SE	SP	Accuracy
A. Sucerquia [27]	95.5 %	96.38 %	95.96 %
A. Sucerquia [28]	99.27 %	99.37 %	99.33 %
L. P. Nguyen [24]	99.62%	98.26%	96.60%
Proposed (SVM-based)	99.94%	100%	99.98%

V. CONCLUSION AND FUTURE WORK

In this study, an efficient fall detection algorithm was proposed which uses a very simple and computationally efficient set of features extracted from a publicly available dataset. The extracted features are used to train and test four machine learning classifiers. Among these classifiers, SVM shows the highest accuracy, i.e., 99.98% which is better than the state-of-the-art techniques as shown in Table III.

The proposed algorithm is efficient to be used in the real-time fall detection system. The future work includes the hardware implementation of the proposed fall detection algorithm in order to secure the independent life of elderly people.

ACKNOWLEDGEMENT

This work was supported by FCT project UID/EEA/50008/2013. The authors would also like to acknowledge the contribution of the COST Actions IC1303 – AAPELE – Architectures, Algorithms and Protocols for Enhanced Living Environments, and CA16226 – Indoor living space improvement: Smart Habitat for the Elderly.

REFERENCES

[1] D. E. Bloom, A. Boersch-Supan, P. McGee, and A. Seike, "Population aging: facts, challenges, and responses," *Benefits Compens. Int.*, vol. 41, no. 1, p. 22, 2011.

[2] W. H. O. Ageing and L. C. Unit, "WHO global report on falls prevention in older age," *World Heal. Organ.*, 2008.

[3] A. T. Özdemir, "An analysis on sensor locations of the human body for wearable fall detection devices: Principles and practice," *Sensors*, vol. 16, no. 8, p. 1161, 2016.

[4] "Falls." [Online]. Available: http://www.who.int/en/news-room/fact-sheets/detail/falls. [Accessed: 07-May-2018].

[5] I. M. Pires, N. M. Garcia, N. Pombo, and F. Flórez-Revuelta, "User Environment Detection with Acoustic Sensors Embedded on Mobile Devices for the Recognition of Activities of Daily Living," *arXiv Prepr. arXiv1711.00124*, 2017.

[6] I. M. Pires, N. M. Garcia, N. Pombo, F. Flórez-Revuelta, and S. Spinsante, "Pattern Recognition Techniques for the Identification of Activities of Daily Living using Mobile Device Accelerometer," *arXiv Prepr. arXiv1711.00096*, 2017.

[7] I. M. Pires, N. M. Garcia, N. Pombo, and F. Flórez-Revuelta, "A Multiple Source Framework for the Identification of Activities of Daily Living Based on Mobile Device Data,"

arXiv Prepr. arXiv1711.00104, 2017.

[8] I. M. Pires, N. M. Garcia, N. Pombo, F. Flórez-Revuelta, S. Spinsante, and M. C. Teixeira, "Identification of activities of daily living through data fusion on motion and magnetic sensors embedded on mobile devices," *Pervasive Mob. Comput.*, vol. 47, pp. 78–93, 2018.

[9] I. M. Pires, N. M. Garcia, N. Pombo, F. Flórez-Revuelta, and N. D. Rodríguez, "Validation Techniques for Sensor Data in Mobile Health Applications," *J. Sensors*, vol. 2016, 2016.

[10] E. Burns and R. Kakara, "Deaths from Falls Among Persons Aged ≥65 Years — United States, 2007–2016," *MMWR. Morb. Mortal. Wkly. Rep.*, vol. 67, no. 18, pp. 509–514, May 2018.

[11] "Age-Adjusted Death Rates* from Unintentional Falls Among Adults Aged ≥65 Years, by Sex — National Vital Statistics System, United States, 2000–2015," *MMWR. Morb. Mortal. Wkly. Rep.*, vol. 66, no. 35, p. 943, Sep. 2017.

[12] N. Deshpande, E. J. Metter, F. Lauretani, S. Bandinelli, J. Guralnik, and L. Ferrucci, "Activity restriction induced by fear of falling and objective and subjective measures of physical function: a prospective cohort study," *J. Am. Geriatr. Soc.*, vol. 56, no. 4, pp. 615–620, 2008.

[13] Y. Dionyssiotis, "Analyzing the problem of falls among older people," *Int. J. Gen. Med.*, vol. 5, p. 805, 2012.

[14] N. El-Bendary, Q. Tan, F. C. Pivot, and A. Lam, "FALL DETECTION AND PREVENTION FOR THE ELDERLY: A REVIEW OF TRENDS AND CHALLENGES.," *Int. J. Smart Sens. Intell. Syst.*, vol. 6, no. 3, 2013.

[15] K. Chaccour, R. Darazi, A. H. El Hassani, and E. Andrès, "From fall detection to fall prevention: A generic classification of fall-related systems," *IEEE Sens. J.*, vol. 17, no. 3, pp. 812–822, 2017.

[16] J. T. Perry, S. Kellog, S. M. Vaidya, J.-H. Youn, H. Ali, and H. Sharif, "Survey and evaluation of real-time fall detection approaches," in *High-Capacity Optical Networks and Enabling Technologies (HONET), 2009 6th International Symposium on*, 2009, pp. 158–164.

[17] R. Igual, C. Medrano, and I. Plaza, "Challenges, issues and trends in fall detection systems," *Biomed. Eng. Online*, vol. 12, no. 1, p. 66, 2013.

[18] C. Medrano, R. Igual, I. García-Magariño, I. Plaza, and G. Azuara, "Combining novelty detectors to improve accelerometer-based fall detection," *Med. Biol. Eng. Comput.*, vol. 55, no. 10, pp. 1849–1858, 2017.

[19] G. Šeketa, J. Vugrin, and I. Lacković, "Optimal Threshold Selection for Acceleration-Based Fall Detection," in *Precision Medicine Powered by pHealth and Connected Health*, Springer, 2018, pp. 151–155.

[20] D. Anderson, R. H. Luke, J. M. Keller, M. Skubic, M. Rantz, and M. Aud, "Linguistic summarization of video for fall detection using voxel person and fuzzy logic," *Comput. Vis. image Underst.*, vol. 113, no. 1, pp. 80–89, 2009.

[21] H. Cao *et al.*, "A fall detection method based on acceleration data and hidden Markov model," in *Signal and Image Processing (ICSIP), IEEE International Conference on*, 2016, pp. 684–689.

[22] J. Howcroft, J. Kofman, and E. D. Lemaire, "Prospective fall-risk prediction models for older adults based on wearable sensors," *IEEE Trans. neural Syst. Rehabil. Eng.*, vol. 25, no. 10, pp. 1812–1820, 2017.

[23] Y. Wang, K. Wu, and L. M. Ni, "Wifall: Device-free fall detection by wireless networks," *IEEE Trans. Mob. Comput.*, vol. 16, no. 2, pp. 581–594, 2017.

[24] L. P. Nguyen, M. Saleh, and R. L. B. Jeannès, "An Efficient Design of a Machine Learning-Based Elderly Fall Detector," in *International Conference on IoT Technologies for HealthCare*, 2017, pp. 34–41.

[25] A. T. Ozdemir, C. Tunc, and S. Hariri, "Autonomic Fall Detection System," in *Foundations and Applications of Self* Systems (FAS* W), 2017 IEEE 2nd International Workshops on*, 2017, pp. 166–170.

[26] H. Wang, M. Li, J. Li, J. Cao, and Z. Wang, "An improved fall detection approach for elderly people based on feature weight and Bayesian classification," in *Mechatronics and Automation (ICMA), 2016 IEEE International Conference on*, 2016, pp. 471–476.

[27] A. Sucerquia, J. D. López, and J. F. Vargas-Bonilla, "SisFall: A fall and movement dataset," *Sensors*, vol. 17, no. 1, p. 198, 2017.

[28] A. Sucerquia, "Real-Life/Real-Time Elderly Fall Detection with a Triaxial Accelerometer," *Sensors (Basel).*, vol. 18, no. 4, 2018.

What Do We Mean by the Validation of Activity Monitoring Devices?

Nuno M. Garcia[*], Nuno Pombo[*] and Ivan Miguel Pires[*,**]
[*] Instituto de Telecomunicações,
Universidade da Beira Interior,
Covilhã, Portugal
[**] Altranportugal,
Lisbon, Portugal
e-mails: ngarcia@di.ubi.pt, ngpombo@di.ubi.pt and impires@it.ubi.pt

Salome Oniani and Ia Mosashvili
Faculty of Informatics and Control Systems,
Georgian Technical University,
Tbilisi, Georgia
e-mail: s.oniani@gtu.ge and i_mosashvili@gtu.ge

Gisele Ferreira de Souza
University of São Paulo,
São Paulo, Brazil
e-mail: semfungos@gmail.com

Abstract—**Various device validation methodologies for activity monitoring are growing in number, but the information about the regulation and rules of recognition for the software and hardware used with these devices is not presented. There are different characteristics that should be evaluated to prove the reliability of these devices, including different security and privacy parameters. Activity monitoring can be performed with mobile devices and other devices whose software versions are updated regularly. That is why these devices should be regulated, including the devices implemented in smart environments, containing the ones implemented in furniture, which are important for the monitoring of ageing people. The regulation of these devices and mobile applications has been discussed, but there are no specific rules. This study presents some possible methods for the regulation of mobile devices and applications for activity monitoring of ageing people, which can also be influenced by environmental conditions.**

Keywords-regulation; mobile technologies; activity monitoring; security; privacy.

I. INTRODUCTION

Activity monitoring is a subject that has been growing with mobile devices and other specific devices. The validation of these devices is important because it is estimated that the number of ageing people and those who need special assistance is increasing [1]. Compared with the need for the validation of the medical devices, these devices need to be validated by several rules for safety and accessible use [1]. Some validation rules of the medical devices have been created by the Food and Drug Administration (FDA) [2] in the United States, and CE Marking [3] in European Union (EU), but only few rules were defined for the validation of the mobile applications according to the severity level of their risks.

There are many studies about the validation of activity monitoring systems, especially wearable technology [4]. Most research in this area has been done without mentioning which regulation and software version was considered.

There are no concrete rules for the validation of the activity monitoring devices and the mobile applications available on the market. In 2010, Unites States of America's (USA) government started the regulation of mobile medical applications. While the suggestion of regulation is rooted in patient safety, concerns about limits on innovation and discovery, as well as the evolving nature of both mobile health and current healthcare delivery have emerged [5]. Currently, the EU countries are working on such laws [6].

Activity monitoring devices are very important for the monitoring of ageing people, where their correct functionality should be validated. In USA, FDA is validating these devices and mobile applications, and this is subject to reimbursement as a medical device [7]. These procedures should be implemented in other countries in order to improve the safety and correct use of this equipment.

The rest of this paper is organized as follows. Section II describes the different methodologies used for the validation of the activity monitoring devices and mobile applications. Section III proposes a validation schema for the mobile applications and devices for activity monitoring. Section IV presents the discussion and conclusions of this study. The acknowledgment and references close the article.

II. METHODS

U.S. Department of Health and Human Services implements a variety of regulations for Products and Medical Procedures, Medical Device Safety, Device Advice, Comprehensive Regulatory Assistance, and Digital Health. Therefore, we are concentrating on Medical Devices which include Mobile Medical Applications [8].

Mobile medical applications are mobile applications that meet the definition of a medical device and are an accessory to a regulated medical device or transform it into a regulated medical device [9]. Some mobile medical apps can diagnose heart rate abnormalities by using an Activity Tracker, whose software versions are updated periodically. For example, the fitness watch Vivosmart HR uses the software Garmin Express for synchronizing the date from devices. It updated from version 2.10 to 4.30, so it is important to clarify which version of the software was used in the research. Also, it is important to control that a device does not update itself during the experimental work.

In 2012, the R package 'fda.usc' was eliminated, which included some utilities for functional data analysis. It also contained functions to compute functional regression models and basic functional principal components analysis [10]. In 2014, an article was published, which shows that "Electronic and mobile systems play pivotal roles in healthcare delivery. A classification system for healthcare applications should be developed that recognizes and delineates the difference between apps that support decision-making, and those which purport to intervene in clinical decisions" [11].

In 2017, the FDA created a pilot study for the validation of some products from large companies, including Apple, Fitbit, Samsung and others [12]. The software and hardware for activity monitoring should be validated according to different perspectives, including Organizational Resource Perspective, Customer Perspective, Learning and Growth Perspective and Process Perspective, based on different principles, including Patient Safety, Product Quality, Clinical Responsibility, Cybersecurity Responsibility and Proactive Culture [13]-[15]. The frequency of the updates of these mobile applications and devices should be reduced to guarantee their correct validation.

FDA was the first agency that started the validation for medical devices and applications during the last years in United States. Currently, in the European Union, the CE Marking started the development of strict rules related to the digital health application and devices [16].

Combining the information mentioned above, some rules will be introduced in the next section related to high-risk and moderate-risk recalls of the mobile devices and applications, especially for the activity monitoring systems for ageing people [22][23].

III. RESULTS

This study presents a proposal of validation rules and regulations for mobile and wearable technology that is used by ageing people.

There is much research showing mobile devices or activity monitoring systems validation, but they usually present only brand names and do not demonstrate exactly which tool was used for the experimental work, what was the device serial number, generation, and date of issue [17]. Thus, it is important to clarify serial number, generation, and date of issue of the user device in the research.

An important fact is that, when researchers validate devices, they do not write about the software version of the tool. Smartwatches use their own operating system and mobile applications for synchronizing the raw data to a server and the server gives us access to work with inputs. If the scientist did not mention which software was used and some reader will check artifacts of the study, the results will not the same because programs of mobile applications and device are updating themselves from time to time. So, it is important for researchers to provide information on the software version of the device and operation program for synchronizing the data.

Commonly, the mobile applications and computer programs are updated from time to time. Sometimes, this activity is happening during a very short period. So, it is natural that the software version is the difference in the start and end periods of the research. This case creates a confusing situation, as the data from start steps is not the same then data from the last stages of the study. Therefore, the results of this type of research with be false, because the start and end stages validation were done using a different version. We suggest stopping software updates during the experimental work of any study.

One example of a validated medical device that may be used for activity monitoring is the Everion device, developed by Biovotion [18]. It passed the rules from FDA and it is validated as a medical device in the USA. However, this validation is not valid worldwide. Therefore, common rules should be developed for all countries.

Based on the validation rules created by FDA, the validation process should be executed in three stages [19], as follows:

1. Process Design;
2. Process Qualification;
3. Continued Process Verification.

First, stage 1 should include the research about the Building and Capturing Process Knowledge and Understanding, and the Establishment of a Strategy for Process Control. Second, stage 2 should include the research about the Design of a Facility and Qualification of Utilities and Equipment, the Process Performance Qualification (PPQ), the PPQ Protocol, and the PPQ Protocol Execution and Report. Finally, stage 3 should guarantee the continuous validation during software and hardware updates. The main rules commonly adopted are described in [19].

Also, Boston Technology Corporation offers an end to end mobile application testing services which include the following [20]:

- Testing Strategy should focus on two factors – reducing testing costs and improving 'Time to Market' for the mobile applications;
- Functional Testing verifies that the Mobile Application meets the functional requirements. This testing step is critical to ensure that the functionality built to meet the stated business requirements and objectives works correctly as designed. Functional testing leverages automation tools, but many of the testing steps

require manual testing to effectively mimic App user behavior;

- Non-Functional Testing covers testing mobile applications for usability, performance, scalability, security, as well as compatibility on different devices and Operating Systems (OS) platforms. This testing is typically done after the application has been tested for functional requirements and provides insight into the production readiness of the application. Non-functional testing can be effectively carried out by using testing tools, unlike functional testing, which is largely manual. For this type of testing to be effective, it is important to create specific measurable test objectives [20].

IV. Discussion and Conclusion

The results and methodology discussed here are not limited to regulation of mobile applications and wearable technology validation. They provide the basis to develop this field in European and Asian countries. The validation rules and schema of this research are based on studies of U.S. FDA Registration [21] and CE Marking [16].

Also, software problems in medical devices are very frequent and have the potential to negatively influence mHealth care. "Premarket regulation has not captured all the software issues that could harm patients, evidenced by the potentially large number of patients exposed to software products later subject to high-risk and moderate-risk recalls" [22][23].

The population using mobile applications and programs for activity monitoring is growing every day. So, it is necessary to address legal aspects for their validation.

The correct validation of these devices will increase the confidence in them by patients and healthcare professionals. The recognition of the activities can be a critical area, because the recognition of the activities can be used for the monitoring of risk situations, including the falling of ageing people. In the future, the institutions for the ageing people can be more proactive, combining several sensors for the recognition of different activities, and this can be implemented with sensors available in the mobile devices and sensors placed in the furniture, among others. The validation of these devices should be specified and adapted to their purpose, as their risks may increase with the creation of intelligent systems to monitor and help ageing people [24].

Acknowledgment

This work was supported by FCT project UID/EEA/50008/2013. The authors would also like to acknowledge the contribution of the COST Actions IC1303 – AAPELE – Architectures, Algorithms, and Protocols for Enhanced Living Environments, and CA16226 – Indoor living space improvement: Smart Habitat for the Elderly.

References

[1] "New regulations", *Danish Medicines Agency*, 2018. [Online]. Available: https://laegemiddelstyrelsen.dk/en/devices/legislation-and-guidance/new-regulations/. [Accessed: 07- Jul- 2018].

[2] Fda.gov, 2018. [Online]. Available: https://www.fda.gov/downloads/MedicalDevices/DeviceRegulationandGuidance/GuidanceDocuments/UCM587819.pdf. [Accessed: 07-Jul- 2018].

[3] "European CE Marking Strategy for Medical Devices", Emergo, 2018. [Online]. Available: https://www.emergobyul.com/services/europe/ce-certification. [Accessed: 07- Jul- 2018].

[4] M. H. Iqbal, A. Aydin, O. Brunckhorst, P. Dasgupta and K. Ahmed, "A review of wearable technology in medicine", Journal of the Royal Society of Medicine, 109(10), pp.372-380, 2016.

[5] A. J. Barton, "The regulation of mobile health applications" BMC medicine, 10(1), p.46, 2012.

[6] Legal: The laws and regulations of wearable devices [Online]. http://www.wearabletechnology-news.com/news/2015/sep/10/where-law-stands-wearable-devices/. [Accessed: 08- Jul- 2018].

[7] J. Barton, B. O'Flynn, and S. Tedesco, "A Review of Physical Activity Monitoring and Activity Trackers for Older Adults", Proceedings AAATE2017, Sheffield, UK, 12-15 Sept, in: Cudd, P. & de Witte, L. (eds.) Studies in Health Technology and Informatics, IOS Press. 242, pp. 748-754. doi: 10.3233/978-1-61499-798-6-748, (2017)

[8] U.S. Department of Health and Human Services [Online]. https://www.fda.gov/MedicalDevices/default.htm [Accessed: 09- Jul-2018].

[9] M. B. Hamel, N. G. Cortez, I. G. Cohen and A. S. Kesselheim, "FDA regulation of mobile health technologies", The New England journal of medicine, 371(4), p.372, 2014.

[10] M. Febrero-Bande, and M. O. de la Fuente, "Statistical computing in functional data analysis: The R package fda. Usc", Journal of Statistical Software, 51(4), pp.1-28, 2012.

[11] E. Charani, E. Castro-Sánchez, L. S. Moore and A. Holmes, "Do smartphone applications in healthcare require a governance and legal framework? It depends on the application!", BMC medicine, 12(1), p.29, 2014.

[12] A. Parmar, S. Baum, A. DeArment and E. Dietsche, "These 9 companies made it to the FDA's pilot digital health program (Updated) - MedCity News", MedCity News, 2018. [Online]. Available: https://medcitynews.com/2017/09/9-companies-made-fdas-pre-cert-pilot-program-digital-health-tech/. [Accessed: 10- Jul-2018].

[13] "Regulations.gov", Regulations.gov, 2018. [Online]. Available: https://www.regulations.gov/document?D=FDA-2017-N-4301-0001. [Accessed: 10- Jul- 2018].

[14] Fda.gov, 2018. [Online]. Available: https://www.fda.gov/downloads/MedicalDevices/DeviceRegulationandGuidance/GuidanceDocuments/UCM587820.pdf. [Accessed: 10-Jul- 2018].

[15] Fda.gov, 2018. [Online]. Available: https://www.fda.gov/downloads/MedicalDevices/NewsEvents/WorkshopsConferences/UCM593860.pdf. [Accessed: 10- Jul- 2018].

[16] "CE Marking of Digital Health Technologies: Stricter Rules for Medical Device Software under the EU MDR - NAMSA", NAMSA, 2018. [Online]. Available: https://www.namsa.com/european-market/mdr-stricter-rules-medical-device-software/. [Accessed: 10-Jul- 2018].

[17] J. E. Sasaki, at al. "Validation of the Fitbit wireless activity tracker for prediction of energy expenditure", Journal of Physical Activity and Health, 12(2), pp.149-154, 2015.

[18] "Everion", Biovotion, 2018. [Online]. Available: https://www.biovotion.com/everion/. [Accessed: 13- Jul- 2018].

[19] Fda.gov, 2018. [Online]. Available: https://www.fda.gov/downloads/drugs/guidances/ucm070336.pdf. [Accessed: 13- Jul- 2018].

[20] Expert verification and validation of mobile apps across various devices and OS platforms. [Online]. Available: http://www.boston-technology.com/testing/ [Accessed: 16 - Jul- 2018].

[21] Fda.gov, 2018. [Online]. Available: https://www.fda.gov/downloads/drugs/guidances/ucm343101.pdf [Accessed: 14 - Jul- 2018].

[22] J. G. Ronquillo, and D.M. Zuckerman, "Software-Related Recalls of Health Information Technology and Other Medical Devices: Implications for FDA Regulation of Digital Health", The Milbank Quarterly, 95(3), pp.535-553, 2017.

[23] J. Shuren, B. Patel, and S. Gottlieb, "FDA Regulation of Mobile Medical Apps", JAMA, 2018.

[24] P. S. Sousa, D. Sabugueiro, V. Felizardo, R. Couto, I. Pires, N.M. Garcia, "mHealth Sensors and Applications for Personal Aid. In: Adibi S. (eds) Mobile Health", Springer Series in Bio-/Neuroinformatics, vol 5. Springer, Cham, (2015)

Temperature Monitoring in Tissue Phantoms via Spatially Resolved Measurement of Longitudinal Wave Speed

Mario Wolf, Lukas Timmermann, André Juhrig,
Katharina Rath, and Elfgard Kühnicke

Solid State Electronics Laboratories
Technical University of Dresden
Dresden, Germany
Email: mario.wolf@tu-dresden.de

Felix Krujatz

Institute of Natural Materials Technology
Technical University of Dresden
Dresden, Germany
Email: felix.krujatz@tu-dresden.de

***Abstract*—To optimize hyperthermia in cancer therapy, a monitoring of temperature in the tumor and in the surrounding tissue is necessary during the therapy. As the use of Computer Tomography (CT) or Magnetic Resonance Imaging (MRI) is hardly possible during the operation, ultrasonic measurements serve as a very good alternative. This contribution introduces a method to measure the longitudinal wave speed spatially resolved by analyzing the reflected ultrasonic signals from small scatterers in a tissue phantom without needing any large reflectors at known positions. The measurements are done with pre-focused annular-arrays and the recorded signals are focused synthetically. This allows to determine the resulting signal amplitude in a fixed time window as a function of the assumed longitudinal wave speed used for focusing. The amplitude becomes maximal if the assumed sound velocity is equal to the actual one. Sliding the analysis window through the whole signal allows to determine the mean longitudinal wave speed for each depth. As the longitudinal wave speed depends on temperature, this gives the temperature distribution along the acoustic axis of the transducer. To qualify the technique, measurements are done on a tissue phantom for constant sound velocity. The capabilities of the method are demonstrated by monitoring the temperature distribution during local heating of a tisuue phantom. Additionally, the reachable accuracy, as well as reachable temporal and local resolution are discussed.**

Keywords–Ultrasound; Temperature Monitoring; Annular Arrays; Tissue phantoms.

I. INTRODUCTION

Hyperthermia for cancer therapy is a promising alternative to the widely spread radio- or chemotherapy [1]. It works by thermal destruction of the tumour, e.g., by High Intensity Focussed Ultrasound (HIFU) or radio frequency ablation. A minimal temperature of $45\ ^{\circ}C$ to $63\ ^{\circ}C$ (according to literature [2][3]) is necessary for a successful therapy. Whereas the temperature in the surrounding tissue should be as low as possible to avoid tissue injury. Especially if there are vessels near the tumour they cause a heat transport resulting in a too low temperature in the tumour and a possible heat accumulation in other tissue. Due to these complications, a temperature monitoring during the hyperthermia surgery is needed. Although imaging techniques like CT or MRI can be used to determine a temperature distribution, they are hardly applicable during the surgery. So, ultrasound is the preferred method.

The classical approach to monitor temperature changes evaluates the displacement of scatterers in the tissue caused by thermal expansion [4]. This approach has some significant drawbacks: First, the sound velocity increases with temperature, which reduces the time of flight of the echo of one reflector. In opposite, the thermal expansion increases the distance and thereby the time of flight. This reduces the sensitivity and in worst case, there is no change in time of flight with a change in temperature. Second, the thermal expansion coefficient is unknown and there is a large variation not only between different types of tissue but also individual. This results in a temperature distribution localised at a wrong position.

This contribution indroduces an approach to monitor the temperature distribution within a tissue phantom. Evaluating the backscattered echoes gained with an annular array, allows a synthetic focussing to determine the longitudinal wave velocity within the phantom locally resolved. As this sound velocity is a function of temperature, the temperature distribution can be determined from the sound velocity profile.

Note that in this contribution sound velocity always means the longitudinal wave speed. Effects of denaturation, which also change the longitudinal wave speed are neglected and will be the objective of future work. Section II describes the used experimental set-up, Section III explains the developed measuring technique and Section IV gives the results of the experiments. Finally, Section V concludes the paper and gives perspectives for future work.

II. EXPERIMENTAL SET-UP

Preliminary examination had been necessary to develop a tissue phantom with acoustic properties similar to tissue, which models the scattering of tissue and which also changes its properties with increasing temperature, when denaturation occurs in tissue. To develop the measuring technique material with stable and reproducible properties had been required, so that using real tissue was not possible. As bulk material we selected a gel of 5%-polyacrylamide, consisting of 26.9% acrylamide, 1.4% bisacrylamide, 71.7% water or egg-white as well as ammonium persulphate and N, N, N', N'-Tetramethylethylendiamine to start polymerisation. As scattering particles we use Chlorella Vulgaris, a robust monocellular green algae, which can be cultivated easily. The resulting gel-phantom is placed in a water basin where it can be heated and where the ultrasonic measurements can be performed. Figure 1 shows a Cross section of algae in the gel, obtained with an optical microscope.

Figure 2 shows the basic set-up with the gel (left) in a water basin and the ultrasound annular array (right). For data acquisition, a measuring board with 8 channels, a sampling rate of 125 MS/s and a samplesize of 14 bit is used.

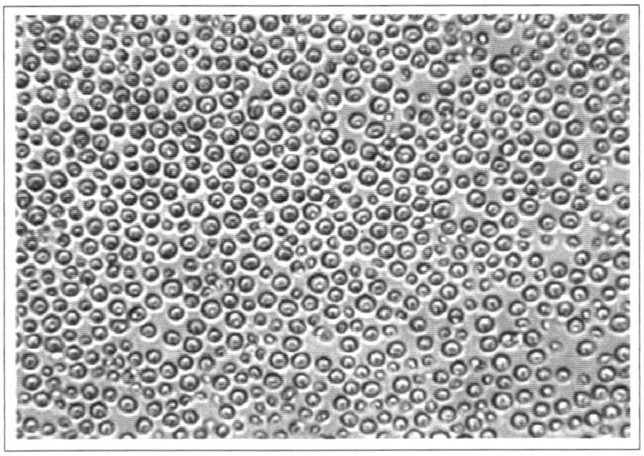

Figure 1. Cross section of the algae in the polyacrylamide-gel, obtained with a optical microscope.

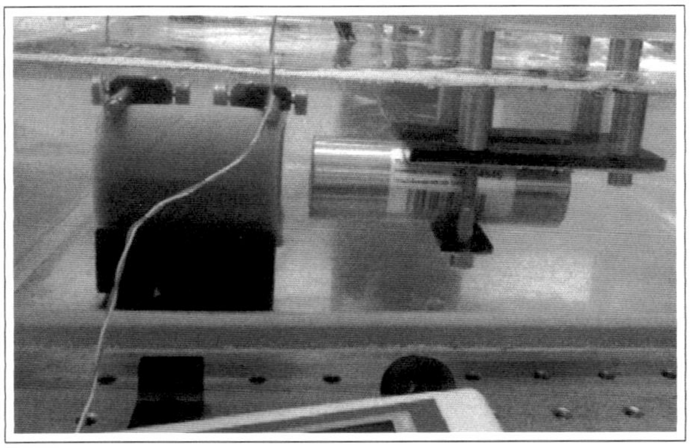

Figure 2. Experimental set-up with gel (left, green) in a water basin and the used annular array, on the right.

A custom-made annular array with a centre frequency of 10 MHz is used. Its structure has been optimized for the measurements and it has been developed for high temperatures as the common ones would not resist them. Figure 3 shows the structure of the array. The whole piezoelectric material is curved spherically with a radius of curvature of 50 mm. All elements have the same active area, and so their natural focus is in the same depth. This is necessary for effective focussing. The inner and outer radii as well as the r and z coordinates, used for focussing, see (2), are given in Table I. Also, the central element is a ring because there is a tube along the rotation axis of the transducer. For some experimental set-ups, gas, which was solved in the water, cumulates in the curvature of the transducer during the heating. The tube can be used to pump off this gas.

If the phantom is placed in a water basin, it can be heated only to an overall temperature, independent of location. An alternative set-up, which allows to generate a temperature gradient, is shown in Figure 4. At the bottom, there is a basin

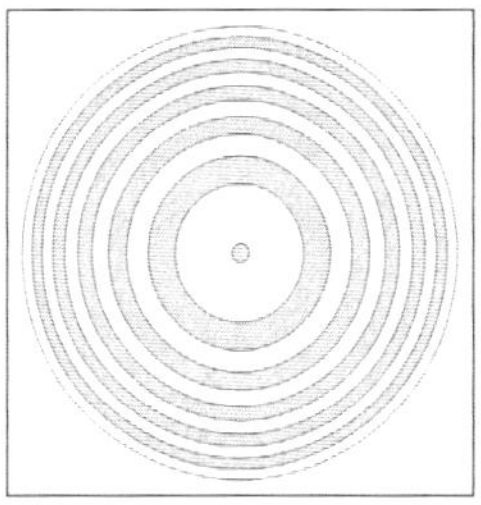

Figure 3. Structure of the used annular array; white: active area, grey: passive area.

TABLE I. RADII OF THE RINGS OF THE ANNULAR ARRAY.

Element-No.	1	2	3	4	5	6
r_i $[mm]$	0,5	5,05	7,13	8,72	10,07	11,25
r_a $[mm]$	3,59	6,18	7,96	9,42	10,68	11,80
r_{eff} $[mm]$	2,56	5,64	7,56	9,08	10,38	11,53
z_{eff} $[mm]$	0,07	0,32	0,57	0,83	1,09	1,37

with water, which is kept at a temperature of 4 $°C$. A second basin filled with the phantom material is placed above. It has a baseplate of metal for a good thermal coupling. On the top, there is a heating surface with a small hole in the middle, where the array can be placed. As the lateral dimensions are much larger than the height of the set-up (diameter of 20 cm and height of 6 cm), a one-dimensional temperature distribution can be assumed near the rotation axis of the gel.

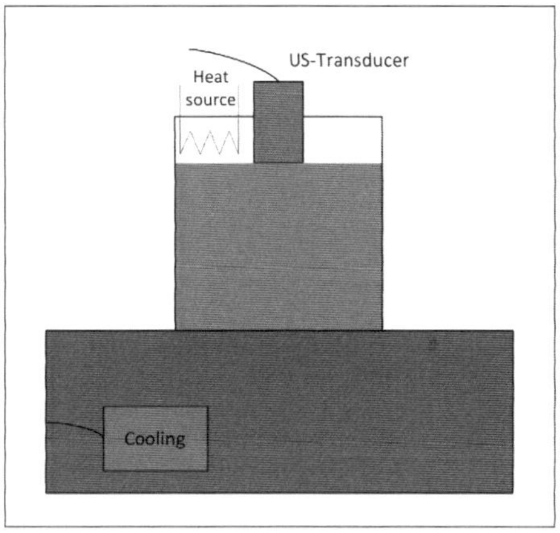

Figure 4. Schematic depiction of the experimental set-up to generate an temperature gradient. There is a cooling at the bottom and a heating surface at the top.

III. MEASURING METHOD

To evaluate the measured data, synthetic focussing is used. This means that each element is driven separately and the reflected wave is recognized on each element. The resulting signal for each element is digitized and stored separately. Although this reduces the signal to noise ratio, it can be used to superpose the recorded signals afterwards, whereby the delay times between the signals can be chosen arbitrarily.

Figure 5 shows an example a signal by emitting and receiving with the central element, averaged over 1000 signals to improve the signal-to-noise ratio (SNR). At the top, the whole signal is shown, including the surface echo from water to gel (42 μs), the back-wall echo from gel to aluminium (105 μs) and a multiple reflection in the aluminium plate (118 μs). Figure 5 (bottom) shows a zoom on the surface echo. Whereas there are no previous echoes, there can be seen many echoes after the surface echo. These echoes are backscattered from the algae. Similar signals are obtained for all 36 combinations of emitters and receivers.

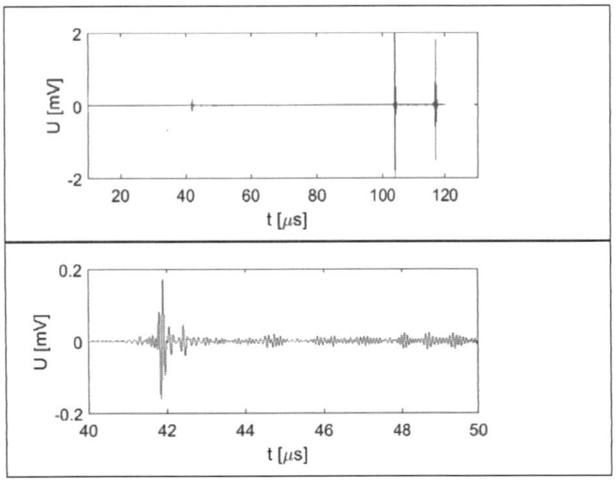

Figure 5. Recorded signal by emitting and receiving with the central ring; top: whole echo including surface echo and back-wall echoes; bottom: signal part including surface echoes and backscattered echoes from the algae

For the following considerations, it shall be assumed that the amplitude of the wave, backscattered from an algae, is proportional to the amplitude of the incident wave. The amplitude becomes maximal if the focus is located at the scatterer.

Figure 7 shows the calculated sound fields for focussing in to different depth, to 35 mm, at the top and to $45mm$ at the bottom. Different focussing regimes are used:

left: $c_{Med} = c_{Fok}$, focussing works correktly;

middle: using focussing regime for $c_{Fok} = 1200\ m/s$ in the same medium, resulting focus is too near at the transducer,

right: focussing with the same regime as at the left, but in a medium wich $c_{Med} = 1200\ m/s$, focus shifts away from transducer

As Figure 7 shows, the resulting focus of an annular array depends on the transducer geometry, the sound velocity of the propagation medium and the used set of delay times and it shows that focussing only works correctly, if the sound velocity used for focussing is similar to the one of the medium.

So, the goal is to find that set of delay times for focussing where the resulting signal amplitude becomes maximal. How the sound velocity is connected to the set of focussing times is described in the following section.

A. Synthetic Focussing

Synthetic focussing means that the signals are superposed with an arbitrary delay time.

$$S_{Fok} = \sum_{n=1}^{6} \sum_{m=1}^{6} S_{mn}(t - \Delta t_m - \Delta t_n + 2\Delta t_1) \qquad (1)$$

where S_{mn} is the signal emitted from element m and received from element n. As the signals are obtained by scattering and not by a specular reflection, it is sufficient to calculate the different propagation path lengths from each element to an arbitrary assigned focus point on the acoustic axis of the array and dividing the differences by the sound velocity, The different propagation paths are illustrated in Figure 6.

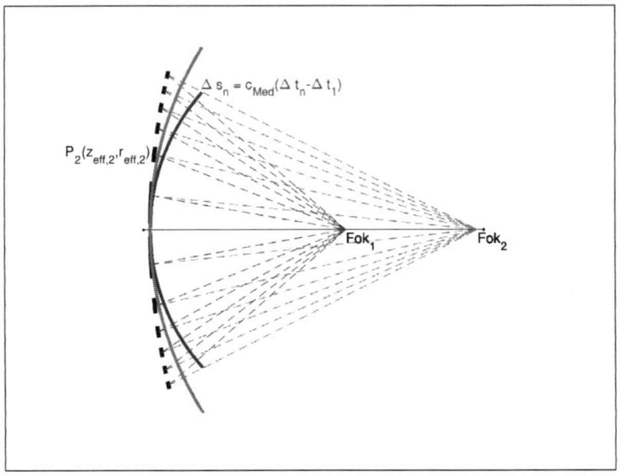

Figure 6. Illustration of the path length differences to generate a virtual curvature.

$$\Delta t_n = \frac{\sqrt{(z_{Fok} - z_{eff,n})^2 + r_{eff,n}^2}}{c_{Med}} \qquad (2)$$

with $z_{eff,n}$ and $r_{eff,n}$ are the coordinates, which are used for ring no. n. They are given in Table I. The resulting times are accumulated in a matrix: the focussing regime F, which only depends on the assigned focus point z_{Fok} and the used (assumed) sound velocity c_{Fok}.

$$F(z_{Fok}, c_{Fok}) = [\Delta t_1, \Delta t_2, ..., \Delta t_N] \qquad (3)$$

Note that the possible focussing range is limited. It involves the range from the near field length of a single element to the near field length of the whole array.

B. Determination of average sound velocity

The determination of the average sound velocity works by the following steps:

- choosing a time frame at an arbitrary position of the signal with a width of about 1 μs
- determination of the time of flight t_{max} where the signal, emitted and received with the central element, has its maximal amplitude
- assumption of a (reasonable) testing sound velocity c_{Test} and of the corresponding position of the scatterer $z_{Test} = c_{Test}\ t_{max}/2$
- focussing all signals using (1) with the para-meters z_{Test} and c_{Test} and determination of resulting signal energy as well as the resulting signal amplitude

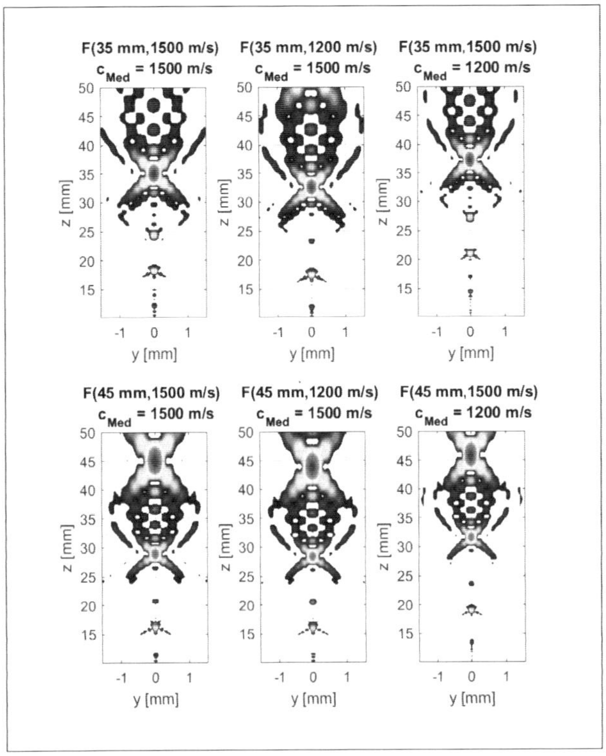

Figure 7. Calculated sound fields for focussing in to different depth; top: 35 mm, bottom: 45mm, for different media und different focussing regimes

- variation of c_{Test} and taking up signal energy $E(c_{Test})$ and Amplitude $A(c_{Test})$ as a function of the testing sound velocity
- determination of the correct average sound velocity by determining the maximum of both of the curves $c_{med,A} = argmax(A(c_{test}))$, $c_{med,E} = argmax(E(c_{test}))$
- plausibility check via comparing the maximal amplitude A_{max} with the averaged amplitude $\bar{A}$ and the requirement $A_{max} > 2\bar{A}$ (if only noise is evaluated they will be nearly similar)
- stepwise shifting of the time frame through the recorded signal and determination of the average sound velocity $c_{av,i}$ locally resolved.

The width of the time frame is determined by the demand that the frame should be much longer than the signal length of about 0.4 μs but not that large, that several echoes are in one window. Also the testing sound velocities should be in a reasonable range. As the sound velocity of tissue is in a range of 1500 m/s to 1700 m/s values below 1000 m/s or above 2500 m/s are not useful.

Figure 8 shows an example of a resulting curve of determined signal energy versus testing sound velocity. If there are not sufficient scatterers in the frame, the resulting energy is nearly constant and there is no significant maximum. In this case, the determined sound velocity is neglected.

After determining the correct average sound velocities $c_{av,i}$ for each frame position, the position z_i of the scattering algae

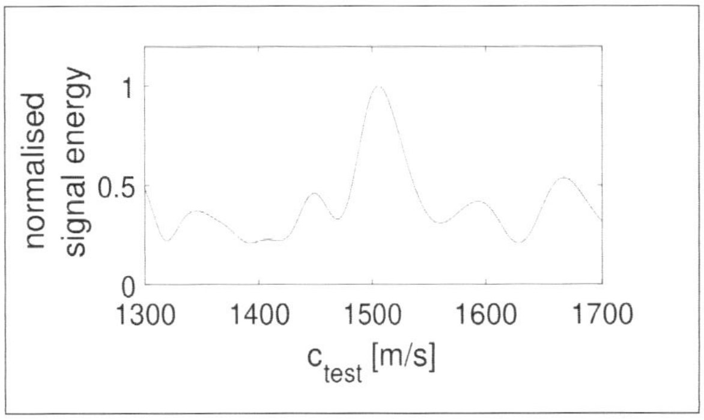

Figure 8. Evaluation of the resulting signal energy as a function of the used testing sound velocity.

can be determined. The value of $c_{av,i}$ is the average sound velocity from the transducer to the corresponding focus depth. To determine the local sound velocity, which is only averaged from one position to the next, (4) can be used:

$$c_{loc,i} = \frac{c_{av,i} z_i - c_{av,i-1} z_{i-1}}{z_i - z_{i-1}} \tag{4}$$

To determine the temperature distribution additionally, only the dependence of sound velocity from temperature is needed.

IV. Results

Figure 9 shows a determined sound velocity profile with sound velocity versus time of flight (top) and sound velocity versus reflector position (bottom). As this is a measurement for constant temperature (and so for constant sound velocity), the observable deviations can be interpreted as the uncertainty of the technique. The measurement uncertainty is about $\pm 15\ m/s$ or 2%, independent if signal energy or signal amplitude are evaluated.

After validating the measurement technique for constant sound velocities, it shall be used to monitor a heating process. The experimental set-up shown in Figure 4 was used to generate a temperature gradient. Measurements were starting with switching on the heat source. One measure was started each 20 s and the introduced algorithm was applied on the measured data. The results are shown in Figure 10. Each column of the picture represents one reconstructed sound velocity profile as it is shown in Figure 9, whereby the sound velocity is colour-coded. So, the y-axis represents the measuring depth and it is directed in a way that the heat source and the transducer would be above and the cooling would be below the picture. The x-axis represents the progressing duration of the measurements. It is easily notable that a sound velocity gradient appears with increasing measurement duration. Note that there is already a small gradient when the measurement starts. The reason is that the bottom is kept to 4 $°C$ whereas the top of the gel-phantom has room temperature of about 20 $°C$.

V. Conclusion

This contribution introduced and qualified a new measurement technique to measure temperatures respectively sound velocity locally and temporarily resolved in tissue phantoms. As an absolute value for the sound velocity is measured, it is not only possible to determine a relative change of temperature,

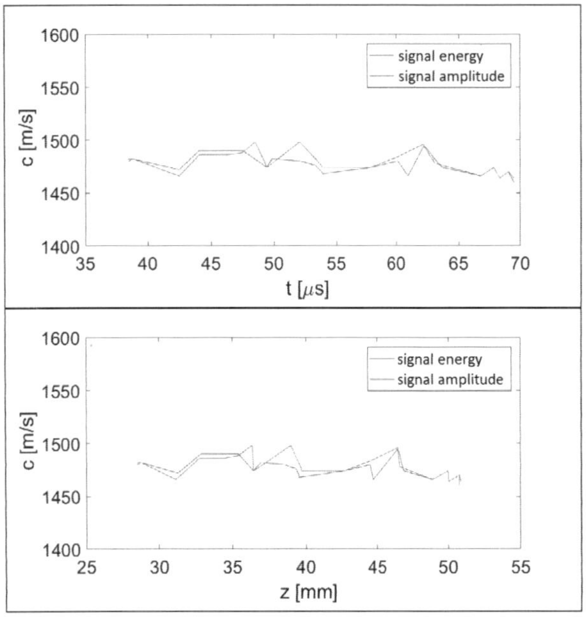

Figure 9. Reconstructed sound velocity profiles, evaluating signal energy (blue) and signal amplitude (red); top: sound velocity versus time of flight, bottom: sound velocity versus measurement depth

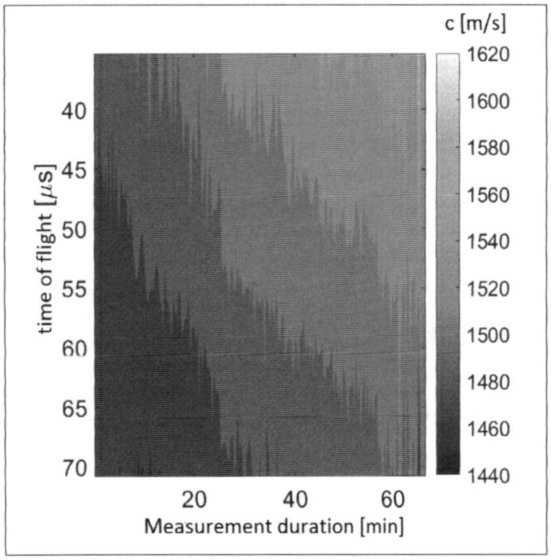

Figure 10. Resulting monitored temperature profile; colour-coded: determined sound velocity, y-axis: time of flight respectively measurement depth, x-axis: duration of the measurements.

like in the classic approach, but it is possible to relate the temperature to fixed measurement positions. The technique works independently of the thermal expansion of the tissue.

Currently, the measurement uncertainty of the technique is about 2% the reachable local resolution is about $1\ mm$ at $10\ MHz$. The temporal resolution depends on the total duration of the experiment. For durations of a few minutes it is possible to measure each second. For longer experiments a measure can be performed each $20\ s$. It is mainly limited by memory capacity and by the available data transfer rates of the measurement hardware.

To improve the reachable accuracy, examination of the used focussing regimes are necessary. Improved regimes result in a smaller focus area, so that the evaluation algorithm is more sensitiv to the sound velocity.

Enhancing the signal to noise ratio of the used electronics, especially of the amplifiers in the receive channels, allows to reduce the necessary number of averaged signals and so to enhance the possible temporal resolution. Examinations with transducers with another frequency range are planned to examine the relation between frequency and local resolution.

ACKNOWLEDGMENT

The authors would like to thank the Deutsche Forschungsgemeinschaft (DFG) for the financial support in the ongoing project: 260366138, and SONAXIS for developing and manufacturing the array transducer for high temperatures.

REFERENCES

[1] G. Shen, Y. Chen, and G. Ren, "An improved tumour temperature measurement and control method for superficial tumour ultrasound hyperthermia therapeutic system," in Journal of Physics: Conference Series, vol. 48, no. 1. IOP Publishing, 2006, p. 653.

[2] H.-Y. Tseng, G.-B. Lee, C.-Y. Lee, Y.-H. Shih, and X.-Z. Lin, "Localised heating of tumours utilising injectable magnetic nanoparticles for hyperthermia cancer therapy," IET nanobiotechnology, vol. 3, no. 2, 2009, pp. 46–54.

[3] D. A. Iero, L. Crocco, and T. Isernia, "Thermal and microwave constrained focusing for patient-specific breast cancer hyperthermia: A robustness assessment," IEEE Transactions on Antennas and Propagation, vol. 62, no. 2, 2014, pp. 814–821.

[4] A. Anand, D. Savery, and C. Hall, "Three-dimensional spatial and temporal temperature imaging in gel phantoms using backscattered ultrasound," IEEE transactions on ultrasonics, ferroelectrics, and frequency control, vol. 54, no. 1, 2007, pp. 23–31.

Spatially-Resolved Determination of Transverse Wave Speed in Tissue Phantoms Using High-Frequent Ultrasound

Lukas Timmermann, Mario Wolf, André Juhrig, Carmen Wolf, Katharina Rath and Elfgard Kühnicke

Technical University Dresden
Solid State Electronics Laboratories
Mommsenstr. 15, 01069 Dresden
Email: lukas.timmermann@tu-dresden.de

Felix Krujatz

Technical University Dresden
Institute of Natural Materials Technology
Bergstr. 120, 01069 Dresden
Email: felix.krujatz@tu-dresden.de

Abstract—**Online temperature measurement in biological tissue would improve the hyperthermia therapy. This contribution presents a novel method for measuring the shear wave speed in biological tissue with very small echo signal amplitudes from scattering particles. Since the tissue's properties change during heating, it is not possible to average measures taken over a long time period to improve Signal-to-Noise-Ratio (SNR). The novel method relies on evaluating the signal's energy as a function of time shifted signals instead of using a cross correlation. For reproducible experiments, a tissue phantom made of polyacrylamide and algae is used.**

Keywords–Ultrasound; Shear Wave Velocity; Scattering Particles; Tissue Phantom.

I. INTRODUCTION

In cancer therapy, malicious tissue can be destructed non-invasively using hyperthermia treatment. To be sure that the destruction is complete, it is important that the whole cancer as well as a security zone reaches a temperature of at least 56 °C [1]. Due to the lack of non-invasive temperature monitoring, the used power and duration of heating is currently selected by the doctor based on his knowledge and experience. Though this method works pretty well, it is very fault-prone if there is a large blood vessel located near the tissue to be destructed. In this case, the vessel may transfer the induced heat away from the tumor, which makes it very difficult to have a good balance between complete destruction of malicious tissue and unintended impairment of surrounding tissue.

Non-invasive, locally resolved online monitoring of the tissue temperature would improve the success of the hyperthermia therapy. Since tissue has very similar acoustic properties compared to water, its longitudinal sound speed c_L is strongly dependent on temperature [2]. The locally resolved temperature measurement is introduced in [3]. However, the investigations in [4] showed that c_L does not only depend on temperature, but also on the tissue's denaturation state. Contrary, the shear wave speed c_S has low sensitivity on temperature, but is sensitive to tissue modification. To be able to measure temperature change and denaturation separately, it is necessary to know both c_L and c_S, spatially and temporally resolved.

This contribution deals with robust measurement of c_S in tissue. Section II describes the experimental setup and used materials. The experimental results are presented in Section III. Since the ultrasound signals backscattered by the tissue's structure are very small, it is indispensable to improve the SNR, which is described in Section IV. Finally, Section V provides a conclusion and an outlook of future research.

II. DESCRIPTION OF EXPERIMENTS

A. Tissue phantoms

To ensure reproducibility, instead of real biological tissue we are using tissue phantoms made of 5 % polyacrylamide gel (26.9 % acrylamide, 1.4 % bisacrylamide, 71.7 % water as well as ammonium persulfate and N,N,N',N'-tetramethylethylenediamine to start polymerization). The gel is doped with Chlorella Vulgaris, single-celled green algae that act as scatter particles. This green alga is a good choice, because it behaves like a real cell, but also is very robust and easy to grow.

B. Measurement setup

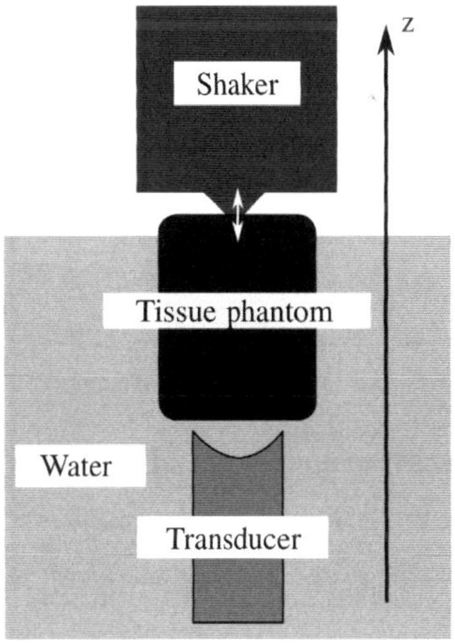

Figure 1. Setup for measuring shear wave speed c_S.

The measurement setup consists of the tissue phantom described in Section II-A, an ultrasound transducer and a shaker, which is in contact with the phantom (Figure 1). For better wave propagation, the transducer and the tissue phantom are stored in water. The oscillation generated by the shaker is coupled into the phantom, where a shear wave starts to propagate. This leads to a movement of scattering particles, such as algae cells, inside the phantom. Since the shear wave velocity is in the range of a few meter per second only, it is possible to observe the cells' movement using longitudinal ultrasound waves with a velocity of $c_L \approx 1500\,\mathrm{m/s}$ and high pulse repetition rates. The shear wave speed c_S is calculated from the observed cell movement in various depths inside the phantom. The positions are selected windowing the ultrasound signal.

To investigate shear wave propagation at different temperatures and degrees of denaturation, the water may be heated by a thermostat. Due to the outgasing of the water, and thus rising air bubbles, the transducer is located beneath the phantom. This ensures that no gas bubbles accumulate in front of the transducer, which would disturb the measurement.

III. MEASUREMENT RESULTS

Using several A-scans, it is possible to observe the shear wave. Figure 2 shows a M-Mode scan of the tissue's movement. It can be clearly seen that the echoes from the tissue phantom's surface show the movement induced by the shear wave. Using the time difference of two matching oscillation states from top and bottom surface (vertical lines in Figure 2) and the sample's thickness, the shear wave speed can be calculated. In the presented experiment, this yields to a mean speed of $c_S \approx 7.8\,\mathrm{m/s}$. This value also matches values from literature, as shown in [5].

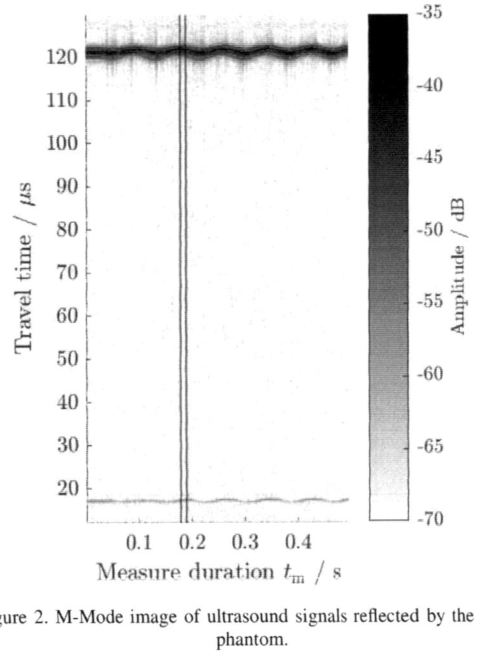

Figure 2. M-Mode image of ultrasound signals reflected by the tissue phantom.

The oscillation of the surfaces can be recovered using a correlation analysis. The maxima of the windowed signal's cross correlation give the surface's position at the arrival time of the signal. This is shown in Figure 3. Fitting a sinus to these data gives information about the current oscillation state, especially the phase.

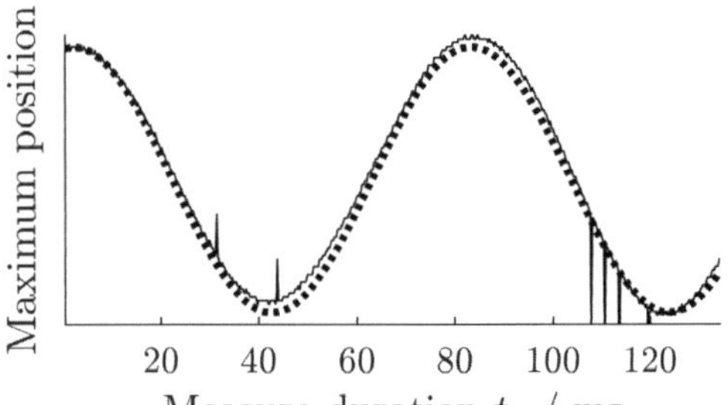

Figure 3. Positions of the cross correlation's maxima of echoes from tissue's bottom surface (solid line) and sinus fit to the data (dotted line).

Unfortunately, this method is only applicable for signals with a good SNR. As shown in Figure 2, this condition is only met on large interfaces with sufficient impedance difference. Since the cell's echo amplitude is only a little bit bigger as the noise amplitude, the cross correlation function is not able to distinguish between signal part and noise and thus provides wrong results. The SNR may be improved by increasing the number of measured cycles with at least one shear wave period and then averaging over these signals. However, the measure time would then increase, which in practice is not acceptable.

IV. EVALUATION OF SIGNALS WITH LOW SNR

In contrast to the cross correlation of the signals, in this section, the signal's energy as a function of time shifted signals will be evaluated. If several similar signals are superimposed, the resulting signal energy will increase while the resulting noise energy decreases. However, this will only work, if both transducer and reflector stay at a constant position over time.

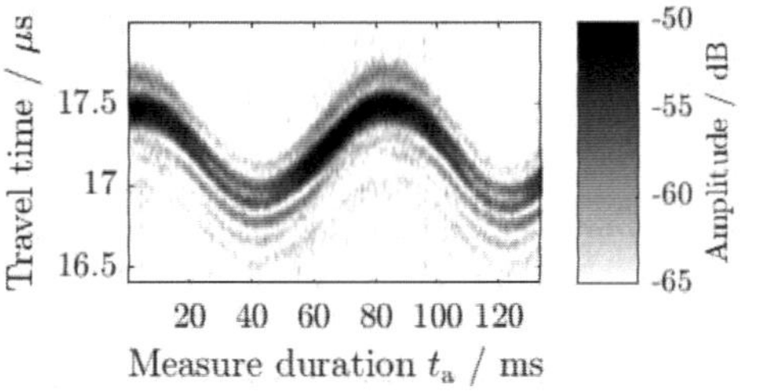

Figure 4. M-Mode picture of ultrasound signals reflected from the phantom's bottom surface.

The signals shown in Figure 4, which is a detail of Figure 2, will not sum up constructively on superimposing along measure duration, because the surface's position does change. To improve SNR as described above, the signals will need to be time-shifted with a time resulting from the shaker's oscillation y_S. The oscillation can be expressed by

$$y_S(t, \varphi) = a_S \sin(\omega_S t + \varphi) \quad (1)$$

where ω_S is the known shaker's angular frequency. The amplitude a_S depends on the phantom's damping and the travel time of the shear wave, however, it may be estimated using the surface's echoes. The time-shift t_{sh} used to align the signals is described in (2).

$$t_{sh}(t_a, \varphi) = \frac{a_S}{c_L} \sin(\omega_S t_a + \varphi) \quad (2)$$

The time t_a is the arrival time of the ultrasound pulse. So, the single parameter left to determine is φ, which may be varied.

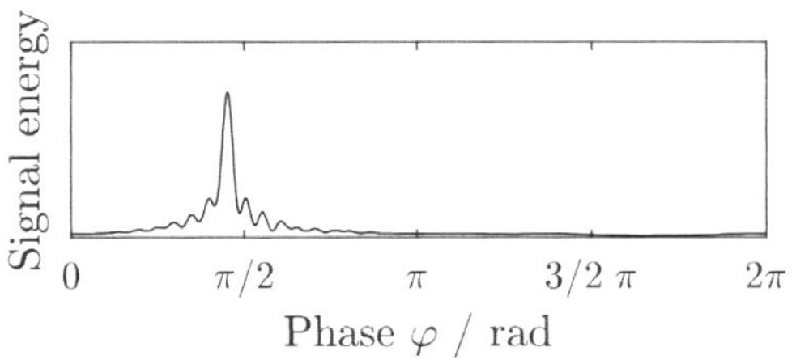

Figure 5. Signal energy as a function of phase shift φ. The maximum marks the current phase φ_m at time t_a. For this example the best phase is $\varphi_m = 1.413\,\text{rad}$

Figure 5 shows the calculated phase dependent signal energy using (2) for the signals shown in Figure 4. The maximum in the signal energy indicates the phase φ_m, where the model described by (1) maps the oscillation in the chosen window best.

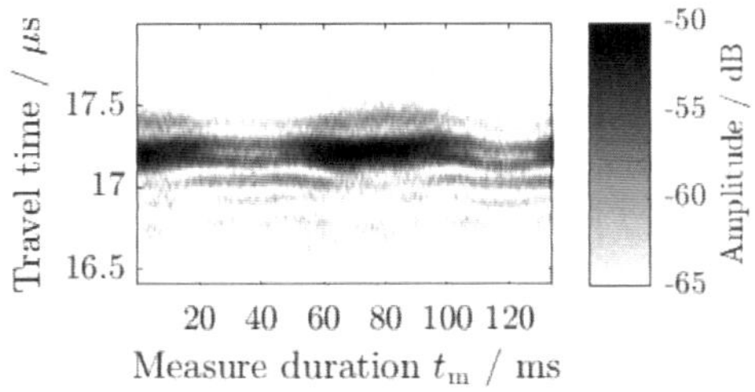

Figure 6. Time-shifted signals from Figure 4 using the phase determined with signal energy method.

The presented method can be tested by shifting the echo signals with the determined phase. This in done in Figure 6. If the model and the determined phase are correct, the figure should show all echo signals at the same travel time displaying horizontal lines. Apparently, this works pretty well in the presented example, although the form of the echo signals varies depending on oscillation state.

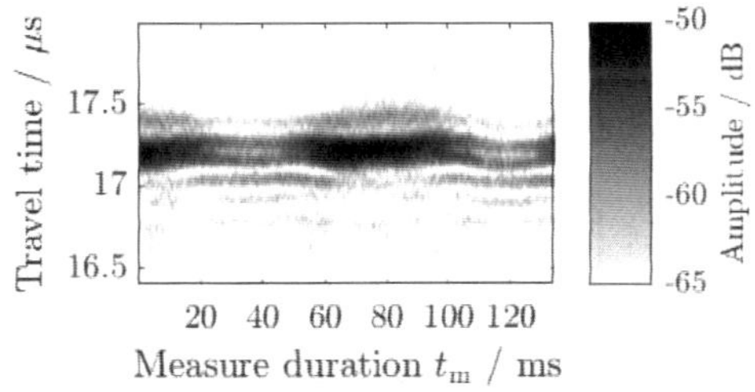

Figure 7. Time-shifted signals from Figure 4 using phase from cross correlation.

For verification, the signal shift shown in Figure 6 is also done with the phase determined by the cross correlation method introduced in Section III and is shown in Figure 7. Since the determined phases ($\varphi_c = 1.411\,\text{rad}$ and $\varphi_m = 1.413\,\text{rad}$ from cross correlation method and signal energy method, respectively) are almost equal, it is consistent that Figures 6 and 7 almost show the same pattern.

When windowing the ultrasound signals, it is possible to determine the shear wave's phase at different depths z. This allows a spatially resolved identification of the shear wave's speed c_S with both methods, but for a low SNR the cross correlation method is not applicable.

V. Conclusion and Outlook

The knowledge of the shear wave's speed may allow to distinguish between the effects of denaturation and temperature change on the longitudinal wave speed c_L. This would improve the non-invasive temperature monitoring and thus enhance quality of hyperthermia therapy.

Due to its slow propagation speed in tissue, shear waves may be observed using high frequent longitudinal ultrasound waves. This contribution proposes a method to determine the shear wave's propagation speed spatially resolved in biological tissue. For better reproducibility, we use a tissue phantom made of polyacrylamide and algae. The shear waves are generated using an external shaker.

Since the shear wave causes moving reflectors, it is not possible to improve the signal quality by recording the same scene multiple times and then averaging to reduce noise. The presented novel method evaluates the energy of superimposed time-shifted signals and is capable to deal with signals that have a low SNR. A comparison with a method using the cross correlation of signals from a big interface confirmed the functionality and accuracy of the presented approach. Currently, we are improving the novel method's robustness to work with signals that have a very poor SNR, such as echoes from moving scattering particles.

Acknowledgment

The authors would like to thank the Deutsche Forschungsgemeinschaft (DFG) for financial support in project 260366138.

References

[1] J. Kormann, D. Ockert, and A. Bunk, "Hochfrequenz-Thermoablation bei Lebertumoren," Zentralblatt für Chirurgie, vol. 126, no. 8, 2001, pp. 576–585.

[2] W. Marczak, "Water as a standard in the measurements of speed of sound in liquids," The Journal of the Acoustical Society of America, vol. 102, no. 5, Nov. 1997, pp. 2776–2779.

[3] M. Wolf et al., "Temperature monitoring in tissue phantoms via spatially resolved measurement of longitudinal wave speed," SENSORDEVICES, 2018.

[4] G. Shin and J. Helfmann, "Die Temperaturabhänginkeit der Ultraschallgeschwingdigkeit in biologischen Medien," Shaker-Verlag, 1997.

[5] L. Sandrin et al., "Shear elasticity probe for soft tissues with 1-d transient elastography," IEEE Transactions on Ultrasonics, Ferroelectrics and Frequency Control, vol. 49, no. 4, Apr. 2002, pp. 436–446.

A Transducer with Inversion Layer Technique for Expanded Lesion Size in HIFU Surgery

Jin Ho Sung, Da Sol Kwon, Eun Young Jeong, Jong Seob Jeong
Department of Medical Biotechnology, Dongguk University
Seoul, 04620, Republic of Korea
madeinjinho@dongguk.edu, kwondas_31@dongguk.edu, chocoeun7@dongguk.edu, jjsspace@dongguk.edu

Abstract—**In High Intensity Focused Ultrasound (HIFU) surgery, benign or malignant tumors can be treated through the thermal and mechanical effects of the focused ultrasound. However, the overall HIFU treatment time is relatively long compared with the open surgery because the irradiation area of the ultrasound beam is very small. In this paper, we present a dual-concentric HIFU transducer with inversion layer technique to extend the focal region in the axial direction. The performance of the proposed technique was demonstrated by Finite Element Analysis (FEA) simulation, and the lesion size was increased by 97% compared with the conventional single element transducer based on the extended -6 dB Depth of Focus (DOF). Therefore, the proposed HIFU transducer can be one of the useful ways to shorten the total treatment time of the HIFU surgery.**

Keywords-finite element analysis; dual-concentric HIFU transducer; high intensity focused ultrasound; inversion layer; phase inversion.

I. Introduction

In High Intensity Focused Ultrasound (HIFU) surgery, one of the main disadvantages is relatively long treatment time, mainly due to the small therapeutic area per sonication [1]. In order to solve this problem, some researchers have developed specially designed HIFU transducers, such as toric or split-aperture transducers [2][3]. However, they can mainly expand the lesion size in the lateral direction rather than the axial direction. In this paper, we propose a dual-concentric HIFU transducer with inversion layer technique that can increase lesion size in the axial direction to treat a deeply located target. The performance of the proposed technique was demonstrated by Finite Element Analysis (FEA) using PZFlex tool (OnScale, Cupertino, CA, USA) [4].

The rest of the paper is structured as follows. In Section II and Section III, the principle of the proposed technique and the simulation results are explained, respectively. The conclusions are drawn in Section IV.

II. Methods

The proposed HIFU transducer consists of disc-type and ring-type elements with the confocal point. Each element is driven by two input signals with opposite phases, i.e., 0° and 180°. In this case, the axial beam pattern with a deep valley can be generated [5]. To complement that deep notch point, multi-frequency ultrasound generated by the inversion layer technique was employed [6]. In other words, a dual-concentric transducer using inversion layer technique can achieve a relatively uniform -6 dB Depth of Focus (DOF). Note that DOF is closely related to the lesion size. In the FEA simulation, PZT4 (Lead Zirconate Titanate) and unloaded epoxy were used for piezoelectric material and kerf filler, respectively. To implement inversion layer technique, two piezoelectric layers with opposite poling direction were employed as shown in Figure 1(b). A conventional single element transducer in Figure 1(a) was also designed to compare the performance of the proposed transducer. The outer diameter of the ring-type element was 31.4 mm, the inner diameter of the disc-type element was 22 mm, and a kerf width was 0.2 mm. The aperture had a concave shape, and the focal length was 35 mm. There was no backing layer to maximize the transmitted energy, and water was chosen as the medium.

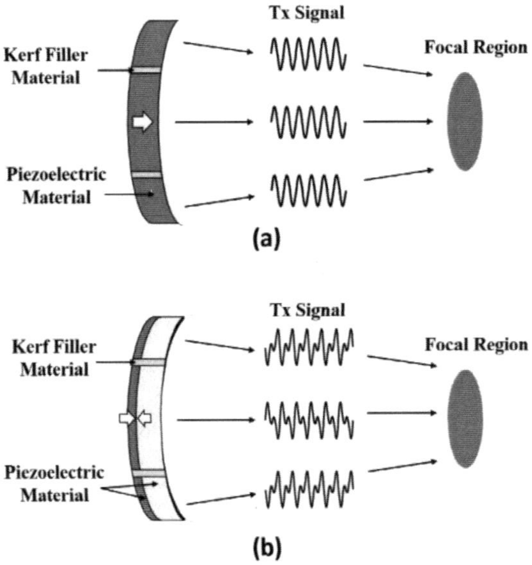

Figure 1. Schematic diagrams of (a) the conventional single element transducer and (b) the proposed transducer. Note that a white arrow indicates polling direction of piezoelectric material.

III. Results

The simulation results of electrical impedance are shown in Figure 2(a) and (b). The conventional single element transducer in Figure 2(a) had single-resonance peak at 3

MHz frequency, and the proposed transducer in Figure 2(b) had dual-resonance peaks at 3 MHz and 6 MHz at the same time. This phenomenon may reduce transmitted power, but it can be compensated by adjusting driving voltage of the input signal. In the sound field simulation, the conventional single element transducer had -6 dB DOF of 5.97 mm as shown in Figure 3(a), while the proposed transducer in Figure 3(b) had -6 dB DOF of 11.74 mm, which is 97% improved compared with the conventional single element transducer. The -6 dB lateral beamwidths of the conventional single element transducer and the proposed transducer were 0.79 mm and 0.72 mm, respectively. The lateral beamwidth of the proposed transducer was slightly reduced (7.7%) compared with the conventional single element transducer. Note that -6 dB lateral beamwidths were obtained based on beam projection scheme while the -6 dB DOF was acquired at maximum pressure in the axial direction.

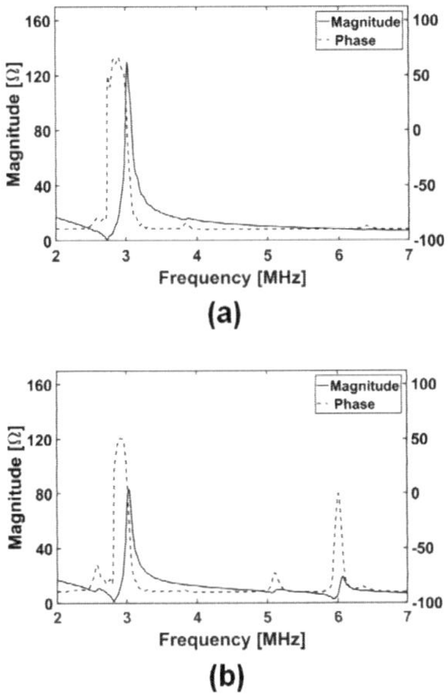

Figure 2. Electrical impedance simulation results: (a) the conventional single element transducer and (b) the proposed transducer (inner disc-type element).

IV. CONCLUSION

In this paper, we propose the dual-concentric HIFU transducer with the inversion layer technique to extend the focal length (i.e., -6 dB DOF). The proposed method can axially increase the focal length related to the lesion size by 97% compared with the conventional single element transducer and thus shorten the total treatment time of the HIFU surgery.

ACKNOWLEDGMENT

This work was supported by the National Research Foundation of Korea (NRF) grant funded by the Korea government (MSIT) (No. 2018R1A2B6004103).

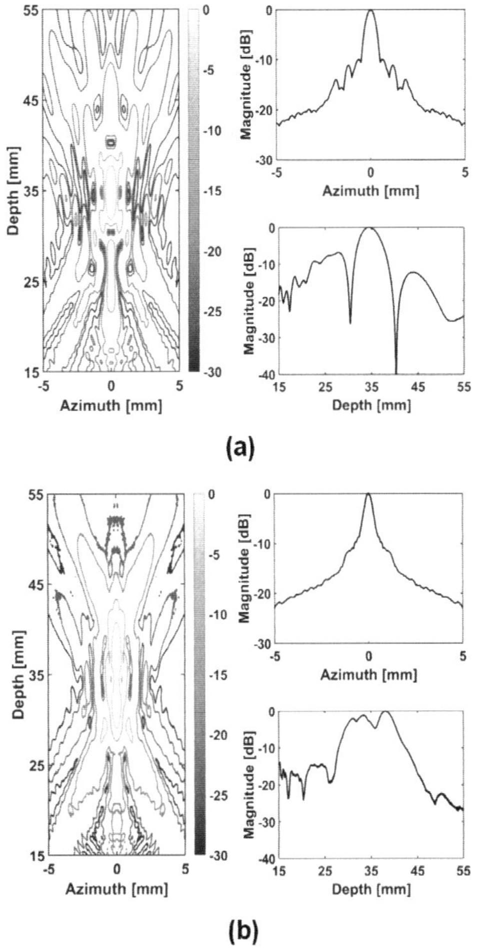

Figure 3. Sound field simulation results including 2D sound field, lateral beam pattern, and axial beam pattern: (a) the conventional single element transducer and (b) the proposed transducer.

REFERENCES

[1] G. T. ter Haar, "Ultrasound focal beam surgery," Ultrasound Med. Biol., vol. 21, no. 9, pp. 1089–1100, 1995.

[2] D. Melodelima et al., "Thermal ablation produced using a surgical toroidal high-intensity focused ultrasound device is independent from hepatic inflow occlusion," Phys. Med. Biol., vol. 54, no. 20, pp. 6353–6369, 2009.

[3] K. Sasaki et al., "Effect of split-focus approach on producing larger coagulation in swine liver," Ultrasound Med. Biol., vol. 29, no. 4, pp. 591–599, 2003.

[4] Onscale Inc. Web Site: https://pzflex.com/software/.

[5] J. S. Jeong, "Dual concentric-sectored HIFU transducer with phase shifted ultrasound excitation for expanded necrotic region: A simulation study," IEEE Trans. Ultrason., Ferroelect., Freq. Control, vol. 60, no. 5, pp. 924–931, 2013.

[6] C. Y. Park, D. S. Kwon, J. H. Sung, and J. S. Jeong, "Dual-frequency ultrasound transducer using inversion layer technique for therapeutic ultrasound surgery," IEEE Sensors J., vol. 17, no. 21, pp. 6859–6866, 2017.

Self-Assembled Plasmonic Sensor Platforms: a Promising Approach for Monitoring Enzymatic Degradation of Thin Gelatin Layers

Markus Weiler and Stefan B. Quint
Department of Biosystems and New Materials,
Max Planck Institute of Intelligent Systems
Stuttgart, Germany

Supratim Basak and Claudia Pacholski
Institute of Chemistry, University of Potsdam
Potsdam, Germany
e-mail: cpachols@uni-potsdam.de

Abstract - **Plasmonic sensors based on periodic hole arrays in metallic films are investigated for monitoring enzymatic degradation of extracellular matrix. Sensors are fabricated using a bottom-up strategy in which soft colloidal lithography is combined with chemical gold film deposition. The resulting plasmonic sensors show extraordinary transmission of light supported by surface plasmon polaritons. These are highly sensitive to refractive index changes in close proximity to the sensor surface and are utilized for the quantitative detection of extracellular matrix degradation.**

Keywords - Optical sensor; bottom-up; enzymes; surface plasmon resonance; real-time monitoring.

I. Introduction

Qualitative and quantitative detection of biomolecular interactions, such as DNA hybridization, antigen/antibody recognition, as well as enzymatic reactions is nowadays routinely achieved by optical biosensors (overview in [1]). These sensor platforms are composed of a recognition layer providing specificity for the target analyte and a transducer converting the recognition events into a measurable optical signal.

A prominent transduction method exploited in these sensors is Surface Plasmon Resonance (SPR) – a resonant oscillation of conduction band electrons occurring at a dielectric/metal interface (reviewed in [2]). The resonance wavelength of SPR depends on the refractive index of the environment in proximity to the metal surface. SPR can be subdivided in Propagating Surface Plasmon Resonance (PSPR) and Localized Surface Plasmon Resonance (LSPR). The latter, LSPR, occurs in metallic nanostructures – especially nanoparticles - and can be directly excited by light. A vital difference between LSPR and PSPR is the field decay length of the SPR. Whereas LSPR in gold nanoparticles can detect refractive index changes only several nanometers (maximal 10 nm – 20 nm) above the gold surface, PSPR are sensitive to refractive index changes several 100 nm above the gold film. However, PSPR cannot be directly excited. In order to match the momentum of incoming light to that of the plasmon, commercial available SPR biosensors employ the so-called Kretschmann configuration in which a thin gold film on a prism is used. Another way to generate SPPs is to introduce a period structure (grating) into the gold film. It has been reported that periodic hole arrays in metallic films show an extraordinary transmission of light (EOT), meaning that more light is transmitted through the sub-wavelength holes than expected from Bethe's law. EOT has been traced back to the excitation of PSPR by the grating [3].

Sensors based on nanohole arrays could offer several advantages in comparison to SPR sensor based on thin metal films on prisms, such as more convenient experimental geometries, higher spatial resolution and greater reproducibility [4]. For example, the presented plasmonic sensor can be operated in transmission mode and therefore could be incorporated in multi-well plates. Thus, multiplexing in combination with the advantages of PSPR sensors could be exploited for detecting target analytes, determining equilibrium binding constants or enzymatic activities. Due to these tremendous advantages over commercial PSPR sensors, optical sensors based on this technology have already been used for the detection of biomolecular interactions in a proof-of-concept study [5]. However, the full potential of these sensor platforms has not been tapped.

Two challenges can be identified for this. On the one hand plasmonic sensors based on hole arrays in metallic films have a lower sensitivity than thin gold films investigated in Kretschman configuration. In order to increase the sensitivity of the hole array sensors, different approaches have been suggested including the deposition of fluorescent material [6] or metallic nanoparticles in the holes [7] of the perforated metal film. On the other hand - on the background of the numerous promising applications - it seems evident that simple, fast and inexpensive techniques to fabricate hole arrays are needed to make them accessible to the many research groups who could benefit from such devices. However, periodic arrays of nanoholes in opaque metal films are commonly fabricated by focused ion beam milling or electron beam lithography. These techniques are expensive and provide only small nanostructured areas at low throughput. An alternative approach is photolithographic fabrication but it suffers from the complicated production of a master and/or the requirement to work in a clean-room.

Only a few attempts have been made to use simpler approaches, like colloidal nanolithography, to fabricate hole arrays in metallic films. However, even in these approaches expensive equipment, such as reactive ion etching machines were used. Recently, our group reported a novel strategy to produce sub-wavelength hole arrays in metallic films, which is solely based on simple chemical techniques [7]. The procedure, which is based on soft colloidal nanolithography and electroless plating, has great advantages over standard fabrication procedures as it allows high throughput, can be easily applied to areas of square centimeters, and requires only standard lab equipment. Furthermore, this method might enable the deposition of periodic hole arrays in metallic films in multiwell plates.

The sensors fabricated by utilizing this 'pure' bottom-up approach showed comparable sensitivity to refractive index changes as nanohole arrays in metal films prepared by more sophisticated and expensive methods. Furthermore, the adsorption of bovine serum albumin to the sensor surface and protein A/IgG interactions could be monitored in real-time using these self-assembled plasmonic sensors. Highly sensitive detection of biomolecular interactions has also been reported for nanohole arrays in metallic films produced by electron beam lithography [5].

However, sensors based on periodic hole arrays in metallic films have not been investigated for determining enzymatic activity – to the best of our knowledge. This fact is quite surprising as biosensors for detecting enzymatic activity were and still are in the focus of biosensor research [8]–[10]. The high interest in this topic is based on the crucial role that certain enzymes (proteases) play in physiological processes, e.g., matrix metalloproteases in cancer development – degradation of extracellular matrix (ECM) [11]–[13]. Consequently, detection of enzymatic activity using biosensors which exploit surface plasmon resonance as transduction method has already been reported. Here, either thin gold films deposited on prisms (Kretschmann configuration) [14] or gold nanoparticles on solid substrates were utilized [15].

In this contribution, we report on the bottom-up fabrication of an optical sensor composed of a periodic hole array in a metallic film, which allows for monitoring enzymatic activity in real-time. The paper is structured in the following way: In Section I an introduction to the topic is given. Afterwards, experimental details on the preparation and characterization of the presented plasmonic sensor platforms are described in Section II. Obtained scientific results on the fabrication and optical behavior of the plasmonic sensors, as well as their sensing performance are presented and discussed in Section III. Finally, the content of the paper is summarized in Section IV (conclusions).

II. EXPERIMENTAL SECTION

A. *Materials & Methods*

All chemicals were used as received without any further purification except of *N*-isopropylacrylamide (NIPAM), which was purchased together with (3-amino-propyl)triethoxysilane (APTES) from Acros Organics. NIPAM was recrystallized from hexane before synthesizing microgels. Tetrachloroauric(III) acid trihydrate, hydroxyl-amine hydrochloride, and sodium citrate were obtained from Sigma Aldrich. Ethanol, *N,N'*-methylene(bisacrylamide) (BIS), hydrochloric acid (fuming), sulfuric acid (96%), calcium chloride dihydrate, glycerol, N-2-HydroxyEthyl Piperazine-N'-2-Ethane Sulphonic acid (HEPES) and glass cover slips (20 × 20 mm or 24 × 24 mm) were received from Carl Roth. Nitric acid (65%) and hydrogen peroxide (30%) were supplied by Merck. Potassium peroxodisulfate (KPS) was obtained from Fluka. Methanol was purchased from BASF. Collagenase, Type III from *Clostridium histolyticum* was purchased from Merck. Water was deionized to a resistance of at least 18.2 MΩ using an Ultra-Pure Water System (TKA, Germany).

Transmission spectra were recorded with a Cary 5000 UV-VIS-NIR spectrometer (Varian, USA) at normal incidence using unpolarized light.

Scanning electron micrographs were taken with a Zeiss Ultra 55 "Gemini" scanning electron microscope.

Atomic force microscopy (AFM) was carried out with a device from Asylum research (MFP-3D-BIO). Commercially available silicon cantilever (Olympus, spring constant 0.02 N /m, resonance frequency 11 kHz) were used for the measurements.

B. *Sensor fabrication*

Plasmonic sensors were prepared according to Quint and Pacholski [7]. In this fabrication method, poly-*N*-isopropylacrylamide (polyNIPAM) beads were employed for colloidal lithography, previously synthesized by aqueous dispersion copolymerization of NIPAM with BIS in the presence of sodium dodecyl sulfate as described elsewhere [16]. Prior to use, the bead dispersion was purified by centrifugation and filtration.

Microscope cover slips were utilized as substrates. To clean them and provide a hydrophilic surface, the glass cover slips were immersed in piranha solution (concentrated sulfuric acid : hydrogen peroxide 3 : 1, v : v) for 1.5 h followed by thorough rinsing with ultra-pure water. The cleaned cover slips were stored in deionized water from 1 to 24 h and were blown dry with nitrogen just before the deposition of polyNIPAM beads.

Deposition of polyNIPAM bead arrays onto glass substrates was achieved by spin coating. Spin coating was carried out using a Laurell WS-400A-6NPP Lite spin coater (Laurell Technologies Corporation, North Wales). Cleaned glass substrates were mounted in the spin coater and a 40 µl droplet of diluted polyNIPAM bead dispersion was placed in the center of the substrate. Subsequently, 5 µl of ethanol were added to facilitate self-assembly of polyNIPAM beads in hexagonal patterns and to obtain a complete substrate wetting. Subsequently, the sample was rotated for 6 min at 500 rpm followed by 1 min at 6000 rpm using an acceleration of 100 rpm/s in both cases. This procedure yielded high ordered arrays of polyNIPAM beads on the glass substrate surface.

In order to allow a binding of gold colloids to the substrate, the glass surface was functionalized with amino groups. To do this, previously spin coated samples were encased in a standard exsiccator together with a small dish containing 40 µl of APTES. The exsiccator was then evacuated until a pressure of 0.3 mbar was reached. The samples were kept under these conditions for 1 h to allow a dense silanization of the glass surface. Afterwards the samples were incubated for 1 h in a drying oven at 80 °C. Subsequently, the sensor surface was wetted with a ~ 12 nM colloidal gold solution [17] and incubated at 40 °C for 30 min to allow gold nanoparticle binding to the free amino groups. Afterwards the samples were rinsed with ultra-pure water.

In the next step, a gold film was formed by electroless deposition. For this purpose, the samples were immersed in an aqueous solution of 0.4mM hydroxylamine hydrochloride and 0.5% $HAuCl_4 \cdot 3H_2O$ [18]. The solution was agitated on a vibrating table to ensure the formation of a homogenous gold film. After 1 h the samples were rinsed with water and blown dry under a nitrogen stream. Finally, the colloidal mask was removed by flame annealing in a propane/butane flame which leads to pyrolysis of the polyNIPAM beads. In an alternative approach, the colloidal mask was removed by ultrasonication after the deposition of gold colloids.

C. *Sensor performance*

1) Deposition of gelatin layer

Spin-coating was employed for obtaining thin films of gelatin. Here, 100 µL of a warm solution of gelatin in ultra-pure water (50 °C) was dropped on a 20 × 20 mm glass substrate, which was rotated at 6000 rpm at this moment and for a further minute after applying the gelatin solution. Thereby, complete drying of the gelatin layer was ensured. In order to control the thickness of the deposited gelatin layer, different concentrations of gelatin in solution were investigated. Moreover, glutardialdehyde was added to the gelatin solution prior to spin-coating in order to cross-link the gelatin. For example, warm gelatin solution (2.5 wt% gelatin) was mixed with 0.5 wt% glutardialdehyde (final concentration) and then immediately spin-coated onto cleaned glass substrates.

2) Monitoring enzymatic reactions

Gelatin coated sensors were mounted in a custom-made flow cell and exposed to buffer solution (50mM HEPES, 10 mM $CaCl_2$, 5% glycerol, pH 7.4). After establishing a constant baseline, the buffer solution was replaced by a solution of collagenase in buffer. Different concentrations of collagenase were tested. Transmission spectra were recorded every 30 s and the position of the transmission minimum in each spectrum was determined by a fitting routine. Briefly, to extract the positions of the transmission minimum, we have used a Matlab script which first determined the absolute minimum. This minimum was taken as starting point. Then, we chose 40 data points, which surrounded this minimum, and fitted these points with the polyfit Matlab function with a degree of $n = 2$ ($f(x) = ax^2 + bx + c$).

III. RESULTS & DISCUSSION

A. *Sensor fabrication and characterizaion*

Three major steps are involved in the presented fabrication method for periodic hole arrays in metallic films (Figure 1). In the first step, a lithographic mask is prepared on a glass cover slip. In contrast to previous colloidal lithographic approaches, polyNIPAM beads are used for the mask production. This allows for directly creating loosely packed, hexagonally ordered arrays of microspheres as polyNIPAM undergoes a reversible phase transition from a swollen to shrunken state upon drying. This property is very advantageous as it supersedes any further treatment of the mask, which is necessary in conventional colloidal nanolithography approaches. The obtained two dimensional hexagonal array can be readily used as a lithographic mask for the fabrication of hole arrays.

In the following step, a homogenous gold film is deposited by electroless plating. The reaction requires Au(0) as nucleation seeds for the chemical reduction of dissolved Au(III) [18]. Thus, the glass surface is functionalized with 3-(aminotriethoxy)silane and subsequently decorated with gold colloids, which serve as seeds for the growth of a homogenous gold-layer by electroless plating. Removal of the colloidal mask was achieved by thermal treatment or ultrasonication. This fabrication process has already been published [7].

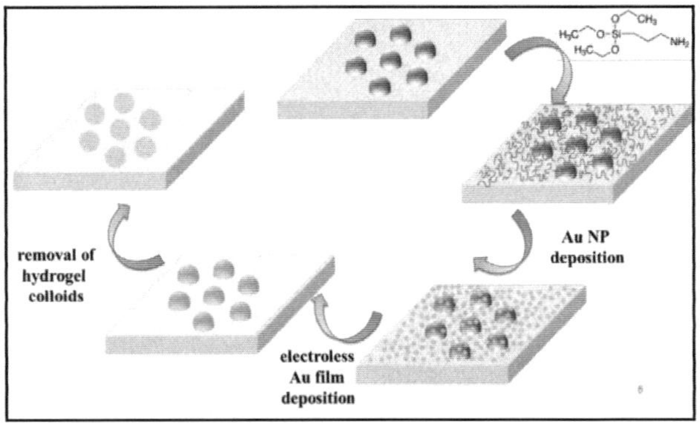

Figure 1. Major steps involved in the fabrication of sub-wavelength holes in gold films.

In Figure 2, a representative scanning electron microscopy (SEM) image of a periodic hole arrays in a gold film, prepared by the previously presented method, is displayed. On the first glance a quasi-hexagonal order of the holes can be noticed. To provide a quantitative measure for the lattice constant of the hole array, we have calculated the radial distribution function by analyzing several SEM images [19].

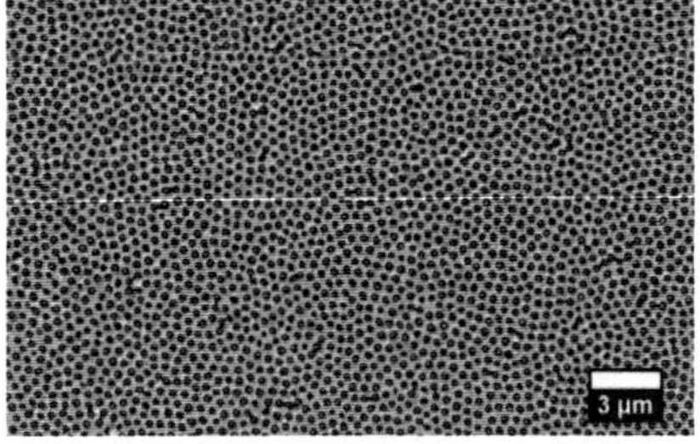

Figure 2. Representative SEM image of a prepared periodic hole array in a metallic film.

For this purpose, we have read out the positions of the holes in Cartesian coordinates with the help of the software ImageJ. In a second step, the pairwise distance r_{ij} of all colloids and then the radial distribution density g (r) was calculated as follows:

$$g(r)=\frac{1}{2\pi r\Delta r\rho}\sum_{i=1}^{N}\sum_{j>i}^{N}\chi(r_{ij}-r) \quad (1)$$

where N is the total number of colloids in the image, ρ the density per μm^2, Δr is the step size and r the considered colloid distance. χ is defined as:

$$\chi(r_{ij}-r)=\begin{cases}1, \mathit{if}\ |r_{ij}-r|\leq\Delta r\\ 0, \mathit{if}\ |r_{ij}-r|>\Delta r\end{cases} \quad (2)$$

The function g (r) thus describes the mean number of colloids in the distance r + Δr, which is found from any colloid. The first maximum in the radial distribution function corresponds to the lattice constant, which was determined to be (470 ± 100) nm in the shown SEM image.

A transmission spectrum of this hole array in a gold film is presented in Figure 3. The spectrum is characterized by two transmission maxima, which can be assigned to the (1,0) gold,glass resonance at ~1200 nm and to the (1,0) gold,air resonance at ~800 nm using the following equation [20]:

$$\lambda_{SPP}=\frac{a_0}{\sqrt{\frac{4}{3}(n^2+nm+m^2)}}\sqrt{\frac{\varepsilon_m\varepsilon_d}{\varepsilon_m+\varepsilon_d}} \quad (3)$$

Where λ_{SPP} is the resonance wavelength, a_0 is the lattice constant, n as well as m are integer numbers, and ε_m and ε_d are the dielectric constants of the metal and the dielectric medium, respectively.

The horizontal line in the spectrum indicates the open area fraction of the particular hole array, determined by the software ImageJ. As the open area fraction is lower than the transmission of the (1,0) Au,glass resonance of the hole arrays, extraordinary transmission of light is observed.

We have determined the sensitivity of the fabricated hole arrays by immersion of the sensors in solutions with different refractive indices. The position of the transmission minimum in the spectrum was evaluated, which can be found at ~ 600 nm in air and is particularly sensitive. The position of this minimum shifted linearly to longer wavelengths with increasing refractive indices of the immersion medium. It shows a sensitivity of 540nm / RIU and is in the same sensitivity range as published for hole arrays fabricated by conventional lithography. Hence, the presented method for preparing periodic hole arrays in metallic films is highly attractive for mass production, as it is simpler as well as more cost- and time-efficient in comparison to approaches using electron beam lithography or focused ion beam milling. Moreover, the presented bottom-up strategy is capable to nanostructure large areas in the range of cm^2.

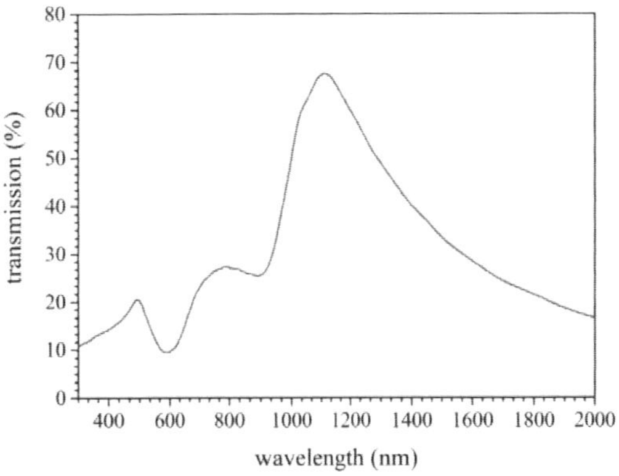

Figure 3. Transmission spectrum of a fabricated optical sensor.

B. Deposition of ECM layer

In order to obtain thin films of gelatin (= ECM), we applied spin-coating. The thickness of gelatin films can be adjusted by varying the gelatin concentration of the gel. As it can be seen from Figure 4, film thickness is an exponential function of the gelatin concentration, when temperature, spinning speed, and suspension volume are kept constant.

To determine the gelatin film thickness we scratched a groove into the film and measured the step height using a white light interferometer. Each data point in Figure 4 coressponds to 6 measured thickness values.

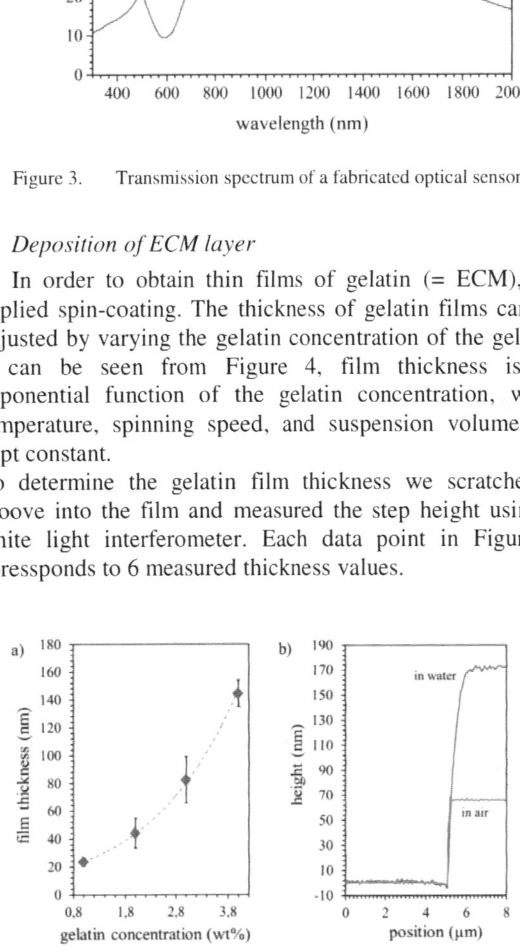

Figure 4. Gelatin films on sensor surface. a) gelatin film thickness in dependence of the gelatin concentration in the soultion used for spin-coating. b) Gelatin film thickness in air and in water determined using atomic force microscopy (AFM).

Gelatin is a network of collagen filaments comprising hydrophilic protein chains. Therefore, gelatin is a highly absorbent polymer matrix, which swells upon immersion in water. The swelling of gelatin depends on the crosslinking density of the gel. Not crosslinked gelatin films can increase roughly tenfold in film weight due to water uptake when stored in a buffer solution. The swelling ratio is important for us because of two reasons. First of all, we would like to tune the thickness of the film in such a way that it matches the penetration depths of the surface plasmons of our sensor. The surface plasmons are only sensitive to changes in the refractive index which are within their penetration depth, which is roughly 100 nm at the resonance minimum we consider for following refractive index changes. If we know the swelling ratio, we can easily estimate the thickness of the film in water after measuring the thickness in air. A measurement in air is much easier to perform than in water, but can give us only relevant information when we know the swelling ratio. Second, the swelling ratio will also have an effect on the refractive index of the film. The more water the film takes up the more the refractive index will be shifted towards that of water. Also, this has an effect on the sensitivity of our sensor.

A way to affect the swelling ratio of gelatin films is cross linking by GluTardiAldehyde (GTA). Therefore, we measured the Swelling Ratio (SR) for different contents of GTA, which were added prior to spin-coating. We used AFM to measure the height profiles of gelatin films in air and in water, and to determine the swelling ratio of thin gelatin films, which is simply the thickness in water divided by the thickness in air. Figure 4 b) shows two typical height profiles for a gelatin film in air and water. A SR of ~2 was determined by using this method in accordance with published values [21].

C. Monitoring ECM degradation

For the degradation experiments the sensor surface was coated with a gelatin layer, which has a thickness of (57 ± 8) nm in the dry state (determined by white light interferometry). Figure 5 shows transmission spectra of a sensor, before and after coating the sensor surface with gelatin, recorded in air.

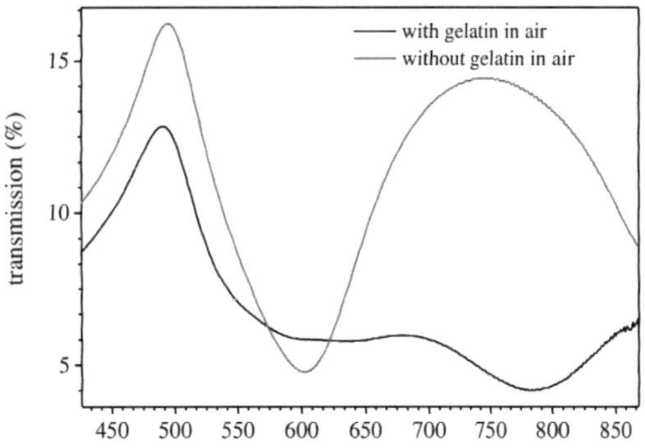

Figure 5. Transmission spectra of a sensor before and after coating with gelatin.

The spectrum of the bare sensor is characterized by a transmission maximum at ~760 nm which can be assigned to the (1,0) gold,air resonance. After coating the sensor with gelatin this maximum shifts to longer wavelengths due to the increase of the refractive index at the sensor surface. In this case, the maximum is close to the wavelength region in which water absorption interferes with measuring reliable spectra for determining the sensor response to refractive index changes. Therefore, we have chosen to monitor the position of the transmission minimum located at ~800 nm after coating the sensor with gelatin.

To carry out the degradation experiments the sensor was mounted in a custom-made flow cell and rinsed with HEPES buffer at 37 °C. Transmission spectra of the sensor were recorded throughout the whole degradation experiment every 30 s. In Figure 6, the position of the transmission minimum on the wavelength scale is plotted versus time. First, a stable baseline in buffer was established for each sensor. Then, at 0 min, a solution composed of collagenase in HEPES buffer was added. An enzyme concentration of 1 units/mL led to a quasi-linear decrease in the peak position until after about 180 min the signal remains almost unchanged. In this case, the same results were obtained under flow and static conditions (red circles and black squares, respectively).

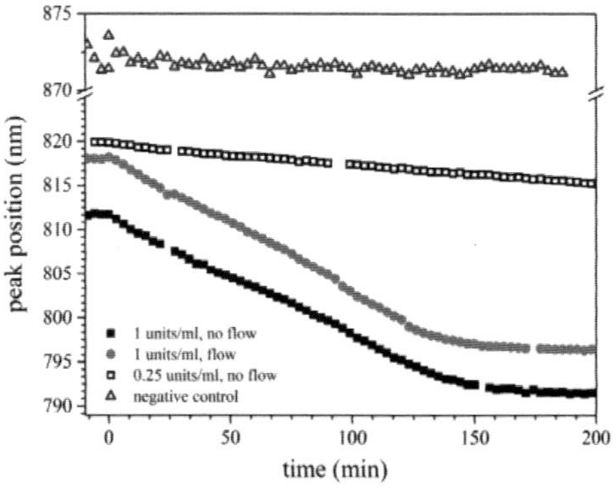

Figure 6. Real-time monitoring of enzymatic activity. At 0 min the enzyme was added to the buffer solution.

If the concentration of the enzyme in the solution was lower (0.25 units/mL) the degradation reaction was much slower – as expected. A negative control experiment was carried out by injecting only HEPES buffer at 0 min into the flow cell. In this case, no degradation of the gelatin layer could be detected by monitoring the transmission minimum position (open blue triangles). Hence, a first proof-of-concept for utilizing periodic hole arrays in metallic films was demonstrated. The enzymatic activity was reliably determined, but the sensitivity of the sensor should be improved for being capable of detecting smaller amounts of enzymes. For this purpose, it is planned to replace the gelatin layer with a more sophisticated layer mimicking ECM.

IV. Conclusions

In summary, periodic hole arrays in metallic films were prepared using a bottom-up strategy and successfully tested as optical sensors for monitoring enzymatic degradation of gelatin layers in real-time.

Fabrication of sensor platforms was achieved by combining soft colloidal lithography with subsequent chemical deposition of a gold film. The resulting periodic hole array in a gold film showed extraordinary transmission of light facilitated by the excitation of surface plasmon resonance by the grating and leading to distinct transmission maxima and minima in their optical spectrum. Surface plasmon resonance is confined to the sensor surface and probes only refractive index changes occurring with a maximum distance of approximately 100-200 nm from the gold film (for the reported sensor). These characteristics of the prepared sensors were successfully exploited for detecting enzymatic activity by following the position of a transmission minimum on the wavelength scale in the optical spectrum.

ACKNOWLEDGMENT

This project was funded by the VolkswagenStiftung, the Heidelberg Academy of Sciences and Humanities, and the Max Planck Society. In addition, C. Pacholski is grateful for funding by the DFG (Heisenberg fellowship / project number: 286735196).

REFERENCES

[1] X. Fan et al., "Sensitive optical biosensors for unlabeled targets: A review," *Anal. Chim. Acta*, vol. 620, no. 1–2, pp. 8–26, Jul. 2008.

[2] J. Homola, S. S. Yee, and G. Gauglitz, "Surface plasmon resonance sensors: review," *Sens. Actuators B Chem.*, vol. 54, no. 1–2, pp. 3–15, Jan. 1999.

[3] T. W. Ebbesen, H. J. Lezec, H. F. Ghaemi, T. Thio, and P. A. Wolff, "Extraordinary optical transmission through sub-wavelength hole arrays," *Nature*, vol. 391, no. 6668, pp. 667–669, Feb. 1998.

[4] A. De Leebeeck et al., "On-Chip Surface-Based Detection with Nanohole Arrays," *Anal. Chem.*, vol. 79, no. 11, pp. 4094–4100, Jun. 2007.

[5] A. G. Brolo, R. Gordon, B. Leathem, and K. L. Kavanagh, "Surface Plasmon Sensor Based on the Enhanced Light Transmission through Arrays of Nanoholes in Gold Films," *Langmuir*, vol. 20, no. 12, pp. 4813–4815, Jun. 2004.

[6] S. Wu, P. Guo, W. Huang, S. Xiao, and Y. Zhu, "Dielectric Thickness Detection Sensor Based on Metallic Nanohole Arrays," *J. Phys. Chem. C*, vol. 115, no. 31, pp. 15205–15209, Aug. 2011.

[7] S. B. Quint and C. Pacholski, "A chemical route to sub-wavelength hole arrays in metallic films," *J. Mater. Chem.*, vol. 19, no. 33, pp. 5906–5908, 2009.

[8] Y. Zhou, S. Jiang, S. Krause, and J.-N. Chazalviel, "Biosensor Arrays Based on the Degradation of Thin Polymer Films Interrogated by Scanning Photoinduced Impedance Microscopy," *Anal. Chem.*, vol. 79, no. 23, pp. 8974–8978, Dec. 2007.

[9] C. Sumner, A. Sabot, K. Turner, and S. Krause, "A Transducer Based on Enzyme-Induced Degradation of Thin Polymer Films Monitored by Surface Plasmon Resonance," *Anal. Chem.*, vol. 72, no. 21, pp. 5225–5232, Nov. 2000.

[10] B. Schyrr, S. Boder-Pasche, R. Ischer, R. Smajda, and G. Voirin, "Fiber-optic protease sensor based on the degradation of thin gelatin films," *Sens. Bio-Sens. Res.*, vol. 3, pp. 65–73, Mar. 2015.

[11] L. A. Liotta et al., "Metastatic potential correlates with enzymatic degradation of basement membrane collagen," *Nature*, vol. 284, no. 5751, pp. 67–68, Mar. 1980.

[12] M. A. Moses et al., "Increased incidence of matrix metalloproteinases in urine of cancer patients," *Cancer Res.*, vol. 58, no. 7, pp. 1395–1399, Apr. 1998.

[13] R. A. Cairns, R. Khokha, and R. P. Hill, "Molecular mechanisms of tumor invasion and metastasis: an integrated view," *Curr. Mol. Med.*, vol. 3, no. 7, pp. 659–671, Nov. 2003.

[14] A. Shoji, M. Kabeya, and M. Sugawara, "Real-time monitoring of matrix metalloproteinase-9 collagenolytic activity with a surface plasmon resonance biosensor," *Anal. Biochem.*, vol. 419, no. 1, pp. 53–60, Dec. 2011.

[15] S.-H. Jung et al., "Rapid analysis of matrix metalloproteinase-3 activity by gelatin arrays using a spectral surface plasmon resonance biosensor," *The Analyst*, vol. 135, no. 5, p. 1050, 2010.

[16] R. H. Pelton and P. Chibante, "Preparation of aqueous latices with N-isopropylacrylamide," *Colloids Surf.*, vol. 20, no. 3, pp. 247–256, Oct. 1986.

[17] J. Turkevich, P. C. Stevenson, and J. Hillier, "A study of the nucleation and growth processes in the synthesis of colloidal gold," *Discuss. Faraday Soc.*, vol. 11, no. 0, pp. 55–75, 1951.

[18] K. R. Brown and M. J. Natan, "Hydroxylamine Seeding of Colloidal Au Nanoparticles in Solution and on Surfaces," *Langmuir*, vol. 14, no. 4, pp. 726–728, Feb. 1998.

[19] S. B. Quint and C. Pacholski, "Getting real: influence of structural disorder on the performance of plasmonic hole array sensors fabricated by a bottom-up approach," *J. Mater. Chem. C*, vol. 2, no. 36, pp. 7632–7638, 2014.

[20] T. Thio, H. F. Ghaemi, H. J. Lezec, P. A. Wolff, and T. W. Ebbesen, "Surface-plasmon-enhanced transmission through hole arrays in Cr films," *J. Opt. Soc. Am. B*, vol. 16, no. 10, p. 1743, Oct. 1999.

[21] C. M. Ofner and H. Schott, "Swelling studies of gelatin. I: Gelatin without additives," *J. Pharm. Sci.*, vol. 75, no. 8, pp. 790–796, Aug. 1986.

Improvement and Application of Sensor Device Capable of Autonomously Keeping Accurate Time Information for Buildings and Civil Infrastructures

Narito Kurata
Faculty of Industrial Technology
Tsukuba University of Technology
Tsukuba City, Ibaraki, Japan
e-mail: kurata@home.email.ne.jp

Abstract - **In this research, sensor devices were developed for application to seismic observation to understand damage conditions after earthquakes and to structural health monitoring for the maintenance of buildings and civil infrastructures. To apply the sensor devices, they must be densely installed in a broad area and measurement data with synchronized time must be obtained. It is desirable that the sensor devices themselves keep accurate time information even in environments with no available network or Global Positioning System (GPS) signals. Therefore, a sensor device was developed that keeps accurate time information autonomously using a Chip Scale Atomic Clock (CSAC), which consumes ultra-low power, can be mounted on a small board, and is an ultra-high precision clock. This paper explains the CSAC and a mechanism to add highly accurate time information to the measured data using the CSAC. Next, the paper discusses the process of development from prototype to practical device as well as improvement results to solve challenges identified in the actual use at a bridge. Finally, the paper demonstrates the usability of the developed sensor device using a case study where seismic observation was implemented by installing the improved devices in an actual building.**

Keywords-Time Synchronization; Chip Scale Atomic Clock; Earthquake Observation; Structural Health Monitoring; Acceleration Sensor.

I. INTRODUCTION

Due to degradation of buildings and civil infrastructures, such as bridges, and highways over time, automation of inspection for their maintenance and management is an urgent social issue. Also, since there are many earthquakes in Japan, it is required to detect the damage of the structure immediately after the earthquake and to grasp the situation of the urban damage. In order to detect those abnormal situations, data collection and analyses by a group of sensors are necessary. Sensors were developed for seismic observation and structural health monitoring applying wireless sensor network technology, and their performance in a skyscraper was demonstrated [1]-[3]. One important challenge in this research was time synchronization among sensors. To analyze a group of data measured by multiple sensors and assess structural safety, time synchronization among the sensors must be kept. In the wireless sensor network system, the time synchronization was materialized through transmission of wireless packets among the sensors [3]. However, the wireless sensor network technology is not practically applied to multiple buildings, long-span structures, such as bridges, or broad urban spaces. If sensors installed in various locations are capable of keeping accurate time information autonomously, this problem can be solved. Using Global Positioning System (GPS) signals is effective for outdoor situations, but it is not available inside buildings, underground, under bridges, or in tunnels. Therefore, a prototype sensor device capable of maintaining accurate time information autonomously was developed using a Chip Scale Atomic Clock (CSAC) [4]-[6], which is a high-precision clock and very accurate compared with crystal resonators [7][8]. Then, the prototype device was upgraded for higher functionality and practical application to develop a practical device [9].

In addition, in order to apply the developed sensor dêvice to earthquake observation, logic to detect the occurrence of an earthquake and store data of only earthquake events was implemented and confirmed its function in shaking table experiment [10][11]. These tests confirmed the performance of the sensor device that can maintain accurate time information autonomously and showed that the device is applicable to seismic observation and structural health monitoring of buildings and civil infrastructures.

In this article, Section 2 shows the existing time synchronization methods and describes their problems and achievement of the development of sensor device proposed in this study. Section 3 describes CSAC and explains the mechanism for providing ultra-high accurate time information to sensor data by the CSAC. Section 4 describes the development of a practical module from its prototype. Section 5 lists problems that were extracted when the practical modules were installed on an actual bridge, and describes details of improvements made to cope with these problems. Further, Section 6 shows actual examples where a developed sensor device is applied to a building structure.

II. STATE OF THE ART

A time synchronizing function is indispensable for sensor devices that are used for seismic observation and structural health monitoring. Unless a data group where time synchronization is ensured is obtained, a time history analysis employing phase information cannot be made. For example, it is difficult to clarify a phenomenon where seismic waves propagate through the ground. Moreover, it is not possible to make a modal analysis or an analysis for damage evaluation of a structure. Many studies have been carried out so far in relation to the time synchronized sensing, including the GPS that makes use of a radio clock or a satellite, and the Network Time Protocol (NTP) [12] designed for time synchronization on the internet. There are also studies where time synchronization is realized by making use of the characteristics of a radio sensor network where a propagation delay is small. For example, time-synchronizing protocols have been studied, which include Reference Broadcast Synchronization (RBS), Timing-sync Protocol for Sensor Networks (TPSN), and Flooding Time synchronization Protocol (FTSP) [13]-[17]. However, although these time synchronizing technologies are widely used even now, they cannot constitute an optimum means for sensor devices for use in seismic observation and structural health monitoring. Specifically, the GPS cannot be used inside a building, and the time synchronizing accuracy of the NTP is not sufficient. The time synchronizing method employing the radio technology is highly useful, but it is not ensured that the radio communication is always available. In particular, if the wireless communication is interrupted at the time of an earthquake, time synchronization cannot be performed.

In this study, a prototype of a sensor module for autonomously keeping accurate time information is developed by making use of a CSAC that is an ultra-high accurate clock, and an improvement is carried out on the prototype for a practical application. Even though a tremendous number of sensors are installed in the buildings and civil infrastructures, in case accurate time information can autonomously be given to the data measured by those sensors, time synchronization can be ensured between the sensors only by collecting the data using an arbitrary means and by realigning the data utilizing the time information. The data group where the time synchronization is ensured by using the sensor device proposed in this paper is available for an analysis intended to grasp a seismic phenomenon or evaluate the damage of a structure.

III. Time Stamping Mechanism Using Chip Scale Atomic Clock

A CSAC has time accuracy equivalent to that of a rubidium atomic clock and is very accurate compared with crystal resonators [4][6]. The CSAC can achieve ultra-precision time measurement at a level of some ten picoseconds, consumes low power and is small enough to be mounted on a circuit board (Table I).

TABLE I. SPECIFICATIONS OF CSAC

Model	SA.45s
RF output	10 MHz
1 PPS output	Rise/fall time: < 10 ns Pulse width: 100 μs
Power consumption	< 120 mW
Outside dimensions (mm)	40 × 35 × 12
Frequency accuracy	$\pm 5 \times 10^{-11}$
Aging	$< 9 \times 10^{-10}$/month

The development of the CSAC started with the support of Defense Advanced Research Projects Agency, and the commercial product was released by an American company in 2011 and is still available for purchase. Recently, ultra-small atomic clock systems, which can be mounted on general communication terminals, such as smart phones, have been proposed, and further downsizing and price reduction are expected. If the sensor device is equipped with a CSAC and a mechanism that adds time stamping for every sample of measured data, the sensor device can create data having high-accuracy time information. Each sensor device autonomously keeps highly accurate time information even if the GPS signals and network communication are unavailable. Therefore, by collecting the measured data by means, such as 3G, Wi-Fi, Ethernet, etc., a data group ensuring time synchronization can be obtained.

To configure a sensing system composed of multiple sensor devices equipped with a CSAC, one device is set as a master device and other devices as slave devices must be synchronized by defining absolute time information. The main controller of each sensor device is equipped with an input/output connector for 1 Pulse Per Second (PPS) of the CSAC. Using this connector, the master device outputs 1 PPS signal, and each slave device inputs it to synchronize and match the phase of the CSAC in each slave device. The CSAC keeps accurate time, but it does not have absolute time information. Therefore, it must be defined separately. At initial settings, the GPS module installed in the main controller is used. Absolute time information is transmitted from the master device to the slave device by the IEEE 1588 standard. Once all the sensor devices are synchronized at the beginning, they continue keeping highly accurate time information autonomously. It is only necessary to install the sensor device in an arbitrary place and collect data. As mentioned above, any means of data collection, such as Ethernet, Wi-Fi, or 3G, are available as the measured data records accurate time stamping. The sensors are also suitable for use as mobile measurement and a mobile sensing system because the sensors can measure and collect data even if GPS signals are not available, and a wireless or wired network cannot be used.

IV. Development of Sensor Device Equipped with CSAC

The general sensor device is composed of a sensor chip, CPU, filter, A/D converter, memory, and network interface, and a crystal oscillator is used as the clock of the CPU. If CSAC is installed in the sensor device and measurement is performed while correcting the clock of the CPU, a delay occurs because CSAC's clocking accuracy is too high. Therefore, a mechanism having a special Field Programmable Gate Array (FPGA) was developed to add time information from the CSAC to the data measured by the sensor directly. The FPGA not only adds the time information of the CSAC to the measured data but can also incorporate logic, such as seismic detection. A prototype device was developed first to identify challenges, and then a practical device that has solved the challenges was developed.

A. Prototype Device

Fig. 1 shows the developed prototype device. The prototype device is composed of a mainboard, sensor board, and wireless communication board. The mainboard incorporates a CSAC, FPGA, CPU, memory, network interface, etc. The sensor board is detachable. Two types of sensor board were developed, one of which is an acceleration sensor board equipped with a microelectromechanical systems (MEMS) accelerometer, temperature sensor, anti-aliasing filter, A/D converter, etc., and the other is an external sensor board that can connect an analog sensor externally via the Bayonet Neill-Concelman (BNC) connector (Fig. 2). The communication board is also detachable and can collect data using wireless network once mounted on the mainboard. Two types of dedicated board equipped with Wi-Fi or 3G were developed.

B. Practical Device

The following improvements were made for high functionality and practical use of the prototype device.

1) *3-channeled external analog sensor input interface*
2) *24-bit A/D converter*

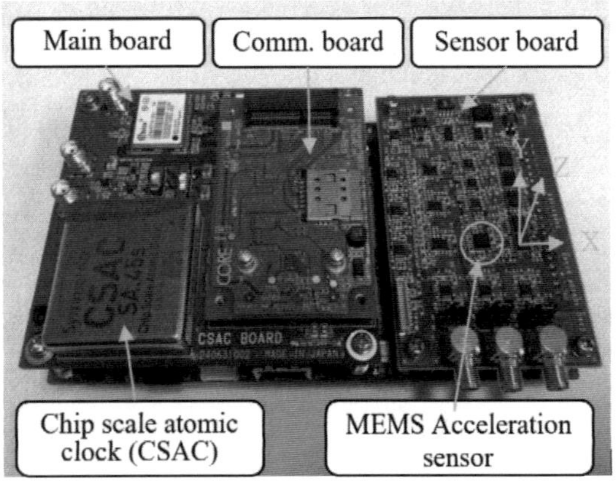

Figure 1. Prototype Device.

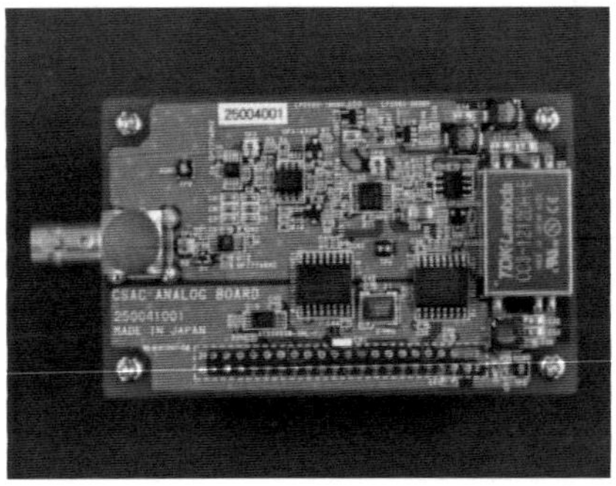

Figure 2. External Sensor Board.

3) *Enhanced FPGA*
4) *Separate wireless communication to use commercially available Raspberry Pi*
5) *Time synchronization by IEEE 1588*

The practical device is composed of a board and Raspberry Pi having a wireless communication function (Fig. 3) and is enclosed in a dedicated case (Fig. 4). As shown in Fig. 3, the board of the practical device is composed of a main control unit and a sensor unit. The main control unit is equipped with a CSAC, FPGA, GPS, CPU, memory, and network interface. The main control unit controls measurement of the sensor while producing time stamping, based on highly accurate time information from the CSAC. The device sends the measurement data via Ethernet or wireless communication to the network after saving data in an SD card. The device saves two types of data, one of which is regularly measured data and the other is extracted seismic event data. The device sends data containing seismic events solely to the network immediately after an earthquake using the FPGA to detect start and end of the earthquake. A GPS is installed in the device to initialize and adjust the time information. The sensor takes measurements following a command from the main control unit. The sensor is equipped with a 3-axis MEMS accelerometer, 3-channel external analog sensor input interface, temperature sensor, anti-aliasing filter, and A/D converter. The wireless communication uses commercially available Raspberry Pi to enable data collection with wireless communication. Either Wi-Fi or 3G is selectively used for the wireless communication.

Compared with the prototype device, the practical device incorporates a 3-channel external analog sensor input interface and 24-bit A/D converter, so it can connect with a sensor requiring a wide dynamic range, such as a servo accelerometer. In addition, the sensor device can be used as a data logger by connecting with three strain sensors, displacement centers, etc. Using Raspberry Pi for the wireless communication, the device can quickly respond to new wireless communication formats. Furthermore, an interface of IEEE 1588 standard for time synchronization of network was incorporated to initialize measurement timing among sensor devices and synchronize them.

V. IMPROVEMENT OF PRACTICAL DEVICE

The developed practical device was installed onto an actual bridge, and measurement was performed for three months to identify challenges in practical use. Based on those challenges, the practical device was improved for higher stability and operability, and the specified performance was confirmed. Improvement items and contents are as follows.

A. Reduction in Built-in SD Card Access

To avoid failures caused by total service life consumed by the number of rewrite cycles resulting from the quality of the SD card (micro SD card) or compatibility issues, the timing to write in the file system was reviewed. By setting the interval of the write timing to the file system from 5 seconds to 240 seconds, access is suppressed to a maximum of 1/48, as shown in Table II.

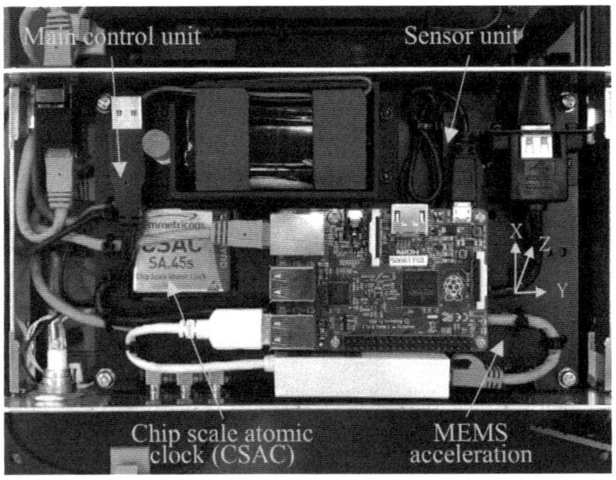

Figure 3. Board Configuration of the Practical Device

Figure 4. Dedicated Case

TABLE II. EFFECTS OF REDUCTION IN ACCESS TO BUILT-IN SD CARD

	Current	After improvement
Frequency of writing	Once per 5 second	Once per 240 second
Data loss during emergency blackout with sampling rate of 100 Hz	Approx. 500 sampling	Approx. 24000 sampling

However, risk of data loss during emergency black out increases, which means it is a trade-off. Table II shows the effects of reduction in access to the built-in SD card.

B. File Compression of Measured Data

In the actual work installed onto the bridge, transmission time for the measured data must be reduced. To reduce the data transmission time and achieve storing long-term measurement data, a file compression function was added. From the viewpoint of durability, it is desirable to use a relatively small capacity SD card, which is considered to be manufactured in a stable production line rather than a large capacity one which might be manufactured in a premature production line. The file compression function is important as a means to materialize long-term data recording in a small capacity SD. The software was improved to compress the measured data to be recorded in the SD card after 75 minutes.

C. Change of Local PC Collecting Display

A tool was developed to collect the measured data saved in the built-in SD card of the practical device placed in the LAN, which was temporarily installed on the site into a local PC using a browser. However, there was a possibility that time information not related to measurement data might be displayed depending on the startup environment in the measurement data download screen (Fig. 5). Specifically, by adjusting the time of Raspberry Pi with the FPGA on the baseboard, improvements were made so that the correct time information of the measurement data is displayed regardless of the activation environment. However, even without this improvement, there is no effect on the high precision time information recorded in the measurement data.

D. Correction of PTP Control Software

The Precision Time Protocol (PTP) defined in the IEEE-1588 standard is a means to synchronize time of computers on a LAN highly accurately. The CSAC is a high precision clock, but it does not keep absolute time information. Therefore, clock adjustment was made with the CSAC and then the absolute time was set to the timer counter of the FPGA by the PTP in the practical device. In the actual work at the bridge, there was a risk that the absolute time set by the PTP may be initialized due to plugging and unplugging of the LAN cable. Such phenomenon is not desirable for the practical device although it follows the standard implementation and specifications of Linux as the PTP must be operated with a LAN cable connected. Therefore, the settings were corrected so that the absolute time would not be initialized and would be kept between two practical devices (master device and slave device) whose absolute time had been set by the PTP even if the Ethernet cable was plugged and unplugged.

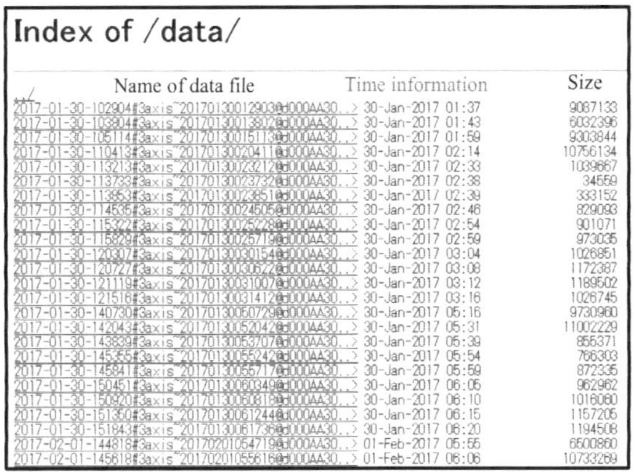

Index of /data/

Name of data file	Time information	Size
../		
2017-01-30-102904#3axis~20170130012903@d000AA30..>	30-Jan-2017 01:37	9087133
2017-01-30-103804#3axis~20170130013802@d000AA30..>	30-Jan-2017 01:43	6032396
2017-01-30-105114#3axis~20170130015113@d000AA30..>	30-Jan-2017 01:59	9303844
2017-01-30-110413#3axis~20170130020411@d000AA30..>	30-Jan-2017 02:14	10756134
2017-01-30-113213#3axis~20170130023212@d000AA30..>	30-Jan-2017 02:33	1039667
2017-01-30-113733#3axis~20170130023732@d000AA30..>	30-Jan-2017 02:38	34559
2017-01-30-113853#3axis~20170130023851@d000AA30..>	30-Jan-2017 02:39	333152
2017-01-30-114535#3axis~20170130024505@d000AA30..>	30-Jan-2017 02:46	829093
2017-01-30-115322#3axis~20170130025228@d000AA30..>	30-Jan-2017 02:54	901071
2017-01-30-115829#3axis~20170130025719@d000AA30..>	30-Jan-2017 02:59	973035
2017-01-30-120307#3axis~20170130030154@d000AA30..>	30-Jan-2017 03:04	1026851
2017-01-30-120727#3axis~20170130030622@d000AA30..>	30-Jan-2017 03:08	1172387
2017-01-30-121119#3axis~20170130031007@d000AA30..>	30-Jan-2017 03:12	1189502
2017-01-30-121516#3axis~20170130031412@d000AA30..>	30-Jan-2017 03:16	1026745
2017-01-30-140730#3axis~20170130050729@d000AA30..>	30-Jan-2017 05:16	9730960
2017-01-30-142043#3axis~20170130052042@d000AA30..>	30-Jan-2017 05:31	11002229
2017-01-30-143839#3axis~20170130053707@d000AA30..>	30-Jan-2017 05:39	855371
2017-01-30-145355#3axis~20170130055242@d000AA30..>	30-Jan-2017 05:54	766303
2017-01-30-145841#3axis~20170130055717@d000AA30..>	30-Jan-2017 05:59	872335
2017-01-30-150451#3axis~20170130060349@d000AA30..>	30-Jan-2017 06:05	962962
2017-01-30-150920#3axis~20170130060818@d000AA30..>	30-Jan-2017 06:10	1016060
2017-01-30-151350#3axis~20170130061244@d000AA30..>	30-Jan-2017 06:15	1157205
2017-01-30-151843#3axis~20170130061736@d000AA30..>	30-Jan-2017 06:20	1194508
2017-02-01-144818#3axis~20170201054719@d000AA30..>	01-Feb-2017 05:55	6500860
2017-02-01-145618#3axis~20170201055616@d000AA30..>	01-Feb-2017 06:06	10733269

Figure 5. Local PC collecting tool display screen.

E. Minimization of Wiring Delay in the FPGA

Depending on the circuit design of the FPGA, the time stamping may not be correctly recorded due to fluctuation of timing to read and write the memory from the FPGA. The wiring delay of the SDRAM control signal in the FPGA was minimized so that the timing to read and write the memory from the FPGA would not fluctuate. The FPGA circuit was redesigned and implemented in the new practical sensor device. It was confirmed that the continuous operation test for 2 months was conducted for the four devices and the time information was correctly displayed.

VI. Application to Actual Building

The developed new practical devices were installed in an actual building and seismic observation started in October 2017. The building is a three-story reinforced concrete building built in Tsukuba, Ibaraki, Japan (Fig. 6). In each floor, one practical device was installed. Fig. 7 shows the plan of 2nd floor of the building and locations of the practical devices installed. Fig. 8 shows how the devices have been installed. As shown in both figures, dedicated installation space was made next to the staircase from 1st to 3rd floors. At each installation location, the device was screwed to the acrylic plate and it was fixed to the floor with an anchor. The device for the rooftop is fixed on the ceiling of the 3rd floor because the rooftop floor is outside.

Figure 6. External appearance of building.

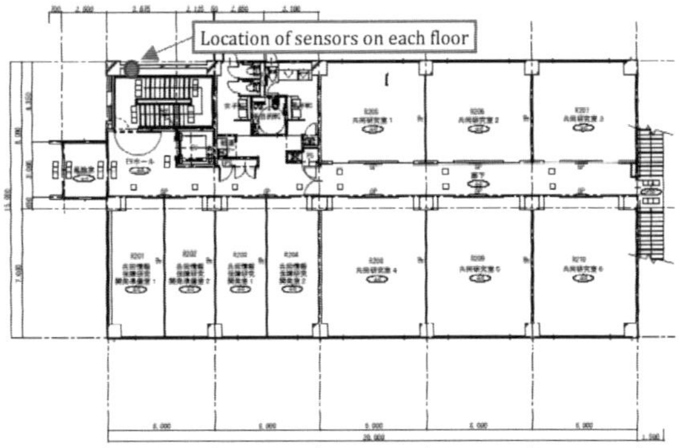

Figure 7. Plan view of 2nd floor of the building and locations of practical device installed.

The sensor device is able to use the built-in MEMS accelerometer and any analog sensor connected to the external input terminal solely. This time, the device is set to use the built-in MEMS accelerometer to measure shaking of small-scale to large-scale earthquakes. Table III shows the specifications of the MEMS accelerometer. This new practical device can detect earthquake occurrence and save seismic event data. The least square calculation for values measured by the accelerometer in each direction is derived by the following equation.

$$l_r = \sqrt{\frac{1}{N}\sum_{i=N-1}^{0}\{(x_i - r_{xi})^2 + (y_i - r_{yi})^2 + (z_i - r_{zi})^2\}}$$

where, r_x, r_y, r_z are correction values of the following zero point.

$$r_x = \frac{1}{N}\sum_{i=N-1}^{0} x_i,\ r_y = \frac{1}{N}\sum_{i=N-1}^{0} y_i,\ r_z = \frac{1}{N}\sum_{i=N-1}^{0} z_i$$

The device was set to judge that an earthquake has occurred when the least square value l_r for 2 seconds exceeds 1 cm/sec^2 and to save the measurement data until the earthquake ends under the condition of a sampling frequency of 100 Hz and a number of correction values of zero point N = 200 in the above equation. The device also saves data 10 seconds before the point that the device judged that the earthquake has occurred and 10 seconds after the earthquake has ended. As shown in Section 3, each practical device is equipped with Ethernet, Wi-Fi, and 3G as communication means and can use any of them. For this time, it was decided to use 3G for data transfer to the data server in order to store only the measurement data at the event of the earthquake.

Table IV shows a list of seismic records observed from October 2017 when the system was installed to November 2017. When an earthquake with Japanese seismic intensity scale of 1 or more occurred, measurements were made reliably. Fig. 9 shows measured acceleration of an earthquake in the building, which occurred on November 3, 2017 (No.8 in Table IV).

TABLE III. Specifications of MEMS Acceleration Sensor

Model	LIS344ALH
Measurement direction	3
Maximum acceleration (± G)	2
Outside dimensions (mm)	4 × 4 × 1.5
Consumption current (mA)	0.68
Stand-by power consumption (μA)	1
Detection sensitivity	660 mV/G ± 5%
Noise characteristics	50 μG/√Hz
Operating temperature (°C)	-40 - +85

(a) Ceiling of 3rd floor (Floor of rooftop)

(b) Floor of 1st floor

Figure 8. Photo of how practical devices are installed.

TABLE IV. LIST OF EARTHQUAKE RECORD MEASURED BY PRACTICAL DEVICES

No	Date	Time	Name of Epicenter	Magnitude/ Depth(km)	Local/Max . Intensity
1	06/10/2017	16:59	Fukushimake n-oki	6.3/57	1/2
2	06/10/2017	23:56	Fukushimake n-oki	5.9/53	2/5 lower
3	07/10/2017	16:20	Ibarakiken-nanbu	3.4/43	1/1
4	12/10/2017	15:12	Fukushimake n-oki	5.2/26	1/2
5	15/10/2017	19:05	Ibarakiken-hokubu	3.0/7	1/1
6	18/10/2017	07:40	Ibarakiken-nanbu	3.7/45	1/2
7	02/11/2017	22:31	Ibarakiken-oki	4.3/74	1/3
8	**03/11/2017**	**21:38**	**Ibarakiken-hokubu**	**4.8/8**	**2/3**
9	05/11/2017	17:40	Ibarakiken-nanbu	2.9/43	1/1
10	15/11/2017	01:21	Ibarakiken-nanbu	3.8/20	1/2
11	26/11/2017	15:55	Ibarakiken-hokubu	3.9/4	1/2
12	30/11/2017	22:02	Ibarakiken-naubu	3.9/42	1/3

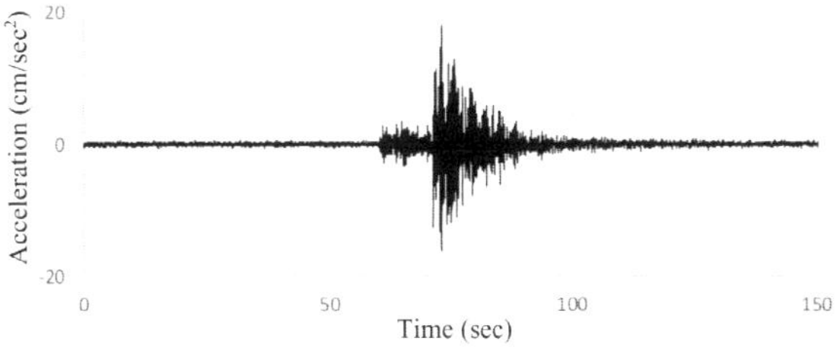

(a) Roof top floor (3rd ceiling)

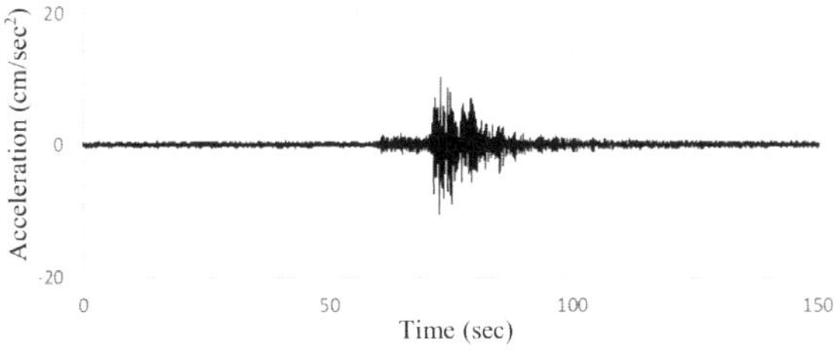

(b) 1st floor

Figure 9. Photo of how practical devices are installed.

Fig. 9 shows measured results of the 1st floor and the 3rd ceiling (floor of the rooftop) in a horizontal direction, respectively. For the 1st floor, an acceleration of 10.2 cm/sec^2 at the maximum is observed. For the rooftop, the vibration of the earthquake is amplified and the maximum value of the acceleration is greater. Function and usability of the improved practical device, which was installed onto an actual building, were verified by the case study of seismic observation.

VII. CONCLUSION

This paper describes research and development on the sensor devices that can keep highly accurate time information autonomously using the built-in Chip Scale Atomic Clock (CSAC) for the purpose of application to seismic observation and structural health monitoring of buildings and civil infrastructure. First, a process of development was explained from the prototype, which uses the mechanism that adds highly accurate time information to the measured data with the CSAC to the practical device. Then, challenges in practical use were identified by the long-term measurement implemented by installing the developed practical device onto a bridge. Based on the challenges, further improvements were made for stability and operability of the practical device, and its performance was confirmed. In addition, the improved practical device was installed onto an actual building, and its usability was verified by the case study of seismic observation.

As one of challenges, the operating method of the sensing system must be considered depending on the objective of measurement because the CSAC is aged over time although it is a highly accurate clock. Another challenge is the high cost of manufacture. The CSAC is expected to be mounted on all computers and smart phones in the near future, but only one American company manufactures and sells it at this time. It is expected that many companies will also participate in the business, and CSACs are actively used in various fields. Further verification will be performed by using the sensing system in actual buildings and civil infrastructures.

ACKNOWLEDGMENT

This research was partially supported by the New Energy and Industrial Technology Development Organization (NEDO) through the Project of Technology for Maintenance, Replacement and Management of Civil Infrastructure, Cross-ministerial Strategic Innovation Promotion Program (SIP). This research was also partially supported by JSPS KAKENHI Grant Number JP16K01283.

REFERENCES

[1] N. Kurata, B. F. Spencer, and M. Ruiz-Sandoval, "Risk Monitoring of Buildings Using Wireless Sensor Network," Journal of Structural Control and Monitoring, vol. 12, Issue 3-4, pp. 315-327, July-Dec. 2005, doi: 10.1002/stc.73.

[2] N. Kurata, M. Suzuki, S. Saruwatari, and H. Morikawa, "Actual Application of Ubiquitous Structural Monitoring System using Wireless Sensor Networks," Proc. the 14th World Conference on Earthquake Engineering (14WCEE) IAEE, Oct. 2008, pp. 1-8, Paper ID:11-0037.

[3] N. Kurata, M. Suzuki, S. Saruwatari, and H. Morikawa, "Application of Ubiquitous Structural Monitoring System by Wireless Sensor Networks to Actual High-rise Building," Proc. the 5th World Conference on Structural Control and Monitoring (5WCSCM) IASCM, July 2010, pp. 1-9, Paper No. 013.

[4] S. Knappe, V. Shah, P. D. D. Schwindt, and J. Kitching, "A microfabricated atomic clock," Applied Physics Letters, vol. 85, Issue 9, pp. 1460-1462, Aug. 2004, doi:10.1063/1.1787942.

[5] Q. Li and D. Rus, "Global Clock Synchronization in Sensor Networks," IEEE Transactions on Computers, vol. 55, Issue 2, pp. 214-226, Jan. 2006, ISSN: 0018-9340.

[6] R. Lutwak, et al., "The Chip-Scale Atomic Clock - Prototype Evaluation," Proc. the 39th Annual Precise Time and Time Interval (PTTI) Meeting, ION, Nov. 2007, pp. 269-290.

[7] N. Kurata, "Disaster Big Data Infrastructure using Sensing Technology with a Chip Scale Atomic Clock," World Engineering Conference and Convention (WECC2015) WFEO/UNESCO/SCJ/JFES, Dec. 2015, pp. 1-5.

[8] N. Kurata, "Basic Study of Autonomous Time Synchronization Sensing Technology Using Chip Scale Atomic Clock," Proc. the 16th International Conference on Computing in Civil and Building Engineering (ICCCBE2016) ISCCBE, July 2016, pp. 67-74.

[9] N. Kurata, "Development of Sensor Module for Seismic and Structural Monitoring with a Chip-Scale Atomic Clock," Proceedings of the 16th. World Conference on Earthquake Engineering (16WCEE) IAEE, Jan. 2017, pp. 1-8, Paper No.583.

[10] N. Kurata, "An Autonomous Time Synchronization Sensor Device Using a Chip Scale Atomic Clock for Earthquake Observation and Structural Health Monitoring," The Eighth International Conference on Sensor Device Technologies and Applications (SENSORDEVICES 2017) IARIA, Sep. 2017, pp. 31-36, ISSN: 2308-3514, ISBN: 978-1-61208-581-4.

[11] N. Kurata, "Development and Application of an Autonomous Time Synchronization Sensor Device Using a Chip Scale Atomic Clock," Sensors & Transducers Journal, Vol. 219, Issue 1, pp.17-25, January 2018, ISSN: 2306-8515, e-ISSN 1726-5479.

[12] D. L. Mills, "Internet time synchronization: the network time protocol," IEEE Transactions on Communications, vol. 39, Issue 10, pp. 1482-1493, Oct. 1991, doi:10.1109/26.103043.

[13] M. Maroti, B. Kusy, G. Simon, and A. Ledeczi, "The Flooding Time Synchronization Protocol," Proc. the 2nd International Conference on Embedded Networked Sensor Systems (SenSys '04), Nov. 2004, pp. 39-49, ISBN:1-58113-879-2.

[14] Q. Li and D. Rus, "Global Clock Synchronization in Sensor Networks," IEEE Transactions on Computers, vol. 55, Issue 2, pp. 214-226, Jan. 2006, ISSN: 0018-9340.

[15] J. Elson, L. Girod, and D. Estrin, "Fine-Grained Network Time Synchronization using Reference Broadcasts," Proc. 5th Symposium on Operating Systems Design and Implementation (OSDI'02), Dec. 2002, pp. 147-163.

[16] S. Ganeriwal, R. Kumar and M. B. Srivastava, "Timing-sync Protocol for Sensor Networks," Proc. the 1st international conference on Embedded networked sensor systems (SenSys '03), Nov. 2003, pp. 138-149.

[17] K. Romer, "Time Synchronization in Ad Hoc Networks," Proc. the 2nd ACM International Symp. on Mobile Ad Hoc Networking & Computing (MobiHoc'01), Oct. 2001, pp. 173-182.

Navigation Cells Based on Visible Light Communication for Indoor Positioning

Paula Louro[1,2], Manuela Vieira[1,2], Manuel A. Vieira[1,2]

[1] ISEL/IPL – Instituto Superior de Engenharia de Lisboa, Instituto Politécnico de Lisboa
R. Conselheiro Emídio Navarro, 1959-007 Lisboa, Portugal
[2]CTS-UNINOVA

[2] Quinta da Torre, Monte da Caparica, 2829-516, Caparica, Portugal
e-mail: plouro@deetc.isel.ipl.pt; mv@isel.pt; mvieira@deetc.isel.ipl.pt

Abstract—**White Light emitting Diodes (LEDs) revolutionized the field of illumination technology, mainly due to energy efficiency. In addition, LEDs can also be used in wireless communication systems when integrated in Visible Light Communication (VLC) systems. Indoor positioning for navigation in large buildings using Global Positioning Service (GPS) systems is limited by signal attenuation. The motivation for this application is also supported by the possibility of taking advantage of an existing lighting and WiFi infrastructure. In this work, we propose an indoor navigation system based on the use of VLC technology. The proposed system includes tri-chromatic white LEDs with the red and blue chips modulated at different frequencies and a pin-pin photodetector with selective spectral sensitivity. Optoelectronic features of both optical sources and photodetector device are analyzed. The photodetector device consists of two pin structures based on a-SiC:H and a-Si:H with geometrical configuration optimized for the detection of short and large wavelengths in the visible range. Its sensitivity is externally tuned by steady state optical bias. The localization algorithm makes use of the Fourier transform to identify the frequencies present in the photocurrent signal and the wavelength filtering properties of the sensor under front and back optical bias to detect the existing red and blue signals. The viability of the system was demonstrated through the implementation of an automatic algorithm to infer the photodetector cardinal direction.**

Keywords- amorphous SiC; optoelectronic; spectral sensitivity; white LEDs; visible light communication; indoor positioning.

I. INTRODUCTION

Indoor lighting is being driven by white LED luminaires that provide high efficiency, low power consumption and long life span [1]. This provided a large development of the LEDs market for lighting purposes. Additionally, LEDs can switch to different light intensity levels at a very fast rate, which can be used for communication where data to be transmitted is encoded in the emitting light supplied by the LED. This is the basis of Visible Light Communication (VLC) [2][3][4], which is a technology holding an increasing importance as the visible light spectrum corresponds to license free bandwidth. Besides, it is a line of sight technology, and consequently not prone to interference. This confers high reliability for secure wireless communication [5]. Moreover, the reuse of the lighting infrastructure for the additional functionality of data communication is a very attractive advantage. Currently, VLC is considered an attractive technology to complement the RF-based mobile communications systems [6][7][8][9].

VLC applications were initially developed to supply access network in homes, but rapidly progressed to support hand-held devices and transport vehicles [10][11][12]. Other fields where VLC is growing include indoor localization, human computer interaction, device-to-device communication and vehicular applications. Outdoor location services are largely dependent on Global Positioning System (GPS). However, for indoor scenarios this technology is no longer feasible due to the strong attenuation of the GPS signal. Thus, alternative solutions are demanded. Currently, indoor localization technology is based on WiFi and VLC. Main difference between the use of these technologies is related to the location accuracy. In WiFi, the accuracy is limited by the number of available wireless access points, while in VLC it is determined by the number of LED luminaires. As, typically in a building, there are 10 times more LED luminaires than the number of WiFi access points, the accuracy is naturally improved using VLC. Most of the location approaches based on VLC described in literature report the use of LED sources transmitting specific identity and location information and receivers that detect the transmitted signal by multiple optical sources. Based on the distance evaluation, trilateration is used for location assessment.

In this paper, we propose an indoor localization system [13] designed with white RGB LEDs and a heterostructure pinpin photodiode based on a-SiC:H/a-Si:H with a simple On-Off modulation scheme. The tri-chromatic LEDs provide three channels for data transmission. Blue and red emitters are modulated at two different specific frequencies that correspond to different cardinal directions. The green emitter is used for identification of the LED transmission unit [14][15]. The photodetector is designed for operation in the visible light spectrum. The different bandgap semiconductors of each active region of the pin structures allow selective absorption of the light spectral components [16][17]. This is used in the decoding strategy to infer the optical signals received by the photodetector [18].

The proposed lighting and positioning/navigation system involves wireless communication, computer-based algorithms, smart sensor and optical sources network, which constitutes a transdisciplinary approach framed in cyber-physical systems.

The rest of the paper is structured as follows. In Section II, the design of the VLC system is described. Section III contains results and respective discussion. Section IV presents main conclusion and a few guidelines for future work.

II. DESIGN OF THE VLC SYSTEM

The proposed VLC system includes an indoor scenario of infrastructure-to-device communication. The LED luminaires are used to perform three tasks, namely, room illumination, position/navigation services and data transmission.

The proposed system is composed by the transmitter and the receiver modules, located respectively at the infra-structure and at the device. The transmitter includes white RGB LEDs, the coder and the modulator. This unit is responsible for the modulated optical transmission of coded data. The receiver consists of the photodetector, the demodulator and the decoder. The transmission channel of the optical link is free space propagation with the constraint of line of sight condition.

The transmitter proposed in this VLC system uses ceiling lamps based on commercial white LEDs with red, green and blue emitters (w-RGB LEDs). Each LED luminaire at the ceiling is composed by four white LEDs framed at the corners of a square (Figure 1).

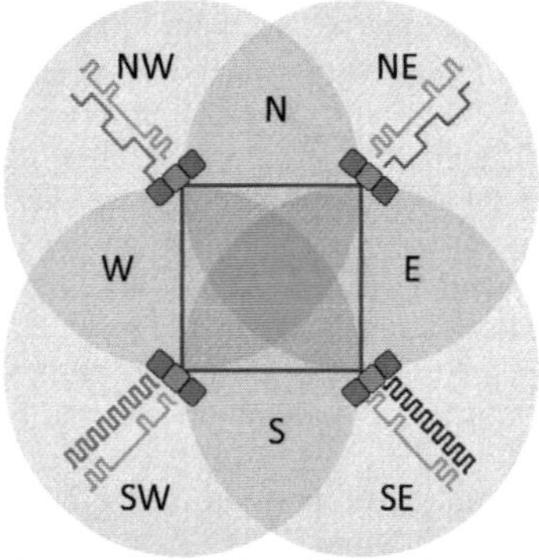

Figure 1. Configuration of the LED luminaire.

Each navigation cell is assigned to a unique identifier supplied by the green emitters that make the correspondence between the device and the emission area. Increased position accuracy within each navigation cell is obtained through the modulation of the blue and red emitters of the luminaire LEDs that map different spatial regions by the correspondent illumination pattern. The top emitters, assigned to the north direction, are modulated at half frequency of the bottom emitters, assigned to the south direction. The left emitters (west direction) are the red emitters while the right emitters (east direction) are the blue chips of the RGB LEDs.

The optical sources used for the dual function of lighting and data transmission through VLC are commercial RGB white LEDs of high intensity light output and wide viewing angle. Data from datasheet specifications indicate peak wavelengths located in the ranges 619 nm – 624 nm, 520 nm – 540 nm and 460 nm – 480 nm for the red, green and blue emitters. The codification of the optical signals includes the transmission of information related to navigation data and to the message to broadcast.

In every transmission channels each frame is a word of 32 bits, divided into four blocks: START SYNC block (4 bits), INFO block (8 bits), MESSAGE block (16 bits) and STOP SYNC BLOCK (4 bits).

An on-off keying modulation scheme was used with a 32-bit codification (logical state 1: light on and logical state 0: light off). A dedicated three channel LED driver with multiple outputs was developed to modulate the optical signals. The modulator converts the coded message of each transmission channel into a modulated driving current signal that actuates the emitters of each tri-chromatic white LED. In every LED, the driving current of each emitter is controlled independently of the other emitters.

The photodetector used for the transduction of the optical signal is a monolithic heterojunction composed by two pin structures built on a glass substrate and sandwiched between two transparent electrical contacts (Figure 2).

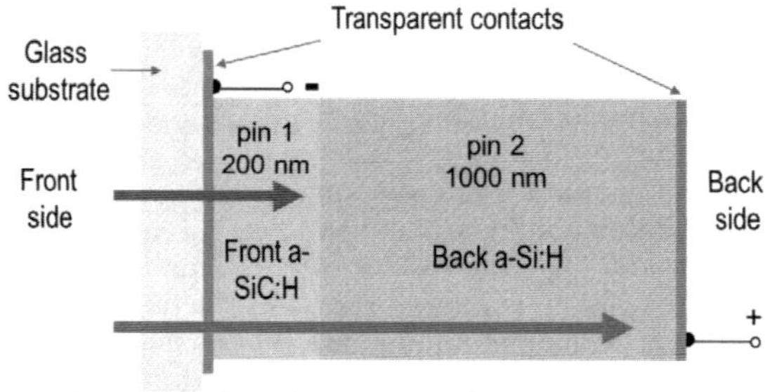

Figure 2. Configuration of the photodetector at the receiver module.

The intrinsic absorbers of the device are based on a-Si:H and a-SiC:H, which provide high sensitivity in the visible range. Both intrinsic layers were designed to detect separately short and long visible wavelengths. The front intrinsic layer is narrow (200 nm) and exhibits a higher bandgap material (2.1 eV, a-SiC:H). The back intrinsic layer is thicker (1000 nm) and has a lower bandgap semiconductor (1.8 eV, a-Si:H). This design confers high absorption of the blue light (shorter wavelengths) and high transparency of the red wavelength to the front absorber (pin 1) and high absorption of longer wavelengths (red light) to the back absorber (pin 2).

The filtering properties of the pinpin photodetector assigned to each pin structure are demonstrated in Figure. 3, that displays the transient photocurrent output of the device under excitation of the RGB white LEDs using different optical biasing conditions (back and front optical bias of 400 nm and no optical bias).

As shown in the graph of Figure 3, the photocurrent signals for each optical excitation show different trends dependent on the optical biasing conditions. Long wavelength light from the red and green emitters are amplified under front optical bias and attenuated (70%) under back optical bias. For the short wavelengths (blue light), the photocurrent signal is increased when the optical excitation is on the back side and attenuated from the front side.

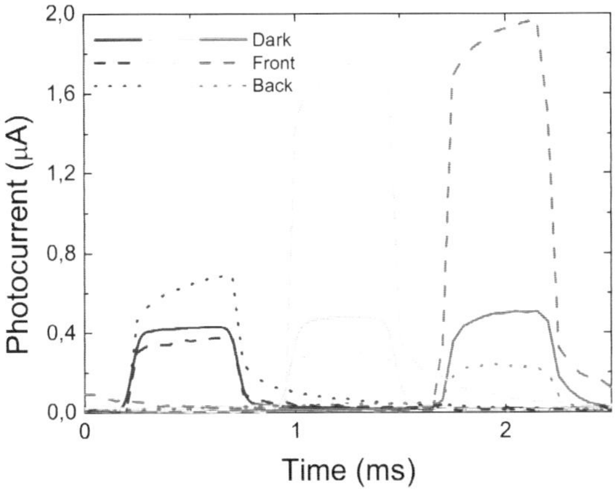

Figure 3. Transient photocurrent output of the photodetector under excitation of the RGB white LEDs using different optical biasing conditions.

The quantification of the signal amplification under front and back bias is determined by the optical gain, defined at each wavelength as the ratio between the signal magnitudes measured with and without optical bias. For the red, green and blue light the front optical gain under violet background light is, respectively, 5, 3.5 and 1.3, while for the back optical gains, the values are 0.6, 0.6 and 1.7.

The decoding unit processes the output signals, measured with front and back optical bias, incoming from the oscilloscope to extract the input optical signals. The decoding strategy starts with the identification of the triggering event, given the idle and start bits, that ensures the synchronization of the process. Then, it follows the identification of the unit navigation cell, which demands the extraction of the green signal from the multiplexed signal. After this identification, the green signal contribution is subtracted from the front and back photocurrent signals. Then, the next 8 bits assigned to the position INFO word of both front and back photocurrents are processed to evaluate the modulus of the complex Fourier coefficients. When the calculated coefficient is above a certain threshold the signal is considered to be present at the respective frequency, otherwise it is discarded. The photocurrent signals measured under front and back optical bias are used to infer, respectively, the red signal and the blue optical signals. This procedure allows the identification of the wavelengths and frequencies assigned to the optical excitations, which corresponds to a specific spatial position. The next 16 bits contain the message transmitted by each emitter channel. It is decoded using the front optical photocurrent to identify the red contribution and the back photocurrent signal to classify the blue excitation.

III. RESULTS AND DISCUSSION

A. *Information coding*

The test case used to validate the proposed communication scheme is displayed in Figure 4 that shows the specific words sent in the Position INFO and DATA blocks of each emitter, which correspond to the second and third blocks, respectively.

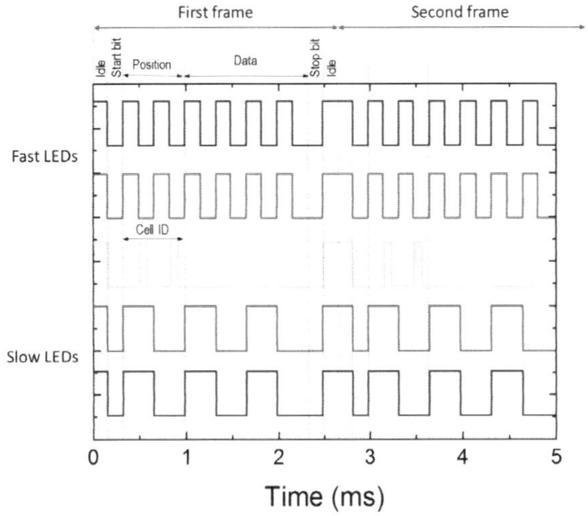

Figure 4. Codification of the optical signals in test conditions.

The Position INFO word is set to the code word 10101010 in the fast emitters, to 11001100 in the slow emitters and to 00100010 in the green emitter, corresponding therefore to the navigation cell located in line 1 and column 1. The DATA word is set to 00000000 in the green channel, as predicted by the adopted codification scheme and to the words 11001100 and 10101010 in the slow and fast emitters, respectively.

Figure 5 displays the acquired photocurrent signal by the pinpin photodiode, biased at -8 V and under variable conditions of optical bias (without and with front/back steady state background light).

The signal was acquired in different positions of the navigation unit cell, exhibiting in each case a different pattern due to different lighting excitations. In all graphs the trigger event allows easy synchronization and identification of each transmitted frame. This is clearly noticeable by the high peaks of the front photocurrent (represented in the graphs by the magenta line), as in the idle bits all emitters are set to ON and this combination results in photocurrent amplification when the device is soaked by steady state illumination from the front side. In contrast, the same signal under back background light is decreased.

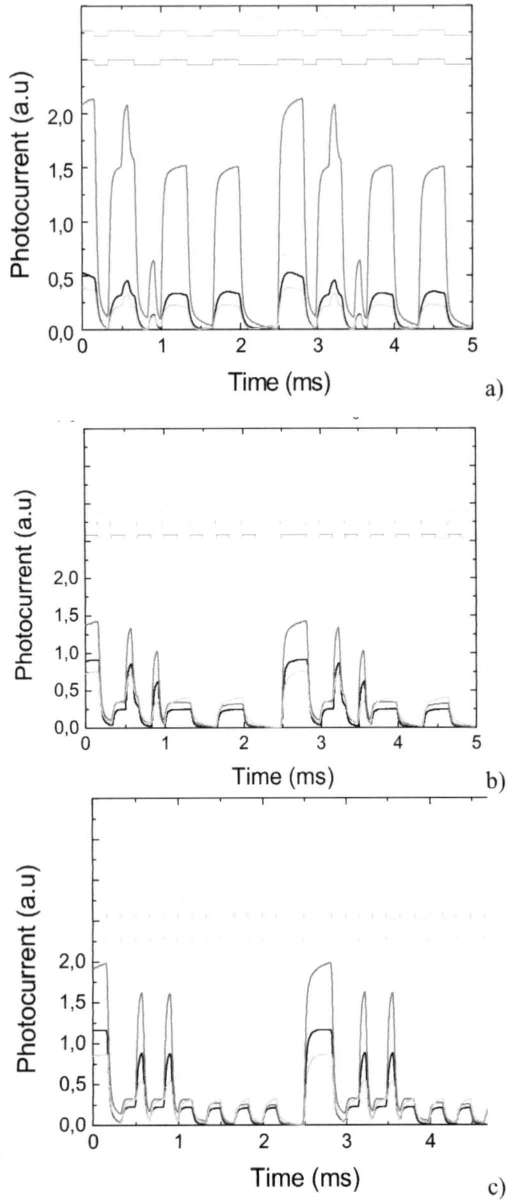

Figure 5. Photocurrent signal by the pinpin photodiode, biased at -8 V and under variable conditions of optical bias (without and with front/back steady state background light).

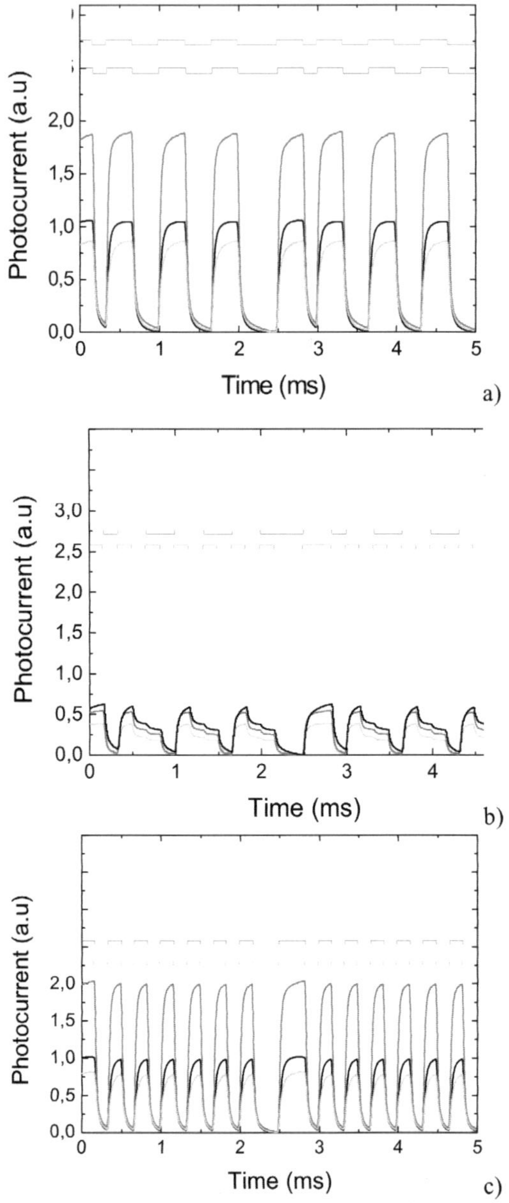

Figure 6. Photocurrent signals without the contribution of the green signal at positions: a) #1, b) #2 and c) #3.

B. Information recovery

Figure 6 displays the photocurrent signals after the removal of the green excitation contribution.

The next step is the identification of the transmitted frequencies, which requires the computation of the modulus of the complex Fourier coefficients over the 8 bits data sent next to the idle and start bits. When the calculated coefficient is above a certain threshold the signal is present at the respective frequency. In this step the front photocurrent is used to identify the red light and the back photocurrent for the blue light.

This procedure enables the identification of the position within the navigation cell, which mixed with the cell identification by the green channel enables the absolute position recognition. The message is decoded using the adjacent 16 bits of the slow and fast emitters. The algorithm assumes that in the front photocurrent the highest levels correspond to the presence of the red light, while the lowest ones to its absence, which allows the immediate recognition of the ON-OFF states for the red channel. Attending to the back-photocurrent signal, the same reason can be used. Here, the highest levels are assigned to the presence of the blue input signal and the lowest levels to its nonexistence, which allows the immediate decoding of the blue channel. Thus, both red and blue channels can be immediately tuned by using adequate biasing light for the background. Using this simple key algorithm, the independent red and blue bit sequences of the message can be decoded.

IV. CONCLUSION AND FUTURE WORK

Simultaneous navigation and data transmission based on visible light communication was presented and discussed. The use of RGB white LEDs and a-SiC:H pinpin photodiodes for indoors navigation was extended to add data transmission functionality to the VLC system. Codification of the optical signals ensured synchronization between frames and was also designed to shield the decoding process from errors that might provide wrong identification of the correspondent spatial position. The transmitted data is encoded in a 32 bits word, but the length can be easily expanded. Future work comprises the analysis of the system in a wider range of optical fluxes, as well as the decoding of different random transmitted messages.

ACKNOWLEDGEMENTS

This work was sponsored by FCT – Fundação para a Ciência e a Tecnologia, within the Research Unit CTS – Center of Technology and systems, reference UID/EEA/00066/2013 and by IPL/2017/SMART_VeDa/ISEL and IPL/2018/LAN4CC/ISEL.

REFERENCES

[1] Y. Tanaka, S. Haruyama, and M. Nakagawa, "Wireless optical transmissions with white colored LED for wireless home links", Personal, Indoor and Mobile Radio Communications, 2000. PIMRC 2000. The 11th IEEE International Symposium on, vol. 2, 2000, pp. 1325-1329.

[2] W. Zhang, S. Chowdhury, and M. Kavehrad, "Asynchronous indoor positioning system based on visible light communications", Optical Engineering 53(4), 045105, April 2014.

[3] W. Zhang, M. Kavehrad, "A 2-D indoor localization system based on visible light LED," in Proc. IEEE Photonics Society Summer Topical Conf.—Optical Wireless Systems Applications, pp. 80–81 ,2012.

[4] Z. Zia, "A visible light communication based hybrid positioning method for wireless sensor networks", Intelligent System Design and Engineering Application (ISDEA) 2012 Second International Conference, pp. 1367-1370, 2012.

[5] D. Karunatilaka, F. Zafar, V. Kalavally, and R. Parthiban, "LED based indoor visible light communications: state of the art", Communications Surveys Tutorials, IEEE, vol. PP, n° 99, pp 1-1, 2015.

[6] E. Ozgur, O. Dinc, and B. Akan, "Communicate to illuminate: State-of-the-art and research challenges for visible light communications", Physical Communication 17 (2015) pp. 72–85, http://dx.doi.org/10.1016/j.phycom.2015.08.003

[7] J. Armstrong, Y. Sekercioglu, and A. Neild, "Visible light positioning: a roadmap for international standardization", Communications IEEE, vol. 51, no. 12, pp. 68-73, 2013.

[8] K. Panta K. and J. Armstrong, "Indoor localisation using white LEDs,"Electron. Lett. 48(4), pp. 228–230 (2012).

[9] T. Komiyama, K. Kobayashi, K. Watanabe, T. Ohkubo, and Y. Kurihara, "Study of visible light communication system using RGB LED lights," in Proceedings of SICE Annual Conference, IEEE, 2011, pp. 1926–1928.

[10] N. Kumar, and N. R. Lourenço, "LED-based visible liht communication system: a brief survey and investigation", Journal of Engineering and Applied Sciences, vol. 5, nº4, pp. 296-307, 2010.

[11] A. Jovicic, J. Li, and T. Richardson, "Visible light communication: opportunities, challenges and the path to market," Communications Magazine, IEEE, vol. 51, no. 12, pp. 26–32, 2013, DOI: 10.1109/MCOM.2013.6685754

[12] Z. Zhou, M. Kavehrad, and P. Deng, "Indoor positioning algorithm using light-emitting diode visible light communications," Opt. Eng. 51(8), 085009 (2012).

[13] P. Louro, V. Silva, M. A.,Vieira and M. Vieira, "Viability of the use of an a-SiC:H multilayer device in a domestic VLC application", Phys. Status Solidi C 11, No. 11–12, pp. 1703–1706 (2014) / DOI 10.1002/pssc.201400035.

[14] P. Louro, V. Silva, J. Costa, M. A. Vieira and M. Vieira, "Added transmission capacity in VLC systems using white RGB based LEDs and WDM devices ", Proc. SPIE 9899, Optical Sensing and Detection IV, 98990F ,April 29, 2016.

[15] M. A. Vieira, M. Vieira, V. Silva and P. Louro "Optical signal processing for indoor positioning using a-SiC:H technology" Proc. SPIE 9891, Silicon Photonics and Photonic Integrated Circuits V, 98911Z (May 13, 2016).

[16] P. Louro et al. "Optoelectronic characterization of a-SIC:H stacked devices", Journal of Non-Crystalline Solids, vol. 338-340, no. 1 SPEC. ISS., 15 June 2004, pp. 345-348.

[17] A. Fantoni, M. Fernandes, P. Louro, and I. Rodrigues, "Stacked n-i-p-n-i-p heterojunctions for image recognition, Materials Research Society Symposium - Proceedings, Volume 762, 2003, pp. 199-204 Materials Research Proceedings: Amorphous and Nanocrystalline Silicon-Based Films – 2003.

[18] P. Louro, J. Costa, M. Vieira, M. A. Vieira and Y. Vygranenko, "Use of VLC for indoors navigation with RGB LEDs and a-SiC:H photodetector", Proc. of SPIE, vol. 10231, Optical sensors 2017 (102310F-2).

Capillary Sensors with Two Coupled LEDs for UV-Forced Degradation and Fluorescence Reading of Chemical Stability of Diesel Fuels

Michal Borecki
Institute of Microelectronics and Optoelectronics
Warsaw University of Technology
Warsaw, Poland
email: borecki@imio.pw.edu.pl

Piotr Doroz
Institute of Microelectronics and Optoelectronics
Warsaw University of Technology
Warsaw, Poland
email: piotr.65@gazeta.pl

Mateusz Gęca
Lublin University of Technology
Lublin, Poland
email: mati.geca@gmail.com

Przemysław Prus
Blue Oak Inventions
Wroclaw, Poland
email: pprus@boinv.com

Michael L. Korwin-Pawlowski
Département d'informatique et d'ingénierie
Université du Québec en Outaouais
Gatineau, Québec, Canada
email: Michael.Korwin-Pawlowski@uqo.ca

Jan Szmidt
Institute of Microelectronics and Optoelectronics
Warsaw University of Technology
Warsaw, Poland
email: j.szmidt@imio.pw.edu.pl

Abstract- **The stability of the diesel fuel is related to the fuel composition that evolved to the modern fuels from the historical ones. The instability of modern diesel fuel is mainly due to the presence of unsaturated components and components with oxygen. Standard laboratory techniques for measuring fuel stability are relatively complex and time consuming. The time of examination of initial stages of degradation is in the rank of a dozen of hours. The fast methods of diesel fuel stability pointing with single ultraviolet (UV) wavelength forced degradation and fluorescence reading have been proposed. The present paper concentrates on the possibility of further reduction of time of examination of the diesel fuel that enables initial and advanced stages of fuel instability indicating. The reduction of time of degradation is expected as two light emitting diodes (LED) working at different wavelengths are implemented in sensor head. The long-wave ultraviolet (UVA) - 365 nm high power light emitted diode and the short-wave ultraviolet (UVC) - 265 nm light emitted diode are selected for examination. The procedure of degradation and examination with signal switching of LEDs has been proposed. Experimental results are presented for the dual LED degradation system in comparison of to the single 265 nm LED degradation system. Obtained characteristics show fluorescence emitted signal at selected wavelength bands dependency of initial, medium and advanced effects of fuel degradation. The results show that using dual LED system increases fuel degradation speed as an advanced effects of fuel instability arise in the time less than one hour.**

Keywords-biodiesel fuel stability; diesel fuel instability; unsaturated hydrocarbons; capillary sensor; LED excited fluorescence; UV degradation.

I. INTRODUCTION

Capillary measurement systems are popular in many chemical laboratories as they enable measurement of complex solutions. Capillary electrophoresis (CE) is one of the highest efficiency small volume separation methods available and laser induced fluorescence (LIF) detection is the most sensitive CE detection method [1]. It should be pointed that, CE is appropriate to examination of conductive solutions. Therefore, CE is not applicable to direct inspection of oils [2][3]. The LIF detecting units are still expensive and dangerous to eyes. Thus, implementation of LIF in sensor is the subject of investigations [4]. Capillary measurement systems are also made with the use of liquid core waveguide (LCW) and LED fluorescence detection unit. A Teflon AF coated fused silica capillary usually serves as the LCW [5]. Therefore, examination of oils is quite difficult. But, implementation of low cost unit for fluorescence examination with dual LED system was proposed. This unit, consisting of one high power LED worked at 365 nm and other worked at 405 nm, seems very interesting and fit for in sensing device application.

A dedicated sensor of diesel fuels stability using a disposable capillary optrode and UV radiation as the fluorescence excitation factor and fuel degradation initiator was investigated [6]. The preliminary results of an examination, using a single wavelength configuration of the sensor, show that it is possible to obtain the first signs of fuel instability in a time less than one hour [7]. Therefore, advances of two wavelength examinations using two LEDs working at UVC and UVA in sensor dedicated to examination of diesel fuel stability are presented in this paper.

A. Modern diesel fuels

There are many types of diesel fuels including petro-diesel, syn-diesel (synthetic) and bio-diesel. The fuel types can be further classified in groups as for example petro-diesels include classical petro-diesel and modern petro diesel groups, while bio-diesels include Fatty-Acid Methyl ester (FAME) or Hydrogenated Vegetable Oil (HVO) components. The syn-diesel main groups cover liquid fuel components. Liquid syn-diesel is produced from any carbonaceous material that was gasified, purified and converted in the Fischer–Tropsch process. Gas syn-diesel is Dimethyl Ether (DME).

Classical petro-diesel fuels are made from stable components of straight run distillate products of crude oil (alkanes) with an addition of improvers [8]. Modern petro-diesel fuels include stable and unstable components.

Stable components are alkanes and cycloalkanes. Unstable components include acyclic and cyclic unsaturated hydrocarbons. Acyclic unsaturated components may include alkynes, alkadienes and alkatrienes, while cyclic unsaturated components may include monocyclic benzene (MAH – Monocyclic Aromatic Hydrocarbon) and Polycyclic Aromatic Hydrocarbons (PAHs). MAH is represented by benzene, a natural liquid constituent of crude oil and one of the elementary petrochemicals. The simplest PAHs are naphthalene (white crystalline solid), having two aromatic rings and the three-ring compounds anthracene (colorless solid) and phenanthrene (white powder). Diesel fuel is expected to contain PAHs particles ranging from three to five ring systems [9], although the harmfulness of PAHs for human health is a known issue. Thus, the volume of PAHs with two or higher number of rings is limited in Europe by the Directive 2003/17/EC to 11 wt%. But, for the defined in Sweden class 1 diesel fuel the limit value for PAHs with three or more rings is 0.02 vol%.

It was historically postulated that classical petro-diesel fuel may be kept in storage for prolonged periods, but also that synthetic diesel and HVO components are generally first class fuels.

On the other hand, modern petro-diesel and FAME are unstable and their degradation is accelerated with oxygen presence, temperature and sunlight, which include ultraviolet radiation [10]-[12]. The results of diesel fuel instability are sediments and gum formation. The results of bio-diesel degradation with polymer and soluble waxes formation is the increase in the diesel fuel viscosity [13]. The changes in molecular composition of the fuel affect its ignition characteristics, which is one of the most important diesel fuel quality parameters. The minimum cetane number of diesel fuel differs by region. For example, in Europe the minimum value is 51, but in some regions of United States it is 40. It should be noted, that obtaining fuel with high cetane number is not simple task.

There are two methods to increase the cetane number. The first method is to reduce the unsaturated content of fuel by hydrogenation - this is usually not done because of a high cost. The second method is using cetane improving additives – this method is preferred due to its low cost [14]. The 2-Ethyl Hexyl Nitrate (2-EHN) is the most popular improver, but it can be an additional cause of the fuel instability. Thus, the extended period diesel fuel storage conditions have to be described with the use of parameters including exposure to air and light with a specified environment temperature.

B. Optoelectronic measurement systems and sensors for diesel fuel testing

There are many standards of fuel testing procedures, but their applications are limited to petrochemical laboratories. New methods and adaptation of examination standards to ordinary laboratory conditions and in-situ examinations are in development. The most popular directions of investigation include fuel type and fuel fit for use classifications [15]-[17]. For such measurement set-ups and corresponding measurement procedures dedicated electronic components [18]-[20] and units [21]-[23] as well as methods of data analysis [24][25] are under development.

Spectrophotometric methods consisting of examinations of light absorption, scattering and fluorescence are popular for diesel fuel testing. Light absorption in infra-red is used in screening analysis to detect specific types of adulteration in diesel/biodiesel blends [26]. Biodiesel content determination in diesel fuel is also possible with the use of fluorescence examination [27].

The Time-Resolved Laser-Induced Fluorescence Spectroscopy (TRLIFS) enables the characterization and identification of different petroleum diesel fuels, biodiesel from different feed stocks and theirs blends. A typical TRLIFS set-up consists of an ultraviolet excitation pulsed laser working at 266 nm wavelength, an acquisition system measuring the dynamic response with a specific time gate width, and software that compares obtained results as: recorded impulse shape, frequency behavior and decay behavior, maximal intensities and the wavelength of the maximal fluorescence intensity to a previously created data base [28]. Similar created databases used with measurement data of Synchronous Scanning Fluorescence Spectroscopy (SSFS) that are processed with multivariate analysis enable the determination of quality parameters of diesel blends [29]. The sample measurement set-up of SSFS includes a fluorescence spectrometer, for example Shimadzu RF-5301, that is equipped with a high power xenon discharge light source that converts about 150 W of power into radiation spectrum for sample excitation with wavelength width equal 1.5 nm scanned from 220 nm to 750 nm, while the recorded wavelength interval is 50 nm.

The literature review may lead to the conclusion that spectrophotometric methods require costly equipment dedicated to a chemical laboratory environment. But fortunately, diesel fuel stability may be considered as a function of most unstable components presence and concentration. These unstable components include multi-unsaturated hydrocarbons are known as fluorophores [30]. For example, anthracene absorbs radiation in the range of 200 nm to 380 nm and emits light mainly in the range of

380 nm to 600 nm with characteristic multi peak spectrum with three major peaks with maximum at 430 nm [31]. For optical detection of such particles presence, the optoelectronic components are available. Such components may be the base of prototyping of rapid in examination and low-cost in use sensors for reliable determination of fuel chemical stability.

The rest of this paper is organized as follows. Section II describes the sensor configuration including the sensor head with the optrode as well as the optoelectronics system set-up. Section III addresses the experimental results of the fluorescent signal analysis. Section IV goes into short conclusions.

II. SENSOR CONFIGURATION

The idea of the sensor was inspired by the need to come up with a low-cost measurement method for a set of diesel fuels utilizing forced UV degradation effects in one system that would require the minimum of automated mechanical elements.

A. *Sensor head*

The sensor's head consists of two functional units: the head base with fixed optical fibers and the capillary optrode, as shown in Figure 1.

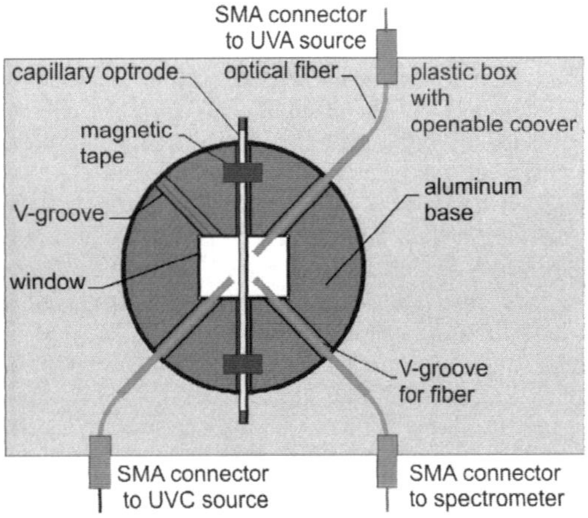

Figure 1. Head of the capillary sensor.

The use of capillary reduces significantly the costs of measurement in a few ways:

First, the measurement of diesel fuel degradation results in adhesive gums generation inside the vessel, thus a disposable vessel is a must. Moreover, diesel and biodiesel fuels affect plastic optical cuvettes made from poly(methyl methacrylate). Therefore, using a capillary glass optrode reduces costs versus classic cuvettes.

Second, the capillary optrode introduces a smaller fluorescent aperture and radiation path compared to classic cuvette holders. Thus, the optical power used for degradation and excitation of fluorescence in the proposed head may be significantly lower (100 times) than when a commercial spectrophotometer is used. Therefore, radiation sources with lower power can be used in the construction of the sensors, for example light emitted diodes instead of laser diodes.

Third, the capillary optrode is filled with the use of capillary force; therefore, pipettes are not used contrary classic set-up.

Thus, the capillary optrode CV7087Q is used here as a replaceable and disposable vessel.

B. *Sensor scheme and measurement procedure*

The set of parameters of interest may be observed using forced UV degradation realized simultaneously at UVC 265 nm and UVA range 366 nm wavelengths. Light emitted diodes can be used as a cost/performance balanced radiation source at these ranges of wavelengths. Commercial LEDs powers at UVA wavelengths are relatively high, as 15 mW at 365 nm are available. What should be noted is that the powers of LEDs in mentioned wavelengths increase with current technological progress. For example, single chip M365F1 LEDs, that represent the state of the art of the last few years, has the maximum power of about 4 mW, while this year's M365FP1e Thorlabs' element's maximum power is about 15 mW. LEDs at UVC and UVB ranges are characterized by significantly lower emitted powers than those for UVA [32]. In the UVC range the single chip LEDs maximum power is about 1.5 mW. Maximum power increase of UVC LEDs is realized with the multi- chip construction as for example in the UVLUX250-HL-5 element. Unfortunately, such construction does not fit well with the fiber optics senor technology.

The sensor scheme designed to realize simultaneous degradation at UVC and UVA and fluorescence reading with excitation at UVC is presented in Figure 2.

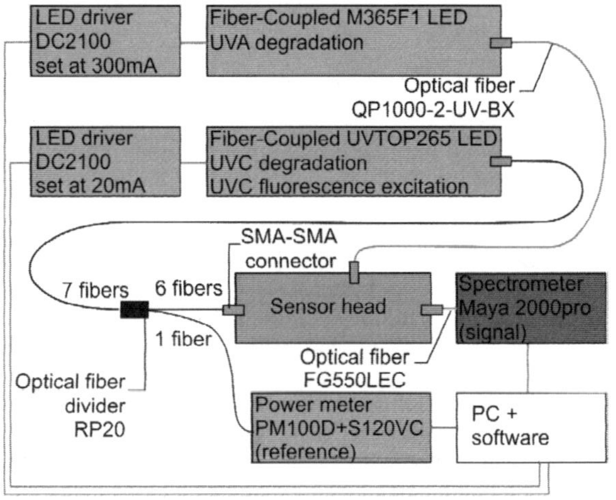

Figure 2. Scheme of the capillary sensor.

The optoelectronic set-up is divided into two parts, the UV radiation sources and the detection unit, both connected to a personal computer equipped with spectra acquisition software and system script designed for measurement automation.

As the UVA source, fiber-coupled LED Thorlabs M365F1 with the 365 nm dominant wavelength was used. As the UVC source, the UVTOP265 from Roithner LaserTechnik was implemented into Thorlabs SM1 micromechanical components to make a fiber-coupled unit. Diodes were connected to DC2100 controllers operating in the constant current mode. In the presented set-up the powers delivered from both sources are not perfect balanced. The source working at 366 nm delivers 1 mW of power, while the source working at 265 nm delivers 300 μW.

The detection unit consists of the power meter (PM100D+S120VC), the optical fiber divider (RP20) and the spectrometer (Maya 2000pro). The RP20 divider is used to divide the UVC signal between the head and the power meter. Thus, UVC radiation can be used for degradation and for fluorescence excitation with a precisely monitored value. This value is used for the calibration of the fluorescence emitted signals. The spectrometer is used for the acquisition of spectra signals. The software on the personal computer enables proper sequencing of the degradation measurement procedure.

Examination procedure resulted in better than 280 [a.u.] absolute measured signal accuracy when full scale range of analyzed signal is 64000 [a.u.].

III. Experimental Results

Experimental results have been obtained for two measurement procedures. The first procedure was with active UVC and UVA sources. The time stamp of first two steps of this procedure is presented in Figure 3.

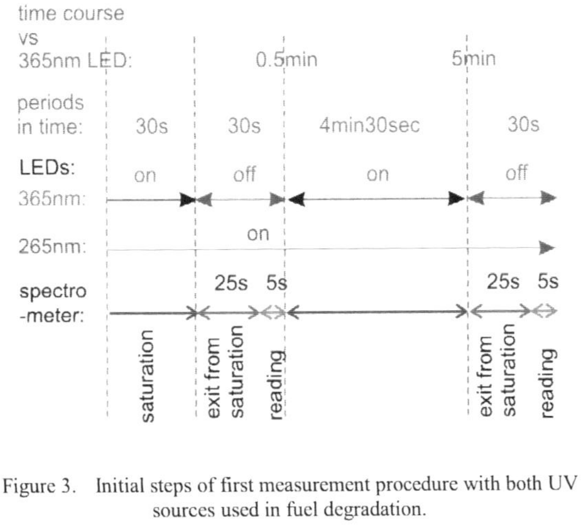

Figure 3. Initial steps of first measurement procedure with both UV sources used in fuel degradation.

The time stamp is calculated versus time of activation of UVA source. The second procedure used for evaluation was performed with only one active UVC source. For the second procedure, the time stamp is provided with the same starting point as for the first procedure. The measurement procedure time events are triggered with 1 second accuracy. The experiments were performed for two winter diesel fuels marked as standard and premium, but both characterized with identical chemical stability according to EN 15751 standard equals 20 hours and 25 g/m^3 base of ISO 12205. Base of both fuels consist of hydrocarbon mixtures that include particles with carbon number from C9 up to C25. Both fuels are characterized by initial boiling points in 175-180°C range and solid state pollution 24 mg/kg according to EN 12662. Examined fuels differ in cetane number, which for premium one is 55 and for standard fuel is 51. The bio-component is not present in premium diesel fuel. The standard fuel includes 93% of petro-diesel and up to 7% of FAME including saturated and unsaturated components with carbon number from C16 to C18.

The premium winter diesel fuels examination with first procedure results are presented in Figure 4, while examination results with the second procedure are presented in Figure 5.

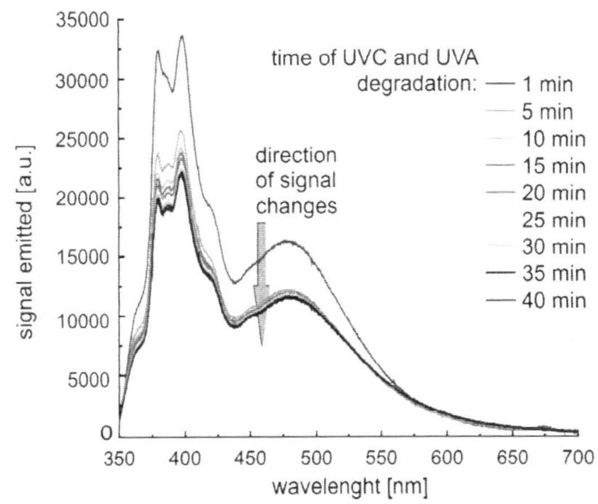

Figure 4. Spectra of first measurement procedure with UVA and UVC sources used for premium winter fuel degradation.

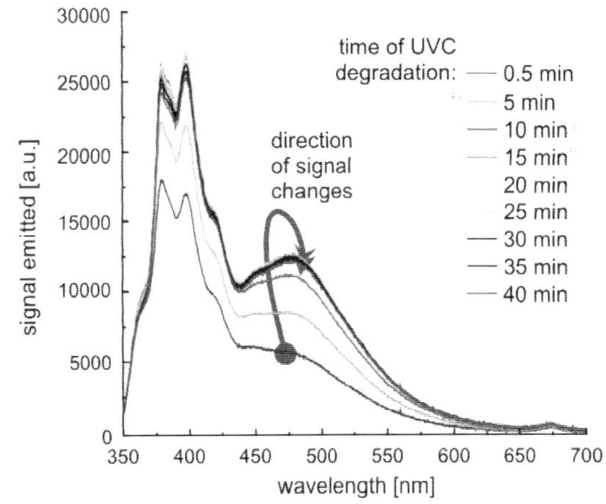

Figure 5. Spectra of second measurement procedure with one UVC source used for premium winter fuel degradation.

The results obtained for two types of winter fuel degradation look similar. The big difference is in the direction of signal changes during degradation. The signal decreases for two UVC and UVA sources degradation, while it first increases and then slowly decreases for single UVC source degradation. Moreover, for two UVC and UVA sources degradation, the absolute emitted signal level is higher than for one UVC source. The shape of saddle between peaks at 380 and 405 nm is also different, pointing that there is a possibility of a new unsaturated hydrocarbon generation for two wavelengths degradation. The small peak of emission at 675 nm can be observed in Figure 4 and Figure 5. For degradation with first procedure the peak disappears while with second procedure the peak presence lasts.

The results of the eco winter fuels examination with the first procedure are presented in Figure 6, while the results for examination with second procedure in which one UVC source is active are present in Figure 7.

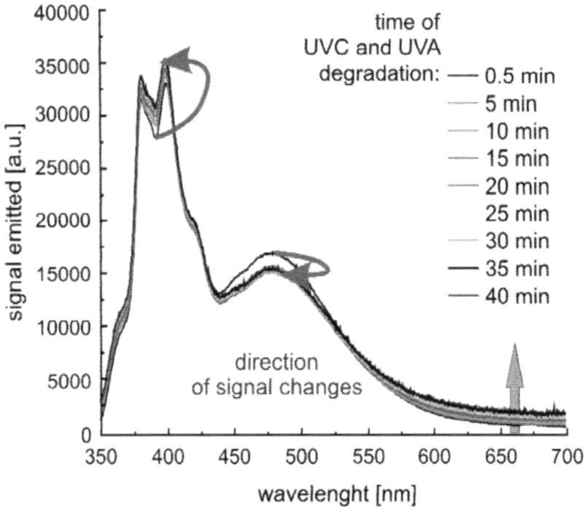

Figure 6. Spectra of first measurement procedure with UVA and UVC sources used for standard winter fuel degradation.

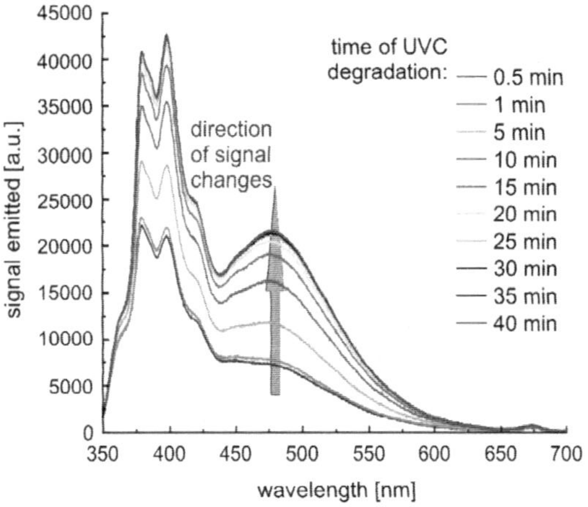

Figure 7. Spectra of second measurement procedure with one UVC source used for standard winter fuel degradation.

In the latter case, the spectra are also similar, but as previously changes of emitted radiation are in different directions. But, the spectral signal increases in range from 550 nm towards 700 nm in the case of UVA and UVC degradation, presented in Figure 6. This is significant for detection of advanced fuel degradation products, as emitted signal presence in this range can be connected with resin development.

IV. CONCLUSIONS

We have examined a capillary sensor of diesel fuel chemical stability with forced UV degradation realized at 265 nm and 365 nm wavelengths with fluorescence reading with excitation at 265 nm. These observation points, that chemical instability of diesel fuel is a result of complex chemical reactions that follow one after the other. Obtained results show emitted signal dependency on degradation grades. The initial grade of degradation can be related to increase of emitted signal in 380 - 420 nm and 450 - 525 nm ranges. The medium grade of degradation can be related with signal saturation in mentioned above ranges as well as disappearance of 675 nm peak. The advance grade of degradation can be related to increase of signal in 550 - 700 nm range.

The analysis of the signals measured during fuel degradation with two radiation sources working at UVA and UVC shows that the emitted signal characteristics saturate faster than in the case of examination with one UVC source. Moreover, in the one-sensor set-up we have shown that depending on the used degradation regime the changes of emitted signal differ for different fuels. Interestingly, for different fuels characterized with identical chemical stability at 475 nm, the saturation time of changes is similar for examinations with two UV sources. Therefore, we conclude that the proposed sensor configuration may lead in future to the reduction of the time of examination of diesel fuel stability. Obtained results, for set-up with two LEDs sources, show the necessity of degradation procedure, parameters optimization as initial stages of fuel degradation are crossed a bit too fast.

ACKNOWLEDGMENT

This work was supported by the WUT grant no. 8956/E-365/S/2017, task 504/03115/1035/40.000105.

REFERENCES

[1] C. A. Monnig and R. T. Kennedy, "Capillary electrophoresis," Anal. Chem., vol. 66, 1994, pp. 280R-314R.

[2] L. Sánchez-Hernández, M. Castro-Puyana, M. Luisa Marina, and A.L. Crego, "Determination of betaines in vegetable oils by capillary electrophoresis tandem mass spectrometry--application to the detection of olive oil adulteration with seed oils," Electrophoresis, vol. 32, 2011 pp. 1394-401.

[3] T. Galeano-Díaz, I. Acedo-Valenzuela, and A. Silva-Rodríguez, "Determination of tocopherols in vegetable oil samples by non-aqueous capillary electrophoresis (NACE) with fluorimetric detection," Journal of Food Composition and Analysis, vol. 25, 2012, pp. 24-30.

[4] A. Van Schepdael, "Recent Advances in Portable Analytical Electromigration Devices," Separations, vol. 3, 2016, pp. 1-12.

[5] G. Song et al., "Capillary scale liquid core waveguide based fluorescence detectors for liquid chromatography and flow analysis," Talanta, vol. 77, 2008, pp. 901–908.

[6] M. Borecki, M. Gęca, M. L. Korwin-Pawlowski, and P. Prus, "Capillary sensor with UV-forced degradation and fluorescence reading of diesel and biodiesel fuel chemical stability," The Eighth International Conference on Sensor Device Technologies and Applications (SENSORDEVICES 2017) IARIA, Aug. 2017, pp. 25-30, ISBN: 978-1-61208-581-4.

[7] M Borecki, M Gęca, ML Korwin-Pawlowski, and P Prus, "Capillary Sensor with UV-Forced Degradation and Examination of Fluorescence for Determination of Chemical Stability of Diesel and Biodiesel Fuels," Sensors & Transducers, vol. 220 (2), 2018, pp. 20-30.

[8] Technical Committee of Petroleum Additive Manufactures in Europe, "Fuel Additives: Use and Benefits," ATC Document, vol. 113, 2013, pp. 1-68.

[9] P. Aakko, T. Harju, M. Niemi, and L. Rantanen-Kolehmainen, "PAH content of diesel fuel and automotive emissions," Research Report VTT, vol. VTT-R-1155-06, 2006, pp. 1-50.

[10] M. A. Wechter and D. R. Hardy, "Insoluble Sediment Formation in Middle-Distillate Diesel Fuel: Evidence Concerning the Role of Fuel Acidity," Energy & Fuels, vol. 3, 1989, pp. 461-464.

[11] S. Jain and M. P. Sharma "Stability of biodiesel and its blends: A review," Renewable and Sustainable Energy Reviews, vol. 14, 2010, pp. 667-678.

[12] M. Borecki and M.L. Korwin-Pawlowski, "Capillary sensor with UV-VIS reading of effects of diesel and biodiesel fuel degradation in storage," Sensors & Transducers, vol. 205, 2016, pp. 1-9.

[13] R. A. Korus, T. L. Mousetis, and L. Lloyd, "Polymerization of vegetable oils," American Society of Agricultural Engineering vol. 4, 1982, pp. 127-137.

[14] T. Herold, "Next Generation Derivered Cetane Analysis: High Precision Enables Refineries to Operate Close to Specifications and Increase Profitability," Petro Industry News, vol. 15, 2014, pp. 6-7.

[15] M. Wlodarski, A. Bombalska, M. Mularczyk-Oliwa M. Kaliszewski, and K. Kopczyński, "Fluorimetric techniques in analysis and classification of fuels," Proc. SPIE vol. 8703, 2012, pp. 87030B.

[16] M. Borecki et al., "Fiber optic capillary sensor with smart optrode for rapid testing of the quality of diesel and biodiesel fuel," IJASM, vol. 7, 2014, pp. 57-67.

[17] M. Borecki et al., "Dynamical capillary rise photonic sensor for testing of diesel and biodiesel fuel," Sensors & Transducers Journal, vol. 193, 2015, pp. 11-22.

[18] A. Baranowska, P. Miluski, M. Kochanowicz, J. Zmojda, and D. Dorosz, "Capillary optical fibre with Sm3+ doped ribbon core," Proc. SPIE, vol. 9662, 2015, pp. 96620Z.

[19] A. Kociubiński, M. Borecki, M. Duk, M. Sochacki, and M. L. Korwin-Pawlowski, "3D photodetecting structure with adjustable sensitivity ratio in UV–VIS range," Microelectronic Engineering, vol. 154, 2016, pp. 48-52.

[20] P Firek and J Szmidt, "MISFET structures with barium titanate as a dielectric layer for application in memory cells," Microelectronics Reliability, vol. 51, 2011, pp. 1187-1191.

[21] S. Y. Yurish, N. V. Kirianaki, and R. Pallàs Areny, "Universal frequency to digital converter for quasi digital and smart sensors: specifications and applications," Sensor Review, vol. 25(2), 2005, pp. 92-99.

[22] P. Doroz, M. Duk, M. L. Korwin-Pawlowski, and M. Borecki, "Amplifiers dedicated for large area SiC photodiodes," Proc SPIE, vol. 10031, 2016, pp. 100311R.

[23] Z. Bielecki, "Readout electronics for optical detectors," Opto-electronics Review, vol. 12, 2004, pp. 129-137.

[24] M. T. Ibrahim et al., "Self-adaptability and man-in-the-loop: a dilemma in autonomic computing systems," Proceedings: 15th International Workshop on Database and Expert Systems Applications (IEEE Computer Society), Los Alamitos, California, USA, 2004, pp. 722-729.

[25] P. Prus, M. Borecki, M. L. Korwin-Pawlowski, A. Kociubiński, and M. Duk, "Automatic detection of characteristic points and form of optical signals in multiparametric capillary sensors," Proc. SPIE, vol. 9290, 2014, pp. 929009.

[26] M. J. Coelho Pontes, C. F. Pereira, M. F. Pimentel, F. V. Cruz Vasconcelos, and A. G. Brito Silva, "Screening analysis to detect adulteration in diesel/biodiesel blends using near infrared spectrometry and multivariate classification," Talanta, vol. 85, 2011, pp. 2159-2165

[27] A. R. L. Caires, V. S. Lima, and S. L. Oliveira, "Quantification of biodiesel content in diesel/biodiesel blends by fluorescence spectroscopy: Evaluation of the dependence on biodiesel feedstock," Renewable Energy, vol. 46, 2012, pp. 137-140.

[28] Z. Fan and J. Krahl, "Characterization and Identification of Diesel Fuels, Biodiesel and their Blends by Time-Resolved Laser Induced Fluorescence Spectroscopy," The 14th International Meeting on Chemical Sensors (IMCS 2012), 2012, pp. 1483-1485.

[29] M. Insausti, C. Romano, M. F. Pistonesi, and B. S. Fernández Band, "Simultaneous determination of quality parameters in biodiesel/diesel blends using synchronous fluorescence and multivariate analysis," Microchemical Journal, vol. 108, 2013, pp. 32-37.

[30] D. Liuet et al, "A Reversible Crystallinity-Preserving Phase Transition in Metal−Organic Frameworks: Discovery, Mechanistic Studies, and Potential Applications," J. Am. Chem. Soc., vol. 137(24), 2015, pp 7740-7746.

[31] S. Reineke and M. A. Baldo, "Room temperature triplet state spectroscopy of organic semiconductors." Scientific Reports vol. 4:3797, 2014, pp. 1-8.

[32] Roithner LaserTechnik, "DUV-OC39," Roithner LaserTechnik data sheet rev. 4.5 (11/2017), pp. 1-4.

Use of Body-Diode for Thermal Monitoring of Power MOSFET

Giovanni Pangallo, Riccado Carotenuto, Demetrio Iero, Massimo Merenda, Francesco Giuseppe Della Corte
Department of Information Engineering, Infrastructure and Sustainable Energy, DIIES
Università degli Studi "Mediterranea"
Reggio Calabria 89122, Italy
e-mail: giovanni.pangallo@unirc.it, r.carotenuto@unirc.it, demetrio.iero@unirc.it, massimo.merenda@unirc.it, francesco.dellacorte@unirc.it

Giovanna Adinolfi, Giorgio Graditi
ENEA – Italian National Agency for New Technologies, Energy, and Sustainable Economic Development Research Center of Portici.
Portici 80055, Naples, Italy
giovanna.adinolfi@enea.it, giorgio.graditi@enea.it.

***Abstract*—The dependence on temperature of the body-drain voltage appearing across a forward-biased body-diode is used to estimate the junction temperature of power Metal-Oxide-Semiconductor Field-Effect Transistors. Moreover, the temperature sensor sensitivity, linearity, resolution, error and output repeatability are accurately discussed. The integrated diodes are characterized in a typical working temperature range, between about 22 °C and 150 °C and for currents between 1 µA and 1 mA. The best trade-off between sensitivity and linearity is found at a low bias current of 21 µA.**

Keywords-Junction temperature; Power MOSFET; Temperature measurement; Temperature sensors; Linear sensors.

I. INTRODUCTION

The monitoring of the junction temperature (T_J) of power semiconductor devices is of paramount importance in many applications. In particular, the measurement of the junction temperature is essential to evaluate the performance of a circuit and of semiconductor devices as it has a strong influence on electrical parameters, reliability and operating lifetime of power devices [1][2].

However, the direct measurement of junction temperature is very difficult, and still an open issue among designers, who have generally to rely on external sensors placed in contact with the observed device metal case.

An alternative way for the monitoring of the junction temperature of a power MOSFET consists in using Temperature-Sensitive Electrical Parameters (TSEPs) of the same device [1][2]. Studies have demonstrated the possibility to monitor the MOSFET junction temperature through TSEPs, *e.g.*, the on-state resistance, turn-on delay of pulse signal, turn-off delay time and gate drive current [3]-[6].

In previous works, we have shown that Schottky and p-i-n diodes can be used as linear temperature sensors thanks to the favorable temperature dependence of their forward bias voltage drop [7][8]. As commercial power MOSFETs include an intrinsic diode (body-diode), formed at the body-drain P-N junction connected between drain and source, the body-drain voltage (V_{BD}) can be considered itself a TSEP, varying almost linearly with temperature when this body-diode is forward biased with a proper DC current.

The aim of this paper is to demonstrate the possibility of monitoring the power MOSFET junction temperature through V_{BD}-T relation. The almost linear dependence between the body-drain voltage and junction temperature has been studied in the MOSFET operative temperature range from room temperature up to 150 °C.

The paper is organized as follows. The Section 2 consists of two parts; first, the linear dependence between voltage and temperature, the electrical circuit and the experimental setup used for measuring the junction temperature are described. The second part reports the experimental results with particular attention to temperature sensor performance, i.e., linearity, sensitivity and temperature error. Finally, conclusions and future works are presented in Section 3.

II. RESULTS AND DISCUSSION

A. Use of Body-Diode as Temperature Sensor

As well-known, the I_D current flowing in a diode at a given applied voltage V_{BD} can be analytically described using the following formula:

$$I_D = I_S\left(e^{\frac{q(V_{BD}-R_S I_D)}{\eta kT}} - 1\right), \qquad (1)$$

where η is the ideality factor, I_S is the saturation current, R_S is the series resistance, q is the electronic charge and k is the Boltzmann constant.

The characterization of the sensor output has been performed under forward bias condition where, at constant DC current, the voltage across the diode is linearly dependent on the temperature. In fact, if $q(V_{BD}-R_S I_D) >> \eta kT$, the voltage drop dependence on temperature can be

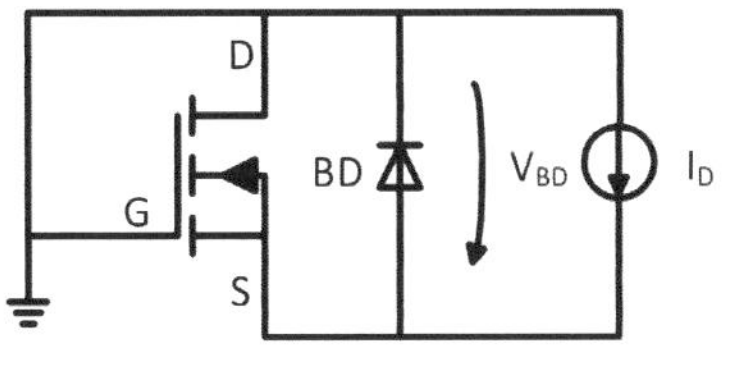

Figure 1. Electrical circuit for the measurement of the body-drain voltage (V_{BD}) in the bias current range from 1 μA up to 1 mA.

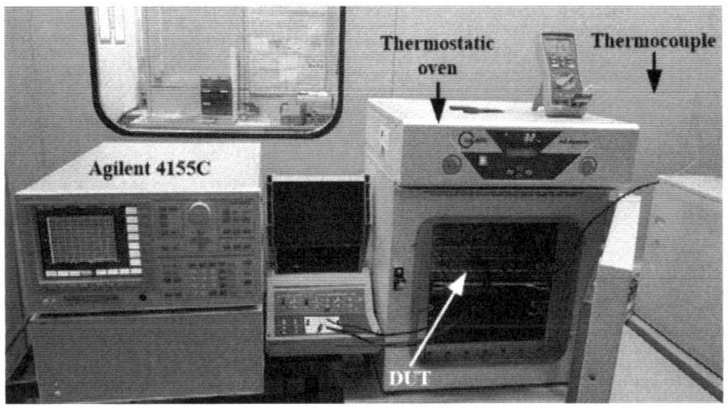

Figure 2. Experimental setup

obtained from (1), yielding:

$$V_{BD} = \frac{kT}{q}\eta \ln\left(\frac{I_D}{I_S}\right) + R_S I_D . \quad (2)$$

As demonstrated in [8], equation (2) makes explicit the linear dependence V_D-T as long as the contribution of the series resistance can be considered negligible. Keeping the diode operating in its exponential region with a low bias current helps meeting this requirement. Moreover, the use of low bias currents allows to avoid both self-heating effects, which can negatively affect the sensor linearity, and excessive power consumption.

In our set-up, the integrated Body-Diode (BD) was biased at a forward constant current (I_D), as schematically reported in Figure 1, while the gate was connected to ground.

It is clear that the use of this technique in a working power circuit, e.g., a static converter, for the real time measure of the internal operating temperature of a switching MOSFET, the so called junction temperature T_j, would require the temporary switch-off of the device and the forcing of the probe I_D current through the body diode. This scheme, however, should not have a serious impact on the circuit performance because of the very limited time interval necessary to proceed with the V_{DB} measurement, of the order of a few milliseconds.

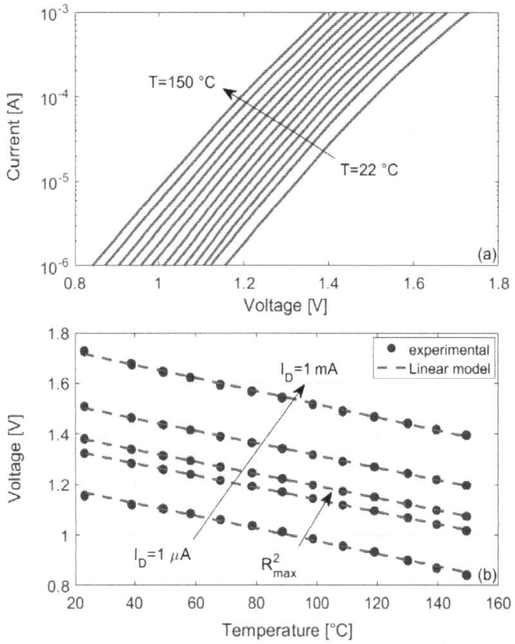

Figure 3. (a) Current-voltage (I_D-V_{BD}) characteristics in the temperature range T=22-150°C in steps of 10 °C. (b) Measured (points) body-drain voltage versus temperature. Experimental data are fitted with the best-calculated linear model.

B. *Temperature Sensor Performance*

The experimental measurements are carried out on a commercial SiC MOSFET (C2M0025120D) [9] having a maximum drain-source voltage of 1200 V, a maximum continuous drain current of 90 A and a drain-source on-state resistance of 25 mΩ. Moreover, the operating junction temperature range is claimed from -55 °C up to 150 °C. The device has been tested in a thermostatic oven (Galli G210F030P) setting the reference temperature through its internal Proportional Integral Derivative (PID) digital microcontroller. A thermocouple (K-type) temperature sensor was placed in contact with the Device Under Test (DUT) in order to monitor, during measurements, the exact temperature set points, gradually varied from (down to) ~22 °C up to (from) 150 °C. By using an Agilent 4155C semiconductor parameter analyzer, tests were made for I_D varied in a range from 1 μA to 1 mA ±(0.12%·I_D+500 nA+2 nA·V_{BD}) accuracy, 100 nA resolution [10], and the corresponding voltage drops V_{BD} across the body-diode were measured. The experimental setup used for temperature measurements is shown in Figure 2.

While the DC bias current, I_D, was varied in the given range, the corresponding voltage drop V_{BD} across the body-diode was measured as reported in Figure 3(a). At each

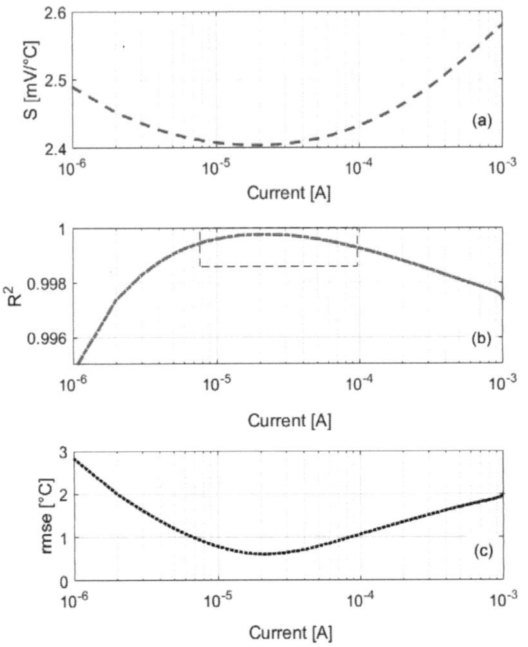

Figure 4. (a) Sensitivity, S; (b) coefficient of determination, R^2; and (c) root mean square error, *rmse*, within the whole temperature range of 22-150 °C and for bias currents in the range I_D=1 μA-1 mA.

temperature, measurements started after waiting for the settling of stable temperatures for several minutes. Moreover, the experimental data are reported at five currents I_D (1 μA, 10 μA, 21 μA, 100 μA and 1 mA).

From I_D–V_{BD}–T measurements, the V_{BD}–T characteristics have been extracted as shown in Figure 3(b), which also reports the linear fitting of data obtained through a proper computer routine.

In our analysis, the coefficient of determination (R^2) [11] has been calculated to evaluate the agreement between the experimental measurements and their linear best fit, $f_L(T)$. In particular, R^2 allows to quantify the sensor linearity goodness by fitting the experimental data with a linear model.

In Figure 3(b), the measured data are fitted with the best-calculated linear model showing a good degree of linearity (R^2 > 0.995) for the considered range of I_D. The sensor sensitivity S can be obtained from the slope of the V_{BD}–T characteristics. When I_D is 1 μA the sensitivity is 2.49 mV/°C and increases to 2.58 mV/°C for I_D=1 mA.

Figures 4(a) and (b) report a detailed analysis of the sensitivity and coefficient of determination for different value of biasing currents I_D. The maximum of R^2~0.9997 has been calculated for I_D=21 μA, corresponding to a sensitivity S=2.41 mV/°C.

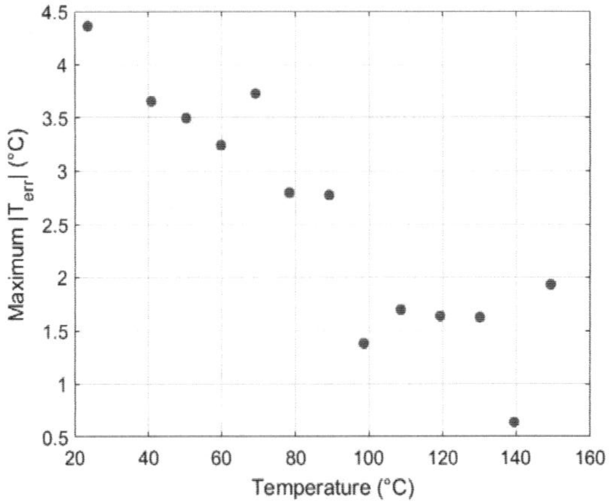

Figure 5. Maximum absolute temperature error between the linear fitting and body-drain voltage (V_{BD}) at bias current of I_D=21 μA

Another important parameter for the characterization of a linear temperature sensor is the root mean square error (rmse) between the calculated linear best-fit and the experimental measurements. The rmse was first calculated and subsequently converted into a temperature error by dividing by the sensitivity.

The obtained plot, rmse versus I_D, for the considered temperature range is reported in Figure 4(c). The root mean square error is always lower than 2.83 °C while a minimum rmse of 0.61 °C is obtained for I_D=21 μA, which also provides the maximum linearity.

As shown in the three graphs of Figure 4, the best bias current range for the sensor is from 8 to 100 μA. In fact, in this range the sensor shows a coefficient of determination higher than 0.9993 (see rectangle of Figure 4(b)). It is worth noting that in this current range the R^2 varies by only 0.016% from the average of R_a^2=0.99953 over the considered temperature range, leading to an integrated temperature sensor with a highly linear behavior also for unwanted variation of the bias current during the short-time sensing phase. The corresponding average values of sensitivity and rmse are S_a=2.42 mV/°C and $rmse_a$=0.83 °C with standard deviations of 0.01 mV/°C and 0.15 °C respectively.

Another important parameter for the characterization of a temperature sensor is the temperature error. In this case, the maximum absolute error $|T_{err}|$ of experimental data was extracted with respect to their linear best fit for different measurement cycles. The obtained values, for the best bias current of I_D=21 μA, are reported in Figure 5. As shown in the graph, the maximum absolute error decreases as the temperature rises. Moreover, for temperatures above 100 °C, which might be considered as a safety threshold to avoid MOSFET malfunctions, the maximum error is less than 2 °C. This appears to be a small maximum error if the target is the monitoring of the operating temperature of a power device, at least compared to other techniques that involve the use of an external sensor, placed in contact with the device case.

III. Conclusion and Future Work

A highly-linear temperature sensor based on body-drain diode integrated within a power MOSFET has been characterized.

The proposed type of sensor allows to monitor the junction temperature of power MOSFETs during their operation. Different cycles of measurements were iterated showing a good output repeatability. Measurements showed a maximum linearity coefficient R^2~0.9997 for I_D=21 μA, corresponding to a sensitivity S=2.41 mV/°C in the temperature range T = 22–150 °C.

Future work will mainly cover the design and realization of a circuit for monitoring the MOSFETs junction temperature in power converter systems. Moreover, the analysis reported in this work will be extended to MOSFETs of various suppliers.

References

[1] D. Blackburn and D. Berning, "Power MOSFET temperature measurements," in 1982 IEEE Power Electronics Specialists conference, June 1982, pp. 400–407. DOI: 10.1109/PESC.1982.7072436

[2] Y. Avenas, L. Dupont, and Z. Khatir, "Temperature Measurement of Power Semiconductor Devices by Thermo-Sensitive Electrical Parameters—A Review," IEEE Trans. Power Electron., vol. 27, no. 6, pp. 3081–3092, dec. 2011. DOI: 10.1109/TPEL.2011.2178433

[3] M. L. Walters and R. D. Lorenz, "Circuit modeling methodology for isolated, high bandwidth junction temperature estimation," in The 2010 International Power Electronics Conference - ECCE ASIA -, June 2010, pp. 970–974. DOI: 10.1109/IPEC.2010.5542176

[4] B. Shi et al., "Junction Temperature Measurement Method for Power MOSFETs Using Turn-On Delay of Impulse Signal," IEEE Trans. Power Electron., vol 33, no 6, pp. 5274–5282, June 2018. DOI: 10.1109/TPEL.2017.2736523

[5] H. Niu and R. Lorenz, "Real-time Junction Temperature Sensing for Silicon Carbide MOSFET with Different Gate Drive Topologies and Different Operating Conditions," IEEE Trans. Power Electron., vol. 33, no. 4, pp. 3424 – 3440, Apr. 2018. DOI: 10.1109/TPEL.2017.2704441

[6] Z. Wang et al., "A High Temperature Silicon Carbide mosfet Power Module With Integrated Silicon-On-Insulator-Based Gate Drive," IEEE Trans. Power Electron., vol. 30, no. 3, pp. 1432–1445, Mar. 2015. DOI: 10.1109/TPEL.2014.2321174

[7] S. Rao, G. Pangallo, and F. G. Della Corte, "4H-SiC p-i-n diode as Highly Linear Temperature Sensor," IEEE Trans. Electron Devices, vol. 63, no. 1, pp. 414–418, Jan. 2016. DOI: 10.1109/TED.2015.2496913

[8] S. Rao, L. Di Benedetto, G. Pangallo, A. Rubino, S. Bellone, and F. G. Della Corte, "85 K to 440 K Temperature Sensor Based on a 4H-SiC Schottky Diode," IEEE Sens. J., vol. 16, no. 17, pp. 6537 - 6542, Sept. 2016. DOI: 10.1109/JSEN.2016.2591067

[9] CREE, C2M0025120D Datasheet, 2015, [Online] Available: https://www.wolfspeed.com/media/downloads/161/C2M0025120D.pdf.

[10] A. Tecnologies, Agilent 4155B/4156B User's Guide, 2000, [Online]. Available:http://eecs.oregonstate.edu/matdev /man /Agilent4155C_4156C_Users_Guide_Vol1.pdf.

[11] N. J. D. Nagelkerke, "A note on a general definition of the coefficient of determination," Biometrika, vol. 78, no. 3, pp. 691–692, Sep. 1991. DOI:10.1093/biomet/78.3.691

Ultra Low Power Consumption Magnetic Microsystem for IoT Applications

Janez Trontelj, Damjan Berčan, Aleksander Sešek
Laboratory for Microelectronics
Faculty of Electrical Engineering, University of Ljubljana
Tržaška cesta 25, 1000 Ljubljana, Slovenia
e-mail: janez.trontelj@fe.uni-lj.si, damjan.bercan@fe.uni-lj.si, aleksander.sesek@fe.uni-lj.si

Abstract— **Smart sensor applications have recently grown at an unprecedented pace. The possibility of monitoring specific situations is further increased by applying Internet of Things (IoT) technology. Many key advances have been triggered by sensors improvements such as extended compatibilities and by the use of wireless communication. This also calls for a battery operation. Ideally, a battery operated sensor should be capable of operating for a minimum of 5 years without battery replacement. At the same time, it should be capable of communicating at the required predefined time or on a particular event. If more and more sensor functions are requested, the challenge is how to realize the sensor device to optimize different requirements regardless of the operation timing of the sensors, their current consumption and wireless communication demands. The presented paper is an attempt to provide some solutions for the optimization of the cost/performance ratio of a magnetic microsystem sensor designed using the 0.35µm Complementary Metal Oxide Semiconductor (CMOS) technology.**

Keywords-ultra low power consumption; magnetic microsystem; IoT applications.

I. INTRODUCTION

In this paper, a magnetic microsystem for various applications is presented. It includes two spatially positioned integrated magnetic sensors [1], which can provide a variety of information of the permanent magnet position relative to the microsystem position by signal processing of both sensor outputs [2]. The integrated circuits and permanent magnets are shown in Figures 1 and 2 as an example of linear and angular movement.

The cost effectiveness of different integrated or discrete magnetic sensors i.e. the standard integrated Hall element, Anisotropic Magnetoresistance (AMR) and Tunnel Magnetoresistance (TMR), including the required signal processing, has been analysed. The main finding was that the highest performance/cost is achieved by using a six terminal

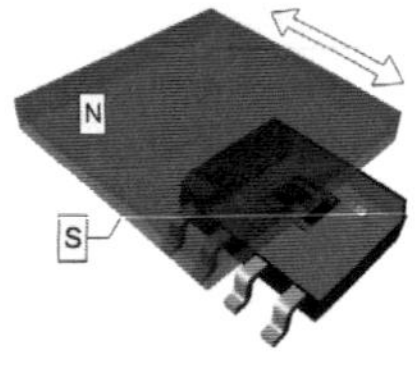

Figure 1. Permanent magnet linear movement.

Figure 2. Permanent magnet angular movement.

Hall sensor array, which has been introduced in 1995 [4] and comprises the on board integrated microcoil for internal generation of the magnetic field.

The rest of the paper is structured as follows. In Section 2, we describe the idea of minimizing the current consumption of the Hall element. In Section 3, we present the microsystem and its design. Finally, we summarize the paper in Section 4.

II. SENSOR CURRENT CONSUMPTION MINIMIZATION

The Hall element sensitivity is directly proportional to the bias current of the Hall element; therefore, its high sensitivity brings the main drawback of the Hall element, which is large power consumption [3]. Most of our microsystem applications target a slow variation of the measured magnetic field. Therefore, the average current consumption should be below µA, when the Hall element bias current is several mA. The refresh rate of the signal should be up to 10Hz. These figures call for measurement duty cycle down to 10^{-4} or 0.1%.

The full measurement cycle should only take a few microseconds. Fortunately, the bandwidth of Hall element is not a limiting factor in this case, however the signal

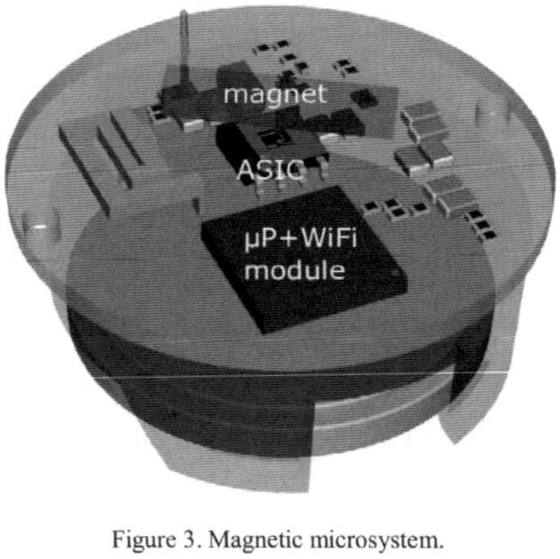

Figure 3. Magnetic microsystem.

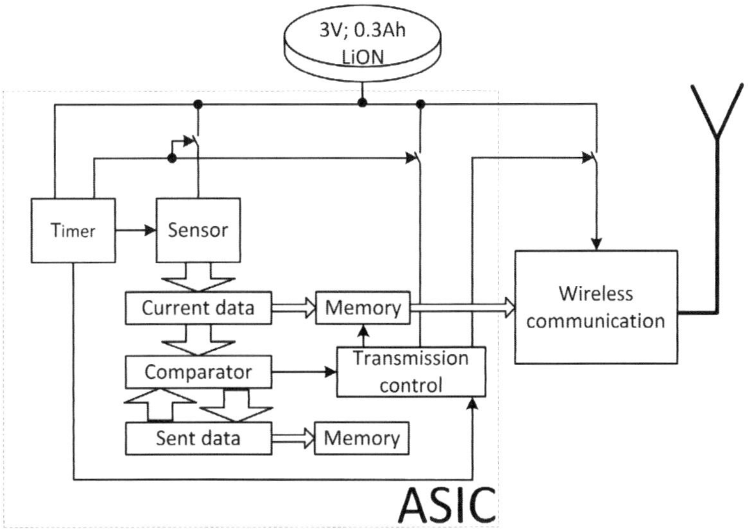

Figure 4. Block diagram of the proposed system.

processing circuitry should be fast, which results in higher power consumption.

III. MICROSYSTEM SYSTEM DESIGN

The magnetic microsystem is shown in Figure 3 with permanent magnet, which is attached to the valve. The valve is not shown in Figure 3. The sensors indicate the position of the valve and returns α as tan^{-1}, where α is the rotation angle of the magnet. The electronic circuit is placed on top of a battery holder, which contains 300mAh 3V lithium coin cell battery.

The block diagram of the Application Specific Integrated Circuit (ASIC) is shown in Figure 4 with external wireless communication module. It consists of extremely low current consumption timer, Hall element sensors and associated circuitry, signal processing unit, digital signal processing and data memory. The strategy for current consumption optimization is the following.

The circuit is divided into two parts. The part which needs to be connected to the battery constantly and the part which can be switched on only a fraction of the time to perform the sensing function and the send and receive function. The part of the circuit which is constantly connected to power supply is further divided into the static part and to the dynamic part. The static part consists of the logic where only leakage current of the parasitic diodes exists. This current accounts for only a small part of the power supply losses of the system, however, special care was taken to minimize the drain area of those nodes.

The dynamic part of the circuit is the main consumer of the supply current. The dynamic current consumption is the sum of the switching current and charging and discharging parasitic capacitance. The dynamic current consumption is given by (1):

$$I = \sum_{i=1}^{n} c_i V_{dd}^2 \cdot f_s, \quad (1)$$

where c_i is parasitic capacitance of nodes, n is the number of nodes, V_{dd} is a power supply voltage and f_S is the switching frequency.

To minimize this dynamic consumption, the layout minimization of node capacitance has been carried out.

In addition, the oscillation frequency has been reduced for further optimization of the current consumption. A large current loss originates also in the cross conducting during the

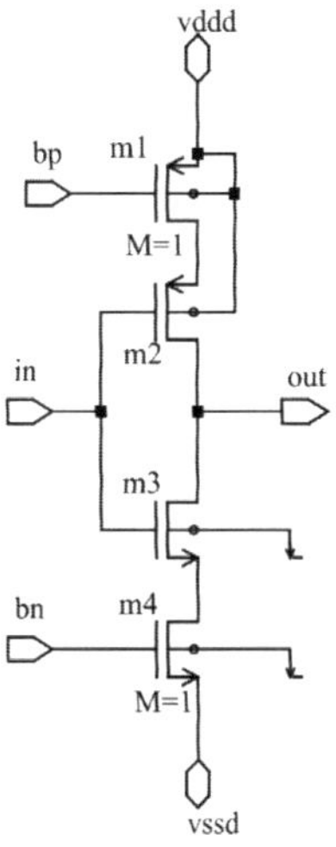

Figure 5. Special low cross-conducting current inverter *invbia*.

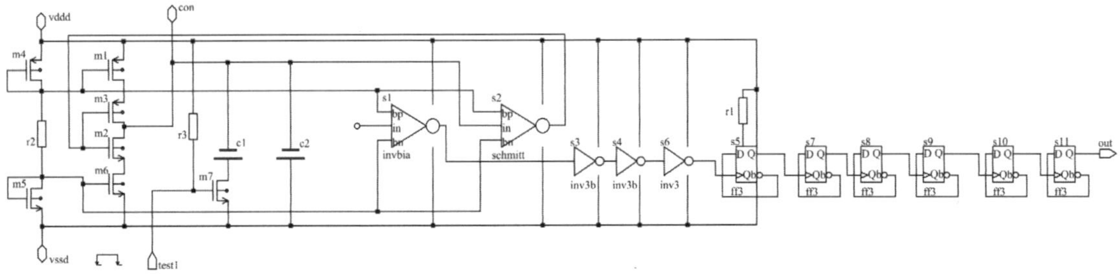

Figure 6. Timer schematic diagram.

slow switching of the logic gates and inverters. Therefore, a special inverter *invbia* we designed for the timer section, shown in Figure 5, to control the cross conduction current. It consists of a current switching approach for the inverters with limited current to only 50nA. *Bp* and *bn* voltages control transistors *m1* and *m4*. *In* and *Out* represent the input and output of the special inverter. *Vddd* and *vssd* are power supply connections. *M* represents the transistor size multiplication factor. With this approach, the average current consumption of the dynamic part of the circuit has been reduced to less than 100nA.

Figure 6 presents a schematic of the timer, which contains the already presented special inverter *invbia*, Schmitt trigger *Schmitt*, D flip-flops *ff3* and inverters *inv3* and *inv3b*. As the resulting capacitance of the parallel connected capacitors *c1* and *c2* is quite large (this means only a few Hz refresh rate), an additional test pin *test1* with pull-up resistor is added. This pin can be used (connected to ground) to speed up the ASIC for testing purposes. In this block, additional six D flip-flops are used in series to scale down the frequency of the timer by 64 to achieve the requested refresh rate. The *con* pin is used

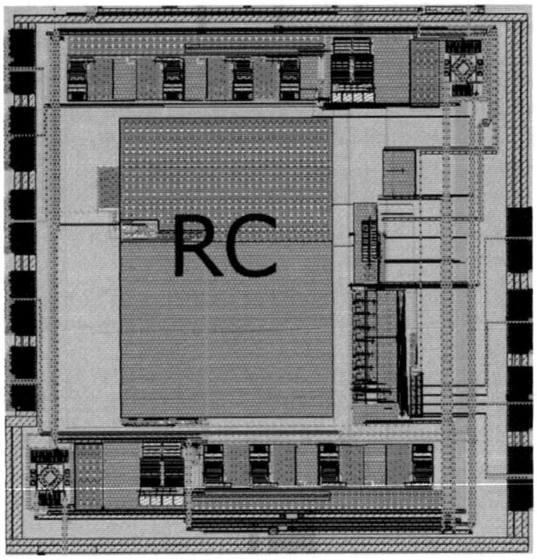

Figure 7. Layout of the ASIC.

only for the simulation test to set the initial condition. The pin *out* represents an output of the timer. *Vddd* and *vssd* are power supply connections. Transistors *m1*, *m3* and *m4* represent P type of MOS transistors and *m2*, *m5*, *m6* and *m7* represent N type of MOS transistors. Resistor *r3* is a pull up resistor, which connects the gate of transistor *m7* to the *vddd*.

As most appropriate, the Resistor-Capacitor (RC) type of the oscillator has been selected. To further minimize the current consumption, the large portion of the ASIC area is occupied by integrated resistor *r2* and capacitor *c1*. Figure 7 presents the layout of the presented ASIC.

As the wireless communication unit used in the system consumes the largest amount of power when transmitting or a bit lower even when the unit is hibernating or in sleep mode, the power consumption of this unit should also be optimized. To minimize the communication unit power consumption, the system turns on the wireless communication only at the maximal required time period, if there is no magnet position change. If there is a change in position, the data is sent out as frequently as specified by the application. Our main targeted application requires measurement refresh rate up to 10 per second and the average position change is a few times per day.

In the ASIC, the constantly measured current position is compared with the last sent data. The transmitter is turned on according to the result of the comparison, therefore a small button type battery provides enough energy to achieve a long life operation of the presented system of over 5 years.

The ASIC is now under evaluation and the measured data are summarized in Table 1. Measurements were done at 3V power supply and 25°C.

TABLE I. MEASUREMENT RESULTS

Function	Simulated	Measured	Units
Current consumption	305	330	nA
Current consumption at measurement	4.9	4.8	mA
Sensitivity	180	200	mV/mT
Magnetic field angle resolution	6.4	6.5	Deg

IV. CONCLUSIONS

A developed magnetic microsystem has been presented and some solutions on how to reduce system power consumption were provided in the paper. The main effort of the design was to achieve average current consumption in the range of μA and retain the measurement cycle of magnet position in the range of microseconds. As the required position data refresh rate, which is transmitted to the main receiver unit, depends on the certain change of the permanent magnet position, and the position is changed only several times daily, the total power consumption could be kept low enough to obtain the long lifetime operation, using a standard button-kind battery.

REFERENCES

[1] A. Sesek and J. Trontelj, "Magnetic microsystem with extended dynamic range and absolute accuracy," ICECS 2008, The 15th IEEE International Conference on Electronics, Circuits and Systems, August 31 - September 3, 2008, The Westin Dragonara Resort, Malta, pp. 882-885, 2008.

[2] J. Trontelj. "A magnetic microsystem on a chip," AASRI 2014, Conference on Sports Engineering and Computer Science, Amsterdam, vol. 8, pp. 93-99, 2014, ISSN 2212-6724.

[3] E. Ramsden, "Hall-Effect Sensors," Theory and Application, Newnes, pp. 272, 2006.

[4] J. Trontelj, R. Opara and A. Pletersek, "Integrirano vezje z magnetnim senzorjem (Integrateted circuit with magnetic sensor)", patent no. SI 9300622 A, Ljubljana, 1995.

Development of a Real-Time Evaluation System For Top Taekwondo Athletes

SPERTA

Pedro Cunha
ALGORITMI Research Centre
Minho University
Guimarães, Portugal
email: id5514@alunos.uminho.pt

Vítor Carvalho
2Ai Lab - EST & ALGORITMI Research Centre
IPCA & Minho University
Barcelos & Guimarães, Portugal
email: vcarvalho@ipca.pt

Filomena Soares
ALGORITMI Research Centre
Industrial Electronics Department
Minho University
Guimarães, Portugal
email: fsoares@dei.uminho.pt

***Abstract* - At any level of sport, evaluating the performance of the athletes is a constant challenge for trainers. In the case of Taekwondo, where there is lack of technological solutions to help the trainer to perform this task, there is a higher difficulty. The system presented in this paper is part of a PhD project, which the main objective is to develop a system reliable and affordable for evaluate in real-time the performance of top Taekwondo athletes. The system consists of a 3D camera Orbbec Astra with RGB and depth sensor and a computer for data acquisition and processing. The data (information of the Cartesian coordinates and speed of the hands and feet movements performed by the athlete) is displayed in real-time either by numerical value or by charts. It is intended to provide an accurate feedback for the correction or improvement of the athlete's technique, allowing an increase in the athlete performance in a shorter period of time. Aiming to evolve the Taekwondo training techniques and the technological development of Taekwondo practice.**

Keywords* - *motion analysis; orbbec astra; performance; real-time; Taekwondo.

I. INTRODUCTION

In today's society, technology has been assimilated as something natural and accessible, being part of the daily routines. The regular use of technology, in the personal, professional and even during the educational journey, comes from the combination of information processing with objects. This combination provides a reality where the extension of computing devices into in everyday life is known as "Ubiquitous Computing" [1]. Ubiquitous computing has been suffering a fast-growing with applications in many areas.

One of these areas is motion analysis where there has been active participation of scientists in the development of technological solutions that do not require markers on the human body for monitor and analyze athletes' movements performed in ordinary environment conditions. The use of these new methods of movement analysis have contributed to for the emergence of motion capture solutions and low-cost and accessible equipment [2].

One of the applications is in sports, where the equipment are used not only to collect, analyze and present athletes performance data from training practices and competitions but also to develop automatic score and refereeing systems [3]. This trend allows the development of athlete's performance feedback systems, by measuring accelerations and forces, recognizing and tracking movements, quantifying the effort applied and many other functionalities. The overall objective is to reduce the time of analysis of the trainer and to accelerate the improvement of the performance of the athlete [4] [5].

Taekwondo was introduced in Portugal in 1974 by Grand Master David Chung Sun Yong [6]. Over the last two decades, it has gained popularity and it became an Olympic Sport in the year 2000 [7]. The number of federated athletes has been increasing, reaching currently more than 4500 athletes in Portugal [8]. Unlike other sports, Taekwondo has not accompanied the technological development regarding training methods. Nowadays, the evaluation methods used by the trainers are mostly made manually, making the assessment of the athletes a slow, and sometimes, inefficient process. The trainer has to analyze all the available data, such as videos, time and number of movements' executions, in order to obtain the information needed to provide a relevant feedback that allows the athletes to improve their performance.

Martial arts and combat sports depend on special activities that expect complex skills and tactical excellence. The movements most executed by the athletes consist of specific stances and dynamic activities (strikes, punches, kicks, throws, blocks, falls, among others) performed individually or in contact with the opponent. The majority of them are characterized by high dynamics, high intensity and very short duration, usually named as ballistic movements [9].

Following this trend, the main objective of the present work is to develop a real-time system to evaluate the performance of the Taekwondo athletes in training environment, taking into account reliability, usability and the cost of the system. The proposed system aims to provide a faster feedback process, contribute to an evolution of the performance of the most effective athlete and add technological development in the practice of taekwondo. This study presents the system structure and the developed software, which allows input data of the athletes training and output data of the Cartesian coordinates and speed of both hands and feet.

This paper is divided in five sections. The Section 2 addresses the state of the art in the field of motion analysis and performance evaluation in sports. The Section 3 presents the methodology used for the development of the technological tool to aid the evaluation of athletes in real time. In Section 4 are disclosed the final remarks of the development process and of the achieved system. The Section 5 reveal the future work regarding the further development and application of the system presented in this paper.

II. State of Art

Motion analysis, over time, has aroused the interest of several areas of scientific research. With the evolution of technology, several devices have emerged that enable the monitoring and analysis of movements performed by the human body. Sports area currently represents a significant part of the research conducted with the aim of contributing to both improving athletes' performance and preventing injury.

For trainers, motion analysis has been a key issue as it can improve technical skills by correcting the trainee's body motion to perform correct movements in any sports.

Some of the research carried out in motion movement aims to study the hands movements and localization, such as the study of Suarez and Murphy [10] that consists in a survey where they resumed the techniques used for hand localization and gesture classification.

Traditional video cameras, when used in low or in unstable lighting and in skin colored objects environments, hamper the correct digital analysis of the image. The depth cameras are the appropriate alternative for image collection in these situations, as they allow to collect depth images that are not dependent on the brightness or color scheme of the environment. The most used depth sensor in scientific research regarding hand localization and gesture classification is the Microsoft Kinect [10]. Microsoft Kinect systems are low cost, portable, do not require markers, are easy to set up, and create 3D images. These 3D video motion systems are used to human movement kinematics analysis of body joints and segments in several areas associated with gait analysis, medical robotics, rehabilitation, biofeedback and sports performance.

Concerning the whole human body gesture recognition Patsadu, Nukoolkit and Watanapa [11] present a study for human gesture recognition using data mining classification methods in video streaming of twenty body-joints positions of the human body collected with the Microsoft Kinect camera. The study recognized gesture patterns as stand, sit down, and lie down. The classification methods adopted for comparison were backpropagation neural network, decision tree, support vector machine and naive Bayes. For this, the researchers used the Microsoft Kinect camera. The results obtained allowed to conclude that backpropagation neural network shows superior performance compared to the other classification methods, recognizing human gestures with 100% accuracy. The average accuracy of all classification methods was 93.72%, confirming the efficiency of the Kinect camera when used in human body recognition applications.

Other study of the Microsoft Kinect was performed by Zerpa et al. [12]. They compared the Microsoft Kinect displacement measures with the Peak Motus marker-based system displacement measures. The results allowed to conclude that the Microsoft Kinect, for being a markless system, was more favorable during the setup, data collection and analysis stages as compared to the Peak Motus.

In their study, VencesBrito et al. describe and compare the variety of modern motion analysis systems used in scientific research as well in the daily work of coaches and athletes in combat sports and martial arts. The authors suggest some applications in scientific research and scope of applications that contribute for optimizing the training process, providing information for non-expert trainers and athletes in the field of biomechanics but interested in motion analysis [13].

Pinto et al. [14] present a real-time evaluation approach that uses a Microsoft Kinect and image processing techniques to recognize and record the number of occurrences of a movement in Taekwondo training environment. The recognition of the movements was made through the calculation of the angles between human body joints and comparing them with the correct values of each movement previously saved in a database.

Further studies are needed, to confirm the reliability and validity of the Microsoft Kinect for human movement kinematics analysis [12]. However Robertson et al. [15] and Corazza et al. [16] both verified and agreed that markerless systems would be a major revolution in the analysis of human motion and significantly would expand the application of human motion capture.

III. Development

The training process in martial arts, just as in other sports, aims to improve the performance of certain techniques and strategic behaviors along with the increase of the physical condition of the athlete, allowing him/her to compete with other athletes and reduce the risk of injury. The analysis of the movements performed by the athletes is a key element in training sessions. In this sense, motion analysis could provide relevant information about the accuracy of the athlete techniques and identify errors, when implemented during the training. The information collected should serve to apply actions that allow the trainers and the athletes to correct the errors and adjust the training plan. Thus, contributing to improve the efficiency of movements and obtain the expected progress [13].

The study exposed in this paper is part of a PhD project, which has the main objective to develop a system where the overall goal is the evaluation of performance of top Taekwondo athletes in real time.

The system developed consists in a 3D camera with RGB and depth sensor, a computer and a software for data processing and storage, as seen in Figure 1. It is intended that the developed system is as portable and easy to use as possible, without neglecting the reliability and robustness.

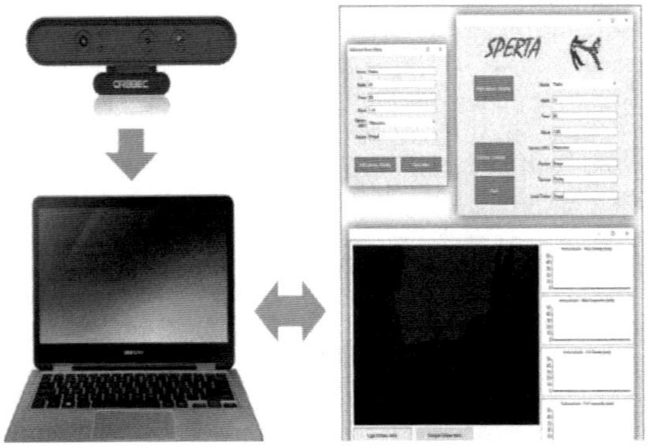

Figure 1. Sperta system architecture

It is provided a graphical environment for the user to interact with the system that allows:

- the trainer to enter the athlete information and training data;
- to store the training data in a database;
- real-time visualization of movements and joints of the athlete;
- view through charts the Cartesian coordinates values of the athlete's hands and feet;
- graphical visualization of the instantaneous velocity of the athlete's hands and feet.

The depth sensor chosen for the development of the system was the 3D camera Orbbec Astra, shown in Figure 2, that provides 640 pixels x 480 pixels at 30 frames per second for depth and RGB image size, a 0.6 to 8 meter range and a field of view of 60° horizontal x 49.5° vertical (73° diagonal). Another relevant aspect to the choice was the small size and ease of use that are important for the usability of the system. Thus, the dimensions of the Orbbec Astra are 165 x 30 x 40 mm, the weight is 300 grams and the power supply and the data interface only require a USB 2.0 port [17]. Comparing with Microsoft Kinect 2, the most used depth sensor in research, Orbbec is smaller, has less weight, with a higher maximum reach distance.

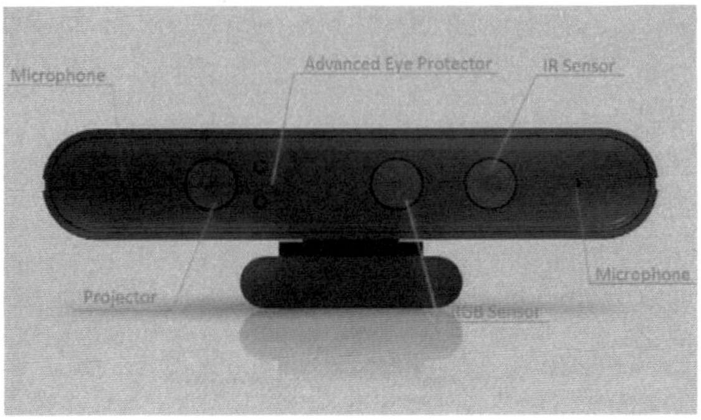

Figure 2. 3D Camera Orbbec Astra [17]

The performance of the computer must be taken into account for the proper functioning of the system. Due to the large amount of data read, processed and stored by the software, the performance of the computer is of utmost importance. The better the processing capacity is, the better the efficiency of the movements' data collection is, either by the motion sensor or by the software where the information is processed. The computer used for the development consists of a portable computer, with 4th generation Intel® Core ™ i7-4720HQ processor with Intel® Turbo Boost Technology 2.0, 8 GB of RAM, AMD Radeon ™ R9 M265X graphics card with 2 GB dedicated and Microsoft Windows 10 64-bit operating system.

A Windows application was developed, so that it can be used by computers running the Windows operating system, the most commonly used operating system in Portugal at the moment [18]. The programming language used was C# along the Microsoft Visual Studio 2017 IDE. Although Orbbec Astra provides a SDK with full body skeleton tracking, Orbbec itself advises the use of Nuitrack ™ that has been developed in partnership with 3DiVi Inc. Nuitrack™ is a 3D skeleton tracking gesture recognition solution middleware enabling Natural User Interface (NUI) capabilities on Android, Windows and Linux platforms [19].

The developed software interface consists of several windows/forms that allow the user to enter and view the information regarding the training performed, visible in Figure 3a). The main window has 3 buttons, one for 'Add athlete', one for 'Begin training', one for 'Exit' application and also fields for data entry of the training to be performed.

When pressed the 'Add athlete' button another window opens, Figure 3b), that allows adding the database athlete data such as name, age, weight, height, gender and team. The 'Begin training' button is pressed after selecting the athlete in the dropdown field 'Name:´, which automatically fills the remaining fields referring to the athlete.

After 'Begin training' is pressed, a new window opens, Figure 3c), that allows to see the depth image and the athlete hands and feet joints movements data in Cartesian coordinates numeric values, Cartesian coordinates line chart and speed line chart, all in real-time as presented in Figure 4.

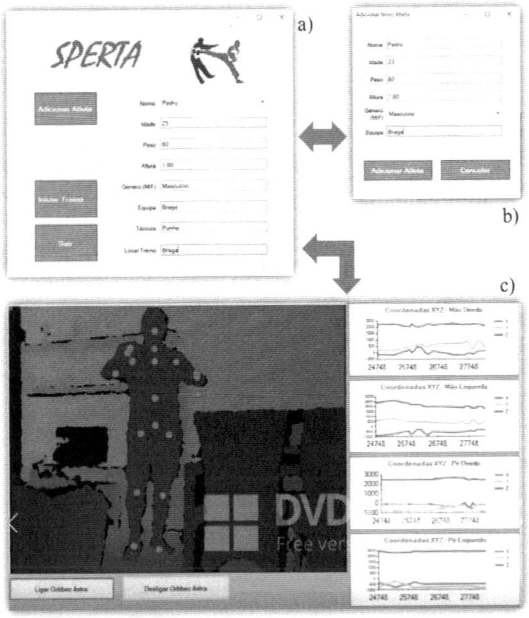

Figure 3. Sperta software interface windows: a) information regarding the training; b) athlete data; and c) depth image and line charts.

The joints Cartesian coordinates are obtained through the Nuitrack™ SDK integrated in the software and their values are presented in millimeters. The values of each one of the joints refer to the X, Y, and Z coordinates relative to the range of the 3D camera Orbbec Astra.

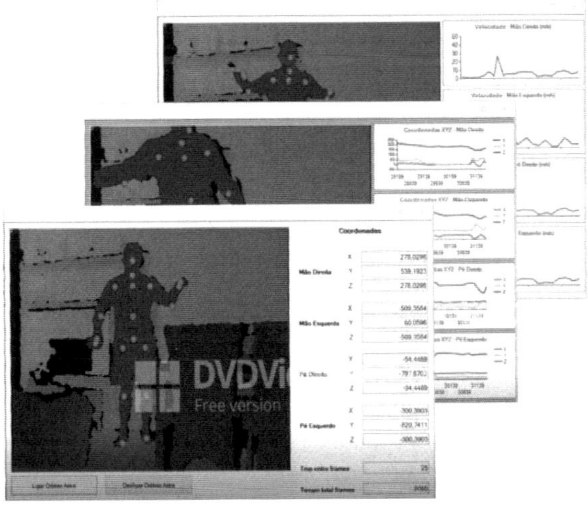

Figure 4. Depth sensor, cartesian coordinates and speed data output in real-time

It is important for the trainer to access the previous training information in order to evaluate the performance evolution of the trainee. The developed software integrates an SQL database where all the training data collected with the system is saved, which structure is presented in Figure 5.

The database is divided into three tables: 'Athlete' table with fields 'IdAthelete', 'name', 'age', 'weight', 'height', 'genre' and 'team'; 'Training' table with fields 'IdTraining', 'dateHour', 'technique, 'place' and foreign key 'trainingAthlete'; 'CoordinatesXYZ' table with fields 'IdCoordinates', 'time', 'handRightX', 'handRightY', 'handRightZ', 'handLeftX', 'handLeftY', 'handLeftZ', 'footRightX', 'footRightY', 'footRightZ', 'footLeftX', 'footLeftY', 'footLeftZ' and foreign key 'coordinatesTraining'.

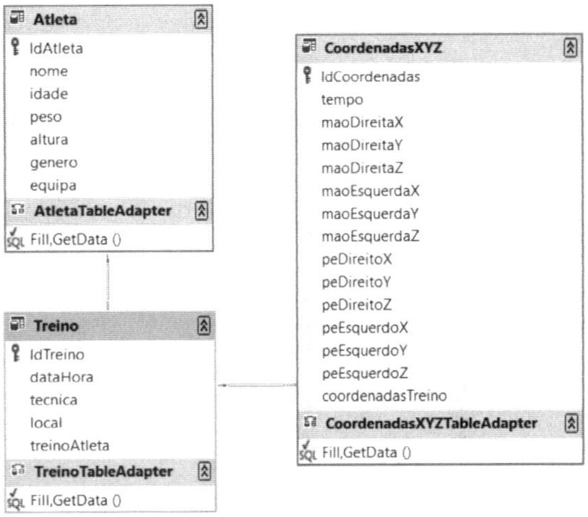

Figure 5. Database tables and data fields (in Portuguese).

The speed of the athlete joints movements is not obtained directly from the SDK Nuitrack. To calculate the speed of the athlete's movements in real-time using the Cartesian coordinates it is necessary to calculate the movement displacement value according to the time elapsed between each reading. For that it was used the distance equation in three-dimensional Euclidean space (1). Where p and q are the current values read and the last read antecedent's values, respectively of the Cartesian coordinates of the joints.

$$d(\mathbf{p},\mathbf{q}) = \sqrt{(p_1 - q_1)^2 + (p_2 - q_2)^2 + (p_3 - q_3)^2} \quad (1)$$

The time elapsed between two adjacent acquisitions was calculated (current coordinate data of the joints of the athlete and the previous coordinates). This calculation was performed through the used computer system clock in milliseconds (2), where t and t_{-1} are the current time value and the time value of the previous Cartesian coordinates read respectively.

$$te = t - t_{-1} \quad (2)$$

After calculating the joints distance between the collected data and the time between data collection, the velocity calculation was performed using (3), where *ds* and *dt* are the derivative of the displacement value of the joint and the derivative of the value of the time elapsed between the displacement, respectively.

$$v = \frac{ds}{dt} \tag{3}$$

The calculated speed values are presented by the software in real-time allowing the trainer to follow the evolution of the training and providing relevant feedback in real-time to the athlete.

In order to verify the accuracy of the system developed, some tests were made, where the recording of the operation and data presented in real-time was performed. The collected (in the database) output graphs of various sections of the training were compared with the charts provided by the system software. The charts of the database were created using the Microsoft Excel worksheet. In Figure 6, it is possible to visualize the comparison between the Cartesian coordinates of the movement realized by the right hand during the period comprised between the 9890 and the 13895 milliseconds of a section of training.

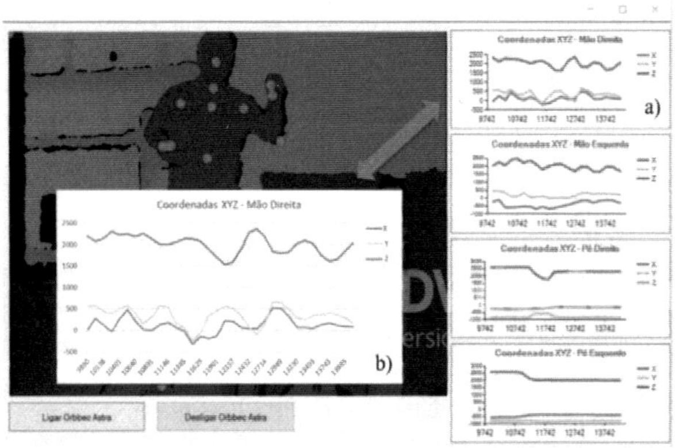

Figure 6. Hand right Cartesian coordinates charts from 9890 to 13895 milliseconds: a) Excel chart of values collected by Orbbec Astra and stored in the database; b) graph of the values presented by the software in real time.

This comparison seeks to visually verify that the values collected in real-time by the Orbbec Astra 3D camera, Figure 6 a), and the values presented by the software in real-time, Figure 6 b), are the same. This allows us to conclude that the system performance is effective and able to provide real-time feedback of the performance of Taekwondo athletes.

IV. CONCLUSION

The development of an accurate, economically affordable and non-invasive solution to monitor in real-time the practice of Taekwondo is of utmost importance [5].

The system presented in this paper intends to accomplish the performance evaluation of taekwondo athletes in real-time in a training environment. The evaluation of the movements of the athlete is performed through motion analysis of the movements, using computer processing of the information collected through the 3D Camera Orbbec Astra, with its depth sensor and the SDK Nuitrack™.

The system developed allows the trainer and athlete to have a real-time feedback of the movements performed during the training and the speed of the movement execution. In fact, the objective is to provide a tool that could be used by both, trainer and athlete, which promotes an increase in the speed of the feedback of the trainer on the performance of the athlete during the training.

Thus, the developed system aims to be an easy-to-use and affordable technology solution and to contribute to the technological development of the performance evaluation of Taekwondo athletes in a training environment.

V. FUTURE WORK

The system presented is part of a larger project and it is still under development. So, it is intended to add other features to the system, such as: output of the movements acceleration and strength in real-time, either in numeric values or charts; output of the speed, acceleration and strength of more human body joints relevant to the evaluation of the athlete performance; create a database with the correctly executed Taekwondo movements Cartesian coordinate's patterns, for use as reference values; identify and count the movements performed by the athlete during the training sessions using deep learning methods, such as backpropagation neural network using as reference values the data previously saved in the database of the correct execution of the movements.

Finally, it will be necessary to test the software in real training environment with Taekwondo top athletes to be able to adjust the system to the real needs of the training, as well as collecting enough data to allow the use of deep learning methods needed to make the system more efficient and accurate in real-time interpretation of data.

ACKNOWLEDGMENT

The authors would like also to express their acknowledgments to COMPETE: POCI-01-0145-FEDER-007043 and FCT – Fundação para a Ciência e Tecnologia within the Project Scope: UID/CEC/00319/2013. Pedro Cunha thanks FCT for PhD scholarship SFRH/BD/121994/2016.

REFERENCES

[1] A. Baca, P. Dabnichki, M. Heller, and P. Kornfeind, "Ubiquitous computing in sports: A review and analysis," Journal of Sports Sciences, vol. 27, pp. 1335-1346, Oct. 2009, doi.org/10.1080/02640410903277427.

[2] B. A. King and L. D. Paulson, "Motion capture moves into new realms," Computer, vol. 40(9), pp. 13–16, Sep. 2007, doi.ieeecomputersociety.org/10.1109/MC.2007.326.

[3] A. Baca and P. Kornfeind, "Rapid feedback systems for elite sports training," IEEE Pervasive Computing, vol. 5 (4), pp. 70–76, Oct. 2006 doi.org/10.1109/MPRV.2006.82.

[4] D. G. Liebermann et al., "Advances in the application of information technology to sport performance," Journal of Sports Science, vol. 20, pp. 755–769, Dec. 2010, doi.org/10.1080/026404102320675611.

[5] P. Cunha, V. Carvalho, and F. Soares, "Real-Time Data Movements Acquisition of Taekwondo Athletes: First Insights," in International Conference on Innovation, Engineering and Entrepreneurship, Cham, Springer, pp. 251-258, Jun. 2018, doi.org/10.1007/978-3-319-91334-6_35.

[6] E. H. A. Costa, "Taekwondo History," [Online]. Available: http://www.dojangabilio-costa.com/home.. [retrieved: june, 2018].

[7] W. T. Organization, "About the Federation," [Online]. Available: http://www.worldtaekwondo.org/about-wt/about-wt/. [retrieved: june, 2018].

[8] I. P. D. J. I.P, " Federated Practitioners - Statistics - Tables," [Online]. Available: http://www.idesporto.pt/conteudo.aspx?id=103. [retrieved: june, 2018].

[9] A. M. VencesBrito, M. A. Rodrigues Ferreira, N. Cortes, O. Fernandes, and P. Pezarat-Correia, "Kinematic and electromyographic analyses of a karate punch," Journal of Electromyography and Kinesiology, vol. 21(6), pp. 1023–1029, Dec. 2011, doi.org/10.1016/j.jelekin.2011.09.007.

[10] J. Suarez and R. R. Murphy, "Hand gesture recognition with depth images: A review," Ro-man, 2012 IEEE, pp. 411-417, Sep. 2012.

[11] O. Patsadu, C. Nukoolkit, and B. Watanapa, "Human gesture recognition using Kinect camera," Computer Science and Software Engineering (JCSSE), 2012 International Joint Conference on. IEEE, pp. 28-32, 2012.

[12] C. Zerpa, C. Lees, P. P., and E. Pryzsucha, "The use of microsoft Kinect for human movement analysis," International Journal of Sports Science, vol. 5(4), pp. 120-127, Oct. 2015, doi:10.5923/j.sports.20150504.02.

[13] A. VencesBrito, M. A. Castro, and O. Fernandes, "Motion analysis systems as optimization training tools in combat sports and martial arts," Revista de Artes Marciales Asiáticas, vol. 10(2), pp. 105-123, 2016, dx.doi.org/10.18002/rama.v10i2.1687.

[14] T. Pinto et al., "Recording of Occurrences Through Image Processing in Taekwondo Training: First Insights," European Congress on Computational Methods in Applied Sciences and Engineering, vol. 27, pp. 427-436, Oct. 2017, doi.org/10.1007/978-3-319-68195-5_47.

[15] D. G. E. Robertson, G. Caldwell, J. Hamill, G. Kamen, and S. N. Whittlesey, "Research methods in biomechanics," in Human Kinetics., Champaign, IL, 2004.

[16] S. Corazza, L. Mundermann, E. Gambaretto, G. Ferrigno, and T. Andriacchi, "Markerless motion capture through visual hull, articulated ICP and subject specific model generation," International Journal of Computer Vision, vol. 87, pp. 156-169, Sep. 2009, doi.org/10.1007/s11263-009-0284-3.

[17] Orbbec, "Orbbec Astra, Astra S & Astra Pro," [Online]. Available: https://orbbec3d.com/product-astra/. [retrieved: june, 2018].

[18] S. GlobalStats, "Operating System Market Share Portugal, June 2017 - June 2018," Statcounter GlobalStats, [Online]. Available: http://gs.statcounter.com/os-market-share/all/portugal. [retrieved: june, 2018].

[19] Nuitrack, "What is Nuitrack™SDK?," 3DiVi Inc., [Online]. Available: http://download.3divi.com/Nuitrack/doc/Overview_page.htm. [retrieved: june, 2018].

Sensors Selection and Detailed Mechanical Design on Developing a Mechatronic System for the Promotion of Physical Activity

Leandro Pereira
Mechanical Engineering Department
University of Minho
Guimarães, Portugal
e-mail: A75901@alunos.uminho.pt

Vítor Carvalho
2Ai Lab
IPCA-EST
Barcelos, Portugal
e-mail: vcarvalho@ipca.pt

Demétrio Matos
ID+
IPCA-ESD
Barcelos, Portugal
e-mail: dmatos@ipca.pt

José Machado
MEtRICs Research Centre
University of Minho
Guimarães, Portugal
e-mail: jmachado@dem.uminho.pt

Filomena Soares
Algoritmi Research Centre
University of Minho
Guimarães, Portugal
e-mail: fsoares@dei.uminho.pt

Abstract— **The increase in the number of elderly people and people with motor limitations takes along concerns to health professionals. A way of helping health professionals and the elderly may be through the development of systems that allow people to maintain their mobility regardless of age and health problems that may arise. This paper presents the studies carried out in the development of a mechatronic system that aims to promote physical activity in people with motor limitations. The proposed mechatronic system consists of a stationary bike, however its architecture is completely different, besides including a game that aims to increase the motivation of its users, in order to make physical activity and rehabilitation more enjoyable. Briefly, this paper presents a description of the proposed solution, followed by an approach to the study of the dimensions of the model taking into account the anthropometric data, so that the system can be used by as many people as possible. Afterwards, a detailed mechanical design of the structure was carried out, as well as the selection of the encoders, sensors and actuators that could be used in the model to obtain the inputs supplied by the user.**

Keywords- Serious Games; Rehabilitation; Modular Design; Sensors and Actuators.

I. INTRODUCTION

Aging and chronic diseases, such as obesity, Parkinson's, hypertension, arthritis, diabetes and even symptoms resulting from strokes are the main factors that force people to gradually lose their autonomy, making it more difficult for performing daily tasks such as bathing, dressing and walking. As many of the above diseases require rehabilitation, some researchers believe that active games (games involving physical activity) can increase adherence to treatment [1]. Over the years, several games have been developed with the purpose of promoting and improving the physical condition of the population in an effective and pleasant way. One of the first games of this type was Foot Craz in 1987 and since then several games have been released, however the device that more success had was the popular Wii console of Nintendo [2].

Nowadays, several equipment of this type is studied and commercialized, with special emphasis on games that use virtual reality through cameras, pressure platforms and simulators. Through the literature review, it was possible to find several studied and commercialized systems, among them: ReaKing, Physioland, Smartfloor, Physiosensing, Twall, GymTop USB, BOBO Balance and Trixter VR [3].

Recent research has integrated serious games as a valuable therapeutic tool in rehabilitation. In fact, virtual reality, especially in the form of serious games, combines therapeutic and recreational challenges. This strategy prevents boredom, making therapy less tiring and discouraging. Serious games can motivate patients to perform exercise and rehabilitation improving adherence to treatment. This ludic and challenging environment is the main aspect that differentiates virtual reality games from traditional physical rehabilitation programs [4].

Despite the wide variety of games on the market that aim to motivate the practice of physical exercise, it can be verified that there is a need to adapt them to allow their use by people with motor limitations. In fact, commercial games do not provide safety and comfort necessary for this people. To improve the practice of physical activity through this type of games by the elderly and/or physical impaired population, it is fundamental to develop rehabilitation games considering their safety and comfort [2].

In order to achieve the main goals of this paper, the respective organization is as follows: in Section 2, the proposed solution is presented; it is also presented some aspects used in the 3D modeling, giving main emphasis to the modular principle that is intended to be implemented and to the study of the dimensions of the model taking into account the anthropometric data, that aims the use of the model by the largest number of people. In Section 3, a detailed mechanical design of the structure of the model is presented, analyzing the forces involved in the course of its use; a numerical analysis of the structure is also performed in this section. In Section 4, it is presented the review of the sensors, encoders and actuators that could be used; it also includes the analysis of the characteristics of each component and a brief comparison between them. Finally, Section 5 presents the conclusions.

II. PROPOSED SYSTEM

The proposed model is presented in Figure 1 and consists of a stationary bike with a didactic component (simulation of a paramotor). This proposed 3D model resulted from an iterative process in which it was intended to choose the appropriated systems and to promote the desired versatility and functionality to the model. It was also intended that this 3D model presented an equipment that: occupied the minimum space as possible; had a chair with adjustment capability; allowed to adjust the loads for different workouts and to provide the necessary comfort and safety to be used by people with motor limitations [4].

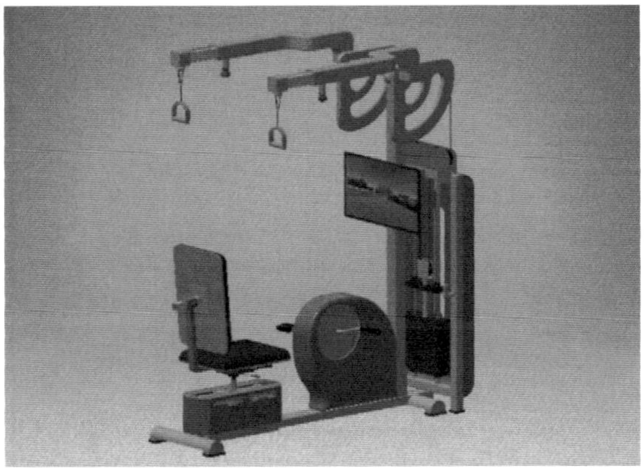

Figure 1. The proposed solution.

A. *Modules of the proposed model*

In order to occupy the smallest space possible, a modular system was adopted. In this way, it was easier to reduce the occupied space when it is fully assembled. Thus, it was decided to divide the system's model into 3 modules - chair module, pedal module and main module. This division into modules, besides allowing the disassembly and division of the equipment, allows the adaptation to any chair, wheelchairs included [2].

B. *Study of the dimensions of the model taking into account the anthropometric data*

This project was aimed at obtaining a 3D model whose dimensions were adequate to any person.

First, it was necessary to define the length of the pedal crank arm. Research has reported that the ideal length of the crank arm can be between 145 and 180 mm [5] [6] [7]. Other studies in the same scope establish pedal performance analyzes according to the lengths of the pedal crank arms. A study carried out in these models shows that the difference is relatively small when using arms of lengths of 170 and 175 mm (commonly used lengths). The difference can be significant in competitive sports [8]. As in the case of the model under study, that it is not a competition sport, the used length is 175 mm.

This study of dimensions aims to allow anyone, in a wheelchair, to use the model, since the wheelchairs are not adjustable, contrary to what happens with the use of the chair module. For this it was also necessary to know the height of the seat of a wheelchair, which was considered 49.5 cm according to the researches carried out in [9]. Table I shows the dimensions for percentile 95 and 5 for both men and women to the following dimensions: buttock-heel length, seated vertical reach, vertical reach of apprehension and body depth maximum [9].

TABLE I. HUMAN DIMENSIONS STUDIED.

	Percentile	Buttock-heel length (cm)	Seated vertical range (cm)	Vertical reach of apprehension (cm)	Maximum body depth (cm)
Men	95	117,1	131,1	224,8	33
Women		124,5	124,7	213,4	
Men	5	100,1	149,9	195,1	25,7
Women		86,4	140,2	185,2	

In order to collect the data presented above, it was considered that the dimensions of wheelchair's users would be close to the dimensions of normal people, since the anthropometric study of people in wheelchairs is more difficult due to some variables, among them: the type of disability, the affected limbs or segments, the spread of paralysis, among others [9].

From the collected data, it was possible to verify the dimensions of the model being studied, taking into account some adjustments. The buttock-heel length varies according to the footwear and knee flexion in the execution of the exercise, so it was decided to reduce 5 cm to this length. In the case study, it can be verified that the handle will be below the maximum vertical seated range, because this measure goes from the seat to the tip of the middle finger with the arm stretched, while the handle will be reached with the hand closed and the arms will not be completely stretched. For this reason, a tolerance of approximately 20 cm this length is adopted. The vertical reach of apprehension is usually made with the individual without shoes, therefore a compensation of 3 cm will be performed in relation to this measure. Finally, it was considered that the horizontal perpendicular distance between the backrest of the wheelchair and the handle should be approximately 1/3 of the maximum body depth (horizontal distance between the most forward point of the body and the point farther back).

III. DETAILED MECHANICAL DESIGN

The following computational tools were used: Autodesk Inventor 2017 and Autodesk Simulation Mechanical 2017 (CAD-CAE).

In order to be able to perform the simulation (CAE) stages, it was necessary to define the initial conditions and the boundaries.

A. *Study of the forces applied to the structural components of the model*

Figure 2 shows the free body diagram of one of the arms of the model structure.

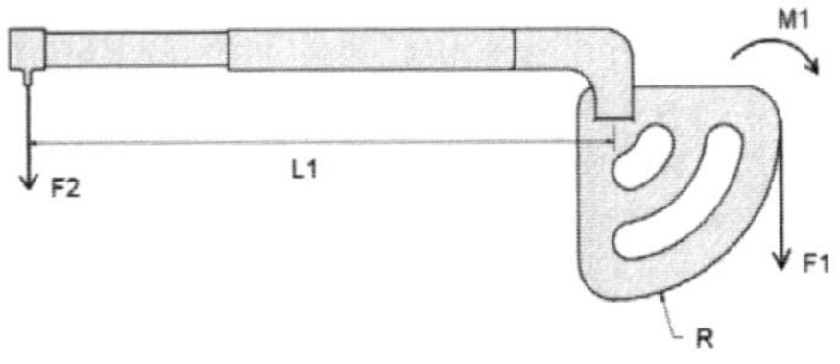

Figure 2. Free body diagram of one of the arms of the model (where F1 represents the load exerted by the weights and F2 represents the force exerted by the user)

For the arm completely stretched and the maximum load *F1* (the maximum force *F1* is half the maximum load of the weights, since this load is divided by two arms) the following values are considered:

- *L1* = 1,225 m
- *R* = 0,35 m
- *F1max* = 368 N

M1 and *F2* are calculated as follows:

- Calculation of the torque produced by the force *F1*:

$$M1 = F1 \times R = 128{,}8 \text{ Nm} \quad (1)$$

- Calculation of the force *F2* that will be required to move the arm:

$$M1 = F2 \times L1 \quad (2)$$

$$F2 = M1/L1 = 105{,}1 \text{ N} \quad (3)$$

In the course of the game, the force exerted by the user will not be constant, since the direction of the force will change with the rotation of the arms. Figure 3 shows the variation of the position of the arms and their applied forces.

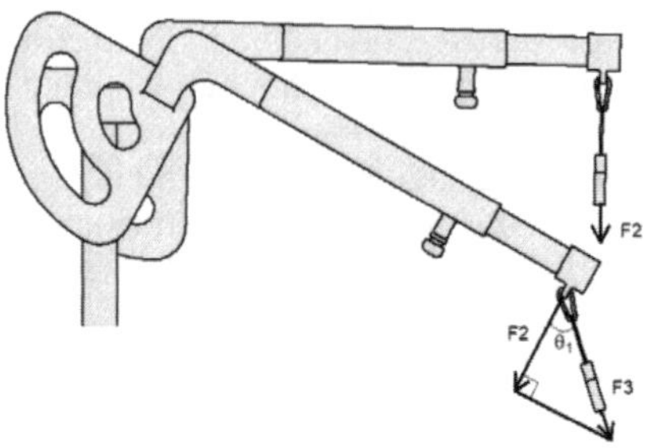

Figure 3. Variation of the position of the arms and their applied forces (where F1 represents the load exerted by the weights and F2 represents the force exerted by the user)

Calculation of F3, considering that the triangle from the Figure 3 is a triangle rectangle:

$$\cos \theta 1 = F2/F3 \quad (4)$$

$$F3 = F2/\cos \theta 1 \quad (5)$$

Figure 4 represents a graph showing the variation of the force *F3* with the variation of angle *θ1*.

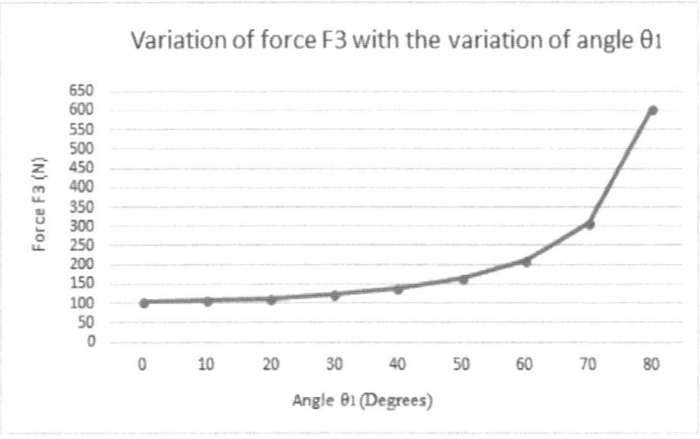

Figure 4. Variation of force F3 with the variation of angle θ1.

B. *Numerical analysis and simulation of the model structure*

In order to verify and study the structure and its behavior, quickly and effectively for different geometries, a numerical analysis was chosen. For the numerical analysis, a finite element analysis software was used (Autodesk Simulation Mechanical 2017). The following are presented the pre-processing and the post-processing performed for the final form of the model.

1) Pre-Processing

With regard to the simulation, the first step corresponds to the selection of the type of analysis. In this case, a linear static analysis was performed, because the structure presents linear behavioral materials, with the exception of the bushings, which, in this case, was neglected.

After defining the type of analysis, the model was discretized (mesh generation). The mesh initially presented was coarse generated, which allowed the first simulation to be faster and to identify the locations of the most critical zones. After the creation of the mesh, the boundary conditions were considered. In this case, it is intended a static model, so it was considered that the base of the structure was embedded with no rotation of the arms. Finally, the materials (AISI 1050 and AISI 304 [2]), the loads and the contacts were defined. In the case of loads, the forces previously obtained (Section III.A) were used for the situation where L1 = 1,225 m, F1 = 368 N and F2 = 105 N for the initial position. In the case of joints, it was considered that all the pieces were bonded. Figure 5 shows the pre-processing representation of the structure model.

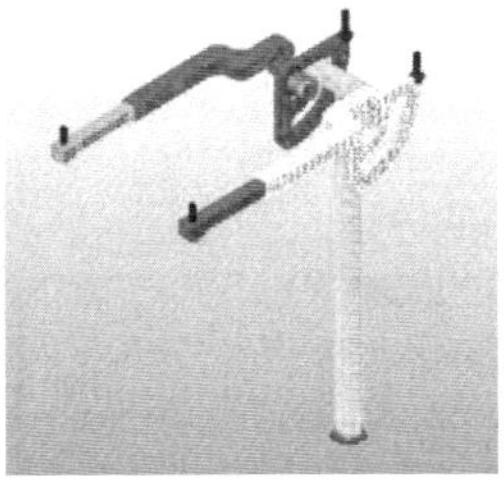

Figure 5. Pre-processing representation of the structure.

2) Post Processing

After the processing step - Solver execution - the results of the maximum displacements and the installed stress were obtained and verified. Figure 6 presents the maximum displacement, whereas Figure 7 presents the stress analysis by the criterion of Von Mises.

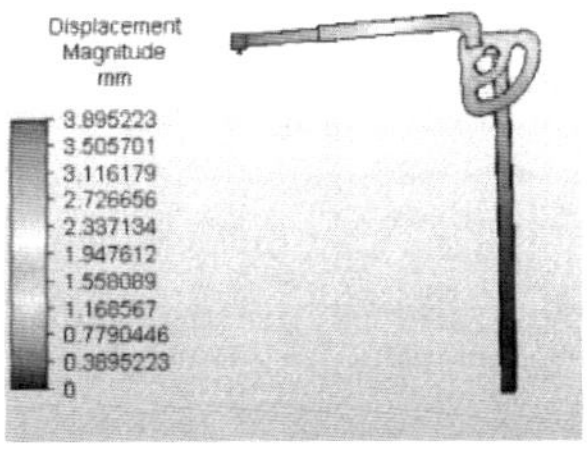

Figure 6. Displacement magnitude results.

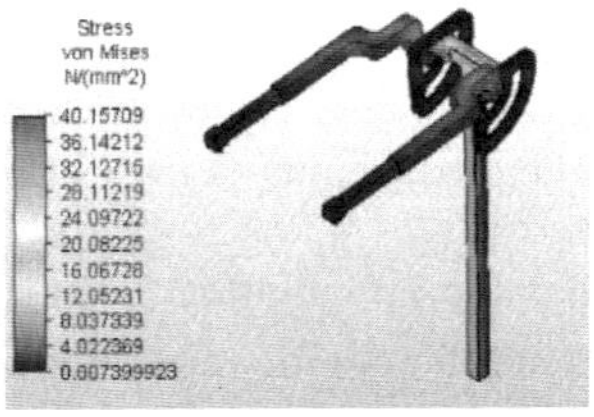

Figure 7. Stress Von Mises results.

From the obtained results, it can be verified that the maximum displacement verified by the software was 3,90 mm. This value can be considered acceptable for the structure. Another important verified aspect was the maximum analyzed stress, in the structure, that presented a value of 40,16 MPa. In addition to these results, a mesh refinement was also carried out in the zone of higher tension. This refinement presented a result of around 42 MPa for the maximum tension. Comparing the maximum installed tension with the yielding tension of the material (415 MPa) it can be stated that the material is adequate for the required loads.

IV. Selection of Sensors

In order to create the game, it is necessary to acquire some inputs: detection of the pedal velocity and detection of the position of the arms of the structure. To obtain this data, it is necessary to use encoders and sensors to measure the position and velocity. In the following section, there are presented the encoders and sensors that will be used for the detection of the pedal speed and the position of the arms of the structure.

A. Detection of position of the structure arms and the pedal speed

For the detection of the position of the arms of the structure, incremental rotary encoders will be used. The incremental encoders are simpler and low-cost when compared to the absolute encoder. This type of encoder generates only pulses and does not have a different combination for each position. In this way, they are manufactured with a quantity of pulses per revolution. The higher the number of pulses per revolution, the higher the encoder resolution. The disadvantage of this type of encoder is in the reading of its data, because as it operates by pulses, the reading of a certain positioning needs an initial reference.

For the detection of the pedal speed it will be used a Reed Switch sensor. The Reed sensors are used as highly effective speed sensors in low speed applications (up to 1000 rpm). A Reed sensor consists of a switch having two ferromagnetic blades contained within a hermetically sealed tubular glass housing. Generally, the gas inside the glass is nitrogen that serves to eliminate the presence of oxygen and to ensure that the contacts do not oxidize. Reed switches are usually activated by a permanent magnet or an electromagnet. This type of sensor allows solutions for detection of proximity, speed, flow, among others. In this way, these sensors are versatile possessing different utilities and forms [10].

B. Selection of encoder for the rotation of the arms of the structure

The following are encoders that can be used in the case under study

1) Rotary Encoder 200 P/R (YUMO)

Figure 8 presents an encoder with 200 pulses per revolution. This encoder produces electrical pulses that can be interpreted using a microcontroller to find the position of the input shaft. This allows the addiction of a feedback to the control system. Encoders of this type are often used in balancing robots. The encoder comes with a set screw coupling that will connect to any 4mm shaft [11]. Table II shows the specifications of the encoder 200 P/R.

Figure 8. Rotary Encoder 200 P/R (YUMO) [11].

TABLE II. SPECIFICATIONS OF ROTARY ENCODER 200 P/R [11]

Resolution	200 Pulse/Rotation
Input Voltage	5 - 12VDC
Maximum speed of rotation	5000 rpm
Permissible radial load	5 N
Permissible axial load	3 N
Cable length	50 cm
Shaft diameter	4 mm

2) Rotary encoder 1024 P/R (YUMO)

Figure 9 presents an encoder with 1024 pulse per rotation; this encoder has an output gray code which can be interpreted using a microcontroller and find out how and in which direction the shaft is turning. This allows to add feedback to the control system. Encoders of this kind are often used in balancing robots and dead reckoning navigation but they can also be used as a precise input knob [12]. Table III shows the specifications of the encoder 1024 P/R.

Figure 9. Rotary encoder 1024 P/R (YUMO) [12].

TABLE III. SPECIFICATIONS OF ROTARY ENCODER 1024 P/R [12]

Resolution	1024 Pulse/Rotation
Input Voltage	5 - 12VDC
Maximum speed of rotation	6000 rpm
Permissible radial load	5 N
Permissible axial load	3 N
Cable length	50cm
Shaft diameter	5mm

3) Encoders comparison

By the analysis of the two encoders presented it can be verified that any of them could be used, however, as the *1024 P/R* rotary encoder presents superior resolution it will give more accurate results.

C. Selection of encoder for the detection of the pedal speed

In the following, there are presented sensors and actuators that can be used in the model being studied.

1) 59150 Flange Mount Sensor and 57150 Actuator

Figure 10 presents a flange mounting reed sensor (28.57mm x 19.05mm x 6.35mm) with a choice of normally open, normally open high voltage, normally closed or changeover contacts. The design of this sensor enables screw or adhesive mounting and the wires exit from top right-hand side. It is also available with left hand exit (59145 Series). It is capable of switching up to 265Vac/300Vdc at 10VA. The 59150 functions best with the matching actuator 57150-000 [13].

Figure 10. 59150 Flange Mount Sensor [13].

Table IV shows the types of sensors (normally open, normally open high voltage, normally closed or changeover contacts) and two sensitivity options for each one of them (These data are based on the use of an actuator 57150).

TABLE IV. SENSITIVITY OPTIONS FOR 59150 FLANGE MOUNT SENSOR WITH 57150 ACTUATOR [13].

		S		V	
	Switch Type	***Pull in AT Range***	***Activate distance - D mm average***	***Pull in AT Range***	***Activate distance - D mm average***
1	Normally open	12-18	13,5	27-33	9
2	High Voltage	-	-	27-33	9
3	Change Over	15-20	11	-	-
4	Normally closed	15-20	11	-	-

2) 59025 Firecracker Reed Sensor and 57025 Actuator

Figure 11 presents a Firecracker Reed Sensor (length=25.4mm and diameter=6.22mm). This sensor has a cylindrical shape with a choice of normally open, normally open high voltage, normally closed or changeover contacts. It is capable of switching up to 265Vac/300Vdc at 10VA. The 59025 Firecracker Reed Sensor is available with a range of sensitivity and cable length options. It functions best with the 57025 actuators [14].

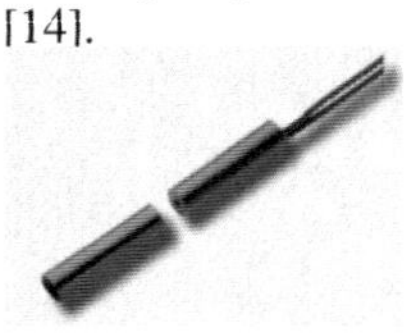

Figure 11. 59025 Firecracker Reed Sensor [14].

Table V shows the types of sensors (normally open, normally open high voltage, normally closed or changeover contacts) and two sensitivity options for each one of them (These data are based on the use of an actuator 57025).

TABLE V. SENSITIVITY OPTIONS FOR FOR 59025 FIRECRACKER REED SENSOR WITH 57025 ACTUATOR [14]

		S		V	
Switch Type		*Pull in AT Range*	*Activate distance - D mm average*	*Pull in AT Range*	*Activate distance - D mm average*
1	Normally open	12 to 18	7,9	27-33	4,2
2	High Voltage	-	-	27-33	4,2
3	Change Over	15 to 20	7,2	-	
4	Normally closed	15 to 20	7,2	-	

3) *Switch Reed sensors comparison*

One of the most important factors for the selection of a reed sensor and its actuator is the sensitivity. The sensitivity of the switch is the amount of magnetic field that is required to actuate the contact into an open or closed mode (Most reed switches have a sensitivity range of 10–30 AT, where 10 AT is more sensitive than 30 AT)

A check that can be made in terms of sensitivity is that for the same variations of sensitivity the distance in the set 59150 Flange Mount Sensor and 57150 Actuator is higher. In addition to the sensitivity, the ease of assembly and adjustment makes the set 59150 Flange Mount Sensor and 57150 Actuator more advantageous.

V. CONCLUSIONS

With this work it was verified the evolution and growth of the serious games over the years, besides it was verified that it is necessary to adapt and create new equipment so that they can be used in physiotherapy and rehabilitation areas. Thus, the development of a mechatronic system was presented, whose main advantages are: being motivating, adjustable, appealing, comfortable and safe.

The system was divided into modules and a study of the dimensions of the model was carried out considering the anthropometric data. A detailed mechanical design study was also conducted.

Finally, it was analyzed the sensors and actuators in the market that could be implemented in the system, among them: Rotary Encoder 200 P / R (YUMO), Rotary encoder 1024 P / R (YUMO), 59150 Flange Mount Sensor, 57150 Actuator, 59025 Firecracker Reed Sensor and 57025 Actuator.

Future work may include: the development of the game scenario, the construction of a prototype for validation and the implementation of the studies performed.

ACKNOWLEDGMENT

The authors would like to express their acknowledgments to COMPETE: POCI-01-0145-FEDER-007043 and FCT – Portuguese Foundation for science and technology within the Project Scope: UID/CEC/00319/2013.

REFERENCES

[1] N. Zeng, Z. Pope, J. Eun, and Z. Gao, "A systematic review of active video games on rehabilitative outcomes among older patients," Journal of Sport and Health Science, vol. 6, no. 1, pp. 33–43, 2017.

[2] L. Pereira, J. Machado, V. Carvalho, F. Soares and D. Matos, "Mechatronic System for the Promotion of Physical Activity in People with Motor Limitations: First Insights," Innovation, Engineering and Entrepreneurship. HELIX2018, vol. 4, pp. 267–274, https://doi.org/10.1007/978-3-319-91334-6_37, 2018.

[3] L. Pereira, J. Machado, V. Carvalho, F. Soares and D. Matos, "Mechatronic system for the promotion of physical activity in people with motor limitations," Accepted for Publication in International Journal of Mechatronics and Applied Mechanics, vol. 3, 2018.

[4] E. Marcelino, G. M. Rossito and Y. S. Júnior, "A serious game developed for physical," European Research in Telemedicine/La Recherche Européenne En Télémédecine, vol 5, no. 2, pp. 45–53. https://doi.org/10.1016/j.eurtel.2016.05.003, 2016.

[5] O. Inbar, R. Dotan, T. Trousil and Z. Dvir, "The effect of bicycle crank length variation upon power performance." Ergonomics, vol 26, no. 12, pp. 1139–1146, 1982.

[6] D. Too and C Williams, "The effect of pedal crank arm length on joint angle and power production in upright cycle ergometry." J Sports Sci, vol. 18, pp. 153–161, 2000.

[7] J. Martin and W. Spirduso, "Determinants of maximal cycling power: crank length, pedalling rate and pedal speed." Eur J Appl Physiol vol.84, pp. 413–418, 2001.

[8] P. MacDermid and A. Edwards, "Influence of crank length on cycle ergometry performance of well-trained female cross-country mountain bike athletes," European Journal of Applied Physiology, vol. 108, no. 1, pp. 177–18, https://doi.org/10.1007/s00421-009-1197-0, 2010.

[9] J. Panero and M. Zelnik, "Human dimension and interior space: A source book of design reference standards," First publish in 1979 in United states and Canada, Book.

[10] LittelFuse, "Product catalog & design guide (Sensors), http://m.littelfuse.com, retrieved: 06, 2018.

[11] Sparkfun start something, Products: rotary encoders https://www.sparkfun.com/products/10932, retrieved: 06, 2018.

[12] Sparkfun start something, Products: rotary encoders https://www.sparkfun.com/products/11102, retrieved: 06, 2018.

[13] LittelFuse, electronics | datasheets | reed_sensors, http://m.littelfuse.com/~/media/electronics/datasheets/reed_sensors/littelfuse_reed_sensors_59150_datasheet.pdf.pdf, Retrieved: 06, 2018.

[14] LittelFuse, electronics | datasheets | reed_sensors, http://m.littelfuse.com/~/media/electronics/datasheets/reed_sensors/littelfuse_reed_sensors_59025_datasheet.pdf.pdf, Retrieved: 06, 2018.

An Approach to Behavioural Distraction Patterns Detection and Classification in a Human-Robot Interaction

Bruno Amaro[1], Vinicius Silva[2]
[1]Dept. of Industrial Electronics
[2]Algoritmi Research Centre
University of Minho
Guimarães, Portugal
e-mail: [a70785, a65312]@alunos.uminho.pt

Filomena Soares[1,2], João Sena Esteves[1,2]
[1]Dept. of Industrial Electronics
[2]Algoritmi Research Centre
University of Minho
Guimarães, Portugal
e-mail: [fsoares, sena]@dei.uminho.pt

***Abstract*—The capacity of remaining focused on a task can be crucial in some circumstances. In general, this ability is intrinsic in a human social interaction and it is naturally used in any social context. Nevertheless, some individuals have difficulties in remaining concentrated in an activity, resulting in a short attention span. In order to recognize human distraction behaviours and capture the user attention, several patterns of distraction, as well as systems to automatically detect them, have been developed. One of the most used distraction patterns detection methods is based on the measurement of the head pose and eye gaze. The present work proposes a system based on a RGB camera, capable of detecting the distraction patterns, head pose, eye gaze, blinks frequency, and the distance of the user to the camera, during an activity, and then classify the user's state using a machine learning algorithm. The goal is to interface this system with a humanoid robot to consequently adapt its behaviour taking into account the individual affective state during an emotion imitation activity.**

Keywords-Human-Robot Interaction; ZECA Robot; Distraction Patterns; Emotional States; Machine Learning.

I. INTRODUCTION

In general, the ability of concentrating on a task for an extended period of time is a paramount skill to develop. As observed by various authors [1][2], when a person tries to reach a particular object, the observer's gaze arrives at the target before the action is completed. Additionally, the predictive gaze provides the time for the observer to plan and execute an action towards a goal.

Following this idea, the attention span and the eye gaze can be very important elements in social interaction, as they can help an individual to perceive the goals of others. However, some individual's present a low attention span, especially children with Autism Spectrum Disorder (ASD) [3] when, for example, focusing on things that do not interest them, i.e., activities that involve shared attention. Additionally, in accordance to the literature [4][5], authors suggest that individuals with ASD attend less to faces than typically developing individuals.

In an attempt to increase and captivate these individuals' interest, authors have been proposing new technological tools in the field of assistive robotics to help users with special needs in their daily activities. Assistive robots are designed to identify, measure, and react to social behaviours, being repeatable and objective offering an exceptional occasion for quantifying social behaviour [6].

They can be a social support to motivate children, socially educate them and beyond that to help transferring knowledge. Furthermore, research with assistive robots have showed that, in general, individuals with ASD express elevated interest while interacting with robots: increase attention [7], recognition and imitation abilities [8], verbal utterances [7], among others. According to studies, it was observed that children with ASD can exhibit certain positive social behaviours when interacting with robots in contrast to what is perceived when interacting with their peers, caregivers, and therapists [9]. Furthermore, few projects worldwide pursue to include robots as part of the intervention program for individuals with autism [10][11].

These robots are presented with different embodiments, varying their physical appearance from simple designs, e.g., four-wheeled mobile robots, to many levels of anthropomorphic forms, including humanoid [12], animal-like [13], and machine-like systems [14].

Recently, the research in the area of assistive robotics have moved to using robots with a humanoid design, since it can promise a great potential for generalisation, especially in tasks of imitation and emotion recognition which can be harder if the robot does not present a human form [11][12][15].

The majority of the systems proposed in the literature are controlled using the Wizard-of-Oz (WOZ) setup, meaning that in fact the robot does not adapt its behaviour to the children's actions as it does not perceive them [16]. Additionally, there have been studies with assistive robots with the goal of measuring the children eye gaze duration [17][18] and direction. However, this analysis is not performed in real-time by the robot, meaning that usually the sessions are recorded, and the metrics are manually quantified during a post-analysis of the videos.

More recently, there has been a concern in developing more adaptive approaches to interact with children with ASD. These recent approaches usually use wearable and non-wearable technologies in order to measure the children affective states.

The work developed by [19] consisted in controlling the robot reactions and responses, by using a combination of hardware, wearable devices, and software algorithms to measure the affective states (e.g., eye gaze attention, facial expressions, vital signs, skin temperature, and skin conductance signals) of children with ASD. The wearable devices that the authors used were a sensorized t-shirt to acquire the subject physiological signals (ECG and respiration rate), wireless electrode bands to collect the user's skin temperature and Electro Dermal Activity (EDA) and the HATCAM, a system composed of a hat with markers and a grid of cameras to estimate the user's gaze. The developed system, FACET, includes a multisensory room in which a psychologist drives a stepwise protocol involving the android FACE and the autistic subject. This interaction between the robot and the subject is tailored by the therapist. A preliminary test was conducted with six male subjects: four individuals with ASD aged between 15 and 22 years old and two typically developing individuals aged between 15 and 17 years old. By analysing the results, the authors conclude that the subjects were calm during the activity and responded well to the robot. Additionally, the results confirmed that the system can be used as an innovative tool during the intervention sessions with subjects with ASD.

Bekele and colleagues [20][21] developed and later evaluated a humanoid robotic system capable of intelligently managing joint attention prompts and adaptively respond based on gaze and attention measurements. The system is composed of a humanoid robot with augmented vision by using a network of cameras for real-time head tracking using a distributed architecture. In order to track the child's head motion, a hat with markers was used. Thus, based on the cues from the child's head motion, the robot adapts its behaviour to generate prompts and reinforcements. A pilot usability study was conducted with six children with ASD. The results allowed to conclude that the children directed their gaze towards the robot when it prompted them with a question. The authors suggested that robotic systems, endowed with enhancements for successfully captivating the child's attention, might be capable to meaningfully enhance skills related to coordinated attention.

Following this trend, the present work proposes the development of a framework that uses a RGB camera to interface with the humanoid robot ZECA (Zeno Engaging Children with Autism). Generally, in order to track the user's attention patterns, the literature approaches combine the use of several wearable sensors, which can be invasive, with non-wearable sensors. Thus, in order to become less invasive, the present approach uses only one camera to estimate eye gaze, head motion, the blinks frequency and the distance of the user to the camera. The proposed system allows to infer children distraction patterns (if any) when performing a task and to adapt the robot behaviour accordingly.

The final goal of the present work is to collect the selected patterns (head pose, eye gaze, blink frequency, and distance of the user to the camera), and based on these patterns classify the user state, attentive or distracted, during a laboratorial activity.

The paper is organized as follows: in Section 2 the experimental set-up is presented. Section 3 presents the experimental methodology describing the system modules as well as the robot behaviour. The results and their discussion are presented in Section 4. The conclusion and future work are addressed in Section 5.

II. EXPERIMENTAL SETUP

The proposed structure (Figure 1) was designed to use only an RGB camera to detect patterns of user distraction in order to adapt the behaviour of the robot during the activity.

In addition to an RGB camera, the experimental setup uses a computer and the ZECA humanoid robot.

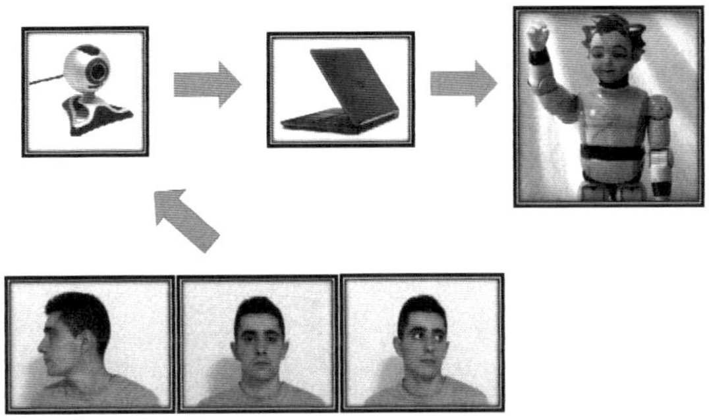

Figure 1. Experimental setup: starting from the left, the RGB camera; in the centre, the computer; and on the right, the humanoid robot ZECA.

The camera used in the present work is a RGB camera, more specifically the Microsoft VX-1000 camera. This device has a minimum resolution of 320 by 240 pixels and a maximum resolution of 640 by 480 pixels. The camera dimensions are 5.5 cm of width, 6.8 cm of height, and 5.3 cm of depth. For a better detection and feature extraction, the camera is placed on the robot chest, being at the same level as the user's face.

The Zeno R50 RoboKind humanoid child-like robot ZECA is a robotic platform that has 34 degrees of freedom: 4 are located in each arm, 6 in each leg, 11 in the head, and 1 in the waist. The robot is capable of expressing facial cues thanks to the servo motors mounted on its face and a special material, Frubber, which looks and feels like human skin, being the major feature that distinguishes Zeno R50 from other humanoid robots.

III. EXPERIMENTAL METHODOLOGY

Since the purpose of this work is to know whether the user is distracted, a study was done to determine which patterns best fit in this evaluation. The following patterns were identified: the eye gaze, the head orientation, the eyes blinking frequency, and the distance of the user to the camera. These patterns will be detected during an emotion imitation activity.

After the extraction of these patterns, the classification was done using an algorithm based on machine learning, thus classifying the user as attentive or distracted.

The design of this activity consists in ZECA displaying a facial expression and asking the child to imitate it. Then, the robot automatically verifies if the answer is correct and responds accordingly. Meanwhile, if the system detects any distraction pattern in the child, the robot adapts its behaviour, encouraging the child to return and participate in the activity.

A. *Affective state detection and classification*

Figure 2 presents the block diagram of the overall system considering the detection of distraction patterns, as well as the classification of the emotional state of the chid during an activity.

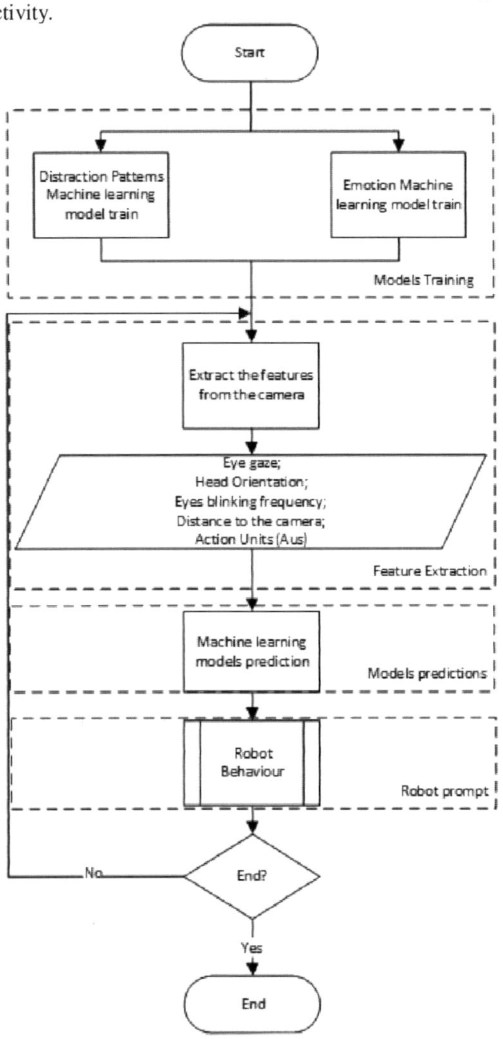

Figure 2. System flowchart highlighting the defined modules for detecting distraction patterns and emotional states: Models training, Feature extraction, Models predictions, and Robot prompt.

The first module, Models Training, consists in training each machine learning model with a previously defined database.

Three other modules are defined: Feature Extraction, Models predictions, and Robot prompt.

For the feature extraction an algorithm based on the OpenFace [22]-[25] library is used to track the face and eyes of the user, as well as the user's Action Units (AUs).

The OpenFace is an open source library that makes available a collection of facial landmarks (a total of 68 facial points) and AUs based on the Facial Action Coding System (FACS). The FACS system, developed by Ekman and Friesen [26], allows researchers to analyse, and classify facial expressions in a standardized framework. This system associates the action of the facial muscles to the changes in facial appearance. The basic metric of the FACS system are the AUs which are actions performed by a muscle or a group of muscles. Ekman also proposed the six basic emotions [26], also considered the six universal emotions – happiness, sadness, anger, surprise, fear, and disgust.

Additionally, OpenCV is also used due to its suitability and applicability in computer vision solutions.

Generally, some researches use machine learning techniques in order to infer the user emotional states [27]. Then, by using machine learning methods, for example Support Vector Machines (SVM) or k-Nearest Neighbours (k-NN), the attention patterns and the user facial expression will be recognized.

Once the patterns corresponding to distraction and emotional states are detected, the robot should trigger the corresponding action (robot prompt module) to acknowledge the emotion, to give reinforcement and, if necessary, to capture the user's attention again.

B. *Robot Behaviour*

The general procedure during an activity is: 1) ZECA greets the researcher and the user; 2) ZECA asks which activity shall be played; 3) The selected activity starts and continues until the experimenter decides to end it.

In the activity, the robot prompts a different behaviour accordingly to the results, the child attentiveness, and response. Thus, according to the classifier output, four conditions may occur:

- the user is attentive and answer to the robot prompt;
- the user is attentive but does not answer to the robot prompt;
- the user is distracted and does not answer to the robot prompt;
- the user is distracted but answer to the robot prompt.

In order to adapt the robot behaviour accordingly to the four different conditions mentioned, a state machine model is proposed [28].

After classification it is necessary to take an action, that is, if the robot classified the user as attentive, then it will continue the activity. Then, ZECA revises the patterns, so as to always know if the user is attentive. If it has previously considered the user inattentive, then it will trigger an action in order to capture the user's attention again.

At the end of the cycle, it is always checked if the activity is complete; if it is accomplished, the robot does not need to revise the defaults; if it is not, then the robot will have to continue to analyse the user defaults. Figure 3 depicts the general procedure that happens during an activity.

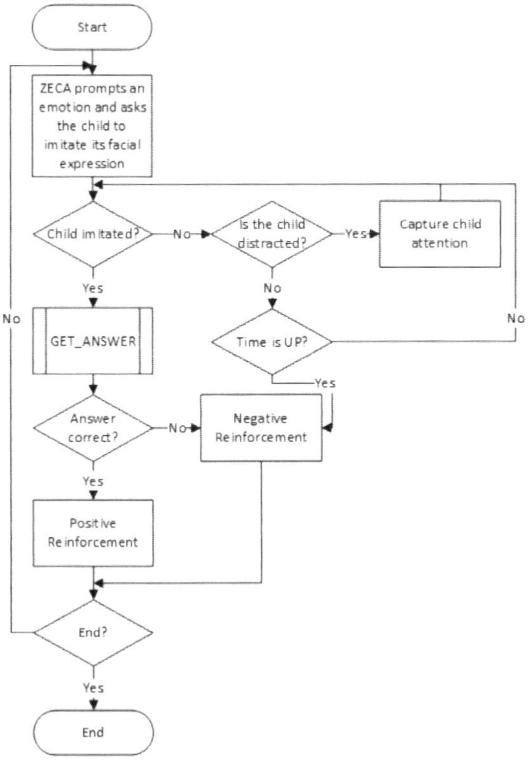

Figure 3. Robot behaviour flowchart.

IV. RESULTS AND DISCUSSION

In order to display the user's information and to monitor the activity, a Graphical User Interface (GUI) was developed. Figure 4 shows the GUI where the head pose angles (pitch, roll, and yaw), the number of blinks, the gaze estimation, the distance of the user to the camera, and the prediction of the classification model are displayed.

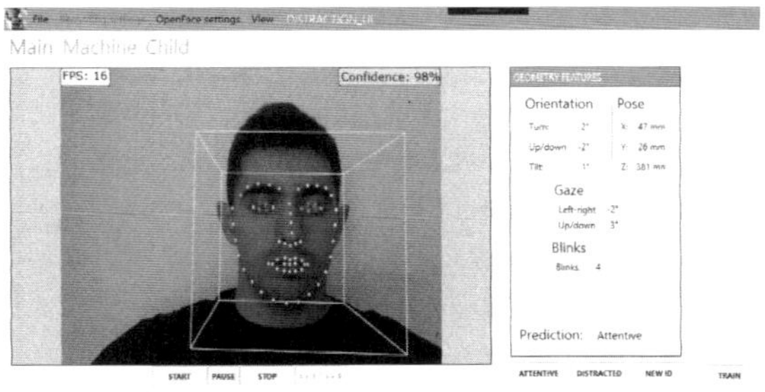

Figure 4. The GUI displaying the webcam feed, the user's eye gaze, the head pose, the number of blinks, the distance of the user to the camera, and the prediction of the classification model.

Several distraction and attention behaviours were simulated in a laboratorial environment, where the user sat in front of the camera. The corresponding patterns were stored in a training database (head pose, eye gaze, blink frequency, distance of the user to the camera). This database was built with six different subjects with 500 samples each. Then, with Accord [29], two classification methods, Gaussian SVM and k-NN [27], were used.

To test the robustness of the system a test database was created and tested with these two methods, in order to find out the best method for this type of classification. This new database was composed by three different subjects and with 100 samples each. The same patterns were stored in the test database (head pose, eye gaze, blink frequency, distance of the user to the camera).

Tables 1 and 2 represent the confusion matrix for the Gaussian SVM method with the two databases created.

TABLE I. CONFUSION MATRIX FOR GAUSSIAN SVM METHOD WITH TRAINING DATABASE.

Predicted Class	Actual Class	
	Attentive	*Distracted*
Attentive	81.0%	5.1%
Distracted	19.0%	94.9%

TABLE II. CONFUSION MATRIX FOR GAUSSIAN SVM METHOD WITH TEST DATABASE.

Predicted Class	Actual Class	
	Attentive	*Distracted*
Attentive	63.5%	0%
Distracted	36.5%	100%

By analysing Table 1, it is possible to see that the results are satisfactory, since the accuracy of the attentive and distracted classes are above 80%. Regarding the confusion matrix with the test database (Table 2), it is possible to see that the accuracy of the distracted class is 100%. Conversely, the accuracy of the attentive class has decreased. Although, in the test database (Table 2), the accuracy of the attentive class decreased, the distracted class accuracy increased, meaning that the system can accurately detect when the user is distracted which is the main goal of the proposed system.

In Tables 3 and 4, it is presented the confusion matrix for the k-NN method with the two databases created.

TABLE III. CONFUSION MATRIX FOR K-NN METHOD WITH TRAINING DATABASE.

Predicted Class	Actual Class	
	Attentive	*Distracted*
Attentive	100%	0%
Distracted	0%	100%

TABLE IV. CONFUSION MATRIX FOR K-NN METHOD WITH TEST DATABASE.

Predicted Class	Actual Class	
	Attentive	*Distracted*
Attentive	65.3%	2.8%
Distracted	34.7%	97.2%

Analysing Table 3, the k-NN performed better in the training step in comparison to the Gaussian SVM method. However, by analysing the performance of the k-NN method in with the test database (Table 4), the performance, in general, decreased.

Tables 5 and 6 present the values of accuracy, the Matthews Correlation Coefficient (MCC), the sensitivity, the specificity, the precision, and the Area Under the Curve (AUC) obtained with the Gaussian SVM and the k-NN methods for the training and test databases, respectively.

TABLE V. METRICS OBTAINED WITH THE GAUSSIAN SVM METHOD FOR THE TRAINING AND TEST DATABASES.

Metrics	**Database**	
	Training	***Test***
Accuracy	88.1%	80.3%
MCC	76.9%	66.6%
Sensitivity	81.0%	63.5%
Specificity	94.9%	100%
Precision	93.8%	100%
AUC	88.0%	81.8%

TABLE VI. METRICS OBTAINED WITH THE K-NN METHOD FOR THE TRAINING AND TEST DATABASES.

Metrics	**Database**	
	Training	***Test***
Accuracy	100%	79.9%
MCC	100%	64.7%
Sensitivity	100%	65.3%
Specificity	100%	97.2%
Precision	100%	96.5%
AUC	100%	81.3%

Analysing both Tables, it is possible to conclude that, in general, the SVM with the Gaussian kernel achieved better results with an accuracy of 80.3% when compared with the k-NN method (accuracy: 79.9%) with the test database. Although the k-NN method obtains excellent results with the training database, the same does not happen with the test database, having lower results in some of the metrics. The Gaussian SVM method, despite obtaining slightly lower results with the training database when compared to the k-NN, the overall performance is slightly better and more consistent than the k-NN method with the test database. Thus, in general, it can be concluded that the results obtained with the test database, using Gaussian SVM method, are overall better than when using the k-NN method.

As the Gaussian SVM trained model showed better results, it was used in a real-time laboratorial environment evaluation. The user sat in front of the camera and performed simulated behaviours, attentive and distracted. The system automatically classified the user state. Some of the results for different positions obtained using this method are shown in Figure 5.

V. CONCLUSION AND FUTURE WORK

The ability of concentrating on a task for an extended period of time is a paramount skill to develop. In general, when a person tries to reach a particular object, the observer's gaze arrives at the target before the action is completed. Thus, the predictive gaze provides the time for the observer to plan and execute an action towards a goal. During a social interaction, the predictive gaze and the attention span can be crucial elements, as they can help an individual to perceive the goals of the others.

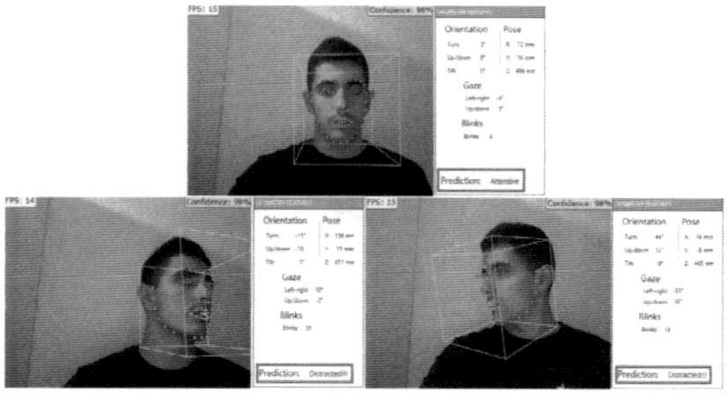

Figure 5. The GUI displaying the classification considering different poses (results using Gausian SVM method). The classifier output is presented in the interface (red rectangles).

However, some individuals present a low attention span, especially children with Autism Spectrum Disorder (ASD), and in general they attend less to faces than typically developing individuals.

Researches have been using robotic platforms for promoting social interaction with individuals with ASD. Furthermore, it has already been proven that the use of robots encourages the promotion of social interaction and skills lacking in children with ASD. However, most of these systems are controlled remotely and cannot adapt automatically to the situation. Even those who are more autonomous still cannot perceive whether or not the user is paying attention to the instructions and the actions of the robot. Additionally, some of these systems use an array of cameras and a hat with markers in order to infer the user gaze.

The present paper concerns the development of a framework to estimate the user/child affective states. The system is based on a camera to detect and follow the face and contours, and extract the user head orientation angles (yaw, pitch, and roll), eye gaze, action units, blinking frequency, and the distance between the user and the camera. It applies an algorithm based on Opencv functions and OpenFace library. Using the features extracted from the user, and a machine learning model (Gaussian SVM or k-NN) it is possible to recognize these patterns and classify the user as distracted or attentive.

In general, the method that registered a better accuracy was the SVM with the Gaussian kernel (accuracy: 80.3%); the k-NN method had slightly lower results (accuracy: 79.9%) both with the test database.

As future work, it is necessary to recognize these patterns (distraction and emotional states) during a triadic emotion imitation activity with children with ASD (child, researcher and robot ZECA), where the child facial expression is recognized through facial features in real-time. Robot behaviour will be constantly adapted taking into account child affective state. Through the use of a friendly interface, the teacher/therapist will be able to access the child's performance as well as to monitor the running intervention activity.

To accomplish this, the developed system is going to be evaluated in different scenarios in order to assess its performance. A first evaluation is going to be conducted in a school environment with typically developing children with the purpose of detecting the system constraints and to tune the conditions of the experimental scheme. After this first validation in a controlled environment, a second test should be developed in a real-world context with individuals with ASD.

ACKNOWLEDGEMENTS

The authors would like to express their acknowledgments to COMPETE: POCI-01-0145-FEDER-007043 and FCT – Fundação para a Ciência e Tecnologia within the Project Scope: UID/CEC/00319/2013. Vinicius Silva also thanks FCT for the PhD scholarship SFRH/BD/ SFRH/BD/133314/2017.

REFERENCES

[1] G. Gredebäck and T. Falck-Ytter, "Eye Movements During Action Observation.," Perspect. Psychol. Sci., vol. 10, no. 5, pp. 591–8, Sep. 2015.

[2] J. R. Flanagan and R. S. Johansson, "Action plans used in action observation," Nature, vol. 424, no. 6950, pp. 769–771, 2003.

[3] C. Chevallier et al., "Measuring social attention and motivation in autism spectrum disorder using eye-tracking: Stimulus type matters," Autism Res., vol. 8, no. 5, pp. 620–628, 2015.

[4] A. Klin, W. Jones, R. Schultz, F. Volkmar, and D. Cohen, "Visual fixation patterns during viewing of naturalistic social situations as predictors of social competence in individuals with autism," Arch. Gen. Psychiatry, vol. 59, no. 9, pp. 809–816, 2002.

[5] G. Dawson, S. J. Webb, and J. Mcpartland, "Understanding the Nature of Face Processing Impairment in Autism: Insights From Behavioral and Electrophysiological Studies," Dev. Neuropsychol., vol. 27, no. 3, pp. 403–424, 2005.

[6] A. Tapus, M. J. Mataric´, and B. Scassellati, "The grand challenges in socially assistive robotics," IEEE Robot. Autom. Mag., vol. 14, no. 1, pp. 35–42, 2007.

[7] E. S. Kim, R. Paul, F. Shic, and B. Scassellati, "Bridging the Research Gap: Making HRI Useful to Individuals with Autism," J. Human-Robot Interact., vol. 1, no. 1, pp. 26–54, 2012.

[8] I. Fujimoto, T. Matsumoto, P. R. S. de Silva, M. Kobayashi, and M. Higashi, "Mimicking and evaluating human motion to improve the imitation skill of children with autism through a robot," Int. J. Soc. Robot., vol. 3, no. 4, pp. 349–357, 2011.

[9] D. J. Ricks and M. B. Colton, "Trends and considerations in robot-assisted autism therapy," in 2010 IEEE International Conference on Robotics and Automation, 2010, pp. 4354–4359.

[10] K. Dautenhahn, "Design issues on interactive environments for children with autism.," 3Th Int. Conf. Disabil. ,Virtual Real. Assoc. Technol., pp. 153–162, 2000.

[11] P. Chevalier et al., "Dialogue Design for a Robot-Based Face-Mirroring Game to Engage Autistic Children with Emotional Expressions," in Lecture Notes in Computer Science (including subseries Lecture Notes in Artificial Intelligence and Lecture Notes in Bioinformatics), 2017, vol. 10652 LNAI, pp. 546–555.

[12] S. C. C. Costa, "Affective robotics for socio-emotional development in children with autism spectrum disorders," Oct. 2014.

[13] E. S. Kim et al., "Social Robots as Embedded Reinforcers of Social Behavior in Children with Autism," J. Autism Dev. Disord., vol. 43, no. 5, pp. 1038–1049, May 2013.

[14] F. Michaud et al., "Autonomous Spherical Mobile Robot for Child-Development Studies," IEEE Trans. Syst. Man, Cybern. - Part A Syst. Humans, vol. 35, no. 4, pp. 471–480, Jul. 2005.

[15] M. Begum et al., "Measuring the Efficacy of Robots in Autism Therapy," in Proceedings of the Tenth Annual ACM/IEEE International Conference on Human-Robot Interaction - HRI '15, 2015, pp. 335–342.

[16] P. Pennisi et al., "Autism and social robotics: A systematic review," Autism Research, vol. 9, no. 2. pp. 165–183, 2016.

[17] B. Robins, K. Dautenhahn, and P. Dickerson, "From Isolation to Communication: A Case Study Evaluation of Robot Assisted Play for Children with Autism with a Minimally Expressive Humanoid Robot," in 2009 Second International Conferences on Advances in Computer-Human Interactions, 2009, pp. 205–211.

[18] S. Costa, H. Lehmann, K. Dautenhahn, B. Robins, and F. Soares, "Using a Humanoid Robot to Elicit Body Awareness and Appropriate Physical Interaction in Children with Autism," Int. J. Soc. Robot., vol. 7, no. 2, pp. 265–278, Apr. 2015.

[19] D. Mazzei et al., "Development and evaluation of a social robot platform for therapy in autism," in 2011 Annual International Conference of the IEEE Engineering in Medicine and Biology Society, 2011, pp. 4515–4518.

[20] E. T. Bekele et al., "A step towards developing adaptive robot-mediated intervention architecture (ARIA) for children with autism," IEEE Trans. Neural Syst. Rehabil. Eng., vol. 21, no. 2, pp. 289–299, 2013.

[21] E. Bekele, J. A. Crittendon, A. Swanson, N. Sarkar, and Z. E. Warren, "Pilot clinical application of an adaptive robotic system for young children with autism.," Autism, vol. 18, no. 5, pp. 598–608, Jul. 2014.

[22] T. Baltrušaitis, P. Robinson, and L. P. Morency, "Constrained local neural fields for robust facial landmark detection in the wild," in Proceedings of the IEEE International Conference on Computer Vision, 2013, pp. 354–361.

[23] T. Baltrusaitis, P. Robinson, and L. P. Morency, "OpenFace: An open source facial behavior analysis toolkit," in 2016 IEEE Winter Conference on Applications of Computer Vision, WACV 2016, 2016.

[24] T. Baltrusaitis, M. Mahmoud, and P. Robinson, "Cross-dataset learning and person-specific normalisation for automatic Action Unit detection," in 2015 11th IEEE International Conference and Workshops on Automatic Face and Gesture Recognition (FG), 2015, pp. 1–6.

[25] E. Wood et al., "Rendering of Eyes for Eye-Shape Registration and Gaze Estimation," in 2015 IEEE International Conference on Computer Vision (ICCV), 2015, pp. 3756–3764.

[26] P. Ekman and W. V. Friesen, "Facial Action Coding System: A Technique for the Measurement of Facial Movement," in Consulting Psychologists Press, 1978.

[27] V. Silva et al., "Real-time emotions recognition system," in 2016 8th International Congress on Ultra Modern Telecommunications and Control Systems and Workshops (ICUMT), 2016, pp. 201–206.

[28] B. Amaro, V. Silva, F. Soares, and J. S. Esteves, "Building a Behaviour Architecture: An Approach for Promoting Human-Robot Interaction," in Lecture Notes in Electrical Engineering, Guimarães: Springer, Cham, 2019, pp. 39–45.

[29] "Accord.NET Machine Learning Framework." [Online]. Available: http://accord-framework.net/. [Accessed: 14-Jul-2018].

Serious Games Assisted By Playware As A Way To Improve Socio-Emotional Skills In Children With Autism Spectrum Disorder

José Azevedo[1], Vinicius Silva[2]
[1]Dept. of Industrial Electronics
[2]Algoritmi Research Centre
University of Minho
Guimarães, Portugal
[email: a70448, a65312]@alunos.uminho.pt

Filomena Soares[1,2], João Sena Esteves[1,2], and Ana Paula Pereira[3]
[3]Research Centre on Education, Institute of Education, University of Minho
Braga, Portugal
[email: fsoares, sena]@dei.uminho.pt, appereira@ie.uminho.pt

***Abstract*—This paper presents a project developed with the aim of promoting emotional skills in children with Autism Spectrum Disorders (ASD). The project involves a serious game and a playware object, which is a physical component that allows the user to interactively play the serious game. The playware object has six buttons, each one showing an emoji with a specific facial expression and communicates via Bluetooth with the serious game app installed in an Android device. The facial expressions used are: happiness, sadness, fear, anger, surprise and neutral/normal. They were applied to the three game activities (imitation, recognition and storytelling). The chain of tests started with an online questionnaire to validate the avatars created to represent the previously mentioned facial expressions in the game, which was followed by a usability test of the application (serious game and playware object) with six typically developing children. Finally, the three game activities were tested with six children with ASD in three/four sessions. Due to the small test group and reduced number of sessions, the primary objective was to assess if the target group accepted the application. In fact, it had a high level of approval regarding both the serious game and the playware object.**

Keywords - Serious Games; Playware; Autism Spectrum Disorder; Emotions.

I. INTRODUCTION

Humans are social by nature. Every interaction is emphasized by the participants' emotions, which are constantly present during their lives. Being unable of "reading" the emotional state of their peers is a very significant deficit for anyone. This is the situation in which children with Autism Spectrum Disorder (ASD) usually find themselves in, since they struggle with emotions interpretation, replication and control. This fact is present throughout their lives but may have a reduced effect if the subject undergoes behavioural intervention and/or receives specialized education.

Several works have been developed in areas, such as robotics and software engineering, in the form of serious games [1]–[6], playware technology [7]–[11] and robots [12]–[19], among others, with the aim of facilitating the assimilation and improvement of emotional skills by children with ASD.

Playware is the term attributed to the use of intelligent technology that aims at producing playful experiences by combining the use of both hardware and software [7].

This project integrates playware and serious games with the objective of delivering an interactive and appellative serious game to the user, allowing him/her to improve his/her socio-emotional skills.

This article is divided into four sections: Section 2 addresses the application, presenting the playware object and the serious game, Section 3 focus on the obtained results and Section 4 presents the concluding thoughts.

II. THE APPLICATION

The application is composed of a serious game and a playware object. The goal was creating a serious game to deliver the information in a "*funny*" way. A playware object was added with the aim of making the game even more attractive and interactive, working as a reinforcement.

A. Playware Object

A playware object was created for this project to act as the intermediary between the user and the Android device (Fig. 1).

Figure 1. The playware object that acts as the game controller

The style chosen for the playware was a panel of six buttons, which is simple, making it easy to assimilate information, acting as an intuitive controller. Furthermore, the fact that all six buttons are visible at once facilitates the task of going through the facial expressions available to choose from and decide upon the one that the user finds more appropriate.

The playware object integrates a microcontroller, which detects which button was pressed and sends the respective signal to the serious game wirelessly through a Bluetooth module.

B. *Serious Game*

The serious game is the core of the application, because it is where all the information is centred. It was developed for Android and, during the test phase, it was played in an Android tablet. Upon the start, the serious game opens the main screen, i.e., the menu (Fig. 2, in Portuguese). From the menu, the user can choose one of the three game modes to play (imitation, recognition or storytelling), access the options menu (to adjust the volume, start the Bluetooth connection or access the scoreboard) or quit the game.

Figure 2. The serious game main menu (in Portuguese) – Imitation, Recognition, Storytelling and Options buttons respectively.

Visually, the serious game has a very simplistic and clean design, not only in the main menu, but also throughout the game itself, so the users' attention will not change its focus towards unnecessary features.

Note that the chosen game language is Portuguese, due to the target group.

1) *Imitation game mode*

In this game mode, several different facial expressions displayed by the avatar are presented to the user, one at a time. After stating what emotion is being displayed, the user him/herself replicates that emotion. This set of instructions is given to the user in a pre-game screen, designed for this purpose.

The game is played side by side with a therapist/teacher that acts as a reinforcement to motivate the user to show the facial expression that matches each emotion. This agent has also the role of evaluating if the correct facial expression is replicated and sending the respective feedback to the serious game.

2) *Recognition game mode*

The instruction screen tells the user how to perform this game mode, which he/she does using the playware object.

The same set of images (avatars) is presented to the player, but the task is different. In this case, the user looks at the display, identifies the emotion that the avatar is portraying and chooses the emoji present in the playware object that more accurately shows that emotion.

3) *Storytelling game mode*

This is the hardest of all three game activities. Throughout the exhibition of 15 images, each displaying a unique scenario with its own narrative, the user listens to the story and, at the end, he/she is prompted to tell what emotion the main character was feeling in that specific situation.

The answer is transmitted to the serious game in the same manner used in the recognition game mode, i.e., by the user, through the playware object.

III. Results

The first test that was performed had the objective of validating the avatars (Fig. 3) that were created to represent each of the six previously mentioned facial expressions. This was possible to achieve due to an on-line questionnaire that was developed for this purpose. After 114 submissions, all avatars had an accuracy of over 90% for the emotion that they meant to portrait. The values were: fear – 94.7%, surprise – 93%, neutral – 95.6%, happiness – 99.1%, sadness – 98.2% and anger – 99.1%.

A usability test of the application was then performed with six typically developing children that were asked to look at the avatars and say what emotion they were representing. After, they looked at the emojis and chose the one that they felt matched that emotion.

It is worth to point out that only two of the six children did not answer correctly to all questions (each failed one emotion).

Figure 3. Avatars used in the serious game

The last round of tests was performed over the course of a maximum of four sessions with children with ASD, with ages ranging between 6 to 10 years old, where data was saved considering the time they took to answer and if that answer was correct or not. For the purpose of anonymity, the children will be referred as subject 1 to 6 (or S1 to S6).

A. *Subject 1*

The teachers considered that the two activities, recognize and imitate facial expressions, would be easy for Subject 1. On the other hand, the storytelling game would be challenging for her.

In fact, as it is visible in Figures 4 to 6, both the imitation activity, as well as the recognition activity were executed flawlessly, and it is possible to see a significant increase in the percentage of correct answers between both sessions for the storytelling game mode.

It is to note that subject 1 was highly participative and stated that she enjoyed these activities very much.

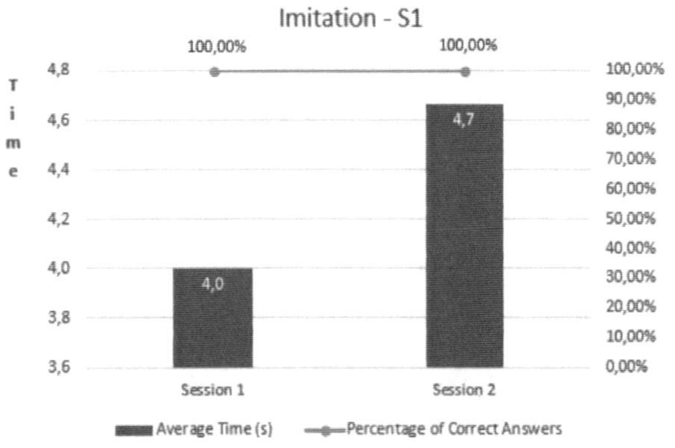

Figure 4. Results for the imitation activity from S1

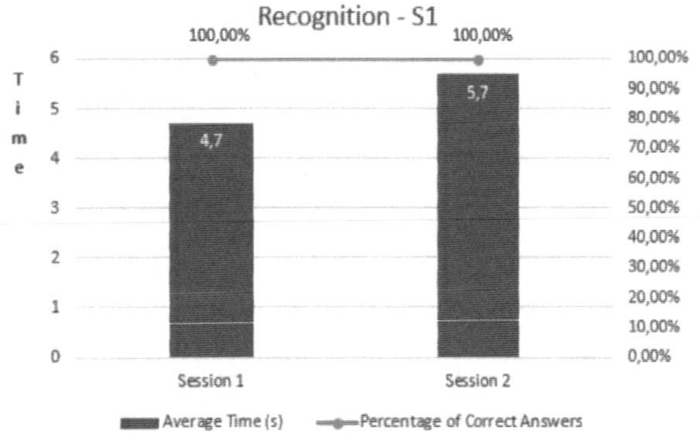

Figure 5. Results for the recognition activity from S1

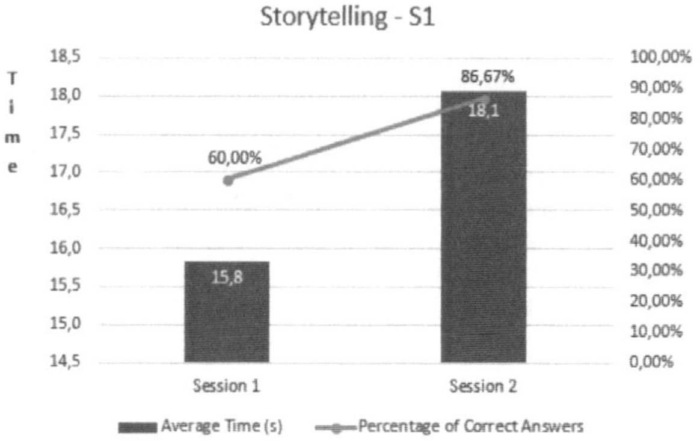

Figure 6. Results for the storytelling activity from S1

B. *Subject 2*

Subject 2 demonstrated a good understanding of the game and it is clearly visible the improvement in both time and percentage of correct answers for the recognition activity (Fig. 7).

The imitation game mode was slightly more difficult, but S2 was able to identify emotions and replicate them, for the most part (Fig. 8).

The storytelling activity was by far the hardest (Fig. 9), which was expected. It should also be mentioned that even though the number of correct answers for this game mode improved in the second session, the therapist needed to be more interventive, which did not happen for the two other game modes, in any of the sessions.

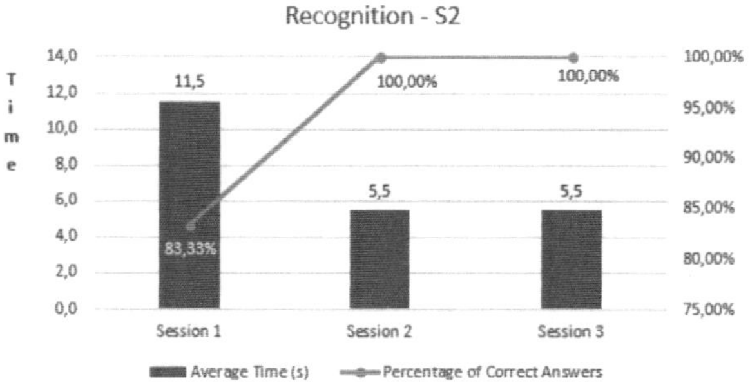

Figure 7. Results for the recognition activity from S2

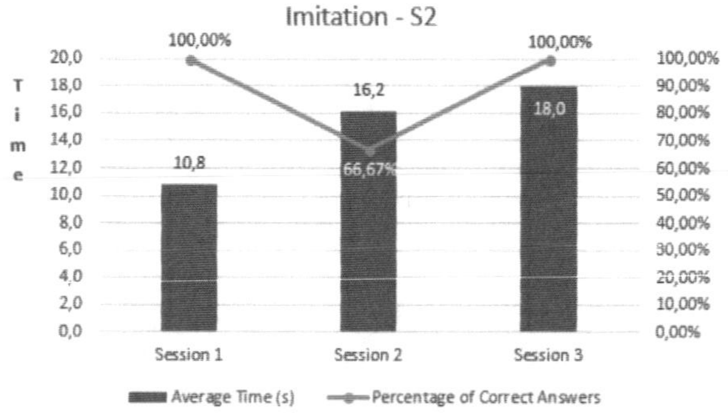

Figure 8. Results for the imitation activity from S2

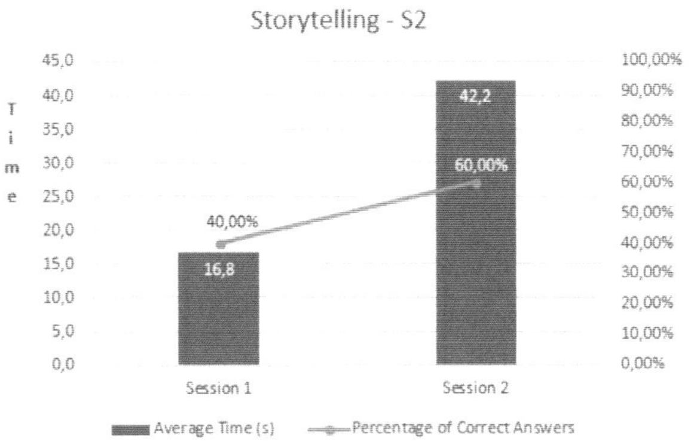

Figure 9. Results for the storytelling activity from S2

C. Subject 3

This child had already studied emotions before and was very participative, which contributed to the good performance demonstrated and visible in Figures 10 to 12. The main issue was the "fear" of giving wrong answers, something that was more present in the last sessions and even led him to quit the activity.

Improvements are very visible, especially in the first two game modes.

The storytelling activity is a particular case, because the data gathered from session 1 is only regarding seven answers. Subject 3 quit the activity at that point and only completed all the fifteen stories on the second session.

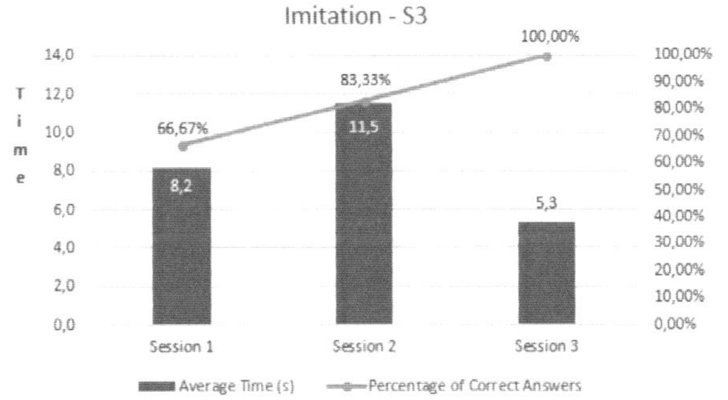

Figure 10. Results for the imitation activity from S3

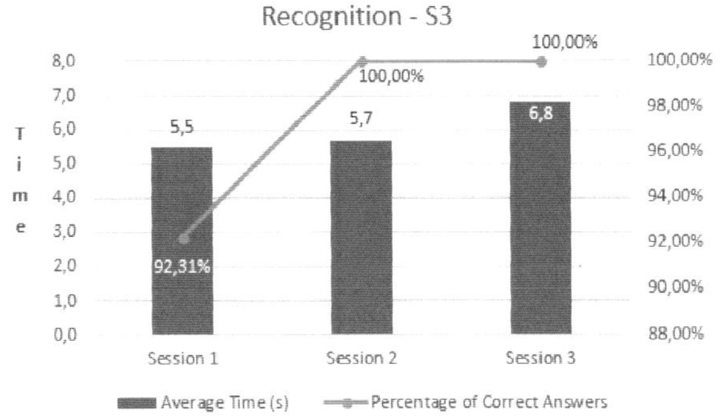

Figure 11. Results for the recognition activity from S3

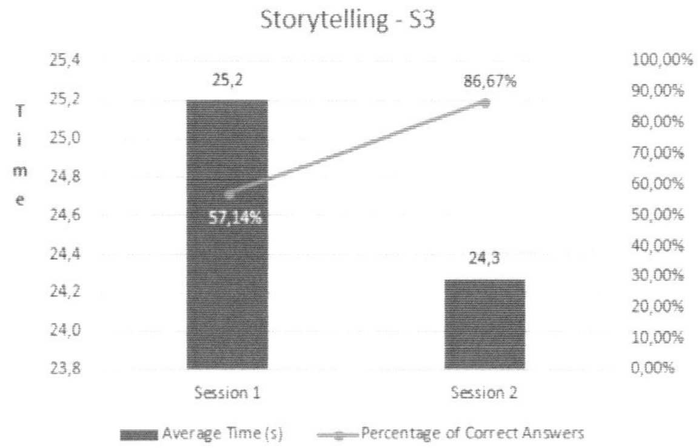

Figure 12. Results for the storytelling activity from S3

D. Subject 4

Subject 4 was very young and had a lot of difficulties playing the game in a correct manner.

Most of the time he was distracted, focusing on the screen of the Android device and trying to touch the avatar face. He could not replicate emotions and did not show any interest in doing so, which led that activity to fail completely.

The recognition game mode followed similar steps. The therapist had to intervene in the session trying to obtain an answer from the child, which was almost always the wrong one.

Since both the imitation and the recognition activities were unsuccessful, the conclusion was that there was no point in keep trying during further sessions, because he would not engage in the activity, due to the lack of attention demonstrated.

E. Subject 5

This child was very participative and autonomous, stating more than once that the game was interesting and funny to play.

Her main difficulty was interpreting emotions, especially when those emotions were shown by the emojis.

In the imitation game mode, she had an easier time replicating the facial expressions than identifying emotions (Fig. 13).

Similarly to the imitation activity, the recognition game was played during all four sessions. The results are visible in Fig.14 and show an improvement in the number of correct answers, even though interlinked with an increase in response time.

The storytelling activity was the one where she showed more difficulties (Fig. 15), what was expected since she would have to interpret specific situations and have a deeper knowledge regarding emotions.

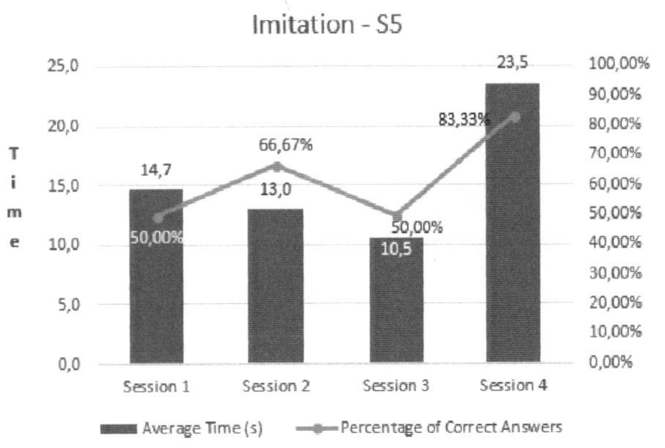

Figure 13. Results for the imitation activity from S5

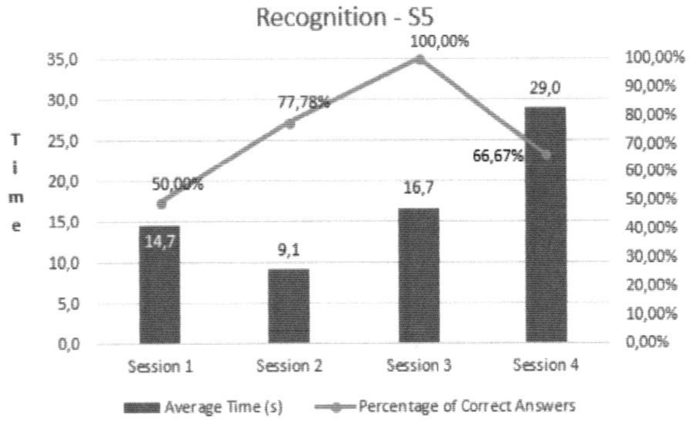

Figure 14. Results for the recognition activity from S5

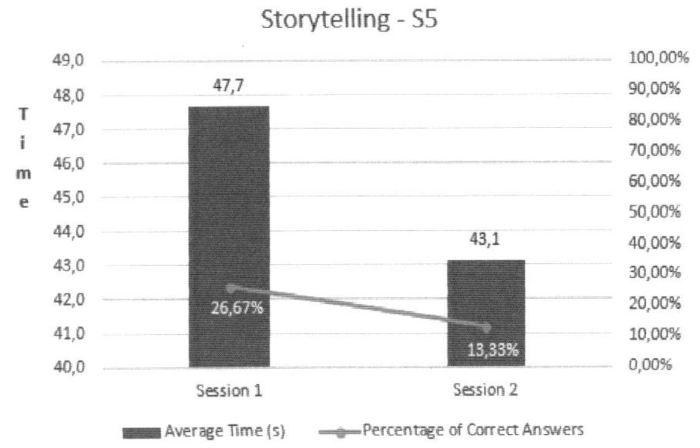

Figure 15. Results for the storytelling activity from S5

F. *Subject 6*

No data was gathered regarding subject 6 because he did not engage in the activity at all.

The lack of attention was the main issue. This child went into the room and shifted his focus between everyone and everything around him. Furthermore, he could not understand the game or even pay attention to the application long enough to start playing.

IV. CONCLUSIONS

This paper presented the work developed using a serious game and a playware object, aimed at improving the socio-emotional skills of children with ASD. The main goal was to determine if this application would be well accepted by the target group and its impact in teaching and/or facilitating the learning of emotions.

After testing it first with six typically developing children and later with six children with ASD (these ones during four sessions), it was noticeable that both the playware and the serious game are intuitive, attractive, and easy to use. The entire application was well received and even though the sample size was too small, improvements were visible, indicating that this type of tool could act as a mediator in the learning of emotional skills.

Future work with the application will be based on more testing, with a larger group and over a larger period. This type of testing allows for a better support and provides more reliability to the results and respective conclusions, consequently determining if this type of tool really acts as a facilitator in the learning of social skills. There is also a high possibility of integrating this application with other works developed by the group Robótica-Autismo (http://robotica-autismo.dei.uminho.pt/) which would involve humanoid robots like ZECA [15]

ACKNOWLEDGMENTS

The authors would like to express their acknowledgments to COMPETE: POCI-01-0145-FEDER-007043 and FCT – Fundação para a Ciência e Tecnologia within the Project Scope: UID/CEC/00319/2013. Vinicius Silva also thanks FCT for the PhD scholarship SFRH/BD/ SFRH/BD/133314/2017. The authors thank the teachers and students of the Elementary School of Gualtar (EB1/JI Gualtar) in Braga for the participation in the tests.

REFERENCES

[1] H. Noor, F. Shahbodin, and N. Pee, "Serious game for autism children: review of literature," *World Acad. Sci.*, vol. 6, no. 4, pp. 554–559, 2012.

[2] A. Z. Hassan *et al.*, "Developing the concept of money by interactive computer games for autistic children," *Proc. - 2011 IEEE Int. Multimedia, ISM 2011*, pp. 559–564, 2011.

[3] A. Anwar, M. M. Rahman, S. M. Ferdous, S. A. Anik, and S. I. Ahmed, "A computer game based approach for increasing fluency in the speech of the autistic children," *Proc. 2011 11th IEEE Int. Conf. Adv. Learn. Technol. ICALT 2011*, pp. 17–18, 2011.

[4] M. Frutos, I. Bustos, B. G. Zapirain, and A. M. Zorrilla, "Computer game to learn and enhance speech problems for children with autism," *Proc. CGAMES'2011 USA - 16th Int. Conf. Comput. Games AI, Animat. Mobile, Interact. Multimedia, Educ. Serious Games*, pp. 209–216, 2011.

[5] S. Bernardini, K. Porayska-Pomsta, and T. J. Smith, "ECHOES: An intelligent serious game for fostering social communication in children with autism," *Inf. Sci. (Ny).*, vol. 264, pp. 41–60, 2014.

[6] Z. S. S. De Urturi, A. M. M. Zorrilla, and B. G. B. G. Zapirain, "Serious Game based on first aid education for individuals with Autism Spectrum Disorder (ASD) using

android mobile devices," *Proc. CGAMES'2011 USA - 16th Int. Conf. Comput. Games AI, Animat. Mobile, Interact. Multimedia, Educ. Serious Games*, pp. 223–227, 2011.

[7] H. H. Lund, T. Klitbo, and C. Jessen, "Playware technology for physically activating play," *Artif. Life Robot.*, vol. 9, no. 4, pp. 165–174, 2005.

[8] G. N. Yannakakis, O. M, J. Hallam, and H. H. Lund, "Comparative Fun Analysis in the Innovative Playware Game Platform," *Proc. 1st World Conf. Fun 'n Games*, pp. 64–70, 2006.

[9] H. H. Lund and P. Marti, "Designing modular robotic playware," *Proc. - IEEE Int. Work. Robot Hum. Interact. Commun.*, pp. 115–121, 2009.

[10] H. H. Lund, L. S. D. Jensen, Y. Ssessanga, S. Cataldo, and K. I. Yahya-Malima, "An approach for a national eHealth implementation - The case of modular interactive tiles for rehabilitation," *2015 IST-Africa Conf. IST-Africa 2015*, pp. 1–10, 2015.

[11] K. Suzuki, "Social Playware: Device-mediated social interaction for therapeutic activities," *Proc. - IEEE Int. Work. Robot Hum. Interact. Commun.*, vol. 2014–Octob, no. October, pp. 69–72, 2014.

[12] S. Costa, F. Soares, and C. Santos, "Facial expressions and gestures to convey emotions with a humanoid robot," *Lect. Notes Comput. Sci. (including Subser. Lect. Notes Artif. Intell. Lect. Notes Bioinformatics)*, vol. 8239 LNAI, pp. 542–551, 2013.

[13] H. Kozima, M. P. Michalowski, and C. Nakagawa, "Keepon: A playful robot for research, therapy, and entertainment," *Int. J. Soc. Robot.*, vol. 1, no. 1, pp. 3–18, 2009.

[14] B. Vanderborght *et al.*, "Using the social robot probo as a social story telling agent for children with ASD," *Interact. Stud.*, vol. 13, no. 3, pp. 348–372, 2012.

[15] S. Costa, F. Soares, A. P. Pereira, C. Santos, and A. Hiolle, "A pilot study using imitation and storytelling scenarios as activities for labelling emotions by children with autism using a humanoid robot," *IEEE ICDL-EPIROB 2014 - 4th Jt. IEEE Int. Conf. Dev. Learn. Epigenetic Robot.*, pp. 299–304, 2014.

[16] P. Chevalier *et al.*, "Dialogue Design for a Robot-Based Face-Mirroring Game to Engage Autistic Children with Emotional Expressions ", "Social Robotics," vol. 7621, 4th International Conference, ICSR 2012, Chengdu, China, October 29-31, 2012., pp. 546–555, 2012.

[17] "Aims & Objectives – DE-ENIGMA." [Online]. Available: http://de-enigma.eu/features/aims-objectives/. [Retrieved: Feb,2018].

[18] A. Ghorbandaei Pour, A. Taheri, M. Alemi, and A. Meghdari, "Human–Robot Facial Expression Reciprocal Interaction Platform: Case Studies on Children with Autism," *Int. J. Soc. Robot.*, pp. 179-198, 2018.

[19] D. O. David, C. A. Costescu, S. Matu, A. Szentagotai, and A. Dobrean, "Developing Joint Attention for Children with Autism in Robot-Enhanced Therapy," *Int. J. Soc. Robot.*, pp. 1-11, 2018.

Real-Time Gesture Classification for Monitoring Elderly Physical Activity Using a Wireless Wearable Device

Alexandre Calado[1], Pedro Leite[1], Filomena Soares[1], Paulo Novais[1] and Pedro Arezes[1]
[1]Algoritmi Centre, University of Minho
Guimarães, Portugal
e-mail: alexandreluiscalado@gmail.com, a66161@alunos.uminho.pt, fsoares@dei.uminho.pt, pjon@di.uminho.pt, parezes@dps.uminho.pt

Filipe Sousa[2] and Joana Silva[2]
[2]Fraunhofer Portugal Research Centre,
Porto, Portugal
e-mail: filipe.sousa@fraunhofer.pt, joana.silva@fraunhofer.pt

***Abstract*—Gestures are part of communication between humans, however, they can also have an important role to play for improving human-machine interaction. Moreover, gesture recognition can have relevant applications for activity monitoring in older adults. This paper proposes the use of the Pandlet (a wearable wireless device that features a 3-axis accelerometer, gyroscope and magnetometer) for the recognition of two distinct throwing movements performed in the Boccia game. The results from this paper will be inserted into the iBoccia framework, created with the aim of monitoring and promoting physical activity on the elderly by playing the game of Boccia. The recognition of throwing gestures shall allow a caregiver to follow the performance of the elder throughout the game and the force associated with each throw, which can be important for identifying muscular diseases. Furthermore, it can be used for the elders to interact with a user interface that displays the current game score. To achieve the goal proposed by this paper, a Support Vector Machine (SVM) was trained with data extracted from eight subjects regarding two types of throws used in the Boccia game and movements performed when the player is not playing. The trained model was afterwards implemented for real-time classification and tested on four subjects. Overall, the average test accuracy was of 75±8%. These results show that the model is able to successfully recognize different throwing gestures and encourages its use on the iBoccia framework.**

Keywords-Gesture Recognition; Activity Monitoring; SVM; Boccia

I. INTRODUCTION

Gestures are an essential part of general human interaction. Whether it involves physical movements of the fingers, hands, arms, head or any other part of the body, gestures are usually performed with the intent of conveying important information to the interlocutor or interacting with the surrounding environment [1].

Gesture recognition can also be used for further improving human-machine interaction. The current trend of applications based on virtual reality demands a more suitable type of interaction that traditional devices, such as mouse and keyboard, cannot cope with [2]. Moreover, it can have an important role to play in a wide range of applications, such as sign language recognition [3], improve airport security [4] and various health applications, such as physical rehabilitation in individuals with motor disabilities [5] or the diagnosis of neurological disorders [6]. However, the focus of this paper will fall on elderly activity monitoring.

The work described by this paper is based on the exploitation of machine learning algorithms for detecting, in real-time, different types of ball-throwing movements performed by elders during a Boccia game. This is intended to be the follow up of previous work [7] and the obtained algorithm will be posteriorly annexed to the iBoccia framework [8][9]. This framework was created with the purpose of monitoring the bio-signals of the elders while they play Boccia, simultaneously motivating them to practice physical activity by enhancing the overall game experience. It comprehends an User Interface (UI) that displays, to the elders, the score of the game in real-time through the use of a computer vision algorithm [10][11] and an UI designed for the caregivers. In the latter, it is possible to keep track of information related with the heartbeat, stress levels and game performance from each of the players throughout several games. The data necessary is acquired using various sensors non-wearable and wearable sensors, including the Pandlet [12], a wireless wearable device developed by Fraunhofer.

In the present paper, this device was used to extract inertial data from various subjects and train a multiclass Support Vector Machine (SVM) model. The trained model was afterwards used for classifying data obtained from the Pandlet in real-time. For this task, three distinct classes were considered: underarm throw, overarm throw and a class dedicated to all the movements performed by the player different from the latter.

Considering the aforementioned remarks, recognizing the players' throwing movements would make possible for the caregiver to identify what type of throws the elder executed throughout the game, along with the force applied in each throw, which is easily computed from the accelerometer data. Most importantly, posterior analysis of this data could allow the caregiver to observe the evolution of the throwing force over time, which could help identifying potential muscular diseases that often occur at an old age.

This paper is structured as follows. Section II presents a brief literature review regarding gesture recognition and activity monitoring in old adults. Section III describes the used methodology for training and testing the SVM model and section IV displays the attained results. Finally, Section V addresses the final remarks and future work.

II. Literature Review

Currently there are three main approaches for gesture recognition: vision based without markers [13][14], using coloured markers [15][16] and using wireless devices integrating inertial sensors, such as the Pandlet. Considering the latter, Hidden Markov Models (HMM) have been frequently used in various works related with gesture recognition. Positive outcomes have been obtained using this model. For instance, Schlömer *et al.* [17] employed a Wii-controller for the recognition of five gestures. The average accuracy was of 90%. On the other hand, Wilson *et al.* [18], compared HMM with Linear Time Warping (LTW) and Dynamic Time Warping methods (DTW), by means of accuracy, for evaluating the classification of seven gestures using a wireless device with inertial sensors. The results showed that HMM proved to be the best approach, achieving an accuracy of 90.43%. Despite HMM's popularity in this type of applications, various other approaches have been explored regarding classification strategies including the use of Artificial Neural Networks (ANN) [19] and SVM [20], which also produced accurate results. Previous work [7] included the use of the latter with a DTW kernel for the offline classification of the overarm and underarm Boccia throwing movements. The accuracies obtained with the data extracted from the Pandlet were, however, shadowed by the accuracies obtained using the Kinect (66.7% and 80%, respectively).

There are five main groups of activity monitoring technology in the elderly [21]: passive infrared sensors, body-worn sensors, video monitoring, sound recognition and multicomponent approaches. Regarding body-worn sensors, the works found in the literature mainly focus on recognizing daily activities performed by the elderly in order to assess their health status [22], based on the premise that mobility is a good health indicator. Najafi *et al.* [23] used a kinematic sensor attached to the chest to detect sitting, standing and lying body positions, along with periods of walking and postural transitions.

Due to the decline of muscular strength, which is characteristic of old age, it is also essential to detect falls, which can be also found abundantly in the literature [24], [25]. For instance, Kang *et al.* [26] used a single 3-axis accelerometer placed on the subject's waist to recognize, besides daily activities as seen in Najafi *et al.*, an emergency state such as a falling situation. This system was tested on five healthy young subjects and the attained detection rate was of 96%.

To the best of the authors' knowledge, no other works regarding the use of gesture recognition applied to Boccia were found in the literature. However, some studies were performed regarding the kinematic analysis of the throwing movement in individuals with cerebral palsy [27][28].

III. Methods

This section addresses the used methodology for acquiring data with the Pandlet, along with a brief description about this device. This is followed by the strategies used for feature selection and training of an SVM. Finally, the used approach for testing the model is described.

A. The Pandlet

As stated in Section 1 of this paper, the Pandlet is a wireless wearable device developed by Fraunhofer. It can be placed on the individual's wrist as an armbrace and embodies a 3-axis accelerometer, gyroscope and magnetometer, enabling the tracking of the user's movements. It also features an Application Programming Interface (API), which allows the communication via Bluetooth with Windows, Linux and Android platforms.

For the purpose of this paper, a 50 Hz sampling was enabled. Furthermore, a total of sixteen attributes were extracted in each acquisition: the orientation, in Euler angles (pitch, yaw and roll) and quaternions, along with the values from the accelerometer, gyroscope and magnetometer for each axis.

B. Data Acquisition

Two throwing gestures were considered, the overarm throw and the underarm throw, which are both depicted in Fig. 1. During a game of Boccia, these gestures are typically used by the player with the intention of hitting the target ball, which is called the *jack* [29].

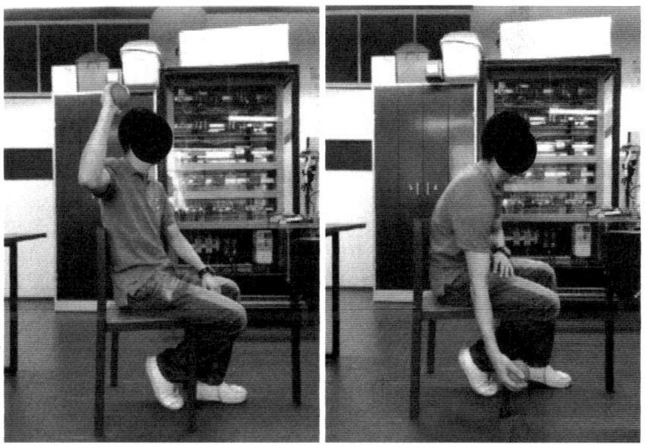

Figure 1. On the left: the overarm throw; On the right: the underarm throw

Eight subjects with 24±1 years of age were selected for the task at hand. Since the elders from the nursing home where the final system will be tested play while sitting, the subjects were asked to sit in a chair. The Pandlet was afterwards placed in the subject's right wrist.

A ball, used to act as the *jack,* was placed about 8 meters away from the sitting subject. The subject was then asked to throw the ball using the underarm throw fifty times and using the overhand throw another fifty times, always with the intent of hitting the *jack* and using the right arm. Every throwing movement was recorded for 2 seconds, immediately after the subject was given a signal to start. Thus, fifty recordings of each movement were obtained for each of the subjects. Moreover, in between the execution of the throws, the natural movements of the player would be recorded. Much like the other classes, fifty recordings of 2 seconds were performed. This was done so that the algorithm could recognize when the user is not currently playing. Overall, a total of 1200 recordings were performed.

C. Training the Model

Regarding the training of the model, ten of the attributes were considered: the orientation in quaternions, plus the acceleration and angular speed for each axis. The 1200 data windows with 2 seconds of length were afterwards used to train, without any further feature extraction, a multi-class SVM with a linear Kernel and Sequential Minimal Optimization (SMO) learning. The decision of using an SVM was based on previous work [7]. Besides, according to the literature, good results have been obtained using an SVM for gesture recognition with wireless devices [30][31][32].

The training of the SVM and its subsequent real-time implementation were performed by using the Accord.NET framework [33]. This framework offers multiple applications for scientific computing in .NET, such as statistical data processing, machine learning and pattern recognition. Moreover, it features a wide selection of classifiers, kernel functions, performance measuring techniques and hypothesis tests.

D. Testing the Model

The training of the model was followed by its real-time implementation. For classification purposes, windows with 2 seconds of length were used with no overlapping.

Testing protocol was similar to what was described in subsection B. In total, four subjects with 24.5±1.0 years of age participated in the test. The subjects selected for testing were different from the ones selected for data acquisition. This was done to test the system's robustness and avoid influence from overfitting.

The subject was invited to sit on a chair and the Pandlet was placed on his/her right wrist. Afterwards he/she was told to execute all throwing movements with the right arm.

Twenty balls were given to the subject and the *jack* was placed about 8 meters in front of him/her. The subject was then asked to throw ten of the twenty balls using the overarm throw movement and the remaining ten using the underarm throw movement, always with intent of hitting the jack. The obtained results are presented in the following section.

IV. RESULTS

Table I presents the average recognition accuracy confusion matrix, considering the computed results from all the subjects during testing. Class A refers to the underarm throw, B to the overarm throw and C to any movement that differs from a throw. All percentages refer to accuracy.

TABLE I. AVERAGE RECOGNITION ACCURACY CONFUSION MATRIX

		Predicted Classes		
		A	*B*	*C*
Actual Classes	*A*	80%	-	20%
	B	-	70%	30%

For evaluation purposes, the classifier's output was only considered when throwing movements were executed by the subject. Thus, each time the subject performed a throw, the output label was noted.

As it can be observed in Table I, during testing, the model did not mislabel any underarm throw as an overarm throw or vice-versa. Instead, when a throwing movement was mislabelled, it was always classified as class C (non-throwing movement).

The obtained average accuracies for each subject can also be observed in Table II.

TABLE II. AVERAGE ACCURACIES OF EACH SUCBJECT

Subject	Accuracy (%)
1	65
2	75
3	85
4	75

Overall, the total average accuracy for throwing gestures recognition was of 75±8%.

V. FINAL REMARKS

The work described in this paper focused on the training of a linear SVM and subsequent implementation for real-time classification. The model, trained with data acquired from eight subjects, was used for the recognition of two throwing movements used in the game of Boccia: the overarm and the underarm throw. Furthermore, it was also used to recognize when the player is idle, i.e., any movement performed by the used that differs from a throw. Thus, this classification problem comprised three classes which, in this paper, were identified as classes A, B or C.

The results from the real-time testing phase showed that classification achieved an average accuracy of 75±8%, showing that the system successfully recognizes and differentiates between the two throwing gestures and other movements performed by the player while "idle".

The system recognized the underarm throw more efficiently, obtaining an 80% accuracy, comparing to the 70% obtained for the overarm throw. This difference could be justified by the fact that, during data acquisition for training, subjects performed the underarm throw more similarly amongst themselves, oppositely to the overarm movement, in which the execution varied from subject to subject.

Another positive aspect is that the classifier did not misclassify class A as class B and vice-versa, which appears to mean that the data from both throws differs sufficiently for the algorithm to not misclassify one for another.

However, the accuracy considerably varies between some of the subjects, which is one of the downsides of the proposed system. This shows that each subject has a different method of throwing, which might differ substantially from the recorded gestures contained in the data set used for training. This might be a constraint for testing the system during a real Boccia game situation, due to the probability of the elders having very different throwing techniques amongst themselves, therefore, it is imperative to have a robust model. Having this into account, the usage of other classification techniques should be used for further improving of the results, such as feature extraction, enable overlapped windows for real-time classification or even using other kernels and classifiers. Furthermore, more data should be acquired from different subjects in order to have a more extensive and variable training set, thus increasing the model's robustness.

Regarding future work, it is intended to implement this system in the iBoccia framework for gesture recognition. As stated in Section I from this paper, this framework comprises two UIs, one for the caregiver to monitor the elder's physical activity and another which displays the game score, in real-time, for the elders. The implemented algorithm for gesture recognition will allow the caregiver to keep track of the different throwing movements performed in each game by the elders. Thanks to the accelerometer data and knowledge of the approximate weight of a Boccia ball (0.275 kg) it is also possible to compute the approximate force applied by the player during the throw and plot this data for later consultation, thus allowing the caregiver to detect decreases in the elder's strength and identify muscular diseases characteristic of old age.

On the other hand, the results from the work described in this paper will be also useful for the elders to interact indirectly with the UI that displays the current game score. By using gesture recognition, it can be possible for the system to automatically detect when a player's turn is over and notify the next player that his/her turn has started by showing the respective elder's photo and name on the screen. This can further motivate the elders to play Boccia by enhancing the game experience.

In addition, the proposed system is predicted to be tested during a Boccia match played in a nursing home. Bearing this in mind, it is pertinent to use data acquired from the elders during the match for adding to the data set used to train the model. The results, as seen in this paper, will be evaluated using accuracy as performance metric.

Overall, the results obtained with the proposed system are encouraging and allow the further development of innovative solutions for monitoring and motivating elder physical activity.

ACKNOWLEDGMENTS

This article is a result of the project Deus Ex Machina: NORTE-01-0145-FEDER-000026, supported by Norte Portugal Regional Operational Program (NORTE 2020), under the PORTUGAL 2020 Partnership Agreement, through the European Regional Development Fund (ERDF).

REFERENCES

[1] S. Mitra and T. Acharya, "Gesture recognition: A survey," *IEEE Trans. Syst. Man Cybern. Part C Appl. Rev.*, vol. 37, no. 3, pp. 311–324, 2007.

[2] R. Hassanpour, S. Wong, and A. Shahbahrami, "Vision - Based Hand Gesture Recognition for Human Computer Interaction : A Review," *IADIS Int. Conf. Interfaces Hum. Comput. Interact.*, pp. 25--27, 2008.

[3] R.-H. L. R.-H. Liang and M. O. M. Ouhyoung, "A real-time continuous gesture recognition system for sign language," *Proc. Third IEEE Int. Conf. Autom. Face Gesture Recognit.*, pp. 558–567, 1998.

[4] G. Saggio, F. Cavrini, and F. Di Paolo, "Inedited SVM application to automatically tracking and recognizing arm-and-hand visual signals to aircraft," *IJCCI 2015 - Proc. 7th Int. Jt. Conf. Comput. Intell.*, vol. 3, no. Ijcci, pp. 157–162, 2015.

[5] Y. J. Chang, S. F. Chen, and J. Da Huang, "A Kinect-based system for physical rehabilitation: A pilot study for young adults with motor disabilities," *Res. Dev. Disabil.*, vol. 32, no. 6, pp. 2566–2570, 2011.

[6] A. Kupryjanow, B. Kunka, and B. Kostek, "UPDRS tests for diagnosis of Parkinson's disease employing virtual-touchpad," *Proc. - 21st Int. Work. Database Expert Syst. Appl. DEXA 2010*, pp. 132–136, 2010.

[7] V. Silva *et al.*, "A wearable and non-wearable approach for gesture recognition – Initial results," *9Th Int. Congr. Ultra Mod. Telecommun. Control Syst.*, pp. 185–190, 2017.

[8] V. Silva *et al.*, "iBoccia: A Framework to Monitor the Boccia Gameplay in Elderly," *Lect. Notes Comput. Vis. Biomech.*, vol. 27, pp. 437-446, 2018.

[9] C. Figueira *et al.*, "iBoccia: Monitoring elderly while playing Boccia gameplay," *ICINCO 2017 - Proc. 14th Int. Conf. Informatics Control. Autom. Robot.*, vol. 1, no. Icinco, pp. 670–675, 2017.

[10] P. Leite, A. Calado, and F. Soares, "Boccia Court Analisys for Real-Time Scoring," *In Press*, 2018.

[11] A. Calado, P. Leite, F. Soares, P. Novais, and P. Are-, "Boccia Court Analysis for Promoting Elderly Physical Activity," *Innov. Eng. Entrep. HELIX 2018. Lect. Notes Electr. Eng.*, vol. 505, pp. 158-164, 2018.

[12] Fraunhofer Portugal AICOS, "Pandlets – Personal Area Dots: Letting Everything Sense," *Innov. Eng. Entrep. HELIX 2018. Lect. Notes Electr. Eng.*, vol. 505, no. 1, 2018.

[13] S. Bhattacharya, B. Czejdo, and N. Perez, "Gesture classification with machine learning using Kinect sensor data," *2012 Third Int. Conf. Emerg. Appl. Inf. Technol.*, pp. 348–351, 2012.

[14] Q. Chen, N. D. Georganas, and E. M. Petriu, "Real-time Vision-based Hand Gesture Recognition Using Haar-like Features," *IEEE Conf IMTC*, pp. 1–6, 2007.

[15] H. Hienz, K. Grobel, and G. Offner , "Real-Time Hand-Arm Motion Analysis using a single Video Camera," *Proc. Second Int. Conf. Autom. Face Gesture Recognition, Kill.*, pp. 165–168, 1996.

[16] C. Joslin, A. El-Sawah, Qing Chen, and N. Georganas, "Dynamic Gesture Recognition," *2005 IEEE Instrumentationand Meas. Technol. Conf. Proc.*, vol. 3, no. May, pp. 1706–1711, 2005.

[17] T. Schlömer, B. Poppinga, N. Henze, and S. Boll, "Gesture recognition with a Wii controller," *Proc. 2nd Int. Conf. Tangible Embed. Interact. - TEI '08*, p. 11, 2008.

[18] D. Wilson and A. Wilson, "Gesture recognition using the XWand," 2004.

[19] R. Xie and J. Cao, "Accelerometer-Based Hand Gesture Recognition by Neural Network and Similarity Matching," *IEEE Sens. J.*, vol. 16, no. 11, pp. 4537–4545, 2016.

[20] Z. He and L. Jin, "Activity recognition from acceleration data based on discrete consine transform and SVM," *Conf. Proc. - IEEE Int. Conf. Syst. Man Cybern.*, no. October, pp.

5041–5044, 2009.

[21] K. K. B. Peetoom, M. A. S. Lexis, M. Joore, C. D. Dirksen, and L. P. De Witte, "Literature review on monitoring technologies and their outcomes in independently living elderly people," *Disabil. Rehabil. Assist. Technol.*, vol. 10, no. 4, pp. 271–294, 2015.

[22] A. M. Khan, Y. K. Lee, S. Lee, and T. S. Kim, "Accelerometer's position independent physical activity recognition system for long-term activity monitoring in the elderly," *Med. Biol. Eng. Comput.*, vol. 48, no. 12, pp. 1271–1279, 2010.

[23] B. Najafi, K. Aminian, A. Paraschiv-Ionescu, F. Loew, C. J. Büla, and P. Robert, "Ambulatory system for human motion analysis using a kinematic sensor: Monitoring of daily physical activity in the elderly," *IEEE Trans. Biomed. Eng.*, vol. 50, no. 6, pp. 711–723, 2003.

[24] M. Luštrek and B. Kaluža, "Fall Detection and Activity Recognition with Machine Learning," *Informatica*, vol. 33, pp. 205–212, 2008.

[25] G. Perolle *et al.*, "Automatic Fall Detection and Activity Monitoring for Elderly," *Proc. MEDETEL*, vol. 41, no. 2, pp. 33–41, 2006.

[26] D. W. Kang, J. S. Choi, J. W. Lee, S. C. Chung, S. J. Park, and G. R. Tack, "Real-time elderly activity monitoring system based on a tri-axial accelerometer," *Disabil. Rehabil. Assist. Technol.*, vol. 5, no. 4, pp. 247–253, 2010.

[27] P. C. Huang, P. J. Pan, Y. C. Ou, Y. C. Yu, and Y. S. Tsai, "Motion analysis of throwing Boccia balls in children with cerebral palsy," *Res. Dev. Disabil.*, vol. 35, no. 2, pp. 393–399, 2014.

[28] R. D. de Arroxellas, R. G. Romano, R. Cymrot, and S. M. Blascovi-Assis, "Bocha adaptada: análise cinemática do arremesso e sua relação com a realidade virtual," *Rev. Bras. Ciencias do Esporte*, vol. 39, no. 2, pp. 160–167, 2017.

[29] BISFed, "BISFed International Boccia Rules (v.2)," 2017.

[30] A. Moschetti, L. Fiorini, D. Esposito, P. Dario, and F. Cavallo, "Recognition of daily gestures with wearable inertial rings and bracelets," *Sensors (Switzerland)*, vol. 16, no. 8, 2016.

[31] J. Wu, G. Pan, D. Zhang, and G. Qi, "Gesture recognition with a 3-d accelerometer," *Proc. 6th Int. Conf. Ubiquitous Intell. Comput.*, vol. 5585, pp. 25–38, 2009.

[32] Z. He, "Accelerometer based gesture recognition using fusion features and SVM," *J. Softw.*, vol. 6, no. 6, pp. 1042–1049, 2011.

[33] C. R. Souza, "The Accord.NET Framework." [Online]. Available: http://accord-framework.net. [Accessed: 26-Jul-2018].

Investigating the Relevance of Sensor Selection: Recognition of ADLs Based on Feet Movement and Posture Information

Rafael de Pinho André, Pedro Henrique Diniz, Hugo Fuks
Department of Informatics
Pontifical Catholic University of Rio de Janeiro
Rio de Janeiro, RJ, Brazil +55 21 3527-1510
Email: randre,pfonseca,hugo@inf.puc-rio.br

Abstract—**In this work, we present an analysis of the relevance of different sensor types for the recognition of activities of daily living based on foot movement and position. By conducting a comprehensive experiment with 12 diverse volunteers that resulted in about 1 million data samples, and employing a machine learning HAR (Human Activity Recognition) classifier developed for a 9-activity classes model, we were able to assess the impact of sensor selection on the activity recognition accuracy. Aiming at a replicable research, we provide full hardware information, system source code and a public domain dataset.**

Keywords–Clothes-based sensors; IoT (Internet of Things) devices; Mobile sensing applications.

I. INTRODUCTION

Human Activity Recognition (HAR) is an active and fast-growing field of research that has seen an intense growth during the last five years, drawing attention of researchers from fields, such as mobile healthcare, sports performance and mass context inference. From the rehabilitation of stroke patients [1] to energy expenditure estimation of Activities of Daily Living (ADL) [2] [3], studies based on feet movement and posture show promising results and interesting applications. Current research works can be grouped into two main approaches for collecting user's feet movement and posture data: (i) image processing and (ii) clothes-based sensors. In this work, we address one of the current challenges of the clothes-based sensors approach: understanding which types of sensors are relevant for the recognition of ADLs. Since clothes-based sensors HAR is a comprehensive filed of research, we focus on feet movement and posture information.

Firstly, we performed a literature review on HAR using Internet of Things (IoT) devices and clothes-based sensors, discussed in Section II, which unfolded the intense growth on the number of publications related to the analysis of feet posture and movement in recent years. Throughout the review, we observed that (i) no previous work thoroughly addressed the relevance of the sensors employed for the assessed activity model, (ii) few works provided public datasets for benchmarking, (iii) there is no sufficient information on sensors deployment, (iv) few works addressed their sample rates and time window size choices and (vi) few works addressed the positioning of the plantar pressure sensors. The lack of published datasets, the insufficient information for the replication of these studies and the overall obliviousness of other work's results points to a lack of maturity of the area.

The main contributions of this work are (i) an analysis of the relevance of different types of sensors for the building of a HAR classifier based on feet movement and posture information, (ii) a comprehensive literature review focused on HAR research using clothes-based sensors for collecting feet movement and posture information and (iii) an IoT device blueprint for HAR research, an insole equipped with all the types of sensors used in the surveyed works along with novel sensors. In Section III, the design of the IoT device, sensors deployment and replication information are shown along with the details of the experiment conducted to collect ADL data. In Section IV, the development of the activity model, the classifier and the experimental results are presented and analyzed. In Section V, we conclude with an assessment of sensor relevance and additional findings.

II. LITERATURE REVIEW

This section presents a comprehensive literature review and meta-data analysis about HAR clothes-based sensors research projects using feet movement and posture information for ADL recognition. The literature review workflow was conducted in the following way: (i) definition of a research question, (ii) crafting of a search query string, (iii) definition of exclusion criteria and (iv) performing quantitative and qualitative data analysis. The research question posed in this review is: What are the clothes-based sensors HAR research projects conducted in recognition of ADL using feet movement and posture information?

This research question was further divided into sub-questions:

- What are the types, quantities and locations of the sensors used?
- How was the sensor mix chosen?
- What activities are present in the activity model?

Based on these questions, we formulated a search query string and refined it by the publication year range filter to exclude works not published during the last 10 years. With over three hundred search results combining the searched databases, we applied a very strict exclusion criteria and obtained 24 articles for analysis. Whenever available, from each article, we collected the (i) types and quantity of sensors used, (ii) activity model and machine learning technique, (iii) number of subjects and samples collected and (iv) test technique and results.

The metadata associated with the IoT devices and clothes-based sensor selection presented by these works is summarized in Table I, where the articles are grouped into three distinct research categories: (i) works using Ground Contact Force (GCF) sensors, (ii) works using Inertial Motion Units (IMUs) sensors and (iii) works employing sensor fusion and other non-conventional sensors.

TABLE I. SUMMARY OF SENSOR SELECTION AND POSITIONING.

Name	*Sensor*	*Positioning*
Crea [4]	FSR	Insole
De Santis [5]	FSR	Insole
Drobny [6]	FSR	Insole
el Achkar [7]	FSR	Insole
Fukahori [8]	FSR	Sock
Holleczek [9]	FSR	Sock
Lin [10]	FSR	Insole
Zhu [11]	FSR	Shoe and Waist
Kong [12]	GCF	Insole
Ugulino [13]	Accelerometers	Waist, Thigh, Arm and Ankle
McCarthy [14]	Gyroscope	Shoe
Doppler [15]	IMU	Insole and Shoe
Ghobadi [16]	IMU	Shoe
Edgar [1]	FSR, IMU	Insole
Lin [17]	FSR, IMU	Insole and Shoe
Tang [18]	FSR, IMU	Insole
Zhang [19]	FSR, IMU	Insole and Shoe
Zhang [20]	FSR, IMU	Insole and External
Noshadi [21]	FSR, Gyroscope and Accelerometers	Insole, Shoe and External
Sazonov [2]	FSR, Accelerometers	Insole and Shoe
Sazonov [22]	FSR, Accelerometers	Insole and Shoe
Jiang [23]	IR	Shoe
Matthies [24]	Capacitive Sensing	Insole
Haescher [25]	Capacitive Sensing	Chest, Leg and Insole

A. Recognition of Common Movement Activities

The recognition of common movement activities, such as walking, standing, sitting, climbing stairs and running, is the most common type of research found in this literature review. Those works, such as [5] [7] [9] [15], rely mostly on plantar Force Sensitive Resistor (FSR) pressure sensors to classify user activity according to a previously elaborated activity model. Other works, such as [6] [14] [16], rely on IMUs located on the user's feet for that purpose. Sensor fusion of FSRs and IMUs is employed by works such as [2] [17] [18] [26], achieving good overall results. Only four of the surveyed works used sensors other than GCF sensors and IMUs: infrared sensors in [23], capacitive sensing technology in [24] [25] and air bladders in [12]. Some works positioned extra sensors in other places beyond the user's feet, such as [13], where extra sensors are positioned onto user's waist, thigh, arm and ankle and [25], where extra sensors are positioned onto user's chest and leg. They all use very similar activity models composed of sitting, standing, running, walking and slope-walking activities, the main differences being the machine learning algorithms used and the context of the experiments. Two of the activity models proposed by the works of this section are more comprehensive than the prevailing standing-walking-running activity models [17] [20]. Both relied on sensor fusion techniques to classify user's activities and obtained promising results.

Many of the surveyed studies were conducted in the recognition of activities related to healthcare and well-being, such as (i) the research presented in [10], that aims at recognizing caregiver's Patient Handling Activities (PHA) and movement activities to help prevent overexertion injuries, (ii) the works presented in [19] [27], that measure activity in people with stroke, (iii) the work presented in [1], that recognizes activities and postures to provide behavioral feedback to patients recovering from a stroke, and (iv) the research proposed by [21], in which researchers present a pair of shoes that offer low-cost balance monitoring outside of laboratory environments using features identified by geriatric motion study experts. The lightweight smart shoes are based on the MicroLEAP wireless sensor platform [28], which uses an IMU and FSR pressure sensors embedded inside each insole for data acquisition. Some other shoe-based wireless sensor platforms, such as the SmartStep [29], were used by many different healthcare-related researches. In [30], the platform was used for developing an Android application to capture data from the IoT device to recognize activities and real time feedback provision. Works, such as [3] [22], employ the SmartShoe platform for energy expenditure estimation after the classification of the activities performed by the user, and in [31] it is used to predict body weight and energy expenditure. The same platform is then used by [27] [32] to identify activity levels and steps in people with stroke. Although the majority of the works focused on healthcare and well-being, some, such as [8], investigated the use of foot-based gestures, known as Foot Plantar-Based (FPB) gestures, to control computing devices.

B. Literature Review Discussion

The measuring of GCFs is the most prevalent approach used by the surveyed works for the task of recognizing user activity, being present in 16 of the 24 studies, while the second most common approach, present in 12 of the 24 studies, is the use of IMUs. Although the challenge of adequately positioning the GCF sensors is recognized as a very important factor by studies, such as [33] [34], it is not thoroughly addressed by most of the surveyed works. Considering the IoT devices presented in the literature, two characteristics impair their reproducibility: (i) the lack of information about the IMUs orientation and the (ii) absence of sensor model information or specification. Most of the works analyzed, 22 out of 24, provided detailed information regarding the models of its activity classifiers, but only 12 studies detailed the test techniques used in the activity classifiers – 7 of which used k-fold cross validation and 5 used leave-one-out. Although most studies stated that tests were performed, they provided no detailed information about these tests. The success rate of ADL recognition of the surveyed works fell into the 80% - 100% range. No work addressed the sensor mix choice besides stating that its selection is commonly found throughout the literature.

It was also observed that 21 out of 24 works provided information on the number of participants, but only 6 of the 24 studies provided information on the dataset size. The main issue detected in the literature review is the absence of publicly available datasets, impairing that way the understanding of the results. Knowledge of datasets is especially important to assess works that use similar (i) sensor selection, (ii) sensor placement and (iii) activity models. As discussed in [11], dataset disclosure is crucial for benchmarking purposes, given that classification algorithms rely heavily on datasets. Beyond dataset size, sample rates and time window durations also affect the understanding of the results. Only 16 of the 24 surveyed works provided information on the sample rates, and 8 of those 16 also provided information on the time window size. The prevailing suggestions for future works and contribution found in the literature are to (i) increase the data set through longer data collection intervals and the diversification of participant's profiles and (ii) adapt the activity model to a specific challenge, such as helping patients to avoid falls. To make the literature review presented in this article replicable, all surveyed publications are available in RIS (Research Information Systems) format in [35].

III. Methods

A. IoT Device Prototyping

In this section, we present the IoT device prototyped to collect user data. Aiming at a highly replicable research, we provide detailed software and hardware information – types, quantities and models of every sensor, along with their exact positioning and orientation, and source code of the embedded software and the application server. Since battery lifetime is a major concern for studies outside of a laboratory environment and the participants came from diverse technological backgrounds, the key design goals were to develop a (i) low power consumption device capable of extended operation that (ii) was easy to use during the experiment. The IoT device comprises two components: an US men's size 8 insole that houses the plantar pressure sensors and an external protective case that houses the microcontroller and the other sensors. The insole component was developed with six GCF sensors, and their placement followed literature's recommendations found in [33] [36]. We used the FSR 402 by Interlink Electronics, a Polymer Thick Film (PTF) device that exhibits a decrease in resistance as the force applied to its active surface increases. Given that each sensor needs a static resistor to create a variable voltage for the microcontroller's Analog to Digital Converter (ADC) inputs, we placed six 10KΩ 1/4W resistors inside the insole next to them. We opted to use a single insole in the experiment to reduce prototyping costs, since the literature suggested that the loss of information when compared to experiments collecting data from both feet is minimal [23]. The external protective case is built around a Particle Electron, a 2G-enabled microcontroller from Particle.io that collects and transmits sensor data to the database. For the accelerometer, gyroscope and magnetometer sensors responsible for monitoring the feet posture, we used the LSM9DS1 by STMicroelectronics, a system-in-package component that is part of the Photon microcontroller board. The LSM9DS1 is a digital sensor, automatically calibrated by its firmware when the device is powered up [37]. The barometer selected for the experiment is the MPL3115A2, by Freescale Semiconductor, a low power, high-precision altitude, pressure and temperature sensor. The MPL3115A2 sensor is factory calibrated for sensitivity, offset for both temperature and pressure measurements, and has a built-in altimeter calculator. Under normal operation, there is no need for further calibration [38]. For the range-finder sensor, we used the VL6180 by STMicroelectronics. Although other sensors are capable of greater sampling rates, the selected range-finder sensor is one of the few distance sensors adequate for the 10 Hz sampling rate used in the experiment. The VL6180 sensor is calibrated using the Very High Voltage (VHV) calibration approach described in [39], and the method for free-calibration usage described by the manufacturer in [40] is also employed. The Electron microcontroller and its board, along with the MPL3115A2 and VL6180 sensors mentioned above, were positioned in the ABS 3D printed external protective case. The prototype is powered by a 2,200 mAh lithium ion battery pack by Sparkfun Electronics, allowing for an easier, faster replacement and improved usability. Its 7-segment LED (Light-Emitting Diode) charge level display helped us plan and execute the experiment session cycles. Since we needed a comprehensive sensor selection to investigate the relevance of sensor types for the recognition of ADLs based on feet movement and posture information, we decided to use all sensor types employed by the surveyed works and a novel sensor, the barometer.

The software model used in this work comprises two components: (i) the embedded software running on the microcontroller, responsible for acquiring, structuring and transmitting raw sensor data over a 2G connection to an iMac application server, and (ii) the application server itself, responsible for processing and logging the streamed data to a NOSQL (Non SQL) cloud database – tasks not suitable for the embedded microcontroller due to its hardware limitations. The authors made available the complete and commented source code of the embedded software and the application server in [35].

B. Procedure

Twelve volunteers carefully selected for their diverse characteristics participated in the experiment. One prevailing limitation of the surveyed works was the employment of young adults only as participants in their experiments. This study tries to circumvent this problem with the participation of people with disabilities, two Class II obesity individuals, two overweight individuals, two knee-injured patients and one ankle-injured patient, a balanced mix of male and female participants and one third of senior adult volunteers. Since the insole and shoes are US men's size 8, we selected participants in the 7.5 to 8.5 shoe size range. We collected 24 hours of activity data, which is 2 hours of feet posture and movement data from each volunteer. Compared to the other studies, the number of subjects in our study is not that different from the others, considering the average of 7 in the surveyed works. However, the number of samples in our study – around 950,000 – is significantly higher than the average number of samples – around 50,000 – found in the surveyed works. We developed a comprehensive activity model for the experiment, since we were aiming at assessing the relevance of different sensor types for the recognition of ADLs based on feet movement and posture information. It comprises 9 activities: walking straight (2km/h), walking slope up (2km/h), walking slope down (2km/h), slow jogging (6km/h), slow jogging slope up (6km/h), slow jogging slope down (6km/h), ascending stairs, descending stairs and sitting. The experiment was conducted in four distinct sessions, where participants performed a subset of the planned activities. Due to their availability, some participants performed more than one session per day. All sessions were performed on a garden area inside the university campus. The first session lasted for 50 minutes, and each participant performed 5 cycles of 10 minutes (8 minutes walking followed by 2 minutes resting). The second session also lasted for 50 minutes and consisted of 5 cycles of 10 minutes (4 minutes slope walking up, 4 minutes slope walking down and 2 minutes resting). In the third session, each participant performed 5 cycles of stair climbing interleaved with sitting for a total of 20 minutes (1 minute ascending stairs, 1 minute resting, 1 minute descending stairs, 1 minute resting). Finally, in the last session, participants performed 3 cycles of slow jogging and sitting – this section was performed two months after the initial experiment, when we added 3 more activities to our activity model, namely: (i) slow jogging (6km/h), (ii) slow jogging slope up (6km/h) and (iii) slow jogging slope down

(6km/h). Subjects were free to perform the activities – the IoT device did not restrict in any way their movement and the instructions provided did not specify how the activities were to be performed. This way we were able circumvent a common limitation of most HAR works in which activities are performed in a non-natural way. It is important to note that we had removed running (8km/h) from the original model, because that would be a deterrent to some of the participants. For the sake of adding the last three activities to the activity model, we had to remove one elder volunteer from the experiment, but kept the injured participants after consulting with a certified health professional. We accompanied all participants during the sessions to log any unusual occurrence.

IV. Data Analysis

In this section, we describe the stages followed to develop the HAR classifier, data acquisition, data processing, feature extraction, feature selection, classification and validation, and our findings regarding sensor relevance. The full dataset is available in [35].

A. Data Acquisition

During the data acquisition stage, a stream of raw, unprocessed signals was acquired from the insole's sensors and stored in the microcontroller in JSON format. This raw data combined the accelerometer, gyroscope, magnetometer, six FSR sensors, altitude, temperature and range-finder sensor signals, resulting in 17-feature set entries to the dataset. We used the 10 Hz sampling rate recommended by [41]. As discussed in [42], we understand that this sample rate may not be adequate for recognizing similar activities or subtle variations within the same activities. However, these concerns were not relevant to our research. To reduce energy consumption and allow for an extended operating time, the JSON formatted data was periodically sent to the application server in small packages of 100KB.

B. Data Processing and Feature Extraction

The data processing stage occurs in three steps. First, data unrelated to the specific planned activities for the experiment is discarded, given that the prototype starts collecting feet movement and posture information immediately after it is powered. Then, the dataset is labelled for supervised learning, and activity class information is appended to each entry according to the activity performed in the experiment. Finally, all sensor data is normalized to make their scales equivalent, partly address sensor drift and reduce the possibility of model overfitting.

In the feature extraction stage, we used descriptive statistics, standard deviation, variance, minimum, maximum and average values, to generate derived features from each of the 17 original features:

- Six FSR sensor readings;
- Three gyroscope axis data;
- Three magnetometer axis data;
- Three accelerometer axis data;
- Altimeter reading; and
- Range-finder sensor reading.

Moreover, (i) the cumulative difference between samples for each feature and (ii) the Euler angles of pitch, roll and yaw were also used to generate additional derived features, for a total of over 100 features for selection.

C. Classification and Validation of the Baseline Model

To build and validate our baseline model, a model that makes use of all sensor raw and derived features, we used the Leave-one-out Cross Validation method, in an attempt to decrease the chances of overfitting. Although there is no evidence to support this assumption, this method at least guarantees that both training and test splits do not share any example data. Different strategies were then experimented to build the classifier for our 9-activities activity model, and the Random Forest Algorithm was selected for classification, given that its average performance of 91.26% was superior to the other ones. The individual validation results for each of the 12 examples were: 89.17%, 90.86%, 92.42%, 94.82%, 97.41%, 90.18%, 79.78%, 94.14%, 95.01%, 88.31%, 91.98% and 91.01%. In total, 12 features were utilized to build the classifier: 2 axis of the gyroscope, 2 axis of the magnetometer, 1 axis of the accelerometer, 4 FSRs, 2 Euler angles and the cumulative difference between samples of the barometer. The features selected for the baseline classifier provided valuable insights for the next step, the analysis of sensor type relevance.

As discussed in [43], after experimenting several time window sizes during the classifier construction, we decided to use a 0.3s one based on our model validation results, registering an accuracy improvement of about 19% when contrasting the selected window (0.3s) and the largest time window experimented (2.0s).

D. Analysis of Sensor Type Relevance

After building the baseline model, we were able to investigate the relevance, correlation of a feature with the average classifier accuracy, of each sensor type for the achieved results. We used Hall's algorithm [44] based on correlation with its default "Best Fit" configuration, a backtracking greedy strategy. This method was selected based on its superior performance when compared to the other feature selection methods found in the surveyed works. Ugulino et al. [13] also use this same method to reduce feature redundancy and still achieve better-than-average results. Based on the results commonly found in the literature, we already expected to see gyroscope, accelerometer and FSR features showing high correlation and being used in the building of the classifier. However, the results achieved by Hall's algorithm suggested which features were relevant and to what extent. Considering the baseline model, the distance sensor showed a very low correlation and was not used in the building of the classifier. Although distance sensors were successfully employed by works such as [23], when presented with a broader sensor selection the classifier did not make use of it. FSRs 5 and 6 showed a medium to low correlation and were not employed, while the remaining FSRs showed a high correlation. Considering that some of the surveyed works also used between three to four FSRs with similar positioning, further investigation could lead to evidence as to where to position the sensors for better recognition accuracy of the selected activities. Euler angles showed a high correlation and were utilized by some of the surveyed works, making a strong case that they should be evaluated during the feature engineering phase for similar activity models. Finally, the barometer provided the feature with the second highest correlation score, suggesting that this type of sensor should also be evaluated for similar activity models. The topic of feature engineering and its methods are beyond the scope of this work, so we used the features employed by the surveyed works in our analysis.

After that initial assessment, we evaluated each sensor, raw and derived features, separately, employing the same methods used to build the baseline classifier: (i) Leave-one-out Cross Validation and (ii) Random Forest Algorithm. The average accuracy results are shown in Table II, where all values are rounded to the nearest whole number and ordered by average accuracy.

TABLE II. SINGLE SENSOR CLASSIFIER ACCURACY.

Sensor	*Model Accuracy*
IMU	66%
FSRs	60%
Barometer	29%
Distance	17%

Following that analysis, we combined the two most successful sensor types, FSRs and IMUs, with all available sensor types. We built and validated a classifier for each combination, and the average accuracy results for the better performing combinations are shown in Table III, where all values are rounded to the nearest whole number and ordered by average accuracy.

TABLE III. SENSOR MIX CLASSIFIER ACCURACY.

Sensor	*Model Accuracy*
IMU (9-axis) and FSRs	81%
FSRs and Barometer	71%
IMU (9-axis) and Barometer	70%
FSRs and Gyroscope	65%
FSRs and Accelerometer	60%
FSRs and Magnetometer	59%
IMU (9-axis) and Distance	57%
FSRs and Distance	55%
Distance	17%

Although the results shown in Table III take into account the combined FSRs, FSR1 to FSR4, we also evaluated FSR5 and FSR6 for the same combinations, achieving less than 1% increase in average accuracy. The experimental results show that (i) 9-Axis IMUs, (ii) 4-FSR arrays and (iii) barometers were the most relevant sensor types for the recognition of ADLs based on feet movement and posture information, when considering a typical activity model with the stand, walk, run and climb stairs activities. Above that, we learned that accuracy can be greatly improved (15%) by the IMU and FSR sensor fusion, so that approach should be considered in future research if it is needed to (i) differentiate between similar activities or (ii) identify subtle variations of the same activity. Lastly, the barometer sensor allowed for an increase of the average accuracy by more than 10%, making a strong case for its adoption whenever possible.

V. CONCLUSION AND FUTURE WORK

In this work, we expanded the research conducted in [42] by (i) enhancing the IoT device's sensor array, (ii) improving the machine learning HAR classifier, (iii) increasing the number of participants and activity classes in the experiment and, above all, (iv) focusing on assessing the relevance of different sensor types for the task of recognizing ADL using foot movement and posture information. The main contributions of this work are:

- An analysis of the relevance of different types of sensors in the building of a HAR classifier based on foot movement and posture information, discussed in Section IV;
- A public domain dataset with about 1 million samples and 9 activity classes, available in [35];
- A comprehensive literature review about clothes-based sensor HAR researches, presented in Section II; and,
- A clothes-based sensor IoT device, presented in Section III, for the data collection of feet movement and posture information.

Despite not taking any measures to address FSRs' drift over time, the overall classifier accuracy was satisfactory - achieving top quartile performance when compared to the surveyed works. After the experiment, we developed a new version of the IoT device with the purpose of helping reduce injury risk during functional exercise sessions. Our goal is to employ sensor fusion and machine learning techniques to provide users with real time feedback of the exercises, helping them to improve and avoid injuries. Currently, we are conducting an outdoor experiment with 18 volunteers - including two sight impaired participants - to investigate the extent to which we can detect correct execution of the exercise routines. We were able to use the lessons learned from the experiment presented in this work to improve the new version of the IoT device developed for the new research, making changes, such as: (i) removing the range-finder sensors, and reducing the number of FSRs to 4, based on our findings, (ii) using sewable connectors for the FSR sensors to withstand the impact of jogging activities – all commercially available connectors disconnected the sensors at some point during the jogging sessions, forcing the session to pause to repair the prototype – and (iii) using Sparkfun Electronics' battery pack to turn the IoT device into a convenient and easy-to-use device that can be deployed outdoors without difficulty.

REFERENCES

[1] S. R. Edgar, T. Swyka, G. Fulk, and E. S. Sazonov, "Wearable shoe-based device for rehabilitation of stroke patients," in Engineering in Medicine and Biology Society (EMBC), 2010 Annual International Conference of the IEEE. IEEE, 2010, pp. 3772–3775.

[2] E. S. Sazonov, G. Fulk, J. Hill, Y. Schutz, and R. Browning, "Monitoring of posture allocations and activities by a shoe-based wearable sensor," IEEE Transactions on Biomedical Engineering, vol. 58, no. 4, 2011, pp. 983–990.

[3] N. Sazonova, R. C. Browning, and E. Sazonov, "Accurate prediction of energy expenditure using a shoe-based activity monitor," Med Sci Sports Exerc, vol. 43, no. 7, 2011, pp. 1312–21.

[4] S. Crea, S. De Rossi, M. Donati, P. Reberšek, D. Novak, N. Vitiello, T. Lenzi, J. Podobnik, M. Munih, and M. Carrozza, "Development of gait segmentation methods for wearable foot pressure sensors," in Engineering in Medicine and Biology Society (EMBC). IEEE, 2012, pp. 5018–5021.

[5] A. De Santis, E. Gambi, L. Montanini, L. Raffaeli, S. Spinsante, and G. Rascioni, "A simple object for elderly vitality monitoring: The smart insole," in Mechatronic and Embedded Systems and Applications (MESA), ASME. IEEE, 2014, pp. 1–6.

[6] D. Drobny, M. Weiss, and J. Borchers, "Saltate!: a sensor-based system to support dance beginners," in CHI'09 Extended Abstracts on Human Factors in Computing Systems. ACM, 2009, pp. 3943–3948.

[7] C. M. El Achkar, F. Massé, A. Arami, and K. Aminian, "Physical activity recognition via minimal in-shoes force sensor configuration," in Pervasive Computing Technologies for Healthcare. ICST, 2013, pp. 256–259.

[8] K. Fukahori, D. Sakamoto, and T. Igarashi, "Exploring subtle foot plantar-based gestures with sock-placed pressure sensors," in Proceedings of the 33rd Annual ACM Conference on Human Factors in Computing Systems. ACM, 2015, pp. 3019–3028.

[9] T. Holleczek, A. Ruegg, H. Harms, and G. Troster, "Textile pressure sensors for sports applications 9th ieee sensors conf," Kona, HI, 2010.

[10] F. Lin, C. Song, X. Xu, L. Cavuoto, and W. Xu, "Sensing from the bottom: Smart insole enabled patient handling activity recognition through manifold learning," in Connected Health: Applications, Systems and Engineering Technologies (CHASE). IEEE, 2016, pp. 254–263.

[11] C. Zhu and W. Sheng, "Multi-sensor fusion for human daily activity recognition in robot-assisted living," in International conference on Human robot interaction. ACM, 2009, pp. 303–304.

[12] K. Kong and M. Tomizuka, "A gait monitoring system based on air pressure sensors embedded in a shoe," IEEE/ASME Transactions on mechatronics, vol. 14, no. 3, 2009, pp. 358–370.

[13] W. Ugulino, D. Cardador, K. Vega, E. Velloso, R. Milidiú, and H. Fuks, "Wearable computing: Accelerometers' data classification of body postures and movements," in Advances in Artificial Intelligence, SBIA. Springer, 2012, pp. 52–61.

[14] M. McCarthy, D. James, J. Lee, and D. Rowlands, "Decision-tree-based human activity classification algorithm using single-channel foot-mounted gyroscope," Electronics Letters, vol. 51, no. 9, 2015, pp. 675–676.

[15] J. Doppler, G. Holl, A. Ferscha, M. Franz, C. Klein, M. dos Santos Rocha, and A. Zeidler, "Variability in foot-worn sensor placement for activity recognition," in Wearable Computers, 2009. ISWC'09. International Symposium on. IEEE, 2009, pp. 143–144.

[16] M. Ghobadi and E. T. Esfahani, "Foot-mounted inertial measurement unit for activity classification," in Engineering in Medicine and Biology Society, EMBC. IEEE, 2014, pp. 6294–6297.

[17] F. Lin, A. Wang, Y. Zhuang, M. R. Tomita, and W. Xu, "Smart insole: A wearable sensor device for unobtrusive gait monitoring in daily life," IEEE Transactions on Industrial Informatics, vol. 12, no. 6, 2016, pp. 2281–2291.

[18] W. Tang and E. S. Sazonov, "Highly accurate recognition of human postures and activities through classification with rejection," IEEE Journal of Biomedical and Health Informatics, vol. 18, no. 1, 2014, pp. 309–315.

[19] T. Zhang, G. D. Fulk, W. Tang, and E. S. Sazonov, "Using decision trees to measure activities in people with stroke," in Engineering in Medicine and Biology Society (EMBC), 2013 35th Annual International Conference of the IEEE. IEEE, 2013, pp. 6337–6340.

[20] Z. Zhang and S. Poslad, "Improved use of foot force sensors and mobile phone gps for mobility activity recognition," IEEE Sensors Journal, vol. 14, no. 12, 2014, pp. 4340–4347.

[21] H. Noshadi, F. Dabiri, S. Ahmadian, N. Amini, and M. Sarrafzadeh, "Hermes: mobile system for instability analysis and balance assessment," ACM Transactions on Embedded Computing Systems (TECS), vol. 12, no. 1s, 2013, p. 57.

[22] E. Sazonov, N. Hegde, R. C. Browning, E. L. Melanson, and N. A. Sazonova, "Posture and activity recognition and energy expenditure estimation in a wearable platform," IEEE journal of biomedical and health informatics, vol. 19, no. 4, 2015, pp. 1339–1346.

[23] X. Jiang, Y. Chen, J. Liu, G. R. Hayes, L. Hu, and J. Shen, "Air: recognizing activity through ir-based distance sensing on feet," in International Joint Conference on Pervasive and Ubiquitous Computing: Adjunct. ACM, 2016, pp. 97–100.

[24] D. J. C. Matthies, T. Roumen, A. Kuijper, and B. Urban, "Capsoles: Who is walking on what kind of floor?" in Proceedings of the 19th International Conference on Human-Computer Interaction with Mobile Devices and Services, ser. MobileHCI '17. New York, NY, USA: ACM, 2017, pp. 9:1–9:14. [Online]. Available: http://doi.acm.org/10.1145/3098279.3098545

[25] M. Haescher, D. J. C. Matthies, G. Bieber, and B. Urban, "Capwalk: A capacitive recognition of walking-based activities as a wearable assistive technology," in Proceedings of the 8th ACM International Conference on PErvasive Technologies Related to Assistive Environments, ser. PETRA '15. New York, NY, USA: ACM, 2015, pp. 35:1–35:8. [Online]. Available: http://doi.acm.org/10.1145/2769493.2769500

[26] N. Hegde, M. Bries, T. Swibas, E. Melanson, and E. Sazonov, "Automatic recognition of activities of daily living utilizing insole based and wrist worn wearable sensors," IEEE journal of biomedical and health informatics, 2017.

[27] G. D. Fulk and E. Sazonov, "Using sensors to measure activity in people with stroke," Topics in stroke rehabilitation, vol. 18, no. 6, 2011, pp. 746–757.

[28] L. K. Au, W. H. Wu, M. A. Batalin, D. H. McIntire, and W. J. Kaiser, "Microleap: Energy-aware wireless sensor platform for biomedical sensing applications," in Biomedical Circuits and Systems Conference. BIOCAS. IEEE, 2007, pp. 158–162.

[29] N. Hegde and E. Sazonov, "Smartstep: A fully integrated, low-power insole monitor," Electronics, vol. 3, no. 2, 2014, pp. 381–397.

[30] N. Hegde, E. Melanson, and E. Sazonov, "Development of a real time activity monitoring android application utilizing smartstep," in Engineering in Medicine and Biology Society (EMBC), 2016 IEEE 38th Annual International Conference of the. IEEE, 2016, pp. 1886–1889.

[31] N. A. Sazonova, R. Browning, and E. S. Sazonov, "Prediction of bodyweight and energy expenditure using point pressure and foot acceleration measurements," The open biomedical engineering journal, vol. 5, 2011, p. 110.

[32] G. D. Fulk, S. R. Edgar, R. Bierwirth, P. Hart, P. Lopez-Meyer, and E. Sazonov, "Identifying activity levels and steps in people with stroke using a novel shoe-based sensor," Journal of Neurologic Physical Therapy, vol. 36, no. 2, 2012, p. 100.

[33] L. Shu, T. Hua, Y. Wang, Q. Li, D. D. Feng, and X. Tao, "In-shoe plantar pressure measurement and analysis system based on fabric pressure sensing array," IEEE Transactions on Information Technology in Biomedicine, vol. 14, no. 3, 2010, pp. 767–775.

[34] U. Manupibul, W. Charoensuk, and P. Kaimuk, "Design and development of smart insole system for plantar pressure measurement in imbalance human body and heavy activities," in Biomedical Engineering International Conference (BMEiCON), 2014 7th. IEEE, 2014, pp. 1–5.

[35] R. De Pinho André, P. H. F. S. Diniz, and H. Fuks, "Iwoar smart insole," https://goo.gl/6ozm26, 2017.

[36] J. Perry and J. M. Burnfield, "Gait analysis: normal and pathological function," Developmental Medicine and Child Neurology, vol. 35, 1993, pp. 1122–1122.

[37] ST, "Lsm9ds1 datasheet," https://www.st.com/resource/en/datasheet/lsm9ds1.pdf, 2018 (retrieved: june, 2018).

[38] NXP, "Mpl3115a2 datasheet," https://www.nxp.com/docs/en/data-sheet/MPL3115A2.pdf, 2018 (retrieved: june, 2018).

[39] ST, "Vl6180x datasheet," https://cdn-learn.adafruit.com/assets/assets/000/037/608/original/VL6180X_datasheet.pdf, 2017 (retrieved: june, 2018).

[40] STMicroelectronics, "Vl6180x product site," https://www.st.com/en/imaging-and-photonics-solutions/vl6180x.html, 2017 (retrieved: june, 2018).

[41] A. Harasimowicz, T. Dziubich, and A. Brzeski, "Accelerometer-based human activity recognition and the impact of the sample size," Advances in Neural Networks, Fuzzy Systems and Artificial Intelligence, 2014, pp. 130–135.

[42] R. De Pinho André, P. H. F. S. Diniz, and H. Fuks, "Bottom-up investigation: Human activity recognition based on feet movement and posture information," in Proceedings of the 4th International Workshop on Sensor-based Activity Recognition and Interaction, ser. iWOAR '17. New York, NY, USA: ACM, 2017, pp. 10:1–10:6. [Online]. Available: http://doi.acm.org/10.1145/3134230.3134240

[43] O. Banos, J.-M. Galvez, M. Damas, H. Pomares, and I. Rojas, "Window size impact in human activity recognition," Sensors, vol. 14, no. 4, 2014, pp. 6474–6499.

[44] M. Hall, "Correlation-based feature subset selection for machine learning," Thesis submitted in partial fulfillment of the requirements of the degree of Doctor of Philosophy at the University of Waikato, 1998.

VehicularVisible Light Communication

I2V2V2I connected cars

Manuel Augusto Vieira, Manuela Vieira, Paula Louro,
ADETC/ISEL/IPL,
R. Conselheiro Emídio Navarro, 1959-007
Lisboa, Portugal
CTS-UNINOVA
Quinta da Torre, Monte da Caparica, 2829-516,
Caparica, Portugal

e-mail: mv@isel.ipl.pt, mv@isel.pt, plouro@deetc.isel.pt,
afantoni@deetc.isel.ipl.pt

Pedro Vieira
ADETC/ISEL/IPL,
R. Conselheiro Emídio Navarro, 1959-007
Lisboa, Portugal
Instituto das Telecomunicações
Instituto Superior Técnico, 1049-001,
Lisboa, Portugal
e-mail: pvieira@isel.pt

***Abstract*—This paper investigates the connected vehicle concept at intersections with traffic signals control and proposes the use of Visible Light Communication (VLC) in Vehicular Communication Systems for vehicle safety applications. A smart vehicle lighting system that combines the functions of illumination, signaling, communications, and positioning is presented. A generic model of cooperative transmissions for vehicular communications services is established. Three specific vehicular communications systems are analyzed. One is for Infrastructure-to-Vehicle communications from the street lamps, located on roadside, to the vehicles; the other is for in line Vehicle-to-Vehicle communications and the last for Vehicle-to-Infrastructure communications from cars to the traffic lights, at the crossroad. An on-off code is used to transmit data. The encoded message contains the ID code of each emitter concomitantly with a traffic message that is received, decoded and resent to another vehicle or to traffic light, in the crossroad. An algorithm to decode the information is established. A phasing traffic flow is presented as a proof of concept.**

Keywords- I2V, V2I and V2V Vehicular communication; Visible Light Communication; white LEDs; SiC photodetectors; OOK modulation; Traffic control.

I. INTRODUCTION

The communication through visible light holds special importance when compared to existing forms of wireless communications. The visible light spectrum is completely untapped for communication and can complement the Radio Frequency (RF)-based mobile communication systems. Modern vehicles are equipped with many electronic sensors, which monitor the vehicle's speed, position, heading, and lateral and longitudinal acceleration. Although the technology already exists, vehicles rarely communicate this information wirelessly to other vehicles or roadside infrastructure [1]. The goal of the Cooperative Intelligent Transport System (C-ITS) is to provide a vehicular communication system that can enable quick, cost-effective means to distribute data in order to ensure safety, traffic efficiency, driver comfort, and so forth. Researchers are anticipating the deployment of wireless vehicle communication to improve safety and reduce congestion [2]. This use case is known as connected vehicles. Recently, the transportation lighting infrastructure such as street lamps, traffic lights, automotive lamps, etc., is changing to Light Emiting Diodes (LEDs). In the case of an ITS based on Visible Light Communication (VLC), it will be possible to make use of the conventional automotive and traffic LEDs. Secondly, the electromagnetic compatibility problem, which is a very serious problem in ITSs based on RF signals, will be minimized since visible light and the conventional RF signals occupy different parts of the electromagnetic spectrum. Compared to RF-based communications, VLC offers robustness against jamming attacks, a smaller interference domain, and a large license-free spectrum [3].

Vehicular Communication Systems are an emerging type of network in which vehicles and roadside units are the communicating nodes, providing each other with information, such as safety warnings and traffic information [4]. The vehicular communication for C-ITS is composed of infrastructure-to-vehicle (I2V), vehicle-to-vehicle (V2V) and vehicle-to-infrastructure (V2I) communications. The I2V applications focus on utilizing the traffic related infrastructure, such as traffic light or streetlight to communicate useful information. So, VLC can be realized as a secondary application in LED arrays that are placed for lighting.

In the recent past, we have developed a Wavelength Division Multiplexing (WDM) device that enhances the transmission capacity of the optical communications in the visible range. The device was based on tandem a-SiC:H/a-Si:H pin/pin light controlled filter with two optical gates to select different channel wavelengths. When different visible signals are encoded in the same optical transmission path

[5], the device multiplexes the different optical channels, performs different filtering processes (amplification, switching, and wavelength conversion) and finally decodes the encoded signals recovering the transmitted information. This device can be used as receiver, and helps developing automated vehicle technologies that allow vehicles to communicate with the surrounding 'environment' [6].

An introduction to the paper is given. The rest of the paper is structured as follows: In Section II, a traffic scenario is established and the transmitters and receivers are characterized. The performance of a cooperative driving system is evaluated in Section III. In Section IV, as proof of concept, a traffic scenario is presented and tested. Finally, in Section V, the conclusions are addressed. The proposed smart vehicle lighting system involves wireless communication, computer based algorithms, smart sensor and optical sources network, which constitutes a transdisciplinary approach framed in cyber-physical systems.

II. Connected Vehicles Model

An infrastructure-to-vehicle followed by vehicle-to-vehicle and by vehicle-to-infrastructure communication was simulated. The illustration of the proposed scenario is displayed in Figure 1, for a light traffic controlled crossroad.

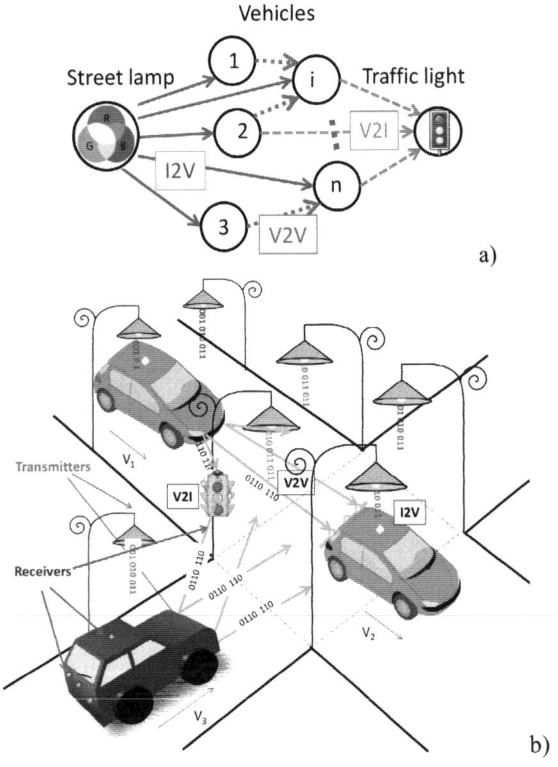

Figure 1. Illustration of the proposed V2V, V2I and I2V communication scenario: a) Generic model for cooperative vehicular communications. b) Connected vehicles communication in a crossroad.

In Figure 1a, the generic cooperative vehicular model is shown and in Figure 1b, the proposed scenario is illustrated. Using the I2V communication, each street lamp (transmitter) sends a message received and analyzed by a SiC receiver, located at the rooftop of the vehicle. Using the headlights as transmitters, the information is resent to a leader vehicle (V2V) or directly to a crossroad receiver (V2I), at the traffic light, interconnected to a local controller that feeds one or more signal heads.

Along the roads, street lamps are distributed in a square topology, for data transmission and lighting purposes. They are based on commercially available violet (V: 400 nm) and white RGB-LEDs. The white LEDs require three separate driver circuits to realize the white light. To decrease this complexity at each node, only one chip of the LED is modulated for data transmission, the Red (R:626 nm), the Green (G:530 nm) or the Blue (B:470 nm) while the other two are provided constant current for illumination.

A four-code assignment for the LEDs was used. The unit cell employs four R, G, B and V LED located at the corners of a square grid, as shown in Figure 2. The estimated distance from the street lamps to the receivers is used to generate a circle around each transmitter (see Figure 2), on which the receiver must be located in order to receive the transmitted information. The grid size was chosen in order to avoid an overlap in the receiver from the data from adjacent grid points. The geometric scenario used for calculation uses, for calibration, a smaller size square grid (2 cm), to improve its practicality. To receive the information from several transmitters, the device must be positioned where the circles from each transmitter overlap, producing, at the receiver, a MUX signal that after demultiplexing, acts twofold as a positioning system and a data transmitter. The nine generated regions, defined onwards as footprints, are presented in Figure 2 [6].

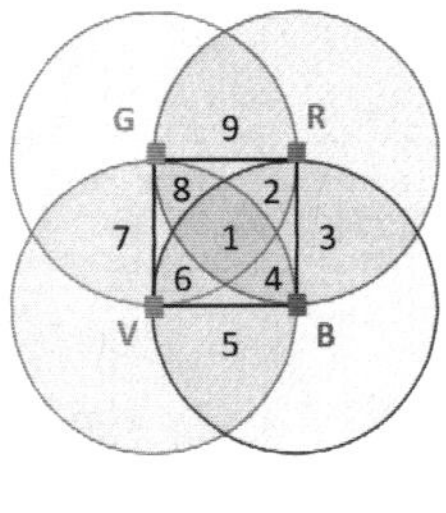

Figure 2. Unit cell (LED array = RGBV color spots).

A large-dimension environment, like a road network surrounding (Figure 1b), is analysed by dividing the space into unit navigation cells (see Figure 2) with an appropriate side length giving the geographical position assigned to each node. The lighting plan and generated joint footprints are illustrated in Figure 3. Two traffic flows are considered, one in the horizontal (W) and the other on the vertical direction (S). Each streetlight sends traffic message that includes the synchronism, its physical ID and traffic information. Each node, X $_{i,j}$, carries its own colour, X, (RGBV), as well as its horizontal and vertical ID position in the surrounding network (*i,j*).

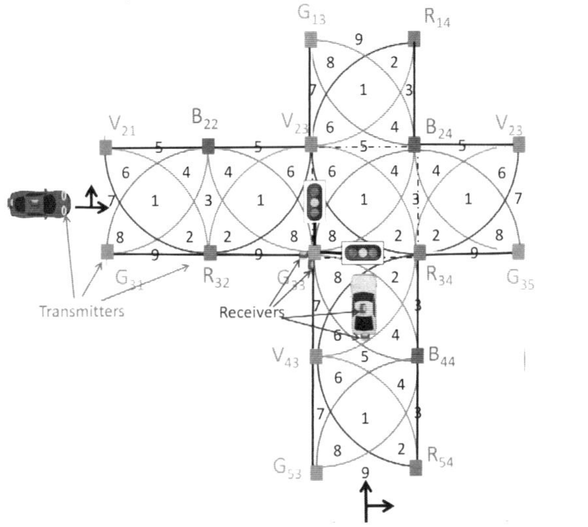

Figure 3. Lighting plan and generated joint footprints in a crossroad.

In the I2V communication, the emitters are located along the roadside. Each lamp transmits data during the time slot it occupies, *i.e.*, the individual LED lamp transmits its own data depending on the area it locates. The transmitted information is received and decoded at an external SiC pi'npin receiver, located on the rooftop of the car (Figure 1b). When a probe vehicle enters the streetlight´s capture range, the receivers respond to light signal and its unique ID and the traffic message are assigned.

To build the V2V system between a leader and a follower vehicle, the follower sends the message that is received by the leader and can be retransmitted to the next car [7] or to the infrastructure. Therefore, each probe vehicle receives two different messages: the one transmitted by the streetlight (I2V) and the one coming from the follow vehicle (V2V) and can compare them. This system uses an approach in which a sequence of cellular locations is matched to a route segment along the road network that appears to be the most probable. All observations for a single section are analysed together to produce an estimate of the lane occupied and travel time along that section.

In the V2I communication, two interconnect receivers are located at the same traffic light, facing the cross roads, and the emitters at the headlights of the moving cars approaching the interception. When a car enters in the infrastructure´s capture range of the receivers, an approach message is received and decoded by the corresponding optical pi'npin receiver. So, each driver, approaching the intersection area from S, W or both sends an approach request, that are compared by the intersection manager (local controller of the traffic light). Those messages contain the assigned ID positions, speeds, and flow direction of the vehicles that approach the intersection. The requests are labelled either with a W (West) or S (South) label, depending on the flow they belong to. The vehicle service time depends on its flow and on the flow of the following vehicle. The problem that the intersection manager has to solve is allocating the reservations among a set of drivers in a way that a specific objective is maximized. In particular, V2V communication is useful to enhance the action space of a driver, e.g., through the option of dynamically joining groups of vehicles, based on the idea of platoons.

III. Coding/Decoding Techniques

A. Modulation scheme

We have considered a network composed of a single access point (vehicle) and several nodes that periodically generate data, at different rates. The optical signals are synchronized and include the transmission of information related to the ID position of the transmitters and the message to broadcast. So, in a time slot, each node has a packet to transmit.

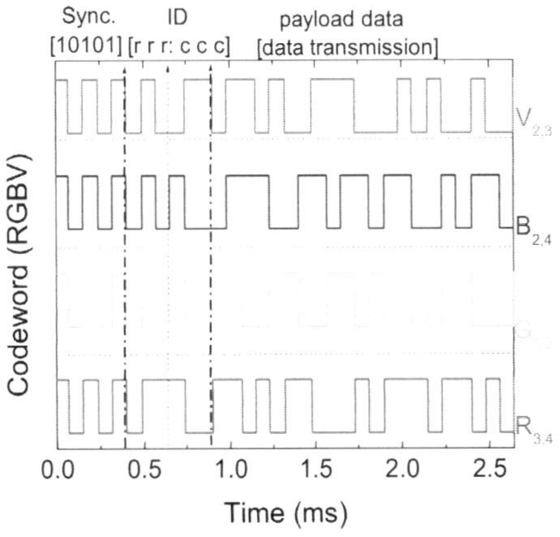

Figure 4. Frame structure. Representation of one original encoded message [10101: rrr ccc: XY….]. $R_{3,4}$, $G_{3,3}$, $B_{2,4}$ and $V_{2,3}$ are the transmitted node packet, in a time slot, from the crossroad in the network.

Each frame is a word of 32 bits, divided into three blocks: the synchronism (5 bits), the binary node address, (6 bits) and the traffic message (payload data). In Figure 4, an example of the codification of the digital optical signals is illustrated. We assigned the first five bits to the synchronization in a [10101] pattern. It corresponds to the simultaneous transmission of the four nodes in a time slot. Each colour signal carries its own ID-BIT [rrr;ccc] where the first three bits give the ID binary code of the line and the next three the ID binary code of the column. For instance, an ID_BIT [011 100] for the $R_{3,4}$ streetlight is sent whereas in case of $G_{3,3}$, an ID_BIT [011 011] is generated by the green LED. Thus, $R_{3,4}$, $G_{3,3}$, $B_{2,4}$ and $V_{2,3}$ are the transmitted node packets, in a time slot, inside the crossroad. With perfect information, this method will give an exact, unique answer, i.e., the unit cell location in the cluster and, for each unit navigation, the correspondent footprint.

B. *The pi´npin receiver*

The VLC receiver is a tandem, p-i'(a-SiC:H)-n/p-i(a-Si:H)-n heterostructure sandwiched between two transparent conductive contacts (TCO). The device configuration and operation is shown in Figure 5. The deposition conditions and optoelectronic characterization of the single layers and device, as well as their optimization were described previously [5] [8].

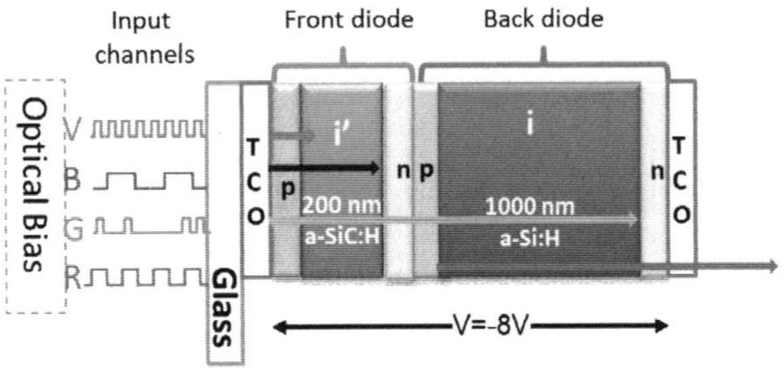

Figure 5. Double pin configuration and device operation.

The device operates within the visible range using for data transmission the modulated light supplied by the violet (V) and by the trichromatic red (R), green (G), blue (B) LED transmitters. The mixture of the modulated optical signal (transmitted data) impinging on the receiver are absorbed accordingly to their wavelengths. The combined optical signal (MUX signal; received data) is analysed by reading out the generated photocurrent. Previous results have shown that the device acts as a Multiplexer/demultiplexer device [5] [9].

C. *Signal decoding and positioning*

In Figure 6, the normalized MUX signal, in a stamp time, is displayed. In Figure 6a, the bit sequence was chosen to allow all the *on/off* sixteen possible combinations of the four channels. On top, the signals used to drive LEDs are shown to guide the eyes into the *on/off* states of each input. In Figure 6b, the MUX signal acquired by the receiver, located at the crossroad, position #1, #9 and #7 (see Figure 3), are displayed. The decoded packet of transmitted information when all the channels are received is presented in the top of the figure.

Results from Figure 6a, show that the MUX signal presents as much separated levels as the *on/off* possible combinations of the input channels, allowing decoding the transmitted information [10]. On the right hand side, the match between MUX levels and the 4 bits binary code ascribed to each level is shown. The MUX signal presented in Figure 6a, is used for calibration purposes.

The signal is decoded by assigning each output level to a 4- digit binary code, [X_R, X_G, X_B, X_V], with X=1 if the channel is *on* and X=0 if it is *off*.

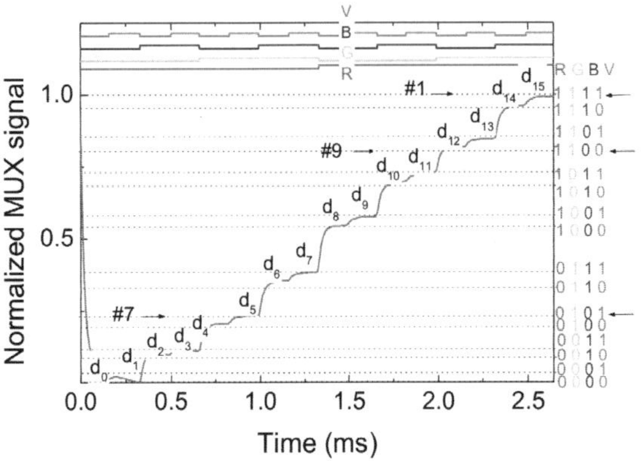

a)

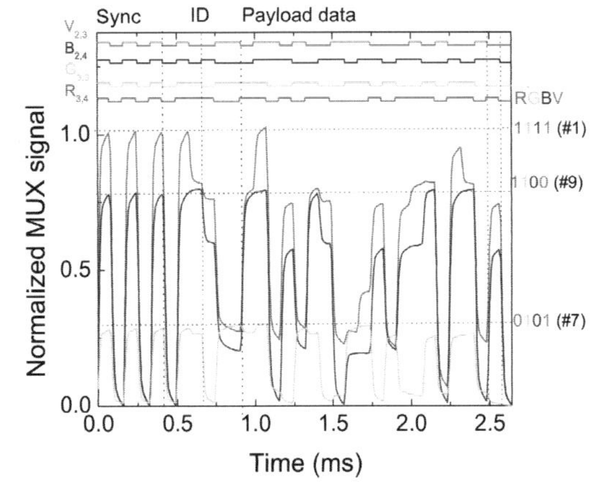

b)

Figure 6. a) MUX/DEMUX signals under 390 nm front irradiation. On the top the transmitted channels packets [R, G, B, V] are decoded. a) Calibration cell. b) MUX signal at positions #1, #7 and #9.

After decoding the MUX signals, the localisation of the mobile target is direct. Taking into account the frame structure (Figure 4), the position of the receiver inside the navigation cell and its ID in the network is revealed. The ID position comes directly from the synchronism block, where all the received channels are, simultaneously, *on* or *off*. The 4-bit binary code ascribed to the higher level identifies the receiver position in the unit cell. Those binary codes are displayed in the right hand of the figure. For instance, the level [1100] corresponds to the level d_5 where the green and the violet channels are simultaneously *on* (see arrow in Figure 6a). The same happens to the other footprints (#1 and #9). Each decoded message carries, also, the node address of the transmitter. So, the next block of six bits gives de ID of the received node. In #7 the location of the transmitters, in the network, are $G_{3,2}$ and $V_{2,3}$ while in #1 the assigned transmitters are $R_{3,4}$, $G_{3,2}$ $B_{2,4}$ and $V_{2,3.}$ The last block is reserved for the transmission of the traffic message (payload data). A stop bit (0) is used at the end of the frame.

IV. COOPERATIVE VLC SYSTEM EVALUATION

A. *I2V communication*

Figure 7a displays the I2V MUX signal received, in three times slots, by a rooftop receiver, moving in the W direction, when the vehicle is located in #3, moves to #1 and arrives to the stop line (#7). In Figure 7b, it moves from south from #5 to #1 and arrives to the cross line (# 9). In the top of both figures, the decoded packet of data sent by the addressed R, G, B and V transmitters are pointed out. On the right sides of the figures, the received channel, and so the footprint position in the navigation cell, are identified by their 4 digit binary code.

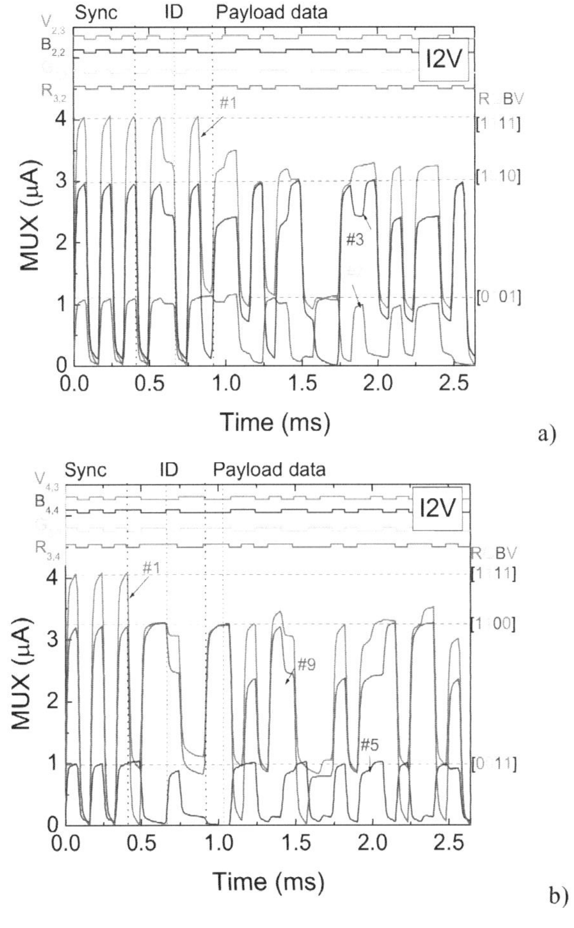

Figure 7. a) Three MUX/DEMUX signals under 390 nm front irradiation. On the top the transmitted channels packets [R, G, B, V] are decoded. a) West flow (#3>#1>#7). b) South flow (#5>#1>#9).

In Figure 7a, the nodes $R_{3,2}$ [...011 010...], $G_{3,3}$ [...011 011...], $B_{2,2}$ [...010 010...] and $V_{2,3}$ [...010 011...] are recognized while in Figure 7b the $R_{3,4}$ [...011 100...], $G_{3,3}$ [...011 011...], $B_{4,4}$ [...100 100...], and $V_{4,3}$ [...100 111...] nodes are identified. In the others positions, only two messages arrive to the receiver. The assigned reference nodes in Figure 7a are: $R_{3,2}$; $B_{2,2}$ (#3) and $G_{3,3}$;$V_{2,3}$ (#7), while in Figure 7b the assigned reference point are: #5 ($B_{4,4}$; $V_{4,3}$) and #9 ($R_{3,4}$; $G_{3,3}$).The vehicle speed can be calculated by measuring the actual distance travelled overtime using ID´s transmitters tracking. The distance is fixed while the elapsed time will be obtained through the instants where the number of received channels changes. As in Figure 3b, at the instant initial, t_0, the receiver moves west from footprint 3 to footprint 1 (Figure 7a). The decoded MUX message changes from two ($R_{3,2}$ $B_{2,2}$) to four ($R_{3,2}$ $G_{3,3}$ $B_{2,2}V_{2,3}$) transmitted channels. After an elapsed time, Δt, footprint 7 is reached and the number of received transmitters changes again to two ($G_{3,3}$ $V_{2,3}$). In the following, this data will be transmitted to another leader vehicle through the V2V communication or to the traffic light through V2I.

B. *Traffic Signal phasing: I2V, V2V and V2I communication*

Signal phasing is the sequence of individual signal phases within a cycle that define the order in which pedestrian and vehicular movements are assigned the right-of-way. The cycle repeats itself continuously over time but the timing of the light switches is made according to the phasing of the traffic light. A brief look is given in Figure 8.

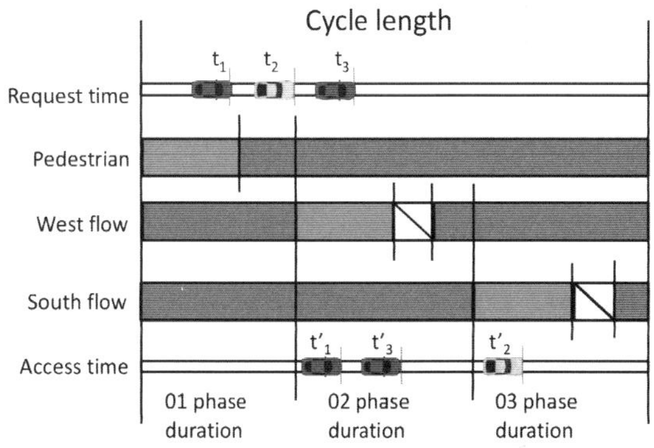

Figure 8. Phasing of traffic flows: phase number 01 (pedestrian phase), phase number 02 (W flow), phase number 03 (S flow).

A traffic scenario was simulated. We consider two flows of vehicles entering the system at the beginning of their respective roads, one from West (W flow), and one from South (S flow). Three vehicles are considered. Vehicle 1 and Vehicle 3 belong to the same flow (W) and Vehicle 2 belongs to the S flow. The phasing of the traffic flows is composed of a pedestrian-only stage (01 phase), and two single-lane road phases crossing at a square intersection area: the W flow stage (02 phase) and the S flow stage (03 phase). Each phase exists as an electrical circuit from the controller to the traffic light and feeds one or more signal heads. A phase can apply to a two aspect head (pedestrians; red or green) or to a three aspect head (vehicles; red or yellow or green). The green and yellow represent the time where it is allowed to pass the traffic light and the red the time not allowed. The traffic pedestrian lights are passively green as long as no vehicle is approaching.

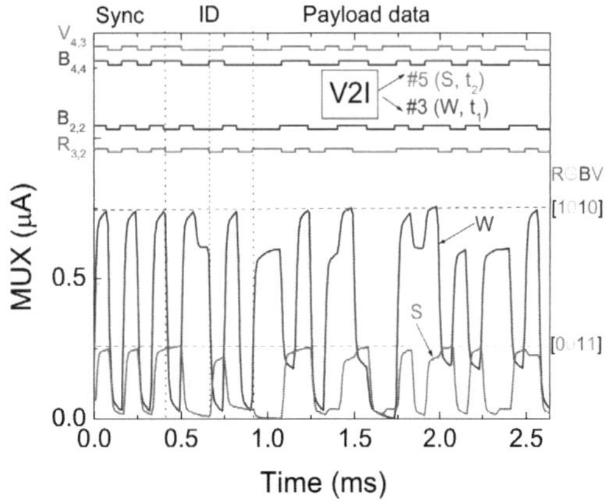

Figure 9. Proof of concept. MUX/DEMUX signals. V2I communication from Vehicles 1 and 2 and the infrastructure. On the top the transmitted channels packets [R, G, B, V] are decoded.

In Figure 9, the V2I communications, in successive moments, are displayed. Three instants are considered to define the phase's duration, t_1, t_2 and t_3 (Figure 8). At t_1 and t_2, Vehicle 1 and Vehicle 2 approaches, respectively, the intersection and contact optically the intersection manager (controller) by sending a request message to the receiver (V2I) located at the traffic light that faces the road (Figure 3b). Vehicle 3, contacts the infrastructure (V2I) at t_3. Those messages contain their positions and approach velocities. The MUX signal at each receiver and the assigned decoded messages (at the top of the figure) are displayed at t_1 and t_2. The position of both vehicles are: $R_{3,2}$ and $B_{2,2}$ (#3, W) for Vehicle 1 and $B_{4,4}$ and $V_{4,3}$ (#5, S) for Vehicle 2.

To model a worst-case situation, vehicles approaching the intersection from different flows are assumed to have a conflicting trajectory. Therefore, three subsequent instants have to be predictable, t'_1, t'_2 and t'_3, as the correspondent access times of the Vehicle 1, Vehicle 2 and Vehicle 3 (Figure 8). From a capacity point of view it is more efficient, if Vehicle 3 is given access at t'_3 before Vehicle 2, t'_2 to the intersection, then, forming a west platoon of vehicles before (t'_2) giving way to the south conflicting flow as stated in Figure 8.

V. CONCLUSIONS

A distributed mechanism for the control and management of a traffic light controlled crossroad network, where connected vehicles receive information from the network (I2V), interact each other (V2V) and with the infrastructure (V2I) was analyzed. A simulated traffic scenario was presented and a generic model of cooperative transmissions for vehicular communications services was established. As a proof of concept, a phasing of traffic flows is suggested.

ACKNOWLEDGEMENTS

This work was sponsored by FCT – Fundação para a Ciência e a Tecnologia, within the Research Unit CTS –, reference UID/EEA/00066/2013 and by projects: IPL/2017/PPGDiode/ISEL, IPL/2017/SMART_VeDa/ISEL and IPL/2017/EmGraph/ISEL.

REFERENCES

[1] N. Kumar, N. Lourenço, D. Terra, L. N. Alves, and R. L. Aguiar, "Visible Light Communications in Intelligent Transportation Systems", IEEE Intelligent Vehicles Symposium, pp. 748-753, 2012.

[2] C. Liu, B. Sadeghi, and E. W. Knightly, "Enabling Vehicular Visible Light Communication (V2LC) networks," Proceedings of the Eighth ACM International Workshop on Vehicular Inter-Networking (VANET '11), ACM, New York, NY, USA, pp. 41-50, 2011.

[3] H. Parth, Pathak, F. Xiaotao, H. Pengfei, and M. Prasant,"Visible Light Communication, Networking and Sensing: Potential and Challenges" September 2015, IEEE Communications Surveys & Tutorials 17(4): Fourthquarter 2015, pp. 2047 – 2077, 2015.

[4] S. Yousefi, E. Altman, R. El-Azouzi, and M. Fathy, "Analytical Model for Connectivity in Vehicular Ad Hoc Networks", IEEE Transactions on Vehicular Technology, vol. 57, pp. 3341-3356 ,2008.

[5] M. Vieira, P. Louro, M. Fernandes, M. A. Vieira, A. Fantoni and J. Costa, "Three Transducers Embedded into One Single SiC Photodetector: LSP Direct Image Sensor, Optical Amplifier and Demux Device" Advances in Photodiodes InTech, Chap.19, pp. 403-425, 2011.

[6] M. A. Vieira, M. Vieira, P. Vieira, and P. Louro, "Optical Signal Processing for a Smart Vehicle Lighting System using a-SiCH technology" Proc. SPIE 10231, Optical Sensors 2017, pp. 102311L , May 16, 2017;

[7] M. A. Vieira, M. Vieira, P. Louro, and P. Vieira, "Smart Vehicle Lighting System in the Visible Range: Vehicle-to-Vehicle Communication" The Eighth International Conference on Sensor Device Technologies and Applications. SENSORDEVICES 2017. - Rome, Italy. pp. 57-62.

[8] M. A. Vieira,, P. Louro, M. Vieira, A. Fantoni, and Steiger-Garção, A., "Light-activated Amplification in Si-C Tandem Devices: A Capacitive Active Filter Model" IEEE Sensor Journal, 12, no. 6, pp. 1755-1762, 2012.

[9] M. A. Vieira, M. Vieira, V. Silva, P. Louro, and J. Costa, "Optical signal processing for data error detection and correction using a-SiCH technology" Phys. Status Solidi C 12, No. 12, pp. 1393–1400 , 2015.

[10] M. A. Vieira, M. Vieira, M., V. Silva, P. Louro, and M. Barata, "Optoelectronic Logic Functions Using Optical Bias Controlled SiC Multilayer Devices". MRS Proceedings, 1536, pp. 91-96, 2013.

ReCal – an Innovative Mathematical Procedure to Determine the Date of Timely Recalibration for Sensor Systems with Metal Oxide Gas Sensors

Rolf Seifert
Institute of Automation and Applied Informatics (IAI)
Karlsruhe Institute of Technology
D-76344 Eggenstein-Leopoldshafen, Germany
e-mail: rolf.seifert@kit.edu

Hubert B. Keller
Institute of Automation and Applied Informatics (IAI)
Karlsruhe Institute of Technology
D-76344 Eggenstein-Leopoldshafen, Germany
e-mail: hubert.keller@kit.edu

Abstract— **Sensor systems with Metal Oxide Gas (MOG) sensors with tin oxide as base material are well established as gas sensing devices for threshold applications like the monitoring of hazardous materials and dangerous situations. However, MOGs have one inherent disadvantage; they are subject to unavoidable aging processes. Therefore, the sensor systems have to be recalibrated regularly. This paper presents an innovative mathematical procedure called ReCal, which is able to determine the proper time for recalibration of the sensor system. The method of ReCal is demonstrated by simulation calculations and it is shown how to determine the parameters in real applications.**

Keywords-sensor system; metal oxide gas sensors; threshold apllications; timely recalibration; date of recalibration; simulation calculations.

I. INTRODUCTION

There is a broad field of economic online and in-situ field analysis applications like the online monitoring of volatile components in chemical and biochemical processes, quality monitoring in food processing, discriminated monitoring of toxic gas leakages, etc. In the field of monitoring hazardous materials and situations, metal oxide gas (MOG) sensors with tin oxide as base material are especially well established as gas sensing devices due to their high sensitivity and low costs. These MOGs can be operated either isothermally or, for example, in a thermo-cyclical mode [1][2]. In the first mode, only one single measurement result is available and thus no substance identification can be performed. In the second mode, a series of measurement results is sampled, which leads to so-called "Conduction over Time Profiles" (CTPs) [3]-[6]. These CTPs can be considered as a "fingerprint" of the substance under consideration and enable substance identification as well as concentration determination, by applying a sophisticated calibration and evaluation procedure like ProSens, which is explicitly described in [7]. As could be shown, ProSens is a powerful tool for substance identification and concentration determination for multi-component gas mixtures even in the case of varying environmental conditions like varying humidity or varying environmental temperature. Figure 1 shows examples of some CTPs of different gases. Figure 1 also clearly shows the specific fingerprints of the various gases.

In previous investigations it was shown that this approach is a very powerful tool for monitoring hazardous materials, for example in the detection of ammonia leakages [8] or cable fires [9].

Other approaches in the field of monitoring hazardous materials in the environment are described in detail in [10].

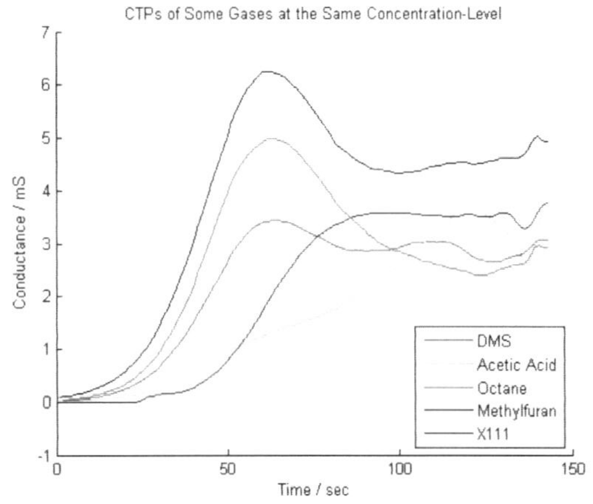

Figure 1. CTPs of different samples at the same concentration level.

Although the MOGs are very powerful gas sensing devices, they have one disadvantage: their long-time stability is often very poor. One possibility to improve this disadvantage is to pre-age the sensors before field application. However, this approach does not solve the problem; it only reduces the rate of decay. The aging process of the sensors may additionally lead to misleading results, causing e.g. no alarm being given in case of hazardous situations. Therefore, the sensor has to be recalibrated from time to time. This raises the issue of choosing the proper time for recalibration.

The necessary recalibration can be easily performed by a recalibration procedure like ProCal, which is explicitly described in [11].

In this paper, we introduce ReCal, a procedure which finds the appropriate time for recalibration of the sensor system. Measurement results are regarded as random variables and simulation calculations will demonstrate the efficacy of this approach.

The rest of this paper is organized as follows. Section II describes the mathematical calibration model and the feature values, which correspond to the gas concentrations. Section III describes the general application scenario. Section IV addresses the mathematical model used in this paper. Section V describes an application of the method using simulation calculations. The conclusions and a section "Future Work" close the article.

II. CALIBRATION MODEL AND FEATURE VALUES

To apply calibration and evaluation procedures for monitoring and alarming, if necessary, in real field applications, the substance under consideration has to be calibrated using calibration measurements. Based on these measurements, the mathematical calibration model can be calculated using calibration procedures like ProSens. In this calibration model, feature values are extracted from the calibration measurements, which allow the evaluation procedure to determine the concentration of a measured sample. The feature values correspond to concentration values and vice versa. For example, there is a feature value, the alarm feature value, for the alarm level that corresponds to a concentration value where an alarm must be given. On the other hand, there is also a feature value, the zero feature value, for the "zero-situation", when no hazardous gas under consideration is present and only the ambient air is measured.

III. APPLICATION SCENARIO

In so-called threshold applications requiring monitoring hazardous materials and situations, the gas under consideration is continuously or frequently measured by the sensor system and an alarm is raised, when the concentration of the gas exceeds a determined value, the threshold value. As mentioned above, there is a one-to-one relation between concentrations and feature values. However, due to the aging process of the sensor, the sensitivity of the sensor will drop over time. That means that the feature values will become lower and will no longer represent the actual gas concentration. When the features have been significantly reduced in amplitude, the sensor has to be recalibrated to guarantee that an alert is still raised when the actual gas concentration exceeds the alarm threshold.

Even though the ambient air does not change, the sensor's measurement of the ambient air changes due to aging. This gradual reduction of the zero feature values goes in hand with the features value reduction for the alarm case, potentially failing to detect dangerous situations.

This reduction of the zero feature values enables the determination of the proper time for recalibration of the sensor system as will be shown in the following chapter.

Of course, varying environmental conditions may also influence the sensor drift. If they are incorporated in the calibration model, sophisticated calibration and evaluation procedures like ProSens can recognize this source of drift. Otherwise, the sensor system has to be recalibrated and the relevant varying conditions have to be incorporated in the calibration model.

IV. MATHEMATICAL MODEL

As mentioned above, features are an appropriate mean to determine the concentration of a gas under consideration. Features are the results of measurements, which are subject to measurement errors. Therefore, features can be considered as random variables F. It is common and, in most cases realistic, to consider these random variables F as normally distributed around the actual concentration with mean μ, variance σ^2 and standard deviation σ, respectively.

That means:

$$F \sim N(\mu,\sigma^2). \quad (1)$$

In case of the "zero-situation", the mean of the random variable is denoted as μ_0 and the corresponding standard deviation as σ_0. In case of an "alarm-situation", the mean of the random variable is denoted as μ_a and the corresponding standard deviation as σ_a.

From the mathematical theory, it is well known that in case of normally distributed random variables, 95% of all realizations (here measurements and the resulting features) of the random variables are within the interval $(\mu-2\sigma, \mu+2\sigma)$. In other words, 5% of the realizations are outside this interval, especially 2.5% of the realizations are lower than $\mu-2\sigma$. That means that if the zero future value is in 2.5% of the measurements smaller than $\mu_0-2\sigma_0$, the sensor system should be recalibrated, because a significant drift of the sensor has likely occurred.

V. APPLICATION AND SIMULATION CALCULATIONS

To demonstrate the application and performance of the procedure ReCal, simulation calculations were performed.

The following assumptions were chosen: the zero feature value F, which corresponds to the zero-measurement, is normally distributed with mean $\mu_0 = 0$ and standard deviation $\sigma_0 = 1$.

In a first step, random variables F were simulated according to the zero measurement case. Next, a drift of -0.01 per measurement was added to these random variables F to simulate a drift of the sensor system. Figure 2 shows the simulated values of random variables in time (Features Zero, pink curve). These values fluctuate around the mean zero line μ_0 (Mean Zero, blue line) and are in mostly within the interval $(\mu_0-2\sigma_0, \mu_0+2\sigma_0)$, which is between the lower threshold and the upper threshold.

In addition, the values of the "manipulated" features (Features Drift, green curve) are also plotted in Figure 2. They fluctuate around the drift line (Mean Drift, black line) and often fall below the lower threshold. This is clear evidence of the sensor drift.

Of course, if the values of the zero feature are lowered, the values of the alarm features are also lowered. This results in the fact that the determination of the gas concentration is too small and an alarm will not be given, even if the alarm level is reached.

Therefore, a timely recalibration must be performed to ensure that the secure applicability of the sensor system can be guaranteed.

In this example, 100 measurements are assumed to be performed over the time. 2.5% of 100 realization are 2,5. That means that if 3 realizations are lower than the lower threshold, the sensor system has to recalibrated to give a timely alarm.

The mathematical procedure ReCal recognizes that in the 55th measurement the according feature value falls for the third time below the lower threshold and indicates that the sensor system should be recalibrated (see Figure 3).

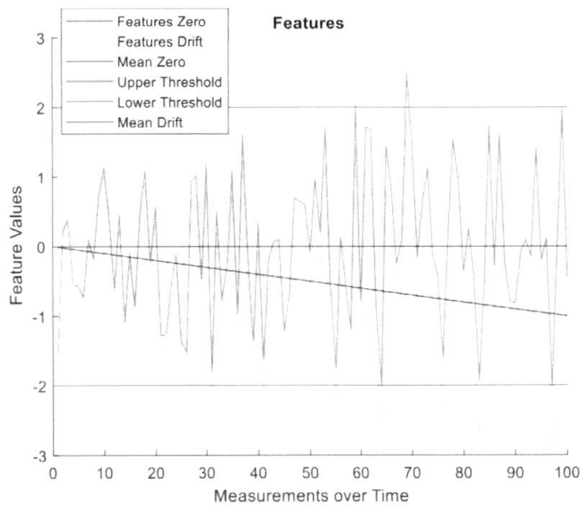

Figure 2. Features and manipulated features of measurements over the time.

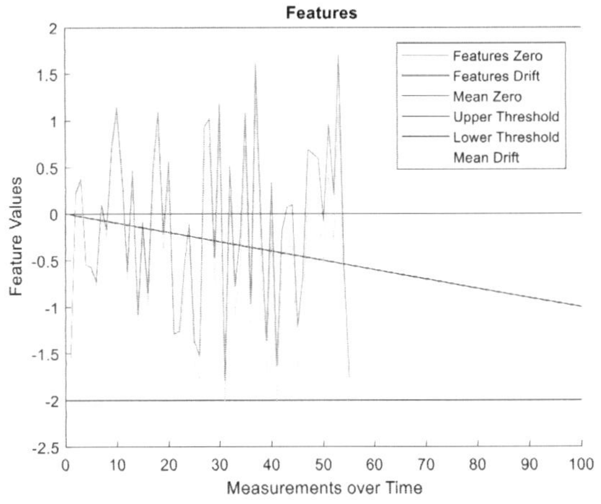

Figure 3. Features and manipulated features of measurements till the time of recalibration.

In real applications, first, it is necesarry to determine the mean μ_0 and the standard deviation σ_0, which is the square root of the variance σ_0^2 of the zero future value F.

As known from the mathematical theory, the mean value of a random variable can be estimated from a population of n identically and independent random variables using the following equation:

$$\mu = 1/n * \Sigma x_i . \quad (1)$$

where x_i are the realizations of the random variables and the sum runs from 1 to n.

The variance σ^2 can be estimated using the following equation (2):

$$\sigma^2 = 1/n * \Sigma (x_i - \mu)^2. \quad (2)$$

where again the sum runs from 1 to n.

To be able to calculate the mean and the standard deviation, samples only containing the ambient air have to be measured by the sensor systems n times.

This is not very costly and time-consuming in respect to the gain of timely detection of a hazardous situation.

VI. CONCLUSIONS

Sensor systems with metal oxide gas sensors with tin oxide as base material are well established as gas sensing devices especially for threshold applications. However, there is an unavoidable drift in the MOG sensors due to their aging process. Therefore, the sensor systems have to be recalibrated from time to time. The mathematical procedure ReCal, introduced in this paper, allows to determine the proper time for recalibration, as was shown by simulation calculations. This is a very important result, because it assures that the sensor systems are suitable for reliable alerting in dangerous situations.

VII. FUTURE WORK

The very promising results obtained by simulation calculations will be tested in a long-term investigation with real measurement data from a real sensor system.

Additionally, a mathematical model will be elaborated, which allows to estimate the drift of other feature values based on the drift of the zero feature values. This approach would enable to recalibrate the sensor system without further calibration measurements. This would be an important progress in the application of sensor systems, because calibration measurements are very time-consuming and costly.

Of course, this approach has also to be verified in a long-term investigation with real measurement data.

REFERENCES

[1] H. Kohler, J. Rober, N. Llink, and I. Bouzid, "New applications of tin oxide gas sensors – I. Molecular recognition by cyclic variation of the working temperature and reasonable numerical analysis", Sensors & Actuators B: pp. 163-169, 1999.

[2] H. Kohler, M. Bauer, and I. Bouzid, "Gas Recognition Using SnO2 Gas Sensors: Analysis of volatile organic substances dissolved in water"; Proceedings Sensor Congress Nürnberg, Vol. I AMA Service, Wunstorf. Germany: pp. 125-128, 1999.

[3] A. Jerger, H. Kohler, F. Becker, H. B. Keller, and R. Seifert, "New applications of tin oxide gas sensors II. Intelligent sensor system for reliable monitoring of ammonia leakages",

Sensors and Actuators B: Chemical, 81, 2-3, pp. 301-307, 2002.

[4] K. Frank et al., “Metal oxide gas sensors for field analysis: Novel SnO2/La2O3 sensor element for analysis of dissolved toluene/ethanol binary mixtures”, Sensor 2005: 12th Internat. Conf., Nürnberg, May, 2005, Proc. Vol. 2, AMA Service GmbH, Wunstorf, pp. 207–209, 2005.

[5] K. Frank et al., “Improving the analysis capability of tin oxide gas sensors by dynamic operation, appropriate additives and an advanced evaluation procedure”, Sensor 2007: 13th Internat.Conf., Nürnberg, May, 2007, Proc. Vol. 1, AMA Service GmbH, Wunstorf, pp. 139–144, 2007.

[6] K. Frank et al., “Chemical Analysis with Tin Oxide Gas Sensors: Choice of Additives, Method of Operation and Analysis of Numerical Signal”, Sensors Letters 6, pp. 908-911, 2008.

[7] R. Seifert, H. B. Keller, K. Frank, and H. Kohler, „ProSens – an Efficient Mathematical Procedure for Calibration and Evaluation of Tin Oxide Gas Sensor Data”, Sensor Letters, Vol. 9/1, pp. 7-10, 2011.

[8] A. Jerger, H. Kohler, F. Becker, H. Keller, and R. Seifert, “New applications of tin oxide gas sensors II. Intelligent Sensor System for Reliable Monitoring of Ammonia Leakages”, Sensors and Actuators B, 81, pp. 301-307, 2002.

[9] R. Seifert, H. Keller, N. Illyaskutty, J. Knoblauch, and H. Kohler, “Numerical Signal Analysis of Thermo-Cyclically Operated MOG Gas Sensor Arrays for Early Identification of Emissions from Overloaded Electric Cables”, Sensors & Transducers journal, Vol. 193, Issue 10, pp.74-79, 2015.

[10] A. D. Wilson, “Review of electronic-nose technologies and algorithms to detect hazardous chemicals in the environment”, Procedia Technol. 2012, 1, pp. 453-463, 2012

[11] R. Seifert, H. B. Keller, K. Frank, and H. Kohler, “Batch-wise Mathematical Calibration of Thermo-CyclicallyOperated Tin Oxide Gas Sensors”, Sensor Letters, Vol. 9/2, pp. 621-624, 2011.

One Year of Wrist Actimetry at One Second Epoch in Real Life

Gianluigi Delucca

Medricerca di Gianluigi Delucca
Rimini, Italy
email: ggdelucca@medricerca.it

Abstract—Quantitative analysis of wrist actigraphy data recorded in real life is a topic of growing interest. For historical reasons, most of that data is collected using a one minute epoch, i.e. the system stores one piece of data each minute, and recordings are limited to a few days. When the data is used for wake/sleep studies, the "gold standard" reference is the Polysomnography (PSG) and little is known about the correlation of actigraphy data with epochs shorter than one minute. It is unknown what is the quantitative impact of infradian rhythms, that could be longer than one year, on shorter recordings. To explore those two areas, the only option is to make longer recordings with shorter epochs. We present a set of data, collected as part of a larger project. For the first time, this paper makes available one year of wrist actimetry in real life, stored at one second epochs. A first evaluation of that data calls for new ways for actimetry analysis and actigraphy display. The raw data is available to the public.

Keywords-Actimetry; Actigraphy; Circadian rhythms.

I. INTRODUCTION

The terms "actimetry" and "actigraphy" are used as synonymous for motion activity measures where "actimetry emphasizes the measurement aspect of the technique and actigraphy emphasizes the descriptive aspects of the technique" [1]. Wrist actigraphy has been used in the past 30 years to monitor motion activity. Clinical guidelines and researches suggest that wrist actimetry is particularly useful in the documentation of circadian rhythms, of sleep disorders, of treatment outcomes and as an adjunct to home monitoring of several pathologies. During the day, it is possible to quantify the physical exercise and (with calibration) recognize some type and intensity of the exercise. Reviews are available in several application areas [2]-[7]. Most published data use a one minute epoch, i.e. the system stores one piece of data each minute, and recordings are limited to a few days. The reasons for that selection of parameters are mainly practical, due to the characteristics of the available instrumentation and the logistic/organizational issues of the recordings, especially in real life.

That selection of parameters sets limits on the possible evaluations of the data. When the data is used for wake/sleep studies, the "gold standard" reference is the Polysomnography (PSG), where data is presented in pages 30s long with signals in the range of 0-100 Hz, so short epochs could allow better correlations. There are infradian rhythms spanning over years and without long continuous recordings it is unknown if and how much those rhythms have an impact on shorter recordings. The technology advances offer today the possibility to record more data and in an easier way, but still few long term recordings are described in literature [8]-[14] and only few groups explore shorter epochs [19]. None of those "extended" recording is available to the public. To explore those two areas, the only option is to make longer recordings with shorter epochs and here we describe one of them.

Section II describes the modality of the recording, the export of the data from the original format and the creation of an activity file of one year. Section III explains the main characteristic of the data and options to study it. Section IV notes the most important findings of those preliminary results. We conclude our work in Section V.

II. MATERIALS AND METHODS

The subject of the recording is the author: age 62 at the start of the recording, male, BMI= 26.3, no known major chronic pathologies. Data is collected using a Motionwatch8 logger (CamNtech Ltd., Cambridge, UK) on the non-dominant wrist. Motionwatch8 is a clinical system extensively used in research [23] and it is a recognized reference in the field. The logger is programmed and data managed using the MotionWare software (CamNtech Ltd – Cambridge – UK). The logger is set to store data in an epoch of one second in "normal" mode. That means that the intensity of the movement on the axis perpendicular to the surface of the unit, is measured by an accelerometer sampled at 50 Hz. Data is transformed in a single value of a custom unit (Counts) each second. The logger acquires also a value of light intensity (Lux) each second. Details are described elsewhere by the manufacturer [15]. A maximum of 36 hours of activity and lights data is stored at 1s epoch in the unit and therefore there is the need for a data download every day. A diary is kept of major events (travels, flu, mismanagements, etc.). As usual in this kind of recordings, it is not possible to know the exact position of the unit on the wrist and if and when the photocell of the unit could be somehow obscured (garments, tools, etc.). The marker available on the logger is used to signal when the unit is not worn.

Using the MotionWare software, the values inside the marked intervals are modified from 0 to "n/a". Then, the recordings are joined in files containing more or less 10 days (one million lines) and exported as .CSV files. Using a spreadsheet (OpenCalc – Apache OpenOffice – Apache Open Foundation), lines with "n/a" are changed to "-1" and the data is divided in 9 columns: year, month, day, hour, minute, seconds, counts, lux integers, lux decimals. That format allows the files to be easily accepted by several software programming languages.

With programs we wrote in Octave [21], activity Counts are extracted, saved as .MAT files and joined in one year long file, for a total of 31.576.501 data lines. The time of the file is continuous, aligned to "summer" time used in Italy in June, at the beginning of the recording (UTC+2: 27 March to 30 October 2016; 26 March to 29 October 2017). Evaluations and graphics of this article are computed from that file using programs we wrote in Octave.

III. RESULTS

Out of 31,576,501 samples, there are 24,936,212 zeros (78.97%), 1,034,485 n/a (3.28%) and 5,605,804 (17.75%) non-zero values. If we compare data stored at one second epoch with data stored at one minute epoch (most used epoch in published articles), we find a completely different ratio between zero and non-zero samples. Over the 1440 minutes of a day, a typical result for one minute epoch would be 555 (39%) zero and 884 (61%) non-zero epochs while for the one second epoch, zeros are about 80 % of the total. How is that possible? The answer is that one minute epochs are computed as the arithmetical sum of 60 one second samples and most of those samples are zero, as shown in Figure 1. For instance, in the lower line, minutes 02.41, 42 and 43 would be counted as 3 active minutes using a one minute epoch, while there are only 5 seconds of movement.

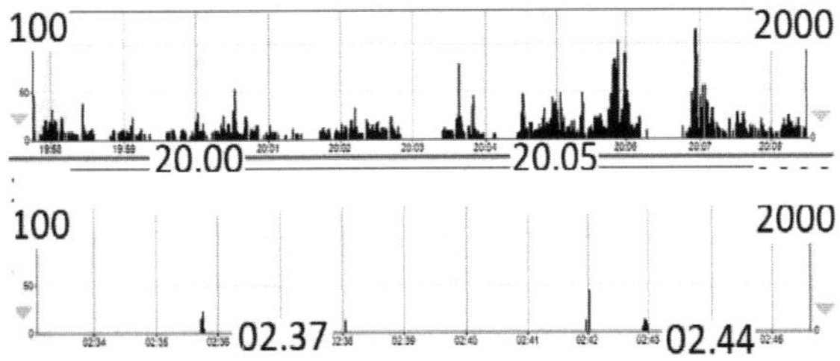

Figure 1. Examples of recordings at epochs of one second: day upper side, night lower. Actimetry in Counts (black) with range on the left, light in Lux (yellow) with range on the right.

Then, we need to extract information from those zero values. A first option for data analysis of zero values could be to consider the percent of zeros inside a time interval. For instance, we may consider one day, divide it in two pieces, like from 10 am to 11. pm and from 11 pm to 10 am, and compute for each day the zero values percent of the two segments. If we plot those values for the full year (Figure 2), the two segments show a quite different behaviour. (Few days with more than 5% of n/a data is removed for a better graph display.). We can get further details if we divide the day in eight segments of 3 hours (Figure 3). It is possible to see that also in that segmentation, a percent of zero values lower than 50% (internal circumference) is exceptional. The circadian behaviour is consistent over the year. The change of the clock to summertime (27 March to 30 October 2016; 26 March to 29 October 2017) may be responsible for some asymmetry that is noted both in Figure 2 and in Figure 3; solar time is from day 135 to day 285.

Another option for data analysis of zero values could be to show not the single epoch values, but the length of the succession of series of zero and non-zero values.

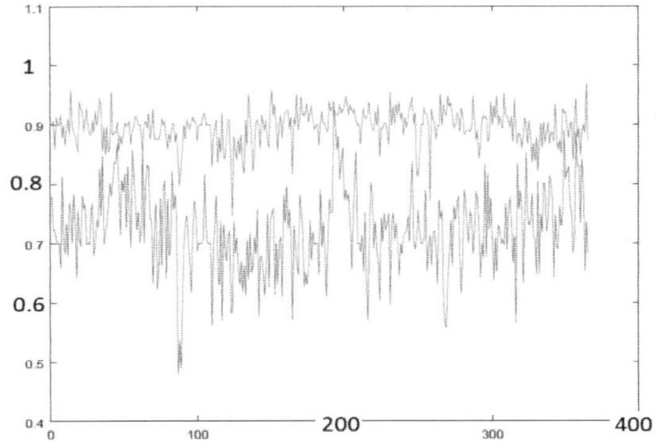

Figure 2. X axis: day of the year - Y axis: zeros percent in the time intervals 10am-11pm (blue) 11pm-10am (red).

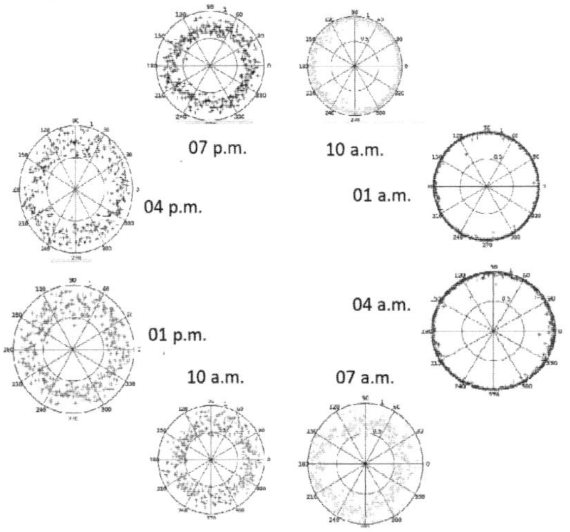

Figure 3. Full year. Zero values percent of 3 hours segments. The time is the start of the 3 hours segment. Circumference is one year, divided in months, 0 is 17 June 2016.

For instance, the sequence ...,0,m,n,0,0,0,p,q,r,0.... will be described using positive and negative integers as ...,2,-3, 3,...In the recorded year, there is a sequence of 1.429.113 zero series and, of course, the same amount of non-zeros ones. The distribution of lengths of series at one second epoch in the year is shown in Figure 4, with non-zero series on the right and zero series on the left. The zero series can be long up to 7400 seconds, the non-zero series up to 623 seconds. There is a peak of several hundred thousand series around few short lengths. If we zoom in Figure 4, we see (Figure 5) that over one year, the number of zero and non-zero series longer than 10 seconds is a small percent of the total.

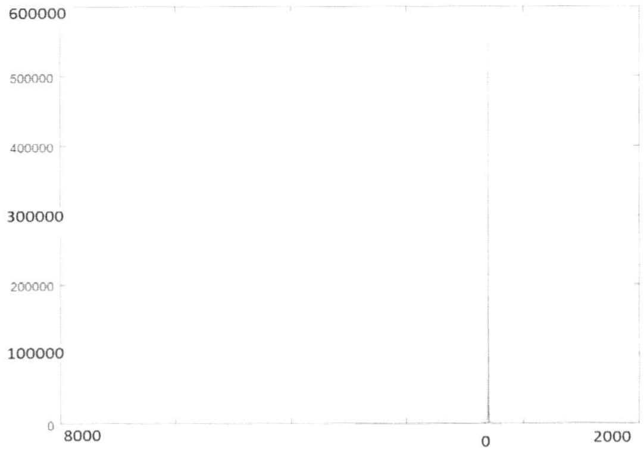

Figure 4. Full year. X axis: length of the series. Zeros series on the left, non-zero series on the right. Y axis: number of series.

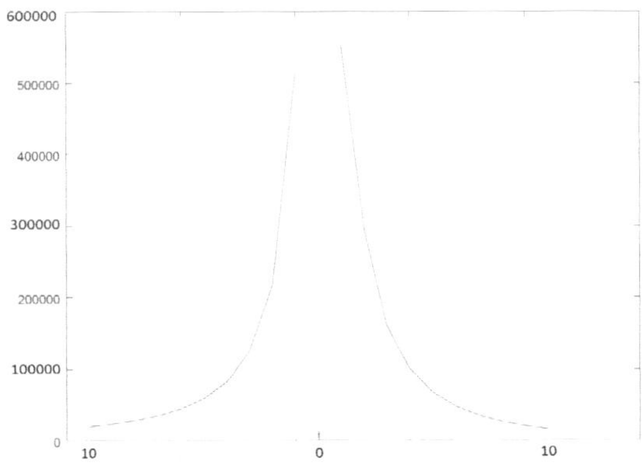

Figure 5. Full year - Zoom of Fig.4 X axis , zeros series on the left, non-zero series on the right Y axis– number of series.

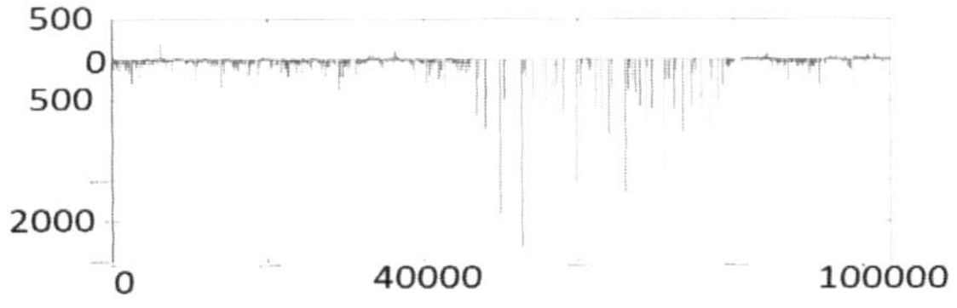

Figure 6. Day one, Start time 09:52:00. X axis: 100,000 seconds – Y-axis: length of the series in seconds: non-zero series up, zero series down.

But, that small percent of lengths are not distributed randomly. If we plot the series, with non-zero series up and zero series down and the distance between the series equal to the length of the series, we get a graph as shown in Figure 6. The pattern is clearly bimodal and that daily profile is consistent over the year.

We may also imagine studying those series as states and search for models of their dynamics. For instance, we may evaluate one step from zero series or from non-zero series. If we plot the length of zero series as negative values and non-zero series that follows them as positive, as in Figure 7, we see that only short zero series can move to long non-zero ones. In the same way, Figure 8 shows that only short non-zero series can move to long zero ones, This suggests that, for instance, a model like the one in Figure 9 and the possibility to make statements on the data dynamics without any a priori hypothesis on the physiology.

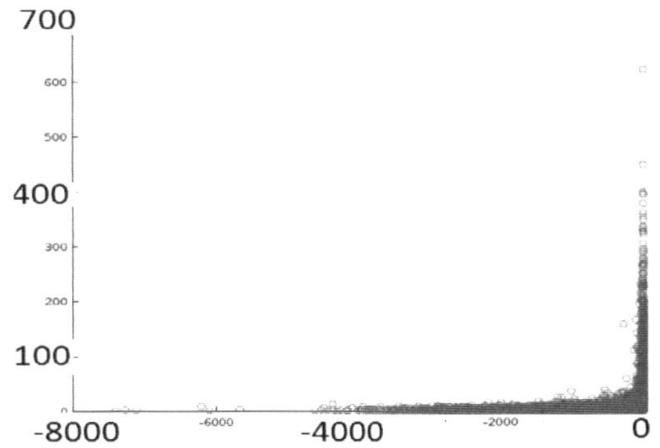

Figure 7. Full year. X axis: zeros series, length in seconds. Y axis : non- zero series that follow, in seconds.

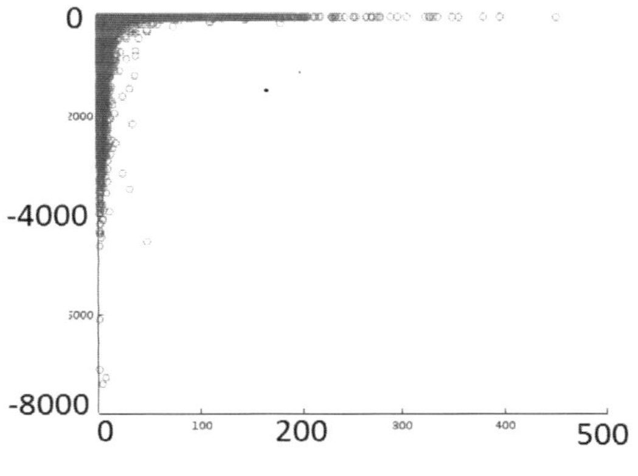

Figure 8. Full year. X axis: non-zeros series, length in seconds. Y axis: non-zero series that follow, length in seconds.

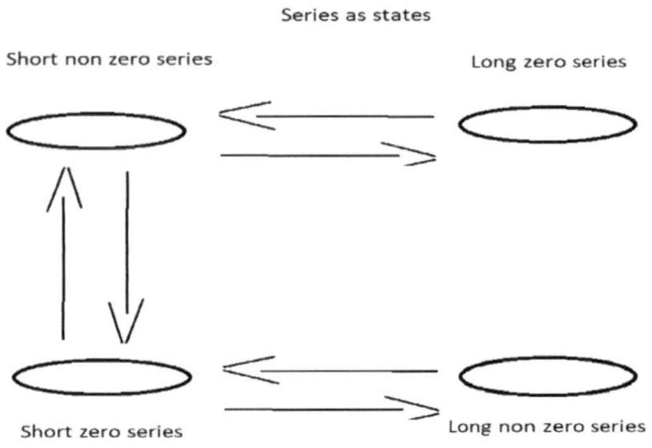

Figure 9. Model of series as states.

IV. DISCUSSION

A first qualitative description of the dataset offers 3 unexpected results. First of all, there is the large number of zero values in the one second epoch recordings compared with the one's with one minute epoch. Traditionally, actigraphy is analysed as a table of a dependent variable (activity counts) and an independent one (time) with fitting methods like Cosinor [16]. That approach is quite difficult when 80% of values are zeros and push to focus on the study of those zero values. Over the years, there were studies on zero values, also called "immobility" [17]. It is one area of studies that is getting new attention [18] and the higher granularity of one second epochs has already shown some potential [19]. The quantity of non-zero values (activity intensity) and quantity of light (light intensity) could provide useful additional information to the study of zero values even if their contribution is based on data more open to artefacts and noise.

The second unexpected result is the permanent circadian distribution of the percent of zero values as shown in Figure 2 and Figure 3. Finding which time interval, and which segmentation of it, would better suit to describe the data, is a research task similar to the well-known Non-Parametric Circadian Rhythm Analysis (NPCRA) method [20].

Last, the pattern in Figure 6 shows, in a different data space, the information of Figure 2 (higher zero percent during the night) but with a more detailed time relationship. It also shows that very long series of zero values, during this year, are allowed only during sleep (personal communication). Their length seems not to be related to sleep stages and co-recording of polygraphic data is needed to explore that relationship. The exploration of series and their dynamics is , as far as I know, a new area of research for actigraphy analysis.

All the above information is easy to see from the proposed graphic displays. That means that there is a very high probability that artificial intelligence algorithms will be able to recognise those patterns and offer better insights (hopefully quantitative) on the data.

V. CONCLUSION AND FUTURE WORK

For the first time, we make available one year of wrist actimetry in real life, stored at one seconds epochs. Most of the activity values stored by the Motionwatch8 are equal to zero. Examples of ways to study those zeros and to display them are introduced. The raw data described in this article are freely available to researchers on the National Sleep Research Resource (NSRR) platform [22]. Hopefully, other researchers will look for new tools to analyse human motor activity and clarify the role of actigraphy in the personalised medicine.

REFERENCES

[1] E. C. Winnebeck, D. Fischer. T. Leise and T. Roenneberg "Dynamics and ultradian structure of human sleep in real life", Current Biology 28, pp.1-11. 2018.

[2] T. Morgenthaler et al., "Practice parameters for the use of actigraphy in the assessment of sleep and sleep disorders: An Update for 2007" Standards of Practice Committee, American Academy of Sleep Medicine SLEEP, vol. 30, No. 4, 2007 pp. 519-529.

[3] Stone, K. L., & Ancoli-Israel, S. Actigraphy. In M. H. Kryger, T. Roth, & W. C. Dement (Eds.), Principles and practice of sleep medicine, 2011, 5th ed., pp.1668–1675.

[4] W. Pan, Y. Song, S. Kwak, S. Yoshida, and Y. Yamamoto "Quantitative evaluation of the use of actigraphy for neurological and psychiatric disorders" Behavioural Neurology vol.2014. Article ID 897282, 6 pages http://dx.doi.org/10.1155/2014/897282.

[5] S. Ancoli-Israel et al., "The SBSM guide to actigraphy monitoring: clinical and research applications" Behavioral Sleep Medicine vol. 13, 2015 - Issue sup1: A Clinical Guide to Actigraphy.pp.S4-S38.

[6] A. Castro, W. M. Anderson and R Nakase-Richardson " Actigraphy reference module in neuroscience and behavioural psychology" Encyclopedia of Sleep 2013, pp. 88–91 Reviewed 20 September 2016.

[7] G. J. Landry, R. S. Falck, M. W. Beets and T. Liu-Ambrose "Measuring physical activity in older adults: calibrating cut-points for the MotionWatch8" Frontiers in Aging Neuroscience, 25 August 2015. https://doi.org/10.3389/fnagi.2015.00165.

[8] E. Werth et al., "Decline in long-term circadian rest-activity cycle organization in a patient with dementia" J Geriatr Psychiatry Neurol, 2002; vol. 15; pp.55-59.

[9] N. Lewis Miller and L. G. Shattuck "Sleep patterns of young men and women enrolled at the United States military academy: Results from Year 1 of a 4-Year Longitudinal Study" Sleep, vol. 28; No. 7; 2005; pp.837–841, https://doi.org/10.1093/sleep/28.7.837.

[10] N. Lewis Miller, L. G. Shattuck and P. Matsangas. "Longitudinal study of sleep patterns of United States military academy cadets" Sleep. 2010 December 1; 33(12): pp.1623–1631.

[11] N. Lewis Shattuck and P. Matsangas, "A 6-month assessment of sleep during naval deployment: a case study of a commanding officer". Aerospace medicine and human performance vol. 86, No. 5 May 2015, pp.481-485.

[12] C. Garbazza et al., "Non-24-hour sleep-wake disorder revisited – a case study". Front. Neurol. 7:17.2016 doi: 10.3389/fneur.2016.00017.

[13] J. Tippin, N. Aksan, J. Dawson, S. W. Anderson and M. Rizzo "Sleep remains disturbed in patients with obstructive sleep apnea treated with positive airway pressure: a three-month cohort study using continuous actimetry" Sleep Medicine, vol. 24, August 2016, pp.24-31.

[14] A. Borbely, T. Rusterholz and P. Achermann "Three decades of continuous motor activity recording:analysis of sleep duration" Poster P041 ESRS 2016 Bologna.

[15] CamNtech Ltd – Cambridge – UK, Info Bulleting No.2, 8/2/2016.

[16] F. Hallberg, F. Caradente, G. Cornelissenand and G. S. Katinas. Glossary of Chronobiology Chronobiologia 4 Suppl 1 February 1977.

[17] A. Huub et al., "Circadian distribution of motor activity and immobility in narcolepsy: assessment with continuous motor activity monitoring", Psychophysiology, vol.32, issue3, May 1995, pp.286-291.

[18] T. Roenneberg et al., "Human activity and rest in situ" Methods of Enzymology, 2014 vol. 552, pp.257-283.

[19] A. Muzet et al., "Assessing sleep architecture and continuity measures through the analysis of heart rate and wrist movement recordings in healthy subjects: comparison with results based on polysomnography", Sleep Medicine May 2016 vol. 21, pp.47–56.

[20] E. J. W. Van Someren et al., "Bright light therapy: improved sensitivity to its effects on rest-activity rhythms in Alzheimer patients by application of nonparametric methods". Chronobiology Int. 1999, 16 (4) pp.505-518.

[21] https://www.gnu.org/software/octave/about.html [accessed August 2018].

[22] https://sleepdata.org/datasets/oya [accessed August 2018].

[23] https://www.camntech.com/products/motionwatch/mw8-biblio [accessed August 2018].